MACROECONOMICS

PRINCIPLES AND POLICY

1998 UPDATE

SEVENTH EDITION

WILLIAM J. BAUMOL
C.V. STARR CENTER FOR APPLIED ECONOMICS
NEW YORK UNIVERSITY

ALAN S. BLINDER
PRINCETON UNIVERSITY

THE DRYDEN PRESS
HARCOURT BRACE COLLEGE PUBLISHERS

FORT WORTH PHILADELPHIA SAN DIEGO NEW YORK AUSTIN ORLANDO SAN ANTONIO
TORONTO MONTREAL LONDON SYDNEY TOKYO

MACROECONOMICS

PRINCIPLES AND POLICY

SEVENTH EDITION

ACQUISITIONS EDITOR	Emily Barrosse
DEVELOPMENTAL EDITOR	Jeanie Anirudhan, Stacey Sims
PROJECT EDITOR	Amy Schmidt, Andrea Wright
ART DIRECTOR	Linda Wooton Miller
PRODUCTION MANAGER	Ann Coburn
ART & LITERARY RIGHTS EDITOR	Annette Coolidge
PRODUCT MANAGER	Kathleen Sharp
MARKETING COORDINATOR	Randa Johnson

PROOFREADER	Teresa Chartos
COMPOSITOR	GTS Graphics, Inc.
TEXT TYPE	10/12 Palatino
COVER AND PART IMAGES	© David Arky Photography, 1995

Address for Orders
The Dryden Press
6277 Sea Harbor Drive
Orlando, FL 32887-6777
1-800-782-4479 or 1-800-433-0001 (in Florida)

Address for Editorial Correspondence
The Dryden Press
301 Commerce Street, Suite 3700
Fort Worth, TX 76102

ISBN for first printing: 0-03-011263-X.
1998 Update ISBN: 0-03-025049-8.
Text has been updated to reflect the most current data.

Library of Congress Catalog Card Number: 95-83621

Printed in the United States of America

7 8 9 0 1 2 3 4 5 6 048 9 8 7 6 5 4 3 2 1

The Dryden Press
Harcourt Brace College Publishers

To my four children, Ellen, Daniel, and now Sabrina and Jim

W.J.B.

To the memory of my father, Morris Blinder, to whom I owe much

A.S.B.

THE DRYDEN PRESS SERIES IN ECONOMICS

BALDANI, BRADFIELD, AND TURNER
Mathematical Economics

BAUMOL AND BLINDER
Economics: Principles and Policy
Seventh Edition (Also available in micro and macro paperbacks)

BAUMOL, PANZAR, AND WILLIG
Contestable Markets and the Theory of Industry Structure
Revised Edition

BERCH
The Endless Day: The Political Economy of Women and Work

BREIT AND ELZINGA
The Antitrust Casebook: Milestones in Economic Regulation
Third Edition

BRUE
The Evolution of Economic Thought
Fifth Edition

DEMMERT
Economics: Understanding the Market Process

EDGMAND, MOOMAW, AND OLSON
Economics and Contemporary Issues
Third Edition

GARDNER
Comparative Economic Systems
Second Edition

GREEN
Macroeconomics: Analysis and Applications

GWARTNEY AND STROUP
Economics: Private and Public Choice
Eighth Edition (Also available in micro and macro paperbacks)

GWARTNEY AND STROUP
Introduction to Economics: The Wealth and Poverty of Nations

HEILBRONER AND SINGER
The Economic Transformation of America: 1600 to the Present
Second Edition

HESS AND ROSS
Economic Development: Theories, Evidence, and Policies

HIRSCHEY AND PAPPAS
Fundamentals of Managerial Economics
Fifth Edition

HIRSCHEY AND PAPPAS
Managerial Economics
Eighth Edition

HYMAN
Public Finance: A Contemporary Application of Theory to Policy
Fifth Edition

KAHN
The Economic Approach to Environmental and Natural Resources

KASERMAN AND MAYO
Government and Business: The Economics of Antitrust and Regulation

KAUFMAN
The Economics of Labor Markets
Fourth Edition

KENNETT AND LIEBERMAN
The Road to Capitalism: The Economic Transformation of Eastern Europe and the Former Soviet Union

KREININ
International Economics: A Policy Approach
Seventh Edition

LOTT AND RAY
Applied Econometrics with Data Sets

MARLOW
Public Finance: Theory and Practice

NICHOLSON
Intermediate Microeconomics and Its Application
Seventh Edition

NICHOLSON
Microeconomic Theory: Basic Principles and Extensions
Sixth Edition

PUTH
American Economic History
Third Edition

RAGAN AND THOMAS
Principles of Economics
Second Edition (Also available in micro and macro paperbacks)

RAMANATHAN
Introductory Econometrics with Applications
Third Edition

RUKSTAD
Corporate Decision Making in the World Economy: Company Case Studies

RUKSTAD
Macroeconomic Decision Making in the World Economy: Text and Cases
Third Edition

SAMUELSON AND MARKS
Managerial Economics
Second Edition

SCARTH
Macroeconomics: An Introduction to Advanced Methods
Third Edition

STOCKMAN
Introduction to Economics
(Also available in micro and macro paperbacks)

THOMAS
Economics: Principles and Applications
(Also available in micro and macro paperbacks)

WALTON AND ROCKOFF
History of the American Economy
Seventh Edition

WELCH AND WELCH
Economics: Theory and Practice
Fifth Edition

YARBROUGH AND YARBROUGH
The World Economy: Trade and Finance
Fourth Edition

PREFACE

The Seventh Edition continues the basic philosophy of its predecessors. In particular, we avoid the fiction, so popular among textbook writers, that everything is of the utmost importance—a pretense that students are sufficiently intelligent to see through in any event. We try, instead, to highlight those important ideas that are likely to be of lasting significance—principles that students will want to remember long after the course is over because they offer insights that are far from obvious, because they are of practical importance, and because they are widely misunderstood by intelligent laymen. Eight of the most important of these ideas are selected as **Ideas for Beyond the Final Exam** and are called to the reader's attention when they occur through the use of the symbol .

While all modern economics textbooks abound with "real world" examples, we try to go beyond this by elevating the examples to preeminence. In our view, the policy issue or everyday economic problem ought to lead the student naturally to the economic principle, not the other way around. For this reason, almost every chapter begins with a real policy issue or a practical problem that may seem puzzling or paradoxical to noneconomists. We then proceed to describe the economic analysis required to remove the mystery.

In so doing, we use technical terminology and diagrams only where there is a clear need for them, never for their own sake. Still, economics is a technical subject, and so this is, unavoidably, a book for the desk and not for the bed. We make, however, strenuous efforts to simplify the technical level of the discussion as much as possible without sacrificing content. Fortunately, almost every important idea in economics can be explained in plain English, and this is what we try to do.

Each edition of this book has been influenced by economic events. Reflecting the growing "globalization" of the world economy, the Fifth Edition was substantially revised to exhibit more clearly the international linkages between the U.S. economy and other economies. The Sixth Edition was written just after the collapse of communism. Since the book has long focused on the market mechanism and how it works, it was easy to incorporate these stunning events into the discussion. Both of these features are retained in the Seventh Edition.

But the Seventh Edition is also affected by another critical development—one that cannot be dealt with so definitively: rising inequality in the world's industrialized countries in general, and in the United States in particular. While overall income continues to grow in these countries, more and more of each nation's income and wealth are going to the most affluent portion of the population, while lower-income groups fall further and further behind. This development is not new; it has been going on for more than a decade. But its very persistence has now made it a subject of urgent concern.

Rising inequality has been accompanied by a sharp and continuing slowdown of growth and by a severe stagnation in the rise of American real wages. Unfortunately, no one is quite sure about the causes of these worrisome developments nor about the means that can be used to ameliorate them. The issues are, therefore, raised at a number of points in this book, and the pertinent facts are reported and discussed. But we are suitably modest in discussing both the underlying causes and the policy issues to which they give rise.

Several new features of this edition are worth noting. Many more "Policy Debate" boxes, a popular feature of the last edition, have been added to this edition. We have also included a new feature that offers students a somewhat more tangible picture of some of the subjects discussed. New boxes called "You Are There" describe a meeting of the Federal Open Market Committee, an antitrust court case, and activities on the floor of the New York Stock Exchange. Finally, the book has undergone extensive and painstaking updating throughout, so that new material could be added without increasing overall length.

As a last personal note, we must mention that most of the Seventh Edition, like the Sixth before it, had to be written under the handicap of a separation between the coauthors. Happily, this separation entailed neither disagreement nor rancor, and is now over. Alan Blinder's sojourn in Washington—first as a Member of the President's Council of Economic Advisers and then as Vice Chairman of the Federal Reserve Board—has undoubtedly contributed to the relevance of this book's materials to the real world. But it has also made communication between us far more challenging.

However, there is a silver lining to this cloud of inconvenience. Blinder reports renewed and enhanced respect for Herbert Stein's sage observation that "most of the economics that is usable for advising on public policy is at about the level of the introductory undergraduate course."

NOTE TO THE STUDENT

We would like to offer one suggestion for success in your economics course. Unlike some of the other courses you may be taking, economics is cumulative—each week's lesson builds upon what you have learned before. You will save yourself both a lot of frustration and a lot of work by keeping up on a week-to-week basis. To assist you in doing so, a chapter summary, a list of important terms and concepts, and a selection of questions to help you with your review are provided at the end of each chapter. Making use of these learning aids will increase your success in your economics course. For additional assistance, see the following list of ancillary materials.

ANCILLARIES

As economic education incorporates new technologies, our extensive learning package has been expanded and improved to accommodate the needs of students and instructors.

- *Study Guide* by Craig Swan, University of Minnesota (for students). Our study guide includes learning objectives, a list of important terms and concepts for every chapter, and a quiz that helps students test their understanding and comprehension of concepts. Also included are multiple-choice tests for self-understanding, a list of supplementary readings and study questions for every chapter, and "Economics in Action" sections that use current news articles to illustrate economic concepts. A new feature, "Economics On-Line," outlines useful Internet and Web sources for economic data and information. Periodic updates of these sources will be provided on the Dryden/Harcourt Web page: www.hbcollege.com.

- *Instructor's Manual/Transparency Masters* by John Isbister, University of California—Santa Cruz. Every chapter in the revised *Instructor's Manual* consists of detailed chapter outlines, teaching tips and suggestions, answers to review questions in the text, and questions for classroom discussion. Multiple-choice questions suitable for quizzes and tests have been added in this edition. The transparency masters include all figures and tables not available as acetates.
- *Macroeconomics Test Bank* by John Dodge, University of Sioux Falls. Consisting of more than 5,000 questions, the test bank helps students understand and comprehend the book's concepts and their applicability to real-world situations. Every question has been checked to ensure the accuracy and clarity of the answers, and we thank Ivan Weinel for assisting with this important task. The true/false, multiple-choice, and short-answer questions, which are organized by section in the text, encourage critical thinking and analytical skills. The test bank is also available in computerized IBM and Windows versions in the *EXAMaster* program. *EXAMaster* allows you to add and edit your own questions, create and edit graphics, print scrambled versions of tests, convert multiple-choice questions to open-ended questions, plus much more.
- *Transparency Acetates.* Full color transparency acetates for all important figures and tables in the text.
- *Weekly News Updates.* Each news update links topics in the text with current economic events and consists of the synopsis of a pertinent article, references to a topic or chapter in the text, and a few discussion questions suitable for classroom use. The news updates are posted on the Harcourt Web page.
- *PowerPoint® Presentation Software.* This user-friendly slide show is suitable for classroom presentations. It consists of important graphs and tables from the text as well as bulleted summaries and chapter outlines. *PowerPoint Viewer* is provided in the package.
- *Tutorial, Analytical, and Graphing (TAG) Software* by Todd Porter and Teresa Riley, Youngstown State University (for students). In addition to an extensive chapter-by-chapter tutorial, a hands-on graphing section in which students are actually required to draw curves (with keystrokes or a mouse), and a practice exam for each section, this tutorial software consists of a number of new and innovative features added for this edition. Annotated multiple-choice questions give students feedback on their answers and explain reasons why a particular answer is right or wrong. The software is now available in a new Windows version.

The Dryden Press may provide complimentary instructional aids and supplements or supplement packages to those adopters qualified under its adoption policy. Please contact your sales representative for more information. If as an adopter or potential user you receive supplements you do not need, please return them to your sales representative or send them to: Attn: Returns Department, Troy Warehouse, 465 South Lincoln Drive, Troy, MO 63379.

NOTE TO THE INSTRUCTOR

In trying to improve the book from one edition to the next, we rely heavily on our experiences as teachers. But our experience using the book is minuscule compared with that of the hundreds of instructors who use it nationwide. If you encounter problems, or have suggestions for improving the book, we urge you to let us know by writing to either one of us in care of The Dryden Press, 301 Commerce Street, Suite 3700, Fort Worth, TX 76102. Such letters are invaluable, and we are glad to receive them, even if they are critical (but not *too* critical!). Many such suggestions accumulated over the past three years found their way into the Seventh Edition.

What follows are suggested course outlines for a one-semester and a one-quarter course.

OUTLINE FOR A ONE-SEMESTER COURSE IN MACROECONOMICS

Chapter Number	Title
1	What Is Economics?
2	The U.S. Economy: Myth and Reality
3	Scarcity and Choice: *The* Economic Problem
4	Supply and Demand: An Initial Look
5	The Realm of Macroeconomics
6	Unemployment and Inflation: The Twin Evils of Macroeconomics
7	Income and Spending: The Powerful Consumer
8	Demand-Side Equilibrium: Unemployment or Inflation?
9	Changes on the Demand Side: Multiplier Analysis
10	Supply-Side Equilibrium: Unemployment *and* Inflation?
11	Managing Aggregate Demand: Fiscal Policy
12	Money and the Banking System
13	Monetary Policy and the National Economy
14	The Debate over Monetary Policy
15	Budget Deficits and the National Debt: Fact and Fiction
16	The Trade-off between Inflation and Unemployment
17	International Trade and Comparative Advantage
18	The International Monetary System: Order or Disorder?
19	Macroeconomics in a World Economy
20	Productivity and Growth in the Wealth of Nations
21	Comparative Economic Systems: What Are the Choices?

OUTLINE FOR A ONE-QUARTER COURSE IN MACROECONOMICS

Chapter Number	Title
1	What Is Economics?
2	The U.S. Economy: Myth and Reality
3	Scarcity and Choice: *The* Economic Problem
4	Supply and Demand: An Initial Look
5	The Realm of Macroeconomics
6	Unemployment and Inflation: The Twin Evils of Macroeconomics
7	Income and Spending: The Powerful Consumer
8	Demand-Side Equilibrium: Unemployment or Inflation?
9	Changes on the Demand Side: Multiplier Analysis
10	Supply-Side Equilibrium: Unemployment *and* Inflation?
11	Managing Aggregate Demand: Fiscal Policy
12	Money and the Banking System
13	Monetary Policy and the National Economy
14	The Debate over Monetary Policy

WITH THANKS

Finally, and with great pleasure, we turn to the customary acknowledgments of indebtedness. Ours have been accumulating now through seven editions. In these days of specialization, not even a pair of authors can master every subject that an introductory textbook must cover. Our friends and colleagues Albert Ando, Charles Berry, Rebecca Blank, William Branson, the late Lester Chandler, Gregory Chow, Avinash Dixit, Robert Eisner, Susan Feiner, the late Stephen Goldfeld, Claudia Goldin, Ronald Grieson, Daniel Hamermesh, Yuzo Honda, Peter Kenen, Melvin Krauss, Herbert Levine, the late Arthur Lewis, Burton Malkiel, Edwin Mills, Janusz Ordover, Uwe Reinhardt, Harvey Rosen, Laura Tyson, and Martin Weitzman have all given generously of their knowledge in particular areas over the course of seven editions. We have learned much from them, and only wish we had learned more.

Many economists and students at other colleges and universities offered useful suggestions for improvements, many of which we have incorporated into the Seventh Edition. We wish to thank Mordechai Kreinin, Michigan State University; David Bradford, University of New Hampshire; Arthur Diamond, University of Nebraska–Omaha; Norman J. Waitzman, the University of Utah; Philip G. King, San Francisco State University; Thomas G. Watkins, Eastern Kentucky University; James E. Bell, Harris-Stowe State College; Donald N. Baum, University of Nebraska—Omaha; Jim Cox, DeKalb College; David N. Weil, Brown University; Ted W. Chiles, Auburn University at Montgomery; Daniel Vencill, San Francisco State University; and Terence J. Alexander, Iowa State University, for their insightful reviews.

We also wish to thank the many economists who responded to our survey; their responses were invaluable in planning this revision: Donald C. Balch, University of South Carolina; John Bockino, Suffolk Community College; Michael J. Smitka, Washington & Lee University; Hassan Y. Aly, Ohio State University—Marion Campus; Carol M. Clark, Guilford College; John A. Edgren, Eastern Michigan University; Michael Dowd, University of Toledo; Colleen Cameron, University of Southern Mississippi; Donald A. Coffin, Indiana University Northwest; Shyam Bhatia, Indiana University Northwest; John W. Dodge, University of Sioux Falls; John Blair, Wright State University; David Bradford, University of New Hampshire; James H. Breece, University of Maine; Nancy R. Fox, Saint Joseph's University; Terence J. Alexander, Iowa State University; George Giu, Tuskegee University; S. N. Gajanan, University of Pittsburgh at Bradford; Steven E. Abraham, University of Northern Iowa; James N. Wetzel, Virginia Commonwealth University; Bruce Carpenter, Mansfield University; Yilma Gebremariam, Southern Connecticut State University; Marie D. Connolly, Chatham College; and Garry Fleming, Roanoke College.

Obviously, the book you hold in your hand was not produced by us alone. An essential role was played by the fine people at The Dryden Press, including Emily Barrosse, Executive Editor for Economics; Jeanie Anirudhan, Developmental Editor; Stacey Sims, Developmental Editor; Amy Schmidt, Project Editor; Linda Miller, Art Director; and Ann Coburn, Production Manager. We would also like to thank Carol Cirulli and Sean Lanham for their role in this edition. We appreciate all of their efforts. William Baumol is grateful to the publisher, and especially to Linda Miller, the book's art director, for the decision to use photographs of Professor Baumol's sculptures as a design feature throughout the volume.

We also thank our intelligent and delightful secretaries and research coworkers at Princeton University and New York University: Phyllis Durepos and Janeece Roderick, who struggled successfully with the myriad tasks involved in completing the manuscript. Above all, Professor Baumol owes an unrepayable debt to his longstanding partner in crime, Sue Anne Batey Blackman, who carried out much of the updating of materials and who contributed draft paragraphs, illustrative items, and far more with her usual insight and diligence. By now, she undoubtedly knows more about the book than the authors do.

And, finally, there are our wives, Hilda Baumol and Madeline Blinder. They have now participated and helped with this project for over 20 years. During that period, this book has quite literally become part of our families. And both their contributions and our affection have grown.

WILLIAM J. BAUMOL
ALAN S. BLINDER

BRIEF CONTENTS

CONTENTS

Chapter 8 Demand-Side Equilibrium: Unemployment or Inflation? 165

Chapter 9 Changes on the Demand Side: Multiplier Analysis 187

CHAPTER 10 SUPPLY-SIDE EQUILIBRIUM: UNEMPLOYMENT *AND* INFLATION? 205

PART III

FISCAL AND MONETARY POLICY 225

CHAPTER 11 MANAGING AGGREGATE DEMAND: FISCAL POLICY 227

William J. Baumol was born and raised in New York City. He received his undergraduate degree in economics with a minor in art from the City University of New York and his Ph.D. in economics from the London School of Economics.

He taught at Princeton University for over forty years, and he is now at New York University, where he is the director of the C.V. Starr Center for Applied Economics.

Professor Baumol has published over five hundred scholarly articles and more than twenty books that have been translated into a dozen languages.

He has been president of four professional societies, including the American Economic Association. He is also a member of the Board of Trustees of the Joint Council on Economic Education and a member of the National Academy of Sciences.

He is married and has two children and two grandchildren. In addition to courses in economics, Professor Baumol also taught wood sculpture at Princeton University.

Alan S. Blinder was born in New York City and earned his A.B. at Princeton University, his M.Sc. at the London School of Economics, and his Ph.D. at Massachusetts Institute of Technology—all in economics.

Since 1971, he has taught at Princeton University, where he is now the Gordon S. Rentschler Memorial Professor of Economics. Professor Blinder chaired the department of economics from 1988 to 1990, and he is also the founder and director of Princeton's Center for Economic Policy Studies.

Professor Blinder is the author of ten books and scores of scholarly articles. He is a member of the American Philosophical Society and the American Academy of Arts and Sciences. From January 1993 through January 1996, he served in Washington—first as a Member of the President's Council of Economic Advisers and then as Vice Chairman of the Board of Governors of the Federal Reserve System.

Professor Blinder is married, has two sons, and resides in Princeton, New Jersey.

MACROECONOMICS

PRINCIPLES AND POLICY

SEVENTH EDITION

PART I

Getting Acquainted with Economics

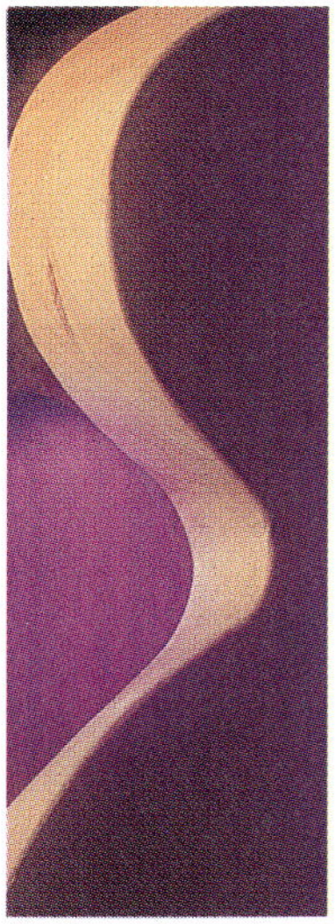

CHAPTER 1

WHAT IS ECONOMICS?

Why does public discussion of economic policy so often show the abysmal ignorance of the participants? Why do I so often want to cry at what public figures, the press, and television commentators say about economic affairs?
Robert M. Solow

Economics is a broad-ranging discipline, both in the questions it asks and the methods it uses to seek answers. Rather than try to define the discipline in a single sentence or paragraph, we will instead introduce you to economics by letting the subject matter speak for itself.

Many of the world's most pressing problems are economic in nature. The first part of the chapter is intended to give you some idea of the sorts of issues that economic analysis helps to clarify and the kinds of solutions that economic principles suggest. The second part briefly introduces the tools that economists use. You are likely to find them useful in your career, personal life, and role as an informed citizen, long after the course is over. Graphs are among these tools, and this book has many of them. For those of you who are unfamiliar with graphs, the appendix to this chapter provides a brief introduction.

IDEAS FOR BEYOND THE FINAL EXAM

As college professors, we realize it is inevitable that you will forget much of what you learn in this course—perhaps with a sense of relief—soon after the final exam. There is not much point bemoaning this fact; elephants may never forget, but people do.

Nevertheless, some economic ideas are so important that you will want to remember them after the course is over. To help you pick out a few of the most crucial concepts, we have selected eight from among the many contained in this book. Some offer key insights into the workings of the economy. Others bear on important policy issues that appear in newspapers. Others point out common misunderstandings that occur among even the most thoughtful lay observers. As the opening quote of this chapter suggests, many learned judges, politicians, and university administrators who have failed to understand or misused these economic principles could have made wiser decisions than they did.

Each of the **Ideas for Beyond the Final Exam** will be discussed in depth as it occurs in the course of the book, so you should not expect to master them after reading this opening chapter. Nonetheless, it is useful to sketch them briefly here to introduce you to economics and to provide a preview of what is to come.

IDEA 1 MUTUAL GAINS FROM VOLUNTARY EXCHANGE

One of the most fundamental ideas of economics is that in a *voluntary exchange both* parties must expect to gain something. Otherwise why would they both agree to trade? This principle seems self-evident. Yet it is amazing how often it is ignored in practice.

For example, it was widely believed for centuries that in international trade one country's gain from an exchange must be the other country's loss (Chapter 17). Analogously, some people feel instinctively that if Ms. A profits handsomely from a deal with Mr. B, then Mr. B must have been exploited. Laws sometimes prohibit mutually beneficial exchanges between buyers and sellers—as when a loan transaction is banned because the interest rate is "too high" (Chapter 6), or when the resale of tickets to sporting events ("ticket scalping") is outlawed even though the buyer is happy to get the ticket that he would not obtain at a lower price (Chapter 4).

In every one of these cases, and many more, well-intentioned but misguided reasoning blocks the mutual gains that arise from voluntary exchange—and thereby interferes with one of the most basic functions of an economic system (see Chapter 3).

IDEA 2 RATIONAL CHOICE AND TRUE ECONOMIC COSTS: THE ROLE OF OPPORTUNITY COST

Despite dramatic improvements in our standard of living since the Industrial Revolution, we have not come anywhere near a state of unlimited abundance, and so we must constantly make choices. If you purchase a new home, you may have to give up a trip you had planned. If a firm decides to retool its factories, it may have to postpone plans for new executive offices. If a government expands its defense program, it may be forced to reduce its outlays on roads or school buildings.

Economists say that the true costs of such decisions are not the number of dollars spent on the house, the new equipment, or the military establishment, but rather *the value of what must be given up in order to acquire the item*—the vacation trip, the new executive offices, the improved roads, and the new schools. These are called **opportunity costs** because they represent the *opportunities* the individual, firm, or government must forgo to make the desired expenditure. Economists maintain that rational decision making requires that opportunity costs be considered as part of the cost of any decision (Chapter 3).

The **OPPORTUNITY COST** of some decision is the value of the next best alternative which you have to give up because of that decision (for example, working instead of going to school).

The cost of a college education provides a vivid example that is probably close to your heart. How much do you think it *costs* to go to college? Most likely you would answer this question by adding together your expenditures on tuition, room and board, books, and the like, and then deducting any scholarship funds you may receive. Economists would not. They would first want to know how much you could be earning if you were not attending college. This may sound like an irrelevant question; but because you give up these earnings by attending college, they must be added to your tuition bill as a cost of your education. Nor would economists accept the university's bill for room and board as a measure of your living costs. They would want to know by how much this exceeds what it would have cost you to live at home, and only this extra cost would be counted as an expense. On balance, a college education probably costs more than you think.

IDEA 3 ATTEMPTS TO REPEAL THE LAWS OF SUPPLY AND DEMAND: THE MARKET STRIKES BACK

When a commodity is in short supply, its price naturally tends to rise. Sometimes disgruntled consumers badger politicians into "solving" the problem by imposing a legal ceiling on the price. Similarly, when supplies are abundant—say, when fine weather produces extraordinarily abundant crops—prices tend to fall. This naturally dismays producers, who often succeed in getting legislation to prohibit low prices by imposing price floors.

But such attempts to repeal the laws of supply and demand usually backfire, and sometimes produce results opposite of those that were intended. Where rent controls are adopted to protect tenants, housing grows scarce because the law makes it unprofitable to build and maintain apartments. When price floors are placed under agricultural products, surpluses pile up.

History provides some spectacular examples of the free market's ability to strike back at attempts to interfere with it. In Chapter 4, we will see that price controls contributed to the hardships of George Washington's army at Valley Forge. Two centuries earlier, when the armies of Spain surrounded Antwerp in 1584, hoping to starve the city into submission, profiteers kept Antwerp going by smuggling food and supplies through enemy lines. However, when the city fathers adopted price controls to end these "unconscionable" prices, supplies dried up and the city soon surrendered.

As we will see in Chapter 4 and elsewhere in this book, such consequences of interfering with the price mechanism are no accident. They follow inevitably from the way free markets work.

IDEA 4 THE TRADE-OFF BETWEEN INFLATION AND UNEMPLOYMENT

Inflation these days is running a bit below 3 percent per year. In 1990, it was just over 5 percent. What made the inflation rate fall? Most economists believe the answer is simple: In mid-1990, the U.S. economy entered a recession that proved to be deeper and longer than policymakers anticipated. The unemployment rate rose from a low of 5 percent in mid-1990 to a peak of nearly 8 percent in mid-1992 and then receded only slowly.

Economists maintain that this conjunction of events—falling inflation and high unemployment—was no coincidence. Owing to features of our economy that we will study in Parts II and III, there is an agonizing *trade-off between inflation and unemployment,* meaning that most policies that lower inflation also cause higher unemployment for a while.

Since this trade-off poses one of the fundamental dilemmas of national economic policy, we will devote all of Chapter 16 to examining it in detail. And we shall also consider some suggestions for escaping from the trade-off, such as supply-side economics (Chapter 10).

IDEA 5 THE ILLUSION OF HIGH INTEREST RATES

Is it more costly to borrow money at 12 percent interest or at 8 percent? That question seems easy, even without a course in economics. But, in fact, it is not. An example will show why.

In 1995, banks were lending money to home buyers at annual interest rates below 8 percent. In 1980, these rates had been over 12 percent. Yet economists maintain that it was actually cheaper to borrow in 1980 than in 1995. Why? Because inflation in 1980 was running at about 10 percent per year while it was just below 3 percent by 1995.

But why is the rate of inflation relevant for deciding how costly it is to borrow? Consider the position of a person who borrows $100 for 1 year at a 12 percent rate of interest when prices are rising at 10 percent per year. At the end of the year the borrower pays back her $100 plus $12 interest. But over that same year her indebtedness declines by $10 *in terms of what that money will buy.* Because the purchasing power of money declines 10 percent, it is as if $10 of her debt had been forgiven. Thus, in terms of *purchasing power,* the borrower really pays only $2 in interest on her $100 loan, or 2 percent.

Now consider someone who borrows $100 at 8 percent interest when inflation is only 3 percent. This borrower pays back the original $100 plus $8 in interest and sees the purchasing power of his debt decline by $3 due to inflation—for a net payment in purchasing-power terms of $5, or 5 percent. Thus, in the economically relevant sense, the 8 percent loan at 3 percent inflation is actually more expensive than the 12 percent loan at 10 percent inflation.

As we will learn in Chapter 6, the failure to understand this principle has caused problems for our tax laws, for the financial system, and for public utilities. In Chapter 15 we will see that it has even led to misunderstanding of the size and nature of the government budget deficit.

IDEA 6 DO BUDGET DEFICITS BURDEN FUTURE GENERATIONS?

The political struggle to reduce the federal budget deficit has been in the news for 15 years now. First President Reagan and then President Bush argued that raising taxes is worse than tolerating the deficit, a claim disputed by many. Critics objected that deficits hold dire consequences—including higher interest rates, more inflation, a stagnant economy, and an irksome burden on future Americans. Finally, during the Clinton administration, a large deficit-reduction package was enacted into law in 1993, and a political brouhaha arose in 1995–1996 over how to balance the budget.

The conflicting claims and counterclaims that have marked this debate are bound to confuse the layperson. Who is right? Are deficits really malign or benign influences on our economy? The answers, economists insist, are so complicated that the only correct short answer is: It all depends. The precise factors on which the answers depend are important enough to merit an entire chapter (Chapter 15). There we will learn that a budget deficit may or may not burden future generations, depending on its size and on the reasons for its existence.

IDEA 7 THE OVERWHELMING IMPORTANCE OF PRODUCTIVITY GROWTH IN THE LONG RUN

In Geneva, a worker in a watch factory now turns out roughly 100 times as many mechanical watches per year as her ancestors did three centuries earlier. The *productivity* of labor (output per hour of work) in cotton production has probably gone up more than 1,000-fold in 200 years. It is estimated that rising labor productivity has increased the standard of living of a typical American worker about 7-fold in the past century. This means that Americans now enjoy about seven times as much clothing, housewares, and luxury goods as did a typical inhabitant of the United States 100 years ago.

Economic issues such as inflation, unemployment, and international trade are important to us all and will receive much attention in this book. But in the long run nothing has as great an effect on our material well-being and the amounts society can afford to spend on hospitals, schools, and social amenities as the rate of growth of productivity. Chapter 20 points out that what appears to be a small increase in productivity growth can have a huge effect on a country's standard of living over a long period of time because productivity compounds like the interest on savings in a bank.

Similarly, a slowdown in productivity growth that persists for a substantial number of years can have a devastating effect on standards of living. After 1973, productivity growth in the United States, like that of other industrial countries, suffered a serious decline. Between 1959 and 1973, the productivity of American workers rose at an annual rate of about 2.85 percent, but since then that growth rate has averaged only about 1.07 percent per year. If productivity growth in the latter period had matched that of the earlier period, average income per person in the United States would now be about 50 percent greater than it actually is!

IDEA 8 THE SURPRISING PRINCIPLE OF COMPARATIVE ADVANTAGE

The Japanese economy produces many products that Americans buy in huge quantities—including cars, TV sets, cameras, and electronic equipment. American manufacturers often complain about the competition and demand protection from the flood of imports that, in their view, threatens American standards of living. Is this view justified?

Economists think not. They maintain that both sides must gain from international trade. But what if the Japanese were able to produce *everything* more cheaply than we can? Would it not then be true that Americans would be thrown out of work and that our nation would be impoverished?

A remarkable result, called the law of *comparative advantage,* shows that even in this extreme case, the two nations can still benefit by trading and that each can gain as a result! We will explain this principle fully in Chapter 17, where we will also note some potentially valid arguments in favor of providing special incentives for particular domestic industries. But for now a simple parable will make the reason clear.

Suppose Sally grows up on a farm and is a whiz at plowing, but she is also a successful country singer who earns $4,000 a performance. Should Sally turn down singing engagements to leave time for plowing? Of course not. Instead she should hire Alfie, a much less efficient farmer, to do the plowing for her. Sally may be a better farmer. But she earns so much more by specializing in singing that it makes sense to leave the farming to Alfie. Alfie, though a less skilled farmer than Sally, is an even worse singer. Thus, Alfie earns a living by specializing in the job at which he at least has a *comparative* advantage (his farming is not as bad as his singing), and both Alfie and Sally gain. The same is true of two countries. Even if one of them is more efficient at everything, both countries can gain by producing the things they do best *comparatively.*

EPILOGUE

These, then, are eight of the more fundamental concepts in this book—ideas that we hope you will retain **Beyond the Final Exam.** There is no need to master them right now, for you will hear much more about each as the book progresses. Instead, keep them in mind as you read—we will point them out to you as they occur—and look back over this list at the end of the course. You may be amazed to see how natural, or even obvious, they will seem then.

INSIDE THE ECONOMIST'S TOOL KIT

Now that you have some idea of the kinds of issues economists deal with, you should know something about the way they grapple with these problems.

ECONOMICS AS A DISCIPLINE

Economics has something of a split personality. Although clearly the most rigorous of the social sciences, it nevertheless looks decidedly more "social" than "scientific" when compared with, say, physics. An economist must be a jack of several trades, borrowing modes of investigation from numerous fields.

Mathematical reasoning is used extensively in economics, but so is historical study. And neither looks quite the same as when practiced by a mathematician or a historian. Statistical inference plays a major role in modern economic inquiry; but economists have had to modify standard statistical procedures to fit the kinds of data they analyze.

An introductory course in economics will not make you an economist; but it should help you approach social problems dispassionately. You will not find solutions to all society's economic problems in this book. But you should learn how to pose questions in ways that will help produce answers that are both useful and illuminating.

THE NEED FOR ABSTRACTION

Some students find economics unduly abstract and "unrealistic." The stylized world envisioned by economic theory seems only a distant cousin to the world they know. There is an old joke about three people—a chemist, a physicist, and an economist—stranded on an island with an ample supply of canned food but no tools to open the cans. The chemist thinks that lighting a fire under the cans would expand their contents and cause the cans to burst. The physicist advocates building a catapult with which they could smash the cans against some nearby boulders. The economist's suggestion? "Assume we have a can opener."

Economic theory *does* make unrealistic assumptions; you will encounter many of them in the pages that follow. But this propensity to abstract from reality results from the incredible complexity of the economic world, not from any fondness economists have for sounding absurd.

Compare the chemist's simple task of explaining the interactions of compounds in a chemical reaction with the economist's complex task of explaining the interactions of people in an economy. Are molecules motivated by greed or altruism, by envy or ambition? Do they ever emulate other molecules? Do forecasts about them influence their behavior? People, of course, do all these things, and many, many more. It is therefore vastly more difficult to predict human behavior than to predict chemical reactions. If economists tried to keep track of every aspect of human behavior, they would never get anywhere. Thus:

Abstraction from unimportant details is necessary to understand the functioning of anything as complex as the economy.

ABSTRACTION means ignoring many details in order to focus on the most important elements of a problem.

To appreciate why economists **abstract** from details, imagine the following hypothetical situation. You have just arrived, for the first time in your life, in Los Angeles. You are now at the Los Angeles Civic Center. This is the point marked *A* in Figures 1-1 and 1-2, which are alternative maps of part of Los Angeles. You

FIGURE 1-1 MAP 1

Map 1 gives complete details of the road system of Los Angeles. If you are like most people, you will find it hard to read and not very useful for figuring out how to get from the Civic Center (point *A*) to the Los Angeles County Museum of Art (point *B*). For this purpose, the map is far too detailed, though for some other purposes (for example, locating some small street in Hollywood), it may be the best map available.

SOURCE: © MCMLXXV by North American Maps, P.O. Box 5850, San Francisco, CA 94101.

want to drive to the Los Angeles County Museum of Art, marked *B* on each map. Which map would you find more useful? You will notice that Map 1 (Figure 1-1) has the full details of the Los Angeles road system. Consequently, it requires a major effort to read it. In contrast, Map 2 (Figure 1-2) omits many minor roads so that the freeways and major arteries stand out more clearly.

Most strangers to the city would prefer Map 2. With its guidance, they are likely to find the museum in a reasonable amount of time, even though they might have found a slightly shorter route by careful calculation and planning using Map 1. Map 2 seems to *abstract* successfully from a lot of confusing details while retaining the essential aspects of the city's geography. Economic theories strive to do the same thing.

Map 3 (Figure 1-3), which shows little more than the major interstate routes that pass through the greater Los Angeles area, illustrates a danger of which all theorists must beware. Armed only with the information provided on this map, you might have a hard time finding the art museum. Instead of a useful idealization of the Los Angeles road network, the map makers have produced a map that is oversimplified for our purpose. Too much has been assumed away. Of course, this map was never intended to be used as a detailed tourist guide, which brings us to an important point:

There is no such thing as one "right" degree of abstraction for all analytic purposes. The proper degree of abstraction depends on the objective of the analysis. A model that is a gross oversimplification for one purpose may be needlessly complicated for another.

FIGURE 1-2

MAP 2

Map 2 shows a different perspective of Los Angeles. Minor roads are eliminated—we might say, *assumed away*—in order to present a clearer picture of where the major arteries and freeways go. As a result of this simplification, several ways of getting from the Civic Center (point *A*) to the Los Angeles County Museum of Art (point *B*) stand out clearly. For example, we can take the Hollywood Freeway west to Alvarado Blvd. south, then west on Wilshire Blvd. The museum is on the right. While we might find a shorter route by poring over the details of Map 1, most of us will feel more comfortable with Map 2.

FIGURE 1-3

Map 3 strips away still more details of the Los Angeles road system. In fact, only major trunk roads and freeways remain. This map may be useful for passing through the city or getting around it, but it will not be of much help to the tourist who wants to see the sights of Los Angeles. For this purpose, too many details are missing.

MAP 3

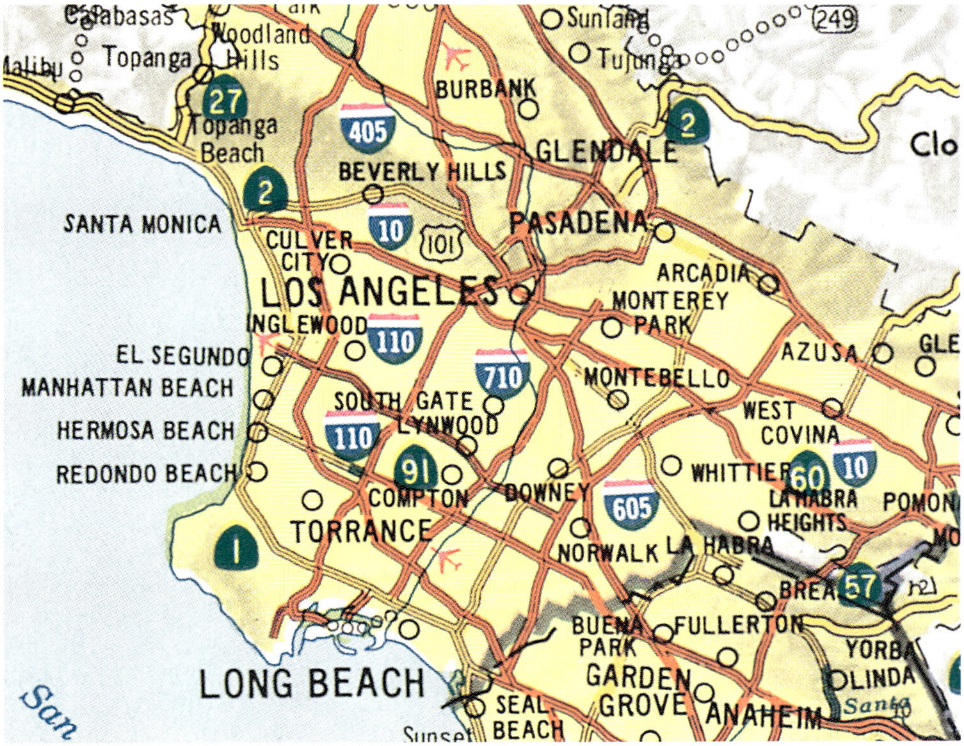

Economists are constantly treading the thin line between Map 2 and Map 3, between useful generalization about complex issues and gross distortions of the pertinent facts. How can they tell when they have abstracted from reality just enough? There is no objective answer to this question, which is why applied economics is as much art as science. One of the things distinguishing good economics from bad economics is the degree to which analysts are able to find the factors that constitute the equivalent of Map 2 (rather than Maps 1 or 3) for the problem at hand. It is not always easy to do.

For example, suppose you want to learn why different people have different incomes, why some are fabulously rich while others are abjectly poor. People differ in many ways, too many to enumerate, much less to study. The economist must ignore most of these details in order to focus on the important ones. While the color of a person's hair or eyes is probably not important, the color of his or her skin certainly is. Height and weight may not matter, but education probably does. Proceeding in this way, we pare Map 1 down to the manageable dimensions of Map 2. But there is a danger of going too far, stripping away some of the crucial factors, and winding up with Map 3.

THE ROLE OF ECONOMIC THEORY

A person "can stare stupidly at phenomena; but in the absence of imagination they will not connect themselves together in any rational way." These words of the renowned American philosopher-scientist C. S. Peirce succinctly express the crucial role of theory in scientific inquiry. What do we mean by a theory?

A **THEORY** is a deliberate simplification of relationships whose purpose is to explain how those relationships work.

To an economist or natural scientist, the word **theory** means something different from what it means in common parlance. In scientific usage, a theory is *not* an untested assertion of alleged fact. The statement that vitamin E provides protection against cancer is not a theory; it is a *hypothesis,* which will prove to be true or false once the right sorts of experiments have been completed.

Instead, a theory is a deliberate simplification (abstraction) of factual relationships that attempts to explain how those relationships work. It is an *explanation* of the mechanism behind observed phenomena. Thus, gravity forms the basis of theories that describe and explain the paths of the planets. Similarly, Keynesian theory (discussed in Parts II and III) seeks to describe and explain how government policies affect the path of the national economy.

Economic theory has acquired an unsavory public image in recent years—partly because of inaccurate predictions by some economists, partly because doctrinal disputes have spilled over into the news media, and partly because some politicians have found it expedient to scoff at economists. This bad image is unfortunate because theorizing is essential to provide a logical structure for organizing and analyzing economic data. Without theory, economists could only "stare stupidly" at the world. With theory, they can attempt to understand it.

People who have never studied economics often draw a false distinction between *theory* and *practical policy.* Politicians and business people, in particular, often reject abstract economic theory as something that is best ignored by "practical" people. The irony of these statements is that:

It is precisely the concern for policy that makes economic theory so necessary and important.

If we could not change the economy through public policy, economics could be a historical and descriptive discipline, asking, for example, what happened in the United States during the Great Depression of the 1930s. But deep concern about public policy forces economists to go beyond historical questions. To analyze policy options, they are forced to deal with possibilities *that have not actually occurred.*

For example, to learn how to prevent economic depressions, they must investigate whether the Great Depression of the 1930s could have been avoided by more astute government policies. As Peirce suggested, not even a lifetime of ogling at real-world data will answer such a question.

Two variables are said to be **CORRELATED** if they tend to go up or down together. But correlation need not imply causation.

Indeed, the facts can sometimes be highly misleading. Data often indicate that two variables move up and down together. But this statistical **correlation** does not prove that either variable *causes* the other. For example, people drive their cars more slowly when it rains, and there are also more traffic accidents. But this correlation does not mean that slow driving causes accidents. Rather, we understand that both phenomena are caused by a common underlying factor—more rain. How do we know this? Not just by looking at the correlation (the degree of similarity) between data on accidents and driving speeds. Data alone tell us little about cause and effect. We must use some simple theory as part of our analysis.

Similarly, most economic issues hinge on some question of cause and effect. So simply observing correlations in data is not enough. Only a combination of theoretical reasoning and data analysis can hope to provide useful answers. We must first proceed deductively from assumptions to conclusions and then test the conclusions against data. In that way, we may hope to understand *how,* if at all, different government policies will lead to a lower unemployment rate.

Statistical correlation need not imply causation. Some theory is usually needed to interpret data.

WHAT IS AN ECONOMIC "MODEL"?

An **ECONOMIC MODEL** is a simplified, small-scale version of some aspect of the economy. Economic models are often expressed in equations, by graphs, or in words.

An **economic model** is a representation of a theory or a part of a theory, often used to gain insight into cause and effect. The notion of a "model" is familiar enough to children; and economists—like other scientists—use the term in much the same way that children do.

A child's model automobile or airplane looks and operates much like the real thing, but it is much smaller and much simpler, and so it is easier to manipulate and understand. Engineers for General Motors and Boeing also build models of cars and planes. While their models are far bigger and much more elaborate than a child's toy, they use them for much the same purposes: to observe the workings of these vehicles "up close," to experiment with them in order to see how they might behave under different circumstances. ("What happens if I do this?") From these experiments, they make educated guesses as to how the real-life version will perform.

Economists use models for similar purposes. A. W. Phillips, the famous engineer-turned-economist who discovered the "Phillips curve" (discussed in Chapter 16), was talented enough to construct a working model of the determination of national income in a simple economy, using colored water flowing through pipes. For years this contraption, depicted in Figure 1-4, has graced the basement

FIGURE 1-4 THE PHILLIPS MACHINE

The late Professor A. W. Phillips, while teaching at the London School of Economics in the early 1950s, built this machine to illustrate Keynesian theory. This is the same theory that we will explain with words and diagrams later in the book; but Phillips's background as an engineer enabled him to depict the theory with the help of tubes, valves, and pumps. Because economists are not very good plumbers, few of them try to build models of this sort; most rely on paper and pencil instead. But the two sorts of models fulfill precisely the same role. They simplify reality in order to make it understandable.

of the London School of Economics. However, most economists lack Phillips's manual dexterity, so economic models are generally built with paper and pencil rather than with hammer and nails.

Because many of the models used in this book are depicted in diagrams, we explain the construction and use of various types of graphs in the appendix to this chapter. But sometimes economic models are expressed only in words. Don't be put off by seemingly abstract models. Think of them as useful road maps. And remember how hard it would be to find your way around Los Angeles without one.

REASONS FOR DISAGREEMENTS: IMPERFECT INFORMATION AND VALUE JUDGMENTS

"If all the earth's economists were laid end to end, they could not reach an agreement," or so the saying goes. Politicians and reporters are fond of pointing out that economists can be found on both sides of many public policy issues. If economics is a science, why do economists quarrel so much? After all, astronomers do not debate whether the earth revolves around the sun or vice versa.

The question reflects a misunderstanding of the nature of science. Disputes are normal at the frontier of any science. For example, astronomers once did argue, and quite vociferously, over whether the earth revolves around the sun. Nowadays, they argue about black holes, gamma-ray bursts, brown dwarfs, and other esoterica. These arguments go mostly unnoticed by the public because few of us understand what they are talking about. But economics is a *social* science, so its disputes are aired in public. All sorts of people are eager to join economic debates about inflation, pollution, poverty, and the like.

Furthermore, the fact is that economists agree on much more than is commonly supposed. Virtually all economists, regardless of their politics, agree that rent controls can ruin a city (Chapter 4), and that free trade among nations is preferable to the erection of barriers through tariffs and quotas (see Chapter 17). The list could go on and on. It is probably true that the issues about which economists agree *far* exceed the subjects on which they disagree.

Finally, many disputes among economists are not scientific disputes at all. Sometimes the pertinent facts are simply unknown. This makes it difficult to agree on a concrete policy proposal.

Another important source of disagreements is that economists, like other people, come in all political stripes: conservative, middle-of-the-road, liberal, radical. Each may have different values and a different view of what constitutes a good society. So each may hold a different view of the "right" solution to a public policy problem, even if they agree on the underlying analysis.

For example, we noted early in this chapter that anti-inflation policies are likely to cause recessions. Using tools we will describe in Part III, many economists believe they can even measure how deep a recession we must endure to reduce inflation by a given amount. Is it worth having 2.6 million more people out of work for a year to cut the inflation rate by 1 percent? An economist cannot answer this any more than a nuclear physicist could have determined whether dropping the atomic bomb on Hiroshima was a good idea. The decision rests on judgments about the moral trade-off between inflation and unemployment, judgments that can be made only by the citizenry through its elected officials.

While economic science can contribute the best theoretical and factual knowledge there is on a particular issue, the final decision on policy questions often rests either on information that is not currently available or on tastes and ethical opinions about which people differ (the things we call "value judgments"), or on both.

Earlier in this chapter, we said that economics cannot provide all the *answers* but can teach you how to ask the right *questions.* Now you know some reasons why. By the time you finish studying this book, you should have a good understanding of when the right course of action turns on disputed facts, when on value judgments, and when on some combination of the two.

LAST WORD: COMMON SENSE IS NOT ALWAYS RELIABLE

Many people think sound decisions are just a matter of "common sense." If that were so—if untrained but intelligent observers could reach the right economic decisions using only their instincts and intuition—there would be little reason to study economics. Unfortunately, common sense is not always a reliable guide in economics.

True, there are many cases where it is not misleading. Most people undoubtedly realize, for example, that a surge in demand for a product is likely to raise its price, at least for a while. They also understand that increases in the prices of American goods will reduce the quantity we can export to foreign countries.

But many economic relationships are counterintuitive. We have seen, for example, that an interest rate of 8 percent under some circumstances may make borrowing more expensive than a 12 percent interest rate under other circumstances. We will see later that rent controls on low-rent apartments may make the lives of the poor more miserable, not less.

We will explain these and many more counterintuitive economic relationships in this book. By the end, you will have a better sense of when common sense works and when it fails. You will be able to recognize common fallacies that are all too often offered as pearls of wisdom by public figures, the press, and television commentators.

SUMMARY

1. To help you get the most out of your first course in economics, we have devised a list of eight important ideas that you will want to remember **Beyond the Final Exam.** Here we list them briefly, indicating where each idea occurs in the book.
   (1) In a **voluntary exchange,** both parties must expect to benefit (Chapters 3 and 17).
   (2) To make a rational decision, the **opportunity cost** of an action must be measured, because only this calculation will tell the decision maker what she has given up (Chapter 3).
   (3) Lawmakers who try to repeal the *"law" of supply and demand* are liable to open a Pandora's box of troubles they never expected (Chapter 4).
   (4) Most government policies that reduce inflation are likely to intensify the unemployment problem, and vice versa—the *inflation-unemployment trade-off* (Chapter 16).
   (5) Interest rates that appear very high may actually be very low if they are accompanied by high inflation (Chapter 6).
   (6) *Budget deficits* may or may not be advisable, depending on the circumstances (Chapter 15).
   (7) In the long run, *productivity* is almost the only thing that matters for a nation's material well-being (Chapter 20).
   (8) Two nations can gain from international trade, even if one is more efficient at making everything—the *law of comparative advantage* (Chapter 17).
2. Economics is a broad-ranging discipline that uses a variety of techniques and approaches to address important social questions.
3. Because of the great complexity of human behavior, economists are forced to **abstract** from many details,

to make *generalizations* that they know are not quite true, and to organize what knowledge they have in terms of some theoretical structure called a "model."

4. **Correlation** need not imply *causation*.
5. Economists use simplified models to understand the real world and predict its behavior, much as a child uses a **model** railroad to learn how trains work.
6. While these models, if skillfully constructed, can illuminate important economic problems, they rarely can answer the questions that confront policymakers. Value judgments are needed for this purpose, and the economist is no better equipped than anyone else to make them.
7. Common sense is often an unreliable guide to the right economic decision.

KEY TERMS

Voluntary exchange
Opportunity cost
Comparative advantage
Productivity
Abstraction and generalization
Theory
Correlation versus causation
Economic model

QUESTIONS FOR REVIEW

1. Think about how you would construct a "model" of how your college is governed. Which officers and administrators would you include and exclude from your model if the objective were:
   a. to explain how decisions on financial aid are made?
   b. to explain the quality of the faculty?

   Relate this to the map example in the chapter.
2. Relate the process of "abstraction" to the way you take notes in a lecture. Why do you not try to transcribe every word the lecturer utters? Why do you not just write down the title of the lecture and stop there? How do you decide, roughly speaking, on the correct amount of detail?
3. Explain why a government policymaker cannot afford to ignore economic theory.

APPENDIX THE GRAPHS USED IN ECONOMIC ANALYSIS[1]

Economic models are frequently analyzed and explained with the help of graphs; and this book is full of graphs. But that is not the only reason for you to study how they work. Most of you will deal with graphs in the future, perhaps frequently. They appear in newspapers. Governments use them to keep track of the amount of money that they owe to foreign countries. Business firms use them to check their profit and sales performance. Persons concerned with social issues use them to examine trends in ethnic composition of cities and the relation of felonies to family income.

Graphs are invaluable because of the way they facilitate interpretation and analysis of both data and ideas. They enable the eye to take in at a glance important relationships that would be far less apparent from prose descriptions or long lists of numbers. But badly constructed graphs can confuse and mislead.

In this appendix we show how to read a graph that depicts a relationship between two variables, we define *slope* and describe how it is measured and interpreted, and finally, we explain how the behavior of three variables can be shown on a two-dimensional graph.

TWO-VARIABLE DIAGRAMS

Graphs are used to depict the behavior of economic variables such as the number of jobs in the United States or the number of computers produced per year.

A **variable** is something measured by a number; it is used to analyze what happens to other things when the size of that number changes (varies).

[1]Students who have a nodding acquaintance with geometry and feel quite comfortable with graphs can safely skip this appendix.

FIGURE 1-5 A DEMAND CURVE FOR NATURAL GAS IN ST. LOUIS

This demand curve shows the relationship between the price of natural gas and the quantity of it that will be demanded. For example, the point labeled *a* indicates that, at a price of $3 per thousand cubic feet (point *P*), the quantity demanded will be 80 billion cubic feet (point *Q*).

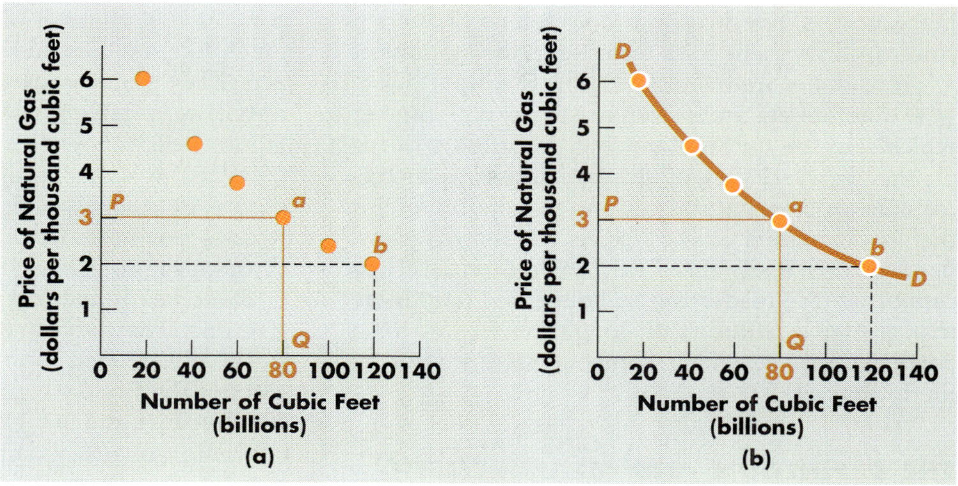

Much of the economic analysis in this and other books requires that we keep track of two variables simultaneously. For example, in studying the operation of markets, we will want to keep one eye on the *price* of a commodity and the other on the *quantity* bought and sold.

For this reason, economists frequently find it useful to display real or imaginary figures in a *two-dimensional graph,* which simultaneously represents the behavior of two economic variables. The numerical value of one variable is measured along the bottom of the graph (called the *horizontal axis*), starting from the point labeled "0," and the numerical value of the other is measured up the side of the graph (called the *vertical axis*), also starting from "0."

The "0" point in the lower left-hand corner of a graph where the two axes meet is called the **origin.** Both variables are equal to zero at the origin.

Figures 1-5(a) and 1-5(b) are typical graphs of economic analysis. They depict an (imaginary) *demand curve,* represented by the orange dots in Figure 1-5(a) and the heavy orange line in Figure 1-5(b). The graphs show the price of natural gas on their vertical axes and the quantity of gas people want to buy at each such price on the horizontal axes. The dots in Figure 1-5(b) are connected by the continuous orange curve labeled *DD.*

Economic diagrams are generally read like latitudes and longitudes on a map. On the demand curve in Figure 1-5, the point marked *a* represents a hypothetical combination of price and quantity demanded in St. Louis. By drawing a horizontal line leftward from that point to the vertical axis, we learn that the average price for gas in St. Louis is $3 per thousand cubic feet. By dropping a line straight down to the horizontal axis, we find that consumers want 80 billion cubic feet at this price, just as the statistics in Table 1-1 show. The other points on the graph give similar information. For example, point *b* indicates that if natural gas in St. Louis cost only $2 per thousand cubic feet, quantity demanded would be higher—it would reach 120 billion cubic feet.

Notice that information about price and quantity is *all* we can learn from the diagram. The demand curve will not tell us about the kinds of people who live in St. Louis, the sizes of their homes, or the

TABLE 1-1

QUANTITIES OF NATURAL GAS DEMANDED AT VARIOUS PRICES

Price (per thousand cubic feet)	$2	$3	$4	$5	$6
Quantity demanded (billions of cubic feet)	120	80	56	38	20

conditions of their furnaces. It tells us about the price and the quantity demanded at that price; no more, no less. Specifically, it does tell us that when price declines there is an increase in the amount of gas consumers are willing and able to buy.

A diagram abstracts from many details, some of which may be quite interesting, in order to focus on the two variables of primary interest—in this case, the price of natural gas and the amount of gas that is demanded at each price. All the diagrams used in this book share this basic feature. They cannot tell the reader the "whole story" any more than a map's latitude and longitude figures for a particular city can make someone an authority on life in that city.

THE DEFINITION AND MEASUREMENT OF SLOPE

One of the most important features of the diagrams of economists is the steepness with which the line, or curve, being sketched runs uphill or downhill as we move to the right. The demand curve in Figure 1-5 clearly slopes downhill (the price falls) as we follow it to the right (that is, if more gas is to be demanded). In such instances we say that *the curve has a negative slope, or is negatively sloped, because one variable falls as the other one rises.*

The *slope of a straight line* is the ratio of the vertical change to the corresponding horizontal change as we move to the right along the line, or as it is often said, the ratio of the "rise" over the "run."

The four panels of Figure 1-6 show all the possible slopes for a straight-line relationship between two unnamed variables called Y (measured along the vertical axis) and X (measured along the horizontal axis). Figure 1-6(a) shows a negative slope, much like our demand curve. Figure 1-6(b) shows a positive slope, because variable Y rises (we go uphill) as variable X rises (as we move to the right). Figure 1-6(c) shows a *zero* slope, where the value of Y is the same irrespective of the value of X. Figure 1-6(d) shows an *infinite* slope, meaning that X does not have to change at all for Y to "leap through the roof."

Slope is a numerical concept, not just a qualitative one. The two panels of Figure 1-7 show two positively sloped straight lines with different slopes. The line in Figure 1-7(b) is clearly steeper. But by how much? The labels should help you compute the answer. In Figure 1-7(a) a horizontal movement, AB, of 10 units (13 − 3) corresponds to a vertical movement, BC, of 1 unit (9 − 8). So the slope is $BC/AB = 1/10$.

In Figure 1-7(b), the same horizontal movement of 10 units corresponds to a vertical movement of 3 units (11 − 8). So the slope is 3/10, which is larger.

By definition, the slope of any particular straight line is the same no matter where on that line we choose to measure it. That is why we can pick any horizontal distance, AB, and the corresponding slope triangle, ABC, to measure slope. But this is not true of lines that are curved.

Curved lines also have slopes, but the numerical value of the slope is different at every point.

The four panels of Figure 1-8 provide some examples of slopes of curved lines. The curve in

FIGURE 1-6 DIFFERENT TYPES OF SLOPE OF A STRAIGHT-LINE GRAPH

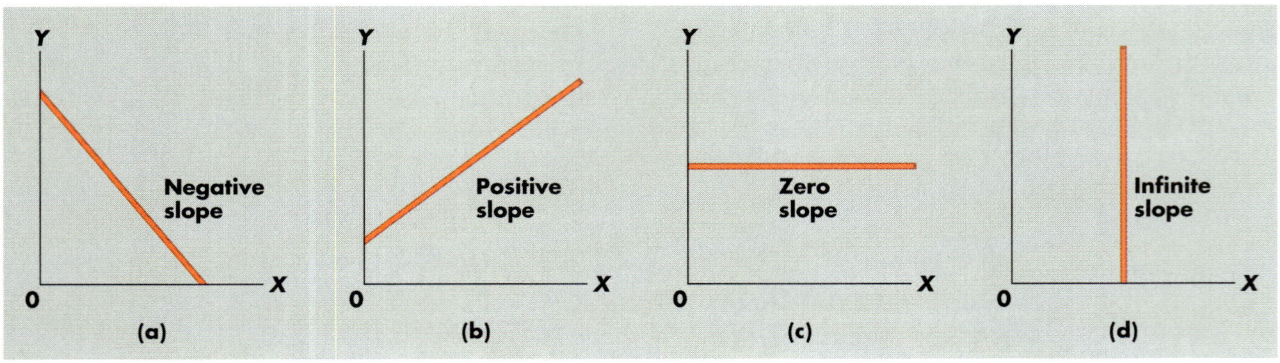

In Figure 1-6(a), the curve goes downward as we read from left to right, so we say it has a negative slope. The slopes in the other figures can be interpreted similarly.

FIGURE 1-7 HOW TO MEASURE SLOPE

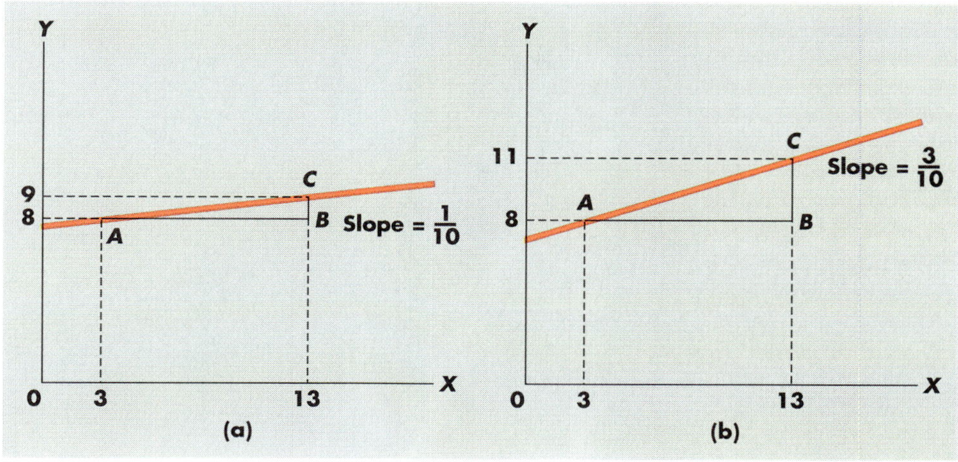

Slope indicates how much the graph rises per unit of movement from left to right. Thus, in Figure 1-7(b), as we go from point *A* to point *B*, we go 13 − 3 = 10 units to the right. But in that interval, the graph rises from the height of point *B* to the height of point *C*; that is, it rises 3 units. Consequently, the slope of the line is *BC*/*AB* = 3/10.

Figure 1-8(a) has a negative slope everywhere, while the curve in Figure 1-8(b) has a positive slope everywhere. But these are not the only possibilities. In Figure 1-8(c) we encounter a curve that has a positive slope at first but a negative slope later on. Figure 1-8(d) shows the opposite case: a negative slope followed by a positive slope.

It is possible to measure the slope of a smooth, curved line numerically *at any particular point*. This is done by drawing a *straight* line that *touches*, but does not *cut*, the curve at the point in question. Such a line is called a *tangent* to the curve.

The slope of a curved line at a particular point is the slope of the straight line that is tangent to the curve at that point.

In Figure 1-9 we have constructed tangents to a curve at two points. Line *tt* is tangent at point *C*, and line *TT* is tangent at point *F*. We can measure the slope of the curve at these two points by applying the definition above. The calculation for point *C*, then, is the following:

$$\text{Slope at point } C = \text{Slope of line } tt = \frac{(\text{Distance } BC)}{(\text{Distance } BA)}$$

$$= \frac{(3-6)}{(3-2)} = \frac{(-3)}{(1)} = -3$$

A similar calculation yields the slope of the curve at point *F*, which, as we can see from Figure 1-9, must be numerically smaller:

FIGURE 1-8 BEHAVIOR OF SLOPES IN CURVED GRAPHS

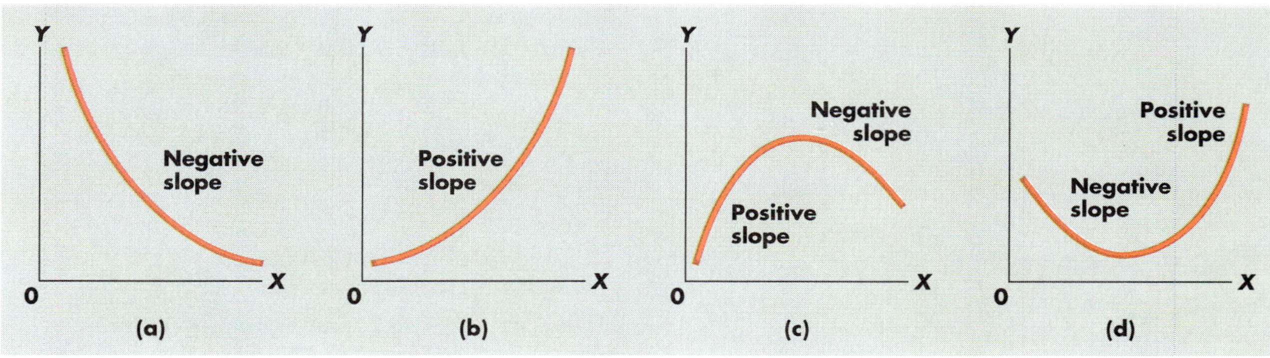

As Figures 1-8(c) and 1-8(d) indicate, where a graph is not a straight line it may have a slope that starts off as positive but that becomes negative farther to the right, or vice versa.

FIGURE 1-9 HOW TO MEASURE SLOPE AT A POINT ON A CURVED GRAPH

To find the slope at point *F*, draw the line *TT*, which is tangent to the curve at point *F*; then measure the slope of the straight-line tangent *TT*, as in Figure 1-7. The slope of the tangent is the same as the slope of the curve at point *F*.

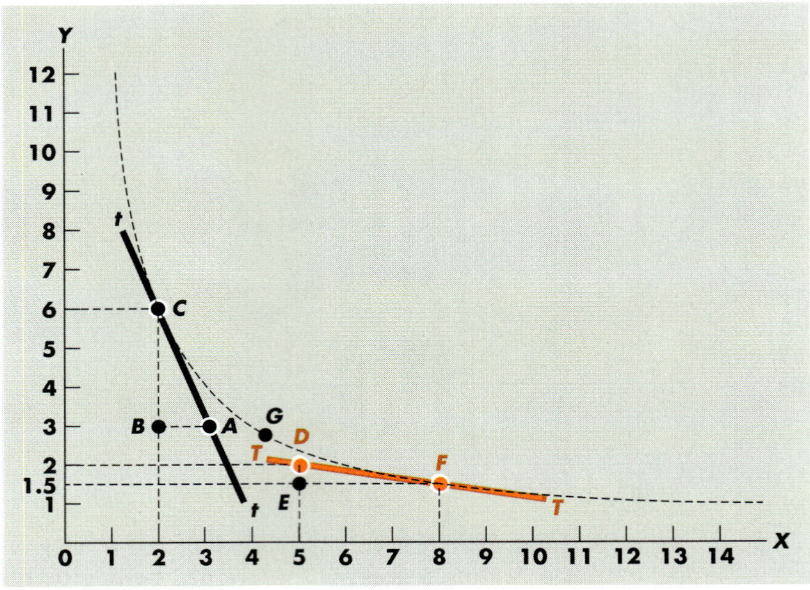

$$\text{Slope at point } F = \text{Slope of line } TT$$

$$= \frac{(1.5 - 2)}{(8 - 5)} = \frac{(-0.5)}{(3)} = -0.16$$

EXERCISE Show that the slope of the curve at point *G* is between −0.16 and −3.

What would happen if we tried to apply this graphical technique to the high point in Figure 1-8(c) or to the low point in Figure 1-8(d)? Take a ruler and try it. The tangents that you construct should be horizontal, meaning that they should have a slope exactly equal to zero. It is always true that where the slope of a smooth curve changes from positive to negative, or vice versa, there will be at least a single point with a zero slope.

Curves that have the shape of a hill, such as Figure 1-8(c), have a zero slope at their *highest* point. Curves that have the shape of a valley, such as Figure 1-8(d), have a zero slope at their *lowest* point.

RAYS THROUGH THE ORIGIN AND 45° LINES

The point at which a straight line cuts the vertical (*Y*) axis is called the *Y-intercept*. For example, the *Y*-intercept of the line in Figure 1-7(a) is a bit less than 8.

Lines whose *Y*-intercepts are zero, that is, lines that emanate from the zero point on a graph, have so many uses that they have been given a special name, a **ray through the origin,** or a **ray.**

Figure 1-10 contains three rays through the origin, and the slope of each is indicated in the diagram. The ray in the center—whose slope is 1—is particularly useful in many economic applications because it marks off points where *X* and *Y* are equal (as long as *X* and *Y* are measured in the same units). For example, at point *A* we have $X = 3$ and $Y = 3$, at point *B*, $X = 4$ and $Y = 4$, and a similar relation holds at any other point on that ray.

How do we know that this is always true for a ray whose slope is 1? If we start from the origin (where both *X* and *Y* are equal to zero) and the slope of the ray is 1, we know from the definition of slope that:

$$\text{Slope} = \frac{\text{(Vertical change)}}{\text{(Horizontal change)}} = 1$$

This implies that the vertical change and the horizontal change are always equal, so the two variables must always remain equal.

Rays through the origin with a slope of 1 are called **45° lines** because they form an angle of 45° with

FIGURE 1-10 RAYS THROUGH THE ORIGIN

Rays are straight lines drawn through the zero point on the graph (the *origin*). Three rays with different slopes are shown. The middle ray, the one with slope = +1, has two properties that make it particularly useful in economics: (1) It makes a 45° angle with either axis, and (2) any point on that ray (for example, point *A*) is exactly equal in distance from the horizontal and vertical axes (length *DA* = length *CA*). So if the items measured on the two axes are in equal units, then at any point on that ray, such as *A*, the number on the *X*-axis (the abscissa) will be the same as the number on the *Y*-axis (the ordinate).

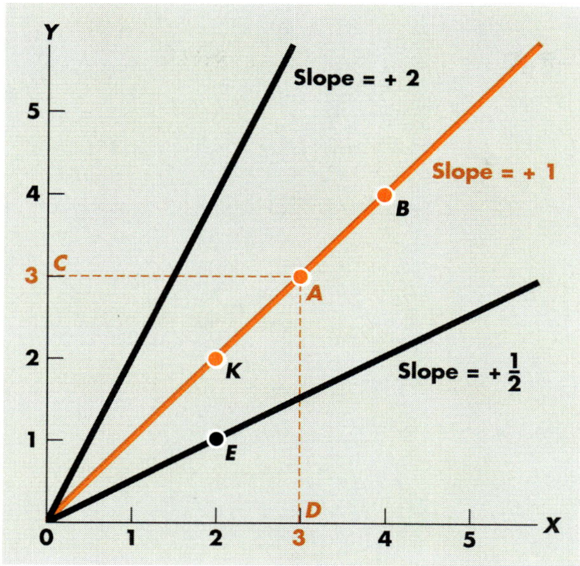

the horizontal axis. A 45° line marks off points where the variables measured on each axis have equal values.[2]

If a point representing some data is above the 45° line, we know that the value of *Y* exceeds the value of *X*. Correspondingly, whenever we find a point below the 45° line, we know that *X* is larger than *Y*.

SQUEEZING THREE DIMENSIONS INTO TWO: CONTOUR MAPS

Sometimes, because a problem involves more than two variables, two dimensions just are not enough, which is unfortunate since paper is only two dimensional. When we study the decision-making process of a business firm, for example, we may want to keep track simultaneously of three variables: how much labor the firm employs, how much raw material it imports from foreign countries, and how much output it creates.

Luckily, there is a well-known device for collapsing three dimensions into two, namely a *contour map*. Figure 1-11 is a contour map of the Grand Teton mountains in the state of Wyoming. On the irregularly shaped "rings" we find numbers (such as 10,000 and 12,400) indicating the height above sea level at that particular spot on the mountain. Thus, unlike the more usual sort of map, which gives only latitudes and longitudes, this contour map exhibits three pieces of information about each point: latiude, longitude, and altitude.

Figure 1-12 looks more like the contour maps encountered in economics. It shows how some third variable, called *Z* (think of it as a firm's output, for example), varies as we change either variable *X* (think of it as a firm's employment) or variable *Y* (think of it as the use of imported raw material). Just like the map of the Grand Tetons, any point on the diagram conveys three pieces of data. At point *A*, we can read off the values of *X* and *Y* in the conventional way (*X* is 30 and *Y* is 40), and we can also note the value of *Z* by checking to see on which contour line point *A* falls. (It is on the *Z* = 20 contour.) So point *A* is able to tell us that 30 hours of labor and 40 yards of cloth produce 20 units of output.

While most of the analyses presented in this book will be based on the simpler, two-variable diagrams, contour maps will find their applications.

[2]The definition assumes both variables are measured in the same units.

FIGURE 1-11

A GEOGRAPHIC CONTOUR MAP

All points on any particular contour line represent geographic locations that are at the same height above sea level.

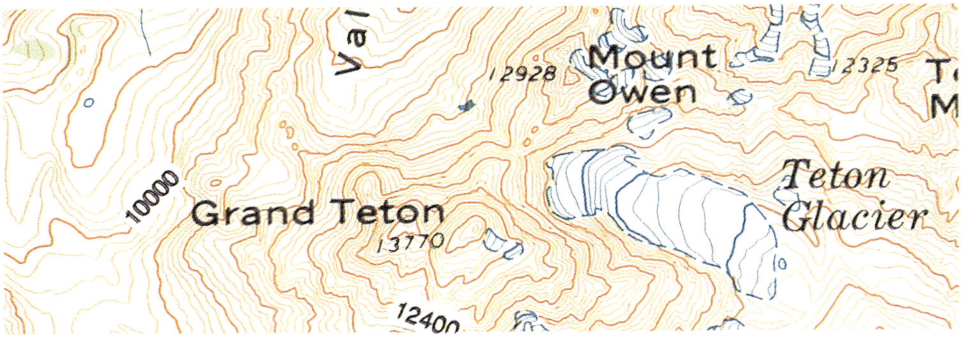

FIGURE 1-12

AN ECONOMIC CONTOUR MAP

In this contour map, all points on a given contour line represent different combinations of labor and raw materials capable of producing a given quantity of output. For example, all points on curve $Z = 20$ represent input combinations that can produce 20 units of output. Point A on that line means that the 20 units of output can be produced using 30 labor hours and 40 yards of cloth. Economists call such maps *production indifference maps*.

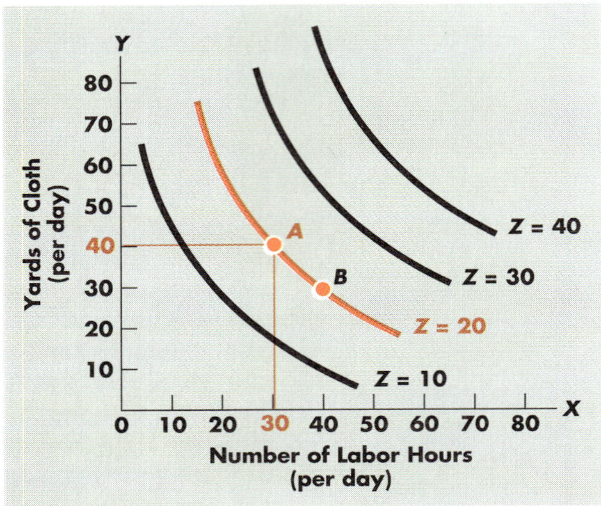

SUMMARY

1. Because graphs are used so often to portray economic models, it is important for students to acquire some understanding of their construction and use. Fortunately, the graphics used in economics are usually not very complex.
2. Most economic models are depicted in *two-variable diagrams*. We read data from these diagrams just as we read the latitude and longitude on a map: Each point represents the values of two **variables** at the same time.
3. In some instances, three variables must be shown at once. In these cases, economists use contour maps, which, as the name suggests, show "latitude," "longitude," and "altitude" all at the same time.
4. Often, the most important property of a line or curve drawn on a diagram will be its slope, which is defined as the ratio of the "rise" over the "run," or the vertical change divided by the horizontal change. Curves that go uphill as we move to the right have *positive slopes*, while curves that go downhill have *negative slopes*.
5. By definition, a *straight line* has the same *slope* wherever we choose to measure it. The *slope of a curved line* changes, but the slope at any point on the curve can be calculated by measuring the slope of a straight line *tangent to the curve* at that point.

KEY TERMS

Variable
Two-variable diagram
Horizontal and vertical axes
Origin (of a graph)
Slope of a straight (or curved) line
Negative, positive, zero, and infinite slope
Tangent to a curve
Y-intercept
Ray through the origin, or ray
45° line
Contour map

QUESTIONS FOR REVIEW

1. Look for a graph in your local newspaper, on the financial page or elsewhere. What does the graph try to show? Is someone trying to convince you of something with this graph?
2. Portray the following hypothetical data on a two-variable diagram:

Enrollment Data: University of Nowhere

Academic Year	Total Enrollment	Enrollment in Economics Courses
1990–1991	3,000	400
1991–1992	3,100	425
1992–1993	3,200	450
1993–1994	3,300	475
1994–1995	3,400	500

Measure the slope of the resulting line, and explain what this number means.

3. From Figure 1-9, calculate the slope of the curve at point G.
4. Sam believes that the number of job offers he will get depends on the number of courses in which his grade is B+ or better. He concludes from observation that the following figures are typical:

Number of grades of B+ or better	0	1	2	3	4
Number of job offers	2	4	5	6	7

Put these numbers into a graph like Figure 1-5(a). Measure and interpret the slopes between adjacent dots.

5. In Figure 1-10, determine the values of X and Y at point K and at point E. What do you conclude?
6. In Figure 1-12, interpret the economic meaning of points A and B. What do the two points have in common? What is the difference in their economic interpretation?

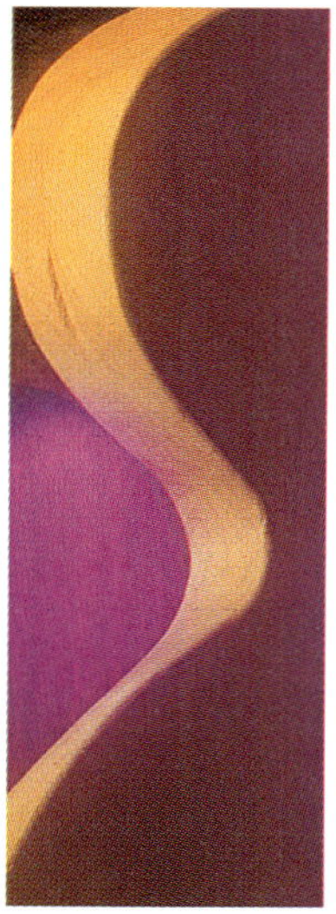

CHAPTER 2

The U.S. Economy: Myth and Reality

E pluribus unum (Out of many, one)
Motto on U.S. currency

This chapter introduces you to the U.S. economy. It might seem that no such introduction is necessary, for you have probably lived your entire life in the United States. Every time you work at a summer or part-time job, pay your college bills, or buy a hot dog, you not only participate in the American economy, but observe something about it.

But the casual impressions we acquire in our everyday lives, while sometimes correct, are often misleading. Experience shows that most Americans—not just students—are either unaware of or harbor grave misconceptions about some of the most basic economic facts. One popular myth holds that America is inundated with imported goods, mostly from Japan. Another is that business profits account for something like a third of the price we pay for a typical good or service. Also, "everyone knows" that federal government jobs have grown rapidly over the last few decades. In fact, none of these things is true.

So, before we begin to study elaborate theories about how the economy works, it is useful to get a more *accurate* picture of what our economy looks like.

THE AMERICAN ECONOMY: A THUMBNAIL SKETCH

The U.S. economy is the biggest national economy on earth, for two very different reasons. First, there are a lot of us. The population of the United States is nearly 264 million—making it the third most populous nation on earth after China and India. That vast total includes children, retirees, full-time students, institutionalized people, and the unemployed, none of whom produce much output. But the *working population* of the United States numbers about 125 million. As long as they are reasonably productive, that many people are bound to produce vast amounts of goods and services. And they do.

But population is not the main reason why the U.S. economy is by far the world's biggest. After all, India has about three and a half times the population of the United States, but its economy is smaller than that of Texas. The second reason why the U.S. economy is so large is that we are a very rich country. Because American workers are among the most productive in the world, our

FIGURE 2-1

POPULATION DENSITIES BY STATE, 1994

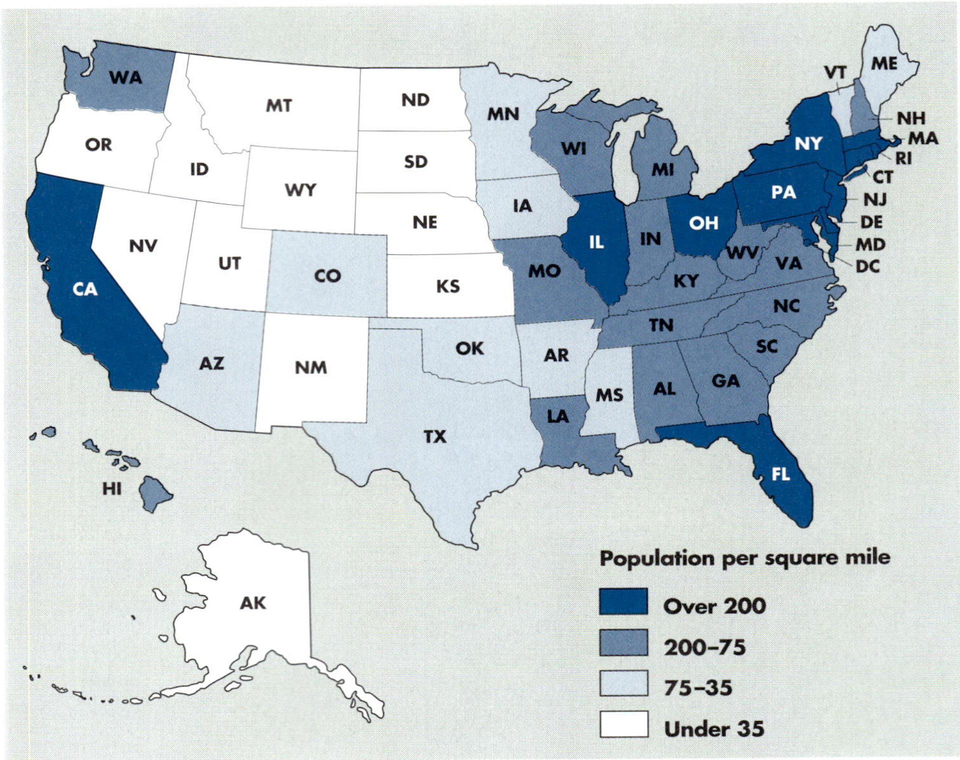

This map divides the United States into four groups according to population density. The most densely populated states (over 200 people per square mile) are displayed in dark blue; they are clearly concentrated in the Northeast. States with intermediate population densities (75 to 200 people and 35 to 75 people per square mile, respectively) are shown in medium blue and light blue. They are found all over the nation, but especially in the Midwest and South. The most sparsely populated states, shown in white, are mainly in the West.

SOURCE: U.S. Bureau of the Census, *Statistical Abstract of the United States: 1995* (115th ed.), Washington, D.C.: U.S. Government Printing Office, 1995.

economy produces almost $28,000 worth of goods and services for every living American. If each of the 50 states was a separate country, California would be the sixth largest national economy on earth!

OUTPUTS are the goods and services that consumers want to acquire.

INPUTS or **FACTORS OF PRODUCTION** are the labor, machinery, buildings, and natural resources used to make outputs.

Why some countries (like the United States) are so rich and others (like India) are so poor is one of the central questions of economics. It is useful to think of an economic system as a machine which takes **inputs** such as labor and other things we call **factors of production** and transforms them into **outputs,** or the things people want to consume. The American economic machine performs this task with extraordinary efficiency, while the Indian machine runs quite inefficiently. Learning why is one of the chief reasons to study economics.

Thus, what makes the American economy the center of world attention is our unique combination of prosperity and population. There are other rich countries in the world, like Germany and Switzerland, and there are other countries with huge populations, like China and India. But no nation combines a huge population with high per-capita income the way the United States does. Japan, with an economy about 65 percent as large as ours, is the only nation that comes close.

While we are a rich and populous country, the 50 states certainly were not created equal. Population density varies enormously—from a high of more than 1,000 people per square mile in crowded New Jersey, to a low of just one person per square mile in Alaska. Figure 2-1 shows where population density is highest and lowest. Income variations are much less pronounced. But, still, the

FIGURE 2-2

DISPOSABLE INCOME PER CAPITA BY STATE, 1994

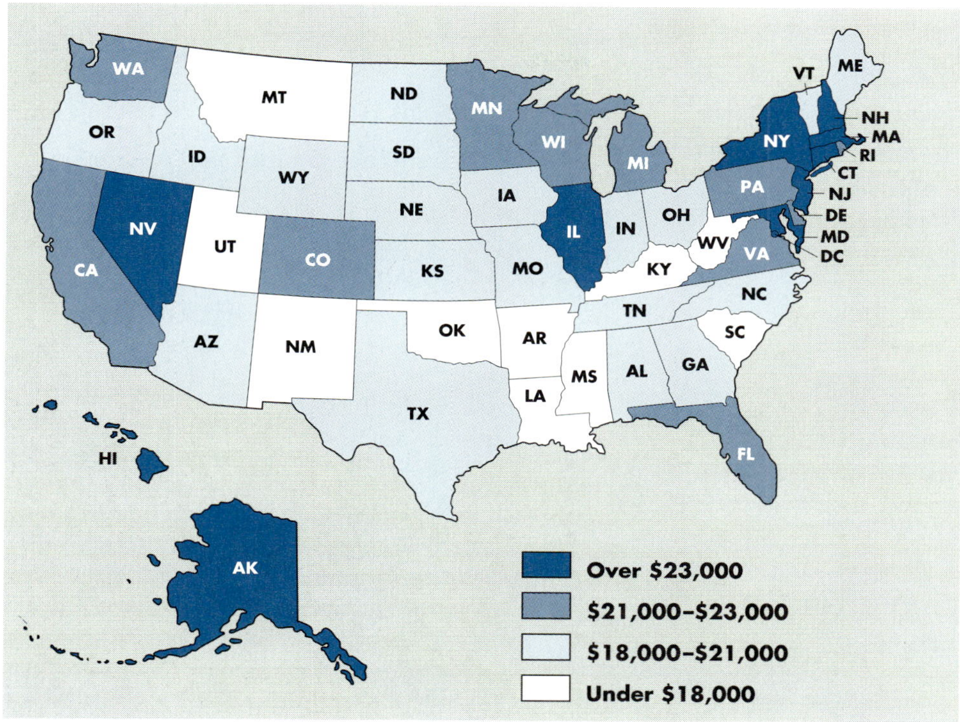

Although the United States is a unified economy, per-capita income nonetheless differs substantially from state to state. The richest states (incomes over $23,000 per capita), shown in dark blue, are concentrated in the Northeast, but also include California, Alaska, and Hawaii. The poorest states (per-capita incomes under $18,000, indicated in white, are found mainly in the South and West.

SOURCE: U.S. Bureau of the Census, *Statistical Abstract of the United States: 1995* (115th ed.), Washington, D.C.: U.S. Government Printing Office, 1995.

average income in Mississippi is only about half that in Connecticut. Figure 2-2 shows how per-capita income varies among the 50 states.

A PRIVATE-ENTERPRISE ECONOMY

Part of the secret of America's economic success is that free markets and private enterprise have flourished here. These days more than ever, private enterprise and capitalism are the rule, not the exception, around the globe. But the United States has taken the idea of the free market further than almost any other country. It remains "the land of opportunity."

Every country has a mixture of public and private ownership of property. Even in the darkest days of communism, Russians owned their own personal possessions. In our country, the post office and Tennessee Valley Authority are enterprises of the federal government, and many cities and states own and operate mass transit facilities and sports stadiums. But the United States stands out among the world's nations as among the most "privatized." Few industrial assets are publicly owned in America. Even many city bus companies, and almost all utilities (such as electricity, gas, and telephones), are run as private companies in the United States; in Europe, they are more often government enterprises.

GROSS DOMESTIC PRODUCT (GDP) is a measure of the size of an economy. It is, roughly speaking, the money value of all the goods and services produced in a year.

We are also one of the most "marketized" economies on earth. The standard measure of the total output of an economy is called **gross domestic product (or GDP),** a term which appears frequently in the news. The share of GDP that passes through markets in the United States is enormous. While government

TABLE 2-1

OPENNESS OF VARIOUS NATIONAL ECONOMIES, 1994 (AVERAGE OF IMPORTS AND EXPORTS, AS A SHARE OF GDP)

The Netherlands	53%
Germany	30%
Canada	25%
United Kingdom	20%
Japan	13%
United States	11%
Mexico	10%
Russia	6%

SOURCE: Central Intelligence Agency, *The World Factbook 1995*, online version (http://www.odci.gov/cia/publications/95fact/index.html).

purchases of goods and services amount to about 17 percent of GDP, much of that is purchased from private businesses. Direct government *production* of goods is extremely rare in our society, and government services amount to only about 11 percent of GDP.

A RELATIVELY "CLOSED" ECONOMY

All nations trade with one another, and we are no exception. Our annual exports exceed $700 billion and our annual imports exceed $800 billion. That's a lot of money. But America's international trade often gets more attention than it deserves. The fact is that we produce most of what we consume and consume most of what we produce.

Among the most severe misconceptions about the U.S. economy is the myth that this country no longer manufactures anything, but rather imports everything from, say, Japan. In fact, only about 12 percent of America's GDP is imported, and only about a fifth of that comes from Japan. Contrary to a second myth, if we include *services* along with *goods* in the total, America's exports—at almost 11 percent of GDP—almost (but not quite) equal imports.

Economists use the terms *open* and *closed* to indicate how important international trade is to a nation. A common measure of "openness" is the average of exports and imports, expressed as a share of GDP. Thus, the Netherlands is considered an extremely **open economy** because it imports and exports about 53 percent of its GDP. (See Table 2-1.) By this criterion, the United States stands out as among the most **closed economies** of the advanced, industrial nations. We export and import a smaller share of GDP than most of the countries listed in the table. Nonetheless, it is important to realize that this U.S. insularity is receding from the peak it attained just after World War II. U.S. exports rose from just 5.5 percent of GDP in 1972 to 9.0 percent in 1982 and 11 percent in 1994. We are increasingly becoming a great trading nation.

An economy is called relatively **OPEN** if its exports and imports constitute a large share of its GDP. An economy is considered relatively **CLOSED** if they constitute a small share.

A GROWING ECONOMY . . . BUT WITH INFLATION

The next salient fact about the U.S. economy is its growth; it gets bigger almost every year. Gross domestic product in 1996 was $7.6 billion, more than 10 times as much as in 1965. Figure 2-3 charts the upward march of GDP in the United States since 1959. The rise looks impressive indeed; GDP increased more than 14-fold over the period. But the impression left by the graph is misleading. There is less here than meets the eye, and we need to understand why.

SOME PERILS IN READING GRAPHS: A DIGRESSION[1]

Graphs like Figure 2-3, in which time is measured horizontally and some economic variable (in this case GDP) is measured vertically, are often used to portray economic data. They are called **time-series graphs** and you will find a number of them in this book as well as in newspapers and magazines. Many of you will routinely read time-series charts in your work after college. So it is vital to understand what they do and do not show.

A **TIME-SERIES GRAPH** is a type of two-variable diagram in which time is the variable measured along the horizontal axis. It shows how some variable changed as time passed.

By summarizing an immense amount of data in compact form, time-series graphs can be invaluable—offering an instant visual grasp of the course of events.

[1]We will deal with some additional problems, beyond those discussed here, in an appendix to this chapter.

FIGURE 2-3 THE GDP OF THE UNITED STATES SINCE 1959

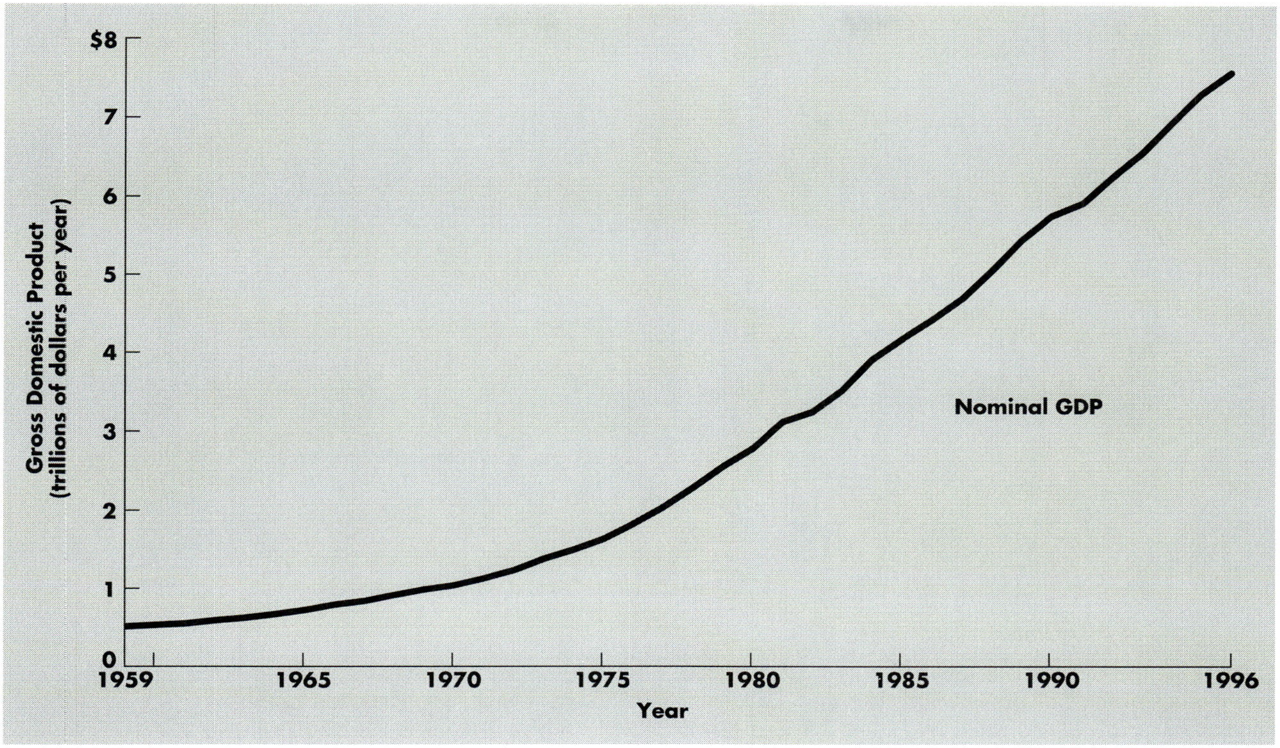

This time-series graph shows that the gross domestic product (GDP) of the United States, measured in dollars, has grown about 14-fold since 1959.

SOURCE: *Economic Report of the President 1997,* Washington, D.C.: U.S. Government Printing Office, 1997.

However, if misused, such graphs are very dangerous. They can easily mislead the inexperienced. Perhaps even more dangerous are the misconceptions perpetrated by people who draw graphs without sufficient care and, as a result, unintentionally mislead themselves and others. Consider Figure 2-3 as an example.

Most of the spectacular growth in GDP over this 36-year period was a reflection of two rather mundane facts. First, the price of almost everything rose between 1959 and 1996 because of **inflation;** in fact, average prices in 1996 were about five times higher than in 1959. Since each dollar in 1996 bought only about one-fifth of what it did in 1959, the dollar makes a rather poor measuring rod for comparing *production* in the two years. Most of the "growth" of GDP depicted in Figure 2-3 reflects inflation, not increases in output.

INFLATION refers to a sustained increase in the average level of prices.

Economists correct for inflation by a process called *deflating by a price index.* Proper deflation leads to the orange line in Figure 2-4, which shows the growth of GDP *in dollars of constant purchasing power.* Economists call this **real GDP.** By this truer measure, we find that output in 1996 was about 3 times as high as in 1959, not 14 times as high.

REAL GDP is the value of all the goods and services produced by an economy in a year, evaluated in dollars of constant purchasing power. Hence, inflation does not raise real GDP.

Second, there were many more Americans alive in 1996 than in 1959—49 percent more to be exact. So output *per person* rose by considerably less than even the orange line in Figure 2-4 indicates. The blue line corrects for *both* inflation *and* population growth by charting the time-series behavior of GDP *per capita* in dollars of constant purchasing power. Americans were indeed richer in 1996 than

FIGURE 2-4 NOMINAL GDP, REAL GDP, AND REAL GDP PER CAPITA, 1959–1996

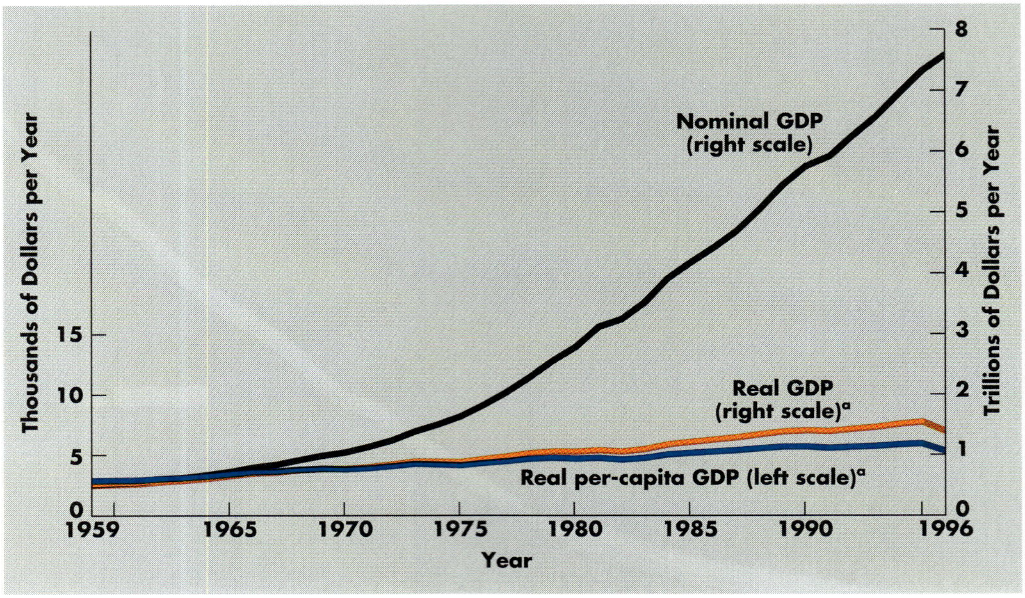

[a]1959 dollars.

The orange line shows that real GDP, that is, GDP measured in dollars of constant purchasing power, has grown much less than GDP in current dollars (black line). Thus, most of the "growth" indicated by Figure 2-3 was just inflation. The blue line takes the next step and corrects for the fact that America was a much bigger place—in terms of population—in 1996 than in 1959. It therefore gives a more accurate picture of the increase in standards of living.

SOURCE: *Economic Report of the President 1997,* Washington, D.C.: U.S. Government Printing Office, 1997.

in 1959, but not by nearly as much as a naïve look at Figure 2-3 might suggest. In fact, the American standard of living roughly doubled over this period, rather than rising 14-fold. How misleading it can be simply to "look at the facts!" There is a general lesson to be learned from this example:

The facts, as portrayed in a time-series graph, most assuredly do not "speak for themselves." Because almost everything grows in a growing economy, one must use judgment in interpreting growth trends. Depending on what kind of data are being analyzed, and for what purpose, it may be essential to correct for population growth, for rising prices, or for other distorting or misleading influences.

BUMPS ALONG THE GROWTH PATH: RECESSIONS

The bird's-eye view offered by Figure 2-4 conceals one more important fact: America's economic growth has been quite irregular. We have experienced alternating periods of good and bad times which are called *economic fluctuations* or sometimes just *business cycles*. In some years—five since 1959, to be exact—GDP actually declined. Such periods of *declining* economic activity are called **recessions.**

A **RECESSION** is a period of time during which the total output of the economy falls.

The bumps along the American economy's historic growth path are visible upon closer inspection of Figure 2-4, but stand out more clearly in Figure 2-5, which displays the same data in a different way. Here we plot not the *level* of real GDP each year, but rather its *growth rate*—the percentage change from one

FIGURE 2-5 THE GROWTH RATE OF REAL GDP IN THE UNITED STATES, 1960–1996

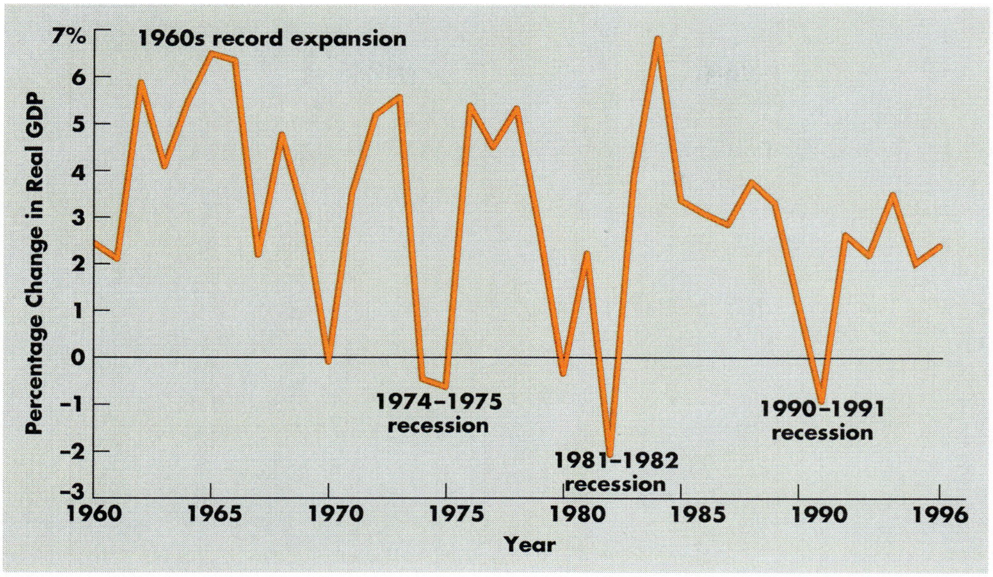

This diagram takes the same data used to construct the orange line in Figure 2-4, but uses it in a different way. Here we show the year-to-year growth rate (percentage increase) in real GDP from 1960 to 1996. Recessions stand out more clearly here as periods of *negative* growth.

SOURCE: *Economic Report of the President 1997,* Washington, D.C.: U.S. Government Printing Office, 1997.

year to the next. Now the booms and busts that delight and distress people—and swing elections—stand out clearly. From 1983 to 1984, for example, real GDP grew by close to 7 percent, which helped ensure the landslide reelection of Ronald Reagan. But from 1990 to 1991, real GDP actually fell by almost 1 percent, which helped Bill Clinton defeat George Bush.

One important consequence of these ups and downs in economic growth is that *unemployment* varies considerably from one year to the next. (See Figure 2-6.)

FIGURE 2-6 THE UNEMPLOYMENT RATE IN THE UNITED STATES, 1929–1996

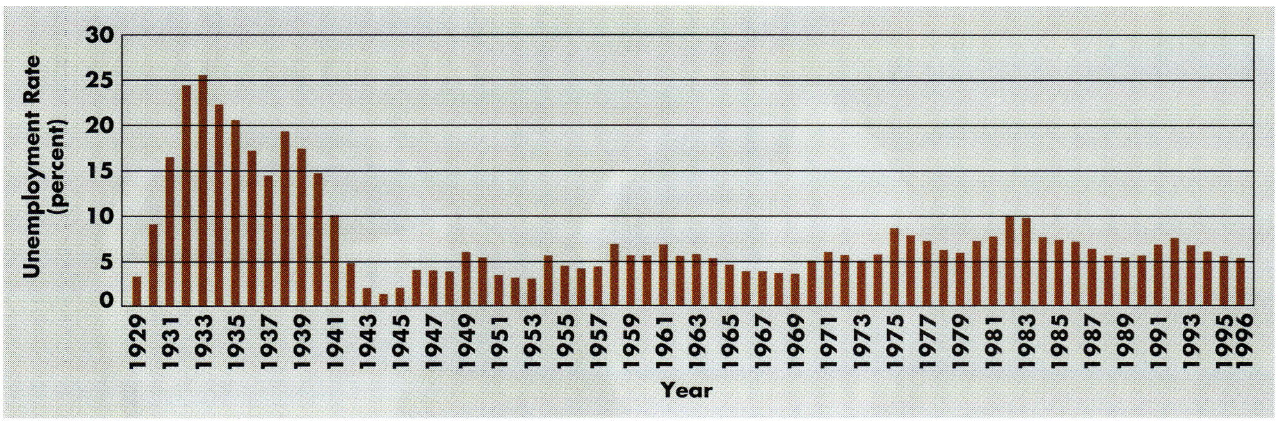

This time-series chart shows the ups and downs of the U.S. civilian unemployment rate annually since 1929.

SOURCE: *Economic Report of the President 1997,* Washington, D.C.: U.S. Government Printing Office, 1997; and Bureau of the Census, *Historical Statistics of the United States, Colonial Times to 1970,* Washington, D.C.: U.S. Government Printing Office, 1975.

During the Great Depression of the 1930s, unemployment ran as high as 25 percent of the work force. But it fell to barely over 1 percent during World War II. Within the last few years, the national unemployment rate has been as low as 5.4 percent (in February 1995) and as high as 7.7 percent (in June 1992). In human terms, that 2.3 percentage point difference meant about 2.6 million *more* jobless workers. Understanding why joblessness varies so dramatically, and what we can do about it, is another major reason for studying economics.

THE INPUTS: LABOR AND CAPITAL

Let us now return to the analogy of an economy as a machine turning inputs into outputs. The most important input is human labor: the men and women who run the machines, work behind the desks, and serve you in the stores.

THE AMERICAN WORK FORCE: WHO IS IT?

We have already mentioned that about 125 million Americans hold jobs. Roughly 54 percent of these workers are men and 46 percent are women. This ratio represents a drastic change from a generation or two ago, when most women worked only at home. (See Figure 2-7.) Indeed, the massive entrance of women into the paid labor force has been one of the major social transformations of American life during the second half of the 20th century. In 1950, just 29 percent of women worked in the marketplace; now more than 46 percent do. The expanding role of women in the labor market has raised many controversial questions—such as whether they are discriminated against (the evidence suggests that they are), whether employers should be compelled to provide maternity leave, and so on.

In contrast to women, teenagers represent a dwindling share of the American work force. (See Figure 2-8.) Young men and women aged 16 to 19 accounted for 8.6 percent of employment in 1974 but only 5.0 percent in 1996. As the baby boom gave way to the baby bust, people under 20 became scarce resources! Still, over 6 million teenagers hold jobs in the U.S. economy today. Most are low-wage jobs at fast-food restaurants, amusement parks, and the like. Relatively few teenagers can be found in the nation's factories.

FIGURE 2-7

THE COMPOSITION OF EMPLOYMENT BY SEX, 1950 AND 1996

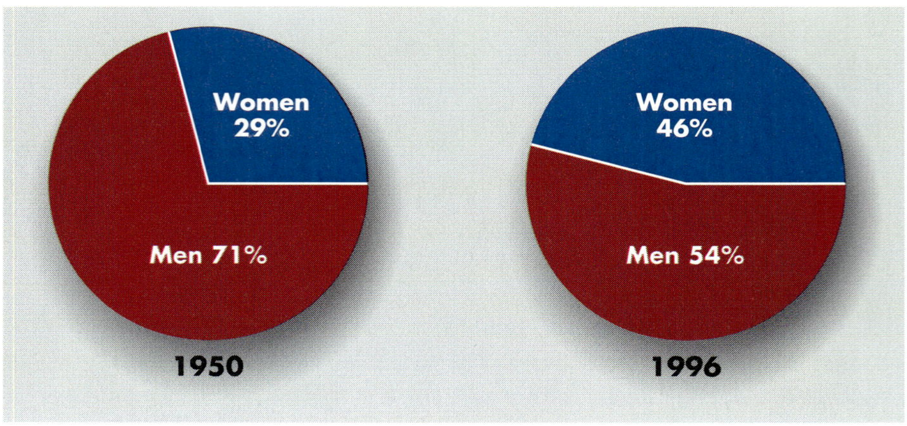

In 1950, just 29 percent of jobs were held by women. By 1996, this share had risen to 46 percent.

SOURCE: *Economic Report of the President 1997*, Washington, D.C.: U.S. Government Printing Office, 1997.

FIGURE 2-8 TEENAGE EMPLOYMENT AS A SHARE OF TOTAL EMPLOYMENT, 1960–1996

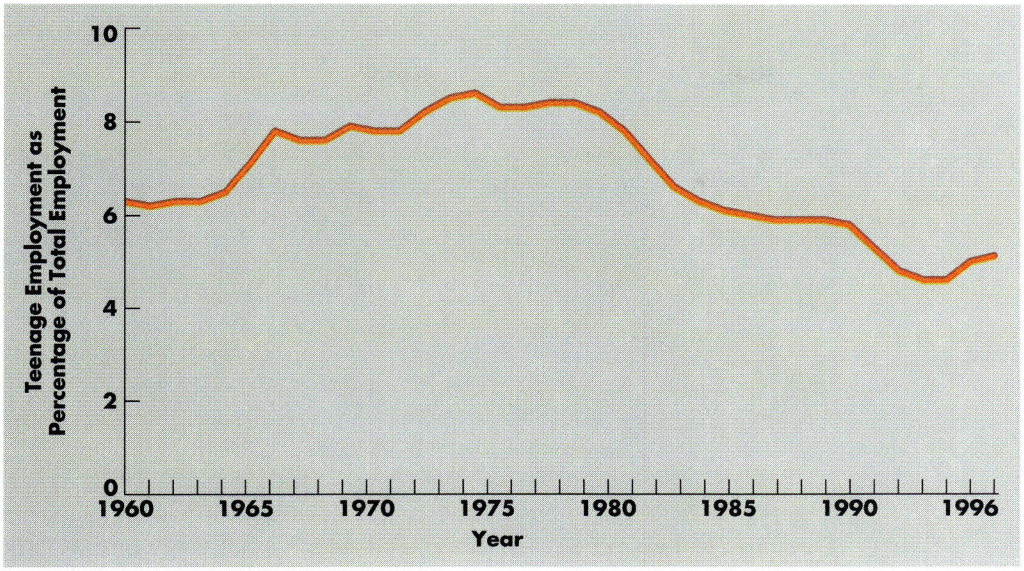

The share of teenagers (ages 16 to 19) in total employment rose from 6.3 percent in 1960 to a peak of 8.4 percent in 1974. Since then, it has largely been falling.

SOURCE: *Economic Report of the President 1997,* Washington, D.C.: U.S. Government Printing Office, 1997.

THE AMERICAN WORK FORCE: WHAT IT DOES

What do these 125 million people in the American work force do? The only real answer is: Almost anything you can imagine. In 1994, America had 656,000 lawyers, 559,000 bank tellers, 867,000 private security guards, 38,000 professional athletes, and 28,000 oil field roustabouts.

Figure 2-9 shows the breakdown by sector. It holds some surprises for most people. The majority of American workers—like workers in all developed countries—produce services, not goods. In 1994, about 90 million people were employed by service industries, including 27 million in retail and wholesale trade, while only 24 million produced goods. The popular image of the typical American worker as a factory hand—Homer Simpson, if you will—is really quite misleading. Manufacturing companies employ only about 18 million people, and almost a third of them work in offices rather than in the factory. Governments at all levels employ about 19 million people. Contrary to another popular misconception, few of these civil servants work for the *federal* government. Federal *civilian* employment is just under 3 million—and has fallen every year since 1990. Finally, about 3.6 million Americans work on farms, and the armed forces employ about 1.7 million soldiers.

THE AMERICAN WORK FORCE: WHAT IT EARNS

All together, these workers earn nearly three-quarters of the income generated by the production process. That figures up to an average hourly wage of about \$12—plus fringe benefits like health insurance and pensions, which can add an additional 30 to 40 percent for people holding what are often called "good jobs." Since the average work week is about 35 hours long, a typical weekly pay check

FIGURE 2-9

CIVILIAN EMPLOYMENT BY SECTOR, 1996

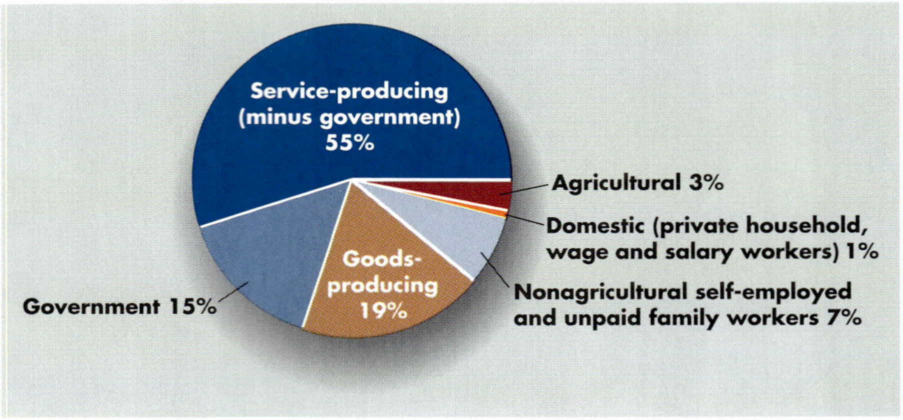

More Americans produce services than goods. In fact, all levels of government now employ more workers than the manufacturing sector.

SOURCE: *Economic Report of the President 1997*, Washington, D.C.: U.S. Government Printing Office, 1997.

is about $420 before taxes. That is hardly a princely sum, and most college graduates can expect to earn more.[2] But that is what wage rates are like in a rich country. Wages in Japan and throughout northern Europe are similar.

CAPITAL AND ITS EARNINGS

After deducting the tiny sliver of income that goes to land and natural resources, most of the remainder accrues to the owners of *capital*—the machines and buildings that make up the nation's industrial plant.

The total market value of American business assets—a tough number to estimate—is believed to be in the neighborhood of $12 trillion. Since that capital earns an average rate of return of about 10 percent before taxes, the total earnings of capital come to about $1,200 billion. Of this, profits are less than half; the rest is mainly interest.

Public opinion polls routinely show that Americans have a distorted view of the level of business profits in our society. The man and woman in the street believe that profits account for about 30 percent of the price of a typical product. In fact, when you spend a dollar in our economy, about 66 cents is for labor costs, 11 cents goes to cover the wear and tear on the capital stock,[3] 13 cents is for taxes, and 4 cents is for interest. That leaves about 6 cents for after-tax profits.

THE OUTPUTS: WHAT DOES AMERICA PRODUCE?

What does all this labor and capital produce? Consumer spending accounts for almost 70 percent of GDP. And what an amazing variety of goods and services it buys! American households spend roughly half of their budgets on goods—ranging from $93 billion per year on new cars to $51 billion on tobacco products. Expenditures on services absorb the other half of household budgets, of which housing commands the largest share. But Americans also spend $68 bil-

---

[2]These days, college graduates typically earn about 65 percent more than those with only high school diplomas.

[3]Economists and accountants call this *depreciation*. It is a well-known cost of doing business.

PUBLIC OPINION ON PROFITS

Most Americans think corporate profits are much higher than they actually are. One public opinion poll, for example, found that the average citizen thought that corporate profits *after tax* amounted to 32 percent of sales for the typical manufacturing company. The actual profit rate at the time was closer to 4 percent! Interestingly, when a previous poll asked how much profit was "reasonable," the response was 26 cents on every dollar of sales—over six times as large as profits actually were.

SOURCE: "Public Attitudes toward Corporate Profits," Opinion Research Corporation, *Public Opinion Index*, Princeton, N.J., June 1986.

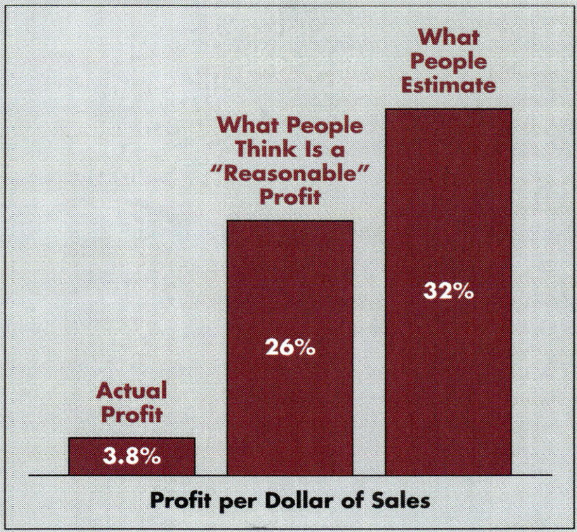

lion annually on their telephone bills, $29 billion on airline tickets, and $39 billion on dentists.

This leaves close to a third of GDP for all nonconsumption uses. The government buys about 17 percent: such things as airplanes, guns, and the services of soldiers, teachers, and bureaucrats. The rest is mainly business purchases of machinery and industrial structures (about 10 percent of GDP) and consumer purchases of new houses (about 4 percent).

THE CENTRAL ROLE OF BUSINESS FIRMS

Calvin Coolidge once said that "the business of America is business." He was largely right. When we peer inside the economic machine that turns inputs into outputs, we see mainly private companies. Astonishingly, the United States has about 21 million business firms—about one for every 13 people!

The owners and managers of these businesses hire people, acquire or rent capital goods, and arrange for the production of the things people want to buy. Sound simple? It isn't. About 75,000 to 80,000 businesses fail every year. A few succeed spectacularly. Some do both. Wang Laboratories, an early entrant into the calculator and word processing business, was founded by a brilliant Chinese immigrant in the 1950s and grew to have annual sales of $3 billion and 30,000 employees by 1984. Eight years later, it was bankrupt. The company's financial condition has improved since 1993, but it is still losing money. Fortunately for the U.S. economy, however, the lure of riches induces hundreds of thousands of people to start new businesses every year—against the odds.

A number of the biggest firms do business all over the world, just as foreign-based *multinational corporations* do business here. Indeed, some people claim that it is now impossible to determine the true "nationality" of a multinational

IS THAT AN AMERICAN COMPANY?

Robert Reich, the secretary of labor in the Clinton administration, has argued that it is almost impossible to define the nationality of a multinational company these days. While many scholars think Reich exaggerates the point, no one doubts that he has one.

Here are some examples:

> What's the difference between an "American" corporation that makes or buys abroad much of what it sells around the world and a "foreign" corporation that makes or buys in the United States much of what it sells? . . . The mind struggles to keep the players straight. In 1990, Canada's Northern Telecom was selling to its American customers telecommunications equipment made by Japan's NTT at NTT's factory in North Carolina.
>
> If you found that one too easy, try this: Beginning in 1991, Japan's Mazda would be producing Ford Probes at Mazda's plant in Flat Rock, Michigan. Some of these cars would be exported to Japan and sold there under Ford's trademark.
>
> A Mazda-designed compact utility vehicle would be built at a Ford plant in Louisville, Kentucky, and then sold at Mazda dealerships in the United States. Nissan, meanwhile, was designing a new light truck at its San Diego, California, design center. The trucks would be assembled at Ford's Ohio truck plant, using panel parts fabricated by Nissan at its Tennessee factory, and then marketed by both Ford and Nissan in the United States and in Japan. Who is Ford? Nissan? Mazda? . . .

SOURCE: Robert B. Reich, *The Work of Nations* (New York: Knopf, 1991), pp. 124, 131.

corporation—which may have factories in ten or more countries, sell its wares all over the world, and have stockholders in dozens of nations. (See the accompanying box.) Most of General Motors' profits are generated abroad, for example. And the Honda you drive was probably made in Ohio.

Firms compete with other companies in their *industry*. Many economists believe that this *competition* is the key to industrial efficiency. The sole supplier of a commodity will find it easy to make money, and may therefore fail to innovate or control costs. Its management is liable to become relaxed and sloppy. But a company besieged by dozens of competitors eager for its business must keep alert at all times. The rewards for success in business can be magnificent. But the punishment for failure is severe.

WHAT'S MISSING FROM THE PICTURE? GOVERNMENT

Thus far we have the following capsule summary of how the U.S. economy works: About 21 million private businesses, energized by the profit motive, employ about 125 million workers and about $12 trillion of capital. These firms bring their enormously diverse wares to market, where they try to sell them to nearly 264 million consumers.

FIGURE 2-10

THE CIRCULAR FLOW OF GOODS AND MONEY

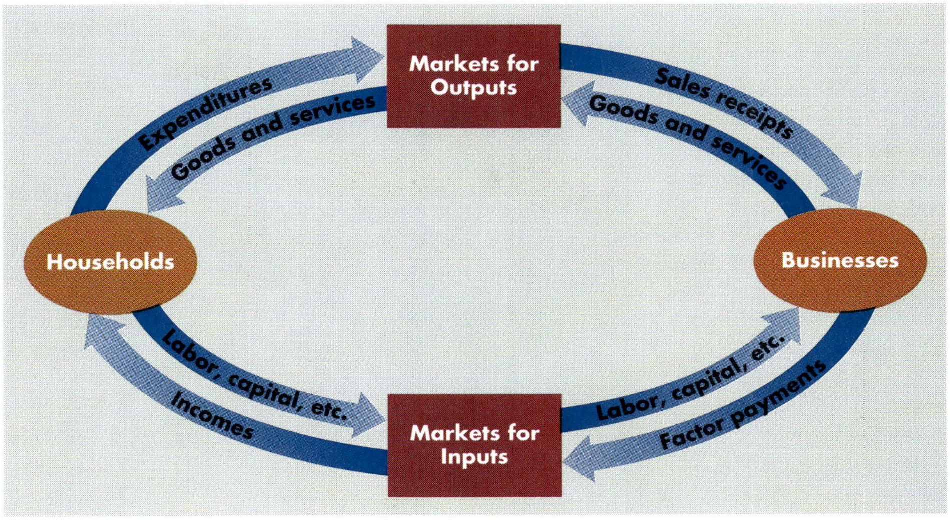

This diagram depicts the ways in which households and firms interact in markets. The upper half signifies the markets for outputs—the goods and services that firms produce and households purchase. The lower half illustrates the markets for inputs like labor and capital that households sell (or rent) to businesses. In each case, the outer loop indicates the flow of money while the inner loop signifies the flow of physical goods and services.

Households and businesses are linked together in a tight circle, depicted in Figure 2-10. Firms use their receipts from sales to pay wages to their employees and interest and profits to the people who provide them with capital. These income flows, in turn, enable consumers to purchase the goods and services that companies produce. This circular flow of money and goods is central to the analysis of how the national economy works. All these activities are linked together by a series of interconnected markets, some of which are highly competitive and others of which are less so.

All very well and good. But the story leaves out something important: the role of *government,* which is pervasive even in our decidedly free-market economy. Just what does government do in the U.S. economy—and why?

While an increasing number of tasks seem to get assigned to the state each year, the traditional role of government in a market economy revolves around five jobs: providing certain goods and services such as national defense, levying taxes to pay for these goods and services, redistributing income, regulating business, and making and enforcing the laws. Every one of these is steeped in controversy and surrounded by intense political debate. We conclude this chapter with a brief look at the role of government.

THE GOVERNMENT AS REFEREE

For the most part, power is diffused in our economy, and people "play by the rules." But, in the scramble for competitive advantage, disputes are bound to arise. Did Company A live up to its contract? Who owns that disputed piece of property? In addition, some unscrupulous businesses are liable to step over the line now and then—via misleading advertising, attempts to monopolize markets, employment of child labor, and the like.

Enter the government as rule maker, referee, and arbitrator. Congress and state and local legislatures pass the laws that define the rules of the economic game. The executive branches of all three levels of government have the responsibility for enforcing them. And the courts interpret the laws and adjudicate disputes.

FIGURE 2-11 THE ALLOCATION OF GOVERNMENT EXPENDITURES

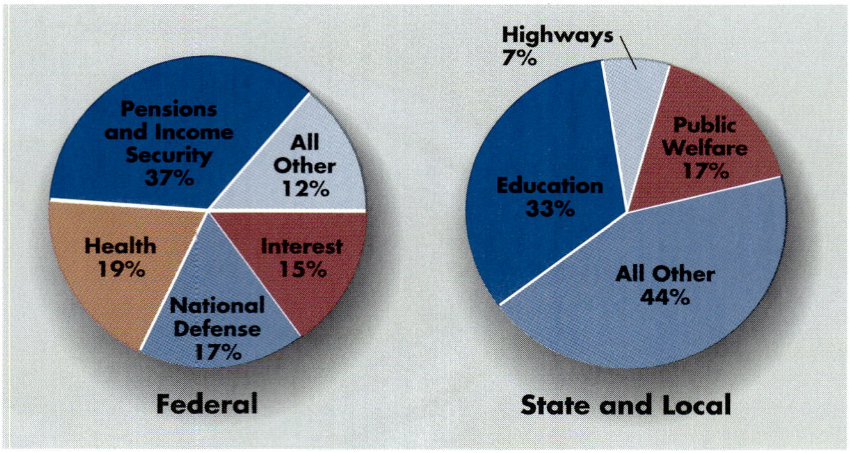

These graphs show how the government spends tax dollars. The federal government spends most of its money on transfer payments to retirees, the poor, the unemployed, and veterans (37 percent) and on national defense (17 percent). The biggest share of state and local government spending goes for education (33 percent), with health and welfare expenditures (17 percent) in second place.

SOURCE: *Economic Report of the President 1997*, Washington, D.C.: U.S. Government Printing Office, 1997.

REGULATING BUSINESS

Nothing is pure in this world of ours. Even in "free-market" economies, governments interfere with the workings of free markets in many ways and for myriad reasons. Some regulations grow out of the rule-making function. For example, America's *antitrust laws* are designed to protect competition against possible encroachment by monopoly. Others are aimed at promoting social objectives to which unfettered markets do not tend; environmental regulations are a particularly clear case. But some economic regulations have *no* persuasive economic rationale at all!

We mentioned earlier that the American belief in free enterprise runs deep. For this reason, the regulatory role of government is more contentious here than in most other countries. It was, after all, Jefferson who said that government is best which governs least. Two hundred years later, Presidents Reagan, Bush, and Clinton pledged to dismantle regulations—and sometimes did.

GOVERNMENT EXPENDITURES

The most contentious political issues often involve taxing and spending because those are the government's most prominent roles. In 1995 and 1996, President Clinton and the Republican-led Congress battled fiercely over the federal budget. Differences over tax policies and spending cuts even led to some temporary shutdowns of the government.

During fiscal year 1996, the federal government spent about $1.5 *trillion*—a sum that is literally beyond comprehension. Figure 2-11 shows where the money went. Over one-third went for *pensions and income security* programs, which include both social insurance programs, like Social Security and unemployment compensation, and programs designed to assist the poor. About 17 percent went for *national defense.* Another 19 percent was absorbed by *health-care* expenditures, mainly on Medicare and Medicaid. Adding in *interest on the national debt,* these four functions alone accounted for about 88 percent of federal spending. The rest went for a miscellany of other purposes including education, transportation, agriculture, housing, and foreign aid.

Government spending at the state and local levels was about $1.4 trillion. Education claimed the biggest share of state and local government budgets (34 percent), with health and public welfare programs in second place (16 percent).

Despite this vast outpouring of public funds, many observers believe that serious social needs remain unmet. Critics claim that our public infrastructure (such as bridges and roads) is inadequate, that our educational system is lacking, that we do not do enough for the poor and homeless, and so on. Many of these claims were echoed during the 1995 budget debate. Other critics argue that government tries to do too much—and does it too inefficiently.

TAXES IN AMERICA

Taxes are required to finance this array of goods and services, and sometimes it seems that the tax collector is everywhere. We have income and payroll taxes withheld from our paychecks, sales taxes added to our purchases, property taxes levied on our homes; we pay gasoline taxes, liquor taxes, and telephone taxes.

Americans have always felt that there are too many taxes and that they are too high. In the 1980s and 1990s, antitax sentiment became a dominant feature of the U.S. political scene. The old slogan "no taxation without representation" gave way to the new slogan "no new taxes." Yet by international standards, Americans are among the most lightly taxed people in the world. Figure 2-12 compares the fraction of income paid in taxes in the United States with those paid by residents of other wealthy nations. Americans shoulder some of the lowest tax burdens in the industrialized world.

How is this money raised? The *personal income tax* is the federal government's biggest revenue source, though the *payroll tax*—a flat-rate tax on wages and salaries up to a certain limit—is not far behind. The rest of federal revenue comes mainly from the *corporate income tax*. Most states and many large cities levy

FIGURE 2-12

THE BURDEN OF TAXATION IN SELECTED COUNTRIES, 1994

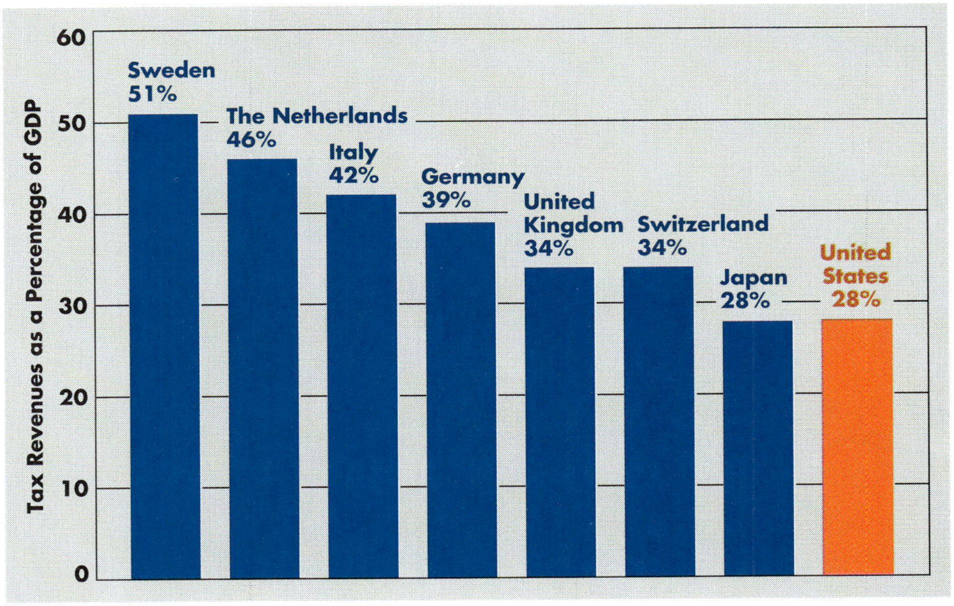

Americans are lightly taxed compared to citizens of other advanced industrial countries. The Swedes and the Dutch, for example, pay far higher taxes than we do.

SOURCE: Organization for Economic Cooperation and Development. Revenue Statistics, 1965–1995, Paris, France.

FIGURE 2-13

SOURCES OF GOVERNMENT REVENUE

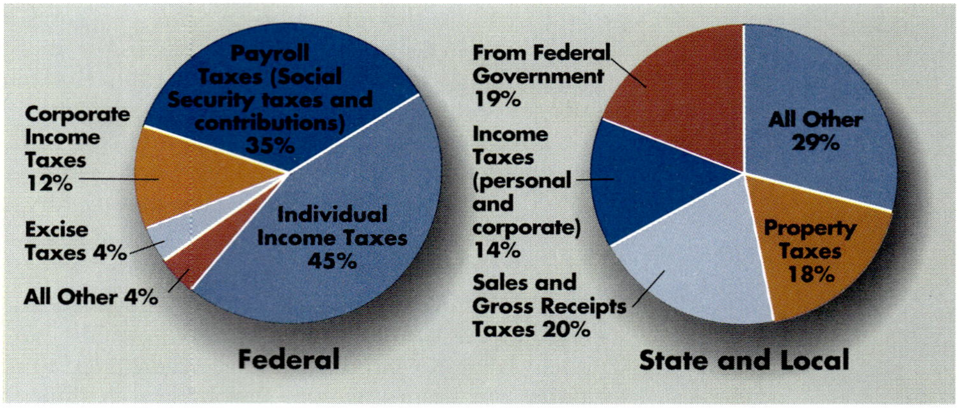

These pie diagrams show the shares of each of the major sources of federal and state and local revenues. Personal income taxes and payroll taxes clearly account for the majority of federal revenues. The states and localities raise money from a potpourri of sources, including the federal government.

SOURCE: *Economic Report of the President 1997*, Washington, D.C.: U.S. Government Printing Office, 1997.

broad-based *sales taxes* on retail purchases, with certain specific exemptions (such as food and rent). Local governments generally raise revenue by levying *property taxes* on homes and business properties. Figure 2-13 shows the breakdown of revenue sources at both the federal and state and local levels.

THE GOVERNMENT AS REDISTRIBUTOR

In a market economy, people earn incomes according to what they have to sell. Unfortunately, many people have nothing to sell but unskilled labor, which commands a paltry price. Others lack even that. Such people fare poorly in unfettered markets. In extreme cases, they are homeless, hungry, and ill. Robin Hood transferred money from the rich to the poor. Some think the government should do the same; others disagree.

If poverty amidst riches offends your moral sensibilities—a personal judgment that each of us must make—there are two basic approaches. The socialist idea is to force the distribution of income to be more equal by overriding the workings of markets. "From each according to his ability, to each according to his needs" was Marx's ideal. In practice, things were not quite so noble under socialism. But there is little doubt that incomes in the old Soviet Union were more equally distributed than those in the United States.

TRANSFER PAYMENTS are sums of money that certain individuals receive as outright grants from the government rather than as payments for services rendered.

A tax is **PROGRESSIVE** if the ratio of taxes to income rises as income rises.

The liberal idea is to let free markets determine the distribution of *before-tax* incomes, but then to use the tax system and **transfer payments** to reduce inequality—just as Robin Hood did. This is the rationale for, among other things, **progressive taxation** and the antipoverty programs colloquially known as "welfare." Americans who support redistribution line up solidly behind the liberal approach. But which ways are the best, and how much is enough? There are no simple answers to these highly contentious questions.

CONCLUSION: THE MIXED ECONOMY

Ideology notwithstanding, all nations at all times blend public and private ownership of property in some proportions. All rely on markets for some purposes; but all also assign some role to government. Hence, people speak of the ubiquity of **mixed economies.** But mixing is not homogenization; different countries can and do blend the state and market sectors in different ways. Even today, the

A **MIXED ECONOMY** is one in which there is some public influence over the workings of free markets. There may also be some public ownership mixed in with private property.

Russian economy is a far cry from the Italian economy, which is vastly different from that of Hong Kong.

While most of you were in middle school, a stunning historical event occurred: Communism collapsed all over Europe. Now the formerly socialist economies are in the midst of a painful transition from a system in which private property, free enterprise, and markets played subsidiary roles to one in which they are central. These nations are changing the mix, if you will—and dramatically so. To understand why this transformation is at once so difficult and so important, we need to explore the main theme of this book: *What does the market do well, and what does it do poorly?* This task begins in the next chapter.

SUMMARY

1. The U.S. economy is the biggest national economy on earth, both because Americans are rich by world standards and because we are a populous nation. Relative to most other advanced countries, our economy is also exceptionally "privatized" and *closed.*
2. The U.S. economy has grown dramatically over the years. But this growth is exaggerated by looking only at dollar figures, which are distorted by both **inflation** and population growth. To get a better understanding of the growth of living standards, we must look at **real GDP** *per capita.*
3. The growth path of the U.S. economy has been interrupted by periodic **recessions,** during which unemployment rises.
4. America has a big, diverse work force whose composition by age and sex has been changing substantially. Relatively few workers these days work in factories or on farms; most work in service industries.
5. Employees take home most of the nation's income. Most of the rest goes, in the forms of interest and profits, to those who provide the capital.
6. Governments at the federal, state, and local levels employ almost one-seventh of the American work force and produce almost a fifth of the GDP. They finance their expenditures by taxes, which account for about 29 percent of GDP. This percentage is one of the lowest in the industrialized world.
7. In addition to raising taxes and making expenditures, the government in a market economy serves as referee and enforcer of the rules, regulates business in a variety of ways, and redistributes income through taxes and **transfer payments.** For all these reasons, we say that we have a **mixed economy** which blends private and public elements.

KEY TERMS

Outputs
Inputs (factors of production)
Gross domestic product (GDP)
Time-series graph
Inflation
Real GDP
Open economy
Closed economy
Recession
Transfer payments
Progressive tax
Mixed economy

QUESTIONS FOR REVIEW

1. Which are the two biggest national economies on earth? Why are they so much bigger than the others?
2. What is meant by a "factor of production?" Have you ever sold any on a market?
3. Do you have any ideas why per-capita income in Connecticut is nearly double that in Mississippi?
4. What is the difference between nominal gross domestic product and real gross domestic product? Why is this distinction important?
5. Roughly speaking, what fraction of U.S. labor works in factories? In service businesses? In government?
6. It sounds paradoxical to say that most American businesses are small, but most of the output is produced by large businesses. How can this be true?
7. What is the role of government in a mixed economy?

APPENDIX FURTHER PERILS IN THE INTERPRETATION OF GRAPHS

The chapter warned you against certain dangers that arise in interpreting time-series graphs. But there are other perils as well. This appendix deals with three of them.

DISTORTING TRENDS BY CHOICE OF THE TIME PERIOD

Users of statistical data must be on guard for distortions of trends caused by an unskillful or unscrupulous choice of the beginning and ending time periods for the graph. This is best explained by an example.

Figure 2-14 shows the behavior of average stock market prices over the period January 1966 to June 1982. The numbers have been corrected for inflation; that is, they are expressed in dollars of constant purchasing power. The graph displays a clear downhill movement that would suggest to anyone not familiar with other information that stocks are a terrible investment.

However, an unscrupulous seller of stocks could use similar stock market statistics for a different group of years to tell exactly the opposite story. Figure 2-15 shows the behavior of average stock prices from 1989 to 1990. Stocks now look like a superb investment.

A much longer and less biased choice of time period (Figure 2-16) gives a less distorted picture. It indicates that investments in stocks are sometimes profitable, sometimes unprofitable. The lesson is that:

You must be on the lookout for distortions resulting from an inadvertent or unscrupulous choice of time period for a graph.

While no ironclad rules can give absolute protection from this difficulty, several precautions can be helpful.

1. Make sure the first date on the graph is not an exceptionally high or low point. Compared to 1966, a year of unusually high stock prices, the years immediately following are bound to give the impression of a downward trend.
2. For the same reason, make sure the graph does not end in a year that is extraordinarily high or

FIGURE 2-14 STOCK PRICES, JANUARY 1966–JUNE 1982

This graph seems to show that stock market prices generally go down.

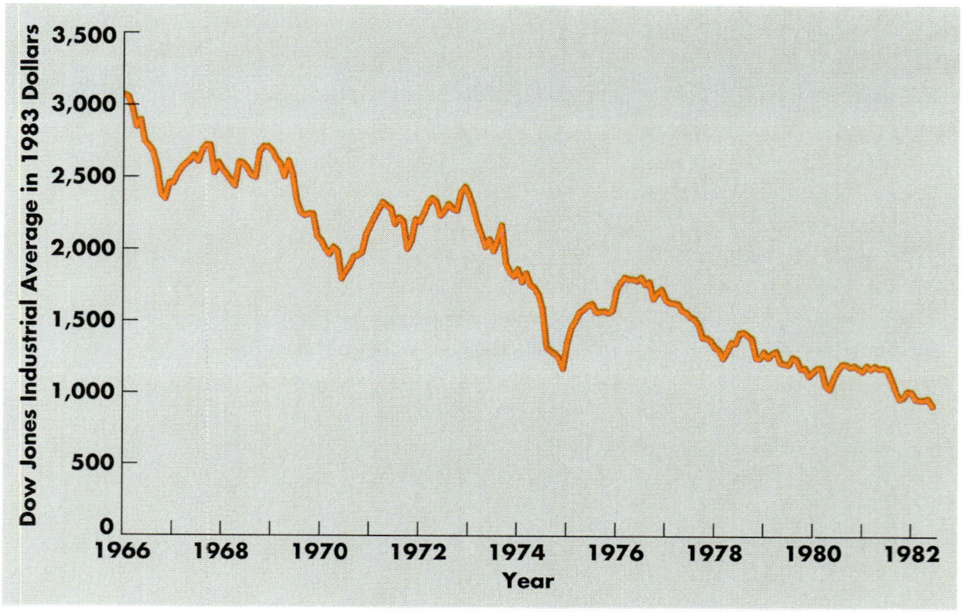

FIGURE 2-15

STOCK PRICES, JANUARY 1989–JULY 1990

This graph seems to indicate that the value of stocks is steadily climbing.

SOURCE: *Economic Report of the President 1991*, Washington, D.C.: U.S. Government Printing Office, 1991.

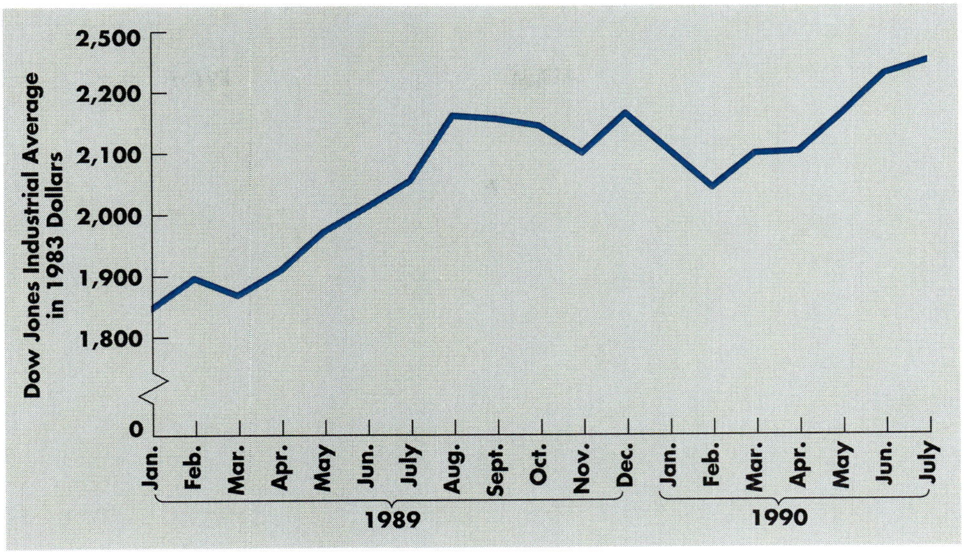

low (although this may be unavoidable if the graph simply ends with the most recent data).

3. Make sure that (in the absence of some special justification) the graph does not depict only a very brief period of time, which can easily be atypical—like Figure 2-15.

DANGERS OF OMITTING THE ORIGIN

Frequently, the value of an economic variable described by a graph does not fall anywhere near zero during the period under consideration. For example, between 1988 and 1992 the civilian unemployment rate never fell below 5 percent. This

FIGURE 2-16

FULL HISTORY OF STOCK PRICES, CORRECTED FOR INFLATION, 1925–MARCH 1997

Here we see that stock prices have lots of *both* ups and downs, and that they have not risen nearly as much, over three quarters of a century, as is popularly supposed—after they have been corrected for the fall in the purchasing power of the dollar that resulted from inflation.

SOURCE: *Economic Report of the President 1997*, Washington, D.C.: U.S. Government Printing Office, 1997.

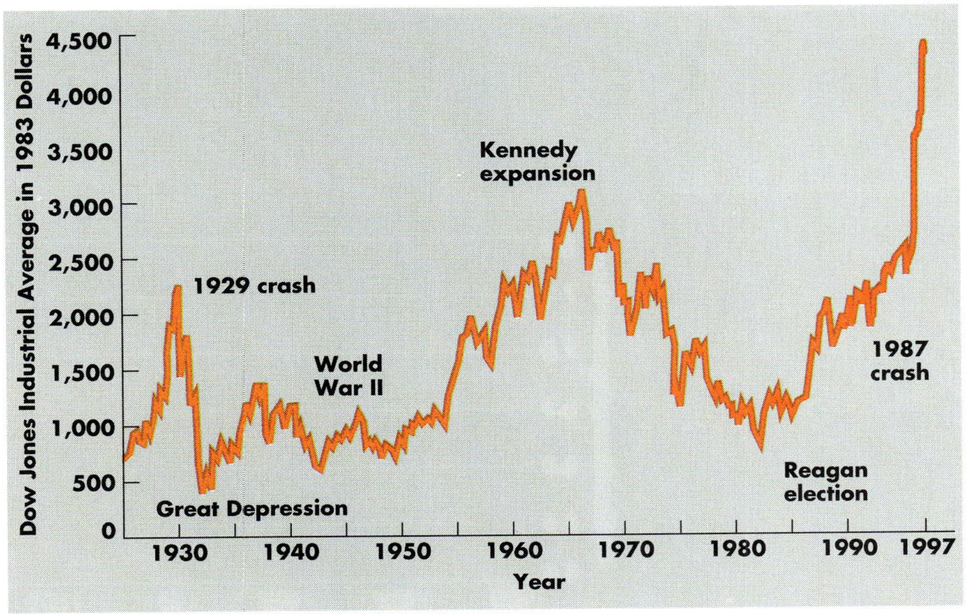

means that a time-series graph showing unemployment over time would have a lot of wasted space between the horizontal axis (where the unemployment rate is zero) and the level of the graph representing 5 percent. There are simply no data points to plot in that range. It is therefore tempting to eliminate this wasted space by beginning the graph at 5 percent, as the magazine *The International Economy* did when it published Figure 2-17 in 1992.

What is wrong with the drawing? Nothing, if you read carefully. But a hasty glance would vastly exaggerate the rise in unemployment. Figure 2-17 makes it look like the United States experienced an economic catastrophe from 1990 to 1992, with unemployment exploding. A less misleading graph, which includes the origin as well as all the "wasted space" in between, is shown in Figure 2-18. Note how this alternative presentation gives a dramatically different visual impression.

Omitting the origin in a graph is dangerous because it exaggerates the magnitudes of the changes that have taken place.

Sometimes, it is true, the inclusion of the origin would waste so much space that it is undesirable to include it. In that case, a good practice is to put a clear warning on the graph to remind the reader that this has been done. Figure 2-19 shows one way to do so.

UNRELIABILITY OF STEEPNESS AND CHOICE OF UNITS

The last pitfall we will consider has consequences similar to the one just discussed. The problem is that we can never trust the visual impression we get from the steepness of a graph. A graph of stock market prices that moves uphill sharply (has a large positive slope) appears to suggest that prices are rising rapidly, while another graph that climbs more slowly seems to imply that prices are going up sluggishly. Yet, depending on how one draws the graph, exactly the same statistics can produce a graph that is rising quickly or slowly.

The reason for this possibility is that, in economics, there are no fixed units of measurement. Coal production can be measured in hundredweights (hundreds of pounds) or in tons. Prices can be measured in cents or dollars or millions of dollars. Time can be measured in days or months or years. Any one of these choices is perfectly legitimate, but it makes all the difference to the speed with which a graph using the resulting figures rises or falls.

An example will bring out the point. Suppose we have the following imaginary figures on daily production from a coal mine, which we measure both in hundredweights and in tons (remembering that 1 ton = 20 hundredweights):

Year	Production in Tons	Production in Hundredweights
1980	5,000	100,000
1985	5,050	101,000
1990	5,090	101,800

Look at Figures 2-20(a) and 2-20(b), one graph showing the figures in tons and the other showing the figures in hundredweights. The line looks quite flat in one panel, but quite steep in the other.

FIGURE 2-17 A GRAPH DISTORTED BY OMISSION OF THE ORIGIN

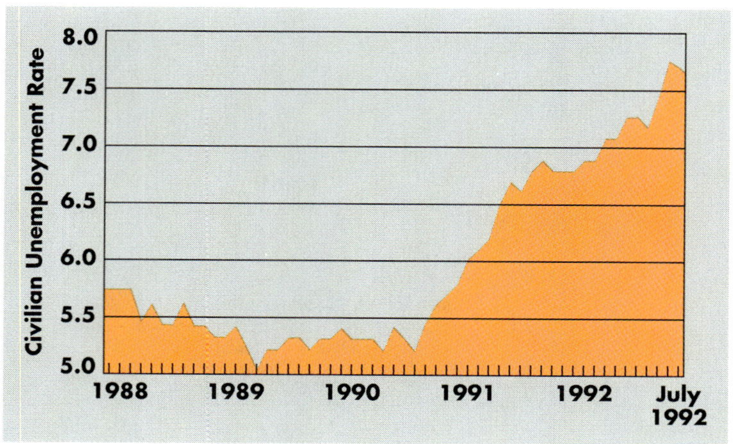

A hasty glance at this figure seems to show that, from mid-1990 to mid-1992, unemployment in the United States soared to disastrous heights.

SOURCE: *The International Economy*, September/October 1992, p. 10.

FIGURE 2-18

THE SAME GRAPH AS FIGURE 2-17, WITH ORIGIN POINT INCLUDED

Extending the previous graph all the way to zero unemployment shows that the rise in unemployment, while significant, was not so enormous as the previous graph suggested.

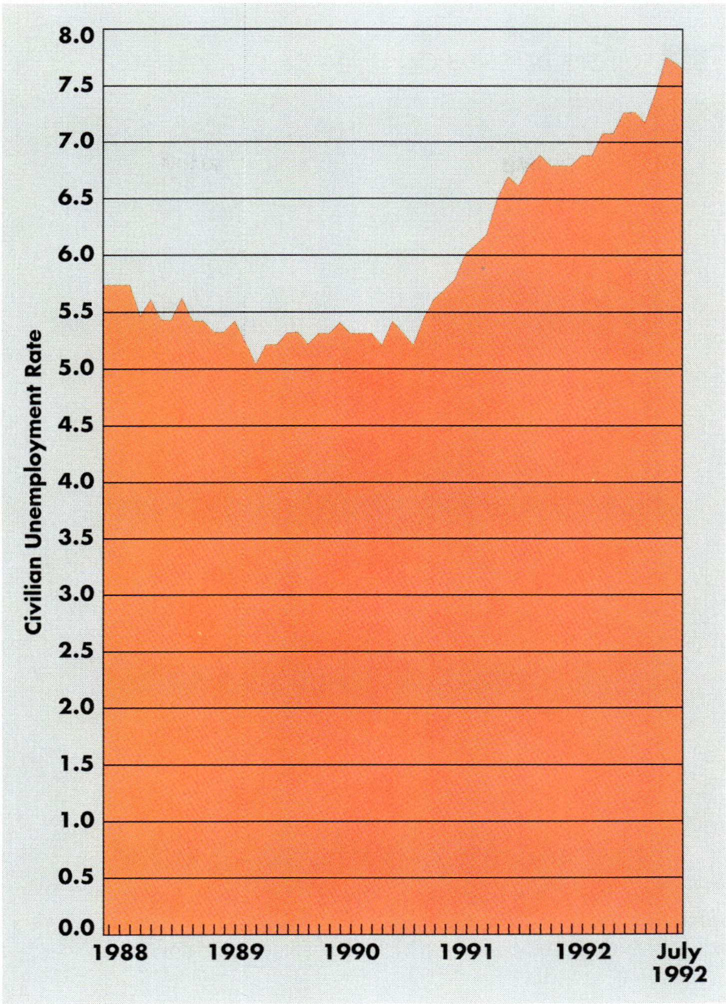

FIGURE 2-19

THE SAME GRAPH AS FIGURE 2-17, WITH A WARNING BREAK

An alternative way to warn the reader that the zero point has been left out is to put a break in the graph, as illustrated here.

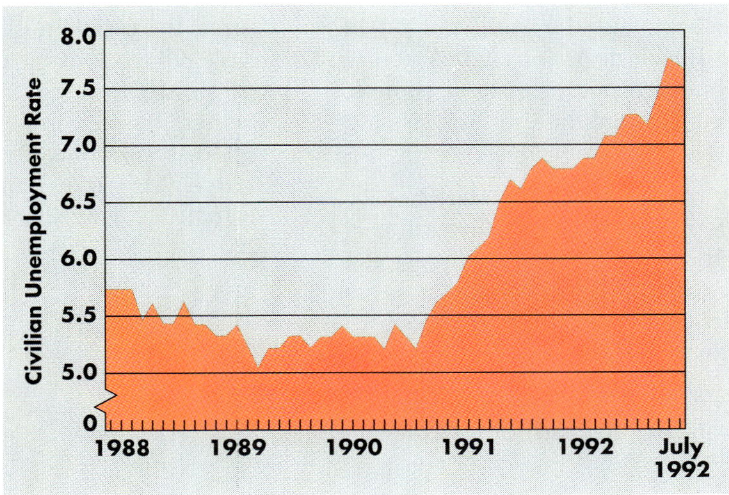

FIGURE 2-20 SLOPE DEPENDS ON UNITS OF MEASUREMENT

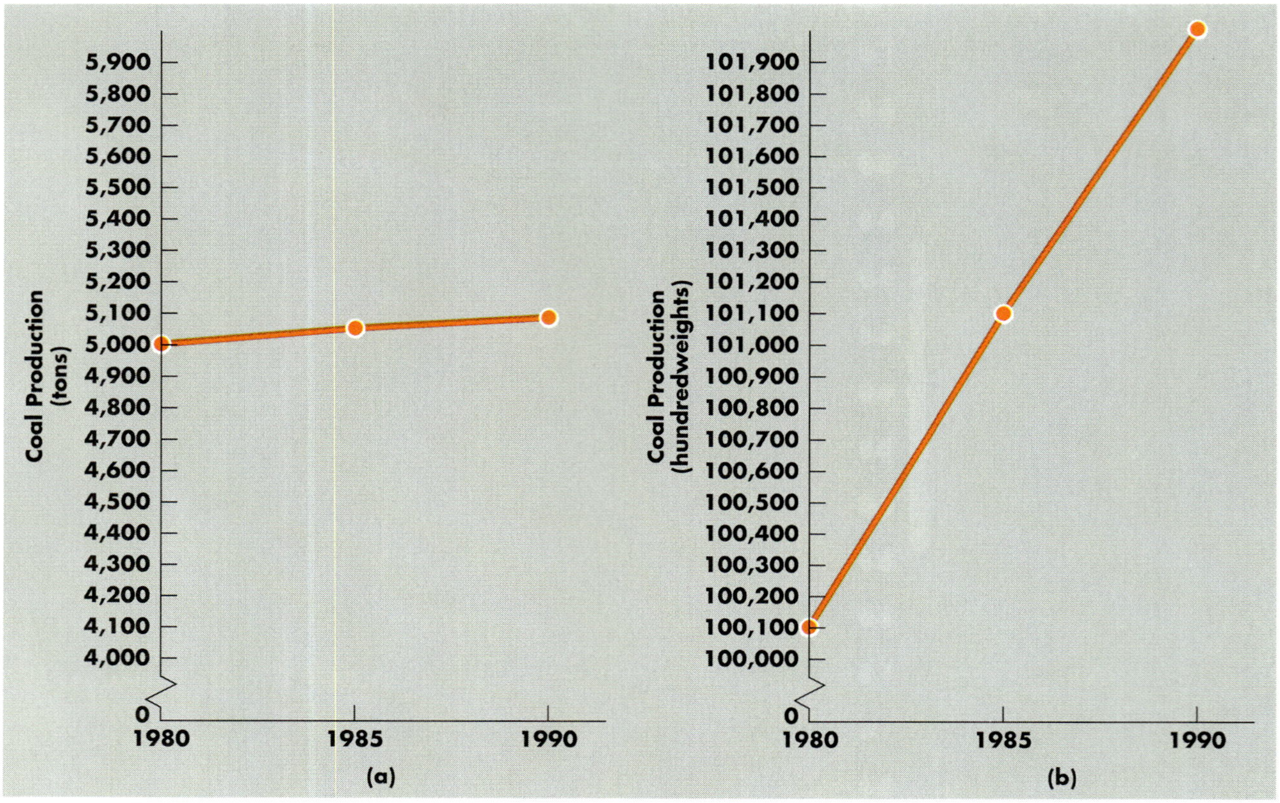

In Panel (a), coal production is measured in tons, and production seems to be rising very slowly. In Panel (b), production is measured in hundredweights (hundred-pound units) so the same facts now seem to say that production is rising spectacularly.

Unfortunately, we cannot solve the problem by agreeing always to stick to the same units of measurement. Pounds may be the right unit for measuring demand for beef, but they will not do in measuring demand for cloth or for coal. A penny may be the right monetary unit for postage stamps, but it is not a very convenient unit for pricing automobiles.

A change in units of measurement stretches or compresses the axis on which the information is represented, which automatically changes the visual slope of a graph. Therefore, we must never place much faith in the apparent implications of the slope of an ordinary graph in economics.

Economists have adopted a useful approach to deal with this problem. Instead of calculating changes in "absolute" terms—like tons of coal—they use as their common unit the *percentage* increase. By using percentages rather than absolute figures, the problem can be avoided. The reason is simple. If we look at our hypothetical figures on coal production again, we see that no matter whether we measure the increase in output from 1980 to 1985 in tons (from 5,000 to 5,050) or in hundredweights (from 100,000 to 101,000), the *percentage* increase was the same. Fifty is 1 percent of 5,000, and 1,000 is 1 percent of 100,000. Since a change in units affects both numbers *proportionately,* the result is a wash; it does not change the percentage calculation.

SUMMARY

1. While time-series graphs are invaluable in helping us condense a great deal of information in a single picture, they can be quite misleading if they are not drawn and interpreted with care.
2. For example, growth trends can be exaggerated by inappropriate choices of units of measurement or by failure to correct for some obvious source of growth (such as rising population). Omitting the origin can make the ups and downs in a time series appear much more extreme than they actually are. Or, by a clever choice of the starting and ending points for the graphs, the same data can be made to tell very different stories. Readers of such graphs—and this includes anyone who ever reads a newspaper—must be on guard for problems like these or they may find themselves misled by "the facts."

QUESTIONS FOR REVIEW

1. Look for a graph in your local newspaper, on the financial page or elsewhere. What does the graph try to show? Is someone trying to convince you of something? Check to see if the graph is distorted in any of the ways mentioned in this chapter.
2. Suppose that between 1995 and 1996 expenditures on dog food rose from $60 million to $70 million, and that the price of dog food went up by 20 percent. What do these facts imply about the popularity of dog food?
3. Suppose that between 1986 and 1996 the U.S. population went up 10 percent and the number of silk neckties imported from Thailand rose from 3,000,000 to 3,600,000. What do these facts imply about the growth in popularity of Thai ties?

CHAPTER 3

SCARCITY AND CHOICE: *THE* ECONOMIC PROBLEM

Our necessities are few but our wants are endless.
Inscription found in a fortune cookie.

The market—what it does well, and what it does badly—is the central issue of this book. But before we delve into this complex subject, we must first ask: What is the basic task that economists expect the market to carry out?

The answer most frequently given is that the market resolves *THE* fundamental problem of the economy: the fact that all decisions are constrained by the scarcity of available resources. A science-fiction writer can depict a world in which everyone travels about in a petroleum-powered yacht, but the earth almost certainly lacks the resources needed to make that dream come true. The scarcity of resources, both natural and man-made, makes it vital that we stretch our limited resources as far as possible. Even millionaires, monarchs, and wealthy nations constantly find themselves frustrated by the fact that their purchasing power, labor, and natural resources are insufficient to let them do everything they would like. Like everyone, they must constantly make hard choices.

Because of scarcity, every economic decision involves a trade-off. Should you use that $5 bill to buy a hoagie or some new diskettes for your computer files? Should Chrysler Corporation invest more money in assembly lines or in research on auto design and fuel efficiency? The key role of the market is to facilitate and guide such decisions, assigning each hour of labor and each kilowatt-hour of electricity to the task where, it is hoped, the input will serve the public most effectively. Scarcity, then, is the fundamental fact with which the market (or the central planner) must grapple.

This chapter introduces a way to analyze the limited choices available to any decision maker. The same sort of analysis, based on the concept of *opportunity cost,* will be shown to apply to the decisions of business firms, governments, and society as a whole. Many of the most basic ideas of economics—such as *efficiency, division of labor, exchange,* and *the role of markets*—are introduced here for the first time. These concepts are useful in analyzing the unpleasant choices forced upon us by scarcity.

PROBLEM: THE "INDISPENSABLE NECESSITY" SYNDROME

It is natural, but not rational, for people to try to avoid facing up to the hard choices that scarcity makes necessary. This happened, for example, when countries such as Russia and Poland were forced by extreme scarcity of foreign currency to tighten their belts sharply during the 1990s. Shortages of foreign currency meant that these governments and their people had to cut down severely on consumer goods and productive inputs purchased from abroad. But most proposals for cuts were met with public demonstrations and the cry that each item slated for reduction was *absolutely* essential.

In the same period, something similar went on in the United States. Taxpayers' revolts made it impossible, politically, for federal, state, and local revenues to increase very much while government services were growing more expensive because of inflation and for other reasons. Belt-tightening was the order of the day. But as politicians and administrators struggled with these decisions, they learned that their constituents often were unwilling to accept *any* reductions. Whether the proposal was to reduce payments to the elderly, expenditures on libraries, outlays on schools, or even defense spending, protest groups argued that the cut in question would destroy American society.

Yet, regrettable as it is to have to give up anything, reduced budgets mean that *something* must go. If everything is declared to be indispensable, the decision maker is in the dark and is likely to end up making ill-advised cuts. When the budget must be reduced, it is critical to determine which cuts are likely to prove *least damaging* to the people affected.

It is nonsense to assign top priority to everything. No one can afford everything. An optimal decision is one that chooses the most desirable alternative *among the possibilities permitted by the quantities of scarce resources available.*

SCARCITY, CHOICE, AND OPPORTUNITY COST

RESOURCES are the instruments provided by nature or by people that are used to create goods and services. Natural resources include minerals, the soil, water, and air. Labor is a scarce resource partly because of time limitations (the day has only 24 hours), and partly because the number of skilled workers is limited. Factories and machines are resources made by people. These three types of resources are often referred to as *land, labor,* and *capital.* They are also called *inputs* or *factors of production.*

One of the basic themes of economics is that the **resources** of decision makers, no matter how large, are always limited, and as a result everyone has to make some hard decisions. The U.S. government has been agonizing over difficult budget decisions for years, though it spends more than a trillion and a half dollars annually! Even Philip II, of Spanish Armada fame and ruler of one of the greatest empires in history, had to cope with frequent rebellions by his troops because he was often unable to pay or supply them with even the most basic provisions.

But far more fundamental than the scarcity of funds is the scarcity of physical resources. The supply of fuel, for example, is not limitless, and some environmentalists claim that we should now be making some hard choices, such as keeping our homes cooler in winter and warmer in summer, living closer to our jobs, or giving up such fuel-using conveniences as dishwashers. While energy is the most widely discussed scarcity these days, the general principle of scarcity applies to all of the earth's resources—iron, copper, uranium, and so on.

Even goods that can be produced are in limited supply because their production requires fuel, labor, and other scarce resources. Wheat and rice can be grown, but nations have nonetheless suffered famines because the land, labor, fertilizer, and water needed to grow these crops were unavailable. We can increase our output of cars, but the increased use of labor, steel, and fuel in auto production will mean that something else, perhaps the production of refrigerators, must be cut back. This all adds up to the following fundamental principle of economics, one we will encounter again and again in this text.

Virtually all resources are *scarce,* meaning that humanity has less of them than we would like. Therefore, choices must be made among a *limited* set of possibilities, in full recognition of the inescapable fact that a decision to have more of one thing means that we will have less of something else.

A **RATIONAL DECISION** is one that best serves the objectives of the decision maker, whatever those objectives may be. Such objectives may include a firm's desire to maximize its profits, a government's desire to maximize the welfare of its citizens, or another government's desire to maximize its military might. The term *rational* connotes neither approval nor disapproval of the objective itself.

In fact, one popular definition of economics is that it is the study of how best to use limited means in the pursuit of unlimited ends. While this definition, like any short statement, cannot possibly cover the sweep of the entire discipline, it does convey the flavor of the type of problem that is the economist's stock in trade.

To illustrate the true cost of an input use, consider the production of additional cars, which requires the production of fewer refrigerators. While the production of a car may cost $15,000 per vehicle, or some other money amount, *its real cost to society is the refrigerators that society must forgo to get an additional car.* If the labor, steel, and fuel needed to make a car are sufficient to make 12 refrigerators, we say that the *opportunity cost* of a car is 12 refrigerators. The principle of opportunity cost is so important that we spend most of this chapter elaborating it.

THE PRINCIPLE OF OPPORTUNITY COST

Economics examines the options available to households, business firms, governments, and entire societies given the limited resources at their command, and it studies the logic of how **rational decisions** can be made from among the competing alternatives. One overriding principle governs this logic—a principle we already introduced in Chapter 1 as one of the **Ideas for Beyond the Final Exam.** With limited resources, a decision to have more of something is simultaneously a decision to have less of something else. Hence, the relevant *cost* of any decision is its **opportunity cost**—the value of the next best alternative that the decision forces one to give up. Rational decision making, be it in industry, government, or households, must be based on opportunity-cost calculations.

OPPORTUNITY COST AND MONEY COST

The **OPPORTUNITY COST** of any decision is the value of the next best alternative that the decision forces the decision maker to forgo.

Since we live in a market economy where (almost) everything "has its price," students often wonder about the connection between the **opportunity cost** of an item and its market price. What we just said seems to divorce the two concepts. We stressed that the true cost of a car is not its market price but the value of the other things (like refrigerators) that could have been made instead. This *opportunity cost* is the true sacrifice that the economy must incur to get a car.

But isn't the opportunity cost of a car related to its money cost? The answer is that the two are usually closely tied because of the way a market economy sets the prices of the steel and electricity that go into the production of cars. Steel is valuable because it can be used to make other goods. If those items are valued highly by consumers, the price of steel will be high. But if the goods that steel can make have little value, the price of steel will be low. Thus, if a car has a high opportunity cost, then a well-functioning price system will assign high prices to the resources that are needed to produce cars, and therefore a car will also have a high *money* cost. In summary:

If the market is functioning well, goods that have high opportunity costs will tend to have high money costs, and goods whose opportunity costs are low will tend to have low money costs.

Yet it would be a mistake to treat opportunity costs and explicit monetary costs as identical. For one thing, there are times when the market does not function well and hence does not assign prices that accurately reflect opportunity costs.

Moreover, some valuable items may not bear explicit price tags at all. We have already encountered one such example in Chapter 1, where we contrasted the opportunity cost of going to college with the explicit money cost. We learned that one important item typically omitted from the money-cost calculation is the *market* value of your time, that is, the wages you could be earning by working instead of attending college. Because you give up these forgone wages in order to acquire an education, they are part of the opportunity cost of your college education just as surely as are tuition payments.

Other common examples are goods and services that are given away "free." You incur no explicit monetary cost to acquire such an item. But you may have to pay implicitly by waiting in line. If so, you incur an opportunity cost equal to the value of the next best use of your time.

SCARCITY AND CHOICE FOR A SINGLE FIRM

The nature of opportunity cost is perhaps clearest in the case of a single business firm that produces two outputs from a fixed supply of inputs. Given current technology and the limited resources at its disposal, the more of one good the firm produces, the less of the other it will be able to produce. Unless management carries out an explicit comparison of the available choices, weighing the desirability of each against the others, it is unlikely that it will make rational production decisions.

Consider the example of a farmer whose available supplies of land, machinery, labor, and fertilizer are capable of producing the various combinations of soybeans and wheat listed in Table 3-1. Obviously, devoting more land and other resources to the production of soybeans means that less wheat will be produced. Table 3-1 indicates, for example, that if only soybeans are produced, the harvest will be 40,000 bushels. But, if soybean production is reduced to 30,000 bushels, the farmer can also grow 38,000 bushels of wheat. Thus, the opportunity cost of obtaining 38,000 bushels of wheat is 10,000 fewer bushels of soybeans. Put another way, the opportunity cost of 10,000 more bushels of soybeans is 38,000 bushels of wheat. The other numbers in Table 3-1 have similar interpretations.

Figure 3-1 is a graphical representation of this same information. Point *A* corresponds to the first line of Table 3-1, point *B* to the second line, and so on. Curves similar to *AE* appear frequently in this

TABLE 3-1

PRODUCTION POSSIBILITIES OPEN TO A FARMER

Bushels of Soybeans	Bushels of Wheat	Label in Figure 3-1
40,000	0	*A*
30,000	38,000	*B*
20,000	52,000	*C*
10,000	60,000	*D*
0	65,000	*E*

FIGURE 3-1 PRODUCTION POSSIBILITIES FRONTIER FOR PRODUCTION BY A SINGLE FIRM

With a given set of inputs, the firm can produce only those output combinations given by points in the shaded area. The production possibilities frontier, *AE,* is not a straight line but one that curves more and more as it nears the axes. That is, when the firm specializes in only one product, those inputs that are especially adapted to the production of the other good lose at least part of their productivity.

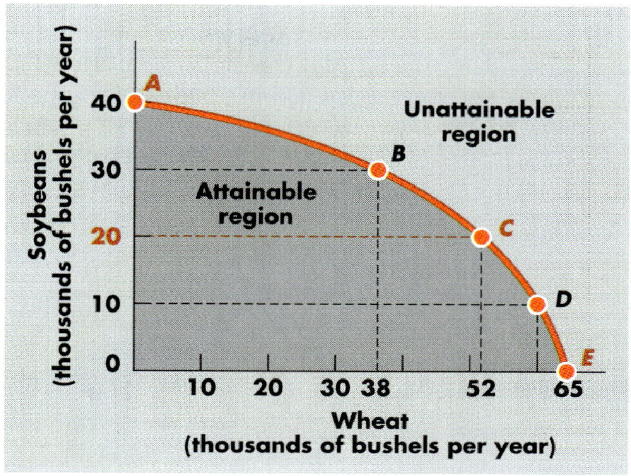

A **PRODUCTION POSSIBILITIES FRONTIER** shows the different combinations of various goods that a producer can turn out, given the available resources and existing technology.

book; they are called **production possibilities frontiers.** Any point *on or inside* the production possibilities frontier is attainable. Points outside the frontier cannot be achieved with the available resources and technology.

Because resources are limited, the production possibilities frontier always slopes downward to the right. The farmer can *increase* wheat production (move to the right in Figure 3-1) only by devoting more of her land and labor to growing wheat. But this simultaneously *reduces* soybean production (moves downward) because less of her land and labor remain available for growing soybeans.

Notice that, in addition to having a negative slope, our production possibilities frontier *AE* has another characteristic—it is "bowed outward." Let us carefully consider what this curvature means.

Suppose that our farmer initially produces only soybeans, using even land that is better suited for wheat cultivation (point *A*). Now, suppose that she decides to switch some of her land from soybean production to wheat production. Which part of her land will she switch? If she is sensible, she will use the part best suited to wheat growing. If she shifts to point *B,* soybean production falls from 40,000 bushels to 30,000 bushels as wheat production rises from zero to 38,000 bushels. A sacrifice of only 10,000 bushels of soybeans "buys" 38,000 bushels of wheat.

Imagine now that the farmer wants to produce still more wheat. Figure 3-1 tells us that the sacrifice of an additional 10,000 bushels of soybeans (from 30,000 down to 20,000) will yield only 14,000 more bushels of wheat (see point *C*). Why? The main reason is that inputs tend to be specialized. As we noted, at point *A* the farmer was using resources for soybean production that were much more suitable for growing wheat. Consequently, their productivity in soybeans was relatively low, and when they were switched to wheat production, the yield was very high. But this cannot continue forever. As more wheat is produced, the farmer must utilize land and machinery that are better suited to producing soybeans and less well-suited to producing wheat. This is why the first 10,000 bushels of soybeans forgone "buys" the farmer 38,000 bushels of wheat while the second 10,000 bushels of soybeans "buys" her only 14,000 bushels of wheat. Figure 3-1 and Table 3-1 show that these returns continue to decline as wheat production expands: The next 10,000-bushel reduction in soybean production yields only 8,000 bushels of additional wheat, and so on.

We can now see that the *slope* of the production possibilities frontier graphically represents the concept of *opportunity cost*. Between points *C* and *B*, for example, the opportunity cost of acquiring 10,000 additional bushels of soybeans is 14,000 bushels of forgone wheat; between points *B* and *A*, the opportunity cost of 10,000 bushels of soybeans is 38,000 bushels of forgone wheat. In general, as we move upward to the left along the production possibilities frontier (toward more soybeans and less wheat), the opportunity cost of soybeans in terms of wheat increases. Putting the same thing differently, as we move downward to the right, the opportunity cost of acquiring wheat by giving up soybeans increases.

THE PRINCIPLE OF INCREASING COSTS

The **PRINCIPLE OF INCREASING COSTS** states that as the production of a good expands, the opportunity cost of producing another unit generally increases.

We have just described a very general phenomenon with applications well beyond farming. The **principle of increasing costs** states that as the production of one good expands, the opportunity cost of producing another unit of this good generally increases.

This principle is not a universal fact; there can be exceptions to it. But it does seem to be a technological regularity that applies to a wide range of economic activities. As our example of the farmer suggests, the principle of increasing costs is based on the fact that resources tend to be specialized, at least in part, so that some of their productivity is lost when they are transferred from doing what they are relatively good at to what they are relatively bad at. In terms of diagrams such as Figure 3-1, the principle simply asserts that the production possibilities frontier is bowed outward.

FIGURE 3-2 PRODUCTION POSSIBILITIES FRONTIER WITH NO SPECIALIZED RESOURCES

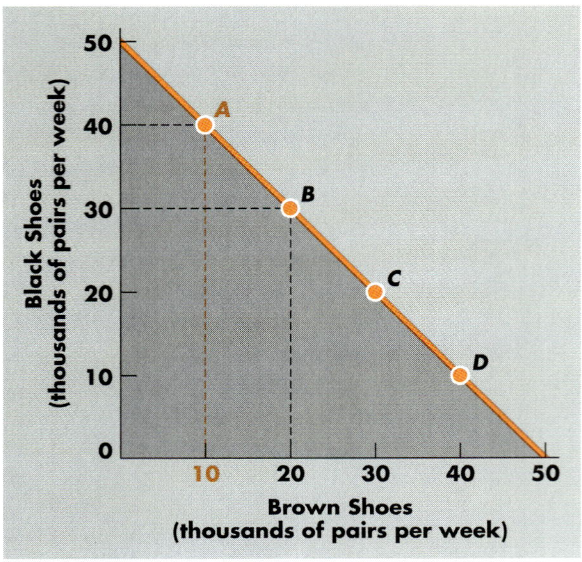

Resources that produce black shoes are just as good at producing brown shoes, so there is no loss of productivity when black-shoe production is decreased in order to increase brown-shoe production. For example, if the firm moves from point *A* to point *B*, black-shoe output falls by 10,000 pairs and brown-shoe output rises by 10,000 pairs. The same would be true if it were to move from point *B* to point *C*, or from point *C* to point *D*. The production possibilities frontier is therefore a straight line.

Perhaps the best way to understand this idea is to contrast it with a case in which there are no specialized resources. Figure 3-2 on the previous page depicts a production possibilities frontier for producing black shoes and brown shoes. Because the labor and capital used to produce black shoes are just as good at producing brown shoes, the frontier is a straight line. If the firm cuts back its production of black shoes by 10,000 pairs, it always gets 10,000 additional pairs of brown shoes. No productivity is lost in the switch because resources are not specialized.

More typically, however, as a firm switches more and more of its productive capacity from Commodity X to Commodity Y, it will eventually be forced to employ in Y production more and more inputs that are better suited to making X. This variation in the *proportions* in which inputs are used is forced on the firm by the limited quantities of some of the inputs it uses. It also explains the typical curvature of the firm's production possibilities frontier.

SCARCITY AND CHOICE FOR THE ENTIRE SOCIETY

Like an individual firm, the entire economy is also constrained by its limited resources and technology. If society wants more aircraft and tanks, it will have to give up some boats and automobiles. If it wants to build more factories and stores, it will have to build fewer homes and sports arenas. In general:

The position and shape of the production possibilities frontier that constrains the choices of the economy are determined by the economy's physical resources, its skills and technology, its willingness to work, and how much it has devoted in the past to the construction of factories, research, and innovation.

Since the debate over reducing military strength has been so much on the agenda of several nations recently (see the box below), let us illustrate the nature of society's choices by an example of choosing between military might (represented by missiles) and civilian consumption (represented by automobiles). Just

A MILITARY-CIVILIAN OUTPUT TRADE-OFF IN REALITY

The arms race may have ground to a halt, but space-age technology that helped keep the peace for 50 years is now being channeled in new directions. Literally hundreds of companies have had to face the new reality: Find other applications for current products, or perish.

The innovations have been spectacular. A rocket parts plant in Colorado developed a racing bike frame made from thermoplastic and reinforced carbon fiber. Composite materials—including boron filaments, graphites, and carbon fibers—have long been principal components in jet aircraft. Today, they are as likely to be found in golf club shafts, tennis rackets, ski poles, and even hockey sticks. Race car companies are trying to take advantage of strong, lightweight materials in car designs.

Spillover benefits haven't been limited to the sports industry. E-Systems, which still does big defense business, demonstrated an innovative touch by adapting spy satellite technology to improve tumor-detection capabilities in mammograms. New uses have even been found for shuttered military

bases. San Francisco's Treasure Island Naval Station, for example, is now being used as a movie studio.

SOURCES: Tim Smart, "Beating Swords into—Golf Clubs?" *Business Week,* April 18, 1994, p. 85; "Uncle Sam's Fire Sales," *U.S. News & World Report,* January 9, 1995; "Aerospace and Defense," *Forbes,* January 3, 1994, p. 106.

FIGURE 3-3 THE PRODUCTION POSSIBILITIES FRONTIER FOR THE ENTIRE ECONOMY

This production possibilities frontier is curved because resources are not perfectly transferable from automobile production to missile production. The limits on available resources place a ceiling, *C*, on the output of one product and a different ceiling, *B*, on the output of the other product.

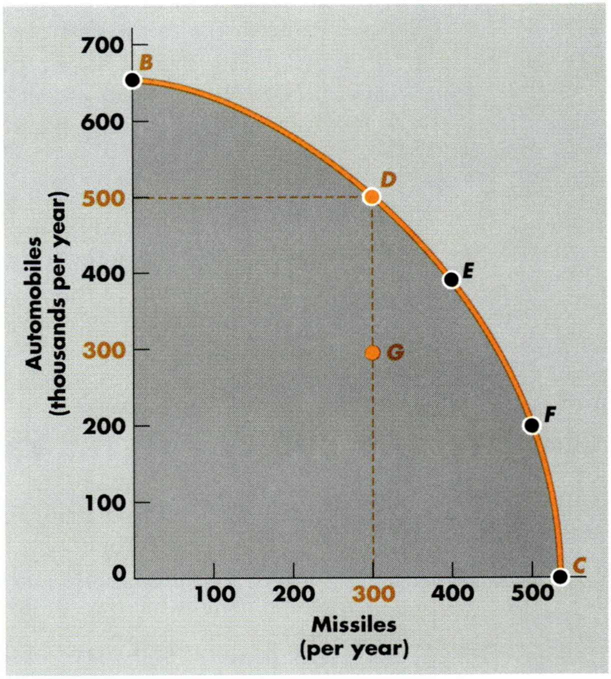

like a single firm, the economy as a whole has a production possibilities frontier for missiles and automobiles determined by its technology and the available resources of land, labor, capital, and raw materials. This production possibilities frontier may look like curve *BC* in Figure 3-3.

If most workers are employed in auto manufacturing, the production of automobiles will be large but the output of missiles will be small. If resources are transferred in the other direction, the mix of output can be shifted toward increased production of missiles at some sacrifice of automobiles (the move from *D* to *E*). However, something is likely to be lost in the transfer process—the seat fabric that went into the cars will not help much in missile production. As summarized in the principle of increasing costs, physical resources tend to be specialized, so the production possibilities frontier probably curves downward toward the axes.

We may even reach a point where the only resources left are items that are not very useful outside auto-building facilities. In that case, even a very large additional sacrifice of automobiles will enable the economy to produce very few more missiles. That is the meaning of the steep segment, *FC*, on the frontier. At point *C* there is very little additional output of missiles as compared to point *F*, even though at *C* automobile production has been given up entirely.

The downward slope of society's production possibilities frontier implies that hard choices must be made. Our civilian consumption (automobiles) can be increased only by decreasing military expenditure, not by rhetoric or by wishing it so. The curvature of the production possibilities frontier implies that, as defense spending increases, it becomes progressively more expensive to "buy" additional military strength ("missiles") by sacrificing civilian consumption.

SCARCITY AND CHOICE ELSEWHERE IN THE ECONOMY

We have stressed that limited resources force hard choices upon business managers and society as a whole. But the same type of choices arise elsewhere—in households, universities, and other nonprofit organizations, as well as the government.

The nature of opportunity cost is perhaps most obvious for a household that must decide how to divide its income among the goods and services that compete for the family's trade. If the Jones family buys an expensive new car, it may be forced to cut back sharply on some of its other purchases. This does not make it unwise to buy the car. But it does make it unwise to buy the car until the full implications of the purchase for the family's overall budget are considered. If the Jones family is to use its limited resources most effectively, it must explicitly acknowledge that the opportunity costs of the car are the things it will actually choose to forgo as a result—for example, a vacation or a new TV set.

Even a rich and powerful nation like the United States or Japan must cope with the limitations implied by scarce resources. The necessity for choice imposed on the governments of these nations by their limited budgets is similar in character to the problems faced by business firms and households. For the goods and services that it buys from others, a government has to prepare a budget similar to that of a very large household. For the items it produces itself—education, police protection, libraries, and so on—it faces a production possibilities frontier much like that of a business firm. Even though the U.S. government will spend about $1.5 trillion in 1996, some of the most acrimonious debates between *every* U.S. president and his critics have centered on allocation of the government's limited resources among competing uses.

APPLICATION: ECONOMIC GROWTH IN THE UNITED STATES AND JAPAN

ECONOMIC GROWTH occurs when an economy is able to produce more goods and services for each consumer.

Among the economic choices that any society must make, there is one extremely important choice that illustrates well the concept of opportunity cost. This choice is embodied in the question "How fast should the economy grow?" At first, the question may seem ridiculous. Since **economic growth** means, roughly speaking, that the average citizen gets larger and larger quantities of goods and services, is it not self-evident that faster growth is always better?

Again, the fundamental problem of scarcity intervenes. Economies do not grow by magic. Scarce resources must be devoted to the process of growth. Cement and steel that could be used to make swimming pools and stadiums must be diverted to the construction of more machinery and factories. Wood that could have been used to make furniture and skis must be used for hammers and ladders instead. Grain that could have been eaten must be used as seed to plant additional acres. By deciding how large a quantity of resources to devote to future needs rather than to current consumption, society in effect *chooses* (within limits) how fast it will grow.

In diagrammatic terms, economic growth means that the economy's production possibilities frontier shifts outward over time—like the move from *FF* to *GG* in Figure 3-4(a). Why? Because such a shift means that the economy can produce more of both of the outputs shown in the graph. Thus, in the figure, after growth has occurred, it is possible to produce the combination of products represented by points like *N*. Before growth had occurred, point *N* was beyond the economy's means because it was outside the production possibilities frontier.

FIGURE 3-4 GROWTH IN TWO ECONOMIES

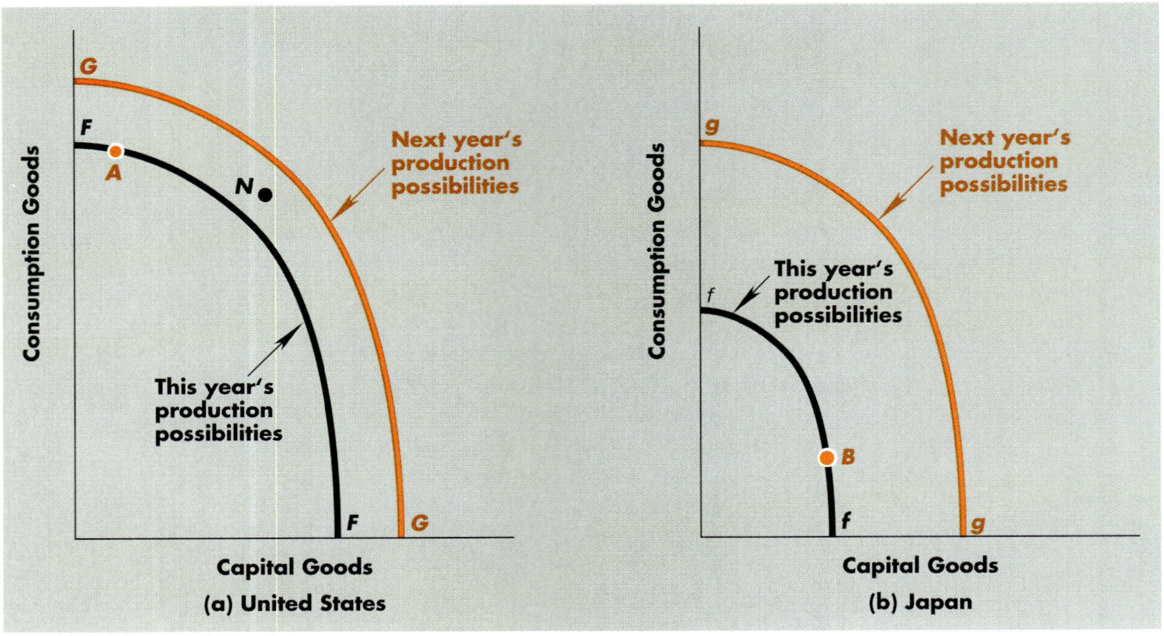

Growth shifts the black production possibilities frontiers, *FF* and *ff*, outward to the orange frontiers, *GG* and *gg*, meaning that each economy can produce more of both goods than it could before. If the shift in both economies occurs in the same period of time, then the Japanese economy [Panel (b)] is growing faster than the U.S. economy [Panel (a)] because the outward shift in (b) is much greater than the one in (a).

How does growth occur? That is, what shifts an economy's production frontier outward? There are many answers. For example, workers may acquire greater skill and learn to produce more output in an hour. Perhaps even more important, the economy may construct more capital goods, temporarily giving up some consumption goods to provide the resources to build the factories and machines. Finally, inventions like the steam engine, AC electricity, and industrial robots can and do increase the economy's productive capacity, thereby shifting its production possibilities frontier outward. However, to increase the supply of new products and new technology, the economy must devote more resources to research and development.

A **CONSUMPTION GOOD** is an item that is available for immediate use by households, one that satisfies wants of members of households without contributing directly to future production by the economy.

A **CAPITAL GOOD** is an item that is used to produce other goods and services in the future, rather than being consumed today. Factories and machines are examples.

Figure 3-4 illustrates, for two different countries, the nature of the choice by depicting production possibilities frontiers for **consumption goods,** which are consumed today (like food and electricity), versus **capital goods,** which can produce larger outputs for future consumption (like drill presses and electricity-generating plants). Figure 3-4(a) depicts a society, such as the United States, that devotes a relatively small quantity of resources to growth, preferring current consumption instead. It chooses a point like *A* on this year's production possibilities frontier, *FF*. At *A*, consumption is relatively high and production of capital is relatively low, so the production possibilities frontier shifts only to *GG* next year.

Figure 3-4(b) depicts a society, such as Japan, that is much more enamored of growth. It selects a point like *B* on its production possibilities frontier, *ff*. At *B*, consumption is much lower and production of capital goods is much higher, so its production possibilities frontier moves all the way to *gg* by next year. Japan grows faster than the United States. But the more rapid growth has a price—an *opportunity cost:* The Japanese must give up some of the current consumption that Americans enjoy.

An economy grows by giving up some current consumption and producing capital goods for the future instead. The more capital it produces, the faster will its production possibilities frontier shift outward over time.

Of course, the production of capital goods is not the only way to shift the economy's production possibilities frontier outward. New technology—the process of invention and innovation—is probably the primary means by which economies have increased the outputs that they can produce with given quantities of resources. Increased education and training of the labor force is generally believed to yield a similar result.

THE CONCEPT OF EFFICIENCY

So far in our discussion of scarcity and choice, we have assumed that either the single firm or the whole economy always operates on its production possibilities frontier rather than *below* it. In other words, we have tacitly assumed that, whatever the firm or economy decides to do, it does *efficiently.* Economists define *efficiency* as the absence of waste. An efficient economy utilizes all of its available resources and produces the maximum amount of output that its technology permits.

To see why any point on the economy's production possibilities frontier in Figure 3-3 represents an efficient decision, suppose for a moment that society has decided to produce 300 missiles. According to the production possibilities frontier, if 300 missiles are to be produced, then the maximum number of automobiles that can be made is 500,000 (point *D* in Figure 3-3). The economy is therefore operating efficiently if it actually produces 500,000 automobiles rather than some smaller amount such as 300,000 (as at point *G*). While point *D* is efficient, point *G* is not. This is so because the economy is capable of moving from *G* to *D,* thereby producing 200,000 more automobiles without giving up any missiles (or anything else). Clearly, failure to take advantage of the option of choosing point *D* rather than point *G* constitutes a wasted opportunity.

Note that the concept of efficiency does not tell us which point on the production possibilities frontier is *best;* it tells us only that any point that is *not* on the frontier cannot be best, because any such point represents wasted resources. For example, should society ever find itself at point *G,* the necessity of making hard choices would (temporarily) disappear. It would be possible to increase production of *both* missiles *and* automobiles by moving to a point such as *E.*

Why, then, would a society ever find itself at a point below its production possibilities frontier? There are a number of ways in which resources are wasted in real life. The most important of them is unemployment. When many workers are unemployed, the economy finds itself at a point like *G,* below the frontier, because by putting the unemployed to work in both industries, the economy could produce both more missiles *and* more automobiles. The economy would then move from point *G* to the right (more missiles) and upward (more automobiles) toward a point such as *E* on the production possibilities frontier. Only when no resources are wasted is the economy on the frontier.

Inefficiency occurs in other ways, as well. One prime example is assigning inputs to the wrong task—as when wheat is grown on land best suited to soybean cultivation, while soybeans are grown on land more appropriate for wheat production. Another important type of inefficiency occurs where large firms produce goods that are best turned out by small enterprises that can pay closer attention to detail, or when small firms produce outputs best suited to large-scale production. Some other examples are the outright waste that occurs because of favoritism (for example, promotion of an incompetent brother-in-law) or restrictive labor practices (for example, requiring a railroad to keep a fireman on a diesel locomotive where there is nothing for him to do).

A particularly serious form of waste is caused by discrimination against African-American, Hispanic, or female workers. When a job is given to a white male in preference to a more qualified African-American woman, output is sacrificed and the entire community is apt to be affected adversely. Every one of these inefficiencies means that the community obtains less output than it could have, given the available inputs.

THE THREE COORDINATION TASKS OF ANY ECONOMY

ALLOCATION OF RESOURCES refers to the society's decision on how to divide up its economy's scarce input resources among the different outputs produced in the economy and among the different firms or other organizations that produce those outputs.

In deciding how to **allocate its scarce resources,** a society must somehow make three sorts of decisions. First, as we have just emphasized, it must figure out *how to utilize its resources efficiently;* that is, it must find a way to reach its production possibilities frontier. Second, it must decide *what combination of goods to produce*—how many missiles, automobiles, and so on; that is, it must select one specific point on the production possibilities frontier. Finally, it must decide *how much of each good to distribute to each person,* doing so in a sensible way that does not assign meat to vegetarians and wine to teetotalers.

Certainly, each of these decisions—*which are often referred to as "how?" "what?" and "to whom?"*—can be made in many ways. For example, a central planner can tell people how to produce, what to produce, and what to consume, as used to be done, at least to some extent, in the former Soviet Union and the other countries of eastern Europe. In a market economy such as the United States, Canada, or the United Kingdom, no one group or individual makes such resource allocation decisions explicitly. Rather, they are made automatically, often unobserved, through a system of prices and markets *whose directions are dictated by the demands of consumers and by the costs of producers.* As the formerly socialist countries have learned, markets can do an impressively effective job in carrying out these tasks. To see how markets can do this, let us consider each task in turn.

SPECIALIZATION, DIVISION OF LABOR, AND EXCHANGE

DIVISION OF LABOR means breaking up a task into a number of smaller, more specialized tasks so that each worker can become more adept at a particular job.

Efficiency in production is one of the economy's three basic tasks. Many features of society contribute to efficiency; others interfere with it. While different societies pursue the goal of economic efficiency in different ways, one source of efficiency is so fundamental that we must single it out for special attention: the tremendous gains in productivity that stem from *specialization* and the consequent **division of labor.**

Adam Smith, the founder of modern economics, first marveled at this mainspring of efficiency and productivity on a visit to a pin factory. In a famous passage near the beginning of his monumental book, *The Wealth of Nations* (1776), he described what he saw:

ADAM SMITH (1723–1790)

Adam Smith, the philosopher of the market system, was born the son of a customs official in 1723 and ended his career in the well-paid post of collector of customs for Scotland. He received an excellent education at Glasgow College, where, for the first time, some lectures were being given in English rather than Latin. A fellowship to Oxford University followed, and for 6 years he studied there mostly by himself, since, at that time, teaching was virtually nonexistent at Oxford.

After completing his studies, Smith was appointed professor of logic at Glasgow College and, later, professor of moral philosophy, a field which then included economics. Fortunately, he was a popular lecturer because, in those days, a professor's pay in Glasgow depended on the number of students who chose to attend his lectures. At Glasgow, Smith was responsible for helping young James Watt find a job as an instrument maker. Watt later invented a key improvement in the steam engine that made its use possible in factories, trains, and ships. In this and many other respects, Smith was present virtually at the birth of the Industrial Revolution, whose prophet he was destined to become.

After 13 years at Glasgow, Smith accepted a highly paid post as a tutor to a young Scottish nobleman with whom he spent several years in France, a customary way of educating nobles in the 18th century. Primarily because he was bored during these years, Smith began working on *The Wealth of Nations*. In 1776, several years after his return to England, the book was published and rapidly achieved popularity.

The Wealth of Nations was one of the first systematic treatises in economics, contributing to both theoretical and factual knowledge about the subject. Among the main points made in the book are the importance for a nation's prosperity of free trade and the division of labor, the dangers of tariffs and government-protected monopolies, and the superiority of self-interest—the instrument of the "invisible hand"—over altruism as a means of making the economy serve the public interest.

The British government was grateful for Smith's ideas on new tax legislation, and to show its appreciation, it appointed him to the lucrative sinecure of collector of customs. The salary from this post, together with the lifetime pension awarded him by his former pupil, left him very well-off financially, although he eventually gave away most of his money to charitable causes.

The intellectual world was small in the 18th century, and Smith's acquaintances included David Hume, Samuel Johnson, James Boswell, Jean Jacques Rousseau, and (probably) Benjamin Franklin. Smith got along well with everyone except Samuel Johnson, who was noted for his dislike of Scots. Smith was absent-minded and apparently timid with women, being visibly embarrassed by the public attention of the eminent ladies of Paris during his visits there. He never married, and he lived with his mother most of his life. When he died, the Edinburgh newspapers recalled only that Smith was kidnapped by gypsies when he was 4 years old. But thanks to his writings, he is remembered for a good deal more than that.

> One man draws out the wire, another straightens it, a third cuts it, a fourth points it, a fifth grinds it at the top for receiving the head; to make the head requires two or three distinct operations; to put it on is a peculiar business, to whiten the pins is another; it is even a trade by itself to put them into the paper.[1]

Smith observed that by dividing the work to be done in this way, each worker became quite skilled in a particular specialty, and the productivity of the group of workers as a whole was enhanced enormously. As Smith related it:

> I have seen a small manufactory of this kind where ten men only were employed. . . . Those ten persons . . . could make among them upwards of forty-eight thousand pins in a day. . . . But if they had all wrought separately and independently . . . they certainly could not each of them have made twenty, *perhaps not one pin in a day*.[2]

In other words, through the miracle of division of labor and specialization, ten workers accomplished what would otherwise have required thousands. This was

[1] Adam Smith, *The Wealth of Nations* (New York: Random House, 1937), p. 4.

[2] Ibid., p. 5.

one of the secrets of the Industrial Revolution, which helped lift humanity out of longstanding abject poverty.

But specialization created a problem. With division of labor, people no longer produced only what they wanted to consume themselves. The workers in the pin factory had no use for the thousands of pins they produced each day; they wanted to trade them for things like food, clothing, and shelter. Specialization thus made it necessary to have some mechanism by which workers producing pins could *exchange* their wares with workers producing such things as cloth and potatoes.

Without a system of exchange, the productivity miracle achieved by the division of labor would have done society little good. With it, standards of living rose enormously. As we observed in Chapter 1, such exchange benefits *all* participants.

MUTUAL GAINS FROM VOLUNTARY EXCHANGE

Unless there is deception or misunderstanding of the facts, a *voluntary* exchange between two parties must make both parties better off. Trading increases production by permitting specialization, as we have just seen. But even if no additional goods are produced as a result of the act of trading, the welfare of society is increased because each individual acquires goods that are more suited to his or her needs and tastes. This simple but fundamental precept of economics is one of our **Ideas for Beyond the Final Exam.**

While goods can be traded for other goods, a system of exchange works better when everyone agrees to use some common item (such as pieces of paper with unique markings printed on them) for buying and selling goods and services. Enter *money*. Then workers in pin factories, for example, can be paid in money rather than in pins, and they can use this money to purchase cloth and potatoes. Textile workers and farmers can do the same.

These two phenomena—specialization and exchange (assisted by money)—working in tandem led to a vast improvement in the well-being of humanity. But what forces induce workers to join together so that the fruits of the division of labor can be enjoyed? Also, what forces establish a smoothly functioning system of exchange so that each person can acquire what she or he wants to consume? One alternative is to have a central authority telling people what to do. But Adam Smith explained and extolled another way of organizing and coordinating economic activity—the use of markets and prices.

MARKETS, PRICES, AND THE THREE COORDINATION TASKS

A **MARKET SYSTEM** is a form of organization of the economy in which decisions on resource allocation are left to the independent decisions of individual producers and consumers acting in their own best interests without central direction.

Smith noted that people are adept at pursuing their own self-interests, and that a **market system** is a fine way to harness this self-interest. As he put it—with pretty clear religious overtones—in doing what is best for themselves, people are "led by an invisible hand" to promote the economic well-being of society as a whole.

People who live in a well-functioning market economy like ours tend to take the achievements of the market for granted, much like the daily rising and setting of the sun. Few bother to think about, say, what makes Florida oranges show up daily in South Dakota supermarkets. While the process by which the market guides the economy to work in such an orderly fashion is far from obvious to most of the public, the general principles are not overly complex.

The market deals effectively with efficiency in production because firms are discouraged by the profit motive from using inputs wastefully. Valuable resources (such as energy) command high prices, and so producers have strong incentives to use them efficiently. The market mechanism also guides firms' output decisions, and hence those of society, matching quantities produced to consumer preferences. A rise in the price of wheat because of increased demand for wheat products, for example, will persuade farmers to produce more wheat and to devote less of their land to soybeans. Finally, a price system distributes goods among consumers in accord with their tastes and preferences, using a series of voluntary exchanges to determine what goods go to which consumers.

Consumers use their incomes to buy the things they like best among those they can afford. But the ability to buy goods is not divided equally. Workers with valuable skills and owners of scarce resources are able to sell what they have at attractive prices. With the incomes they earn, they can then purchase the goods and services they want most, within the limits of their budgets. Those who are less successful in selling what they own receive lower incomes, and so they cannot afford to buy much. In some cases, they suffer severe deprivation.

This, in broad terms, is how a market economy solves the three basic problems facing any society: how to produce any given combination of goods efficiently, how to select an appropriate combination of goods to produce, and how to distribute these goods sensibly among people. As we proceed through the following chapters, you will learn much more about these issues. You will see that they constitute the central theme that permeates not only this text, but the work of economists, in general. As you progress through the book, keep in mind two questions: *What does the market do well, and what does it do poorly?* There are numerous answers to both questions, as you will learn in subsequent chapters.

1. Society has many important goals. Some of them, such as producing goods and services with maximum efficiency (minimum waste), can be achieved extraordinarily well by letting markets operate more or less freely.
2. Free markets will not, however, achieve all of society's goals. For example, they often have trouble keeping unemployment and inflation low. In fact, there are even some goals—such as protection of the environment—for which the unfettered operation of markets may be positively harmful. Many observers also believe that markets do not necessarily lead to equitable distributions of income.
3. But even in cases where markets do not perform at all well, there may be ways of harnessing the power of the market mechanism to remedy its own deficiencies, as you will learn in later chapters.

LIBERAL AND CONSERVATIVE GOALS CAN BOTH BE SERVED BY THE MARKET MECHANISM

Since economic debates often have political and ideological overtones, we think it important to close this chapter by emphasizing that the central theme that we have just outlined is neither a defense of nor an attack on the capitalist system, nor is it a "conservative" position. One does not have to be a conservative to recognize that the market mechanism can be an extraordinarily helpful instrument for the pursuit of economic goals. Most of the formerly staunch socialist countries of Europe are now working hard to "marketize" their economies, and even the People's Republic of China is moving in that direction.

The point is not to confuse means and ends in deciding how much to rely on market forces. Liberals and conservatives surely have different goals, and they may also differ in the means they advocate to pursue these goals. But means should be chosen on the basis of how effective they are in achieving the adopted goals, not on some ideological prejudgments.

Even Karl Marx recognized, indeed emphasized, that the market is a remarkably efficient mechanism for producing an abundance of goods and services unparalleled in pre-capitalist history. Such wealth can be used to promote conservative goals, such as reducing tax rates, or it can be used to facilitate the achievement of the goals of liberals or even radicals, such as more generous public support of the impoverished, the construction of more public schools and hospitals, and the provision of amenities such as national parks and museums.

Certainly, there are economic problems with which the market cannot deal. Indeed, we have just noted that the market is the *source* of a number of significant problems. But the evidence leads economists to believe that many economic problems are best handled by market techniques. The analysis in this book is intended to help you identify the objectives the market mechanism can reliably achieve, and those that it will fail to promote, or at least not promote very effectively. We urge you to forget the slogans you have heard—whether from the left or from the right—and make up your own mind after learning the material in this book.

SUMMARY

1. Supplies of all **resources** are limited. Because resources are scarce, a **rational decision** is one that chooses the best alternative among the options that are possible with the available resources.
2. It is irrational to assign highest priority to everything. No one can afford everything, and so hard choices must be made.
3. With limited resources, a decision to obtain more of one item is also a decision to give up some of another. What we give up is called the **opportunity cost** of what we get. The opportunity cost is the true cost of any decision. This is one of the **Ideas for Beyond the Final Exam.**
4. When the market is functioning effectively, firms are led to use resources efficiently and to produce the things that consumers want most. In such cases, opportunity costs and money costs (prices) correspond closely. When the market performs poorly, or when important costly items do not get price tags, opportunity costs and money costs can be quite different.
5. A firm's **production possibilities frontier** shows the combinations of goods that the firm can produce with a designated quantity of resources, given the state of technology. The frontier usually is not a straight line, but is bowed outward because resources tend to be specialized.
6. The **principle of increasing costs** states that as the production of one good expands, the opportunity cost of producing another unit of that good generally increases.
7. The economy as a whole has a production possibilities frontier whose position is determined by its technology and by the available resources of land, labor, capital, and raw materials.
8. If a firm or an economy ends up at a point below its production possibilities frontier, it is using its resources inefficiently or wastefully. This is what happens, for example, when there is unemployment.
9. **Economic growth** means there is an outward shift in the economy's production possibilities frontier. The faster the growth, the faster this shift occurs. But growth requires a sacrifice of current consumption; this is its opportunity cost.
10. *Efficiency* is defined by economists as the absence of waste. It is achieved primarily by gains in productivity brought about through *specialization,* **division of labor,** and a *system of exchange.*
11. If an exchange is voluntary, both parties must benefit, even if no additional goods are produced. This is another of the **Ideas for Beyond the Final Exam.**

12. Every economic system must find a way to answer three basic questions: How can goods be produced most efficiently? How much of each good should be produced? How should goods be distributed?
13. The **market system** works very well in solving some of society's basic problems, but it fails to remedy others and may, indeed, create some of its own. Where and how it succeeds and fails constitute the theme of this book and characterize the work of economists, in general.

KEY TERMS

Resources
Scarcity
Choice
Rational decision
Opportunity cost
Outputs
Inputs (means of production)
Production possibilities frontier
Principle of increasing costs
Economic growth
Consumption good
Capital good
Allocation of resources
Efficiency
Specialization
Division of labor
Exchange
Market system
Three coordination tasks

QUESTIONS FOR REVIEW

1. Discuss the resource limitations that affect
   a. The poorest person on earth
   b. The richest person on earth
   c. A firm in Switzerland
   d. A government agency in China
   e. The population of the world.
2. If you were president of your college, what would you change if your budget were cut by 10 percent? By 25 percent? By 50 percent?
3. If you were to drop out of college, what things would change in your life? What, then, is the opportunity cost of your education?
4. A person rents a house for which she pays the landlord $12,000 a year. The house can be purchased for $100,000, and the tenant has this much money in a bank account that pays 4 percent interest per year. Is buying the house a good deal for the tenant? Where does opportunity cost enter the picture?
5. Construct graphically the production possibilities frontier for the Grand Republic of Glubstania, using the data given in the following table. Does the principle of increasing cost hold in the Glubstanian economy?

Glubstania's 1998 Production Possibilities

Pork Muffins (millions per year)	Noodle Machines (thousands per year)
75	0
60	6
45	11
30	15
15	18
0	20

6. Consider two alternatives for Glubstania in the year 1998. In case (a), its inhabitants eat 60 million pork muffins and build only 6,000 noodle machines. In case (b), the population eats only 15 million pork muffins but builds 18,000 noodle machines. Which case will lead to a more generous production possibilities frontier for Glubstania in 1999? (**Note:** In Glubstania, noodle machines are used to produce pork muffins.)
7. Sarah's Snack Shop sells two brands of potato chips. Brand X costs Sarah 60 cents per bag, and Brand Y costs Sarah $1. Draw Sarah's production possibilities frontier if she has $60 budgeted to spend on potato chips. Why is it not "bowed out"?
8. To raise chickens, it is necessary to use many types of feed, such as corn and soy meal. Consider a farm in the former Soviet Union, and try to describe how decisions on the number of chickens to be raised, and the amount of each feed to use in raising them, were made under the old communist regime. If the farm is now a private enterprise, how does the market guide the decisions that used to be made by the central planning agency?
9. The United States is one of the world's wealthiest countries. Think of a recent case in which the decisions of the U.S. government were severely constrained by scarcity. Describe the trade-offs that were involved. What were the opportunity costs of the decisions that were actually made?

CHAPTER 4

SUPPLY AND DEMAND: AN INITIAL LOOK

The free enterprise system is absolutely too important to be left to the voluntary action of the marketplace.
Richard Kelly, Congressman from Florida, 1979

If the issues of scarcity, choice, and coordination constitute the basic *problem* of economics, then the mechanism of supply and demand is its basic investigative *tool*. Whether your course concentrates on macroeconomics or microeconomics, you will find that the so-called *law of supply and demand* is the fundamental tool of economic analysis. Economists use supply and demand analysis to study issues as diverse as inflation and unemployment, the international value of the dollar, government regulation of business, and protection of the environment. So careful study of this chapter will pay rich dividends, both in this course and in any other economics courses you may take.

The chapter describes the rudiments of supply and demand analysis in steps. We begin with demand, then add supply, and finally put the two sides together. *Supply and demand curves*—graphs that relate price to quantity supplied and quantity demanded, respectively—are explained and used to show how prices and quantities are determined in a free market. Influences that shift either the demand curve or the supply curve are catalogued briefly, and the analysis is used to explain why airlines often run "sales" and how computers found their way into the home.

One major theme of the chapter is that governments around the world and throughout recorded history have tampered with the price mechanism. We will see that these bouts with Adam Smith's invisible hand often have produced undesired side effects that surprised and dismayed the authorities. These unfortunate effects were no accidents; rather they were inherent consequences of interfering with the operation of free markets. The invisible hand fights back!

Finally, a word of caution. This chapter makes heavy use of graphs such as those described in the appendix to Chapter 1. If you encounter difficulties with these graphs, we suggest that you review pages 18–23 before proceeding.

FIGHTING THE INVISIBLE HAND

Adam Smith was a great admirer of the price system. He marveled at its intricacies and extolled its accomplishments—both as a producer of goods and as a guarantor of individual freedom. Many people since Smith's time have shared his enthusiasm, but many others have not. His contemporaries in the American colonies, for example, were often unhappy with the prices produced by free markets and thought they could do better by legislative decree. (They could not, as the box below shows.) And there have been countless other instances in which the public's sense of justice was outraged by the prices charged on the open market, particularly when the sellers of the expensive items did not enjoy great popularity. Landlords, money lenders, and oil companies are good examples.

Attempts to control interest rates (which are the price of borrowing money) go back hundreds of years before the birth of Christ, at least to the code of laws compiled under Hammurabi in Babylonia about 1800 B.C. Our historical legacy also includes a rather long list of price ceilings on foods and other products imposed in the reign of Diocletian, emperor of the declining Roman Empire.

PRICE CONTROLS AT VALLEY FORGE

George Washington, the history books tell us, was beset by many enemies during the winter of 1777 to 1778—including the British, their Hessian mercenaries, and the merciless winter weather. But he had another enemy that the history books ignore, an enemy that meant well but almost destroyed his army at Valley Forge. As the following excerpt explains, that enemy was the Pennsylvania legislature.

> In Pennsylvania, where the main force of Washington's army was quartered . . . the legislature . . . decided to try a period of price control limited to those commodities needed for use by the army. . . . The result might have been anticipated by those with some knowledge of the trials and tribulations of other states. The prices of uncontrolled goods, mostly imported, rose to record heights. Most farmers kept back their produce, refusing to sell at what they regarded as an unfair price. Some who had large families to take care of even secretly sold their food to the British who paid in gold.
>
> After the disastrous winter at Valley Forge when Washington's army nearly starved to death (thanks largely to these well-intentioned but misdirected laws), the ill-fated experiment in price controls was finally ended. The Continental Congress on June 4, 1778, adopted the following resolution:
>
> "Whereas . . . it hath been found by experience that limitations upon the prices of commodities are not only ineffectual for the purposes proposed, but likewise productive of very evil consequences . . . resolved, that it be recommended to the several states to repeal or suspend all laws or resolutions within the said states respectively limiting, regulating or restraining the Price of any Article, Manufacture or Commodity."

SOURCE: Robert L. Schuettinger and Eamonn F. Butler, *Forty Centuries of Wage and Price Controls* (Washington, D.C.: Heritage Foundation, 1979), p. 41. Reprinted by permission.

More recently, Americans have been offered the "protection" of a variety of price controls. Ceilings have been placed on some prices (such as rents) to protect buyers, while floors have been placed under other prices (such as farm products) to protect sellers.

Many if not most of these measures were adopted in response to popular opinion, and there was a great outcry whenever it was proposed that any of them be weakened or eliminated. Yet, somehow, everything such regulation touches seems to end up in even greater disarray than it was before. Despite rent controls, rents in New York City have soared. Despite laws against ticket "scalping," tickets for popular shows and sports events sell at tremendous premiums—tickets to the Super Bowl, for example, are often scalped for $1,000 or more. Taxis cost much more in New York City (where they are tightly regulated) than in Washington, D.C. (where they are not). The list could go on.

Still, legislators continue to turn to controls whenever the economy does not work to their satisfaction, just as they did in 1777. The 1970s and 1980s saw a return to rent controls in many American cities, a brief experiment with overall price controls by a Republican administration that had vowed never to turn to them, a web of controls over energy prices, and a revival of agricultural price supports. In the 1990s, the Clinton administration also flirted with price controls as part of its efforts to curb health-care costs.

INTERFERENCES WITH THE "LAW" OF SUPPLY AND DEMAND

Public opinion frequently encourages legislative attempts to "repeal the law of supply and demand" by controlling prices. The consequences usually are quite unfortunate, exacting heavy costs from the general public and often aggravating the problem the legislation was intended to cure. This is another of the **Ideas for Beyond the Final Exam,** and it will occupy our attention throughout this chapter.

To understand what goes wrong when markets are tampered with, we must first learn how they operate when they are unfettered. This chapter takes a first step in that direction by studying the machinery of supply and demand. Then, at the end of the chapter, we return to the issue of price controls, illustrating the problems that can arise by case studies of rent controls in New York City and price supports for sugar.

Every market has both buyers and sellers. We begin our analysis on the consumers' side of the market.

DEMAND AND QUANTITY DEMANDED

People commonly think of consumer demands as fixed amounts. For example, when the production of a new model of computer is proposed, management asks "What is its market potential?" Similarly, government bureaus conduct studies to determine how many engineers the work force will require in succeeding years.

Economists respond that such questions are not well posed—that there is no *single* answer to such a question. Rather, they say, the "market potential" for computers or the number of engineers that will be "required" depends on a great number of things, *including the price that will be charged for each.*

The **QUANTITY DEMANDED** is the number of units that consumers want to buy over a specified period of time.

The **quantity demanded** of any product normally depends on its price. Quantity demanded also has a number of other determinants, including population size, consumer incomes, tastes, and the prices of other products.

Because of the central role of prices in a market economy, we begin our study of demand by focusing on the dependence of quantity demanded on price. Shortly, we will bring the other determinants of quantity demanded back into the picture.

Consider, as an example, the quantity of milk demanded. Almost everyone purchases at least some milk. However, if the price of milk is very high, its "market potential" may be very small. People will find ways to get along with less milk, perhaps by switching to tea or coffee. If the price declines, people will be encouraged to drink more milk. They may give their children larger portions or switch away from juices and sodas. Thus:

There is no *one* demand figure for milk, for computers, or for engineers. Rather, there is a different quantity demanded for each possible price.

THE DEMAND SCHEDULE

A **DEMAND SCHEDULE** is a table showing how the quantity demanded of some product during a specified period of time changes as the price of that product changes, holding all other determinants of quantity demanded constant.

Table 4-1 displays this information for milk in what we call a **demand schedule.** It indicates how much consumers are willing and able to buy at different possible prices during a specified period of time. Specifically, the table shows the quantity of milk that will be demanded in a year at each possible price ranging from $1 to 40 cents per quart. We see, for example, that at a relatively low price, like 50 cents per quart, customers wish to purchase 70 billion quarts per year. But if the price were to rise to, say, 90 cents per quart, quantity demanded would fall to 50 billion quarts.

Common sense tells us why this happens.[1] First, as prices rise, some customers will reduce their consumption of milk. Second, higher prices will induce some customers to drop out of the market entirely—for example, by switching to soda or juice. On both counts, quantity demanded will decline as the price rises.

As the price of an item rises, the quantity demanded normally falls. As the price falls, the quantity demanded normally rises.

A **DEMAND CURVE** is a graphical depiction of a demand schedule. It shows how the quantity demanded of some product during a specified period of time will change as the price of that product changes, holding all other determinants of quantity demanded constant.

THE DEMAND CURVE

The information contained in Table 4-1 can be summarized in a graph like Figure 4-1, which is called a **demand curve.** Each point in the graph corresponds to a line in the table. For example, point *B* corresponds to the second line in the table, indicating that at a price of 90 cents per quart, 50 billion quarts per year will be demanded. Since the quantity demanded declines as the price increases, the demand curve has a negative slope.[2]

Notice the last phrase in the definitions of the demand schedule and the demand curve: "holding all other determinants of quantity demanded constant."

[1]This common-sense answer is examined more fully in later chapters.

[2]If you need to review the concept of *slope,* refer back to the appendix to Chapter 1.

TABLE 4-1

DEMAND SCHEDULE FOR MILK

Price (dollars per quart)	Quantity Demanded (billions of quarts per year)	Label in Figure 4-1
1.00	45	*A*
0.90	50	*B*
0.80	55	*C*
0.70	60	*E*
0.60	65	*F*
0.50	70	*G*
0.40	75	*H*

We will examine these "other things" later in the chapter. First, however, let's look at the sellers' side of the market.

SUPPLY AND QUANTITY SUPPLIED

The **QUANTITY SUPPLIED** is the number of units that sellers want to sell over a specified period of time.

Like quantity demanded, the quantity of milk that is supplied by dairy farmers is not a fixed number; it also depends on many things. Obviously, we expect more milk to be supplied if there are more dairy farms, or more cows per farm. Cows may give less milk if bad weather deprives them of their feed. As before, however, let's turn our attention first to the relationship between **quantity supplied** and one of its major determinants—the price of milk.

Economists generally suppose that a higher price calls forth a greater quantity supplied. Why? Remember our analysis of the principle of increasing cost in Chapter 3 (page 54). According to that principle, as more of any farmer's (or the nation's) resources are devoted to milk production, the opportunity cost of

FIGURE 4-1

DEMAND CURVE FOR MILK

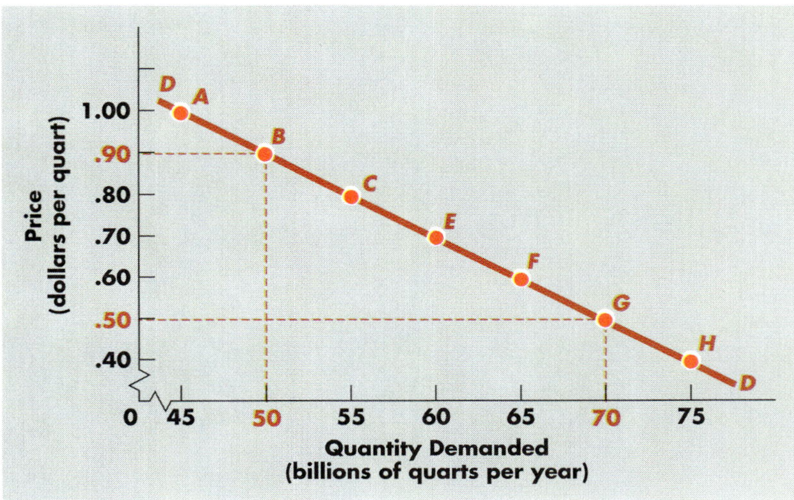

This curve shows the relationship between price and quantity demanded. To sell 70 billion quarts per year, the price must be only 50 cents (point *G*). If, instead, the price is 90 cents, only 50 billion quarts will be demanded (point *B*). To sell more milk, the price must be reduced. That is what the negative slope of the demand curve means.

TABLE 4-2

SUPPLY SCHEDULE FOR MILK

Price (dollars per quart)	Quantity Supplied (billions of quarts per year)	Label in Figure 4-2
1.00	90	*a*
0.90	80	*b*
0.80	70	*c*
0.70	60	*e*
0.60	50	*f*
0.50	40	*g*
0.40	30	*h*

obtaining another quart of milk increases. Farmers will therefore find it profitable to raise milk production only if they can sell the milk at a higher price—high enough to cover the additional costs incurred to expand production.

In other words, it normally will take higher prices to persuade farmers to raise milk production. This idea is quite general and applies to the supply of most goods and services.[3] As long as suppliers want to make profits and the principle of increasing costs holds:

A **SUPPLY SCHEDULE** is a table showing how the quantity supplied of some product during a specified period of time changes as the price of that product changes, holding all other determinants of quantity supplied constant.

As the price of an item rises, the quantity supplied normally rises. As the price falls, the quantity supplied normally falls.

THE SUPPLY SCHEDULE AND THE SUPPLY CURVE

A **SUPPLY CURVE** is a graphical depiction of a supply schedule. It shows how the quantity supplied of some product during a specified period of time will change as the price of that product changes, holding all other determinants of quantity supplied constant.

Table 4-2 shows the relationship between the price of milk and its quantity supplied. Tables like this are called **supply schedules;** they show how much sellers are willing to provide during a specified period at alternative possible prices. This particular supply schedule shows that a low price like 50 cents per quart will induce suppliers to provide only 40 billion quarts, while a higher price like 80 cents will induce them to provide much more—70 billion quarts.

As you might have guessed, when information like this is plotted on a graph, it is called a **supply curve.** Figure 4-2 is the supply curve corresponding to the supply schedule in Table 4-2. It slopes upward because quantity supplied is higher when price is higher. Notice again the same phrase in the definition: "holding all other determinants of quantity supplied constant." We will return to these "other determinants" later. But first we are ready to put demand and supply together.

EQUILIBRIUM OF SUPPLY AND DEMAND

To analyze how price is determined in a free market, we must compare the desires of consumers (demand) with the desires of producers (supply) and see whether the two plans are consistent. Table 4-3 and Figure 4-3 help us do this.

Table 4-3 brings together the demand schedule from Table 4-1 and the supply schedule from Table 4-2. Similarly, Figure 4-3 puts the demand curve from

[3]This analysis is carried out in much greater detail in later chapters.

FIGURE 4-2

This curve shows the relationship between the price of milk and the quantity supplied. To stimulate a greater quantity supplied, price must be increased. That is the meaning of the positive slope of the supply curve.

SUPPLY CURVE FOR MILK

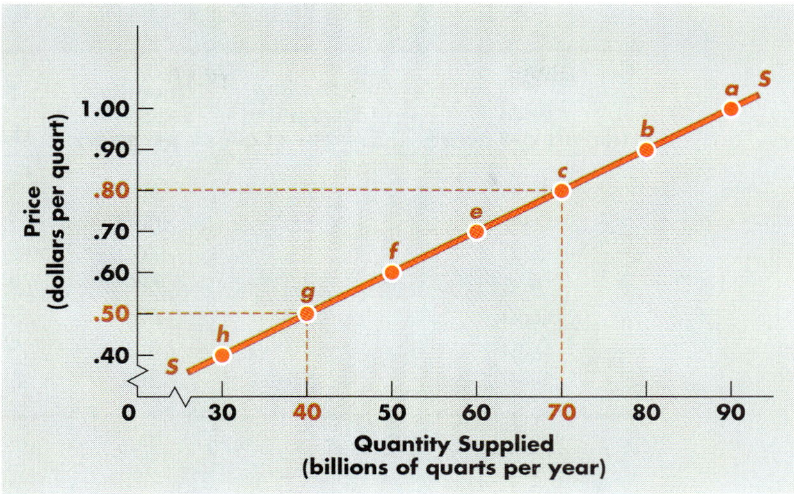

A **SUPPLY-DEMAND DIAGRAM** graphs the supply and demand curves together. It depicts the equilibrium price and quantity.

Figure 4-1 and the supply curve from Figure 4-2 on a single graph. Such graphs are called **supply-demand diagrams,** and you will encounter many of them in this book. Notice that, for reasons already discussed, the demand curve has a negative slope and the supply curve has a positive slope. That is generally true of supply-demand diagrams.

There is only one point in Figure 4-3, point *E,* at which the supply curve and the demand curve intersect. At the price corresponding to point *E,* which is 70 cents per quart, the quantity supplied and the quantity demanded are both 60 billion quarts per year. This means that, at a price of 70 cents per quart, consumers are willing to buy exactly what producers are willing to sell.

FIGURE 4-3

In a free market, price and quantity are determined by the intersection of the supply curve and the demand curve. In this example, the equilibrium price is 70 cents and the equilibrium quantity is 60 billion quarts of milk per year. Any other price is inconsistent with equilibrium. For example, at a price of 50 cents, quantity demanded is 70 billion (point *G*), while quantity supplied is only 40 billion (point *g*), so that price will be driven up by the unsatisfied demand.

SUPPLY-DEMAND EQUILIBRIUM

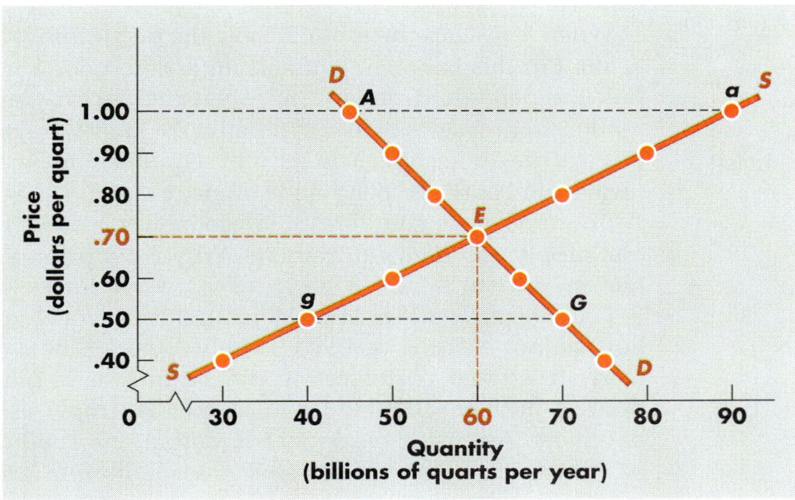

TABLE 4-3

DETERMINATION OF THE EQUILIBRIUM PRICE AND QUANTITY OF MILK

Price (dollars per quart)	Quantity Demanded (billions of quarts per year)	Quantity Supplied (billions of quarts per year)	Surplus or Shortage?	Price Will
1.00	45	90	Surplus	Fall
0.90	50	80	Surplus	Fall
0.80	55	70	Surplus	Fall
0.70	60	60	Neither	Remain the same
0.60	65	50	Shortage	Rise
0.50	70	40	Shortage	Rise
0.40	75	30	Shortage	Rise

A **SHORTAGE** is an excess of quantity demanded over quantity supplied. When there is a shortage, buyers cannot purchase the quantities they desire.

A **SURPLUS** is an excess of quantity supplied over quantity demanded. When there is a surplus, sellers cannot sell the quantities they desire to supply.

An **EQUILIBRIUM** is a situation in which there are no inherent forces that produce change. Changes away from an equilibrium position will occur only as a result of "outside events" that disturb the status quo.

At any lower price, such as 50 cents, only 40 billion quarts of milk will be supplied (point *g*) whereas 70 billion quarts will be demanded (point *G*). Thus, quantity demanded will exceed quantity supplied. There will be a **shortage** equal to 70 minus 40, or 30 billion quarts. Alternatively, at a higher price like $1, quantity supplied will be 90 billion quarts (point *a*) while quantity demanded will be only 45 billion (point *A*). Quantity supplied will exceed quantity demanded, so there will be a **surplus** equal to 90 minus 45, or 45 billion quarts.

Since 70 cents is the price at which quantity supplied and quantity demanded are equal, we say that 70 cents per quart is the *equilibrium price* in this market. Similarly, 60 billion quarts per year is the *equilibrium quantity* of milk. The term *equilibrium* merits a little explanation, since it arises so frequently in economic analysis.

An **equilibrium** is a situation in which there are no inherent forces that produce change. Think, for example, of a pendulum at rest at its center point. If no outside force (such as a person's hand) comes to push it, the pendulum will remain exactly where it is; it is therefore in *equilibrium*. But if you give the pendulum a shove, its equilibrium will be disturbed and it will start to move upward.

When it reaches the top of its arc, the pendulum will, for an instant, be at rest again. But this is not an equilibrium position, for a force known as gravity will pull the pendulum downward. Thereafter, gravity and friction will govern its motion from side to side. Eventually, we know, the pendulum will return to its original position, which is its only equilibrium. At any other point, inherent forces will cause the pendulum to move.

The concept of equilibrium in economics is similar and can be illustrated by our supply and demand example. Why is no price other than 70 cents an equilibrium price in Table 4-3 or Figure 4-3? What forces will change any other price?

Consider first a low price like 50 cents, at which quantity demanded (70 billion quarts) exceeds quantity supplied (40 billion). If the price were this low, many frustrated customers would be unable to purchase the quantities they desired. In their scramble for the available supply of milk, some would offer to pay more. As customers sought to outbid one another, the market price would be forced up. Thus, a price below the equilibrium price cannot persist in a free market because a shortage sets in motion powerful economic forces that push price upward.

Similar forces operate if the market price is *above* the equilibrium price. If, for example, the price should somehow get to be $1, Table 4-3 tells us that quantity supplied (90 billion quarts) would far exceed quantity demanded (45 billion). Producers would be unable to sell their desired quantities of milk at the prevailing price, and some would undercut their competitors by reducing price. Such competitive price-cutting would continue as long as the surplus remained, that is, as long as quantity supplied exceeded quantity demanded. Thus, a price above the equilibrium price cannot persist indefinitely.

We are left with a clear conclusion. The price 70 cents per quart and the quantity 60 billion quarts per year is the *only* price-quantity combination that does not sow the seeds of its own destruction. It is thus the only *equilibrium* for this market. Any lower price must rise, and any higher price must fall. It is as if natural economic forces place a magnet at point *E* that attracts the market just like gravity attracts a pendulum.

The pendulum analogy is worth pursuing further. Most pendulums are more frequently in motion than at rest. However, unless they are repeatedly buffeted by outside forces (which, of course, is exactly what happens to pendulums used in clocks), pendulums gradually return to their resting points. The same is true of price and quantity in a free market. Markets are not always in equilibrium, but, if they are not interfered with, experience shows that they normally *move toward equilibrium.*

THE LAW OF SUPPLY AND DEMAND

In a free market, the forces of supply and demand generally push the price toward its equilibrium level, the price at which quantity supplied and quantity demanded are equal. Like most economic "laws," the **law of supply and demand** is occasionally disobeyed. Markets sometimes display shortages or surpluses for long periods of time. Prices sometimes fail to move toward equilibrium. But the "law" is a fair generalization that is right far more often than it is wrong.

The **LAW OF SUPPLY AND DEMAND** states that, in a free market, the forces of supply and demand generally push the price toward the level at which quantity supplied and quantity demanded are equal.

The last interesting aspect of the pendulum analogy concerns the "outside forces" of which we have spoken. A pendulum that is blown by the wind or pushed by a hand does not remain in equilibrium. Similarly, many outside forces can disturb equilibrium in a market. In 1990 to 1991, the world oil market was disturbed by a war in the Persian Gulf. In 1993 and 1995, severe floods in the Midwest damaged the nation's grain harvests. Often these outside influences *change the equilibrium price and quantity* by shifting either the supply curve or the demand curve. If you look again at Figure 4-3, you can see clearly that any event that causes *either* the demand curve *or* the supply curve to shift will also change the equilibrium price and quantity. Such events constitute the "other things" that were held constant in our definitions of supply and demand curves. We are now ready to analyze how these outside forces affect the equilibrium of supply and demand, beginning on the demand side.

SHIFTS OF THE DEMAND CURVE

The quantity of milk demanded is influenced by a variety of things other than the price of milk. Changes in population, consumer incomes, and the prices of alternative beverages such as soda and orange juice presumably change the quantity of milk demanded even if the price of milk is unchanged.

FIGURE 4-4 MOVEMENTS ALONG VERSUS SHIFTS OF A DEMAND CURVE

If quantity demanded increases because the price of a commodity falls, the market moves along a fixed demand curve such as D_0D_0 (see the movement from C to F). If, on the other hand, quantity demanded increases due to a change in one of its other determinants (such as consumer tastes or incomes), the entire demand curve shifts outward, as shown here by the shift from D_0D_0 to D_1D_1.

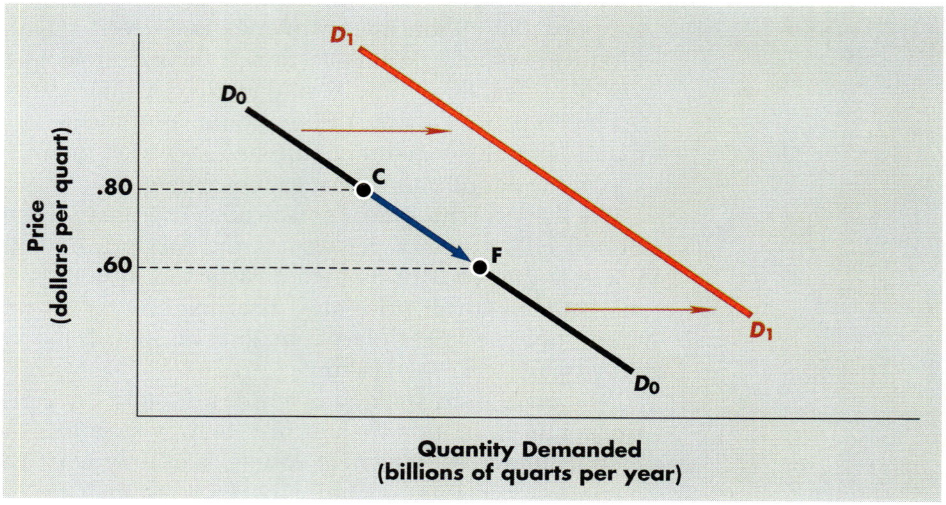

Since the demand curve for milk depicts only the relationship between the quantity of milk demanded and the price of milk, holding all other factors constant, a change in any of these other factors produces a *shift of the entire demand curve.* More generally:

A change in the price of a good produces a *movement along a fixed demand curve.* By contrast, a change in any other variable that influences quantity demanded produces a *shift of the entire demand curve.* If consumers want to buy *more* at any given price than they wanted previously, the demand curve shifts to the right (or outward). If they desire *less* at any given price, the demand curve shifts to the left (or inward).

Figure 4-4 shows this distinction graphically. If the price of milk falls from 80 cents per quart to 60 cents, and quantity demanded rises accordingly, we move *along demand curve* D_0D_0 from point C to point F, as shown by the blue arrow. If, on the other hand, consumers suddenly decide that they like milk better than they did formerly, *the entire demand curve shifts outward from* D_0D_0 to D_1D_1, as indicated by the *orange* arrows. To make this general idea more concrete, and to show some of its many applications, let us consider some specific examples.

1. *Consumer incomes.* If average incomes rise, consumers will purchase more of most goods, including milk, even if the prices of those goods remain the same. That is, *increases in income normally shift demand curves outward to the right,* as depicted in Figure 4-5(a). In this example, the quantity demanded at the old equilibrium price of 70 cents increases from 60 billion quarts per year (point E on the demand curve D_0D_0) to 75 billion (point R on the demand curve D_1D_1). We know that 70 cents is no longer the equilibrium price, since at this price quantity demanded (75 billion quarts) exceeds quantity supplied (60 billion). To restore equilibrium, the price must rise. The diagram shows that the new equilibrium occurs at point T, where the price is 80 cents per quart and both quantities demanded and supplied are 70 billion quarts per year. This illustrates a general result:

FIGURE 4-5 THE EFFECTS OF SHIFTS OF THE DEMAND CURVE

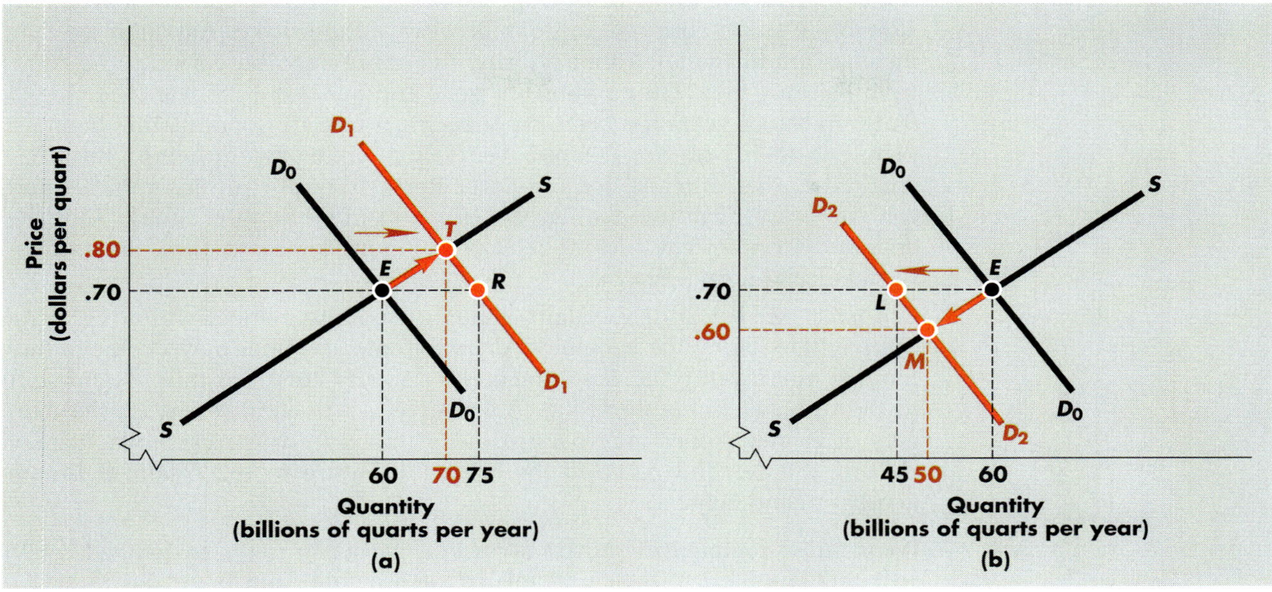

A shift of the demand curve will change the equilibrium price and quantity in a free market. In Panel (a), the demand curve shifts outward from D_0D_0 to D_1D_1. As a result, equilibrium moves from point *E* to point *T;* both price and quantity rise. In Panel (b), the demand curve shifts inward from D_0D_0 to D_2D_2, and equilibrium moves from point *E* to point *M;* both price and quantity fall.

Any factor that makes the demand curve shift outward to the right, and does not affect the supply curve, will raise the equilibrium price and the equilibrium quantity.[4]

For example, when incomes rise rapidly in many developing countries, the demand curves for a variety of consumer goods shift rapidly outward to the right. In Malaysia, for example, auto sales rose by 290 percent between 1987 and 1991—and falling prices were not the driving force.

Everything works in reverse if consumer incomes fall. Figure 4-5(b) depicts a leftward (inward) shift of the demand curve that results from a decline in consumer incomes. For example, the quantity demanded at the previous equilibrium price (70 cents) falls from 60 billion quarts (point *E*) to 45 billion (point *L* on the demand curve D_2D_2). The initial price is now too high and must begin to fall. The new equilibrium will eventually be established at point *M*, where the price is 60 cents and both quantity demanded and quantity supplied are 50 billion quarts. In general:

Any factor that shifts the demand curve inward to the left, and does not affect the supply curve, will lower both the equilibrium price and the equilibrium quantity.

[4]This statement, like many others in the text, assumes that the demand curve is downward sloping and the supply curve is upward sloping.

2. *Population.* Population growth affects quantity demanded in more or less the same way as increases in average incomes. A larger population will presumably want to consume more milk, even if the price of milk and average incomes are unchanged, thus shifting the entire demand curve to the right, as in Figure 4-5(a). The equilibrium price and quantity both rise. The United States in recent years has been experiencing a miniature population boom of people in their mid-20s. Dubbed Generation X, this fast-growing group has sparked higher demand for big-ticket items like sport-utility vehicles and contemporary furniture. Similarly, a decrease in population should shift the demand curve for milk to the left, as in Figure 4-5(b), making the equilibrium price and quantity fall.
3. *Consumer preferences.* If the dairy industry mounts a successful advertising campaign extolling the benefits of drinking milk, families may decide to buy more at any given price. If so, the entire demand curve for milk would shift to the right, as in Figure 4-5(a). Alternatively, a medical report on the dangers of kidney stones may persuade consumers to drink less milk, thereby shifting the demand curve to the left, as in Figure 4-5(b). Again, these are general phenomena:

   If consumer preferences shift in favor of a particular item, its demand curve will shift outward to the right, raising both equilibrium price and quantity, as in Figure 4-5(a). Conversely, if consumer preferences shift against a particular item, its demand curve will shift inward to the left, lowering both equilibrium price and quantity, as in Figure 4-5(b).

   An interesting example of this phenomenon occurred in 1994 when the Italian fashion industry decided that mohair was "in." Consumers snapped up anything in mohair, from bikinis to backpacks, and the price of mohair tripled.
4. *Prices and availability of related goods.* Because soda, orange juice, and coffee are popular drinks that compete with milk, a change in the price of any of these other beverages would be expected to shift the demand curve for milk. If any of these alternative drinks become cheaper, some consumers will switch away from milk. Thus, the demand curve for milk will shift to the left, as in Figure 4-5(b). Other price changes shift the demand curve for milk in the opposite direction. For example, suppose that cookies, which are often consumed with milk, become less expensive. This may induce some consumers to drink more milk and thus shift the demand curve for milk to the right, as in Figure 4-5(a). In general:

   Increases in the prices of goods that are substitutes for the good in question (as soda is for milk) move the demand curve to the right, thus raising both the equilibrium price and quantity. Increases in the prices of goods that are normally used together with the good in question (such as cookies and milk) shift the demand curve to the left, thus lowering both the equilibrium price and quantity.

   This is just what happened when a frost wiped out almost half of Brazil's coffee bean harvest in 1995. The three biggest U.S. coffee producers raised their prices by 45 percent, and, as a result, the demand curve for alternative beverages like tea shifted to the right.

While the preceding list does not exhaust the possible influences on quantity demanded, enough has been said to indicate the principles involved. Let us therefore turn to a concrete example.

FIGURE 4-6

During seasons of slack demand for air travel, the demand curve shifts leftward from D_0D_0 to D_1D_1. In consequence, the market equilibrium point shifts from *E* to *A*, causing both price and quantity to decline.

SEASONAL CHANGES IN AIRLINE FARES

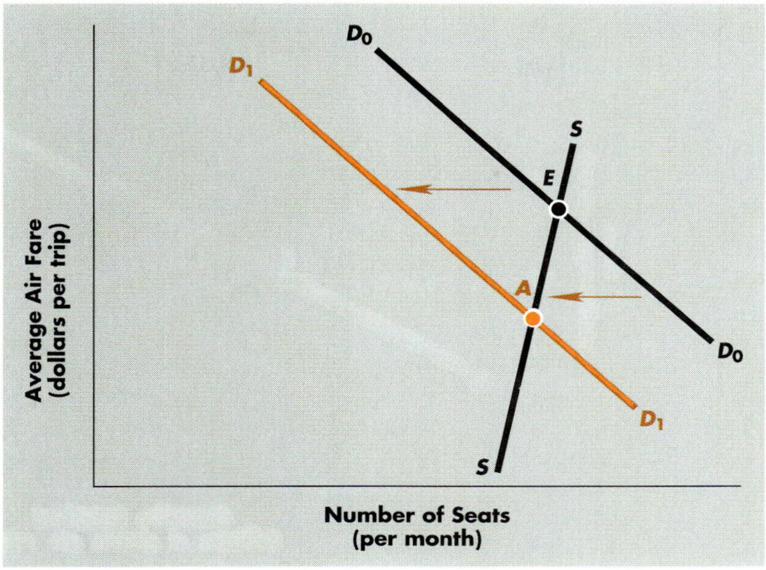

APPLICATION: WHY AIRLINES RUN SALES

Anyone who travels knows that airline companies reduce fares sharply to attract more customers at certain times of the year—particularly in winter (excluding the holiday period), when air traffic is light. There is no reason to think that air transportation gets cheaper in winter. Why, then, do airlines run such "sales"? Simple supply and demand analysis provides the answer.

Given the number of planes in airlines' fleets, the supply of seats is relatively fixed, as indicated by the steep supply curve *SS* in Figure 4-6, and is more or less the same in summer and winter. During seasons when people want to travel less, the demand curve for seats shifts leftward from its normal position, D_0D_0, to a position such as D_1D_1. Hence, equilibrium in the air-traffic market shifts from point *E* to point *A*. Thus, both price and quantity decline at certain times of the year, not because flying gets cheaper or airlines get more generous, but because of the discipline of the market.

SHIFTS OF THE SUPPLY CURVE

Like quantity demanded, the quantity supplied in a market typically responds to many influences other than price. The weather, the cost of feed, the number and size of dairy farms, and a variety of other factors all influence how much milk will be brought to market. Since the supply curve depicts only the relationship between the price of milk and the quantity of milk supplied, holding all other factors constant, a change in any of these other factors will cause the entire supply curve to shift. That is:

A change in the price of the good causes a *movement along a fixed supply curve.* But price is not the only influence on quantity supplied. If any of these other influences change, the *entire supply curve shifts.*

FIGURE 4-7 MOVEMENTS ALONG VERSUS SHIFTS OF A SUPPLY CURVE

If quantity supplied rises because the price increases, we move along a fixed supply curve such as S_0S_0 (see the blue arrow from point *f* to point *c*). If, on the other hand, quantity supplied rises because some other factor influencing supply improves, the entire supply curve shifts outward to the right from S_0S_0 to S_1S_1 (see the orange arrows).

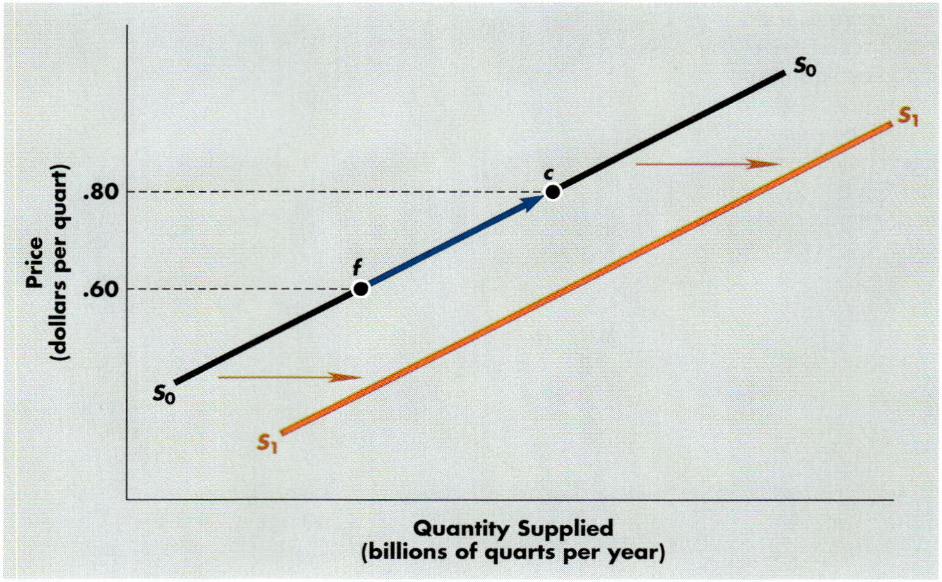

Figure 4-7 once again depicts the distinction graphically. A rise in price from 60 cents to 80 cents will raise quantity supplied by *moving along supply curve* S_0S_0 from point *f* to point *c*. But any rise in quantity supplied attributable to a factor other than price will *shift the entire supply curve outward to the right* from S_0S_0 *to* S_1S_1, as shown by the orange arrows. Let us consider what some of these other factors are, and how they shift the supply curve.

1. *Size of the industry*. We begin with the most obvious factor. If more farmers enter the milk industry, the quantity supplied at any given price will increase. For example, if each farm provides 600,000 quarts of milk per year at a price of 70 cents per quart, then 100,000 farmers provide 60 billion quarts, but 130,000 farmers provide 78 billion. Thus, when more farms are in the industry, the quantity of milk supplied will be greater at any given price—and hence the supply curve will be farther to the right.

   Figure 4-8(a) illustrates the effect of an expansion of the industry from 100,000 farms to 130,000 farms—a rightward shift of the supply curve from S_0S_0 to S_1S_1. Notice that at the initial price of 70 cents, the quantity supplied after the shift is 78 billion quarts (point *I* on the supply curve S_1S_1), which is 30 percent more than the original quantity demanded of 60 billion (point *E* on the supply curve S_0S_0). We can see from the graph that the price of 70 cents is too high to be the equilibrium price; the price must fall. The diagram shows that the new equilibrium point is *J*, where the price is 60 cents per quart and the quantity is 65 billion quarts per year. In general:

   Any factor that shifts the supply curve outward to the right, and does not affect the demand curve, will lower the equilibrium price and raise the equilibrium quantity.

   This must *always* be true if the industry's demand curve has a negative slope, because the greater quantity supplied can be sold only if price is decreased

FIGURE 4-8 EFFECTS OF SHIFTS OF THE SUPPLY CURVE

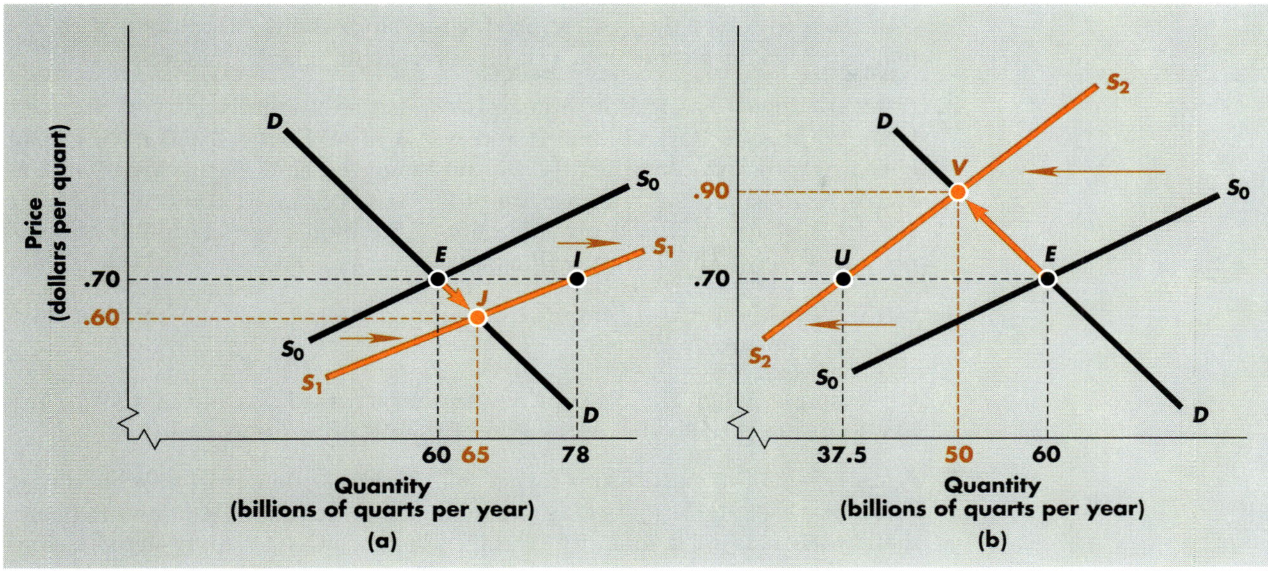

A shift of the supply curve will change the equilibrium price and quantity in a market. In Panel (a), the supply curve shifts outward to the right, from S_0S_0 to S_1S_1. As a result, equilibrium moves from point *E* to point *J;* price falls as quantity increases. Panel (b) illustrates the opposite case—an inward shift of the supply curve from S_0S_0 to S_2S_2. Equilibrium moves from point *E* to point *V,* which means that price rises as quantity falls.

to induce customers to buy more.[5] The cellular phone industry is a case in point. As more providers have entered the industry, the cost of cellular service has plummeted. Many cellular carriers have even started giving away telephones as sign-up bonuses.

Figure 4-8(b) illustrates the opposite case: a contraction of the industry from 100,000 farms to 62,500 farms. The supply curve shifts inward to the left and equilibrium moves from point *E* to point *V,* where price is 90 cents and quantity is 50 billion quarts per year. In general:

Any factor that shifts the supply curve inward to the left, and does not affect the demand curve, will raise the equilibrium price and reduce the equilibrium quantity.

Even if no farmers enter or leave the industry, results like those depicted in Figure 4-8 can be produced by expansion or contraction of the existing farms.

2. *Technological progress.* Another factor that shifts supply curves is technological change. Suppose some enterprising farmer discovers that cows produce more milk if Mozart is played during milking. Thereafter, at any given price, farms will be able to produce more milk; that is, the supply curve will shift outward to the right, as in Figure 4-8(a). This, again, illustrates a general influence that applies to most industries:

Technological progress that reduces costs will shift the supply curve outward to the right.

---

[5]Graphically, whenever a positively sloped curve shifts to the right, its intersection point with a negatively sloping curve must always move lower. Just try drawing it yourself.

Thus, as Figure 4-8(a) shows, the usual consequences of technological progress are lower prices and greater output. Auto makers, for example, have been able to lower the cost of production since the development of robots that can be programmed to work on several different car models.

3. *Prices of inputs.* Changes in input prices also shift supply curves. Suppose farm workers become unionized and win a raise. Farmers will have to pay higher wages and consequently will no longer be able to provide 60 billion quarts of milk profitably at a price of 70 cents per quart (point *E* in Figure 4-8[b]). Perhaps they will provide only 37.5 billion quarts (point *U* on supply curve S_2S_2). This example illustrates that:

Increases in the prices of inputs that suppliers must buy will shift the supply curve inward to the left.

For example, when the price of newsprint increased sharply in 1994, many newspapers opted to shrink the size of their daily editions.

4. *Prices of related outputs.* Dairy farms sell products other than milk. If cheese prices rise sharply, farmers may decide to use some raw milk to make cheese, thereby reducing the quantity of milk supplied. On a supply-demand diagram, the supply curve would then shift inward, as in Figure 4-8(b).

Similar phenomena occur in other industries, and sometimes the effect goes the other way. For example, suppose that the price of beef goes up, which increases the quantity of meat supplied. That, in turn, will raise the number of cowhides supplied even if the price of leather does not change. Thus, a rise in the price of beef will lead to a rightward shift in the supply curve of leather. In general:

A change in the price of one good produced by a multiproduct industry may be expected to shift the supply curves of all the other goods produced by that industry.

APPLICATION: A COMPUTER IN EVERY HOME?

Twenty-five years ago, no one owned a home computer. Now there are tens of millions of them, and enthusiasts look forward to the day when computers will be as commonplace as television sets. What brought the computer from the laboratory into the home? Did Americans suddenly develop a craving for computers?

Hardly. What actually happened is that scientists in the 1970s invented the microchip—a stunning technological breakthrough that sharply reduced both the size and cost of computers. Within a few years, microcomputers were in commercial production. As the technology continued to improve, the cost of computers fell and fell and fell. Today, $1,500 will buy you more computing power than a multimillion-dollar computer could deliver two decades ago—and the machine will play games, and maybe even talk to you, too!

In terms of our supply and demand diagrams, the rapid technological improvement in computer manufacturing shifted the supply curve dramatically to the right. As Figure 4-9 shows, a large outward shift of the supply curve should lower the equilibrium price and raise the equilibrium quantity—which is just what happened to the computer industry. It was not the *demand curve* that shifted out, but the *supply curve.*

FIGURE 4-9

THE EFFECTS OF RAPID TECHNOLOGICAL CHANGE ON THE COMPUTER MARKET

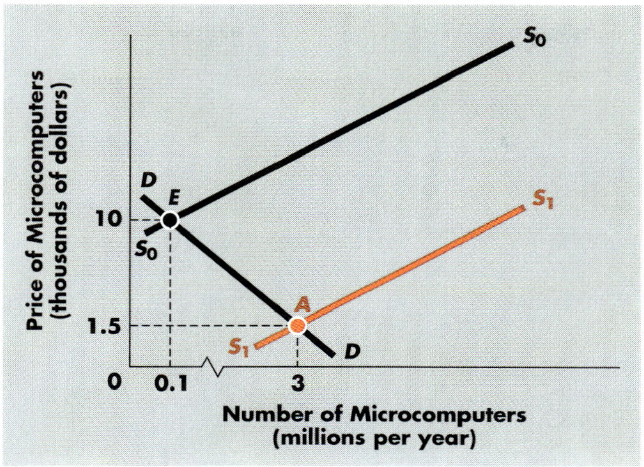

The invention of the microchip and other technological breakthroughs caused the supply curve of computers to shift outward to the right—moving from S_0S_0 to S_1S_1. Consequently, equilibrium shifted from point *E* to point *A*. The price of microcomputers fell from $10,000 to $1,500, and the quantity increased from 100,000 to 3 million per year.

RESTRAINING THE MARKET MECHANISM: PRICE CEILINGS

As we have noted already, lawmakers and rulers have often been dissatisfied with the outcomes of free markets. From Rome to Pennsylvania and from biblical times to the space age, they have battled the invisible hand. Sometimes, rather than trying to make adjustments in the workings of the market, governments have tried to raise or lower the prices of specific commodities *by decree.* In many such cases, the authorities felt that market prices were, in some sense, immorally low or immorally high. Penalties were therefore imposed on anyone offering the commodities in question at prices above or below those established by the authorities.

A **PRICE CEILING** is a legal maximum on the price that may be charged for a commodity.

But the market has proven itself a formidable foe that strongly resists attempts to circumvent its workings. In case after case where legal **price ceilings** are imposed, virtually the same set of consequences ensues:

1. *A persistent shortage develops.* Queuing, direct rationing, or any of a variety of other devices, usually inefficient and unpleasant, must substitute for the distribution process provided by the price mechanism. *Example:* Rampant shortages in Eastern Europe and the former Soviet Union helped precipitate the revolts that ended communism.
2. *An illegal, or "black," market often arises to supply the commodity.* There are usually some individuals who are willing to take the risks involved in meeting unsatisfied demands illegally. *Example:* Although most states ban the practice, ticket "scalping" occurs at most popular sporting events and rock concerts.
3. *The prices charged on illegal markets are almost certainly higher than those that would prevail in free markets.* After all, lawbreakers expect some compensation for the risk of being caught and punished. *Example:* Illegal drugs are normally quite expensive. (See the Policy Debate box on the next page.)
4. *A substantial portion of the price falls into the hands of the illicit supplier instead of going to those who produce the good or who perform the service. Example:* A

POLICY DEBATE: ECONOMIC ASPECTS OF THE WAR ON DRUGS

For years now, the U.S. government has engaged in a highly publicized "war on drugs." Billions of dollars have been spent on trying to stop illegal drugs at the border. In some sense, interdiction has succeeded: Federal agents have seized literally tons of cocaine and other drugs. Yet these efforts have made barely a dent in the flow of drugs to America's city streets. Simple economic reasoning explains why.

When drug interdiction works, it shifts the supply curve of drugs to the left, thereby driving up street prices. But that, in turn, raises the rewards for potential smugglers and attracts more criminals into the "industry," which shifts the supply curve back to the right. The net result is that increased shipments of drugs to our shores replace much of what the authorities confiscate. This is why many economists believe that any successful antidrug program must concentrate on reducing *demand*, which would lower the street price of drugs, not on reducing *supply*, which can only raise it.

Some people suggest that the government should go even further and *legalize* many drugs. While this remains a highly controversial position that few are ready to endorse, the reasoning behind it is straightforward. A stunningly high fraction of all the violent crimes committed in America—especially robberies and murders—are drug-related. One major reason is that street prices of drugs are so high that addicts must steal to get the money, and drug traffickers are all too willing to kill to protect their highly profitable "businesses."

How would things differ if drugs were legal? Since South American farmers earn pennies for drugs that sell for hundreds of dollars on the streets of Los Angeles and New York, we may safely assume that legalized drugs would be vastly cheaper. In fact, according to one estimate, a dose of cocaine would cost less than 50 cents. That, proponents point out, would reduce drug-related crimes dramatically. When, for example, was the last time you heard of a gang killing connected with the distribution of cigarettes or alcoholic beverages?

The argument against legalization of drugs is largely moral: Should the state sanction potentially lethal substances? But there is also an economic aspect. The vastly lower street prices of drugs that would surely follow legalization would increase drug use. Thus, while legalization would almost certainly reduce crime, it would also produce more addicts. The key question here—to which no one has a good answer—is: How many more addicts? If you think the increase in quantity demanded would be large, you are unlikely to find legalization an attractive option.

constant complaint in the series of hearings that marked the history of theater ticket price controls in New York City was that the "ice" (the illegal excess charge) fell into the hands of ticket scalpers rather than going to those who invested in, produced, or acted in the play.

5. *Investment in the industry generally dries up.* Because price ceilings reduce the returns that investors can earn, less capital will be invested in industries subject to price controls. Even fear of impending price controls can have this effect. *Example:* Price controls on farm products in Zambia have prompted peasant farmers and large agricultural conglomerates alike to cut back pro-

FIGURE 4-10 SUPPLY-DEMAND DIAGRAM FOR RENTAL HOUSING

When market forces are permitted to set rents, the quantity of dwellings supplied will equal the quantity demanded. But when a rent ceiling forces rent below the market level, the number of dwellings supplied (point *C*) will be less than the number demanded (point *B*). Thus, rent ceilings induce housing shortages.

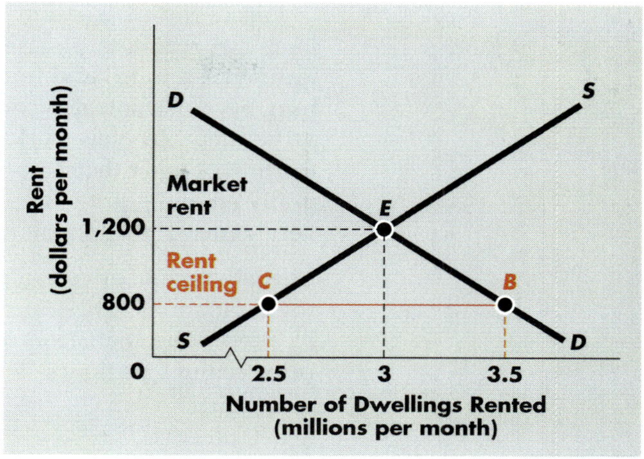

duction rather than grow crops at a loss. The result has been thousands of lost jobs and widespread food shortages.

A CASE STUDY: RENT CONTROLS IN NEW YORK CITY

These points and others are best illustrated by considering a concrete example of price ceilings. New York is the only major city in the United States that has had rent controls continuously since World War II. The objective of rent control is, of course, to protect the consumer from high rents. But most economists believe that rent control does not help the cities or their residents and that, in the long run, it makes almost everyone worse off. Elementary supply-demand analysis shows us why.

Figure 4-10 is a supply-demand diagram for rental units in New York. Curve *DD* is the demand curve and the curve *SS* is the supply curve. Without controls, equilibrium would be at point *E*, where rents average $1,200 per month and 3.0 million units are occupied. If rent controls are effective, they must set a ceiling price *below* the equilibrium price of $1,200. But with a low rent ceiling, such as $800, the quantity of housing demanded will be 3.5 million units (point *B*) while the quantity supplied will be only 2.5 million units (point *C*).

The diagram shows a shortage of 1 million apartments. This theoretical concept of a "shortage" manifests itself in New York City as an abnormally low vacancy rate—typically about half of the national urban average. Naturally, rent controls have spawned a lively black market in New York. The black market raises the effective price of rent-controlled apartments in many ways, including bribes, "key money" paid to move up on the waiting list, and requirements that force prospective tenants to purchase worthless furniture at inflated prices.

According to the diagram, rent controls reduce the quantity supplied from 3.0 million to 2.5 million apartments. How does this show up in New York? First, some property owners, discouraged by the low rents, have converted apartment buildings into office space or other uses. Second, some apartments have been inadequately maintained. After all, rent controls create a shortage which makes even dilapidated apartments easy to rent. Third, some landlords have actually abandoned their buildings rather than pay rising tax and fuel bills. These abandoned buildings rapidly become eyesores and eventually pose threats to public health and safety.

With all of these problems, why do rent controls persist in New York City? And why do other cities sometimes move in the same direction?

Part of the explanation is that most people simply do not understand the problems that rent controls create. Another part is that landlords are unpopular politically. But a third, and important, part of the explanation is that not everyone is hurt by rent controls—and those who benefit from controls fight hard to preserve them. In New York, for example, many tenants pay rents that are only a fraction of what their apartments would fetch on the open market. They are, naturally enough, quite happy with this situation. This last point illustrates another very general phenomenon:

Virtually every price ceiling or floor creates a class of people who benefit from the regulations. These people use their political influence to protect their gains by preserving that *status quo*, which is one reason why it is so hard to eliminate price ceilings or floors.

RESTRAINING THE MARKET MECHANISM: PRICE FLOORS

A **PRICE FLOOR** is a legal minimum on the price that may be charged for a commodity.

Interferences with the market mechanism are not always designed to keep prices *low*. Agricultural price supports and minimum wages are two notable examples in which the law keeps prices *above* free-market levels. **Price floors** are typically accompanied by a standard set of symptoms:

1. *A surplus develops as sellers cannot find enough buyers. Example:* Surpluses of various agricultural products have been a persistent—and costly—problem for the U.S. government. The problem is even worse in the European Union, where the so-called *common agricultural policy* holds prices even higher. Fortunately, agricultural price supports are scheduled to come down under the world trade agreement that took effect in 1995.
2. *Where goods, rather than services, are involved, the surplus creates a problem of disposal.* Something must be done about the excess of quantity supplied over quantity demanded. *Example:* The U.S. government has often been forced to purchase, store, and then dispose of large amounts of surplus agricultural commodities.
3. To get around the regulations, *sellers may offer discounts in disguised—and often unwanted—forms. Example:* When airline fares were regulated by the government, airlines offered more and better food and stylish uniforms for flight attendants instead of lowering fares. Today, the food is worse, but tickets cost much less.
4. *Regulations that keep prices artificially high encourage overinvestment in the industry.* Even inefficient businesses whose high operating costs would doom them in an unrestricted market can survive beneath the shelter of a generous price floor. *Example:* This is why the airline and trucking industries both went through painful "shake outs" of the weaker companies in the 1980s.

Once again, a specific example is useful.

A CASE STUDY: SUGAR PRICE SUPPORTS

America's extensive program of farm price supports began in 1933 as a "temporary method of dealing with an emergency": Farmers were going broke in droves. It is still with us today, even though the farm population of the United

FIGURE 4-11 SUPPORTING THE PRICE OF SUGAR

By inducing domestic producers to grow less sugar, and by limiting imports, the government shifts the supply curve inward to the left from S_0S_0 to S_1S_1. The predictable result is a higher price in the United States.

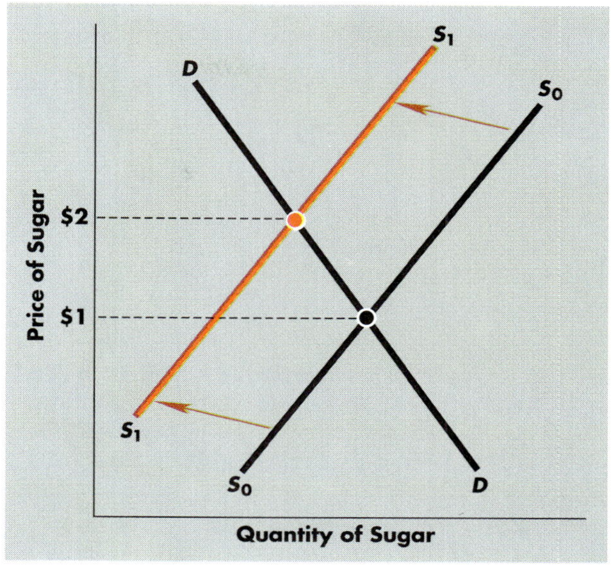

States is less than a sixth of what it was then.[6] One of the more controversial farm price supports involves the sugar industry. Sugar producers receive low-interest loans from the federal government and a guarantee that the price of sugar will not fall below a certain level.

But in a market economy like ours, Congress cannot simply set prices by decree; it must take some action to enforce the price floor. In the case of sugar, that "something" is limiting both domestic production and foreign imports, thereby shifting the supply curve inward to the left. Figure 4-11 displays the mechanics. Government policies shift the supply curve inward from S_0S_0 to S_1S_1 and drive the U.S. price up from \$1 to \$2 per pound. The more the supply curve shifts inward, the higher the price.

The sugar industry obviously benefits from the price-control program. But consumers pay for it in the form of higher prices for sugar and sugar-filled products such as soft drinks, candy bars, and cookies. Estimates vary, but the federal sugar price support program costs consumers somewhere around \$1.5 billion a year.

If all of this sounds a bit abstract to you, take a look at the ingredients of a U.S.-made soft drink. Instead of sugar, you will likely find "high-fructose corn syrup" listed as a sweetener. Foreign products generally use sugar. But in the United States, sugar is simply too expensive to be used for this purpose.

A CAN OF WORMS

Our two case studies—rent controls and sugar price supports—illustrate some of the major side effects of price floors and ceilings, but barely hint at others. There are difficulties that we have not even mentioned, for the market

[6]Under major legislation passed in 1996, many agricultural price supports are being phased out over a seven-year period.

mechanism is a tough bird that imposes suitable retribution on those who seek to circumvent it by legislative decree. Here is a partial list of other problems that may arise when prices are controlled.

FAVORITISM AND CORRUPTION

When price ceilings or floors create shortages or surpluses, someone must decide who gets to buy or sell the limited quantity that is available. This can lead to discrimination along racial or religious lines, political favoritism, or corruption in government. For example, many prices were held at artificially low levels in the former Soviet Union, making queuing for certain goods quite common. But, somehow, Communist party officials and other favored groups were able to purchase the scarce commodities that others could not get.

UNENFORCEABILITY

Attempts to limit prices are almost certain to fail in industries with numerous suppliers, simply because the regulating agency must monitor the behavior of so many sellers. People will usually find ways to evade or violate the law, and something akin to the free-market price will generally reemerge. But there is an important difference: Since the evasion mechanism, whatever its form, will have some operating costs, those costs must be borne by someone. Normally, that someone is the consumer.

AUXILIARY RESTRICTIONS

Fears that a system of price controls will break down invariably lead to regulations designed to shore up the shaky edifice. Consumers may be told when and from whom they are permitted to buy. The powers of the police and the courts may be used to prevent the entry of new suppliers. Occasionally, an intricate system of market subdivision is imposed, giving each class of firms a protected sphere in which others are not permitted to operate. For example, there are laws banning conversion of rent-controlled apartments to condominiums in New York City.

LIMITATION OF VOLUME OF TRANSACTIONS

To the extent that controls succeed in affecting prices, they can be expected to reduce the volume of transactions. Curiously, this is true regardless of whether the regulated price is *above* or *below* the free-market equilibrium price. If it is set above the equilibrium price, quantity demanded will be below the equilibrium quantity. On the other hand, if the imposed price is set below the free-market level, quantity supplied will be cut down. Since sales volume cannot exceed either the quantity supplied or the quantity demanded, a reduction in the volume of transactions is the result.[7]

MISALLOCATION OF RESOURCES

Departures from free-market prices are likely to result in misuse of the economy's resources because the connection between production costs and prices is broken. For example, Russian farmers used to feed their farm animals bread instead of unprocessed grains because price ceilings kept the price of bread ludicrously low. In addition, just as more complex locks lead to more sophisticated

[7]See Review Question 9 at the end of the chapter.

burglary tools, more complex regulations lead to the use of yet more resources for their avoidance.

Economists put it this way. Free markets are capable of dealing with the three basic coordination tasks outlined in Chapter 3: deciding *what* to produce, *how* to produce it, and *to whom* the goods should be distributed. Price controls throw a monkey wrench into the market mechanism. Though the market is surely not flawless, and government interferences often have praiseworthy goals, good intentions are not enough. Any government that sets out to repair what it sees as a defect in the market mechanism runs the risk of causing even more serious damage elsewhere. As a prominent economist once quipped, societies that are too willing to interfere with the operation of free markets soon find that the invisible hand is nowhere to be seen.

A SIMPLE BUT POWERFUL LESSON

The lessons you have learned in this chapter may seem elementary, even obvious. In many respects, they are. But they are also very important, indeed, indispensable. Although the law of supply and demand is one of the simplest principles in economics, it is also one of the most powerful. Astonishing as it may seem, many people in authority fail to understand the law of supply and demand or cannot apply it to concrete situations.

For example, a few years ago *The New York Times* carried a dramatic front page picture of the president of Kenya setting fire to a large pile of elephant tusks that had been confiscated from poachers. The accompanying story explained that the burning was intended as a symbolic act to persuade the world to halt the ivory trade.[8] Economists claim no expertise on the likely psychological effect of burning elephant tusks, though one may doubt that it touched the hearts of criminal poachers. However, one economic effect was clear. By reducing the supply of ivory on the world market, the burning of tusks forced up the price of ivory, which raised the illicit rewards reaped by those who slaughter elephants. That could only encourage more poaching—precisely the opposite of what the Kenyan government sought to accomplish.

[8] *The New York Times,* July 19, 1989.

SUMMARY

1. The quantity of a product that is demanded is not a fixed number. Rather, **quantity demanded** depends on such factors as the price of the product, consumer incomes, and the prices of other products.
2. The relationship between quantity demanded and price, holding all other things constant, can be displayed graphically on a **demand curve.**
3. For most products, the higher the price, the lower the quantity demanded. So the demand curve usually has a negative slope.
4. The quantity of a product that is supplied also depends on its price and many other influences. A **supply curve** is a graphical representation of the relationship between **quantity supplied** and price, holding all other influences constant.
5. For most products, the supply curves have positive slopes, meaning that higher prices call forth greater quantities supplied.
6. A market is said to be in **equilibrium** when quantity supplied is equal to quantity demanded. The equilibrium price and quantity are shown by the point on a graph where the supply and demand curves intersect. The **law of supply and demand** states that price and quantity tend to gravitate to this point in a free market.

7. A change in quantity demanded that is caused by a change in the price of the good is represented by a *movement along a fixed demand curve.* A change in quantity demanded that is caused by a change in any other determinant of quantity demanded is represented by a *shift of the demand curve.*
8. This same distinction applies to the supply curve: Changes in price lead to *movements along a fixed supply curve;* changes in other determinants of quantity supplied lead to *shifts of the whole supply curve.*
9. Changes in consumer incomes, tastes, technology, prices of competing products, and many other influences cause shifts in either the demand curve or the supply curve and produce changes in price and quantity that can be determined from **supply-demand diagrams.**
10. An attempt by government regulations to force prices above or below their equilibrium levels is likely to lead to **shortages** or **surpluses,** to black markets in which goods are sold at illegal prices, and to a variety of other problems. This is one of the **Ideas for Beyond the Final Exam.**

KEY TERMS

Quantity demanded
Demand schedule
Demand curve
Quantity supplied
Supply schedule
Supply curve
Supply-demand diagram
Shortage
Surplus
Equilibrium price and quantity
Equilibrium
Law of supply and demand
Shifts in versus movements along supply and demand curves
Price ceiling
Price floor

QUESTIONS FOR REVIEW

1. How often do you rent videos? Would you do so more often if a rental cost half as much? Distinguish between your demand curve for home videos and your "quantity demanded" at the current price.
2. What shapes would you expect for demand curves for the following:
   a. A medicine that means life or death for a patient?
   b. French fries in a food court with stands offering many types of food?
3. The following are the assumed supply and demand schedules for hamburgers in Collegetown:

Demand Schedule		Supply Schedule	
Price	Quantity Demanded (per year)	Price	Quantity Supplied (per year)
$2.00	6,000	$2.00	15,000
1.75	8,000	1.75	14,000
1.50	10,000	1.50	13,000
1.25	12,000	1.25	12,000
1.00	14,000	1.00	11,000
0.75	16,000	0.75	10,000

   a. Plot the supply and demand curves and indicate the equilibrium price and quantity.
   b. What effect would a decrease in the price of beef (a factor of production) have on the equilibrium price and quantity of hamburgers, assuming all other things were to remain constant? Explain your answer with the help of a diagram.
   c. What effect would an increase in the price of pizza (a substitute commodity) have on the equilibrium price and quantity of hamburgers, assuming again that all other things were held constant? Use a diagram in your answer.
4. Suppose the supply and demand schedules for bicycles are as follows:

Price	Quantity Demanded (per year)	Quantity Supplied (per year)
$ 80	20	12
100	18	14
120	16	16
140	14	18
160	12	20
180	10	22

   a. Graph these curves and show the equilibrium price and quantity.
   b. Now suppose that it becomes unfashionable to ride a bicycle, so the quantity demanded at each price falls by 4 million bikes per year. What is the new equilibrium price and quantity? Show this solution graphically. Explain why the quantity falls by less than 4 million bikes per year.

c. Suppose *instead* that several major bicycle producers go out of business, thereby reducing the quantity supplied by 4 million bikes at every price. Find the new equilibrium price and quantity, and show it graphically. Explain again why quantity falls by less than 4 million.

d. What are the equilibrium price and quantity if the shifts described in Review Questions 4(b) and 4(c) happen at the same time?

5. The table below summarizes information about the market for principles of economics textbooks:

Price	Quantity Demanded (per year)	Quantity Supplied (per year)
$30	2,100	100
40	1,100	300
50	600	600
60	350	1,000
70	225	1,500

a. What is the market equilibrium price and quantity of textbooks?

b. In order to quell outrage over tuition increases, the college places a $40 limit on the price of textbooks. How many textbooks will be sold now?

c. While the price limit is still in effect, automated publishing increases the efficiency of textbook production. Show graphically the likely effect of this innovation on the market price and quantity.

6. Show how the following demand curves are likely to shift in response to the indicated changes:

a. The effect of a drought on the demand curve for umbrellas.

b. The effect of higher popcorn prices on the demand curve for movie tickets.

c. The effect on the demand curve for coffee of a decline in the price of Dr Pepper soda.

7. Discuss the likely effects of:

a. Rent ceilings on the market for apartments.

b. Floors under wheat prices on the market for wheat.

Use supply-demand diagrams to show what may happen in each case.

8. U.S. government price supports for milk lead to a chronic surplus of milk. In an effort to reduce the surplus about a decade ago, Congress offered to pay dairy farmers to slaughter cows. Use two diagrams, one for the milk market and one for the meat market, to illustrate how this policy should have affected the price of meat. (Assume that meat is sold in an unregulated market.)

9. On page 88, it is claimed that either price floors or price ceilings reduce the actual quantity exchanged in a market. Use a diagram or diagrams to support this conclusion, and explain the common sense behind it.

10. The same rightward shift of the demand curve may produce a very small or a very large increase in quantity, depending on the slope of the supply curve. Explain with diagrams.

11. In 1981, when regulations were holding the price of natural gas below its free-market level, then-Congressman Jack Kemp of New York said the following in an interview with *The New York Times:* "We need to decontrol natural gas, and get production of natural gas up to a higher level so we can bring down the price."[9] Evaluate the congressman's statement.

12. From 1979 to 1989 in the United States, the number of working men grew 12 percent while the number of working women grew 29 percent. During this time, average wages for men fell slightly while average wages for women rose about 7 percent. Which of the following two explanations seems most consistent with the data?

a. Women decided to work more, raising their relative supply (relative to men).

b. Discrimination against women declined, raising the relative (to men) demand for female workers.

13. The two diagrams on the next page show supply and demand curves for two substitute commodities: tapes and compact discs (CDs).

a. On the right-hand diagram, show what happens when rising raw material prices make it costlier to produce tapes.

b. On the left-hand diagram, show what happens to the market for CDs.

14. (More difficult) Consider the market for milk discussed in this chapter (Tables 4-1 through 4-3 and Figures 4-1 through 4-3). Suppose that the government decides to fight kidney stones by levying a tax of 30 cents per quart on sales of milk. Follow these steps to analyze the effects of the tax:

a. Construct the new supply schedule (to replace Table 4-2) that relates quantity supplied to the price that consumers pay. (*Hint:* Before the tax, when consumers paid 70 cents, farmers supplied 60 billion quarts. With a 30 cent tax, when consumers pay 70 cents, farmers will receive only 40 cents. Table 4-2 tells us that they will provide only 30 billion quarts at this price. This is one point on the new supply curve. The rest of the curve can be constructed in the same way.)

b. Graph the new supply curve constructed in Review Question 14(a) on the supply-demand diagram depicted in Figure 4-3. What are the new equilibrium price and quantity?

---

[9]*The New York Times*, December 23, 1981.

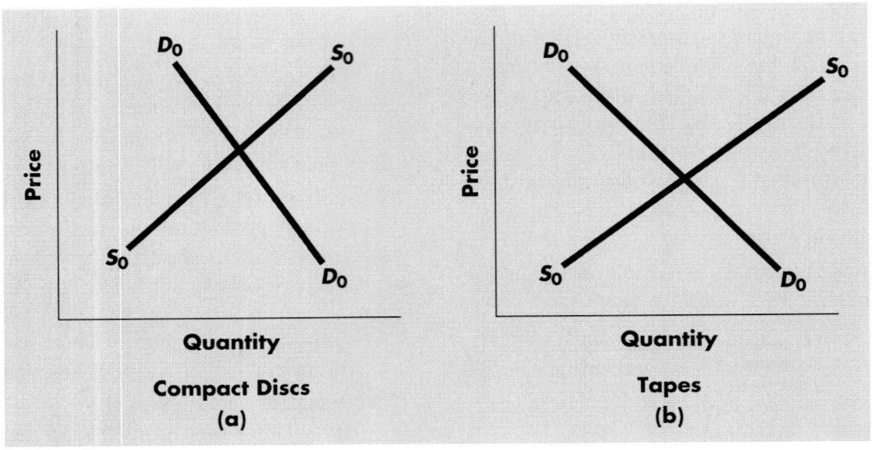

c. Does the tax succeed in its goal of reducing the consumption of milk?
d. How much does the equilibrium price increase? Is the price rise greater than, equal to, or less than the 30 cent tax?
e. Who actually pays the tax, consumers or producers? (This may be a good question to discuss in class.)

15. (More difficult) The demand and supply curves for T-shirts in Touristown, U.S.A., are given by the following equations:

$$Q = 24{,}000 - 500P \qquad Q = 6{,}000 + 1{,}000P$$

where P is measured in dollars and Q is the number of T-shirts per year.

a. Find the equilibrium price and quantity algebraically.
b. If tourists decide they do not really like T-shirts that much, which of the following might be the new demand curve?

$$Q = 21{,}000 - 500P \qquad Q = 27{,}000 - 500P$$

Find the equilibrium price and quantity after the shift of the demand curve.

c. If, *instead,* two new stores that sell T-shirts open up in town, which of the following might be the new supply curve?

$$Q = 3{,}000 + 1{,}000P \qquad Q = 9{,}000 + 1{,}000P$$

Find the equilibrium price and quantity after the shift of the supply curve.

PART II

THE MACROECONOMY: AGGREGATE SUPPLY AND DEMAND

CHAPTER 5

THE REALM OF MACROECONOMICS

Where the telescope ends, the microscope begins. Which of the two has the grander view?
Victor Hugo

By long-standing tradition, economics is divided into two fields: *microeconomics* and *macroeconomics.* These inelegant words are derived from the Greek, where "micro" means something small and "macro" means something large. Chapters 3 and 4 introduced you to microeconomics. This chapter does the same for macroeconomics.

We begin the chapter by exploring the dividing line between microeconomics and macroeconomics: How do the two branches of the discipline differ and why? Next, we stress a key fact: that, while macroeconomists and microeconomists study different issues, *they use nearly identical tools.* Supply and demand provide the basic organizing framework for constructing macroeconomic models, just as they do for microeconomic models. Third, we define some important macroeconomic concepts, such as recession, inflation, and gross domestic product. Fourth, we briefly review American economic history to get some idea of the prevalence and seriousness of the macroeconomic problems of recession and inflation. Finally, we preview what is to come in subsequent chapters by introducing the idea of government management of the economy.

DRAWING A LINE BETWEEN MACROECONOMICS AND MICROECONOMICS

In microeconomics, *we study the behavior of individual decision-making units.* For example, the dairy farmers of Chapter 4 are individual decision makers; so are the consumers who purchase milk. How do they decide what actions are in their own best interests? How are these millions of decisions coordinated by the market mechanism, and with what consequences? Questions like these lie at the heart of microeconomics.

Although Plato and Aristotle might wince at the abuse of their language, microeconomics applies to the decisions of some astonishingly large units. Exxon and the American Telephone and Telegraph Company, for instance, have annual sales that exceed the total production of many nations. Yet someone who studies the pricing policies of AT&T is a microeconomist, whereas someone who studies inflation in Monaco is a macroeconomist. The micro-versus-macro distinction in economics is certainly not based solely on size.

What, then, is the basis for this time-honored distinction? Whereas microeconomics focuses on the decisions of individual units (no matter how large), *macroeconomics concentrates on the behavior of entire economies* (no matter how small). Rather than look at the price and output decisions of a single company, macroeconomists study the overall price level, unemployment rate, and other things that we call *economic aggregates.*

AGGREGATION AND MACROECONOMICS

An "economic aggregate" is nothing but an *abstraction* that people use to describe some salient feature of economic life. For example, while we observe the prices of gasoline, telephone calls, and movie tickets every day, we never actually see "the price level." Yet many people—not just economists—find it meaningful to speak of "the cost of living." In fact, the government's attempts at measuring the cost of living are widely publicized by the news media each month.

Among the most important of these abstract notions is the concept of *domestic product,* which represents the total production of a nation's economy. The process by which real objects like hairpins, baseballs, and theater tickets get combined into an abstraction called total domestic product is **aggregation,** and it is one of the foundations of macroeconomics. We can illustrate it by a simple example.

AGGREGATION means combining many individual markets into one overall market.

Imagine a nation called Agraria, whose economy is far simpler than the U.S. economy: Business firms in Agraria produce nothing but foodstuffs to sell to consumers. Rather than deal separately with all the markets for pizzas, candy bars, hamburgers, and so on, macroeconomists group them all into a single abstract "market for output." Thus, when macroeconomists in Agraria announce that output in Agraria rose 10 percent last year, are they referring to more potatoes or hot dogs, more soybeans or green peppers? The answer is: They do not care. In the aggregate measures of macroeconomics, output is output, no matter what form it takes.

Amalgamating many markets into one means ignoring distinctions among different products. Can we really believe that no one cares whether the national output of Agraria consists of $800,000 worth of pickles and $200,000 worth of ravioli rather than $500,000 each of lettuce and tomatoes? Surely this is too much to swallow! Macroeconomists certainly do not believe that no one cares; instead, they rest the case for aggregation on two foundations:

1. While the *composition* of demand and supply in the various markets may be terribly interesting and important for *some* purposes (such as how income is distributed and what kinds of diets people enjoy or endure), it may be of little consequence for the economy-wide issues of inflation and unemployment—the issues that concern macroeconomists.
2. During economic fluctuations, markets tend to move up or down together. When demand in the economy rises, there is more demand for potatoes *and* tomatoes, more demand for artichokes *and* pickles, more demand for ravioli *and* hot dogs.

Although there are exceptions to these two principles, both seem serviceable enough as approximations. In fact, if they were not, there would be no discipline called macroeconomics, and a full-year course in economics could be reduced to a half-year. Lest this cause you a twinge of regret, bear in mind that many people feel that unemployment and inflation would be far more difficult to control without macroeconomics. And that would be even more regrettable.

THE LINE OF DEMARCATION REVISITED

These two principles—that markets normally move together and that the composition of demand and supply may be unimportant for some purposes—enable us to draw a different kind of dividing line between microeconomics and macroeconomics.

In macroeconomics, we typically assume that most details of resource allocation and income distribution are of secondary importance to the study of the overall rates of inflation and unemployment. In microeconomics, we typically ignore inflation and unemployment and focus instead on how individual markets allocate resources and distribute income.

To use a well-worn metaphor, the macroeconomist analyzes the determination of the size of the economic "pie," paying scant attention to what is inside it or to how it gets divided among the dinner guests. A microeconomist, on the other hand, assumes that the pie is of the right size and shape, and frets over its ingredients and its division. If you have ever baked or eaten a pie, you will realize that either approach alone is a trifle myopic.

Similarly, the division of economics into macroeconomics and microeconomics is maintained largely for the sake of pedagogical clarity. In reality, the crucial interconnection between macroeconomics and microeconomics is with us all the time. There is, after all, only one economy.

SUPPLY AND DEMAND IN MACROECONOMICS

Some economics students take courses that concentrate on macroeconomics while others focus their studies on microeconomics. The discussion of supply and demand in Chapter 4 serves as an invaluable introduction to both fields because supply and demand analysis is just as fundamental to macroeconomics as it is to microeconomics.

Figure 5-1 shows two diagrams that should look familiar from Chapter 4. In Figure 5-1(a), there is a downward-sloping demand curve, labeled *DD,* and an upward-sloping supply curve, labeled *SS.* The axes labeled "Price" and "Quantity" do not specify what commodity they refer to because this is a multipurpose diagram. To start on familiar terrain, first imagine that this is a picture of the market for milk, so the price axis measures the price of milk while the quantity axis measures the quantity of milk demanded and supplied. As we know, if there are no interferences with the operation of a free market, equilibrium will be at point *E* with a price P_0 and a quantity of output Q_0.

Next, suppose that something happens to shift the demand curve outward. For example, we learned in Chapter 4 that an increase in consumer incomes might have this effect. Figure 5-1(b) shows this shift as a rightward movement of the demand curve from D_0D_0 to D_1D_1. Equilibrium shifts from *E* to *A,* so both price and output rise.

Now let us reinterpret Figure 5-1 as representing the abstract market for "domestic product." This is one of those abstractions—an economic aggregate—

FIGURE 5-1 TWO INTERPRETATIONS OF A SHIFT IN THE DEMAND CURVE

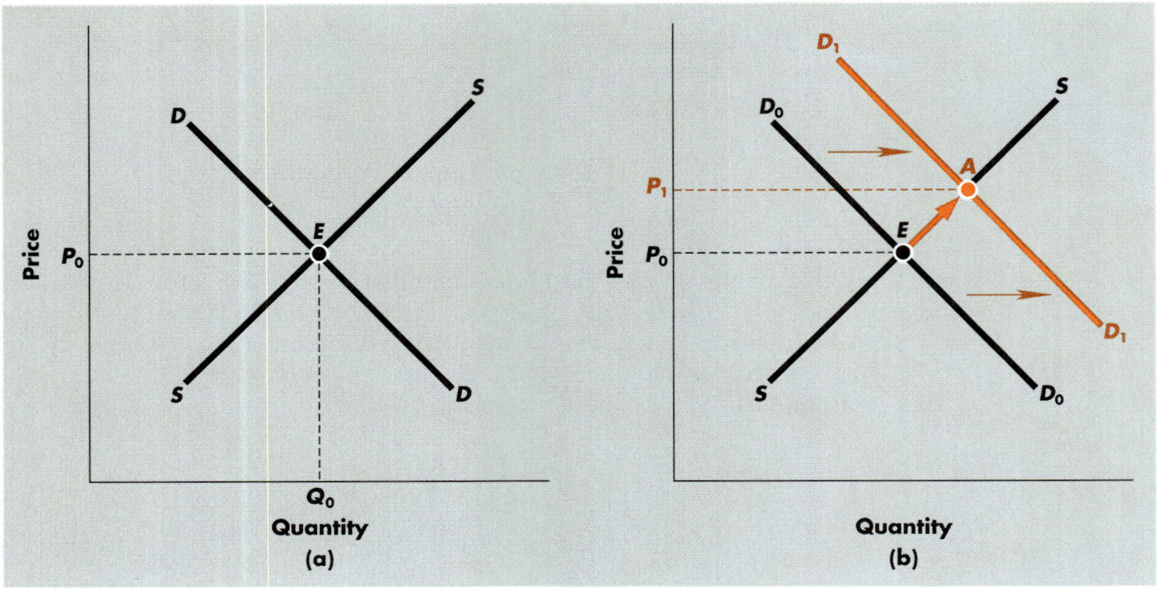

Panel (a) shows an equilibrium at point *E*, where the demand curve *DD* intersects the supply curve *SS*. Panel (b) shows how this equilibrium moves from point *E* to point *A* if the demand curve moves outward. If this graph represents the market for milk, as it did in Chapter 4, then it shows an increase in the price of milk. But if the graph represents the aggregate market for "domestic product," then it shows inflation—a rise in the general price level.

The **AGGREGATE DEMAND CURVE** shows the quantity of domestic product that is demanded at each possible value of the price level.

The **AGGREGATE SUPPLY CURVE** shows the quantity of domestic product that is supplied at each possible value of the price level.

INFLATION refers to a sustained increase in the general price level.

A **RECESSION** is a period of time during which the total output of the economy declines.

that we described earlier. No one has ever seen, touched, or eaten a unit of domestic product, but these kinds of abstractions are the foundations of macroeconomic analysis. Consistent with this reinterpretation, think of the price measured on the vertical axis as being another abstraction—the overall price index, or "cost of living."[1] Then the curve *DD* in Figure 5-1(a) is called an **aggregate demand curve,** and the curve *SS* is called an **aggregate supply curve.** We will derive these curves explicitly from economic theory in Chapters 7–10. As we shall see there, the curves are rather different from the microeconomic counterparts we encountered in Chapter 4. With this reinterpretation, Figure 5-1(b) can depict the macroeconomic problem of **inflation.**

We see from the figure that the outward shift of the aggregate demand curve, whatever its cause, pushes the price level up. If aggregate demand keeps shifting out month after month, the economy will suffer from inflation, that is, a sustained increase in the general price level.

The other principal problems of macroeconomics, recession and unemployment, also can be illustrated on a supply-demand diagram, this time by shifting the demand curve in the opposite direction. Figure 5-2 repeats the supply and demand curves of Figure 5-1(a) and in addition depicts a leftward shift of the aggregate demand curve from D_0D_0 to D_2D_2. Equilibrium now moves from point *E* to point *B* so that domestic product (total output) declines. This is what we normally mean by a **recession**—a period of time during which production falls.

[1]The appendix to Chapter 6 explains how such price indexes are calculated.

FIGURE 5-2 AN ECONOMY SLIPPING INTO A RECESSION

In this aggregate supply-demand diagram, there is an initial equilibrium at point *E*, where the demand curve D_0D_0 intersects the supply curve *SS*. When the demand curve shifts inward from D_0D_0 to D_2D_2, equilibrium moves to point *B*, and output falls from Q_0 to Q_2.

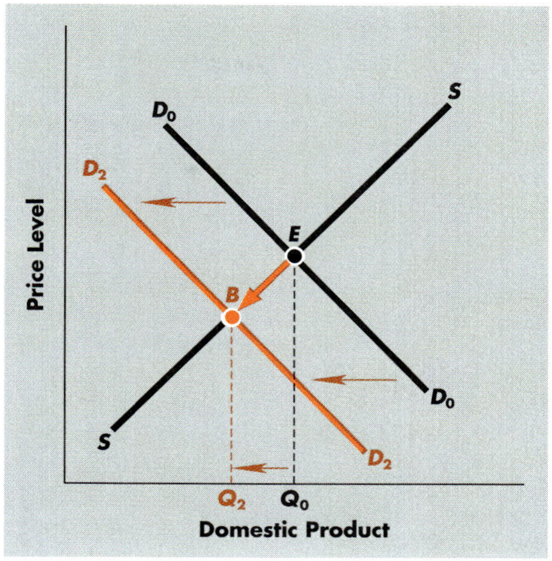

GROSS DOMESTIC PRODUCT

GROSS DOMESTIC PRODUCT (GDP) is the sum of the money values of all final goods and services produced in the domestic economy during a specified period of time, usually 1 year.

The economy's total output is one of the major variables of concern to macroeconomists. While there are several ways to measure it, the most popular choice undoubtedly is the **gross domestic product,** a term you have probably encountered in the news media. The gross domestic product, or GDP for short, is the most comprehensive measure of the output of all the factories, offices, and shops in the United States. Specifically, it is the sum of the *money values* of all *final* goods and services *produced in the domestic economy* within the year.

Several features of this definition need to be underscored.[2] First, you will notice that:

We add up the *money values* of things.

The GDP consists of a bewildering variety of goods and services: mousetraps and computers, tanks and textbooks, ballet performances and rock concerts. How can we combine all of these into a single number? To an economist, the natural way to do this begins by converting every good and service into *money* terms. If we want to add 10 apples and 20 oranges, we first ask: How much *money* does each cost? If apples cost 20 cents and oranges cost 25 cents, then the apples count for $2 and the oranges for $5, so the sum is $7 worth of "output." The market *price* of each good or service is used as an indicator of its *value* to society for a simple reason: *Someone* is willing to pay that much money for it.

NOMINAL GDP is calculated by valuing all outputs at current prices.

This decision raises the question of what prices to use in valuing different outputs. The official data offer two choices. First, we can value each good and service at the price at which it was actually sold during the year. If we do this, the resulting measure is called **nominal GDP,** or *money GDP,* or *GDP in current*

[2]Certain exceptions to the definition are dealt with in the appendix to Chapter 7, especially on page 158. Some instructors may prefer to take up that material here.

dollars. This seems like a perfectly sensible choice. But as a measure of output, it has one serious drawback: Nominal GDP rises when prices rise, even if there is no increase in actual production. For example, if hamburgers cost $2.00 this year but cost only $1.50 last year, then 100 hamburgers will contribute $200 to this year's nominal GDP though they contributed only $150 to last year's. But 100 hamburgers are still 100 hamburgers—output has not grown.

For this reason, government statisticians have devised alternative measures that correct for inflation by valuing goods and services produced in *different* years at *the same* set of prices. For example, if the hamburgers were valued at $1.50 each in both years, $150 worth of hamburger output would be included in GDP *in each year.* In practice, such calculations can be done in several ways, and the details can become quite complicated. But such details need not detain us in an introductory course. Suffice it to say that, when the calculations are done, we obtain **real GDP** or *GDP in constant dollars.* The news media often refer to it as "GDP corrected for inflation." Throughout most of this book, and certainly when we are discussing the nation's output, we will be concerned with *real* GDP. The distinction between nominal and real GDP leads us to a working definition of a *recession* as a period in which *real* GDP declines. For example, between 1990 and 1991, nominal GDP rose from $5,744 billion to $5,917 billion, but real GDP *fell* from $6,139 billion to $6,079 billion.

REAL GDP is calculated by valuing outputs of different years at common prices. Therefore, real GDP is a far better measure than nominal GDP of changes in total production.

The next important aspect of the definition of GDP is that:

The GDP for a particular year includes only goods and services produced during that year. Sales of items produced in previous years are explicitly excluded.

For example, suppose that you buy a perfectly beautiful 1983 Dodge next week and are overjoyed by your purchase. The national income statistician will not share your glee because she had counted your car in the GDP in 1983, when it was first produced and sold. The car will never be counted again. The same holds true of houses. Unlike old cars, old houses often sell for more than their original price; yet the resale values of houses do not count in GDP since they were already counted in the years they were built.

Third, you will note the use of the phrase **final goods and services** in the definition of gross domestic product. The adjective *final* is the key word here. For example, when a supermarket buys milk from a farmer, the transaction is not included in the GDP because the supermarket does not want the milk for itself. It buys milk only for resale to consumers. Only when the milk is sold to consumers is it considered a final product. When the supermarket buys it, economists consider it an **intermediate good.** The GDP excludes sales of intermediate goods and services because, if they were included, we would wind up counting the same outputs several times.[3] For example, if milk sold to grocers were included in GDP, we would count the same container of milk when it was sold to the store and then again when it was sold to a consumer.

FINAL GOODS AND SERVICES are those that are purchased by their ultimate users.

An **INTERMEDIATE GOOD** is a good purchased for resale or for use in producing another good.

Fourth, the adjective *domestic* connotes production within the geographic boundaries of the United States. Some Americans work abroad, and many American companies have offices or factories in foreign countries. All of these people and businesses produce valuable outputs, but none of this is counted in the GDP of the United States. (It is counted, instead, in the GDPs of the foreign countries.) On the other hand, quite a number of foreigners and foreign companies produce

---

[3]Actually, there is another way to add up the GDP by counting a portion of each intermediate transaction. This is explained in the appendix to Chapter 7, especially pages 162–163.

goods and services in the United States. All of this activity does count in our GDP.[4]

Finally, although the definition does not state this explicitly:

For the most part, only goods and services that pass through organized markets count in the GDP.

This restriction, of course, excludes many economic activities. For example, illegal activities are not included in the GDP. Thus, gambling services in Atlantic City are part of GDP, but gambling services in Chicago are not. The definition reflects the statisticians' confession that they cannot possibly measure the value of many of the economy's most important activities, such as housework, do-it-yourself repairs, and leisure time. While these are certainly economic activities that result in currently produced goods or services, they all lack that important measuring rod—a market price.

This omission results in certain oddities. For example, suppose that each of two neighboring families hires the other to clean house, generously paying $1,000 a week for the services. Each family can easily afford such generosity since it collects an identical salary from its neighbor. Nothing real has changed, but GDP goes up by $104,000 a year. If this example seems trivial, you may be interested to know that, according to one estimate, America's GDP would be 44 percent higher if unpaid housework were valued at market prices.[5]

LIMITATIONS OF THE GDP: WHAT GDP IS NOT

Having seen in some detail what the GDP *is*, it is worth examining what it *is not*. In particular:

Gross domestic product is not a measure of the nation's economic well-being.

The GDP is not intended to measure economic well-being, and does not do so for several reasons:

1. *Only market activity is included in GDP.* As we have just seen, a great deal of work done in the home contributes to the nation's well-being but is not measured in the GDP because it has no price tag. One important implication of this exclusion arises when we try to compare the GDPs of developed and less developed countries. Americans are always surprised to learn that the per-capita GDPs of the poorest African countries are less than $250 a year. Surely, no one could survive in America on $5 a week. How can Africans do it? Part of the answer, of course, is that these people are incredibly poor. We will study their plight in Chapter 20. But another part of the answer is that:

   International GDP comparisons are vastly misleading when the two countries differ greatly in the fraction of economic activity that each conducts in organized markets.

---

[4]There is another concept, called gross *national* product, which counts the goods and services produced by all Americans, regardless of where they work. For consistency, the outputs produced by foreigners working in the United States are not included in GNP. In practice, the two measures—GDP and GNP—are very close.

[5]Ann Chadeau, "What Is Households' Non-market Production Worth?" *OECD Economic Studies* No. 18.

This fraction is relatively large in the United States and relatively small in the less developed countries, so when we compare their respective measured GDPs, we are not comparing the same economic activities at all. Many things that get counted in the U.S. GDP are not counted in the GDPs of less developed nations because they do not pass through markets. It is ludicrous to think that these people, poor as they are, survive on what to Americans would amount to $5 a week.

A second implication is that GDP statistics take no account of the so-called "underground economy." This includes not just criminal activities, but a great deal of legitimate business activity that is conducted in cash or by barter to escape the tax collector. Naturally, we have no good data on the size of the underground economy, but some observers think that it may amount to 10 percent or more of U.S. GDP. In some foreign countries, it is surely a much bigger share than this.

2. *GDP places no value on leisure.* As a country gets richer, its citizens normally take more and more leisure time. If that is true, a better measure of national well-being that includes the value of leisure time would display faster growth than conventionally measured GDP. For example, the length of the typical workweek in the United States fell steadily for many decades, which means that growth in GDP systematically *underestimated* the growth in national well-being. But some scholars claim that this trend has stopped, and may even have reversed. (See the box on the next page.) However, there are also reasons why the GDP *overstates* how well-off we are. For example:

3. *"Bads" as well as "goods" get counted in GDP.* Suppose that there is a natural disaster—such as the devastating Los Angeles earthquake in 1994. Surely the well-being of the United States was diminished by this catastrophe. People were killed and injured; many homes and businesses were destroyed. Yet the disaster probably raised U.S. GDP. Consumers spent more to clean up and replace lost homes and possessions. Businesses spent more to rebuild and repair damaged stores and plants. The government spent more for disaster relief and cleanup. Yet no one would think America was better off for its higher GDP.

   Wars represent an extreme example. Mobilization for a war fought on some other nation's soil always causes a country's GDP to rise rapidly. But men and women serving in the military could be producing civilian output. Factories assigned to produce armaments could instead be making cars, washing machines, and televisions. A country at war is surely worse off than a country at peace, but this fact will not be reflected in its GDP.

4. *Ecological costs are not netted out of the GDP.* Many of the activities in a modern industrial economy that produce goods and services also have undesirable side effects on the environment. Automobiles provide enjoyment and a means of transportation, but they also despoil the atmosphere. Factories pollute rivers and lakes while manufacturing valuable commodities. Almost everything seems to produce garbage, which creates a serious disposal problem. None of these ecological costs are deducted from the GDP in an effort to give us a truer measure of the *net* increase in economic welfare that our economy produces. Is this foolishness? Not if we remember the job that national income statisticians are trying to do: they are measuring the economic activity conducted through organized markets, not national welfare. However, the government is currently engaged in a multiyear effort to esti-

ARE AMERICANS WORKING MORE?

According to conventional wisdom, the workweek in the United States is steadily shrinking, leaving Americans with more and more leisure time to enjoy. But, in a 1991 book, economist Juliet Schor argued that this view is wrong: Americans are really working longer and longer hours. Her findings are both provocative and controversial.

> In the last twenty years the amount of time Americans have spent at their jobs has risen steadily. . . . Americans report that they have only sixteen and a half hours of leisure a week, after the obligations of job and household are taken care of. . . . If present trends continue, by the end of the century Americans will be spending as much time at their jobs as they did back in the nineteen twenties.
>
> The rise in worktime was unexpected. For nearly a hundred years, hours had been declining. . . . Equally surprising, but also hardly recognized, has been the deviation from Western Europe. After progressing in tandem for nearly a century, the United States veered off into a trajectory of declining leisure, while in Europe work has been disappearing. . . . U.S. manufacturing employees currently work 320 more hours [per year]—the equivalent of over two months—than their counterparts in West Germany or France. . . . We have paid a price for prosperity. . . . We are eating more, but we are burning up those calories at work. We have color televisions and compact disc players, but we need them to unwind after a stressful day at the office. We take vacations, but we work so hard throughout the year that they become indispensable to our sanity.

SOURCE: Juliet B. Schor, *The Overworked American* (New York: Basic Books, 1991), pp. 1–2, 10–11.

mate what has been called "green GDP," that is, GDP adjusted for environmental damage and for depletion of resources. (See the box on the next page.)

THE ECONOMY ON A ROLLER COASTER

Having defined several of the basic concepts of macroeconomics, let us breathe some life into them by perusing the economic history of the United States. Figure 5-3 charts the growth rate of U.S. real GDP since 1870. It is almost always positive, indicating that the main feature of this 125-year period has been *economic growth.* In fact, the average annual growth rate over this period was about 3.3 percent. This growth—or, more precisely, the excess of real GDP growth over population growth—is the fundamental source of the ever-higher living standards that have been such a conspicuous feature of American history.

But there have been occasional setbacks, periods of falling real GDP, along the way. Such recessions have been a persistent feature of American economic performance, as the figure shows. Especially before the Korean war, the graph gives the impression of an economy on a roller coaster. The ups and downs that are apparent in Figure 5-3 are called *economic fluctuations,* or sometimes *business cycles.*

DEFLATION refers to a sustained decrease in the general price level.

The history of the inflation rate displayed in Figure 5-4 (on page 106) also shows more positive numbers than negative ones—more inflation than **deflation.** Although the price level has risen about 14-fold since 1869, the upward trend is of rather recent vintage. Prior to World War II, Figure 5-4 shows periods of inflation and deflation, with little or no tendency for one to be more common than the other. Indeed, prices in 1940 were barely higher than those at the close of the Civil War. However, the figure does show some large gyrations in the inflation rate, including sharp bursts of inflation during and right after the two world wars and dramatic deflations in the 1870s, 1880s, 1921 to 1922, and 1929 to 1933.

"GREEN" GDP

GDP as conventionally measured does not net out the costs of pollution or the depletion of renewable resources like forests, nor does it "charge" for using up nonrenewable mineral resources. The consequence, some critics argue, is that GDP overstates economic well-being. The government is currently developing experimental measures that will adjust for each of these factors, and the first phase of its research turned up some surprising results.

Statisticians valued the U.S. stock of mineral resources annually from 1958 to 1991. The idea was to estimate how much had been consumed. However, despite the fact that the U.S. economy used enormous amounts of minerals over the 33-year period, the statisticians discovered that proven supplies barely declined. How can this be?

In a purely physical sense, of course, it cannot be. America certainly had fewer actual mineral deposits in the ground in 1991 than in 1958. However, new sources of minerals were discovered during the period, and new technologies made it possible to mine in places previously viewed as either inaccessible or uneconomic. When mineral use was netted against new discoveries, *proven* reserves barely fell over the 33-year period. Therefore, making an adjustment for the depletion of mineral resources would hardly change the official GDP numbers at all.

In sum, although both real GDP and the price level have grown a great deal over the past 125 years, neither has grown smoothly. The ups and downs of both real growth and inflation have been important economic events that need to be explained. Parts II and III develop a macroeconomic theory designed to do precisely that.

As you look at these graphs, the Great Depression of the 1930s is bound to catch your eye. The decline in economic activity from 1929 to 1933 indicated in Figure 5-3 was the most severe in our nation's history, and the rapid deflation in Figure 5-4 was most unusual. The Depression is but a dim memory now, but those who lived through it—including some of your grandparents—will never forget it.

Statistics usually conceal the true drama of economic events. But this is not so of the Great Depression—instead they stand as bitter testimony to its severity. The production of goods and services dropped 30 percent, business investment almost dried up entirely, and the unemployment rate rose ominously from about 3 percent in 1929 to 25 percent in 1933. One person in four was jobless. From the data alone, you can conjure up pictures of soup lines, beggars on street corners, closed factories, and homeless families. (See the box on page 107.)

FIGURE 5-3 THE GROWTH RATE OF REAL GROSS DOMESTIC PRODUCT OF THE UNITED STATES, 1870–1996

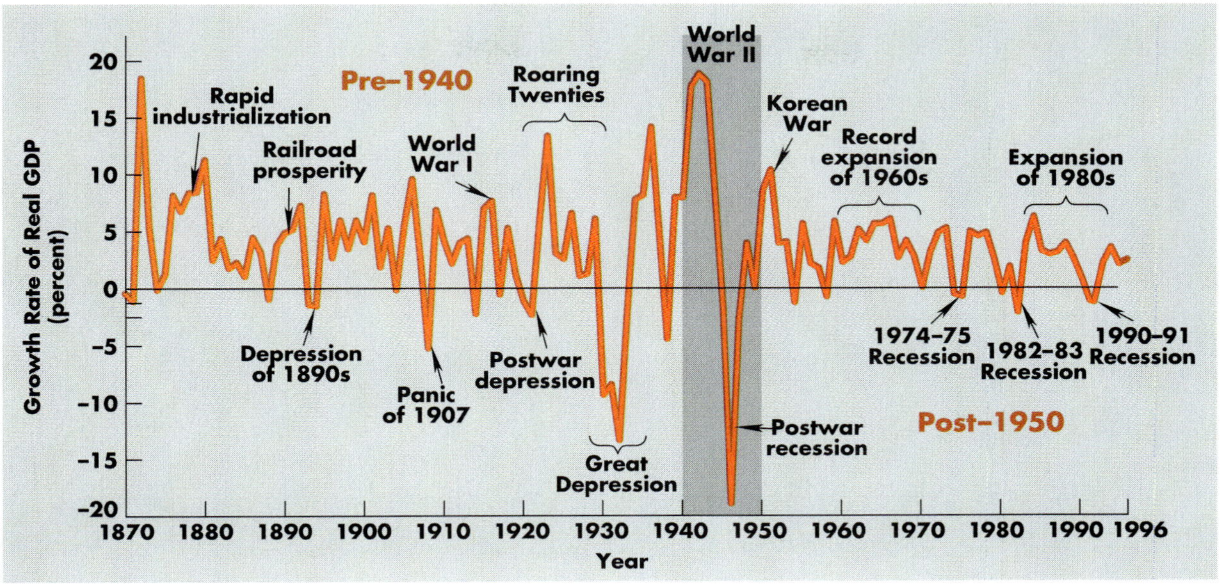

This time-series chart displays the growth rate of real gross domestic product in the United States from 1870 to 1996. (Here real GDP is measured in 1992 prices.) The Great Depression (1929–1939) stands out vividly. The years during and just after World War II are shaded. Does the growth rate look smoother to the right of this shaded area?

SOURCE: Constructed by the authors from Commerce Department data for 1929–1996. Data for 1869–1928 are based on research by Professor Christina Romer.

The Great Depression was a worldwide event. No country was spared its ravages, which literally changed the histories of many nations. In Germany, it facilitated the ascendancy of Nazism. In the United States, it enabled Franklin Roosevelt's Democratic party to engineer one of the most dramatic political realignments in history and to push through a host of political and economic reforms.

The worldwide depression also caused a much-needed revolution in the thinking of economists. Up until the 1930s, the prevailing economic theory held that a capitalist economy occasionally misbehaved but had a natural tendency to cure recessions or inflations by itself. The roller coaster bounced around but did not normally run off the tracks. This optimistic view was not confined to academia. Most political and business leaders shared it, as well. As the great American humorist Will Rogers remarked with characteristic sarcasm:

> It's almost been worth this depression to find out how little our big men knew. Mayby [sic] this depression is just "normalcy" and we don't know it. It's made a dumb guy as smart as a smart one. . . . Depression used to be a state of mind, now it's a state of coma, now it's permanent. Last year we said, "Things can't go on like this," and they didn't, they got worse.[6]

---

[6]From *Sanity Is Where You Find It* by Will Rogers, edited by Donald Day; copyright 1955 by Rogers Company; reprinted by permission of Houghton Mifflin Company; pages 120–121.

FIGURE 5-4 THE INFLATION RATE IN THE UNITED STATES, 1870–1996

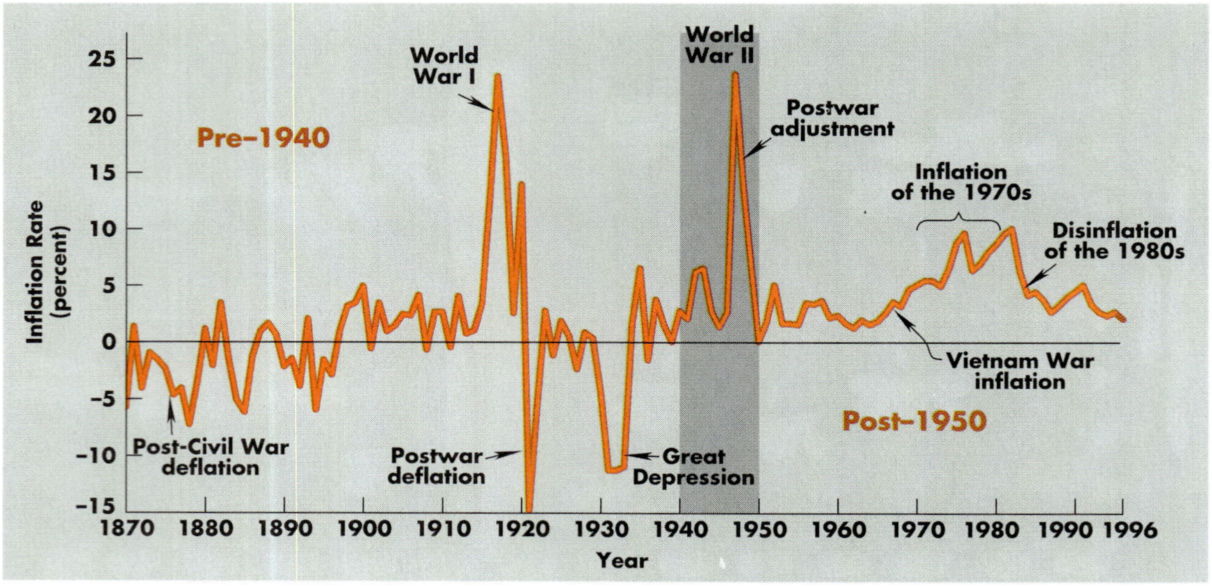

This time-series chart portrays the behavior of the U.S. inflation rate from 1870 to 1996. (The specific price index used is called the *GDP deflator*, and it is defined as the ratio of nominal GDP divided by real GDP.) The difference between the 1870 to 1940 period and the 1950 to 1996 period is pronounced.

SOURCE: Constructed by the authors from Commerce Department data for 1929–1996. Data for 1869–1928 were kindly provided by Professor Christina Romer.

The stubbornness of the Great Depression shook almost everyone's faith in the ability of the economy to correct itself. In Cambridge, England, this questioning attitude led John Maynard Keynes, one of the world's most reknowned economists, to write *The General Theory of Employment, Interest, and Money* (1936). Probably the most important economics book of the 20th century, it carried a rather revolutionary message. Keynes rejected the idea that the economy always gravitated toward high levels of employment, asserting instead that—if a pessimistic outlook led business firms and consumers to curtail their spending plans—the economy might be condemned to years of stagnation.

While this doleful prognosis sounded all too realistic at the time, Keynes closed his book on a hopeful note. For he showed how government actions might prod the economy out of its depressed state. The lessons he taught the world then are among the lessons we will be learning in Parts II and III (along with many qualifications that economists have learned since). These lessons show how governments can manage their economies so that recessions will not turn into depressions and depressions will not last as long as the Great Depression.

While Keynes was working on *The General Theory,* he wrote his friend George Bernard Shaw that, "I believe myself to be writing a book on economic theory which will largely revolutionize . . . the way the world thinks about economic problems." In many ways he was right, though parts of the Keynesian message remain controversial to this day.

LIFE IN "HOOVERVILLE"

During the worst years of the Great Depression, unemployed workers often congregated in shantytowns on the outskirts of many major cities. Conditions in these slums were deplorable. With a heavy dose of irony, these communities were known as "Hoovervilles," in honor of the president of the United States who preached rugged individualism. A contemporary observer described a Hooverville in New York City as follows:

> It was a fairly popular "development" made up of a hundred or so dwellings, each the size of a dog house or chickencoop, often constructed with much ingenuity out of wooden boxes, metal cans, strips of cardboard or old tar paper. Here human beings lived on the margin of civilization by foraging for garbage, junk, and waste lumber. I found some splitting or sawing wood with dull tools to make fires; others were picking through heaps of rubbish they had gathered before their doorways or cooking over open fires or battered oilstoves. Still others spent their days improving their rent-free homes, making them sometimes fairly solid and weather-proof. . . . Most of them, according to the police, lived by begging or trading in junk; when all else failed they ate at the soup kitchens or public canteens. They were of all sorts, young and old, some of them rough-looking and suspicious of strangers. They lived in fear of being forcibly removed by the authorities, though the neighborhood people in many cases helped them and the police tolerated them for the time being.

SOURCE: Mathew Josephson, *Infidel in the Temple* (New York: Knopf, 1967), pp. 82–83.

FROM WORLD WAR II TO 1973

The Great Depression finally ended when the country mobilized for war in the early 1940s. With government spending at extraordinarily high levels, the economy boomed, and the unemployment rate fell as low as 1.2 percent during the war.

Wartime spending of this magnitude usually leads to inflation, but much of the potential inflation during World War II was contained by price controls. With prices held below the levels at which quantity supplied equaled quantity demanded, many goods had to be rationed, and shortages of consumer goods were common. All of this ended with a burst of inflation when controls were lifted after the war.

The period from the end of the war until the early 1960s was one of strong growth marred by several short recessions. Moderate but persistent inflation also became a fact of life. When the economy emerged from recession in 1961, it

JOHN MAYNARD KEYNES (1883–1946)

John Maynard Keynes was something of a child prodigy. After an outstanding scholastic career at Eton and Cambridge, Keynes took the civil service examination. Ironically, his second-place score was not good enough to land him the position he wanted—in the Treasury. Some years later, reflecting on the fact that his lowest score on the exam was in the economics section, he suggested with characteristic immodesty that, "The examiners presumably knew less than I did." He was probably right.

During World War I, Keynes was called to the Treasury to assist in planning the financial aspects of the war. There his unique combination of daring and intellect quickly established him as a dominant figure. At the war's end, he represented the British Treasury at the peace conference in Versailles. The conference was a turning point in Keynes's life, though it was one of his few failures. He tried unsuccessfully to persuade the Allies to take a less punitive attitude toward the vanquished Germans, and then stormed out of the conference to write his *Economic Consequences of the Peace* (1919), which created a furor. In that work, Keynes argued that the Germans could never meet the harsh economic terms of the treaty, and that its viciousness posed the threat of continued instability and perhaps another war in Europe.

No longer welcome in government, Keynes returned to Cambridge and to his circle of literary and artistic friends in London's Bloomsbury district—a remarkable group that included Virginia Woolf, Lytton Strachey, and E. M. Forster. In 1925, he married the beautiful ballerina Lydia Lopokova, who gave up her stage career for him (though she later acted in a theater that Keynes himself established).

Between the wars, Keynes devoted himself to making money, to economic theory, and to political economy. He managed to make both himself and King's College rich by speculating in international currencies and commodities—allegedly by studying the newspapers while still in bed each morning! In 1936, he published his masterpiece, *The General Theory of Employment, Interest, and Money,* on which much of modern macroeconomics is based.

A heart attack in 1937 reduced Keynes's activities, but he returned to the Treasury during World War II to conduct several delicate financial negotiations with the Americans. Then, as the capstone to a truly remarkable career, he represented Great Britain—and by all accounts dominated the proceedings—at the 1944 conference in Bretton Woods, New Hampshire, that established an international financial system that served the Western world for 27 years. (See Chapter 18.)

He died at home of a heart attack as Lord Keynes, Baron of Tilton, a man who had achieved almost everything that he sought, and who had only one regret: he wished he had drunk more champagne.

entered a period of unprecedented—and noninflationary—growth which was credited widely to the success of what came to be called "The New Economics," a term the media created for the economic policies that Keynes had prescribed in the 1930s. For a while, it looked as if we could avoid both unemployment and inflation. But the optimistic verdicts were premature on both counts.

Inflation came first, beginning about 1966. Its major cause was high levels of wartime spending, as it had been so many times in the past. This time it was the Vietnam war. Unemployment followed when the economy ground to a halt in 1969. Despite a short and mild recession, inflation continued at 5 to 6 percent a year.

Faced with persistent inflation, President Richard Nixon stunned the nation by instituting wage and price controls in 1971, the first time this had ever been done in peacetime. The controls program, which will be discussed in Chapter 16, held inflation in check for a while. But inflation worsened dramatically in 1973, mainly because of an explosion in food prices caused by poor harvests around the world.

THE GREAT STAGFLATION, 1973–1980

Then things began to get much worse, not only for the United States, but for all oil-importing nations. A 1973 war between Israel and the Arab nations led to a quadrupling of the price of oil by the Organization of Petroleum Exporting Countries (OPEC). At the same time, continued poor harvests in many parts of the globe pushed world food prices higher. Prices of other raw materials also skyrocketed. Naturally, higher costs of fuel and other materials soon were reflected in the prices of manufactured goods.

By unhappy coincidence, these events came just as wage and price controls were being lifted. Just as had happened after World War II, the elimination of controls led to a temporary acceleration of inflation as prices that had been held artificially below equilibrium levels were allowed to rise. For all of these reasons, the inflation rate in the United States soared to above 12 percent during 1974.

Meanwhile, the U.S. economy was slipping into what was, up to then, its longest and most severe recession since the 1930s. Real GDP fell between late 1973 and early 1975, and the unemployment rate rose to nearly 9 percent. With both inflation and unemployment unusually virulent in 1974 and 1975, a new term—**stagflation**—was coined to refer to the simultaneous occurrence of economic *stag*nation and rapid in*flation*.

STAGFLATION is inflation that occurs while the economy is growing slowly ("stagnating") or having a recession.

Thanks partly to government actions, but mostly to natural economic forces, a sustained recovery from recession began in 1975. Inflation tumbled rapidly as the adjustment to the end of price controls ended and food and energy prices stopped soaring. The severity of the recession also put a brake on inflation, just as it had in the past. In total, the inflation rate tumbled from over 12 percent back down to the 6 percent range.

But the price of oil soared again in 1979 following a revolution in Iran, bringing stagflation back. This time, inflation hit the astonishing rate of 16 percent during the first half of 1980 and the government clamped on credit controls. The controls broke the back of the economy and output fell at an extraordinarily rapid pace. But credit controls remained in effect for only a few months, and by late 1980 recovery was under way.

REAGANOMICS AND ITS AFTERMATH

When President Ronald Reagan assumed office in January 1981, the U.S. economy was showing signs of reviving, but the inflation rate seemed stuck near 10 percent. The new president promised to change things with a package of policies called "supply-side economics."[7]

At first, things did change dramatically—but not in the way President Reagan wanted. While inflation fell remarkably to only about 4 percent in 1982, the lowest rate in a decade, the economy slumped into its worst recession since the Great Depression. When the 1981–1982 recession hit bottom, the unemployment rate was approaching 11 percent, the financial markets were in disarray, and the word *depression* had reentered the American vocabulary. The U.S. government also had a huge budget deficit, bigger than anyone had dreamed possible only a few years before. This problem, as we shall see in subsequent chapters, is still with us.

---

[7]Supply-side economics is discussed further in Chapter 11.

However, the recovery that began in the winter of 1982–1983 proved to be one of the most vigorous and long-lasting in our history. Unemployment fell more or less steadily for about 6 years, eventually dropping below 5-1/2 percent. Meanwhile, inflation remained tame. All of this provided an ideal economic platform on which George Bush ran to succeed Reagan—and to continue Reagan's policies.

Unfortunately for President Bush, the good times did not keep rolling. Shortly after he took office, inflation began to accelerate a bit, economic growth began to sputter, and Congress enacted a deficit-reduction package (including a tax increase) not entirely to the president's liking. Then, in 1990–1991, the U.S. economy slumped into another recession—precipitated, according to some observers, by yet another spike in oil prices before the Persian Gulf war.

While the 1990–1991 recession was relatively mild, the economy had not recovered by the time of the 1992 election. In fact, the growth rate during George Bush's presidency was the weakest of any 4-year period since World War II. This fact was not lost on candidate Bill Clinton, who hammered away at the lackluster economic performance of the period from 1989 to 1992. Most observers believe that the weak economy was the main factor behind George Bush's electoral defeat.

CLINTONOMICS: DEFICIT REDUCTION AND THE RESUMPTION OF GROWTH[8]

President Clinton ran on a detailed economic platform that concentrated on two objectives: spurring economic growth and increasing public investment. But, even before his inauguration in January 1993, the yawning budget deficit forced the new president to deemphasize new spending and concentrate on deficit reduction. A politically contentious package of substantial tax increases and major spending cuts passed the Congress in August 1993 without a single Republican vote. Since then, deficit reduction has been the major economic issue on the American political landscape.

Whether by cause or coincidence, the national economy improved dramatically in the first 2 years of the Clinton presidency. Business perked up, unemployment fell rapidly, and inflation remained remarkably well contained—in the 3 percent range. By the spring of 1996, macroeconomic conditions were the best in a generation: The economic expansion was more than 5 years old, unemployment was about 5-1/2 percent, and inflation was still below 3 percent.

THE PROBLEM OF MACROECONOMIC STABILIZATION: A SNEAK PREVIEW

STABILIZATION POLICY is the name given to government programs designed to prevent or shorten recessions and to counteract inflation (that is, to *stabilize* prices).

This brief look at the historical record shows that our economy has not generally produced steady growth without inflation. Rather, it has been buffeted by periodic bouts of unemployment or inflation, and sometimes has been plagued by both. There was also a hint that government policies may have had something to do with this performance. Let us now expand briefly upon this hint—a subject that will be developed further in subsequent chapters.

We can provide a preliminary analysis of **stabilization policy,** the name given to government programs designed to prevent or shorten recessions and to coun-

[8]One of the authors of this book was a member of President Clinton's original Council of Economic Advisers.

FIGURE 5-5

STABILIZATION POLICY TO FIGHT UNEMPLOYMENT

This diagram duplicates Figure 5-1(b), but here we assume that point *E*—the intersection of the demand curve D_0D_0 and the supply curve *SS*—corresponds to high unemployment. With the kind of policy tools that we will study in later chapters, the government could shift the aggregate demand curve outward to D_1D_1. This would raise output and lower unemployment.

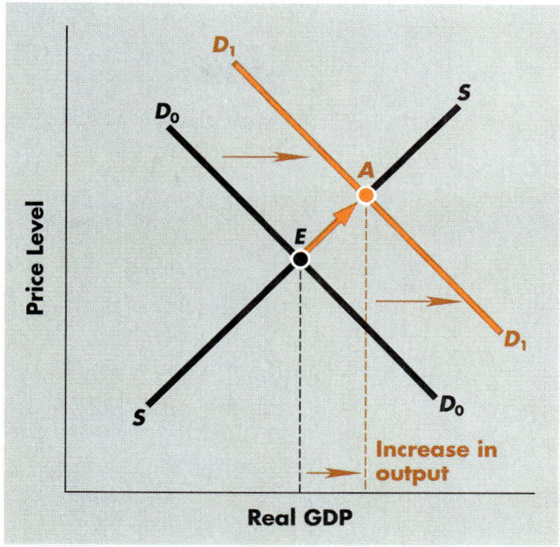

teract inflation, by using the basic tools of aggregate supply and aggregate demand analysis. To facilitate this, we have reproduced as Figures 5-5 and 5-6 two diagrams found earlier in this chapter, but we now give them slightly different interpretations.

Figure 5-5 offers a simplified view of government policy to fight unemployment. Suppose that, in the absence of government intervention, the economy would reach an equilibrium at point *E*, where the demand curve D_0D_0 crosses the supply curve *SS*. Now if the output corresponding to point *E* is so low that many workers are unemployed, *the government can reduce unemployment by increasing aggregate demand.* Chapter 11 will consider in detail how the

FIGURE 5-6

STABILIZATION POLICY TO FIGHT INFLATION

This diagram duplicates Figure 5-2, but here we assume that point *E*—the equilibrium that the economy would attain without government intervention—represents high inflation (that is, the price level corresponding to point *E* is far above last year's price level). By using its policy instruments to shift the aggregate demand curve inward to D_2D_2, the government can keep this year's price level lower than it would otherwise have been; in other words, the government can reduce inflation.

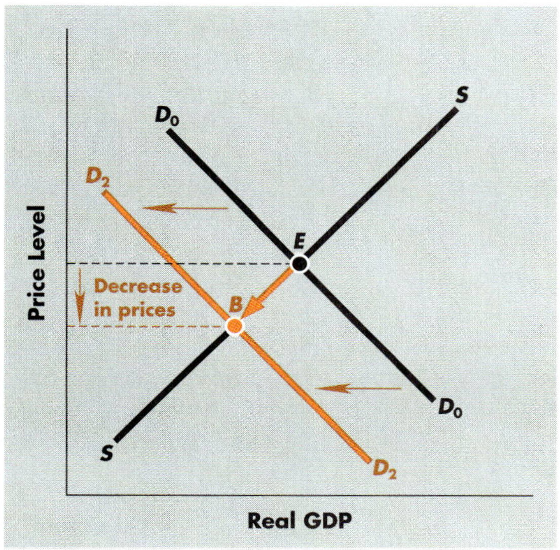

government might do this. In the diagram, such an action would shift the demand curve to D_1D_1, causing equilibrium to move to point A. In general:

Recessions and unemployment are often caused by insufficient aggregate demand. When this occurs, government policies that successfully augment demand—such as increases in government spending—can be an effective way to increase output and reduce unemployment.

The opposite type of demand management is called for when inflation is the main macroeconomic problem. Figure 5-6 illustrates this case. Here again, point E, the intersection of the demand curve D_0D_0 and the supply curve SS, is the equilibrium that would be reached in the absence of government policy. But now we suppose that the price level corresponding to point E is considered "too high," meaning that the *change* in the price level from the previous period to this one would be too rapid if the economy moved to point E. A government program that reduces demand from D_0D_0 to D_2D_2 (for example, a reduction in government spending) can keep prices down and thereby reduce inflation. Thus:

Inflation is frequently caused by aggregate demand racing ahead too fast. When this is the case, government policies that reduce aggregate demand can be effective anti-inflationary devices.

This, in brief, summarizes the intent of stabilization policy. When aggregate demand fluctuations are the source of economic instability, the government can limit both recessions and inflations by pushing aggregate demand ahead when it would otherwise lag, and restraining it when it would otherwise grow too quickly.

Does it work? Can the government actually stabilize the economy? That is a matter of some debate, a debate we will take up in Part III. But a look back at Figures 5-3 and 5-4 may be enlightening right now. First, cover the portions of Figures 5-3 and 5-4 that deal with the period after 1940, the portions from the shaded area rightward in each figure. The picture that emerges for the 1870 to 1940 period is of an economy with frequent and sometimes quite pronounced fluctuations.

Now do the reverse. Cover the data before 1950 and look only at the postwar period. There is, indeed, a difference. Instances of negative real GDP growth are less common and business fluctuations look less severe. While perfection has not been achieved, things do look much better. When we turn to inflation, however, things look rather worse. Gone are the periods of deflation and price stability that occurred before World War II. Prices now seem only to rise.

This quick tour through the data suggests that something has changed. The U.S. economy behaved differently from 1950 to 1995 than it did from 1870 to 1940. Although there is controversy on this point, many economists attribute this shift in the economy's behavior to lessons the government has learned about managing the economy—lessons we will be learning in Part III.

When you look at the prewar data, you are looking at an unmanaged economy that went through booms and recessions for "natural" economic reasons. The government did little about either. When you examine the postwar data, on the other hand, you are looking at an economy that has been increasingly managed by government policy—sometimes successfully and sometimes unsuccessfully. While the recessions are less severe, this improvement has come at a cost: The economy appears to be more inflation-prone than it was in the more distant past. These two changes in our economy may be connected. But, to understand why, we will have to provide some relevant economic theory. That is the task of the rest of Part II.

SUMMARY

1. *Microeconomics* studies the decisions of individuals and firms, how these decisions interact, and how they influence the allocation of society's resources and the distribution of income. *Macroeconomics* looks at the behavior of entire economies and studies the pressing social problems of inflation and unemployment.
2. While they focus on different subjects, microeconomics and macroeconomics rely on virtually identical tools. Both use the supply and demand analysis introduced in Chapter 4.
3. Macroeconomic models use abstract concepts like "the price level" and "domestic product" that are derived by amalgamating many different markets into one. This process is known as **aggregation;** it should not be taken literally but rather viewed as a useful approximation.
4. The best specific measure of the nation's economic output is **gross domestic product (GDP),** which is obtained by adding up the money values of all **final goods and services** produced in a given year. These outputs can be evaluated year by year at current market prices (to get **nominal GDP**) or at some common set of prices (to get **real GDP**). Neither **intermediate goods** nor transactions that take place outside organized markets are included in GDP.
5. The GDP is meant to be a measure of the *production* of the economy, not of the increase in its *well-being*. For example, the GDP places no value on housework and other do-it-yourself activities or on leisure time. On the other hand, even commodities that might be considered as "bads" rather than "goods" are counted in the GDP (for example, activities that harm the environment).
6. America's economic history is one of growth punctuated by periodic **recessions,** that is, periods in which real GDP declined. While the distant past included some periods of falling prices (**deflation**), more recent history shows only rising prices (**inflation**).
7. The Great Depression of the 1930s was the worst in our country's history. It had profound effects both on our nation and on countries throughout the world, and it led also to a revolution in economic thinking, thanks to the work of John Maynard Keynes.
8. From World War II to the early 1970s, the American economy exhibited much steadier growth than it had shown in the past. Many observers attributed this to the implementation of the **stabilization policies** that Keynes suggested. At the same time, however, the price level seems only to rise, never to fall, in the modern economy. The economy seems to have become more "inflation-prone."
9. Since 1973, the U.S. economy has suffered through several serious recessions. Between 1973 and about 1981, inflation was also unusually virulent. This unhappy combination of economic stagnation with rapid inflation was nicknamed "**stagflation.**" Since 1982, however, inflation has been low and fairly steady.
10. One major cause of inflation is that **aggregate demand** may grow more quickly than **aggregate supply.** In such a case, a government policy that reduces aggregate demand may be able to stem the inflation.
11. Similarly, recessions often occur because aggregate demand grows too slowly. In this case, a government policy that stimulates demand may be an effective way to fight the recession.

KEY TERMS

Microeconomics
Macroeconomics
Aggregation
Aggregate demand curve
Aggregate supply curve
Inflation
Recession
Gross domestic product (GDP)
Nominal GDP
Real GDP
Final goods and services
Intermediate good
Deflation
Stagflation
Stabilization policy

QUESTIONS FOR REVIEW

1. Which of the following problems are likely to be studied by a microeconomist and which by a macroeconomist?
   a. The growth of Microsoft Corporation
   b. Why unemployment in the United States fell in 1993 and 1994
   c. Why Japan's economy grew so much faster than the United States' economy for several decades, but has failed to do so thus far in the 1990s
   d. Why university budgets have come under stress in recent years
2. You probably use "aggregates" frequently in everyday discussions. Try to think of some examples. (Here is one: Have you ever said, "The students at this college generally think . . ."? What, precisely, did you mean?)
3. Use an aggregate supply and demand diagram to study what would happen to an economy in which the aggregate supply curve never moved while the aggregate demand curve shifted outward year after year.
4. Try asking a friend who has not studied economics in which year he or she thinks prices were higher: 1870 or 1900? 1920 or 1940? (In both cases, prices were higher in the earlier year.) Most people your age think that prices have always risen. Why do you think they have this opinion?
5. Which of the following transactions are included in gross domestic product, and by how much does each raise GDP?
   a. Smith pays a carpenter $15,000 to build a garage.
   b. Smith purchases $3,000 worth of materials and builds himself a garage, which is worth $15,000.
   c. Smith goes to the woods, cuts down a tree, and uses the wood to build himself a garage that is worth $15,000.
   d. The Jones family sells its old house to the Reynolds family for $100,000. The Joneses then buy a newly constructed house from a builder for $150,000.
   e. You purchase a used computer from a friend for $200.
   f. Your university purchases a new mainframe computer from IBM, paying $200,000.
   g. You win $1,000 in an Atlantic City casino.
   h. You make $1,000 in the stock market.
   i. You sell a used economics textbook to your college bookstore for $25.
   j. You buy a new economics textbook from your college bookstore for $50.
6. Give some reasons why gross domestic product is not a suitable measure of the well-being of the nation. (Have you noticed newspaper accounts in which journalists seem to use GDP for this purpose?)

CHAPTER 6

UNEMPLOYMENT AND INFLATION: THE TWIN EVILS OF MACROECONOMICS

When men are employed, they are best contented.
Benjamin Franklin

Inflation is repudiation.
Calvin Coolidge

Among the many trials faced by Odysseus, the hero of Homer's *Odyssey,* one of the most difficult was to steer his fragile boat through a narrow strait. On one side lay the rock of the monster Scylla, which threatened to break his craft into pieces; on the other was the menacing whirlpool of Charybdis. The makers of national economic policy face a similarly difficult task in trying to chart a middle course between the Scylla of unemployment and the Charybdis of inflation. If they steer the economy far from the rocks of unemployment, they run the risk of being swept up in the swift currents of inflation. But if they maintain a safe distance from inflation, they may smash against the rocks of unemployment.

In Parts II and III, we will explain how economic planners attempt to strike a balance between high employment and low inflation, why these goals cannot be attained with machine-like precision, and why improvement on one front generally spells deterioration on the other. We will pay a great deal of attention to both the *causes* of and *cures* for inflation and unemployment.

But before getting involved in such weighty issues of theory and policy, we pause in this chapter to take a close look at the twin evils themselves. Why does a rise in unemployment cause such social distress? Why is inflation so loudly deplored? Can we measure the costs of unemployment and inflation? The answers to some of these questions may seem obvious at first. But we will see that there is more to them than meets the eye.

The chapter is divided into two parts. The first deals with unemployment. After discussing the human and economic costs of high unemployment, we explain how government statisticians measure unemployment. Then we consider how the elusive concept of "full employment" can be defined. We conclude by investigating our country's system of unemployment insurance.

The second part of the chapter is devoted to inflation. We begin by dispelling some persistent myths about inflation. But the costs of inflation are not all mythical. For example, inflation capriciously redistributes income and wealth from one group of people to another, and certain laws make inflation impose economic damage that could be avoided if the laws were written differently. This last cost stems from failure to understand one of the **Ideas for Beyond the Final Exam:** the effect of inflation on interest rates. Finally, we contrast the costs of low versus high inflation and dispel yet another myth: that low inflation inevitably gives way to high inflation.

An appendix at the end of this chapter explains how inflation is measured.

THE COSTS OF UNEMPLOYMENT

The human costs of unemployment are probably sufficiently obvious. Years ago, loss of a job meant not only enforced idleness and a catastrophic drop in income, it often led to hunger, cold, ill health—even death. This is the way one unemployed worker during the Great Depression described his family's plight in a mournful letter to the governor of Pennsylvania:

> I have been out of work for over a year and a half. Am back almost thirteen months and the landlord says if I don't pay up before the 1 of 1932 out I must go, and where am I to go in the cold winter with my children? If you can help me please for God's sake and the children's sakes and like please do what you can and send me some help, will you, I cannot find any work. . . . Thanksgiving dinner was black coffee and bread and was very glad to get it. My wife is in the hospital now. We have no shoes to were [sic]; no clothes hardly. Oh what will I do I sure will thank you.[1]

Nowadays, unemployment does not hold quite such terrors for most families, although its consequences remain dire enough. Our system of unemployment insurance (discussed later in the chapter) has taken out part of the sting of unemployment, and there are other social welfare programs to support the incomes of the poor. Yet most families still suffer painful losses of income and, often, severe noneconomic consequences when a breadwinner becomes unemployed.

Even families that are well-protected by unemployment compensation suffer when joblessness strikes. Ours is a work-oriented society. A man's place has always been in the office or shop, and lately this has become true for many women, as well. A worker forced into idleness by a recession endures a psychological cost that is no less real for our inability to measure it. Martin Luther King put it graphically: "In our society, it is murder, psychologically, to deprive a man of a job. . . . You are in substance saying to that man that he has no right to exist."[2] High unemployment has been linked to psychological and even physical disorders, divorces, suicides, and crime.

Furthermore, accumulated work experience is a valuable asset. When forced into idleness, workers not only cease accumulating experience, but lengthy peri-

[1]From *Brother, Can You Spare a Dime? The Great Depression 1929–1933,* by Milton Meltzer, p. 103. Copyright 1969 by Milton Meltzer. Reprinted by permission of Alfred A. Knopf, Inc.

[2]Quoted in Coretta Scott King (ed.), *The Words of Martin Luther King* (New York: Newmarket Press, 1983), p. 45.

ods of unemployment may make them "rusty," and thus less productive when they are reemployed. Short periods of unemployment exact different kinds of costs. A record of steady employment is important in applying for a new job, and a worker who has frequently been laid off will lack this record.

The **UNEMPLOYMENT RATE** is the number of unemployed people, expressed as a percentage of the labor force. The labor force is the number of people holding or seeking jobs.

It is important to realize that these costs, whether large or small in total, are distributed most unevenly across the population. In 1996, for example, the **unemployment rate** among all workers averaged 5.4 percent. But, as Figure 6-1 shows, 10.5 percent of black workers were unemployed, as were 8.2 percent of women who maintained families. For teenagers, the situation was worse still, with unemployment at 16.7 percent, and that of black teenagers about 34 percent. Married men had the lowest rate—about 3.0 percent. Overall unemployment varies from year to year, but these relationships are typical:

In good times and bad, married men suffer the least unemployment and teenagers suffer the most; nonwhites are unemployed much more often than whites; blue-collar workers have above-average rates of unemployment; well-educated people have below-average unemployment rates.

THE ECONOMIC COSTS OF HIGH UNEMPLOYMENT

Some of the human costs of high unemployment are, as we just noted, intangible. But others can be translated directly into dollars and cents because:

When the economy does not generate enough jobs to employ all those who are willing to work, a valuable resource is lost. Potential goods and services that might have been enjoyed by consumers are lost forever. This is the real economic cost of high unemployment.

And these costs are hardly negligible. Table 6-1 summarizes the idleness of workers and machines, and the resulting loss of national output, for some of the

FIGURE 6-1

UNEMPLOYMENT RATES FOR SELECTED GROUPS, 1996

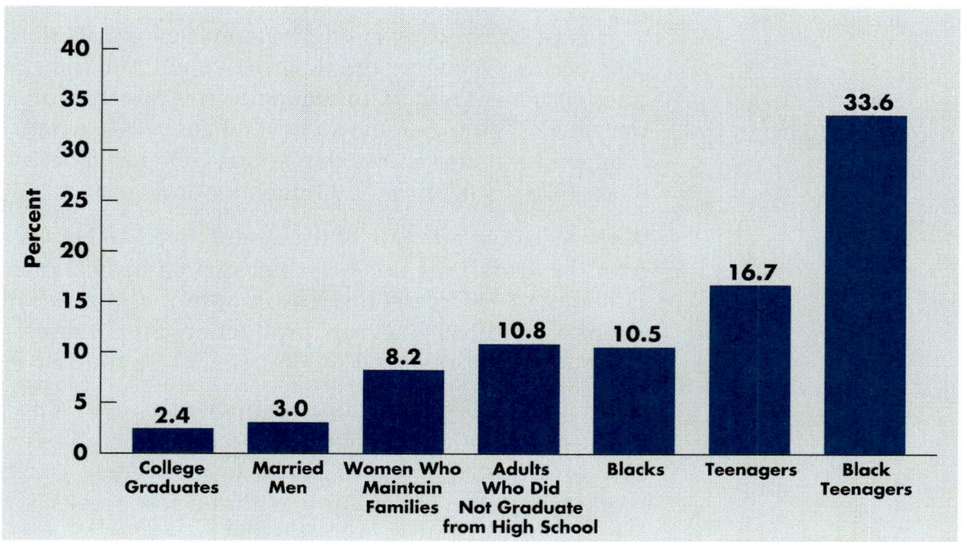

This figure shows that, in 1996, unemployment rates for specific demographic groups varied widely. Similar patterns hold in most years.

SOURCE: Bureau of Labor Statistics.

TABLE 6-1 THE ECONOMIC COSTS OF HIGH UNEMPLOYMENT

Year	Civilian Unemployment Rate (percent)	Capacity Utilization Rate (percent)	Percentage of Real GDP Lost Due to Idle Resources
1958	6.8	75.0	4.4
1961	6.7	77.3	3.3
1975	8.5	72.3	4.6
1982	9.7	70.3	7.4
1992	7.5	79.5	1.6
1995	5.6	82.9	−0.1
1996	5.4	83.1	−0.5

SOURCES: Bureau of Labor Statistics; Federal Reserve System; and the authors' calculations.

years of lowest economic activity in recent decades. The second column lists the civilian unemployment rate, and thus measures unused labor resources. The third lists the percentage of industrial capacity that U.S. manufacturers were actually using, and thus indicates the extent of unused plant and equipment. The fourth column is an estimate of how much more output (real GDP) could have been produced if these labor and capital resources had been fully employed. For comparison, the bottom line shows the situation in 1996, a year of approximately full utilization of resources. We see that unemployment has cost the people of the United States as much as a 7-1/2 percent reduction in their real incomes.

POTENTIAL (GDP) is the real GDP that the economy would produce if its labor and other resources were fully employed.

While Table 6-1 shows extreme examples, inability to utilize all of the nation's available resources has been a recurrent problem for our economy since 1973. The orange line in Figure 6-2 shows actual real GDP in the United States from 1954 to 1996, while the black line shows the real GDP we *could have* produced if "full employment" had been maintained. This last statement defines a concept called **potential GDP.** The graph shows that actual GDP has at times fallen short of potential GDP of the economy.

It *is* possible to push employment beyond its normal full-employment level. This occurs whenever the unemployment rate dips below the "full-employment unemployment rate." Consequently, it *is* possible for actual GDP to exceed potential GDP. Figure 6-2 shows several instances where this happened, shaded in orange. But it also shows that actual GDP has fallen short of potential GDP often since 1973—sometimes by huge amounts. In fact:

A conservative estimate of the cumulative gap between actual and potential GDP over the years 1974 to 1996 (all evaluated in 1992 prices) is approximately $1,600 billion. At 1996 levels, this loss in output as a result of unemployment would be about 3 months' worth of production. And there is no way to redeem these losses. The labor wasted in 1991 cannot be utilized in 1997.

Those who argue that unemployment is nothing to worry about today because of unemployment insurance, or because unemployment is concentrated among certain kinds of workers (such as teenagers), or because many unemployed workers become reemployed within a few weeks, should ponder Figure 6-2. Is the loss of this much output really no cause for worry? Would these optimists

FIGURE 6-2 ACTUAL AND POTENTIAL GDP IN THE UNITED STATES, 1954–1996

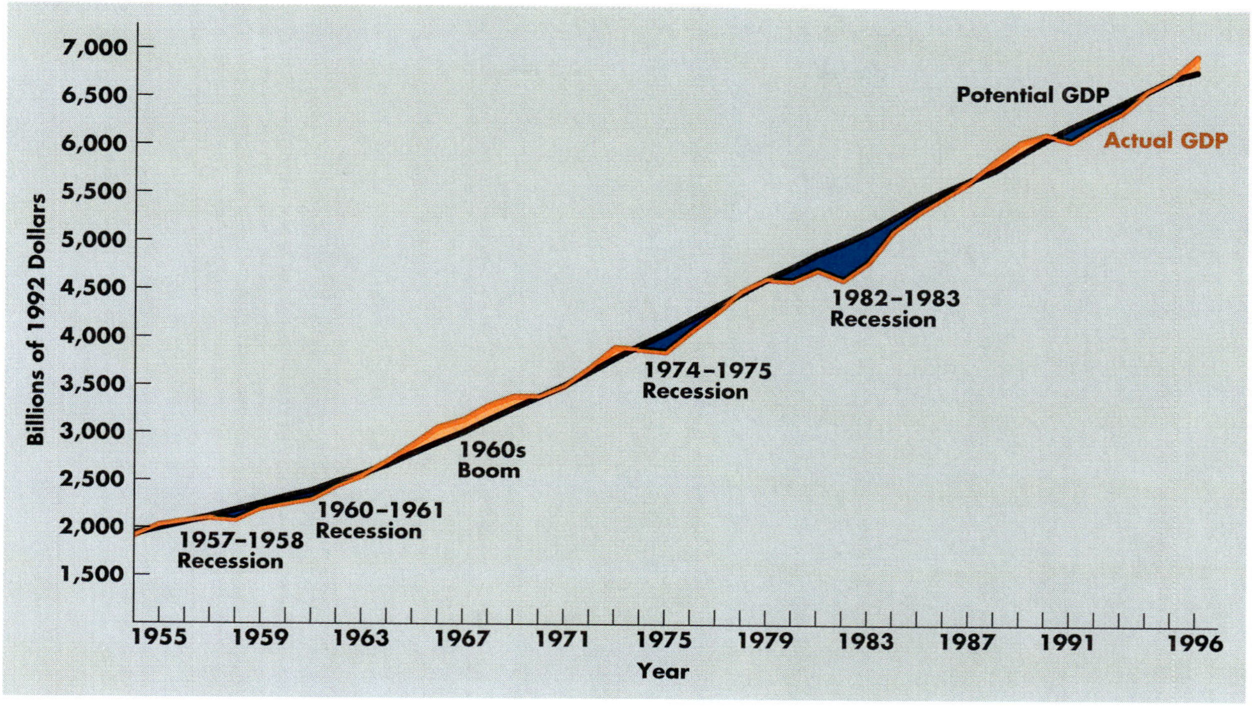

This chart compares the growth of actual GDP (orange line) with that of potential GDP (black line). There have been two lengthy periods during which real GDP remained below its potential (1957 to 1963 and 1974 to 1987), but only one lengthy period during which GDP remained above its potential (1965 to 1970). The large shortfalls of GDP from its potential in the early 1980s stand out.

SOURCE: U.S. Department of Commerce and the authors' calculations.

react the same way if the government collected a fraction of the output of every factory in America and dumped it into the sea? Waste is waste no matter who ultimately pays the cost.

COUNTING THE UNEMPLOYED: THE OFFICIAL STATISTICS

We have been using figures on unemployment without considering where they come from or how accurate they are. The basic data come from a monthly survey of over 50,000 households conducted for the Bureau of Labor Statistics (BLS). The census-taker asks several questions about the employment status of each member of the household and, on the basis of the answers, classifies each person as *employed, unemployed,* or *not in the labor force.*

The first category is the simplest to define. It includes everybody currently working at a job, including part-time workers. Although some part-timers work less than a full week by choice, others do so only because they cannot find suitable full-time jobs. Nevertheless, these workers are counted as employed, even though many would consider them "underemployed."

The second category is a bit trickier. For those not currently working, the BLS first determines whether they are temporarily laid off from a job to which they expect to return. If so, they are counted as unemployed. The remaining workers are asked whether they actively sought work during the previous 4 weeks. If they did, they are also counted as unemployed. But if they did not, they are classified as *out of the labor force;* that is, since they failed to look for a job, they are not considered unemployed.

This seems a reasonable way to draw the distinction—after all, we do not want to count college students who work during the summer months as unemployed between September and May. Yet, there is a problem: Research has shown that many unemployed workers give up looking for jobs after a time. These so-called **discouraged workers** are victims of poor job prospects, just like the officially unemployed. But, ironically, when they give up hope, measured unemployment declines! Some critics have therefore argued that an estimate should be made of the number of discouraged workers and that these people should be added to the rolls of the unemployed. The BLS estimated that about 400,000 people fell into this category in 1996.

A **DISCOURAGED WORKER** is an unemployed person who gives up looking for work and is therefore no longer counted as part of the labor force.

Involuntary part-time work, loss of overtime or shortened work hours, and discouraged workers are all examples of "hidden" or "disguised" unemployment. Those who are concerned about these phenomena argue that we should include them in the official unemployment rate because, if we do not, the magnitude of the problem will be underestimated. Others, however, argue that measured unemployment overestimates the problem because, to count as unemployed, a person need only *claim* to be looking for a job, even if he or she is not really interested in finding one.

TYPES OF UNEMPLOYMENT

Providing jobs for those willing to work is one principal goal of macroeconomic policy. How are we to define this goal? One clearly *incorrect* answer would be "a zero measured unemployment rate." Ours is a dynamic, highly mobile economy. Households move from one state to another. Individuals quit jobs to seek better positions or retool for more attractive occupations. These and other phenomena produce some minimal amount of unemployment—people who are literally *between* jobs. Economists call this the level of **frictional unemployment.**

FRICTIONAL UNEMPLOYMENT is unemployment that is due to normal turnover in the labor market. It includes people who are temporarily between jobs because they are moving or changing occupations, or for similar reasons.

The critical distinguishing feature of frictional unemployment is that it is short-lived. A frictionally unemployed person has every reason to expect to find a new job soon. People tend to think of frictional unemployment as irreducible, but that is not true. During World War II, for example, unemployment in this country fell below 2 percent—substantially below the frictional level.

Frictional unemployment is irreducible only in the sense that—under normal circumstances—it is socially undesirable to do so. Geographic and occupational mobility play important roles in our market economy, enabling people to search for better jobs. Similarly, waste is avoided by allowing inefficient firms, or firms producing items no longer in demand, to be replaced by new firms. Inhibiting either of these phenomena would hamper the workings of the market economy. But, if these adjustment mechanisms are allowed to operate, there will always be some temporarily unemployed workers looking for jobs, and there will always be some firms with unfilled positions looking for workers. This is the genesis of frictional unemployment.

STRUCTURAL UNEMPLOYMENT refers to workers who have lost their jobs because they have been displaced by automation, because their skills are no longer in demand, or for similar reasons.

A second type of unemployment is often difficult to distinguish from frictional unemployment, but it has very different implications. **Structural unemployment** arises when jobs are eliminated by changes in the structure of the economy, such as automation or permanent changes in demand. The crucial difference between frictional and structural unemployment is that, unlike frictionally unemployed workers, structurally unemployed workers cannot realistically be considered "between jobs." Instead, they may find their skills and experience unwanted in the changing economy in which they live. They are thus faced with either prolonged periods of unemployment or the necessity of making major changes in their occupations. For older workers, learning a new occupation may be nearly impossible.

CYCLICAL UNEMPLOYMENT is the portion of unemployment that is attributable to a decline in the economy's total production. Cyclical unemployment rises during recessions and falls as prosperity is restored.

The remaining type of unemployment, **cyclical unemployment,** will occupy most of our attention. Cyclical unemployment rises when the level of economic activity declines, as it does in a recession. Thus, when economists speak of maintaining "full employment," they do not mean achieving zero measured unemployment, but rather limiting unemployment to its frictional and structural components. A key question, therefore, is: How much measured unemployment is that?

HOW MUCH EMPLOYMENT IS "FULL EMPLOYMENT"?

President John F. Kennedy first committed the federal government to a specific numerical goal for unemployment. Looking at experience in the prosperous early 1950s, he picked a 4 percent target. But the 4 percent goal was rejected as outmoded during the 1970s—for three major reasons.

First, some economists argued that the 4 percent target had to be raised because the composition of the labor force had changed. Specifically, there were many more young workers in the 1970s than in the 1950s, and teenagers always have higher rates of unemployment than adults.

Second, they suggested, the increased generosity of unemployment compensation (which is discussed just below) had reduced the incentive to get off the unemployment rolls. The logic here is simple. Since unemployment insurance reduces the income gap between those who work and those who collect unemployment benefits, it must therefore dull the incentive to look for and then accept a job. And the more generous the benefits, the weaker the incentive.

A third reason stems from the short-run *trade-off between inflation and unemployment,* a notion which was mentioned in Chapter 1 and will be studied in depth in Chapter 16. Economic research conducted in the 1970s suggested that the original 4 percent unemployment target was too low—even for the 1960s—in a very specific sense: that inflation will rise if unemployment remains this low.

While the 4 percent unemployment target was abandoned, no new number was put in its place. Instead, a debate began over exactly how much measured unemployment corresponds to *full employment*—a debate that continues to this day. In the 1980s, some economists argued that full employment came at a measured unemployment rate above 6 percent. Others pointed out that the main factors that had raised the full-employment unemployment rate in the 1970s were reversed in the 1980s. For example, the teenage labor force dwindled, and unemployment benefits went to a smaller percentage of the unemployed.

As is so often the case, actual events helped settle the issue—though not definitively. Measured unemployment fell below 6 percent late in the 1980s and remained there until the end of 1990. And, just as this was happening, inflation started to accelerate. This conjunction of events persuaded many economists that full employment comes at an unemployment rate near 6 percent. Then, in 1994 to 1996, inflation remained stable while unemployment hovered just above 5-1/2

POLICY DEBATE DOES THE MINIMUM WAGE CAUSE UNEMPLOYMENT?

Elementary economic reasoning—summarized in the simple supply-demand diagram below—suggests that setting a minimum wage (*W* in the graph) above the free-market wage (*w* in the graph) must cause unemployment. In the graph, unemployment is the horizontal gap between the quantity of labor supplied (point *B*) and quantity demanded (point *A*) at the minimum wage. Indeed, the conclusion seems so elementary that generations of economists took it for granted. Earlier editions of this book, for example, confidently told students that a higher minimum wage must lead to higher unemployment.

But some surprising economic research published in the 1990s casts serious doubt on this conventional wisdom.* For example, Princeton economists David Card and Alan Krueger compared employment changes at fast-food restaurants in New Jersey and nearby Pennsylvania after New Jersey, but not Pennsylvania, raised its minimum wage in 1992. To their surprise, the New Jersey stores did more net hiring than their Pennsylvania counterparts. Similar results were found for fast-food stores in Texas after the federal minimum wage was raised in 1991, and in California after the statewide minimum wage was increased in 1988.

In none of these cases did a higher minimum wage seem to reduce employment—in contrast to the implications of simple economic theory. Thus, a policy question previously deemed closed now seems to be open: Does the minimum wage cause unemployment?

Resolution of this debate is of more than academic interest. In 1995, the Clinton administration recommended an increase in the federal minimum wage—justifying its request, in part, by the new research suggesting that unemployment would not rise as a result. But the Republican Congress, adhering to the conventional view that a higher minimum wage would raise unemployment, refused to go along.

*See David Card and Alan Krueger, *Myth and Measurement: The New Economics of the Minimum Wage* (Princeton, N.J.: Princeton University Press, 1995).

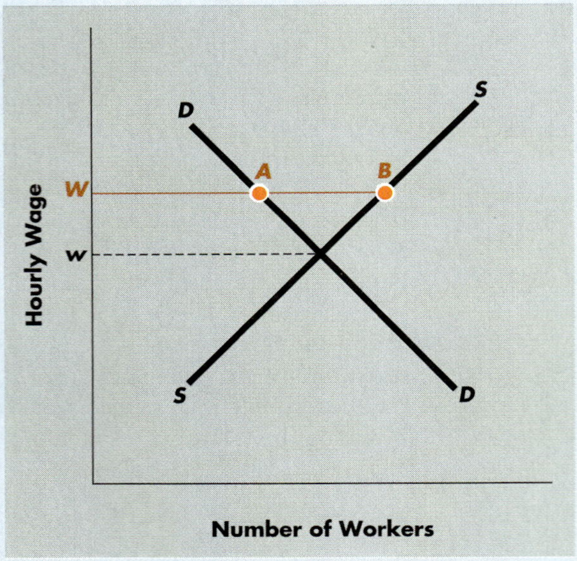

percent, leading many economists to adopt 5-1/2 percent as a working definition of full employment.

UNEMPLOYMENT INSURANCE: THE INVALUABLE CUSHION

One main reason why America's unemployed workers no longer experience the complete loss of income that devastated so many during the 1930s is our system of *unemployment insurance*—one of the most valuable institutional innovations to emerge from the trauma of the Great Depression.

Each of the 50 states now administers an unemployment insurance program under federal guidelines. While the precise amounts vary, the average weekly benefit check in 1995 was about $187, which amounted to about 47 percent of average earnings. Though a 53 percent drop in earnings still poses serious problems, the importance of this 47 percent income cushion can scarcely be exaggerated, especially since it may be supplemented by funds from other welfare programs. Families that are covered by unemployment insurance rarely go hungry or are dispossessed from their homes when they lose their jobs.

Who is eligible to receive these benefits? Precise criteria vary by state, but some stipulations apply quite generally. Only experienced workers qualify; so persons just joining the labor force (such as recent graduates of high schools and colleges) or reentering after prolonged absences (such as women resuming work after years of child rearing) cannot collect benefits. Neither can those who quit their jobs, except under unusual circumstances. Also, benefits end after a stipulated period of time, normally 6 months. For all of these reasons, only about one-third of the 8 million people who were unemployed in an average week in 1994 actually received benefits. Many of the rest received no government support.

The importance of unemployment insurance to the unemployed is obvious. But there are also significant benefits to citizens who never become unemployed. During recessions, many billions of dollars are paid out in unemployment benefits, and since recipients probably spend most of their benefits, unemployment insurance limits the severity of recessions by providing additional purchasing power when and where it is most needed.

The unemployment insurance system is one of several "cushions" that have been built into our economy since 1933 to prevent another Great Depression. By giving money to those who become unemployed, the system helps prop up aggregate demand during recessions.

While the U.S. economy is now probably "depression proof," this should not be a cause for too much rejoicing, for the recession of 1990–1991 amply demonstrated that we are far from "recession proof."

UNEMPLOYMENT INSURANCE AND THE COSTS OF UNEMPLOYMENT

The fact that unemployment insurance and other social welfare programs replace a significant fraction of lost income has led some skeptics to claim that unemployment is no longer a serious problem. But the fact is that:

Unemployment insurance is just what the name says—an *insurance* program. And insurance can never prevent a catastrophe from occurring; it can only *spread the costs* of a catastrophe among many people instead of letting all the costs fall on the shoulders of those few unfortunate souls who it affects directly.

Fire insurance is an example. If your family is covered by fire insurance and your house burns down, you will probably suffer only a small financial loss because the insurance company will pay most of the expenses. But it does not get the money out of thin air. Rather, it must have collected the funds from the many other families who purchased insurance but did not suffer any fire damages. Thus, one family's loss of perhaps $100,000 is covered by the insurance payments of 500 families each paying $200 a year. In this way, the costs of the catastrophe are spread among hundreds of families, and in the process, made much more bearable.

But despite the insurance, the family whose house is destroyed by fire suffers anguish and inconvenience. No insurance policy can eliminate this. Furthermore, society loses a valuable resource—a house. It will take much wood, cement, nails, paint, and labor to replace the burnt-out home. *An insurance policy cannot insure society against losses of real resources.*

The case is precisely the same with insurance against unemployment. All workers and employers pay for the insurance policy by a tax that the government levies on wages and salaries. With the funds so collected, the government compensates the victims of unemployment. Thus, instead of letting the costs of unemployment fall entirely on the minority of workers who lose their jobs:

Our system of payroll taxes and unemployment benefits *spreads* the costs of unemployment over the entire population. But it does not eliminate the basic economic cost.

THE COSTS OF INFLATION

Both the human and economic costs of inflation are less obvious than the costs of unemployment. But this does not necessarily make them any less real, for if one thing is crystal clear about inflation, it is that people do not like it.

Public opinion polls show that, except when inflation is extremely low, it ranks high on people's list of major national problems—generally even ahead of unemployment. Surveys also find that inflation, like unemployment, causes a deterioration in consumers' sense of well-being—it makes people unhappy. Finally, studies of elections suggest that voters penalize the party that occupies the White House when inflation is high.

The fact is beyond dispute: People consider inflation to be something bad. The question is: Why?

INFLATION: THE MYTH AND THE REALITY

The **PURCHASING POWER** of a given sum of money is the volume of goods and services that it will buy.

At first, the question may seem ridiculous. During times of inflation people keep paying higher prices for the same quantities of goods and services they had before. So more and more income is needed just to maintain the same standard of living. Is it not obvious that this erosion of **purchasing power**—that is, the decline in what money will buy—makes everyone worse off?

This would indeed be the case were it not for one very significant fact. The wages that people earn are also prices—prices for labor services. During a period of inflation, wages also rise, and, in fact, the average wage typically rises more or less in step with prices. Thus, contrary to popular myth, workers as a group are not usually victimized by inflation.

The **REAL WAGE RATE** is the wage rate adjusted for inflation. It indicates the volume of goods and services that money wages will buy.

The purchasing power of wages—what is called the **real wage rate**—is not systematically eroded by inflation. Sometimes wages rise faster than prices, and sometimes prices rise faster than wages. The fact is that, in the long run, wages tend to outstrip prices as new capital equipment and innovation increase output per worker.

Figure 6-3 illustrates this simple fact. The orange line shows the annual rate of increase of consumer prices in the United States for each year since 1948, while the black line shows the annual rate of wage increase. The difference between the two indicates the rate of growth of *real* wages. Generally, wages rise faster than prices, reflecting the steady advance of technology and of labor productivity; therefore, real wages rise. (But this is not always the case; the graph shows that real wages fell several times in the 1980s.)

The feature of Figure 6-3 that virtually jumps off the page is the way the two lines dance together. Wages normally rise rapidly when prices rise rapidly, and

FIGURE 6-3

RATES OF CHANGE OF WAGES AND PRICES IN THE UNITED STATES, 1948–1996

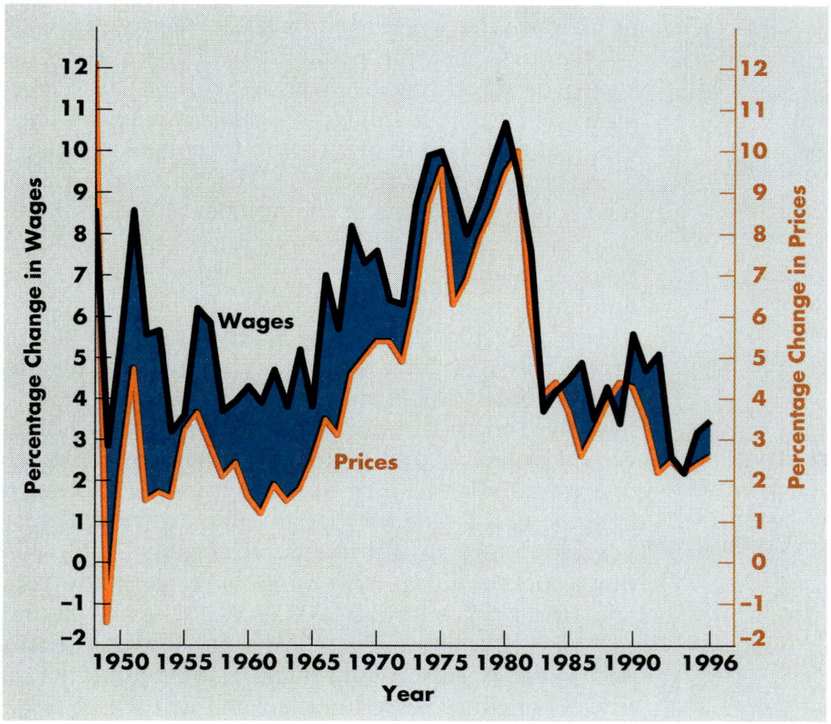

This chart compares the rate of price inflation (orange line) with the rate of growth of nominal wages (black line) in the postwar period. The patterns are clearly quite similar, with wages and prices normally accelerating or decelerating together. Notice that wage increases generally outstrip price increases; that is, *real* wages normally rise from year to year. (*Note:* Data on both wages and prices pertain to the private business sector.)

SOURCE: Bureau of Labor Statistics.

they rise slowly when prices rise slowly. But you should not draw any hasty conclusions from this association. It does not, for example, tell us whether rising prices cause rising wages or rising wages cause rising prices. Remember the warnings given in Chapter 1 about trying to infer causation just by looking at data. But analyzing cause and effect is not our purpose right now. We merely want to dispel the myth that inflation inevitably erodes real wages.

Why is this myth so widespread? Imagine a world without inflation in which wages are rising 2 percent a year because of the increasing productivity of labor. Now imagine that, all of a sudden, inflation sets in and prices start rising 3 percent a year but that nothing else changes. Figure 6-3 suggests that, with perhaps a small delay, wage increases will accelerate to 2 plus 3, or 5 percent a year.

Will workers view this change with equanimity? Probably not. To each worker, the 5 percent wage increase will be seen as something he earned by the sweat of his brow. In his view, he *deserves* every penny of his 5 percent raise. In a sense, he is right because "the sweat of his brow" earned him a 2 percent increment in real wages that, when the inflation rate is 3 percent, can only be achieved by increasing his money wages by 5 percent. An economist would divide the wage increase in the following way:

Reason for Wage Increase	Amount
Higher productivity	2%
Compensation for higher prices	3
Total	5%

"Sure, you're raising my allowance. But am I actually gaining any purchasing power?"

But the worker will probably keep score differently. Feeling that he earned the entire 5 percent by his own merits, he will view inflation as having "robbed" him of three-fifths of his just desserts. The higher the rate of inflation, the more of his raise the worker will feel has been stolen from him.

Of course, nothing could be further from the truth. Basically, the economic system is rewarding the worker with *the same 2 percent real wage increment for higher productivity regardless of the rate of inflation.* The "evils of inflation" are often exaggerated because of a failure to understand this point.

A second reason for misunderstanding the effects of inflation is that people tend to think in terms of the number of dollars it takes to buy something rather than in terms of the *purchasing power* of these dollars. For example, if inflation doubles both prices and wages, workers will have to labor exactly the same amount of time as before to earn the price of a loaf of bread. But because they now pay $2 a loaf instead of $1, they feel that the price of bread is scandalously high. In fact, nothing really has changed; but people cling to an outmoded idea of what bread *should* cost.

An item's **RELATIVE PRICE** is its price in terms of some other item rather than in terms of dollars.

A third misperception results from failure to distinguish between a *rise in the general price level* and a change in **relative prices,** that is, a rise in the price of one commodity relative to that of another. To see the distinction most clearly, imagine first a *pure inflation* in which *every* price rises by 10 percent during the year, so that relative prices do not change. Table 6-2 gives an example in which movie tickets go up from $6.00 to $6.60, candy bars from 50 cents to 55 cents, and automobiles from $9,000 to $9,900. After the inflation, just as before, it will still take 12 candy bars to buy a movie ticket, 1,500 movie tickets to buy a car, and so on. A person who manufactures candy bars in order to purchase movie tickets is neither helped nor harmed by the inflation. Neither is a car dealer with a sweet tooth.

But real inflations are not like this. When there is 10 percent general inflation—meaning that the "average price" rises by 10 percent—some prices may jump 20 percent or more while others actually fall.[3] Suppose that, instead of the price increases shown in Table 6-2, prices rise as shown in Table 6-3. Movie prices go up by 25 percent, but candy prices do not change. Surely, candy manufacturers who love movies will be disgruntled because it now costs 15 candy bars instead of 12 to get into the theater. They will blame inflation for raising the price of movie tickets, even though their real problem stems from the *increase in the price of movies relative to candy.* (They would have been hurt as much if movie tickets had remained at $6 while the price of candy fell to 40 cents.)

TABLE 6-2

Item	Last Year's Price	This Year's Price	Percentage Increase
Candy bar	$ 0.50	$ 0.55	10
Movie ticket	6.00	6.60	10
Automobile	9,000	9,900	10

[3]The way statisticians figure out "average" price increases is discussed in the appendix to this chapter.

TABLE 6-3

Item	Last Year's Price	This Year's Price	Percentage Increase
Candy bar	$ 0.50	$ 0.50	0
Movie ticket	6.00	7.50	25
Automobile	9,000	9,450	5

Since car prices have risen by only 5 percent, theater owners in need of new cars will be delighted by the fact that an auto now costs only 1,260 movie admissions—just as they would have cheered if car prices had fallen to $7,560 while movie tickets remained at $6.00. However, they are unlikely to attribute their good fortune to inflation—as indeed they should not. What has actually happened is that *cars became cheaper relative to movies.*

Because real-world inflations proceed at *uneven* rates, relative prices are constantly changing. There are gainers and losers, just as some would gain and others lose if relative prices were to change without any general inflation. Inflation, however, gets a bad name because losers often blame inflation for their misfortune while gainers rarely credit inflation for their good luck.

These three kinds of misconceptions may go a long way toward explaining why respondents to public opinion polls consistently list inflation as a major national issue, why higher inflation rates depress consumers, and why voters express their ire at the polls when inflation is high.

Inflation does not systematically erode the purchasing power of wages. Nor does it lead to "unfair" prices. Nor is it usually to blame when some goods become more expensive relative to others.

But not all of the costs of inflation are mythical. Let us now turn to some of the real costs.

INFLATION AS A REDISTRIBUTOR OF INCOME AND WEALTH

We have just seen that the *average* person is neither helped nor harmed by inflation. But almost no one is exactly average! Some people gain from inflation and others lose. It is hard to say anything more systematic than this about the effects of inflation on particular prices and wages.

But inflation does have systematic effects on the distribution of income and wealth. Senior citizens trying to scrape by on pensions or other fixed incomes suffer badly from inflation. Since they earn no wages, it is little solace to them that wages keep pace with prices. Their pension incomes do not.[4]

This example actually illustrates a much more general problem. Think of pensioners as people who "lend" money to an organization (the pension fund) when they are young in order to be "paid back" with interest when they are old.

[4]This is not, however, true of Social Security benefits, which are automatically increased to compensate recipients for changes in the price level.

Because of the rise in the price level during the intervening years, the unfortunate pensioners get paid back in less valuable dollars than those they originally loaned. In general:

Those who lend money are apt to be victimized by inflation.

While lenders may lose heavily, borrowers may do quite well. For example, homeowners who borrowed money from banks in the form of mortgages back in the 1950s, when interest rates were 3 or 4 percent, gained enormously from the surprisingly virulent inflation of the 1970s. They paid back dollars of much lower value than those that they borrowed. The same is true of other borrowers.

Borrowers often gain from inflation.

Since the redistribution caused by inflation generally benefits borrowers at the expense of lenders, and since both lenders and borrowers can be found at every income level, we conclude that:

Inflation does not always steal from the rich to aid the poor, nor does it always do the reverse.

Why, then, is the redistribution caused by inflation so widely condemned? Because its victims are selected capriciously. Nobody legislates the redistribution. Nobody enters into it voluntarily. The gainers do not earn their spoils, and the losers do not deserve their fate. Moreover, there are particular classes of people who inflation systematically robs of purchasing power year after year—people living on private pensions, families who save money and "lend" it to banks, and workers on long-term contracts or whose wages and salaries do not adjust easily for some other reason. Even if the average person suffers no damage from inflation, that offers little consolation to those who are hurt by it persistently and systematically. This is one fundamental indictment of inflation.

Inflation redistributes income in an arbitrary way. The actual income distribution should reflect the interplay of the operation of free markets and the purposeful efforts of government to alter that distribution. Inflation interferes with and distorts this process.

REAL VERSUS NOMINAL INTEREST RATES

But wait. Must inflation always rob lenders to bestow gifts upon borrowers? If both parties see inflation coming, won't lenders demand that borrowers pay a higher interest rate as compensation for the coming inflation? Indeed they will. For this reason, economists draw a sharp distinction between inflation that is *expected* and inflation that comes as a *surprise*.

What happens when inflation is fully expected by both parties? Suppose that Diamond Jim wants to borrow $1,000 from Scrooge, and both agree that, in the absence of inflation which erodes the purchasing power of money, a fair rate of interest would be 3 percent on a 1-year loan. This means that Diamond Jim would pay back $1,030 at the end of the year for the privilege of having $1,000 now.

If both expect prices to increase by 6 percent, Scrooge may reason as follows: "If Diamond Jim pays me back $1,030 a year from today, that money will buy less than what $1,000 buys today. Thus, I'll really be *paying him* to borrow from me! I'm no philanthropist. Why don't I charge him 9 percent instead? Then he'll pay back $1,090 at the end of the year. With prices 6 percent higher, this will buy roughly what $1,030 is worth today. So I'll get the same 3 percent increase in purchasing power that we would have agreed on in the absence of inflation, and won't be any worse off. That's the least I'll accept."

Diamond Jim may follow a similar chain of logic. "With no inflation, I was willing to pay $1,030 a year from now for the privilege of having $1,000 today, and Scrooge was willing to lend it. He'd be crazy to do the same with 6 percent inflation. He'll want to charge me more. How much should I pay? If I offer him $1,090 a year from now, that will have roughly the same purchasing power as $1,030 today, so I won't be any worse off. That's the most I'll pay."

This kind of thinking may lead Scrooge and Diamond Jim to write a contract with a 9 percent interest rate—3 percent as the increase in purchasing power that Diamond Jim pays to Scrooge and 6 percent as compensation for expected inflation. Then, if the expected 6 percent inflation actually materializes, neither party will be better or worse off than was expected at the time the contract was signed.

The **REAL RATE OF INTEREST** is the percentage increase in purchasing power that the borrower pays to the lender for the privilege of borrowing. It indicates the increased ability to purchase goods and services that the lender earns.

The **NOMINAL RATE OF INTEREST** is the percentage by which the money the borrower pays back exceeds the money that he borrowed, making no adjustment for any fall in the purchasing power of this money that results from inflation.

This example illustrates a general principle. The 3 percent increase in purchasing power that Diamond Jim agrees to hand over to Scrooge is called the **real rate of interest.** The 9 percent contractual interest charge that Diamond Jim and Scrooge write into the loan agreement is called the **nominal rate of interest.** The nominal rate of interest is arrived at by adding the *expected rate of inflation* to the real rate of interest. Expected inflation is added to compensate the lender for the loss of purchasing power that he expects to suffer as a result of inflation. Because of this:

Inflation that is accurately predicted need not redistribute income between borrowers and lenders. If the *expected* rate of inflation that is embodied in the nominal interest rate closely approximates the *actual* rate of inflation, no one gains and no one loses. However, to the extent that expectations prove incorrect, inflation will still redistribute income.[5]

It need hardly be pointed out that errors in predicting the rate of inflation are the norm, not the exception. Published forecasts bear witness to the fact that economists have great difficulty in predicting the rate of inflation. The task is no easier for businesses, consumers, and banks. This is one reason why inflation is so widely condemned as unfair and undesirable. It sets up a guessing game that no one likes.

INFLATION AND THE TAX SYSTEM[6]

Inflation imposes costs on society because it is hard to predict. But other costs arise from inflation even when it is predicted accurately. These costs stem from the fact that many laws and regulations were designed for an inflation-free economy and may malfunction when inflation is high.

The tax system is probably the most important example. The law does not recognize the distinction between *nominal* and *real* interest rates; it simply taxes

[5]EXERCISE: Who gains and who loses if the inflation turns out to be only 4 percent instead of the 6 percent that Scrooge and Diamond Jim expected? What if the inflation rate is 8 percent?

[6]This section contains somewhat more difficult material that may be omitted from shorter courses.

TABLE 6-4 INFLATION AND THE TAXATION OF INTEREST INCOME

(1) Inflation Rate (percent)	(2) Nominal Interest Rate (percent)	(3) Interest Income (dollars)	(4) Loss of Purchasing Power Due to Inflation (dollars)	(5) Real Interest Income (dollars)	(6) Taxes Paid (dollars)	(7) Real Income After Tax (dollars)	(8) Real Income After Tax (as percentage of $1,000 loan)	(9) Effective Rate of Taxation (percent)
0	3	30	0	30	10	20	2	33⅓
6	9	90	60	30	30	0	0	100

nominal interest regardless of how much real interest it represents. As a result, strange things happen when there is high inflation. Our example of Scrooge's loan to Diamond Jim will illustrate the problem.

The top line of Table 6-4 shows how taxation affects the loan agreement when there is no inflation and the nominal and real interest rates are both 3 percent. Scrooge earns $30 in nominal interest income (Column 3). Since there is no inflation, this also represents $30 in real interest income (Column 5). If Scrooge pays one-third of his income in taxes, his tax bill rises by $10 (Column 6), leaving him with $20 after tax (Column 7). This $20 amounts to 2 percent of the $1,000 originally loaned (Column 8). Because his $10 tax payment is one-third of his $30 in real interest income, Scrooge's effective tax rate is 33-1/3 percent (Column 9), just as Congress intended.

Now let's consider the same transaction when the inflation rate is 6 percent and Scrooge and Diamond Jim settle on a 9 percent nominal interest rate. Scrooge collects $90 in interest (Column 3). But, with 6 percent inflation, the purchasing power of the $1,000 he lends declines by $60 (Column 4). Thus, his real interest income is again $30 (Column 5). However, the tax collector taxes the $90 *nominal* interest income, not the $30 *real* interest income, so Scrooge must pay $30 (one-third of $90) in taxes (Column 6). As we can see in Column 7, his after-tax real income on the loan is zero since the tax collector takes all of his real income. Thus, the effective tax rate on Scrooge's real interest income is 100 percent (Column 9), far larger than the 33-1/3 percent rate intended by Congress. In effect, Scrooge is being taxed on "phantom profits" that, in purchasing-power terms, he never received.

So a tax system that works well at zero inflation misfires at 6 percent inflation because it taxes nominal, rather than real, interest. This little example illustrates a pervasive and serious problem:

Because it fails to recognize the distinction between nominal and real interest rates, our tax system levies high, and presumably unintended, tax rates on interest income when there is high inflation. Similar problems arise in the taxation of capital gains, corporate profits, and other items. Some economists feel that these high tax rates discourage saving, lending, and investing and that high inflation therefore retards economic growth.

A **CAPITAL GAIN** is the difference between the price at which an asset is sold and the price at which it was bought.

A particularly acute version of this problem arises in the taxation of **capital gains**—the difference between the price at which an investor sells an asset and the price that she paid for it. An example will bring out the point. Between 1979 and 1997 the price level doubled, approximately. Consider some stock that was purchased for $5,000 in 1979 and sold for $7,500 in 1997. The investor actually *lost* purchasing power in the transaction because $7,500 in 1997 purchased less than $5,000 in 1979. Yet, since the law levies taxes on nominal capital gains, with no correction for inflation, the investor will be taxed on the $2,500 nominal capital gain as though there had been a profit rather than a loss.

Many economists have proposed that this, presumably unintended, feature of the law be changed by taxing only capital gains that exceed inflation. But, up to now, Congress has not agreed.

INTEREST RATE CEILINGS AND OTHER IMPEDIMENTS

These two quirks of the tax law illustrate a more general problem:

Many of the laws that govern our financial system become extremely counterproductive in an inflationary environment, causing problems that were never intended by the legislators.

Here are two more examples of laws that malfunction under inflation:

USURY LAWS Usury laws, which set *maximum* permissible interest rates on particular types of loans, date back to biblical days. But they can have strange and unintended consequences under inflation because they place ceilings on *nominal* interest rates rather than on *real* interest rates. In effect, limits on nominal interest rates make some activities which are perfectly legal at low or zero inflation illegal in inflationary environments. In fact, usury laws created so much havoc during the period of double-digit inflation in 1979–1980 that Congress took drastic action to curtail them.

REGULATION OF PUBLIC UTILITIES When the rate of inflation rose above 12 percent in 1980, there was a public uproar after regulated utilities asked the regulatory agencies to permit them to earn a rate of return closer to 11 percent—a *negative* real rate of return! They frequently found that their requests were considered exorbitant by the commissions and by the general public. The consequence was that many utilities could not afford to borrow the money needed to serve expanding public demand.

Thus, failure to understand that high *nominal* interest rates can signify low *real* interest rates has been known to make the tax code misfire, to impoverish savers, to inhibit borrowing and lending, and to make it nearly impossible for public utilities to raise the capital they need to serve rising consumer demands—with power shortages the predictable results. It is important to note that *these costs of inflation are not purely redistributive.* Society as a whole loses when mutually beneficial transactions are prohibited by obsolete legislation.

Why, then, do such laws stay on the books? One reason is a general lack of understanding of the difference between real and nominal interest rates. People fail to understand that it is normally the *real* rate of interest that matters in an economic transaction because only that rate reveals how much borrowers pay and lenders receive *in terms of the goods and services that money can buy.* They focus on the high *nominal* interest rates caused by inflation, even when these rates correspond to low real interest rates.

THE ILLUSION OF HIGH INTEREST RATES

The difference between real and nominal interest (and profit) rates, and the fact that the real rate matters economically while the nominal rate is politically significant, are matters that are of the utmost importance and yet are understood by very few people, including many who make public policy decisions in these areas.

This concept is one of our **Ideas for Beyond the Final Exam,** and if you remember it 10 years from now, you will truly have gotten a great deal out of studying economics.

OTHER COSTS OF INFLATION

Another cost of inflation is that rapidly changing prices make it risky to enter into long-term contracts. In an extremely severe inflation, the "long term" may be only a few days. But even moderate inflations can have remarkable effects on long-term loans. Suppose that a corporation wants to borrow $1 million to finance the purchase of some new equipment and needs the loan for 20 years. If inflation averages 4 percent over this period, the $1 million it repays at the end of 20 years will be worth $456,387 in today's purchasing power. If inflation averages 8 percent instead, it will be worth only $214,548. Lending or borrowing for this long a period is obviously a big gamble. With the stakes this high, the outcome may be that neither lenders nor borrowers want to get involved in long-term contracts. But without long-term loans, business investment often becomes impossible. The economy stagnates.

Inflation also makes life difficult for the shopper. You probably have a group of stores that you habitually patronize because they carry the items you want to buy at (roughly) the prices you want to pay. This knowledge saves you a great deal of time and energy. But when prices are changing rapidly, your list quickly becomes obsolete. You return to your favorite clothing store to find that the price of jeans has risen drastically. Should you buy? Should you shop around at other stores? Will they have also raised their prices? Business firms have precisely the same problem with their suppliers. Rising prices force them to shop around more, which imposes costs on the firms and, more generally, reduces the efficiency of the whole economy.

Shopping costs may sound frivolous and unimportant, but they are not. Arthur Okun, who chaired the Council of Economic Advisers under President Johnson, suggested an ingenious mental exercise that illustrates the importance of shopping costs. Ask yourself how much you would have to be paid to promise never again to buy anything from any of the stores you have patronized in the past. When you ponder this for a while, you realize the great value of having normal places to shop. Inflation takes some of this value away.

THE COSTS OF LOW VERSUS HIGH INFLATION

The preceding litany of the costs of inflation alerts us to one very important fact: *predictable inflation is far less burdensome than unpredictable inflation.* When is inflation most predictable? When it proceeds year after year at a modest and more or less steady rate. Thus, the *variability of the inflation rate* is a crucial factor. Inflation of 3 percent a year for three consecutive years will exact lower social costs than inflation that is 2 percent in the first year, zero in the second, and 7 percent in the third. In general:

Steady inflation is more predictable than variable inflation and therefore has smaller social and economic costs.

But the *average level of the inflation rate* is also important. Partly because of the interest rate illusions mentioned above and partly because of the more rapid breakdown in normal customer relationships that we have just mentioned, a steady inflation of 6 percent a year does more damage than a steady inflation of 3 percent a year.

Economists distinguish between *low inflation,* which is a modest economic problem, and *high inflation,* which can be a devastating one, partly on the basis of the average level of inflation and partly on its variability. If inflation remains steady and low, prices may rise for a long time, but at a moderate and fairly constant pace, allowing people to adapt. From 1982 to 1996 in the United States, for example, prices climbed a total of 58 percent, for an average annual inflation rate of 3.3 percent. And the pace of inflation was remarkably steady, never dropping below 2.1 percent or rising above 4.4 percent.

Very high inflations typically last for shorter periods of time and are often marked by highly variable inflation rates from month to month or year to year. In recent decades, for example, countries ranging from Argentina to Israel to Russia have experienced bouts of inflation exceeding 100 percent or even 1,000 percent per year. (See the box on Nicaragua on the next page.) Each of these episodes severely disrupted the country's economy.

The German hyperinflation after World War I is perhaps the most famous episode of runaway inflation. Between December 1922 and November 1923, when a hard-nosed reform finally broke the spiral, wholesale prices in Germany increased by almost 100 million percent! But even this experience was dwarfed by the great Hungarian inflation of 1945–1946, the greatest inflation of them all. For a period of 1 year, the *monthly* rate of inflation averaged about 20,000 percent. In the final month, the price level skyrocketed 42 quadrillion percent!

If you review the costs of inflation that have been discussed in this chapter, you will see why the distinction between low and high inflation is so fundamental. Many economists think we can live rather well in an environment of steady, low inflation. No one believes we can survive very well under extremely high inflation.

When inflation is steady and low, the rate at which prices rise is relatively easy to predict. It then can be taken into account in setting interest rates (as long as the law allows). Under high inflation, especially if prices are rising at ever-increasing or highly variable rates, this is extremely difficult, and perhaps impossible, to do. The potential redistributions become monumental and, as a result, lending and borrowing may cease entirely.

Any inflation makes it difficult to write long-term contracts. Under low, creeping inflation, the "long term" may be 20 years, or 10 years, or 5. But under high, galloping inflation, the "long term" may be measured in days or weeks. Restaurant prices may change daily. Air fares may go up while you are in the middle of your journey. When it is impossible to enter into contracts of any duration longer than a few days, economic activity becomes paralyzed. We conclude that:

The horrors of hyperinflation either are absent in low, steady inflations or are present in such muted forms that they can scarcely be considered horrors.

HYPERINFLATION AND THE PIGGY BANK

While mild inflations are barely noticeable in everyday life, hyperinflation makes all sorts of normal economic activities more difficult and transforms a society in strange and unexpected ways. This article, excerpted from the *New York Times*, illustrates some of the problems that hyperinflation created for Nicaraguans in 1989.

For generations, Nicaraguans have guarded their savings in piggy banks. . . . But no longer. In a country where inflation recently reached 161 percent for a 2-week period, a penny saved is a penny spent. "No one wants a bank now," said a potter who has given over his kilns to making beer mugs. "We've given up even making them."

The demise of the piggy bank is only the least of the complications that have vexed the public as inflation and Government efforts to combat it have sent the value of the Nicaraguan córdoba fluctuating wildly.

After inflation became unbearable, the Government replaced all of its currency in February 1988 at a new rate of 10 córdobas to a dollar. But by December, the new money had reached 4,500 to the dollar, and despite months of harsh austerity measures, it has now surged upward again, reaching 26,250 to the dollar.

That kind of uncertainty has left the banking system in shambles, despite savings accounts that offer up to 70 percent interest a month. . . . And it has left a legacy of quirks that now extends throughout the country's daily life. . . .

In many parts of the country, enterprising mechanics have converted the nation's once-precious stock of coins into something more valuable: metal washers to fit the nuts and bolts of rapidly deteriorating machinery. . . .

In Managua, it is still necessary to deposit a copper-colored 1-córdoba coin to make a pay phone call. But . . . not everybody even remembers what a 1-córdoba coin looks like, and fewer still actually own one. That is probably just as well for the phone system, because if anyone bothered to carry the coins, they could make about 26,250 phone calls for a dollar. . . .

Beating the exchange rates is particularly trying for restaurant owners who must have any price increases approved by the Government Institute of Tourism. Since that process consumes precious amounts of time, restaurant owners must aim high with their requests in the anticipation that new inflation will make their prices competitive, but still profitable, at some future date.

When exchange rates are changing, therefore, prices at a given restaurant can shoot far out of sight, emptying it of patrons for days or weeks. Then, as has happened recently, a new devaluation can make the same prices absurdly low in dollar terms. A steak dinner for two at one of Managua's leading restaurants on a recent weekend cost a little over $3, if you could get a table.

SOURCE: Mark A. Uhlig, "Is Nicaraguan Piggy Bank an Endangered Species?" *New York Times*, June 24, 1989.

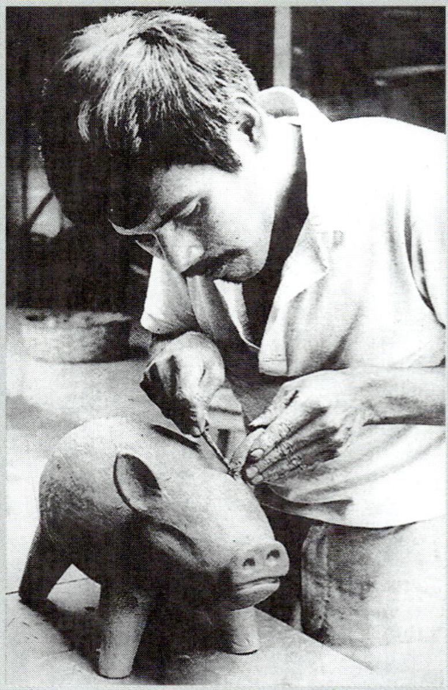

LOW INFLATION DOES NOT NECESSARILY LEAD TO HIGH INFLATION

We noted earlier that inflation is surrounded by a mythology that bears precious little relation to reality. It seems appropriate to conclude this chapter by disposing of one particularly persistent myth: that low inflation is a slippery slope that invariably leads to high inflation.

There is neither statistical evidence nor theoretical support for the myth that low inflation inevitably leads to high inflation. To be sure, inflations sometimes accelerate. But at other times they slow down.

While creeping inflations have many causes, runaway inflations have occurred only when the government has printed incredible amounts of money, usually to finance wartime expenditures. In the German inflation of 1923, the government

These children in Germany during the hyperinflation of the 1920s are building a pyramid with cash, worth no more than the sand or sticks used by children elsewhere.

finally found that its printing presses could not produce enough paper money to keep pace with the exploding prices. Not that it did not try. By the end of the inflation, the *daily* output of currency was over 400 quadrillion marks! The Hungarian authorities in 1945 to 1946 tried even harder. The average growth rate of the money supply was more than 12,000 percent *per month.* Needless to say, these are not the kind of inflation problems that are likely to face the United States in the foreseeable future.

But this should not be interpreted to imply that there is nothing wrong with low inflation. Much of this chapter has been spent analyzing the very real costs of any inflation, no matter how low. A case against even moderate inflation can indeed be built, but it does not help this case to shout foolish slogans like "Creeping inflation always leads to galloping inflation." Fortunately, it is simply not true.

SUMMARY

1. Unemployment exacts heavy financial and psychological costs from those who are its victims, costs that are borne quite unevenly by different groups in the population.
2. In recent decades, the U.S. economy often has produced less output than it could have produced were it operating at full employment, that is, at **potential GDP.**
3. **Frictional unemployment** arises when people are between jobs for normal reasons. Thus, most frictional unemployment is desirable.
4. **Structural unemployment** is due to shifts in the pattern of demand or to technological change that makes certain skills obsolete.
5. **Cyclical unemployment** is the portion of unemployment that rises in recessions and falls when the economy booms.
6. President Kennedy first enunciated the goal of 4 percent unemployment in 1961. But few economists think this is a realistic target for the 1990s. Most now think that *full employment* comes at an unemployment rate between 5.5 and 6.0 percent.
7. *Unemployment insurance* replaces nearly one-half of the lost income of unemployed persons who are insured. But only about one-third of the unemployed collect benefits, and no insurance program can bring back the lost output that could have been produced had these people been working.
8. People have many misconceptions about inflation. For example, many people believe that inflation systematically erodes **real wages,** are appalled by rising prices even when wages are rising just as fast, and blame inflation for any unfavorable changes in **relative prices.** All of these are myths.
9. Other costs of inflation are real, however. For example, inflation often redistributes income from lenders to borrowers.
10. This redistribution can be ameliorated by adding the *expected rate of inflation* to the interest rate. But expectations often prove to be inaccurate.
11. The **real rate of interest** is the **nominal rate of interest** minus the expected rate of inflation.
12. Since the real rate of interest indicates the command over real resources that the borrower surrenders to the lender, it is of primary economic importance.
13. Yet public attention often is riveted on nominal rates of interest, and this confusion can lead to costly policy mistakes when inflation converts high nominal interest rates into low real interest rates. This is one of the **Ideas for Beyond the Final Exam.**
14. Because nominal, not real, interest is taxed, our tax system levies heavy taxes on interest income when inflation is high.
15. Low inflation which proceeds at moderate and fairly predictable rates year after year carries far lower social costs than high and/or variable inflation. But even low, steady inflations entail costs.
16. The notion that low inflation inevitably accelerates into high inflation is a myth with no foundation in economic theory and no basis in historical fact.

KEY TERMS

Unemployment rate
Potential GDP
Labor force
Discouraged worker
Frictional unemployment
Structural unemployment
Cyclical unemployment
Full employment
Unemployment insurance
Purchasing power
Real wage rate
Relative price
Redistribution by inflation
Real rate of interest
Nominal rate of interest
Capital gain
Expected rate of inflation
Inflation and the tax system
Low versus high inflation

QUESTIONS FOR REVIEW

1. Why may it not be as terrible to become unemployed nowadays as it was during the Great Depression?
2. "Unemployment is no longer a social problem because unemployed workers receive unemployment benefits and other benefits that make up for most of their lost wages." Comment.
3. Using what you learned about aggregate demand and aggregate supply in the last chapter, try to explain why the U.S. economy has failed so frequently to produce up to its potential. (You will learn more about this question in later chapters, so don't worry if you find the question difficult now.)
4. Why is it so difficult to define *full employment*? What unemployment rate should the government be shooting for today?
5. Show why each of the following complaints is based on a misunderstanding about inflation:
   a. "Inflation must be stopped because it robs workers of their purchasing power."
   b. "Inflation is a terrible social disease. It leads to unconscionably high prices for basic necessities."
   c. "Inflation makes it impossible for working people to afford many of the things they were hoping to buy."
   d. "Inflation must be stopped today, for if we do not stop it, it will surely accelerate to ruinously high rates and lead to disaster."
6. What is the *real interest rate* paid on a credit-card loan bearing 14 percent nominal interest per year, if the rate of inflation is
   a. zero?
   b. 2 percent?
   c. 6 percent?
   d. 14 percent?
   e. 18 percent?
7. Suppose that you agree to lend money to your friend on the day you both enter college, at what you both expect to be a zero *real* rate of interest. Payment is to be made at graduation, with interest at a fixed *nominal* rate. If inflation proves to be *lower* during your 4 years in college than what you both had expected, who will gain and who will lose?
8. You have lived almost your entire life under moderate inflation. Can you think of some costs that inflation has imposed on you personally? How do these costs relate to the material in this chapter?
9. Add a third line to Table 6-4 showing what would happen if the inflation rate went to 12 percent and the real interest rate remained at 3 percent.

APPENDIX — HOW STATISTICIANS MEASURE INFLATION

INDEX NUMBERS FOR INFLATION

Inflation is generally measured by the change in some index of the general price level. For example, between 1973 and 1995, the Consumer Price Index (CPI) rose from 44.4 to 152.4, an increase of 243 percent. The meaning of the *change* is clear enough. But what are the meanings of the 44.4 figure for 1973 and the 152.4 figure for 1995? These numbers are *index numbers*.

An **index number** expresses the cost of a market basket of goods *relative to its cost in some "base" period.*

Since the CPI currently uses 1982–1984 as its base period, the CPI of 152.4 for 1995 means that it costs $152.40 to purchase the same basket of goods and services that cost $100 in 1982 to 1984.

Now, the particular basket of consumer goods and services under scrutiny really did not cost $100 in

1982 to 1984. When constructing index numbers, it is conventional to set the index at 100 in the base period. How is this conventional figure used in obtaining index numbers of other years? Very simply. Suppose that the budget needed to buy the roughly 250 items included in the CPI was \$2,000 per month in 1982 to 1984 and \$3,048 per month in 1995. Then the index is defined by the following rule:

$$\frac{\text{CPI in 1995}}{\text{CPI in 1982–1984}} = \frac{\text{Cost of the market basket in 1995}}{\text{Cost of the market basket in 1982–1984}}$$

Since the CPI in 1982–1984 is set at 100:

$$\frac{\text{CPI in 1995}}{100} = \frac{\$3{,}048}{\$2{,}000} = 1.524$$

or

$$\text{CPI in 1995} = 152.4$$

Exactly the same sort of equation enables us to calculate the CPI in any other year. We have the rule:

$$\text{CPI in given year} = \frac{\text{Cost of market basket in given year}}{\text{Cost of market basket in base year}} \times 100$$

Of course, not every combination of consumer goods that cost \$2,000 in 1982 to 1984 rose to \$3,048 by 1995. For example, a color TV set that cost \$400 in 1983 might still have cost \$400 in 1995, but a \$400 hospital bill in 1983 might have ballooned to \$1,200.

Since no two families buy precisely the same bundle of goods and services, no two families suffer precisely the same increase in their cost of living unless all prices rise at the same rate. Economists refer to this phenomenon as the **index number problem.**

When relative prices are changing, there is no such thing as a "perfect price index" that is correct for every consumer. Any statistical index will understate the increase in the cost of living for some families and overstate it for others. At best, the index can represent the situation of an "average" family.

THE CONSUMER PRICE INDEX

The *Consumer Price Index (CPI)*, which is calculated and announced each month by the Bureau of Labor Statistics (BLS), is surely the most closely watched price index. When you read in the newspaper or see on television that the "cost of living rose by 0.3 percent last month," chances are the reporter is referring to the CPI.

TABLE 6-5

RESULTS OF STUDENT EXPENDITURE SURVEY, 1983

Item	Average Price	Average Quantity Purchased per Month	Average Expenditure per Month
Hamburger	\$ 0.80	70	\$ 56
Jeans	24.00	1	24
Movie ticket	5.00	4	20
		Total	\$100

The **Consumer Price Index (CPI)** is measured by pricing the items on a list representative of a typical urban household budget.

To know what items to include and in what amounts, the BLS conducts an extensive survey of spending habits roughly once every decade. This means that the *same* bundle of goods and services is used as a standard for 10 years or so, whether or not spending habits change.[7] Of course, spending habits do change, and this introduces a small error into the CPI's measurement of inflation.

A simple example will help us understand how the CPI is constructed. Imagine that college students purchase only three items—hamburgers, jeans, and movie tickets—and that we want to devise a cost-of-living index (call it SPI, or "student price index") for them. First, we would conduct a survey of spending habits in the base year. (Suppose it is 1983.) Table 6-5 represents the hypothetical results. You will note that the frugal students of that day spent only \$100 per month: \$56 on hamburgers, \$24 on jeans, and \$20 on movies.

Table 6-6 presents hypothetical prices of these same three items in 1996. Each price has risen by a different amount, ranging from 25 percent for jeans up to 50 percent for hamburgers. By how much has the SPI risen? Pricing the 1983 student budget at 1996 prices, we find that what once cost \$100 now

[7]Economists call this a *base-period weight index* because the relative importance it attaches to the price of each item depends on how much money consumers actually chose to spend on the item during the base period.

TABLE 6-6

PRICES IN 1996

Item	Price	Percentage Increase over 1983
Hamburger	$ 1.20	50
Jeans	30.00	25
Movie ticket	7.00	40

TABLE 6-7

COST OF 1983 STUDENT BUDGET IN 1996 PRICES

70 hamburgers at $1.20	$ 84
1 pair of jeans at $30	30
4 movie tickets at $7	28
Total	$142

costs $142, as the calculation in Table 6-7 shows. Thus, the SPI, based on 1983 = 100, is:

$$\text{SPI} = \frac{\text{Cost of budget in 1996}}{\text{Cost of budget in 1983}} \times 100$$

$$= \frac{\$142}{\$100} \times 100 = 142$$

So the SPI in 1996 stands at 142, meaning that students' cost of living has increased 42 percent over the 13 years.

HOW TO USE A PRICE INDEX TO "DEFLATE" MONETARY FIGURES

One of the most common uses of price indexes is in the comparison of monetary figures relating to two different points in time. The problem is that, if there has been inflation, the dollar is not a good measuring rod because it can buy less now than it did in the past.

Here is a simple example. Suppose that the average student spent $100 per month in 1983 but $130 per month in 1996. If there was an outcry that students had become spendthrifts, how would you answer the charge?

The obvious answer is that a dollar in 1996 does not buy what it did in 1983. Specifically, our SPI shows us that it takes $1.42 in 1996 to purchase what $1 would purchase in 1983. To compare the spending habits of students in the 2 years, we must divide the 1996 spending figure by 1.42. Specifically, *real* spending per student in 1996 (where "real" is defined by 1983 dollars) is:

$$\text{Real spending in 1996} = \frac{\text{Nominal spending in 1996}}{\text{Price index of 1996}}$$

Thus,

$$\text{Real spending in 1996} = \frac{\$130}{1.42} = \$91.55$$

This calculation shows that, despite appearances to the contrary, the change in nominal spending from $100 to $130 actually represented a *decrease* in real spending.

This calculation procedure is called *deflating by a price index,* and it serves to translate noncomparable monetary figures into more directly comparable real figures.

Deflating is the process of finding the real value of some monetary magnitude by dividing by some appropriate price index.

A good practical illustration is the real wage, a concept we have discussed in this chapter. Average hourly earnings in the U.S. economy were $8.02 in 1983 and $11.46 in 1995. Since the CPI in 1995 was 152.4 (with 1982–1984 as the base period), the real wage in 1995 (expressed in 1982–1984 dollars) was:

$$\text{Real wage in 1995} = \frac{\text{Money wage in 1995}}{\text{Price index of 1995}}$$

$$= \frac{\$11.46}{152.4} \times 100 = \$7.52$$

Thus, by this measure, the real wage fell 6.2 percent over the 12 years.

THE GDP DEFLATOR

In macroeconomics, one of the most important of the monetary magnitudes that we have to deflate is the nominal gross domestic product (GDP).

The price index used to deflate GDP is called the **GDP deflator.**

YOUR PERSONAL CPI

Inflation impacts people differently because everyone has somewhat unique spending habits. For example, many senior citizens spend heavily on medical care, but their homes have long been paid off. Many young professionals, on the other hand, have heavy mortgage payments but almost no doctor bills. Thus, in principle, everyone has his or her own personal CPI.

Use the accompanying chart to calculate yours for the year 1994. Just enter the percentage of your spending that you allocated to each category shown in the table. National inflation figures are based on the assumption that the typical household allocates 41 percent of its spending to housing. But if you spent only 30 percent on housing, enter 30 in the second column and multiply it by the inflation rate for housing listed in the third column. Enter the result in the far right column. Then add up the final column to obtain your personal inflation rate. The national inflation rate for 1994 was around 3 percent. How did you do?

Expenditure Category	Percentage You Spend per Category	Inflation Rate for This Item	Contribution to Your Inflation Rate
Food and beverages		2.3%	
Housing		2.5	
Apparel		0.7	
Transportation		3.3	
Medical care		4.7	
Entertainment		2.5	
Miscellaneous		4.4	
Total			

SOURCE: "What's Your Inflation Rate?" *Kiplinger's Personal Finance Magazine*, January 1995, p. 59.

Our general principle for deflating a nominal magnitude tells us how to go from nominal GDP to real GDP:

$$\text{Real GDP} = \frac{\text{Nominal GDP}}{\text{GDP deflator}} \times 100$$

As with the CPI, the 100 simply serves to establish the base of the index as 100, rather than 1.00.

Some economists consider the GDP deflator to be a better measure of overall inflation in the economy than the Consumer Price Index. The main reason for this is that the two price indexes are based on different market baskets. As already mentioned, the CPI is based on the budget of a typical urban family. By contrast, the GDP deflator is constructed from a market basket that includes *every* item in the GDP—that is, every final good and service produced by the economy. Thus, in addition to prices of consumer goods, the GDP deflator includes the prices of airplanes, lathes, and other goods purchased by businesses. It also includes government services. For this reason, the measures of inflation that these two indexes give are rarely the same. Usually their disagreements are minor. But sometimes they can be substantial, as in 1980 when the CPI recorded a 13.5 percent inflation rate over 1979 while the GDP deflator recorded only 9.2 percent.

SUMMARY

1. Inflation is measured by the percentage increase in an **index number** of prices, which shows how the cost of some basket of goods has changed over a period of time.
2. Since relative prices are changing all the time, and since different families purchase different items, no price index can represent precisely the change in the cost of living for every family.
3. The **Consumer Price Index (CPI)** tries to measure the cost of living for an "average" urban household by pricing a "typical" market basket every month.
4. Price indexes like the CPI can be used to **deflate** monetary figures to make them more comparable. This amounts to dividing the monetary magnitude by the appropriate price index.
5. The **GDP deflator** is a better measure of economy-wide inflation than the CPI because it includes the prices of all goods and services in the economy.

KEY TERMS

Index number
Index number problem
Consumer Price Index
Deflating
GDP deflator

QUESTIONS FOR REVIEW

1. Just below, you will find the yearly average values of the Dow Jones Industrial Average, the most popular index of stock market prices, for 4 different years. The Consumer Price Index for each year (on a base of 1982–1984 = 100) can be found on the inside back cover of this book. Use these numbers to deflate all four stock market values. In which year were stocks really worth the most?

Year	Dow Jones Industrial Average
1964	834
1972	951
1987	2,276
1994	3,794

2. Just below you will find nominal GDP and the GDP deflator for 1974, 1984, and 1994.
   a. Compute real GDP for each year.
   b. Compute the percentage change in nominal and real GDP from 1974 to 1984, and from 1984 to 1994.
   c. Compute the percentage change in the GDP deflator over these two periods.

GDP Statistics	1974	1984	1994
Nominal GDP (billions of dollars)	1,497	3,902	6,931
GDP Deflator	38.5	75.9	105.0

3. Fill in the blanks in the following table of GDP statistics:

	1992	1993	1994
Nominal GDP	6,244		6,931
Real GDP	6,244	6,384	
GDP Deflator		102.6	105.0

4. Use the following data to compute the College Price Index for 1996 using the base 1972 = 100.

Item	Price in 1972	Quantity per Month in 1972	Price in 1996
Button-down shirts	$10	1	$25
Loafers	25	1	55
Sneakers	10	3	35
Textbooks	12	12	40
Jeans	12	3	30
Restaurant meals	5	11	14

5. Average hourly earnings in the U.S. economy during several past years were as follows:

1964	1974	1984	1994
$2.36	$4.24	$8.32	$11.13

Use the CPI numbers provided on the inside back cover to calculate the real wage (in 1982–1984 dollars) for each of these years. Which decade had the fastest growth of money wages? Which had the fastest growth of real wages?

6. The example in the appendix showed that the Student Price Index (SPI) rose by 42 percent from 1983 to 1996. You can understand the meaning of this better if you:
   a. Use Table 6-5 to compute the fraction of total spending accounted for by each of the three items in 1983. Call these the "expenditure weights."
   b. Compute the weighted average of the percentage increases of the three prices shown in Table 6-6, using the expenditure weights you have just computed.
   c. You should get 42 percent as your answer. This shows that "inflation," as measured by the SPI, is a weighted average of the percentage price increases of all the items that are included in the index.

CHAPTER 7

INCOME AND SPENDING: THE POWERFUL CONSUMER

Men are disposed, as a rule and on the average, to increase their consumption as their income increases, but not by as much as the increase in their income.
John Maynard Keynes

In Chapter 5, we noted that the strength of aggregate demand influences the performance of the economy. When aggregate demand is growing briskly, the economy is likely to be booming, though it may also be having trouble with inflation. When aggregate demand stagnates, a recession may follow.

This chapter begins our detailed study of the theory of income determination, the tool economists use to analyze issues like these. The theory is based on the concepts of aggregate demand and supply. In this and the next two chapters, we construct a simplified model of aggregate demand and learn where the *aggregate demand curve* of Chapter 5 comes from. Then Chapter 10 completes the model by adding the *aggregate supply curve.*

This first model of the macroeconomy can teach us much about the causes of unemployment and inflation. But it is too simple to deal with policy issues because the government and the financial system are largely ignored. We remedy these omissions in Part III, where we give government spending, taxation, and interest rates appropriately prominent roles. The influence of the exchange rate between the U.S. dollar and foreign currencies is considered in Part IV.

We build our model in steps. Since consumer spending accounts for the lion's share of total demand, it is natural to begin there. First, we need some definitions of alternative concepts of economic activity—distinguishing carefully among total *spending* (aggregate demand), total *output,* and total *income.* Next, we turn to the interactions among these three concepts, using a convenient pictorial device that shows how they are all related. The bulk of the chapter, however, is devoted to describing and analyzing the important relationship between consumer income and consumer spending. Finally, we discuss some complications that arise from the fact that consumer income, though crucial, is not the *only* factor governing consumer spending.

A PUZZLE: DEMAND MANAGEMENT AND THE ORNERY CONSUMER

We suggested in Chapter 5 that the government sometimes wants to shift the aggregate demand curve. There are a number of ways in which it can try to do so. One direct approach is to alter its own spending, becoming extravagant when private demand is weak and miserly when private demand is strong. But the government can also take a more indirect route by using taxes and other policy tools to influence *private* spending decisions. Since consumer expenditures constitute about two-thirds of gross domestic product, the consumer presents the most tempting target.

While there are many things it can do to alter consumer spending, the government's principal weapon is the personal income tax. Many of you already have encountered Form 1040, the unwelcome New Year's greeting that every taxpayer receives from the federal government each January. Many more of you probably have been on a payroll and seen a share of your wages deducted and sent to the Internal Revenue Service. It should be no mystery, then, how changes in personal taxes affect consumer spending. Any reduction in personal taxes leaves consumers with more after-tax income to spend. Any increase in taxes leaves less.

The linkage from taxes to spendable income to consumer spending seems direct and unmistakable, and, in a certain sense, it is. But a look at the history of some major tax changes aimed at altering consumer spending is sobering. The varying degrees of success both of the measures themselves and of the predictions of their effects explain why economic research into the relationship between taxes and consumption continues.

CASE 1: THE 1964 TAX CUT

The year 1964 was a good one for economists. For years they had been proclaiming that a cut in personal income taxes would be an excellent way to stimulate a stagnating economy. But the plea fell on deaf ears until President John F. Kennedy was persuaded of the basic logic of the argument and his successor, Lyndon Johnson, pushed the legislation through Congress. The 1964 tax cut was designed to spur consumer spending, and it succeeded admirably. Consumers reacted just about as the textbooks of the day predicted, the economy improved rapidly and markedly, and economists smiled knowingly.

CASE 2: THE 1975 TAX CUT

The next major attempt to stimulate the economy by cutting taxes met with much less success. In the spring of 1975, as the economy hit the bottom of a recession, President Gerald Ford and Congress agreed on a temporary tax cut to spur consumer spending: They refunded to each taxpayer part of the taxes paid in 1974, and reduced income tax rates for the rest of 1975. However, consumers confounded the wishes of the president and Congress by saving a good deal of their rebates rather than spending them.

CASE 3: THE 1981–1984 TAX CUTS

When President Ronald Reagan was elected in 1980, one of the first things he did was to push a series of reductions in personal income tax rates through Congress. Tax rates fell by about 23 percent between 1981 and 1984, and consumer

AGGREGATE DEMAND is the total amount that all consumers, business firms, and government agencies are willing to spend on final goods and services.

spending increased by more or less the amounts that economists predicted, thereby contributing to the long economic expansion of the 1980s.

Thus, tax policy did more or less what it was expected to do in 1964 and 1981 to 1984 but seemed to be less effective in 1975. Why? This chapter will attempt to provide some answers. But before getting involved in such complicated issues, we must build some vocabulary and learn some basic concepts. Then, at the end of the chapter, we will see what went wrong in 1975.

AGGREGATE DEMAND, DOMESTIC PRODUCT, AND NATIONAL INCOME

CONSUMER EXPENDITURE, symbolized by the letter ***C,*** is the total amount spent by consumers on newly produced goods and services (excluding purchases of new homes, which are considered investment goods).

INVESTMENT SPENDING, symbolized by the letter ***I,*** is the sum of the expenditures of business firms on new plant and equipment and households on new homes. Financial "investments" are not included, nor are resales of existing physical assets.

GOVERNMENT PURCHASES, symbolized by the letter ***G,*** refer to the goods (such as airplanes and paper clips) and services (such as school teaching and police protection) purchased by all levels of government.

NET EXPORTS, symbolized by ***(X − IM),*** is the difference between U.S. exports and U.S. imports. It indicates the difference between what we sell to foreigners and what we buy from them.

First, the vocabulary. We have already introduced the concept of *gross domestic product* as the standard measure of the economy's total output.[1] For the most part, goods are produced in a market economy only if firms think they can sell them. **Aggregate demand,** another concept encountered in Chapter 5, is the total amount that all consumers, business firms, government agencies, and foreigners wish to spend on all U.S. final goods and services.

The downward-sloping aggregate demand curve of Chapter 5 alerted us to the fact that *aggregate demand is a schedule, not a fixed number.* The actual numerical value of aggregate demand depends on the price level, and several reasons for this dependence will emerge in coming chapters.

But the level of aggregate demand also depends on a variety of other factors like consumer incomes, various government policies, and events in foreign countries. We can understand the nature of aggregate demand best if we break it up into its major components.

Consumer expenditure (*consumption* for short) is simply the total demand for all consumer goods and services. This is the focus of the current chapter, and we represent it by the letter *C.* Consumer expenditure constitutes about two-thirds of total spending.

Investment spending, represented by the letter *I,* is the amount that firms spend on factories, machinery, and the like, plus the amount that families spend on new houses. Notice that this usage of the word *investment* differs from common parlance. Most people speak of "investing" in the stock market or in a bank account. This kind of "investment" merely swaps one form of financial asset (such as money) for another form (such as a share of stock). When economists speak of "investment," they mean instead the purchase of some *new, physical* asset, like a drill press or an oil rig or a house. It is only these kinds of investments that lead directly to additional demand for newly produced goods and, subsequently, to greater productive capacity.

The third major component of aggregate demand is **government purchases** of goods and services—items like paper, computers, airplanes, ships, and labor that are bought by all levels of government. We will use the symbol *G* for this variable.

The final component of aggregate demand is **net exports,** which are simply defined as U.S. exports *minus* U.S. imports. The reasoning here is simple. Part of the demand for American goods and services originates beyond our borders—as when foreigners buy our wheat, our computers, and our banking services. So this must be added to domestic demand. Similarly, some items included in *C*

[1]See Chapter 5, pages 99–103.

and *I* are not American made. Think, for example, of German beer, Japanese cars, and Korean textiles. So these must be subtracted if we want to measure total spending on U.S. products. The addition of exports, which we represent by the symbol ***X***, and the subtraction of imports, ***IM***, leads us to the following shorthand definition of aggregate demand:

NATIONAL INCOME is the sum of the incomes that all individuals in the economy earned in the forms of wages, interest, rents, and profits. It excludes transfer payments and is calculated before any deductions are taken for income taxes.

Aggregate demand is the sum $C + I + G + (X - IM)$.

The last concept we need for our vocabulary is a way to measure the total *income* of all individuals in the economy. There are two versions of this: one for before-tax incomes, called **national income,** and one for after-tax incomes, called **disposable income.**[2] The term *disposable income,* which we will abbreviate *DI*, will play a prominent role in this chapter because it tells us how many dollars consumers actually have available to spend or to save.

THE CIRCULAR FLOW OF SPENDING, PRODUCTION, AND INCOME

DISPOSABLE INCOME is the sum of the incomes of all the individuals in the economy after all taxes have been deducted and all transfer payments have been added.

Enough definitions. How do these three concepts—domestic product, total expenditure, and national income—interact in a market economy? We can answer this best with a rather elaborate diagram (Figure 7-1). For obvious reasons, Figure 7-1 is called a *circular flow diagram*. It depicts a large, circular tube in which an imaginary fluid is circulating in a clockwise direction. There are several breaks in the tube where either some of the fluid leaks out or additional fluid is injected in.

Let us examine this system, beginning on the far left. At point 1 on the circle, we find consumers. Disposable income (*DI*) is flowing into them, and two things are flowing out: consumption (*C*), which stays in the circular flow, and saving (*S*), which "leaks out." This depicts the fact that consumers normally spend less than they earn and save the balance. The "leakage" to savings, of course, does not disappear, but flows into the financial system via banks, mutual funds, and so on. We postpone consideration of what happens there until Chapter 12.

The upper loop of the circular flow represents expenditures, and as we move clockwise to point 2, we encounter the first "injection" into the flow: investment spending (*I*). The diagram shows this as coming from "investors"—a group that includes both business firms and consumers.[3] As the circular flow moves past point 2, it is bigger than it was before: Total spending has increased from *C* to $C + I$.

At point 3, there is yet another injection. The government adds its demand for goods and services (*G*) to those of consumers and investors ($C + I$). Now aggregate demand is up to $C + I + G$.

The final leakage and injection come at point 4. Here we see export spending entering the circular flow from abroad and import spending leaking out. The net effect of these two forces may increase or decrease the circular flow, depending on whether net exports are positive or negative. In either case, by the time we pass point 4, we have accumulated the full amount of aggregate demand, $C + I + G + (X - IM)$.

---

[2]More detailed information on these and other concepts is provided in the appendix to this chapter.

[3]You are reminded that expenditure on housing is part of *I*, not part of *C*.

FIGURE 7-1

THE CIRCULAR FLOW OF EXPENDITURES AND INCOME

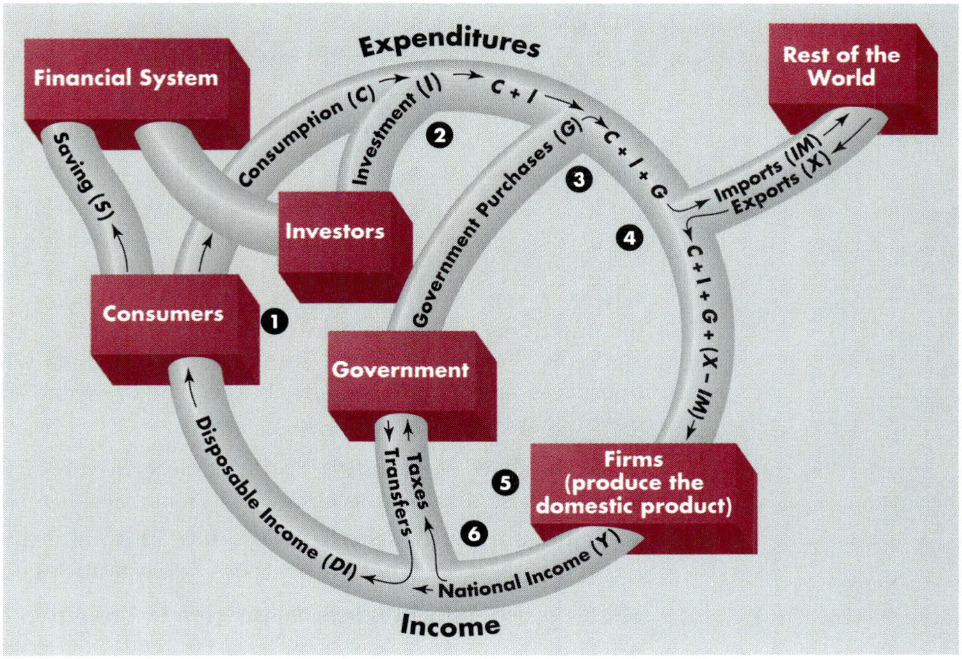

The upper part of this circular flow diagram depicts the flow of expenditures on goods and services that comes from consumers (point 1), investors (point 2), government (point 3), and foreigners (point 4); that flow goes to the firms that produce the output (point 5). The lower part of the diagram indicates how the income paid out by firms (point 5) flows to consumers (point 1), after some is siphoned off by the government in the form of taxes and part of this is replaced by transfer payments (point 6).

The circular flow diagram shows this aggregate demand for goods and services arriving at the business firms, which are located at point 5. Responding to this demand, firms produce the domestic product. As the circular flow emerges from the firms, however, we have renamed it *national income*. Why? The reason is that, except for some complications explained in the appendix:

National income and domestic product must be equal.

Why is this so? When a firm produces and sells $100 worth of output, it pays most of the proceeds to its workers, to people who have lent it money, and to the landlord who owns the property on which it is located. All of these payments are *income* to some individuals. But what about the rest? Suppose, for example, that the firm pays wages, interest, and rent totaling $90 million and it sells its output for $100 million. What happens to the remaining $10 million? The answer is that the owners of the firm receive it as *profits*. Since these owners are citizens of the country, their incomes also count in national income.[4] Thus, when we add up all the wages, interest, rents, *and profits* in the economy to obtain the national *income*, we must arrive at the *value of output*.

TRANSFER PAYMENTS are sums of money that certain individuals receive as outright *grants* from the government rather than as payments for services rendered to employers. Some common examples are Social Security and unemployment benefits.

The lower loop of the circular flow diagram traces the flow of income by showing national income leaving the firms and heading for consumers. But there is a detour along the way. At point 6, the government does two things. First, it siphons off a portion of the national income in the form of taxes. Second, it adds back government **transfer payments,** like unemployment compensation and

[4]Some of the income paid out by American companies goes to non-citizens. Similarly, some Americans earn income from foreign firms. This complication is dealt with in the chapter appendix.

Social Security benefits, which are funds that certain individuals receive as outright *grants* from the government rather than as payments for goods or services rendered.

By subtracting taxes from GDP and adding transfer payments, we obtain disposable income.[5]

$$\begin{aligned} DI &= \text{GDP} - \text{Taxes} + \text{Transfer payments} \\ &= \text{GDP} - (\text{Taxes} - \text{Transfers}) \end{aligned}$$

or

$$DI = Y - T$$

where Y represents GDP and T represents taxes *net of transfers*. Disposable income flows unimpeded to consumers at point 1, and the cycle repeats.

Figure 7-1 raises several complicated questions which we pose now but will not try to answer at this early stage. The answers will be made clear in subsequent chapters.

1. Is the flow of spending and income growing larger or smaller as we move clockwise around the circle? Why?

2. Is the output that the firms produce at point 5 (the GDP) equal to aggregate demand? If so, what makes these two quantities equal? If not, what happens?

The next chapter provides the answers to these two questions.

3. Are the government's accounts in balance, so that what flows in at point 6 (taxes minus transfers) is equal to what flows out at point 3 (government purchases)? What happens if they are not?

This important question is first addressed in Chapter 11 and then recurs many times, especially in Chapter 15, which is devoted to discussing budget deficits.

4. Is our international trade balanced, so that exports equal imports? More generally, what factors determine net exports and what are the consequences of trade deficits or surpluses?

We take up these questions briefly in the next two chapters and then consider them fully in Part IV, which is devoted to international economic issues.

However, we cannot discuss any of these issues profitably until we first understand what goes on at point 1, where consumers make decisions. We turn next, therefore, to the determinants of consumer spending.

CONSUMER SPENDING AND INCOME: THE IMPORTANT RELATIONSHIP

Recall that we started the chapter with a puzzle: Why did consumers respond more or less as expected to tax changes in 1964 and the early 1980s, but not in 1975? An economist interested in predicting how consumer spending will respond to a change in personal income tax payments must first ask how C is related to disposable income; for an increase in taxes is a decrease in after-tax income, and a reduction in taxes is an increase in after-tax income. This section, therefore, will examine what we know about the response of consumer spending to a change in disposable income.

[5]This definition omits a few minor details, which are explained in the appendix to this chapter.

FIGURE 7-2

CONSUMER SPENDING AND DISPOSABLE INCOME

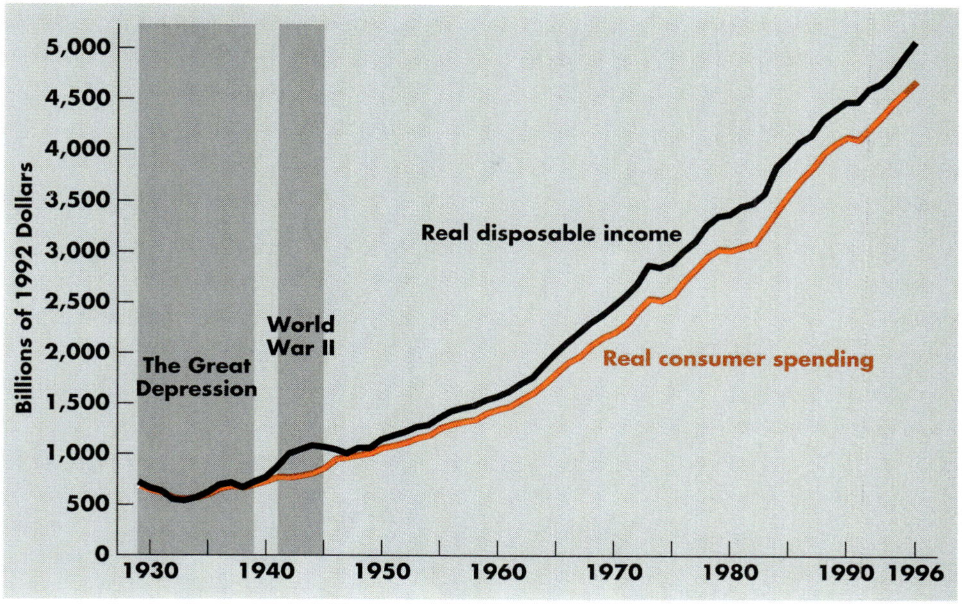

This time-series chart shows the behavior of consumer spending and disposable income in the United States since 1929. Except for the World War II years, the correspondence between the two variables is remarkably close. The distance between the two lines represents consumer saving, which was obviously quite small during the Great Depression of the 1930s and quite large during World War II.

SOURCE: U.S. Department of Commerce.

Figure 7-2 depicts the historical paths of *C* and *DI* for the United States since 1929. The association is obviously rather close and certainly suggests that consumption will rise whenever disposable income does, and fall whenever income falls. The difference between the two lines is personal saving. Notice how little saving consumers did during the Great Depression of the 1930s, where the two lines are very close together, and how much they did during World War II, when many consumer goods were either unavailable or rationed, leaving little on which to spend money.

Of course, knowing that consumer expenditures, *C,* will move in the same direction as disposable income, *DI,* is not enough for policy planners. They need to know *how much* one will go up when the other rises a given amount. Figure 7-3 presents the same data as in Figure 7-2, but in a way designed to help answer the "how much" question.

A **SCATTER DIAGRAM** is a graph showing the relationship between two variables (such as consumer spending and disposable income). Each year is represented by a point in the diagram. The coordinates of each year's point show the values of the two variables in that year.

Economists call such pictures **scatter diagrams,** and these diagrams are very useful in predicting how one economic variable (in this case, consumer spending) will change in response to a change in another economic variable (in this case, disposable income). Each dot in the diagram represents the data on *C* and *DI* corresponding to a particular year. For example, the point labeled "1976" shows that real consumer expenditures in 1976 were $2,714 billion (which we read off the vertical axis), while real disposable incomes amounted to $3,008 billion (which we read off the horizontal axis). Similarly, each year from 1929 to 1995 is represented by its own dot in Figure 7-3.

How can such a diagram assist the fiscal policy planner? Imagine that this is 1963 and you must decide whether to recommend to Congress a tax cut of $5 billion, $10 billion, or $15 billion. You have forecasts of what consumer expenditures are expected to be if taxes are not reduced. This, plus other forecasts of investment, government spending, and net exports has led you to conclude that aggregate demand in 1964 will be insufficient if taxes are not reduced.

FIGURE 7-3

This diagram shows the same data as depicted in Figure 7-2 but in a different manner. Each point on the diagram represents the data for both consumer spending and disposable income during a particular year. For example, the point labeled "1976" indicates that in that year consumer spending was $2,714 billion while disposable income was $3,008 billion. Diagrams like this one are called *scatter diagrams.*

SCATTER DIAGRAM OF CONSUMER SPENDING AND DISPOSABLE INCOME

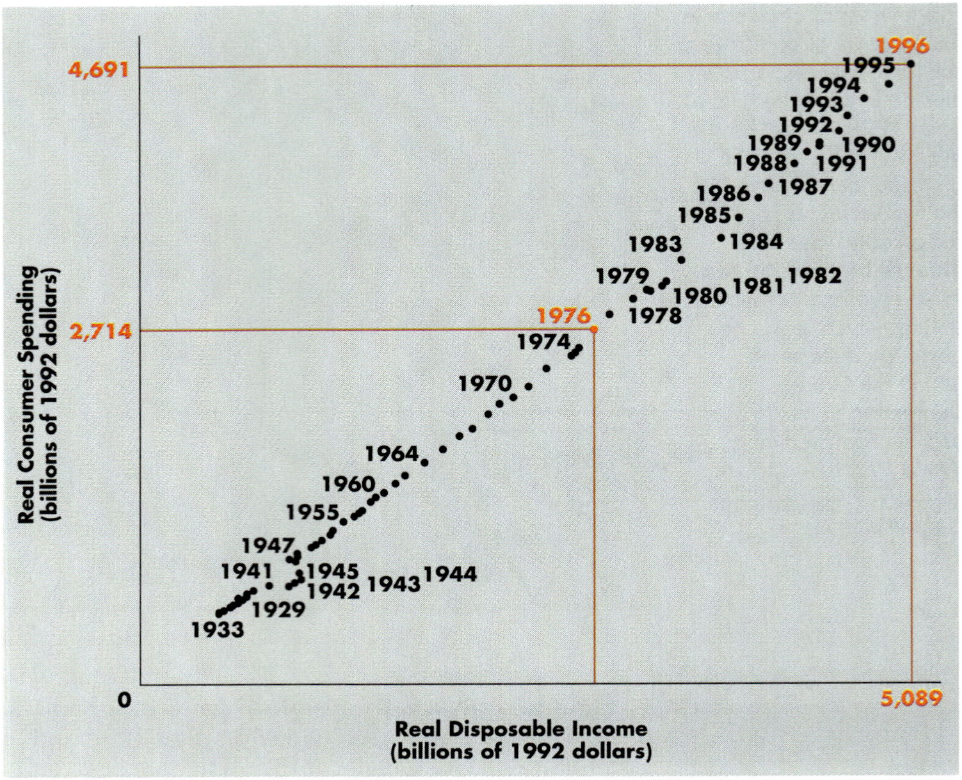

To assist your imagination, another scatter diagram is given in Figure 7-4. This one removes the points for 1964 through 1996, which appear in Figure 7-3; after all, these were not known in 1963. Years prior to 1947 have also been removed because, as Figure 7-2 showed, both the Great Depression and wartime rationing seriously disturbed the normal relationship between *DI* and *C* during that period. With the training in economics that you have right now, what would you do?

One rough-and-ready approach is to get a ruler, set it down on Figure 7-4, and sketch a straight line that comes as close as possible to hitting all the points. That has been done for you in the figure, and you can see that it comes remarkably close to touching all of the points. The line summarizes, in a very rough way, the consumption-income relationship that is the focus of this chapter. The two variables do indeed appear to be closely related.

The *slope* of the straight line in Figure 7-4 is very important.[6] Specifically, we note that it is:

$$\text{Slope} = \frac{\text{Vertical change}}{\text{Horizontal change}} = \frac{\$90 \text{ billion}}{\$100 \text{ billion}} = 0.90$$

Since the horizontal change involved in the move from *A* to *B* represents a rise in disposable income of $100 billion (from $1,300 billion to $1,400 billion), and

[6]To review the concept of *slope,* turn back to page 18.

FIGURE 7-4 SCATTER DIAGRAM OF CONSUMER SPENDING AND DISPOSABLE INCOME, 1947–1963

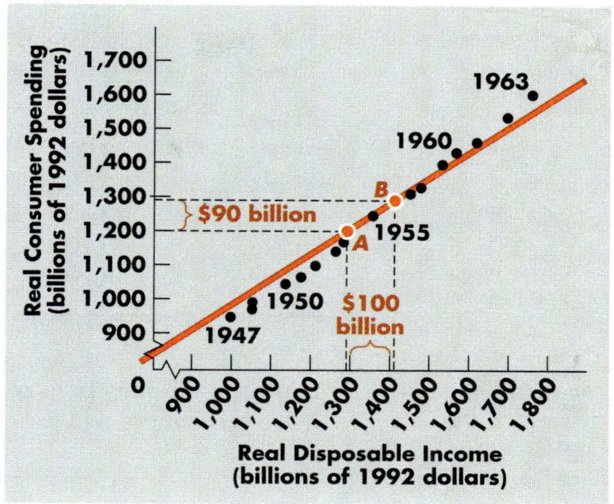

This scatter diagram omits some of the data found in Figure 7-3 and thereby indicates the information that policy planners might have used in deciding upon the size of the 1964 income tax cut. The straight line in orange comes about as close as possible to fitting all the data points.

the corresponding vertical change represents the associated $90 billion rise in consumer spending (from $1,200 billion to $1,290 billion), the slope of the line indicates how spending responds to changes in disposable income. In this case, we see that each additional $1 of income leads to 90 cents of additional spending.

In terms of the policy issue of 1964, this line can therefore help provide an answer to the question: How much more consumer spending will be induced by tax cuts of $5 billion, $10 billion, or $15 billion, if the effects are similar to those observed in the past? First, we need to keep in mind that each dollar of tax cut increases disposable income by $1. Then we apply the finding from Figure 7-4 that each additional dollar of disposable income increases consumer spending by 90 cents to conclude that proposed tax cuts of $5 billion, $10 billion, or $15 billion would be expected to increase consumer spending by $4.5 billion, $9.0 billion, and $13.5 billion, respectively. Similar questions addressed by economists in 1964 led to a decision to cut taxes by about $9 billion.

THE CONSUMPTION FUNCTION AND THE MARGINAL PROPENSITY TO CONSUME

The **CONSUMPTION FUNCTION** is the relationship between total consumer expenditures and total disposable income in the economy, holding all other determinants of consumer spending constant.

It has been said that economics is just systematized common sense. Let us, then, try to organize and generalize what has been a completely intuitive discussion thus far. One thing we have learned is that there is a close and apparently reliable relationship between consumer spending, *C*, and disposable income, *DI*. Economists call this relationship the **consumption function.**

A second fact we have picked up from these figures is that the *slope* of the consumption function is fairly constant. We infer this from the fact that the straight line in Figure 7-4 comes so close to touching every point. If the slope of the consumption function had changed a lot, it would not be possible to do so well with a single straight line.[7] Because of its importance in such applications as the tax-cut example, economists have given a special name to this slope—the

TABLE 7-1 CONSUMPTION AND INCOME IN MACROLAND

Year	(1) Consumption, *C* (billions of dollars)	(2) Disposable Income, *DI* (billions of dollars)	(3) Marginal Propensity to Consume, MPC
1992	2,700	3,200	
1993	3,000	3,600	0.75
1994	3,300	4,000	0.75
1995	3,600	4,400	0.75
1996	3,900	4,800	0.75
1997	4,200	5,200	0.75

The **MARGINAL PROPENSITY TO CONSUME (MPC)** is the ratio of the change in consumption to the change in disposable income that produces the change in consumption. On a graph, it appears as the slope of the consumption function.

marginal propensity to consume, or **MPC** for short. The MPC tells us how much more consumers will spend if disposable income rises by $1.

$$\text{MPC} = \frac{\text{Change in C}}{\text{Change in } DI \text{ that produces the change in C}}$$

The MPC is best illustrated by an example, and for this purpose we turn away from U.S. data for a moment and look at the consumption and income data of a hypothetical country called Macroland (see Table 7-1). The data for Macroland resemble those for the United States, except that in Macroland, *C* and *DI* figures happen to be nice round numbers, which facilitates computation.

Columns 1 and 2 of Table 7-1 show annual consumer expenditure and disposable income from 1992 to 1997. These two columns constitute Macroland's consumption function and are plotted in Figure 7-5. Column 3 in the table shows the marginal propensity to consume (MPC), which is the slope of the line in Figure 7-5; it is derived from the first two columns. We can see that between 1994 and 1995, *DI* rose by $400 billion (from $4,000 billion to $4,400 billion) while *C* rose by $300 billion (from $3,300 billion to $3,600 billion). Thus, the MPC was:

$$\frac{\text{Change in C}}{\text{Change in } DI} = \frac{\$300}{\$400} = 0.75$$

As you can easily verify, the MPC between any other pair of years in Macroland is also 0.75. This explains why the slope of the line in Figure 7-4 was so crucial in estimating the effect of a tax cut. This slope, which we found to be 0.90, is nothing but the MPC for the United States. It is the MPC that tells us how much *additional* spending will be induced by each dollar *change* in disposable income. For each $1 of tax cut, economists expect consumption to rise by $1 times the marginal propensity to consume.

To estimate the *initial* effect of a tax cut on consumer spending, economists must first estimate the MPC and then multiply the amount of the tax cut by the estimated MPC. But since they never know the true MPC with certainty, this prediction is always subject to some margin of error.[8]

[7]Figure 7-4 is limited to 17 years of data, but try fitting a single straight line to all the data in Figure 7-3. You will find that you can do remarkably well.

[8]The word *initial* in the first sentence is an important one. Later chapters explain why the effects discussed in this chapter are only the beginning of the story.

FIGURE 7-5

THE CONSUMPTION FUNCTION OF MACROLAND

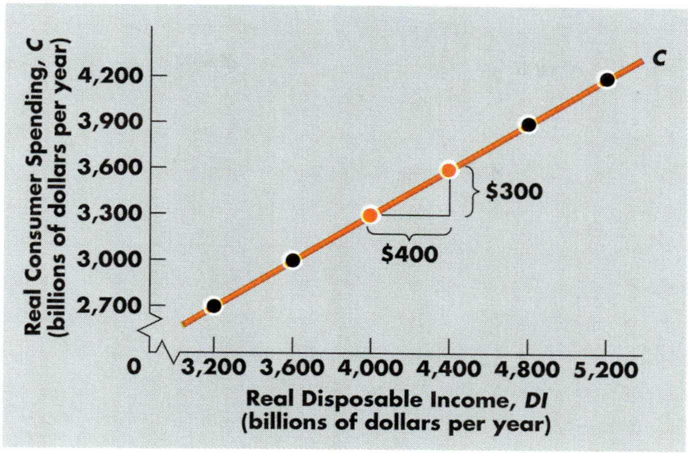

This diagram is similar to Figure 7-4, except that it applies to the hypothetical (and blissfully simple!) economy of Macroland. As can be seen, a straight-line consumption function passes through every point exactly. The slope of this line is 0.75, which is the marginal propensity to consume in Macroland.

In 1963, for example, economists multiplied the anticipated $9 billion tax cut by the estimated MPC of 0.90 and concluded that consumer spending would rise initially approximately $8 billion. Their estimate seems to have been quite accurate.

MOVEMENTS ALONG VERSUS SHIFTS OF THE CONSUMPTION FUNCTION

Unfortunately, this sort of calculation does not always yield such precise results. Among the most important reasons is that the consumption function does not always stand still. Sometimes it shifts.

You will recall from Chapter 4 the important distinction between a *movement along* a demand curve and a *shift* of the curve. A demand curve depicts the relationship between quantity demanded and *one* of its many determinants—price. Thus, a change in price causes a *movement along the demand curve,* but a change in any other factor that influences quantity demanded causes a *shift of the entire demand curve.*

Because consumer spending is influenced by factors other than disposable income, a similar distinction is vital to understanding real-world consumption functions. Look back at the definition of the consumption function in the margin of page 149. A change in disposable income leads to a *movement along the consumption function* precisely because the consumption function depicts the relationship between *C* and *DI*. (See the orange arrow in Figure 7-6.) This is what we have been considering so far. But consumption also has other determinants, and a change in any of these will *shift the entire consumption function*—as indicated by the blue arrows in Figure 7-6. These shifts account for many of the errors in forecasting consumption. To summarize:

Any change in disposable income moves us *along* a given consumption function. But a change in any of the other determinants of consumption *shifts* the entire consumption schedule (see Figure 7-6).

Let us now list some of these "other determinants" that can shift the consumption function.

FIGURE 7-6 SHIFTS OF THE CONSUMPTION FUNCTION

An increase in disposable income causes a movement along a fixed consumption function, such as the movement from point *A* to point *B* on consumption function C_0 (see the orange arrow). But a change in any other determinant of consumer spending will cause the whole consumption function to shift upward (C_1) or downward (C_2).

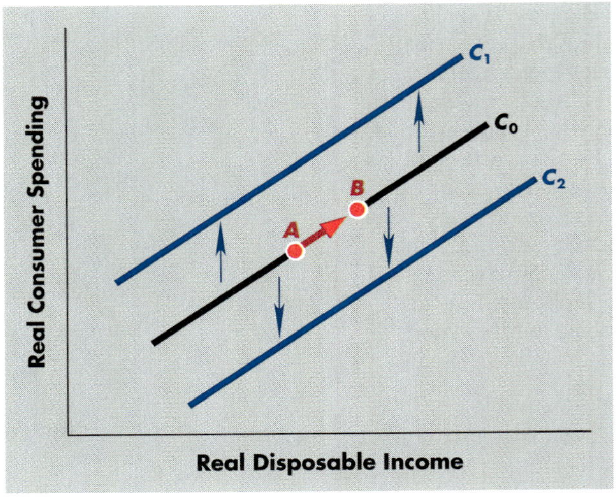

OTHER DETERMINANTS OF CONSUMER SPENDING

WEALTH

One factor affecting consumption is consumers' *wealth*, which is a source of purchasing power in addition to income. Wealth and income are different things. For example, a wealthy person who does not work, but has a healthy bank account, may have little current *income*. Similarly, a high-income individual who spends all she earns will not accumulate wealth. To appreciate the importance of the distinction, consider two consumers, both earning $35,000 this year. One of them has $100,000 in the bank, while the other has no assets at all. Who do you think will spend more this year? Presumably the one with the big bank account.

The general point is that current income is not the only source of funds that households have; they can also finance spending by withdrawals from their bank accounts or by cashing in other forms of wealth. A stock market boom may therefore raise the consumption function (see the shift from C_0 to C_1 in Figure 7-6), while a collapse of stock prices may lower it (see the shift from C_0 to C_2).

THE PRICE LEVEL

A good deal of consumer wealth is held in forms whose values are fixed in money terms. Cash itself is the most obvious example of this, but government bonds, bank accounts, and corporate bonds are all assets with fixed face values in money terms. The purchasing power of any *money fixed asset* obviously declines whenever the price level rises, which means that the asset can buy less. For example, if the price level rises by 10 percent, a $1,000 government bond will buy about 10 percent less than it could when prices were lower. Consequently:

Higher prices decrease the demand for goods and services by eroding the purchasing power of consumer wealth.

This is no trivial matter. Consumers in the United States hold money fixed assets worth over $5 *trillion,* so that each 1 percent rise in the price level reduces the purchasing power of consumer wealth by over $50 billion, a tidy sum. The process, of course, operates equally well in reverse. Since a decline in the price level increases the purchasing power of money fixed assets:

Lower prices increase the demand for goods and services by enhancing the purchasing power of consumer wealth.

For these reasons, a change in the price level will shift the entire consumption function. Specifically:

A higher price level leads to lower real wealth and therefore to less spending *at any given level of real income.* Thus, a higher price level leads to a lower consumption function (such as C_2 in Figure 7-6). Conversely, a lower price level leads to a higher consumption function (such as C_1 in Figure 7-6).

Students often get confused on this point, so it is worth repeating that the depressing effect of the price level on consumer spending works through real *wealth,* not through real *income.* The consumption function is a relationship between *real consumer income* and *real consumer spending.* Thus, any decline in real income, regardless of its cause, moves the economy leftward *along a fixed consumption function;* it does not shift the consumption function.[9] By contrast, any decline in *real wealth* will *shift the whole consumption function downward,* meaning that there is less spending at any given level of real income.

THE INFLATION RATE

Prices may be high and rising slowly, or they may be low but rising rapidly. Therefore, the depressing effect of a high *price level* on real consumer spending must be distinguished from any effect on spending of the *rate of inflation* (that is, the rate at which prices are rising).

If inflation has any effect on consumer spending, it must be small. Economists are not even sure whether inflation stimulates or depresses spending. It used to be thought that high rates of inflation induce consumers to spend faster to "beat" the higher prices that loom on the horizon. But changes in consumer behavior when inflation rose in the 1970s and then fell in the 1980s belied this idea. Consumers have actually spent a *higher* fraction of their disposable incomes since the 1980s, when inflation was lower, than they did in the inflationary 1970s.

Because there is no strong evidence that the rate of inflation shifts the consumption function systematically in one direction or the other, we shall assume that the position of the consumption function is influenced by the *price level,* but not by the *inflation rate.*

THE REAL RATE OF INTEREST

A higher real rate of interest raises the rewards for saving. For this reason, many people believe it is "obvious" that higher real interest rates must encourage saving, and therefore discourage spending. Statistical studies of this relationship suggest otherwise, however. With very few exceptions, they show that interest

[9]This is true even if a rise in the price level lies behind the decline in real income. However, wages and prices normally move together, so there is no reason to expect real wages to fall when the price level rises.

POLICY DEBATE **USING THE TAX CODE TO SPUR SAVING**

Compared to the citizens of most industrial nations, Americans save rather little—only about 5 percent of disposable income in recent years. Many policymakers consider this a serious problem, so they have proposed numerous changes in the tax laws to increase incentives to save. During the 1995 session of Congress alone, for example, bills were discussed (but not passed) to do each of the following:

- Expand Individual Retirement Accounts ("IRAs"), which allow taxpayers to shelter some earnings from income tax by saving it
- Replace the income tax with a tax on consumer spending
- Change the current income tax into a "flat tax" that exempts interest and dividends from taxation

Each of these proposals, and others like them, would increase the after-tax return on saving. For example, under the current tax system, if you put away money at a 6 percent rate of interest and your income is taxed at a 30 percent rate, your after-tax rate of return on saving is just 4.2 percent (70 percent of 6 percent). But, if interest were tax-free, you would keep the full 6 percent. Members of Congress who advocate tax incentives for saving argue that they will induce Americans to save more.

The idea is eminently reasonable and has many supporters. Unfortunately, the evidence is squarely against it. Economists have conducted many studies of the effect of higher rates of return on saving. With very few exceptions, they detect little or no effect. Although the evidence fails to support the "common-sense" solution to the undersaving problem, the debate goes on. Many people, it seems, refuse to believe the evidence.

rates have virtually no effect on consumption decisions in the United States. Hence, in developing our model of the economy, we will assume that changes in interest rates do not shift the consumption function. (See the Policy Debate box, above.)

EXPECTATIONS OF FUTURE INCOMES

It is hardly earth shattering to suggest that consumers' expectations about future incomes may affect how much they spend today. This final determinant of consumer spending turns out to hold the key to resolving the puzzle posed at the beginning of the chapter: Why did tax policy succeed so well in 1964 and the early 1980s, but fail to alter consumer spending much in 1975?

WHY TAX POLICY FAILED IN 1975

To understand how expectations of future incomes affect current consumer expenditures, consider the abbreviated life histories of three consumers given in Table 7-2. (The reason for giving our three imaginary individuals such odd names will be apparent shortly.) The consumer named "No Change" earned $100 in each of the 4 years considered in the table. The consumer named "Temporary Rise" earned $100 in 3 of the 4 years, but had a good year in 1975. The consumer named "Permanent Rise" enjoyed a permanent increase in income in 1975 and was clearly the richest.

Now let us use our common sense to figure out how much each of these consumers might have spent in 1975. Temporary Rise and Permanent Rise had the same income that year. Do you think they spent the same amount? Not if they had some ability to foresee their future incomes, because Permanent Rise was richer in the long run.

Now compare No Change and Temporary Rise. Temporary Rise had 20 percent higher income in 1975 ($120 versus $100) but only 5 percent more over the entire 4-year period ($420 versus $400). Do you think his spending in 1975 was

TABLE 7-2 INCOMES OF THREE CONSUMERS

	Incomes in Each Year				
Consumer	**1974**	**1975**	**1976**	**1977**	**Total Income**
No change	100	100	100	100	400
Temporary rise	100	120	100	100	420
Permanent rise	100	120	120	120	460

closer to 20 percent above No Change's or closer to 5 percent above it? Most people guess the latter.

The point of this example is that it is reasonable for consumers to decide on their *current* consumption spending by looking at their *long-run* income prospects. This should come as no surprise to a college student. Are you spending only what you earn this year? Probably not. But that does not make you a foolish spendthrift. On the contrary, you know that your college education gives you a reasonable expectation of a much higher income in the future, and you are spending with that in mind.

Now let us see what all this has to do with the failure of the 1975 income tax cut. For this purpose, imagine that the three rows in Table 7-2 now represent the entire economy under three different government policies. Recall that 1975 was the year of the temporary tax cut. The first row (No Change) shows the unchanged path of disposable income if no tax cut was enacted. The second (Temporary Rise) shows an increase in disposable income attributable to a tax cut *for 1 year only*. The bottom row (Permanent Rise) shows a policy that increases *DI* in *every future year* by cutting taxes permanently in 1975. Which of the two lower rows do you imagine would have generated more consumer spending in 1975? The bottom row (Permanent Rise), of course. What we have concluded, then, is this:

Permanent cuts in income taxes cause greater increases in consumer spending than do temporary cuts of equal magnitude.

The application of this analysis to the case of the 1975 tax cut is immediate. The tax rebates were clearly one-time increases in income like that experienced by Temporary Rise in Table 7-2. No future income was affected, and so consumers did not increase their spending as much as government officials had hoped. The general lesson is:

A permanent increase in income taxes provides a greater deterrent to consumer spending than does a temporary increase of equal magnitude.

We have, then, what appears to be a general principle, backed up both by historical evidence and common sense. Permanent changes in income taxes have a more significant impact on consumer spending than do temporary changes. Though it may now seem obvious, this is not a lesson you would have learned from the introductory textbooks of 25 years ago. It is one that we learned the hard way, through bitter experience.

THE PREDICTABILITY OF CONSUMER BEHAVIOR

We have now learned enough to see why the economist's problem in predicting how consumers will react to an increase or decrease in taxes is not nearly as simple as suggested earlier in this chapter.

The principal problem seems to be anticipating how taxpayers will view any changes in the income tax law. If the government *says* that a tax cut is permanent, will consumers *believe* it and increase their spending accordingly? Perhaps not, if the government has a history of raising taxes after promising to keep them low. Similarly, when (as in 1975) the government explicitly announces that a tax cut is temporary, will consumers always believe this? Or might they greet such an announcement with a hefty dose of skepticism? This is quite possible if there is a history of "temporary" tax changes that stayed on the books indefinitely.

Thus, the effectiveness of any *future* tax policy move may well depend on the government's *past* track record. A government that repeatedly uses a succession of so-called "permanent" tax cuts and tax increases for short-run stabilization purposes may find consumers beginning to ignore the tax changes entirely. The story of the boy who cried wolf should probably be required reading for fiscal policy planners.

Nor is this the only problem. Consumer spending may be influenced by large and rapid accumulations of wealth (as happened immediately after World War II) or by sizable losses of wealth (such as the drastic decline in the stock market in 1987). Poor forecasts of future prices may lead consumption forecasts astray. Also, there are other hazards that we have not even mentioned here. For example, economists still do not understand why household saving fell (that is, why spending rose) so much in the mid-1980s. Economic predictions are inexact, and predictions of consumption illustrate this well.

There is much more that could be said about the determinants of consumption, but it is best to leave the rest to more advanced courses. For we are now ready to apply our knowledge of the consumption function to the construction of the first model of the whole economy. While it is true that income determines consumption, the consumption function in turn helps to determine the level of income. If that sounds like circular reasoning, read the next chapter!

SUMMARY

1. **Aggregate demand** is the total volume of goods and services purchased by consumers, businesses, government units, and foreigners. It can be expressed as the sum $C + I + G + (X - IM)$, where C is **consumer spending,** I is **investment spending,** G is **government purchases,** and $X - IM$ is **net exports.**
2. Aggregate demand is a schedule: the aggregate quantity demanded depends (among other things) on the price level. But, for any given price level, aggregate demand is a number.
3. Economists reserve the term *investment* to refer to purchases of newly produced factories, machinery, and houses.
4. Domestic product is the total volume of final goods and services produced in the country. It is most commonly measured by the gross domestic product.
5. **National income** is the sum of the *before-tax* wages, interest, rents, and profits earned by all individuals in the economy. By necessity, it must be approximately equal to domestic product.
6. **Disposable income** is the sum of the incomes of all individuals in the economy *after taxes and transfers.* It is the chief determinant of consumer expenditures.
7. All of these concepts, and others, can be depicted in a *circular flow diagram* that shows expenditures on all four sources flowing into business firms and national income flowing out.

8. The close relationship between consumer spending, *C*, and disposable income, *DI*, is called the **consumption function.** Its slope, which is used to predict the change in consumption that will be caused by a change in income taxes, is called the **marginal propensity to consume (MPC).**
9. Changes in disposable income move us *along a given consumption function*. Changes in any of the other variables that affect *C shift the entire consumption function*. Among the most important of these other variables are total consumer wealth, the price level, and expected future incomes.
10. Because consumers hold so many money fixed assets, they lose purchasing power when prices rise, which leads them to reduce their spending.
11. The government often has tried to manipulate aggregate demand by influencing private consumption decisions, usually through changes in the personal income tax. Although this policy seemed to work well in 1964 and 1981, it did not work well in 1975.
12. Future income prospects help explain these disparate events. The 1975 tax cut was temporary, and therefore left future incomes unaffected. By contrast, the 1964 and 1981–1984 tax cuts were permanent, and affected future as well as current incomes. It is no surprise, then, that the 1964 and 1981 actions had stronger effects on spending than did the 1975 action.

KEY TERMS

Aggregate demand
Consumer expenditure (*C*)
Investment spending (*I*)
Government purchases (*G*)
Net exports ($X - IM$)
$C + I + G + (X - IM)$
National income
Disposable income (*DI*)
Circular flow diagram
Transfer payments
Scatter diagram
Consumption function
Marginal propensity to consume (MPC)
Movements along versus shifts of the consumption function
Money fixed assets
Temporary versus permanent tax changes

QUESTIONS FOR REVIEW

1. What are the four components of aggregate demand? Which of these is the largest? Which is the smallest?
2. What is the difference between "investment" as the term is used by most people and "investment" as defined by an economist? Which of the following acts constitute investment according to the economist's definition?
   a. IBM opens a new factory to assemble personal computers.
   b. You buy 100 shares of IBM stock.
   c. A small computer company goes bankrupt, and IBM purchases its factory and equipment.
   d. Your family buys a newly constructed home from a developer.
   e. Your family buys an older home from another family. (*Hint:* Are any *new* products demanded by this action?)
3. What would the circular flow diagram (Figure 7-1, page 145) look like in an economy with no government? Draw one for yourself.
4. The marginal propensity to consume (MPC) for the nation as a whole is roughly 0.90. Explain in words what this means. What is your personal MPC?
5. Look at the scatter diagram in Figure 7-3 (page 148). What does it tell you about what was going on in this country in the years 1942 to 1945?
6. What is a consumption function, and why is it a useful device for government economists planning a tax cut?
7. On a piece of graph paper, construct the consumption function for Simpleland from the data given below and determine the MPC.

Year	Consumer Spending	Disposable Income
1991	1,200	1,500
1992	1,440	1,800
1993	1,680	2,100
1994	1,920	2,400
1995	2,160	2,700

8. In which direction will the consumption function for Simpleland shift if the price level rises? Show this on your graph.
9. Explain why permanent tax cuts are likely to lead to bigger increases in consumer spending than are temporary tax cuts.

10. (More difficult) Between 1990 and 1991, real disposable income (in 1992 dollars) rose only from $4,485 billion to $4,486 billion, owing to a recession. Use the data on real consumption expenditures given on the inside front cover of this book to compare the change in C to the change in DI. Explain why dividing the two does *not* give a good estimate of the marginal propensity to consume.

11. In 1995, several tax bills were debated in Congress that would have provided greater tax incentives for saving. (None were enacted.) If such saving incentives had been enacted, and had been successful, how would the consumption function have shifted?

APPENDIX NATIONAL INCOME ACCOUNTING

The type of macroeconomic analysis presented in this book dates from the publication of John Maynard Keynes's *The General Theory of Employment, Interest, and Money* in 1936. But at that time there was really no way to test Keynes's theories because the necessary data did not exist. It took some years for the theoretical notions used by Keynes to find concrete expression in real-world data.

The system of measurement devised for expressing data is called **national income accounting.**

The development of this system of accounts ranks as a great achievement in applied economics, perhaps as important in its own right as Keynes's theoretical work. Without it the practical value of Keynesian analysis would be severely limited. Economists spent long hours wrestling with the many difficult conceptual questions that arose in translating the theory into numbers, but they had one acknowledged leader: the late Professor Simon Kuznets, who was subsequently awarded the Nobel Prize in economics for his contributions to economic measurement techniques. Along the way some more-or-less arbitrary decisions and conventions had to be made. You may not agree with all of them, but the accounting framework that was devised is eminently serviceable, though, inevitably, it has some limitations that must be understood.

DEFINING GDP: EXCEPTIONS TO THE RULES

We first encountered the concept of gross domestic product (GDP) in Chapter 2.

Gross domestic product (GDP) is the sum of the money values of all final goods and services produced during a specified period of time, usually 1 year.

However, the definition of GDP has certain exceptions that we have not yet noted.

First, the treatment of government output involves a minor departure from the principle of using market prices. Outputs of private industries are sold on markets, so their prices are observed. But "outputs" of government offices are not sold; indeed, it is sometimes even difficult to define what those outputs are. Lacking prices for outputs, national income accountants fall back on the only prices they have: prices for the inputs from which the outputs are produced. Thus:

Government outputs are valued at the cost of the inputs needed to produce them.

This means, for example, that if a clerk at the Department of Motor Vehicles earns $10 an hour and spends one-half hour torturing you with explanations of why you cannot get a driver's license, that particular government "service" is considered as being worth $5, and it increases GDP by that amount.

Second, some goods that are produced during the year but not yet sold are nonetheless counted in that year's GDP. Specifically, goods that firms add to their *inventories* count in the GDP even though they do not pass through markets.

National income statisticians treat inventories as if they were "bought" by the firms that produced them, even though this "purchase" does not take place.

Finally, the treatment of investment goods runs slightly counter to the rule that only final goods are to be counted. In a broad sense, factories, generators, machine tools, and the like might be considered as intermediate goods. After all, their owners want them only for use in producing other goods, not for any innate value that they possess. But this would present a real problem. Since factories and machines normally are never sold to consumers, when would we count them in GDP? National income statisticians avoid this problem by defining investment goods as final products demanded by the firms that buy them.

Now that we have a more complete definition of what the GDP is, let us turn to the problem of actually measuring it. National income accountants have devised three ways to perform this task, and we consider each in turn.

GDP AS THE SUM OF FINAL GOODS AND SERVICES

The first way to measure GDP seems to be the most natural, since it follows so directly from the circular flow diagram in this chapter. It also turns out to be the most useful definition for macroeconomic analysis. We simply add up the final demands of all consumers, business firms, government, and foreigners. Using the symbols Y, C, I, G, and $(X - IM)$ just as we did in the text, we have:

$$Y = C + I + G + (X - IM)$$

The I that appears in the actual U.S. national accounts is called **gross private domestic investment.**

The word *gross* will be explained presently. *Private* indicates that government investment is considered part of G, and *domestic* just means that machinery sold by American firms to foreign companies is included in exports rather than in I. Gross private domestic investment in the United States has three components: business investment in plant and equipment, residential construction (home building), and inventory investment. We repeat again that *only* these three things are *investment* in national income accounting terminology.

As defined in the national income accounts, *investment* includes only newly produced capital goods, such as machinery, factories, and new homes. It does not include exchanges of existing assets.

The symbol G, for government purchases, represents the *volume of current goods and services purchased by all levels of government*. Thus, anything that the government pays to its employees is counted in G, as are all of its purchases of goods.

Few citizens realize, however, that *most of what the federal government spends its money on is not for purchases of goods and services*. Instead, it is on *transfer payments*—literally, giving away money—either to individuals or to other levels of government.

The importance of the conceptual distinction lies in the fact that G represents the part of the national product that government uses up for its own purposes—to pay for armies, bureaucrats, paper, and ink—whereas transfer payments merely represent shuffling of purchasing power from one group of citizens to another group. Except for the administrators needed to run the programs, real economic resources are not used up in this process.

In adding up the nation's total output as the sum of $C + I + G + (X - IM)$, we are summing the shares of GDP that are used up by consumers, investors, government, and foreigners, respectively. Since transfer payments merely give someone the capability to spend on C, it is logical to exclude them from our definition of G, including in C only the portion of these transfer payments that is spent. If we included them in G, the same spending would get counted twice: once in G and then again in C.

The final component of GDP is net exports, which are simply exports of goods and services minus imports of goods and services. Table 7-3 shows GDP for 1995, in both nominal and real terms, computed as the sum of $C + I + G + (X - IM)$. You will note that the numbers for net exports in the table are actually negative. We will have much to say about America's trade deficit in Part IV.

GDP AS THE SUM OF ALL FACTOR PAYMENTS

There is another way to count up the GDP—by *adding up all the incomes in the economy*. Let's see how this method handles some typical transactions. Suppose that General Electric builds a generator and sells it to General Motors for $1 million. The first method of calculating GDP simply counts the $1 million as part of I. The second method asks: What incomes resulted from the production of this generator? The answer might be something like this:

Wages of GE employees	$400,000
Interest to bondholders	50,000
Rentals of buildings	50,000
Profits of GE stockholders	100,000

TABLE 7-3

GROSS DOMESTIC PRODUCT IN 1995 AS THE SUM OF FINAL DEMANDS

Item	Amount (billions of current dollars)	Amount (billions of 1992 dollars)
Personal consumption expenditures (*C*)	4,924.3	4,578.5
Gross private domestic investment (*I*)	1,065.3	1,011.5
Government purchases of goods and services (*G*)	1,358.5	1,260.7
Net exports (*X* − *IM*)	−102.3	−114.2
Exports (*X*)	804.5	774.8
Imports (*IM*)	906.7	888.9
Gross domestic product (*Y*)	7,245.8	6,739.0

SOURCE: U.S. Department of Commerce. Totals do not add up precisely due to rounding.

The total is $600,000. The remaining $400,000 is accounted for by inputs that GE purchased from other companies: steel, circuitry, tubing, rubber, and so on.

But if we traced this $400,000 back further, we would find that it is accounted for by the wages, interest, and rentals paid by these other companies, *plus* their profits, *plus* their purchases from other firms. In fact, for *every* firm in the economy, there is an accounting identity that says:

Revenues from sales = Wages paid + Interest paid + Rentals paid + Profits earned + Purchases from other firms

Why must this always be true? Because profits are the balancing item; they are what is *left over* after the firm has made all its other payments. In fact, this accounting identity is really just a reorganization of the definition of profits: sales revenue less all costs of production.

Now apply this accounting identity to *all firms in the economy*. Total purchases from other firms are precisely what we call *intermediate goods*. What, then, do we get if we subtract these intermediate transactions from both sides of the equation?

Revenues from sales *minus* Purchases from other firms = Wages paid + Interest paid + Rentals paid + Profits earned

On the right-hand side, we have the sum of all factor incomes: payments to labor, land, and capital. On the left-hand side, we have total sales minus sales of intermediate goods. This means that we have only sales of *final* goods, which is precisely our definition of GDP. Thus, the accounting identity for the entire economy can be rewritten as:

GDP = Wages + Interest + Rents + Profits

and this gives national income accountants another way to measure the GDP.

Table 7-4 shows 1995's GDP measured by the sum of all incomes. Once again, we have omitted a few details in our discussion. The sum of wages, interest, rents, and profits actually adds up to only $5,799 billion (whereas GDP is $7,246 billion). We call this sum *national income* because it is the sum of all factor payments. But the actual selling prices of goods include another category of expense that we have ignored so far: sales taxes, excise taxes, and the like.

National income statisticians call these taxes *indirect business taxes*, and when we add them to national income, we obtain the **net national product (NNP).**

Notice here the use of the adjective *national* rather than *domestic*. When we add up all the wages, interest, rents, and profits received by Americans, we will inevitably include some payments derived from production in other countries. Similarly, some of the factor payments made by American businesses go to citizens of other countries.

If we subtract the former and add back the latter, we change net *national* product into **net domestic product (NDP).**

TABLE 7-4

GROSS DOMESTIC PRODUCT IN 1995 AS THE SUM OF INCOMES

Item	Amount (billions of dollars)	
Compensation of employees (wages)	4,209.1	
plus		
Net interest	401.0	
plus		
Rental income	122.2	
plus		
Profits	1,066.9	
Corporate profits		588.6
Proprietors' income		478.3
equals		
National income	5,799.2	
plus		
Indirect business taxes and miscellaneous items	612.4	
equals		
National net product	6,411.6	
minus		
income received from other countries	206.7	
plus		
income paid to other countries	215.0	
equals		
Net domestic product	6,419.9	
plus		
Depreciation	825.9	
equals		
Gross domestic product	7,245.8	

SOURCE: U.S. Department of Commerce. Totals do not add up precisely due to rounding.

Now we are almost at the GDP. The only difference between GDP and NDP is depreciation of the nation's capital stock.

Depreciation is the value of the portion of the nation's capital equipment that is used up within the year. It tells us how much output is needed just to keep the economy's capital stock intact.

The difference between gross and net simply refers to whether depreciation is included or excluded. We add depreciation to NDP to get GDP. Thus, GDP is a measure of all final output, taking no account of the capital used up in the process (and therefore in need of replacement). NDP deducts the required replacements to arrive at a *net* production figure.

From a conceptual point of view, most economists feel that NDP is a more meaningful indicator of the economy's output than GDP. After all, the depreciation component of GDP represents the output that is needed just to repair and replace worn-out factories and machines; it is not available for anybody to consume.[10] Therefore, NDP seems to be a better measure of well-being than GDP. But, alas, GDP is much easier to measure because depreciation is a particularly tricky item. What fraction of his tractor did Farmer Jones "use up" last year? How much did the Empire State Building depreciate during 1996? If you ask yourself these difficult questions, you will understand why most economists feel that GDP is measured more accurately

[10]If the capital stock is used for consumption, it will decline, and the nation will wind up poorer than before.

than is NDP. For this reason, most economic models are based on GDP.

In Table 7-4, you can hardly help noticing the preponderant share of employee compensation in total national income—almost 73 percent. Labor is by far the most important factor of production. The return on land is just 2 percent of national income, and interest accounts for about 7 percent. Profits account for the remaining 18 percent, though the size of corporate profits (less than 9 percent of GDP) is much less than the public thinks. If, by some magic stroke, we could eliminate all corporate profits without upsetting the performance of the economy, the average worker would get a raise of about 11 percent!

GDP AS THE SUM OF VALUES ADDED

It may strike you as strange that national income accountants include only *final* goods and services in GDP. Aren't *intermediate* goods part of the nation's product? They are, of course. The problem is that, if all intermediate goods were included in GDP, we would wind up double and triple counting things and therefore get an exaggerated impression of the actual level of economic activity.

To explain why, and to show how national income accountants cope with this difficulty, we must introduce a new concept, called *value added.*

The **value added** by a firm is its revenue from selling a product minus the amount paid for goods and services purchased from other firms.

The intuitive sense of the concept is clear: if a firm buys some inputs from other firms, does something to them, and sells the resulting product for a price higher than it paid for the inputs, we say that the firm has "added value" to the product. If we sum up the values added in this way by all the firms in the economy, we must get the total value of all final products. Thus:

GDP can be measured as the sum of the values added by all firms.

To verify this, look back at the second accounting identity on page 160. The left-hand side of this equation, sales revenue minus purchases from other firms, is precisely the firm's value added. Thus:

$$\text{Value added} = \text{Wages} + \text{Interest} + \text{Rents} + \text{Profits}$$

Since the second method we gave for measuring GDP is to add up wages, interest, rents, and profits, we see that the value-added approach must also yield the same answer.

The value-added concept is useful in avoiding double counting. Often, however, it is hard to distinguish intermediate goods from final goods. Paint bought by a painter, for example, is an intermediate good. But paint bought by a do-it-yourselfer is a final good. What happens, then, if the professional painter buys some paint to refurbish his own garage? The intermediate good becomes a final good. You can see that the line between intermediate goods and final goods is a fuzzy one in practice.

If we measure GDP by the sum of values added, however, it is not necessary to make such subtle distinctions. In this method, *every* purchase of a new good or service counts, but we do not count the entire selling price, only the portion that represents value added.

To illustrate this idea, consider the data in Table 7-5 and how they would affect GDP as the sum of final products. Our example begins when a farmer who grows soybeans sells them to a mill for $3 a bushel. This transaction does *not* count in the GDP, because the miller does not purchase the soybeans

TABLE 7-5 AN ILLUSTRATION OF FINAL AND INTERMEDIATE GOODS

Item	Seller	Buyer	Price
Bushel of soybeans	Farmer	Miller	$ 3
Bag of soy meal	Miller	Factory	4
Gallon of soy sauce	Factory	Restaurant	8
Gallon of soy sauce used as seasoning	Restaurant	Consumers	$10
			Total: $25

Addendum: Contribution to GDP: $10

TABLE 7-6 AN ILLUSTRATION OF VALUE ADDED

Item	Seller	Buyer	Price	Value Added
Bushel of soybeans	Farmer	Miller	$ 3	$ 3
Bag of soy meal	Miller	Factory	4	1
Gallon of soy sauce	Factory	Restaurant	8	4
Gallon of soy sauce used as seasoning	Restaurant	Consumers	10	2
			Total: $25	$10

Addendum: Contribution to GDP

Final products	$10
Sum of values added	$10

for his own use. The miller then grinds up the soybeans and sells the resulting bag of soy meal to a factory that produces soy sauce. The miller receives $4, but GDP still has not increased because the ground beans are also an intermediate product. Next, the factory turns the beans into soy sauce, which it sells to your favorite Chinese restaurant for $8. Still no effect on GDP.

But then the big moment arrives: The restaurant sells the sauce to you and other customers as a part of your meals, and you eat it. At this point, the $10 worth of soy sauce becomes a final product and is included in the GDP. Notice that if we had also counted the three intermediate transactions (farmer to miller, miller to factory, factory to restaurant), we would have come up with $25—2-1/2 times too much.

Why is it too much? The reason is straightforward. Neither the miller, the factory owner, nor the restaurateur values the product we have been considering *for its own sake.* Only the customers who eat the final product (the soy sauce) have had an increase in their material well-being, so only this last transaction counts in the GDP. However, as we shall now see, value-added calculations enable us to come up with the right answer ($10) by counting only *part* of each transaction. The basic idea is to count at each step only the contribution to the value of the ultimate final product that is made at that step, excluding the values of items produced at earlier steps.

Ignoring the minor items (such as fertilizer) that the farmer purchases from others, the entire $3 selling price of the bushel of soybeans is new output produced by the farmer; that is, the whole $3 is value added. The miller then grinds the beans and sells them for $4. He has added $4 minus $3, or $1 to the value of the beans. When the factory turns this soy meal into soy sauce and sells it for $8, it has added $8 minus $4, or $4 more in value. Finally, when the restaurant sells it to hungry customers for $10, a further $2 of value is added.

The last column of Table 7-6 shows this chain of creation of value added. We see that the total value added by all four firms is $10, exactly the same as the restaurant's selling price. This is as it must be, for only the restaurant sells the soybeans as a final product.

SUMMARY

1. Gross domestic product (GDP) is the sum of the money values of all final goods and services produced during a year and sold on organized markets. There are, however, certain exceptions to this definition.
2. One way to measure the GDP is to add up the final demands of consumers, investors, government, and foreigners: GDP $= C + I + G + (X - IM)$.
3. A second way to measure the GDP is to start with all the factor payments—wages, interest, rents, and profits—that constitute the national income and then add indirect business taxes and depreciation.
4. A third way to measure the GDP is to sum up the values added by every firm in the economy (and then once again add indirect business taxes and depreciation).
5. Except for possible bookkeeping and statistical errors, all three methods must give the same answer.

KEY TERMS

National income accounting
Gross domestic product (GDP)
Gross private domestic investment
Government purchases
Transfer payments
Net exports
National income
Net national product (NNP)
Net domestic product (NDP)
Depreciation
Value added
Personal income
Disposable income (*DI*)

QUESTIONS FOR REVIEW

1. Which of the following transactions are included in the gross domestic product, and by how much does each raise GDP?
   a. You buy a new Chevrolet, paying $12,000.
   b. You buy a new Toyota, imported from Japan, paying $17,000.
   c. You buy a used Chevrolet, paying $3,000.
   d. Ford builds a $100 million factory to make cars.
   e. Your grandmother receives a government Social Security check for $1,200.
   f. Chrysler manufactures 1,000 automobiles at a cost of $12,000 each. Unable to sell them, it holds them as inventories.
   g. Mr. Black and Mr. Blue, each out for a Sunday drive, have a collision in which their cars are destroyed. Black and Blue each hire a lawyer to sue the other, paying the lawyers $3,000 each for services rendered. The judge throws the case out of court.
   g. You sell a used refrigerator to your friend for $40.
2. Explain the difference between final goods and intermediate goods. Why is it sometimes difficult to apply this distinction in practice? In this regard, why is the concept of value added useful?
3. Explain the difference between government spending and government purchases of goods and services (*G*). Which is larger?
4. Explain why national income and gross domestic product would be essentially equal if there were no depreciation and no indirect business taxes.
5. The following outline provides a complete description of all economic activity in Trivialand for 1996. Draw up versions of Tables 7-3 and 7-4 for Trivialand showing GDP computed in two different ways.
   a. There are thousands of farmers but only two big business firms in Trivialand: Specific Motors (an auto company) and Super Duper (a chain of food markets). There is no government and no depreciation.
   b. Specific Motors produced 1,000 small cars, which it sold at $6,000 each, and 100 trucks, which it sold at $8,000 each. Consumers bought 800 of the cars, and the remaining 200 cars were exported to the United States. Super Duper bought all the trucks.
   c. Sales at Super Duper markets amounted to $14 million, all of it sold to consumers.
   d. All the farmers in Trivialand are self-employed and sell all their wares to Super Duper.
   e. The costs incurred by all the businesses were as follows:

	Specific Motors	Super Duper	Farmers
Wages	$3,800,000	$4,500,000	$2,000,000
Interest	100,000	200,000	700,000
Rent	200,000	1,000,000	2,000,000
Purchases of food	0	7,000,000	0

6. (More difficult) Now complicate Trivialand in the following ways and answer the same questions. In addition, calculate national income and disposable income.
   a. The government bought 50 cars, leaving only 150 cars for export. In addition, the government spent $800,000 on wages and it made $1,200,000 in transfer payments.
   b. Depreciation for the year amounted to $600,000 for Specific Motors and $200,000 for Super Duper. (The farmers had no depreciation.)
   c. The government levied sales taxes amounting to $500,000 on Specific Motors and $200,000 on Super Duper (none on farmers). In addition, the government levied a 10 percent income tax on all wages, interest, and rental income.
   d. In addition to the food and cars mentioned in Review Question 5, consumers in Trivialand imported 500 computers from the United States at $2,000 each.

CHAPTER 8

DEMAND-SIDE EQUILIBRIUM: UNEMPLOYMENT OR INFLATION?

Investment . . . is a flighty bird, which needs to be controlled.
J. R. Hicks

We learned in Chapter 5 that the interaction of aggregate demand and aggregate supply determines whether the economy will stagnate or prosper, whether our labor and capital resources will be fully employed or unemployed. And we learned in Chapter 7 that aggregate demand has four components: consumer expenditure (C), investment (I), government purchases (G), and net exports ($X - IM$). It is now time to start building a theory that puts all the pieces together.

Our approach is sequential. Since it is necessary to walk before you can run, we imagine in this chapter that the price level, the rate of interest, and the international value of the dollar are all constant. None of these assumptions are true, of course, and we will dispense with each later. But these three unrealistic assumptions enable us to construct a simple but useful model of how the state of aggregate demand influences the level of gross domestic product (GDP). In this simple model, only C is variable; the other three components of spending—I, G, and $X - IM$—are all assumed to be fixed.

Subsequent chapters will drop the three unrealistic assumptions in turn. In Chapter 10, we will bring in the supply side of the economy, which enables us to treat the price level as variable rather than constant. In Chapter 13, we will see how interest rates—and hence investment—are determined. Finally, Chapters 18 and 19 bring the exchange rate into the picture and study the determination of net exports.

But first things first. This chapter begins by examining the most volatile component of aggregate demand: investment. What factors determine investment spending, and why is it so variable and hard to predict?[1] Then we add net exports and

[1]We repeat the warning given in the previous chapter about the meaning of the word *investment*. It *includes* spending by businesses and individuals on *newly produced* factories, machinery, and houses. But it *excludes* sales of used industrial plants, equipment, and homes, and it *also excludes* purely financial transactions, such as the purchases of stocks and bonds.

government purchases to the model. Treating *I*, *G*, and *X* − *IM* as constants, we next see how equilibrium is established on the demand side of the economy. Finally, we consider a question of great importance to policymakers: Can the economy be expected to achieve full employment of its resources if the government does not intervene?

A PUZZLE: WHY DOES THE MARKET PERMIT UNEMPLOYMENT?

Economists are fond of pointing out—with some awe—the amazing achievements of free markets. Without central direction, they somehow get businesses to produce just the goods and services that consumers want—and to do so cheaply and efficiently. If consumers want less meat and more fish, markets respond; if people subsequently change their minds, markets respond again. Free markets seem to coordinate literally millions of decisions effortlessly and seamlessly.

Yet for hundreds of years and all over the globe, market economies have stumbled over one particular coordination problem: the periodic bouts of mass unemployment that we call *recessions* and *depressions*. Widespread unemployment represents a failure to coordinate economic activity in the following sense. If the unemployed were hired, they would be able to buy the goods and services that businesses cannot sell; revenues from those sales would, in turn, allow firms to pay the workers. So a seemingly straightforward "deal" offers jobs for the unemployed and sales for the firms. But somehow this deal is not consummated. Workers remain unemployed and firms get stuck with unsold output.

Thus, free markets, which somehow get rough diamonds dug out of the ground in South Africa and turned into beautiful rings that are bought for brides in Los Angeles, cannot seem to solve the coordination problem posed by unemployment. Why not? For centuries, economists puzzled over this question. By the end of the chapter, you will be well on the way toward providing an answer.

THE EXTREME VARIABILITY OF INVESTMENT

The first thing to be said about investment spending is that it is extraordinarily variable.

In Chapter 7, we learned that consumer spending follows movements in disposable income with great (though not perfect) reliability. Investment spending is quite different: It swings from high to low levels with astonishing speed. For example, when the U.S. economy declined a scant 1 percent (as measured by real GDP) between 1990 and 1991, real investment spending dropped a hefty 9.7 percent. Then, when the overall economy "boomed" at a 3.5 percent rate from 1993 to 1994, investment soared 14.3 percent. (See the box on the next page.) What accounts for these wide swings in investment spending?

BUSINESS CONFIDENCE AND EXPECTATIONS ABOUT THE FUTURE

While many factors influence business people's desires to invest, Keynes stressed the importance of the *state of business confidence*, which in turn depends on *expectations about the future.*

THE INVESTMENT BOOM OF THE NINETIES

Since the U.S. economy emerged from the recession of 1990–1991, investment spending has been rising at rates rarely seen since World War II. Between 1992 and 1994, outlays for such things as high-tech plants and computer-driven machinery jumped 20 percent. This surge in investment helped to boost productivity and fuel economic growth.

The last time investment spending rose at such a rapid pace was the 1960s, a time when the United States was the unquestioned powerhouse of the world economy. But back then, businesses were mainly looking for ways to increase production. Now the emphasis is on competing in the global market. Companies know they must efficiently create the highest-quality goods or services, create them on time, and exactly to customer specifications. If they do not, there are plenty of foreign and domestic firms ready to take their business away.

Technology is also fueling the boom. Although it may not be good news to some workers, many service companies have found that capital investments make more sense than maintaining large staffs. With modern equipment, factories and offices function better, faster, and more cheaply. Factories are being transformed through investments in new software and automation equipment. By embracing the latest technology, firms are becoming leaner and more efficient producers.

SOURCE: Joseph Spiers, "The Most Important Economic Event of the Decade," *Fortune*, April 3, 1995, p. 33.

While tricky to measure, it does seem obvious that businesses will build more factories and purchase more new machines when they are optimistic. Conversely, their investment plans will be very cautious if the economic outlook appears bleak. Keynes pointed out that psychological perceptions like these are subject to abrupt shifts, so that fluctuations in investment can be a major cause of instability in aggregate demand. Hence Hicks's analogy to a "flighty bird" in the chapter's opening quotation.

Unfortunately, neither economists nor, for that matter, psychologists have many good ideas about how to *measure*—much less *control*—business confidence. Therefore, economists usually focus on several more objective determinants of investment—determinants that are easier to quantify and, perhaps even more important, are more easily influenced by government policy.

THE LEVEL AND GROWTH OF DEMAND

Firms have strong incentives to invest when demand is pressing against capacity. Under these circumstances, business executives are likely to feel that new factories and machinery can be employed profitably. So, for example, firms like Intel and Motorola have recently been investing heavily in new plants to produce microchips. By contrast, if there is a great deal of unused machinery, empty factories, and the like, managers may not find investment opportunities very attractive.

Because it takes a substantial amount of time to order machinery or to build a factory, *investment plans are made with an eye on the future.* Even when pressures on current capacity are not particularly severe, a firm that is expecting rapid growth in sales may start investing now in order to have adequate capacity for the future. Furthermore, briskly growing sales are likely to make business people more optimistic. Conversely, slow growth of output will discourage investment. In sum:

High levels of sales relative to current capacity and expectations of rapid economic growth create an atmosphere favorable to investment. Low levels of sales and slow anticipated growth are likely to discourage investment.

Government stabilization policy thus has an indirect handle on investment spending. By stimulating aggregate demand, it can induce business firms to invest more, though the precise amount may be hard to predict.

TECHNICAL CHANGE AND PRODUCT INNOVATION

Some investments are driven by technology. New investment opportunities suddenly appear when a new product like the mobile telephone is invented, or when a technological breakthrough makes an existing product much cheaper or better, as happened with microcomputers. In our capitalist market system, entrepreneurs seize these opportunities quickly, building new factories, stores, and offices. These new investments need not be "high tech." The VCR, for example, spawned an entire service industry of video rental shops that now dot the American landscape. Two decades ago, such stores did not even exist.

THE REAL RATE OF INTEREST

The real interest rate is the determinant of investment that will play the pivotal role in later chapters. When interest rates rise, investment falls, and it is not hard to see why. A good deal of business investment is financed by borrowing, and the interest rate indicates how much firms pay for that privilege. Some investment projects that yield a profit at an interest rate of 6 percent will be money-losers if the firm has to pay 10 percent.

The amount that businesses will want to invest depends on the real interest rate they must pay on their borrowings. The lower the real rate of interest, the more investment spending there will be.

In Chapter 13, we will study in some detail how the government can influence the rate of interest. Since interest rates affect investment, policymakers have another handle on aggregate demand—a handle they do not hesitate to use. The point is that—unlike business confidence, expectations, and technology—interest rates are visible and can be manipulated. Therefore, even if investment is much more sensitive to changes in confidence than to changes in interest rates, interest rates are nonetheless a more important instrument of government policy. But this is a topic for later in the book.

TAX PROVISIONS

The government has still another important way to influence investment spending—by altering various provisions of the tax law. For example, President Clinton and the Republican Congress locked horns in 1995 over the advisability of reducing the tax rate on *capital gains*—the profit earned by selling an asset for more than you paid for it. Perhaps the principal argument on the Republican side was that lower capital gains taxes would lead to greater investment spending. But Democrats disputed that claim, and no changes were made.

In addition, there is a *tax on corporate profits,* which the government can reduce to spur investment—as it did in 1986. There are other, more complicated, tax provisions, as well. To summarize:

The tax law gives the government several ways to influence business spending on investment goods. But influence is far from control. Investment remains a "flighty bird."

THE DETERMINANTS OF NET EXPORTS

Another highly variable source of demand for U.S. products is foreign purchases of U.S. goods—our *exports.* However, as we learned in Chapter 7, to obtain the net contribution of foreigners to aggregate demand in the United States we must subtract *imports,* which is the portion of domestic demand that is satisfied by foreign producers.

NATIONAL INCOMES

While both exports and imports depend on many factors, the predominant one is *national income.* When consumption and investment spending by American consumers and firms rise, some of the increased spending is on foreign goods. Therefore:

Our imports rise when our GDP rises and fall when our GDP falls.

Similarly, our *exports* are the *imports* of other countries, so it is natural to assume that our exports depend on *their* GDPs, not on our own. Thus:

Our exports are relatively insensitive to our own GDP, but are quite sensitive to the GDPs of other countries.

Putting these two ideas together leads to a clear implication: When our economy grows faster than those of our trading partners, our net exports tend to shrink. Conversely, when foreign economies grow faster than ours, our net exports tend to rise.

RELATIVE PRICES AND EXCHANGE RATES

While GDP levels at home and abroad are important influences on a country's net exports, they are not the only relevant factors. International price differences matter, too. To make things concrete, let us focus on trade between the United States and Japan. Suppose that the prices of American goods rise while Japanese prices are constant. Then U.S. products become more expensive *relative to Japanese goods.* If American consumers react to the new relative prices by buying more Japanese goods, our *imports rise.* If Japanese consumers react to the same relative price changes by buying fewer American products, our *exports fall.* Both reactions reduce America's net exports.

Naturally, the effects of a decline in American prices are precisely the opposite: Exports are stimulated and imports are discouraged, so net exports rise. Thus:

A rise in the prices of a country's goods will lead to a reduction in that country's net exports. Analogously, a fall in the prices of a country's goods will raise that country's net exports.

Since trade patterns are governed by the prices of one country's goods *relative to* those of other countries, precisely the same logic applies to changes in Japanese prices. If Japanese prices fall while U.S. prices remain constant, Americans will import more and export less, so net exports ($X - IM$) will decline. By similar reasoning, rising Japanese prices increase U.S. net exports. Thus:

Price increases abroad raise a country's net exports while price decreases abroad have the opposite effect.

This simple idea holds the key to understanding how rates of exchange among the world's currencies influence exports and imports—a topic we will consider in depth in Chapters 18 and 19. The reason is that exchange rates translate foreign prices into terms that customers are familiar with—their own currencies.

Consider, for example, Americans interested in buying British sweaters that cost £30. If the British pound is worth $1.50, the sweaters cost potential American buyers $45 each. But, if the pound is worth $2.00, those same sweaters cost Americans $60, and consumers are likely to buy fewer. These sorts of responses help explain why American auto makers won back market share from Japanese imports when the yen soared in the mid-1990s.

THE MEANING OF EQUILIBRIUM GDP

The preceding discussion accounts for three of the four main components of total spending. The fourth, government purchases of goods and services (G), is determined in the political arena by our elected representatives. Let us now put the four pieces together and see how they interact, using as our organizing framework the circular flow diagram introduced in the last chapter.

In doing so, we will at first ignore the possibility—raised in Chapter 5—that the government might vary its taxes (T) and spending (G) to steer the economy in some desired direction. Aside from pedagogical simplicity, there is an important reason for doing this. One of the crucial questions surrounding government stabilization policy is whether the economy would *automatically* gravitate toward full employment if the government would simply leave it alone. Keynes, contradicting the teachings of generations of economists before him, claimed that it would not. But Keynes's views remain controversial to this day. We can study the issue best by imagining an economy in which the government never tried to manipulate aggregate demand. This is just what we do in this chapter.

Look now at Figure 8-1, which repeats Figure 7-1 of the last chapter. We can use this circular flow diagram to begin the construction of a simple model of the determination of national income. But first we must understand what is meant by "equilibrium income."

As we explained in the last chapter, total *production* and total *income* must, of necessity, be equal. But the same need not be true of total *spending*. Imagine that, for some reason, the total expenditures, $C + I + G + (X - IM)$, being made after

FIGURE 8-1

THE CIRCULAR FLOW DIAGRAM

Here we repeat the circular flow of income and expenditures that we introduced in Chapter 7. Equilibrium occurs when $C + I + G + (X - IM)$ is equal to Y.

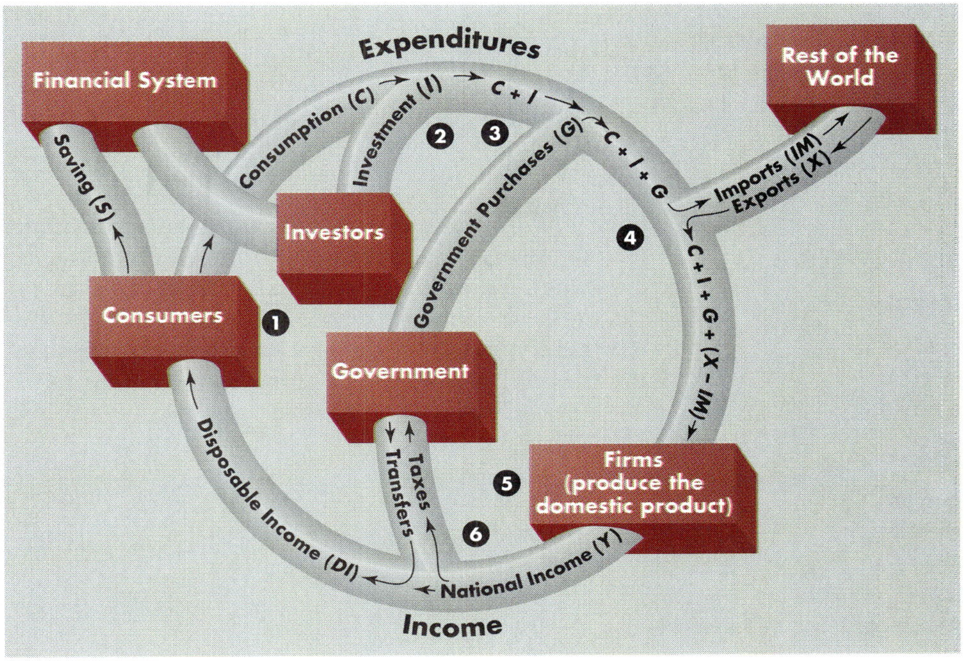

point 4 in the figure are greater than the value of the output being produced by the business firms at point 5.

Two things may happen in such a situation. Since consumers, businesses, government, and foreigners together are buying more than firms are producing, businesses are being forced to take goods out of their warehouses to meet customer demands. Thus, inventory stocks are falling. These inventory reductions are a signal to retailers of a need to increase their orders and to manufacturers of a need to step up their production. Consequently, production is likely to rise.

At some later date, if there is evidence that the high level of spending is not just a temporary aberration, either manufacturers or retailers (or both) may also respond to the buoyant sales performances by raising their prices. Economists therefore say that neither output nor the price level is in **equilibrium** when total spending exceeds the value of current production.

EQUILIBRIUM refers to a situation in which neither consumers nor firms have any incentive to change their behavior. They are content to continue with things as they are.

It is clear from the definition of *equilibrium* that the economy cannot be in equilibrium when total spending exceeds production, for the falling inventories demonstrate to firms that their production and pricing decisions were not quite appropriate.[2] Thus, since we normally use GDP to measure output:

The equilibrium level of GDP cannot be one at which total spending exceeds the value of output because firms will notice that inventory stocks are being depleted. They may first decide to increase production sufficiently to meet the higher demand. Later they may decide to raise prices, as well.

[2]All the models in this book assume, strictly for simplicity, that firms want constant inventories. Deliberate changes in inventories are treated in more advanced courses.

Now imagine the other case, in which the flow of spending reaching firms falls short of current production. Some output cannot be sold and winds up as additions to inventories. (This is just what happened to Nintendo and Sega when the demand for video games sagged in 1994.) The inventory pile-up acts as a signal to firms that at least one of their decisions was wrong. Once again, they will probably react first by cutting back on production, causing GDP to fall. If the imbalance persists, they may also lower prices to stimulate sales. But they certainly will not be happy with things as they are. Thus:

The equilibrium level of GDP cannot be one at which total spending is less than the value of output, because firms will not allow inventories to continue to pile up. They may decide to decrease production, or they may decide to cut prices in order to stimulate demand. Normally, firms are reluctant to cut prices until they are certain that the low level of demand is not a temporary phenomenon, so they rely more heavily on reductions in output.

EQUILIBRIUM ON THE DEMAND SIDE OF THE ECONOMY

We have now determined, through a process of elimination, the level of output that is consistent with people's desires to spend. We have reasoned that GDP will rise whenever it is below total spending, $C + I + G + (X - IM)$, and that GDP will fall whenever it is above $C + I + G + (X - IM)$. Equilibrium can occur, then, only when there is just enough spending to absorb the current level of production. Under such circumstances, producers conclude that their price and output decisions are correct. They therefore have no incentive to change those decisions. We conclude that:

The *equilibrium level of GDP on the demand side* is the one at which total spending equals production. In such a situation, firms find their inventories remaining at desired levels, so there is no incentive to change output or prices.

Thus, the circular flow diagram has helped us to understand the concept of equilibrium GDP on the demand side. It has also shown us how the economy is driven toward this equilibrium. It leaves unanswered, however, three important questions:

1. How large is the equilibrium level of GDP?
2. Will the economy suffer from unemployment, inflation, or both?
3. Is the equilibrium level of GDP on the demand side also consistent with firms' desires to produce? That is, is it also an equilibrium on the *supply* side?

The first two questions will occupy our attention in this chapter; the third question is reserved until Chapter 10.

CONSTRUCTING THE EXPENDITURE SCHEDULE

Our first objective is to determine precisely the equilibrium level of GDP and to see what factors it depends upon. To make the analysis more concrete, we turn to a numerical example. Specifically, we examine the relationship between total spending and GDP in Macroland, the hypothetical economy that was introduced in the last chapter.

TABLE 8-1 TOTAL EXPENDITURE IN MACROLAND (billions of dollars)

(1) GDP (Y)	(2) Consumption (C)	(3) Investment (I)	(4) Government Purchases (G)	(5) Net Exports ($X - IM$)	(6) Total Expenditure
4,800	3,000	900	1,300	−100	5,100
5,200	3,300	900	1,300	−100	5,400
5,600	3,600	900	1,300	−100	5,700
6,000	3,900	900	1,300	−100	6,000
6,400	4,200	900	1,300	−100	6,300
6,800	4,500	900	1,300	−100	6,600
7,200	4,800	900	1,300	−100	6,900

Columns 1 and 2 of Table 8-1 repeat the consumption function of Macroland that we first encountered in Table 7-1. They show how consumer spending, C, depends on GDP, which we symbolize by the letter Y. Columns 3 to 5 provide the other three components of total spending, I, G, and $X - IM$, through the simplifying assumptions that each is just a fixed number regardless of the level of GDP. Specifically, we assume that investment spending is $900 billion, government purchases are $1,300 billion, and net exports are −$100 billion—meaning that in Macroland, as in the United States at present, imports exceed exports.

By adding together Columns 2 through 5, we calculate $C + I + G + (X - IM)$, or total expenditure, which is displayed in Column 6. Columns 1 and 6 are shaded to highlight how total expenditure depends on income in Macroland. We call this relationship the **expenditure schedule.**

An **EXPENDITURE SCHEDULE** shows the relationship between national income (GDP) and total spending.

Figure 8-2 shows the construction of the expenditure schedule graphically. The black line labeled C is the consumption function of Macroland. It plots on a graph the numbers given in Columns 1 and 2 of Table 8-1.

The orange line, labeled $C + I$, displays our assumption that investment is fixed at $900 billion, regardless of the level of GDP. It lies a fixed distance (corresponding to $900 billion) above the C line. If investment were not always $900 billion, the two lines would either move closer together (at income levels at which investment was below $900 billion) or grow farther apart (at income levels at which investment was above $900 billion). For example, our list of determinants of investment spending suggested that I might be larger at higher levels of GDP. Because of this added investment—which is called **induced investment**—the resulting $C + I$ schedule would have a steeper slope than the C schedule.

INDUCED INVESTMENT is the part of investment spending that rises when GDP rises and falls when GDP falls.

The blue line, labeled $C + I + G$, adds in government purchases. Since they are assumed to be $1,300 billion regardless of the size of GDP, the blue line is parallel to the orange line and $1,300 billion higher.

Finally, the burgundy line labeled $C + I + G + (X - IM)$ adds in net exports. It is parallel to the blue line and $100 billion lower, reflecting our assumption that net exports in Macroland are always −$100 billion. Once again, if imports depended on GDP, as our previous discussion suggested, the $C + I + G$ and $C + I + G + (X - IM)$ lines will not be parallel.

FIGURE 8-2 CONSTRUCTION OF THE EXPENDITURE SCHEDULE

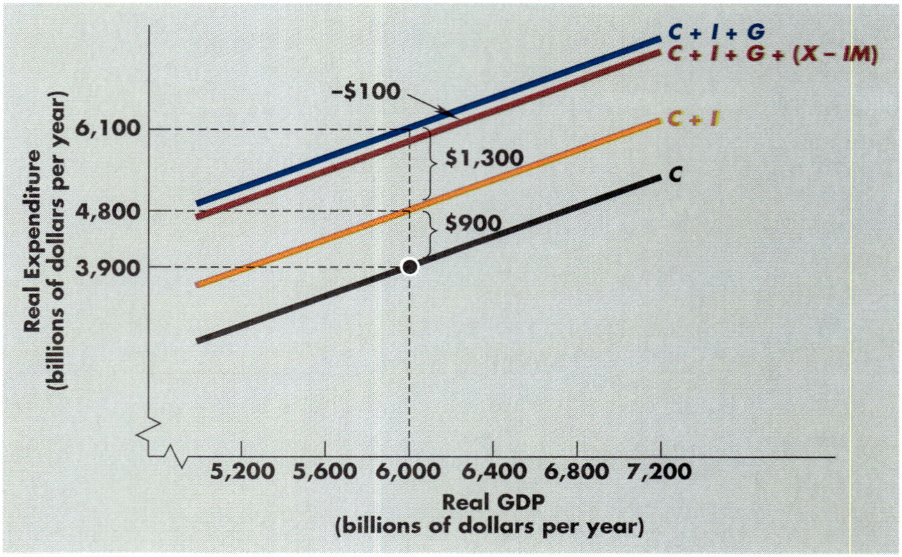

This figure shows in a diagram what Table 8-1 showed numerically—the construction of a total expenditure schedule from its components. Line *C* is the consumption function that we first encountered in Figure 7-5. Line *C* + *I* adds investment (assumed always to be $900 billion in this example), and line *C* + *I* + *G* adds government purchases (which are $1,300 billion). Line *C* + *I* + *G* + (*X* – *IM*) is the expenditure schedule and is obtained by adding net exports to *C* + *I* + *G*. For example, when GDP is $6,000, *C* is $3,900, *I* is $900, *G* is $1,300, and (*X* – *IM*) is –$100, for a total of $6,000.

THE MECHANICS OF INCOME DETERMINATION

We are now ready to determine demand-side equilibrium in Macroland. Look first at Table 8-2, which presents the logic of our circular flow argument in tabular form. The first two columns of this table reproduce the expenditure schedule that was constructed in Table 8-1. The other columns explain the process by which equilibrium is approached. Let us see why a GDP of $6,000 billion must be the equilibrium level.

Consider first any output level below $6,000 billion. For example, at output level Y = $5,200 billion, total expenditure is $5,400 billion (Column 2), which is $200 billion more than production. With spending greater than output (Column 3), inventories will be falling (Column 4). As the table suggests, this will be a signal to producers to raise their output (Column 5). Clearly, then, no output level below Y = $6,000 billion can be an equilibrium. Output is too low.

A similar line of reasoning can eliminate any output level above $6,000 billion. Consider, for example, Y = $6,800 billion. The table shows that total spending would be $6,600 billion if national income were $6,800 billion, so $200 billion of the GDP would go unsold. This would raise producers' inventory stocks and signal them that their rate of production was too high.

Just as we concluded from our circular flow diagram, equilibrium will be achieved only when total spending, $C + I + G + (X - IM)$, is equal to GDP (Y). In symbols, our condition for equilibrium GDP is:

$$Y = C + I + G + (X - IM)$$

The table shows that this occurs only at a GDP of $6,000 billion. This, then, must be the equilibrium level of GDP.

TABLE 8-2 THE DETERMINATION OF EQUILIBRIUM OUTPUT

(1) Output (*Y*) (billions of dollars)	(2) Total Spending [*C* + *I* + *G* + (*X* − *IM*)] (billions of dollars)	(3) Balance of Spending and Output	(4) Inventories Are:	(5) Producers Will Respond by:
4,800	5,100	Spending exceeds output	Falling	Producing more
5,200	5,400	Spending exceeds output	Falling	Producing more
5,600	5,700	Spending exceeds output	Falling	Producing more
6,000	6,000	Spending = output	Constant	Not changing production
6,400	6,300	Output exceeds spending	Rising	Producing less
6,800	6,600	Output exceeds spending	Rising	Producing less
7,200	6,900	Output exceeds spending	Rising	Producing less

Figure 8-3 shows this same conclusion graphically, by adding a 45° line to Figure 8-2. Why a 45° line? Recall from the appendix to Chapter 1 that a 45° line marks all points on a graph at which the value of the variable measured on the horizontal axis is equal to the value of the variable measured on the vertical axis. In this convenient graph of the expenditure schedule, gross domestic product (Y) is measured on the horizontal axis and total expenditure, $C + I + G + (X - IM)$, is measured on the vertical axis. So the 45° line shows all the points at which output and spending are equal; that is, where $Y = C + I + G + (X - IM)$. *The 45° line therefore displays all the points at which the economy can possibly be at equilibrium,* for if total spending is not equal to production, firms will not be content with current output levels.

FIGURE 8-3 INCOME-EXPENDITURE DIAGRAM

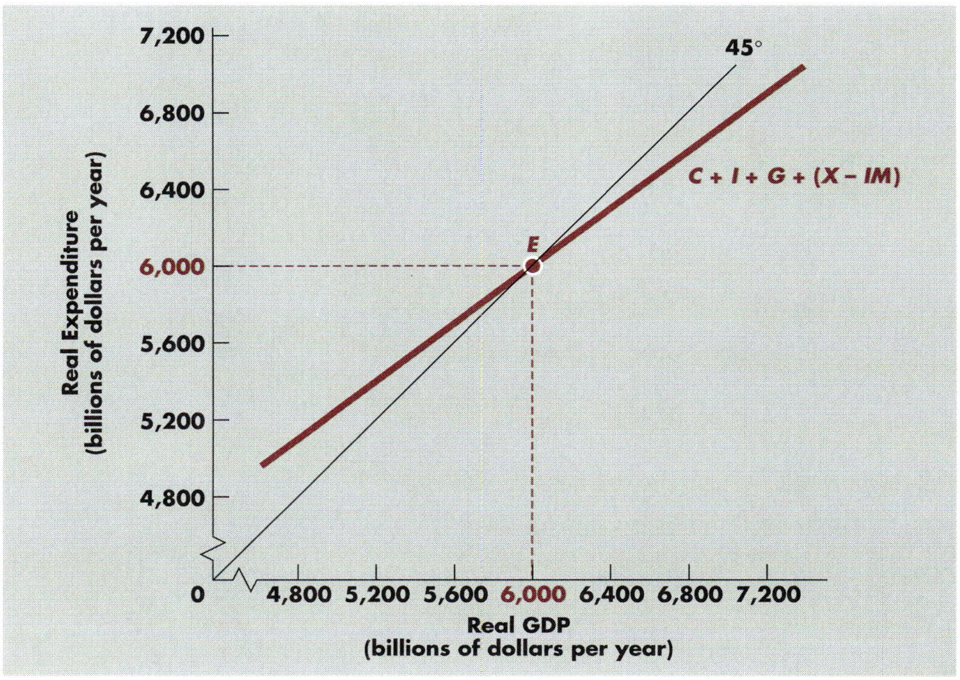

This figure adds a 45° line—which marks off points where expenditure and output are equal—to Figure 8-2. Since the condition for equilibrium GDP is that expenditure and output must be equal, this line can be used to determine the equilibrium level of GDP. In this example, equilibrium is at point *E*, where GDP is $6,000 billion—precisely as we found in Table 8-2.

Now we must compare these *potential* equilibrium points with the *actual* combinations of spending and output that the economy can attain, given the behavior of consumers and investors. That behavior, as we have seen, is described by the $C + I + G + (X - IM)$ line in Figure 8-3, which shows how total expenditure varies as income changes. Thus, *the economy will always be on the expenditure line* because only points on the $C + I + G + (X - IM)$ line are consistent with the spending plans of consumers and investors. Similarly, *if* the economy is in equilibrium, it *must* be on the 45° line. As Figure 8-3 shows, these two requirements together imply that the only viable equilibrium is at point *E*, where the $C + I + G + (X - IM)$ line intersects the 45° line. Only this point is consistent both with equilibrium and with the actual desires to consume and invest.

Notice that to the left of the equilibrium point, *E*, the expenditure line lies above the 45° line. This means that total spending exceeds total output, as we have already noted in words and with numbers. Hence, inventories will be falling and firms will conclude that they should increase production. Thus, production will rise toward the equilibrium point, *E*. The opposite is true to the right of point *E*. Here spending falls short of output, inventories are rising, and firms will cut back production—thereby moving closer to *E*.

An **INCOME-EXPENDITURE DIAGRAM,** also called a **45° LINE DIAGRAM,** plots total real expenditure (on the vertical axis) against real income (on the horizontal axis). The 45° line marks off points where income and expenditure are equal.

In other words, whenever production is above the equilibrium level, market forces will drive output down. And whenever production is below equilibrium, market forces will drive output up. Thus, in either case, deviations from equilibrium will be eliminated.

Diagrams like this one will recur so frequently in this and the next several chapters that it will be convenient to have a name for them. Let us therefore call them **income-expenditure diagrams** since they show how expenditures vary with income. Sometimes we shall also refer to them simply as **45° line diagrams.**

THE AGGREGATE DEMAND CURVE

Chapter 5 sketched a framework for macroeconomic analysis by introducing aggregate demand and aggregate supply curves, which relate aggregate quantities demanded and supplied to the price level. The expenditure schedule graphed in Figure 8-3 is certainly not the aggregate demand curve, for we have yet to bring the price level into our discussion. It is now time to remedy this omission and derive the aggregate demand curve.

Fortunately, no further mechanical apparatus is required. We can bring the price level into our income-expenditure analysis by recalling something we learned in the last chapter: At any given level of real income, higher prices lead to lower real consumer spending. The reason, you will recall, is that consumers own many assets whose values are fixed in money terms, and which therefore lose purchasing power when prices rise.[3] With real wealth lower, consumers spend less. Therefore, total spending in the economy falls *even with no change in real income.*

In terms of our 45° line diagram, a rise in the price level will pull down the consumption function depicted in Figure 8-2 and, hence, will pull down the total expenditure schedule, as well. Conversely, a fall in the price level will raise both the *C* and $C + I + G + (X - IM)$ schedules in the diagram. The two parts of Figure 8-4 illustrate both of these shifts.

---

[3]The money in your bank account is a prime example. If prices rise, it will buy less.

FIGURE 8-4 THE EFFECT OF THE PRICE LEVEL ON EQUILIBRIUM AGGREGATE QUANTITY DEMANDED

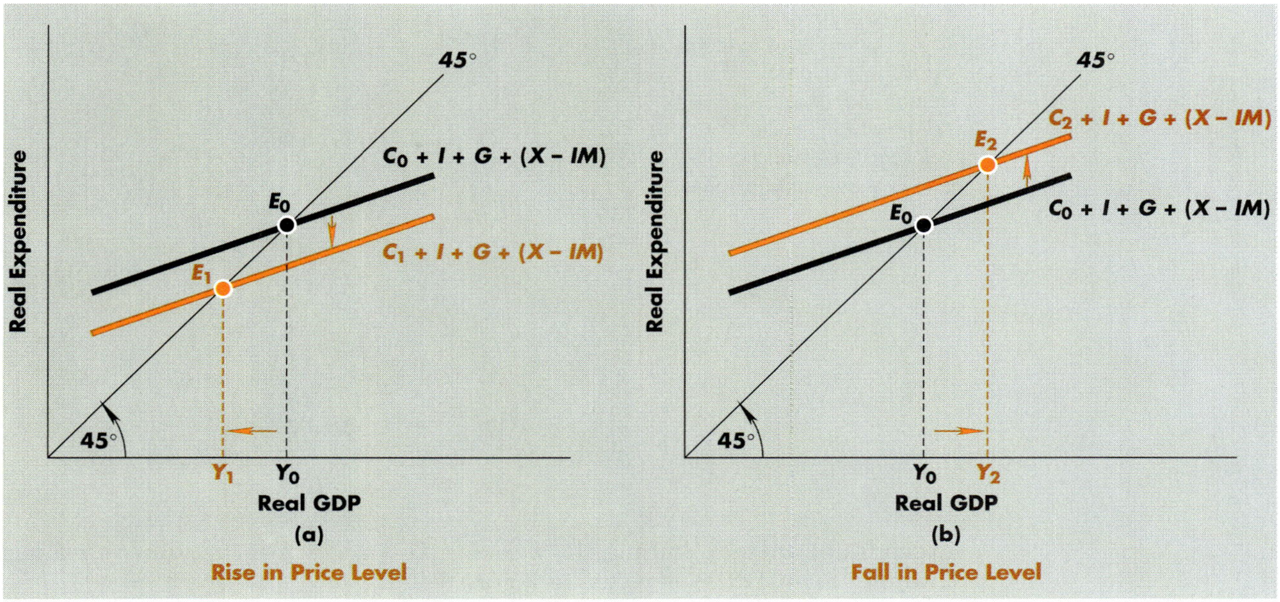

Because a change in the price level causes the expenditure schedule to shift, it changes the equilibrium quantity of real GDP demanded. Panel (a) shows what happens when the price level rises, causing the expenditure schedule to shift downward from $C_0 + I + G + (X - IM)$ to $C_1 + I + G + (X - IM)$. Equilibrium quantity demanded falls from Y_0 to Y_1. Panel (b) shows what happens when the price level falls, causing the expenditure schedule to shift upward from $C_0 + I + G + (X - IM)$ to $C_2 + I + G + (X - IM)$. Equilibrium quantity demanded rises from Y_0 to Y_2.

What, then, do changes in the price level do to the equilibrium level of real GDP on the demand side? Common sense says that, with lower spending, equilibrium GDP should fall, and Figure 8-4 shows that this conclusion is correct. Panel (a) shows that a rise in the price level, by shifting the expenditure schedule downward from $C_0 + I + G + (X - IM)$ to $C_1 + I + G + (X - IM)$ leads to a reduction in the equilibrium quantity of real GDP demanded from Y_0 to Y_1. Panel (b) shows that a fall in the price level, by shifting the expenditure schedule upward from $C_0 + I + G + (X - IM)$ to $C_2 + I + G + (X - IM)$, leads to a rise in the equilibrium quantity of real GDP demanded from Y_0 to Y_2. In summary:

A rise in the price level leads to a lower equilibrium level of real aggregate quantity demanded. This relationship between the price level and the equilibrium quantity of real GDP demanded is depicted in Figure 8-5 on the next page and is precisely what we called the *aggregate demand curve* in earlier chapters. It comes directly from the 45° line diagrams in Figure 8-4. Thus, points E_0, E_1, and E_2 in Figure 8-5 correspond precisely to the points bearing the same labels in Figure 8-4.

The effect of higher prices on consumer wealth is just one of several reasons why the aggregate demand curve relating the price level to real GDP demanded slopes downward. A second reason comes from international trade. In our discussion of the determinants of net exports (see pages 169–170), we pointed out that higher U.S. prices will depress exports (X) and stimulate imports (IM), provided that foreign prices are held constant. That means that, other things equal, a higher U.S. price level will reduce the $(X - IM)$ component of total

FIGURE 8-5 THE AGGREGATE DEMAND CURVE

The graphic analysis in Figure 8-4 showed that higher prices lead to lower aggregate quantity demanded. This relationship is called the *aggregate demand curve* and is shown in this figure.

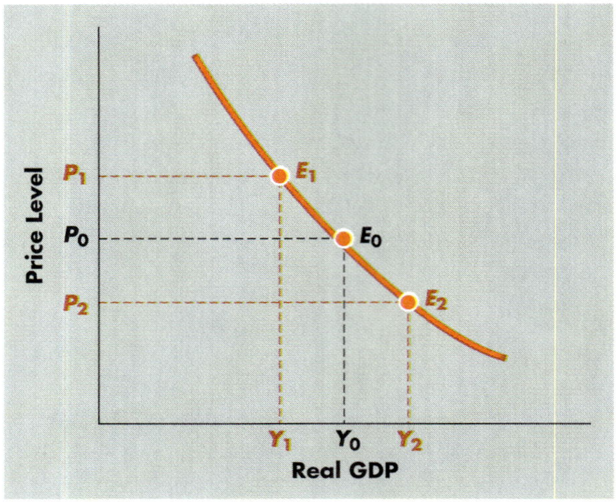

expenditure, thereby shifting the $C + I + G + (X - IM)$ line downward and lowering real GDP, as depicted in Figure 8-4(a).

Later in the book, after we have studied interest rates and exchange rates, we will encounter still more reasons for a downward-sloping aggregate demand curve. All of them imply that:

An income-expenditure diagram like Figure 8-3 can be drawn up only for a *specific* price level. At different price levels, the $C + I + G + (X - IM)$ schedule will be different and, hence, the equilibrium quantity of GDP demanded will be different.

As we shall now see, this finding is critical to understanding the genesis of unemployment and inflation.

DEMAND-SIDE EQUILIBRIUM AND FULL EMPLOYMENT

We now turn to the second major question of this chapter: Will the economy achieve an equilibrium at full employment without inflation, or will there be unemployment, inflation, or both? This is one of the crucial questions surrounding government stabilization policy, for if the economy always gravitates toward full employment *automatically,* then the government should simply leave it alone.

In the income-expenditure diagrams used so far, the equilibrium level of GDP demanded has been shown as the intersection of the expenditure schedule and the 45° line, regardless of whatever level of GDP might correspond to full employment. However, as we will see now, when equilibrium GDP falls above full employment, the economy probably will be plagued by inflation, and when equilibrium falls below full employment, there will be unemployment and recession.

This remarkable fact was one of the principal messages of Keynes's *General Theory of Employment, Interest, and Money.* Writing during the Great Depression, it was natural for him to focus on the case in which equilibrium falls short of full employment so that there are unemployed resources. Figure 8-6 illustrates

FIGURE 8-6

A RECESSIONARY GAP

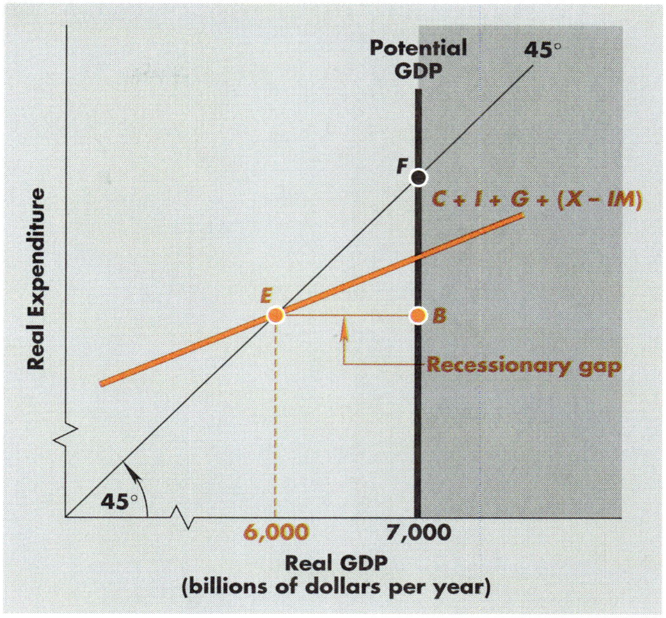

Sometimes equilibrium GDP may fall below potential GDP, so that some workers are unemployed. This diagram illustrates such a case. The horizontal distance *EB* between equilibrium GDP and potential GDP is called the *recessionary gap*.

this possibility. A vertical line has been drawn at the full-employment level of GDP (called *potential GDP*), which is assumed to be $7,000 billion in the example. We see that the $C + I + G + (X - IM)$ curve cuts the 45° line at point E, which corresponds to a GDP (Y = $6,000 billion) below potential GDP. In this case, the expenditure curve is too low to lead to full employment.

Such a situation might arise because consumers or investors are unwilling to spend at normal rates, because government spending is low, because foreign demand is weak, or because the price level is "too high." Any of these would depress the $C + I + G + (X - IM)$ curve. Unemployment must then occur because not enough output is demanded to keep the entire labor force at work.

The **RECESSIONARY GAP** is the amount by which the equilibrium level of real GDP falls short of potential GDP.

The distance between the *equilibrium* level of output demanded and the *full-employment* level of output (that is, potential GDP) is called the **recessionary gap**—and is shown by the horizontal distance from E to B. While Figure 8-6 is entirely hypothetical, real-world gaps of precisely this sort were shown shaded blue in Figure 6-2 (page 119). They are a pervasive feature of recent U.S. economic history.

It is clear from Figure 8-6 that full employment can be reached only by raising the total spending schedule to eliminate the recessionary gap. Specifically, the $C + I + G + (X - IM)$ schedule must move upward until it cuts the 45° line at point F. Can this happen without government intervention? We know that a sufficiently large drop in the price level can do the job. But is that a realistic prospect? We shall return to this question after we bring the supply side into the picture. But first let us consider the other case, in which equilibrium GDP exceeds full employment.

Figure 8-7 illustrates this possibility. Now the expenditure schedule intersects the 45° line at point E, where GDP is $8,000 billion. But this exceeds the full-employment level, Y = $7,000 billion. A case like this can arise when consumer or investment spending is unusually buoyant, when foreign demand is

FIGURE 8-7

AN INFLATIONARY GAP

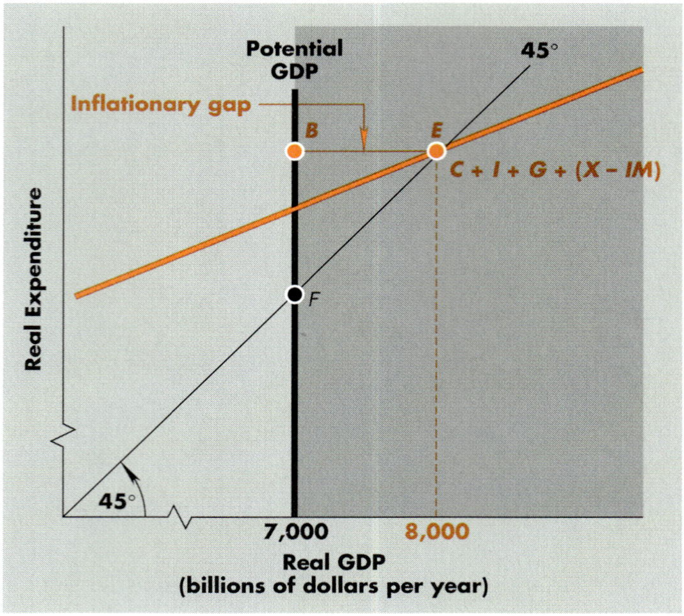

Sometimes equilibrium GDP may lie above potential GDP, meaning that there are more jobs than required for full employment. This diagram illustrates such a case. The horizontal distance *BE* between potential GDP and equilibrium GDP is called the *inflationary gap*. It is gradually eliminated by rising prices, which pull the $C + I + G + (X - IM)$ schedule down until it passes through point *F*.

particularly strong, when the government spends too much, or when a "low" price level pushes the $C + I + G + (X - IM)$ curve upward.

To reach an equilibrium at full employment, the price level would have to rise enough to drive the expenditure schedule *down* until it passed through point *F*. The horizontal distance *BE*—which indicates the amount by which the quantity of GDP demanded exceeds potential GDP—is called the **inflationary gap.** If there is an inflationary gap, a higher price level or some other means of reducing total expenditure is necessary to reach an equilibrium at full employment. Real-world inflationary gaps were shown shaded orange in Figure 6-2.

The **INFLATIONARY GAP** is the amount by which equilibrium real GDP exceeds the full-employment level of GDP.

In sum, only if the price level and spending plans are "just right" will the expenditure curve intersect the 45° line precisely at full employment, so that neither a recessionary gap nor an inflationary gap occurs. Are there reasons to expect this outcome? Does the economy have a self-correcting mechanism that automatically eliminates recessionary or inflationary gaps and propels it toward full employment? And how is it that inflation and unemployment sometimes occur together?

These are questions that we are not ready to address because we have not yet brought *aggregate supply* into the picture. And as we learned in Chapter 5, the price level is determined by the interaction of *both* aggregate demand *and* aggregate supply. However, it is not too early to get an idea about why things can go wrong, why the economy can find itself far away from full employment.

THE COORDINATION OF SAVING AND INVESTMENT

To understand what goes wrong in a recession, it is useful to pose the following question: Must the full-employment level of GDP be an equilibrium? Decades

FIGURE 8-8

A SIMPLIFIED CIRCULAR FLOW

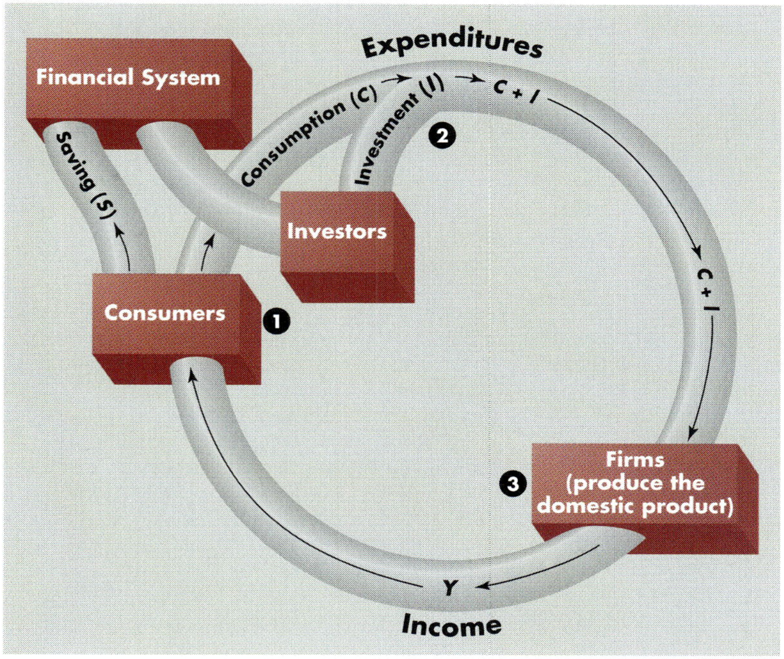

Here we show a simplified version of the circular flow of income and expenditures shown in Figure 8-1. The simplification amounts to shutting off the pipes leading into and out of the government and those into and out of the rest of the world. Thus, this circular flow represents an economy with no government and no foreign trade.

ago, economists thought the answer was *yes*. Since Keynes, most economists believe the answer is *not necessarily*.

To help us understand why, Figure 8-8 offers a simplified circular flow diagram that ignores exports, imports, and the government. In this version, there is just one place for income to "leak out" of the circular flow: at point 1, where consumers save some of their income. Similarly, there is just one place for this lost spending to be replaced: at point 2, where investment enters the circular flow.

What happens if firms produce exactly the full-employment level of GDP at point 3 in the diagram? Will this income level be maintained as we move around the circle, or will it shrink or grow? The answer is that full-employment income will be maintained only if the spending by investors at point 2 exactly balances the saving done by consumers at point 1. In other words:

The economy will reach an equilibrium at full employment only if the amount that consumers wish to save out of full-employment incomes happens to be equal to the amount that investors want to invest. If these two magnitudes are unequal, then full employment will not be an equilibrium for the economy.

Specifically, we can see from the circular flow diagram that, if saving exceeds investment at full employment, the total demand received by firms (point 3) will fall short of total output because the added investment spending will not be enough to replace the leakage to saving. With demand inadequate to support production at full employment, GDP must fall below potential. There will be a recessionary gap. Conversely, if investment exceeds saving when the economy is at full employment, then total demand will exceed potential GDP and production will rise above the full-employment level. There will be an inflationary gap.

UNEMPLOYMENT AND INFLATION AS COORDINATION FAILURES

The idea that unemployment stems from a *lack of coordination* between the decisions of savers and investors may seem abstract. But we encounter coordination failures all the time. The following familiar example may bring the idea down to earth. Picture a crowd watching a football game. Now something exciting happens and the fans rise from their seats. People in the front rows begin standing first, and those seated behind them are forced to stand if they want to see the game. Soon everyone in the stadium is on their feet. But with everyone standing, no one can see any better than when everyone was sitting. And the fans are enduring the further discomfort of being on their feet. (Never mind that stadium seats are uncomfortable!) Everyone in the stadium would be better off if everyone sat down. Sometimes this happens. But the crowd rises to its feet again on every exciting play. There is simply no way to coordinate the individual decisions of tens of thousands of football fans.

Unemployment poses a similar coordination problem. During a deep recession, workers are unemployed and businesses cannot sell their wares. Figuratively speaking, everyone is "standing" and unhappy about it. If only the firms could agree to hire more workers, those newly employed people could afford to buy more of the goods and services the firms want to produce. But, as at the football stadium, there is no central authority to coordinate these millions of decisions.

The coordination failure idea also helps to explain why it is so hard to stop inflation. Virtually everyone prefers stable prices to rising prices. But now think of yourself as the seller of a product. If everyone else in the economy would hold their prices steady, you would happily hold yours steady, too. But, if you believe that others will continue to raise their prices at, say, 5 percent per year, you may find it dangerous not to increase yours apace. Hence, society may get stuck with 5 percent inflation even though everyone agrees that zero inflation is better.

Now this discussion does nothing but restate what we already know in different words.[4] But these words hold the key to understanding why the economy can find itself stuck below full employment (or above it, for that matter), for *the people who do the investing are not the same people who do the saving*. In a modern capitalist economy, investing is done by one group of individuals (primarily corporate executives and home buyers) while saving is done by another group.[5] It is easy to imagine that their plans may not be well-coordinated. If they are not, we have just seen how either unemployment or inflation can occur.

Neither of these problems would arise if the acts of saving and investing were not separated in time or space. Imagine a primitive economy of farmers, each of whom invests only in his own farm. There is no borrowing or lending and no financial system. In this world, any farmer wanting to buy a new plow or tractor (that is, wanting to *invest*) would have to refrain from consuming part of his income (that is, would have to *save*). Therefore, the amount that farmers planned to *save* out of full-employment income would have to be equal to the amount they planned to *invest*. Total spending and production would always have to be equal at full employment.

Almost the same holds true in a centrally planned economy. There the state decides how much will be invested and has a great deal of leverage over how much saving people do. If the planners do their calculations correctly, they can force saving to be equal to investment at full employment. Consequently, busi-

[4] In symbols, our equilibrium condition without government or foreign trade is $Y = C + I$. If we note that Y is also the sum of consumption plus saving, $Y = C + S$, it follows that $C + S = C + I$, or $S = I$, is a restatement of the equilibrium condition.

[5] In a modern economy, it is not only households that save. Businesses save also in the form of retained earnings. Nonetheless, households are the ultimate source of the saving needed to finance investment.

ness fluctuations were not historically major problems for the economies of China and the former Soviet Union. (They had plenty of others!) However, as these two countries liberalized their economies, they found that they had to deal with the inflation and unemployment problems that have long plagued the West.

The analysis in the box on the opposite page raises a tantalizing possibility. If both high unemployment and high inflation arise from *coordination failures,* might the government be able to do something about it? Keynes suggested that it could, and we will examine this idea in detail in later chapters. But the football analogy reminds us that a central authority may not find it easy to solve the coordination problem.

SUMMARY

1. *Investment* is the most volatile component of aggregate demand, largely because it is tied so closely to the state of business confidence and to expectations about the future performance of the economy.
2. Government policy cannot influence business confidence in any reliable way, so policies designed to alter investment spending are aimed at more objective, though possibly less important, determinants of investment. Among these are interest rates, the overall state of aggregate demand, and tax incentives.
3. *Net exports* depend on GDPs and relative prices both here and abroad.
4. The **equilibrium** level of national income on the demand side is the level at which total spending just equals the value of production (GDP). Since total spending is the sum of consumption, investment, government purchases, and net exports, the condition for equilibrium is $Y = C + I + G + (X - IM)$.
5. Income levels below equilibrium are bound to rise because, when spending exceeds output, firms will see their inventory stocks being depleted and will react by stepping up production.
6. Income levels above equilibrium are bound to fall because, when total spending is insufficient to absorb total output, inventories will pile up and firms will react by curtailing production.
7. The determination of the equilibrium level of GDP on the demand side can be portrayed on a convenient **income-expenditure diagram** as the point at which the **expenditure schedule**—defined as the sum of $C + I + G + (X - IM)$—crosses the 45° line. The 45° line is significant because it marks off points at which spending and output are equal—that is, at which $Y = C + I + G + (X - IM)$—and this is the basic condition for equilibrium.
8. An income-expenditure diagram can only be drawn up for a specific price level, however. Thus, the equilibrium GDP so determined depends on the price level.
9. Because higher prices reduce the purchasing power of consumers' wealth and hence reduce their spending, equilibrium real GDP demanded is lower when prices are higher. This downward-sloping relationship is known as the *aggregate demand curve.*
10. Equilibrium GDP can be above or below *potential GDP,* which is defined as the GDP that would be produced if the labor force were fully employed.
11. If equilibrium GDP exceeds potential GDP, the difference is called an **inflationary gap.** If equilibrium GDP falls short of potential GDP, the resulting difference is called a **recessionary gap.**
12. Such gaps can occur because the saving that consumers want to do at full-employment income levels may differ from the investing that investors want to do. This problem of *coordination failure* is not likely to arise in a planned economy or in a primitive economy.

KEY TERMS

Investment
Net exports
Equilibrium
Expenditure schedule
Induced investment
$Y = C + I + G + (X - IM)$
Income-expenditure (or 45° line) diagram
Aggregate demand curve
Full-employment level of GDP (or potential GDP)
Recessionary gap
Inflationary gap
Coordination of saving and investment
Coordination failure

QUESTIONS FOR REVIEW

1. For more than 15 years now, imports have consistently exceeded exports in the U.S. economy. This is often considered a major problem. Does this chapter give you any hints about why? (You may want to discuss this issue with your instructor. We will certainly learn more about it in later chapters.)

2. Why is not any arbitrary level of GDP an equilibrium for the economy? (Do not give a mechanical answer to this question. Explain the economic mechanism involved.)

3. From the following data, construct an expenditure schedule on a piece of graph paper. Then use the income-expenditure (45° line) diagram to determine the equilibrium level of GDP.

Income	Consumption	Investment	Government Purchases	Net Exports
$3,600	$3,220	$240	$120	$40
3,700	3,310	240	120	40
3,800	3,400	240	120	40
3,900	3,490	240	120	40
4,000	3,580	240	120	40

4. From the following data, construct an expenditure schedule on a piece of graph paper. Then use the income-expenditure (45° line) diagram to determine the equilibrium level of GDP. Compare your answer with your answer to Review Question 3.

Income	Consumption	Investment	Government Purchases	Net Exports
$3,600	$3,280	$180	$120	$40
3,700	3,340	210	120	40
3,800	3,400	240	120	40
3,900	3,460	270	120	40
4,000	3,520	300	120	40

5. Suppose that investment spending is always $250, government purchases are $100, net exports are always $50, and consumer spending depends on the price level in the following way:

Price Level	Consumer Spending
90	$740
95	720
100	700
105	680
110	660

On a piece of graph paper, use these data to construct an aggregate demand curve. Why do you think this example supposes that consumption declines as the price level rises?

6. Does the economy this year seem to have an inflationary gap or a recessionary gap? (If you do not know the answer from reading the newspaper, ask your instructor.)

7. Why were there no recessions in the former Soviet Union?

8. (More difficult)[6] Consider an economy in which the consumption function takes the following simple algebraic form:

$$C = 300 + 0.75DI$$

and in which investment (I) is always 900 and net exports are always 100. Government purchases are fixed at 1,300 and taxes are fixed at 1,200. Find the equilibrium level of GDP and compare your answer to Table 8-2 and Figure 8-3. (*Hint:* Remember that in this case disposable income is GDP minus taxes: $DI = Y - T = Y - 1{,}200$.)

9. (More difficult) An economy has a consumption function:

$$C = 100 + 0.8DI$$

The government budget is balanced with government purchases and taxes both fixed at 500. Net exports are 100. Investment is 400. Find equilibrium GDP.

[6]The answer to this question is provided in the appendix to this chapter.

APPENDIX THE SIMPLE ALGEBRA OF INCOME DETERMINATION

The model of demand-side equilibrium that the chapter presented graphically and in tabular form can also be handled with some simple algebra. Written as an equation, the consumption function in our example is:

$$\begin{aligned} C &= 300 + 0.75DI \\ &= 300 + 0.75(Y - T) \end{aligned}$$

since, by definition, $DI = Y - T$. This is simply the equation of a straight line with a slope of 0.75 and an intercept of $300 - 0.75T$. Since $T = 1{,}200$ in our example, the intercept is -600 and the equation can be written more simply as:

$$C = -600 + 0.75Y$$

Investment in the example was assumed to be 900, regardless of the level of income, government purchases were 1,300, and net exports were -100. So the sum $C + I + G + (X - IM)$ is:

$$\begin{aligned} &C + I + G + (X - IM) \\ &= -600 + 0.75Y + 900 + 1{,}300 - 100 \\ &= 1{,}500 + 0.75Y \end{aligned}$$

which describes the expenditure curve in Figure 8-3. Since the equilibrium quantity of GDP demanded is defined by:

$$Y = C + I + G + (X - IM)$$

we can solve for the equilibrium value of Y by substituting $1{,}500 + 0.75Y$ for $C + I + G + (X - IM)$ to get:

$$Y = 1{,}500 + 0.75Y$$

To solve this equation for Y, first subtract $0.75Y$ from both sides to get:

$$0.25Y = 1{,}500$$

Then divide both sides by 0.25 to obtain the answer:

$$Y = 6{,}000$$

This, of course, is precisely the solution we found by graphical and tabular methods in the chapter.

We can easily generalize this algebraic approach to deal with any set of numbers in our equations. Suppose that the consumption function is:

$$C = a + bDI = a + b(Y - T)$$

(In the example, $a = 300$, $T = 1{,}200$, and $b = 0.75$.) Then the equilibrium condition that $Y = C + I + G + (X - IM)$ implies that:

$$\begin{aligned} Y &= a + bDI + I + G + (X - IM) \\ &= a - bT + bY + I + G + (X - IM) \end{aligned}$$

Subtracting bY from both sides leads to:

$$(1 - b)Y = a - bT + I + G + (X - IM)$$

and dividing through by $1 - b$ gives:

$$Y = \frac{a - bT + I + G + (X - IM)}{1 - b}$$

This formula, which is certainly *not* to be memorized, is valid for any numerical values of a, b, T, G, I, and $(X - IM)$ (so long as b is between zero and 1).

QUESTIONS FOR REVIEW

1. Find the equilibrium level of GDP demanded in an economy in which investment is always \$400, net exports are always \$150, the government budget is balanced with purchases and taxes both equal to \$600, and the consumption function is described by the following algebraic equation:

$$C = 50 + 0.75DI$$

(*Hint:* Do not forget that $DI = Y - T$.)

2. Do the same for an economy in which investment is \$450, net exports are zero, government purchases and taxes are both \$500, and the consumption function is:

$$C = 250 + 0.5DI$$

3. In each of the above cases, how much saving is there in equilibrium? (*Hint:* Income not consumed must be saved.) Is saving equal to investment?

4. Imagine an economy in which consumer expenditure is represented by the following equation:

$$C = 100 + 0.75DI$$

Imagine also that investors want to spend 1,000 at every level of income (I = 1,000), net exports are zero ($X - IM = 0$), government purchases are 600, and taxes are 400.

a. What is the equilibrium level of income?
b. If the full-employment level of income is 6,000, is there a recessionary or inflationary gap? If so, how much?
c. What will happen to the equilibrium level of income if investors become optimistic about the country's future and raise their investment to 1,200?
d. Is there a recessionary or inflationary gap now? How much?

5. Ivyland has the following consumption function:

$$C = 50 + 0.8DI$$

Firms in Ivyland always invest \$350 and net exports are zero, initially. The government budget is balanced with spending and taxes both equal to \$250.

a. Find the equilibrium level of GDP.
b. How much is saved? Is saving equal to investment?
c. Now suppose that an export-promotion drive succeeds in raising net exports to \$50. Answer (a) and (b) under these new circumstances.

CHAPTER 9

CHANGES ON THE DEMAND SIDE: MULTIPLIER ANALYSIS

A definite ratio, to be called the *Multiplier,* can be established between income and investment.
John Maynard Keynes

In the last chapter, we derived the economy's *aggregate demand curve,* which shows how the equilibrium quantity of real GDP demanded depends on the price level—holding all other factors constant. But often these "other factors" do not remain constant, and, as a consequence, the entire aggregate demand curve shifts. This chapter is the first of several that are devoted to enumerating these "other factors" and explaining how and why they make the aggregate demand curve shift.

The central concept of this short chapter is the *multiplier*—the idea that an increase in spending will bring about an *even larger* increase in equilibrium GDP. We approach this idea from three different perspectives, each of which provides different insights into the multiplier process. First, we illustrate the multiplier graphically using the income-expenditure diagram from Chapter 8. Next, we reach the same conclusion through the use of a numerical example, and finally, we offer an algebraic statement. Each of these is an expression of the remarkable multiplier result. Near the end of the chapter, we use multiplier analysis to explain how economic developments abroad affect the U.S. economy and why a drive to increase national saving might not succeed.

CASE STUDY: HOW DID KANSAS DO IT?

In 1989, the Kansas state legislature voted to spend $2.6 billion over the next several years to make long overdue repairs on some 135,000 miles of highway. Everyone knew that spending on that scale would give a big boost to the state's construction industry. But Kansans were in for a pleasant surprise. Within 3 years, all sorts of industries, including many with no obvious connection to road building, were booming in Kansas. Personal income in the state was growing at twice the national average. And the state's unemployment rate was the fourth-lowest in the nation.

Did spending on road repair contribute to the boom in other industries? If so, how? This chapter will provide some answers.

THE MAGIC OF THE MULTIPLIER

Because it is subject to such abrupt swings, investment spending is often the cause of business fluctuations in the United States and elsewhere. So let us ask what would happen to equilibrium income in our fictitious country, Macroland, if firms there suddenly decided to spend more on investment goods. As we shall see, such a decision would have a *multiplied* effect on GDP in Macroland; that is, each $1 of additional investment spending would add more than $1 to GDP. The same would be true in Kansas, or in the entire U.S. economy.

For simplicity, we continue to assume that the price level is fixed—an assumption we will drop in the next chapter. Refer first to Table 9-1, which looks very much like Table 8-1 (page 173). The only difference is that we assume here that, for some reason, firms in Macroland now want to invest $200 billion more than they previously did—for a total of $1,100 billion.

The **MULTIPLIER** is the ratio of the change in equilibrium GDP (*Y*) divided by the original change in spending that causes the change in GDP.

The **multiplier** principle says that Macroland's GDP will rise by more than the $200 billion increase in investment. Specifically, the multiplier is defined as the ratio of the change in equilibrium GDP (*Y*) to the original change in spending that causes GDP to change. In shorthand, when we deal with the multiplier for investment (*I*), the formula is:

$$\text{Multiplier} = \frac{\text{Change in } Y}{\text{Change in } I}$$

Let us verify that the multiplier is indeed greater than 1. Table 9-1 shows how to derive a new expenditure schedule by adding up C, I, G, and $(X - IM)$ at each level of Y, just as we did in Chapter 8. If you compare the last column of Table 9-1 with that of Table 8-1, you will see that the new expenditure schedule lies uniformly above the old one by $200 billion.

Figure 9-1 illustrates this shift graphically. The schedule marked $C + I_0 + G + (X - IM)$ is derived from the last column of Table 8-1, while the higher schedule marked $C + I_1 + G + (X - IM)$ is derived from the last column of Table 9-1. The two expenditure lines are parallel and $200 billion apart.

TABLE 9-1 TOTAL EXPENDITURE AFTER A $200 BILLION RISE IN INVESTMENT SPENDING (billions of dollars per year)

(1) Income (*Y*)	(2) Consumption (*C*)	(3) Investment (*I*)	(4) Government Purchases (*G*)	(5) Net Exports (*X* − *IM*)	(6) Total Expenditure
4,800	3,000	1,100	1,300	−100	5,300
5,200	3,300	1,100	1,300	−100	5,600
5,600	3,600	1,100	1,300	−100	5,900
6,000	3,900	1,100	1,300	−100	6,200
6,400	4,200	1,100	1,300	−100	6,500
6,800	4,500	1,100	1,300	−100	6,800
7,200	4,800	1,100	1,300	−100	7,100

This table shows the construction of a total expenditure schedule for Macroland after investment has risen to $1,100 billion. As indicated by the shaded numbers, only income level Y = $6,800 billion is an equilibrium on the demand side of the economy because only at this level is total spending, $C + I + G + (X - IM)$, equal to production (Y).

FIGURE 9-1

ILLUSTRATION OF THE MULTIPLIER

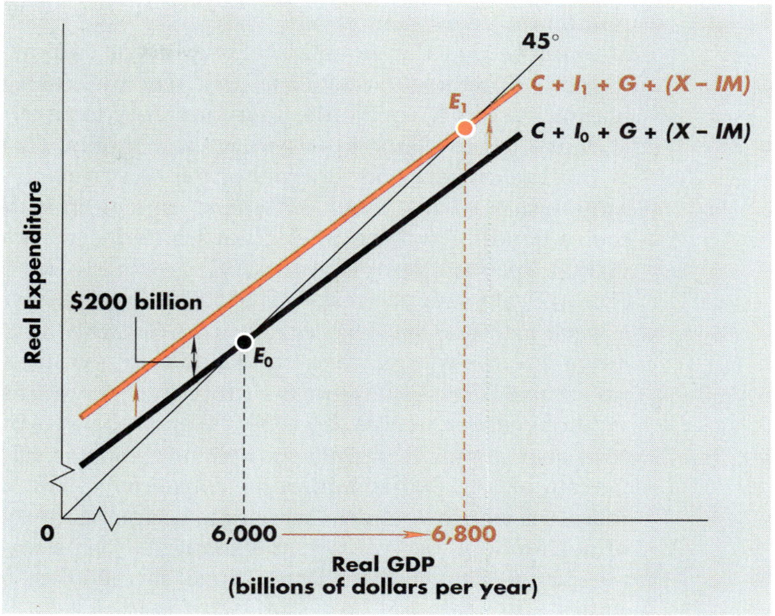

This figure depicts the multiplier effect of a rise in investment spending of \$200 billion. The expenditure schedule shifts upward from $C + I_0 + G + (X - IM)$ to $C + I_1 + G + (X - IM)$, thus moving equilibrium from point E_0 to point E_1. The rise in income is \$800 billion, so the multiplier is \$800/\$200 = 4.

So far no act of magic has occurred—things look just as you might expect. But one more step will bring the multiplier rabbit out of the hat. Let us see what the upward shift of the expenditure line does to equilibrium income. In Figure 9-1, equilibrium moves outward from point E_0 to point E_1; that is, from \$6,000 billion to \$6,800 billion. The difference is an increase in national income of \$800 billion. All this from a \$200 billion stimulus to investment? That is the magic of the multiplier.

Because the change in I is \$200 billion and the change in equilibrium Y is \$800 billion, by applying our definition, the multiplier is:

$$\text{Multiplier} = \frac{\text{Change in } Y}{\text{Change in } I} = \frac{\$800}{\$200} = 4$$

This tells us that, in our example, every additional dollar of investment demand will add \$4 to equilibrium GDP!

This does indeed seem mysterious. Can something be created from nothing? Let us first check that the graph has not deceived us. The first and last columns of Table 9-1 show in numbers what Figure 9-1 shows in a picture. Notice that equilibrium now comes at Y = \$6,800 billion. This equilibrium level of GDP is \$800 billion higher than the \$6,000 billion level found in the last chapter, when investment was only \$900 billion. Thus, a \$200 billion rise in investment leads to an \$800 billion rise in equilibrium GDP. The multiplier really is 4.

DEMYSTIFYING THE MULTIPLIER: HOW IT WORKS

The multiplier result seems implausible at first, but it loses its mystery once we remember the circular flow of income and expenditure, and the simple fact that one person's spending is another person's income. To illustrate the logic of the multiplier and see why it is exactly 4 in our model economy, let us look more closely at what actually happens if businesses decide to spend an additional $1 million on investment goods.

Suppose that Generous Motors—a major corporation in Macroland—decides to spend $1 million to retool a factory to manufacture cars powered by compressed natural gas. Its $1 million expenditure goes to construction workers and owners of construction companies as wages and profits. That is, it becomes their *income.*

But the owners and workers of the construction firms will not keep their $1 million in the bank. They will spend most of it. If they are "typical" consumers, their spending will be $1 million times the marginal propensity to consume (MPC). In our example, the MPC is 0.75. So let us assume that they spend $750,000 and save the rest. *This $750,000 expenditure is a net addition to the nation's demand for goods and services exactly as Generous Motors' original $1 million expenditure was.* So, at this stage, the $1 million investment has already pushed GDP up some $1.75 million. But the process by no means stops here.

Shopkeepers receive the $750,000 spent by construction workers, and they in turn also spend 75 percent of their new income. This accounts for $562,500 (75 percent of $750,000) in additional consumer spending in the "third round." Next follows a fourth round in which the recipients of the $562,500 spend 75 percent of this amount, or $421,875, and so on. At each stage in the spending chain, people spend 75 percent of the additional income they receive, and the process continues. Consumption grows in each round.

Where does it all end? Does it all end? The answer is that it does, indeed, eventually end—with GDP a total of $4 million higher than it was before Generous Motors spent the original $1 million. The multiplier, is, indeed, 4.

Table 9-2 displays the basis for this conclusion. In the table, "round 1" represents Generous Motors' initial investment, which creates $1 million in income for construction workers; "round 2" represents the construction workers' spending which creates $750,000 in income for shopkeepers. The rest of the table proceeds accordingly; each entry in Column 2 is 75 percent of the previous entry. Column 3 tabulates the running sum of Column 2.

We see that after 10 rounds of spending, the initial $1 million investment has mushroomed to $3.77 million, and the sum is still growing. After 20 rounds, the total increase in GDP is over $3.98 million—near its eventual value of $4 million. While it takes quite a few rounds of spending before the multiplier chain is near 4, we see from the table that it hits 3 rather quickly. If each income recipient in the chain waits, say, 2 months before spending his new income, the multiplier will reach 3 in only about 10 months.

Figure 9-2 provides a graphical presentation of the numbers in the last column of Table 9-2. Notice how the multiplier builds up rapidly at first and then tapers off to approach its ultimate value (4 in this example) gradually.

While this is only a hypothetical example, the same thing occurs every day in the real world. For instance, a burst of new housing starts has a multiplier effect on everything from appliances and furniture to carpeting and insulation. Similarly, when a large company like AT&T makes an investment in a developing country, the multiplier effect boosts business activity in many sectors.

TABLE 9-2

THE MULTIPLIER SPENDING CHAIN

This table shows how the multiplier unfolds through time. Round 1 is Generous Motors' initial spending, which leads to $1 million in additional income to construction workers. Round 2 shows the construction workers spending 75 percent of this amount, since the marginal propensity to consume is 0.75. The other rounds proceed accordingly, with spending in each successive round equal to 75 percent of that in the previous round. Technically, the full multiplier of 4 is reached only after an "infinite" number of rounds. But, as can be seen, we are very close to the full amount after 20 rounds.

(1) Round Number	(2) Spending in This Round	(3) Cumulative Total
1	$1,000,000	$1,000,000
2	750,000	1,750,000
3	562,500	2,312,500
4	421,875	2,734,375
5	316,406	3,050,781
6	237,305	3,288,086
7	177,979	3,466,065
8	133,484	3,599,549
9	100,113	3,699,662
10	75,085	3,774,747
⋮	⋮	⋮
20	4,228	3,987,317
⋮	⋮	⋮
"Infinity"	0	4,000,000

FIGURE 9-2

HOW THE MULTIPLIER BUILDS

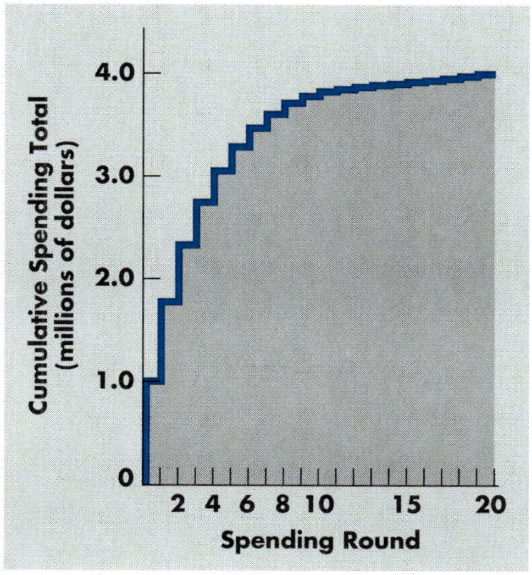

This diagram portrays the numbers from Table 9-2 and shows how the multiplier builds through time. Notice how the effect grows quickly at first and how the full effect is almost reached after 10 rounds.

ALGEBRAIC STATEMENT OF THE MULTIPLIER

Figure 9-2 and Table 9-2 probably make a persuasive case that the multiplier eventually reaches 4. But for the remaining skeptics we offer a simple algebraic proof.[1] Most of you learned about something called an *infinite geometric progression* in high school. This term refers to an infinite series of numbers, each one of which is a fixed fraction of the previous one. The fraction is called the *common ratio.* A geometric progression beginning with 1 and having a common ratio of 0.75 would look like this:

$$1 + 0.75 + (0.75)^2 + (0.75)^3 + \ldots.$$

More generally, a geometric progression beginning with 1 and having a common ratio R would be:

$$1 + R + R^2 + R^3 \ldots.$$

A simple formula enables us to sum such a progression as long as R is less than 1.[2] The formula is:[3]

$$\text{Sum of infinite geometric progression} = \frac{1}{1 - R}$$

Now we can recognize that the multiplier chain in Table 9-2 is just an infinite geometric progression with 0.75 as its common ratio. That is, each \$1 spent by Generous Motors leads to a $(0.75) \times \$1$ expenditure by construction workers, which in turn leads to a $(0.75) \times (0.75 \times \$1) = (0.75)^2 \times \$1$ expenditure by the shopkeepers, and so on. Thus, for each initial dollar of investment spending, the progression is:

$$1 + 0.75 + (0.75)^2 + (0.75)^3 + (0.75)^4 + \ldots.$$

Applying the formula for the sum of such a series, we find that:

$$\text{Multiplier} = \frac{1}{1 - 0.75} = \frac{1}{0.25} = 4$$

Notice how this result can be generalized. If we did not have a specific number for the marginal propensity to consume, but simply called it MPC, the geometric progression in Table 9-2 would have been:

$$1 + \text{MPC} + (\text{MPC})^2 + (\text{MPC})^3 + \ldots$$

---

[1]Students who blanch at the sight of algebra should not be put off. Anyone who can balance a checkbook (even many who cannot!) will be able to follow the argument.

[2]If R exceeds 1, nobody can possibly sum it—not even with the aid of a modern computer—because the sum is not a finite number.

[3]The proof of the formula is simple. Let the symbol S stand for the (unknown) sum of the series:

$$S = 1 + R + R^2 + R^3 + \ldots.$$

Then, multiplying by R,

$$RS = R + R^2 + R^3 + R^4 + \ldots.$$

By subtracting RS from S, we obtain:

$$S - RS = 1 \qquad \text{or} \qquad S = \frac{1}{1 - R}$$

which has the MPC as its common ratio. Applying the same formula for summing a geometric progression to this more general case gives us the following general result:

OVERSIMPLIFIED FORMULA FOR THE MULTIPLIER

$$\text{Multiplier} = \frac{1}{1 - \text{MPC}}$$

We call this formula "oversimplified" because it ignores many factors that are important in the real world. One of them is *international trade*—in particular, the fact that a country's imports depend on its GDP. We deal with this complication in Appendix B. A second factor is *inflation*, a complication we will address in the next chapter. A third is *income taxation*, a point we will elaborate in Chapter 11. The last important influence arises from the *financial system* and, after we discuss money and banking in Chapters 12 and 13, we will explain it in Chapter 14. As it turns out, each of these factors *reduces* the size of the multiplier.

We can begin to appreciate just how unrealistic the "oversimplified" formula is by considering some real numbers for the U.S. economy. The marginal propensity to consume (MPC) has been estimated many times and is about 0.9. From our oversimplified formula, then, it would seem that the multiplier should be:

$$\text{Multiplier} = \frac{1}{1 - 0.9} = \frac{1}{0.1} = 10$$

An **INDUCED INCREASE IN CONSUMPTION** is an increase in consumer spending that stems from an increase in consumer incomes. It is represented on a graph as a movement along a fixed consumption function.

In fact, the actual multiplier for the U.S. economy is believed to be less than 2. This is quite a discrepancy! But it does not mean that anything we have said about the multiplier so far is incorrect. Our story is simply incomplete. As we progress through this and subsequent chapters, you will learn why the multiplier is below 2 even though the MPC is close to 0.9. For now, we simply point out that:

While the multiplier is larger than 1 in the real world, it cannot be calculated with any degree of accuracy from the oversimplified formula. The actual multiplier is *much lower* than the formula suggests.

THE MULTIPLIER EFFECT OF CONSUMER SPENDING

Business firms that invest are not the only ones that can work the magic of the multiplier; so can consumers. To see how the multiplier works when the process is initiated by an upsurge in consumer spending, we must distinguish between two types of change in consumer spending.

An **AUTONOMOUS INCREASE IN CONSUMPTION** is an increase in consumer spending without any increase in incomes. It is represented on a graph as a shift of the entire consumption function.

When C rises because income rises—that is, when consumers move outward *along a fixed consumption function*—we call the increase in C an **induced increase in consumption.** However, if instead C rises because the entire consumption function *shifts up*, we call this an **autonomous increase in consumption.** The name indicates that consumption changes independently of income, and Chapter 7's discussion pointed out that a number of events, such as a change in the price level or in the value of the stock market, can initiate such a shift.

Let us suppose that, for some reason, consumer spending rises autonomously by $200 billion. In this case, we would revise our table of aggregate demand to

TABLE 9-3 TOTAL EXPENDITURE AFTER CONSUMERS DECIDE TO SPEND $200 BILLION MORE (billions of dollars per year)

(1) Income (*Y*)	(2) Consumption (*C*)	(3) Investment (*I*)	(4) Government Purchases (*G*)	(5) Net Exports (*X* − *IM*)	(6) Total Expenditure
4,800	3,200	900	1,300	−100	5,300
5,200	3,500	900	1,300	−100	5,600
5,600	3,800	900	1,300	−100	5,900
6,000	4,100	900	1,300	−100	6,200
6,400	4,400	900	1,300	−100	6,500
6,800	4,700	900	1,300	−100	6,800
7,200	5,000	900	1,300	−100	7,100

This table shows the construction of the total expenditure schedule for Macroland following an autonomous increase of $200 billion in consumption rather than in investment. Notice that Columns 2 and 3 differ from the corresponding columns in Table 9–1, but Column 6 is the same in both tables. Thus, the expenditure schedule in the 45° line diagram is the same as in the earlier example.

look like Table 9-3. Comparing this to Table 9-1 on page 188, we note that each entry in Column 2 is $200 billion *higher* than the corresponding entry in Table 9-1 (because consumption is higher), and each entry in Column 3 is $200 billion *lower* (because investment is lower).

The equilibrium level of income is clearly Y = $6,800 billion once again. Indeed, the entire expenditure schedule (Column 6) is the same as it was in Table 9-1. The initial rise of $200 billion in spending leads to an ultimate rise of $800 billion in GDP, just as occurred in the case of higher investment spending. In fact, Figure 9-1 applies directly to this case once we note that the upward shift is now caused by an autonomous change in C rather than in I. The multiplier for autonomous changes in consumer spending, then, is also 4 (= $800/$200).

The reason is straightforward. It does not matter who injects an additional dollar of spending into the economy, whether it is business investors or consumers. Wherever it comes from, 75 percent of it will be respent if the MPC is 0.75, and the recipients of this second round will, in turn, spend 75 percent of their additional income, and so on and on. And that is what constitutes the multiplier process.

THE MULTIPLIER EFFECT OF GOVERNMENT PURCHASES

What about the third component of total spending, government purchases (G)? Since we now know that the multiplier process is the same no matter who injects the additional dollar of spending into the economy, we conclude that G has to have the very same multiplier as I and C. Figure 9-1 can again be used to illustrate the conclusion graphically—just think of the upward shift as being caused by a change in G this time.

The multipliers are identical because the logic behind them is identical. The multiplier spending chain set in motion when Generous Motors spent $1 million to build a factory could equally well have been kicked off by the government buying $1 million worth of new cars from Generous Motors. Thereafter, each recipient of additional income would spend 75 percent of it (the assumed marginal propensity to consume), until $4 million in new income had eventually been created.

The idea that changes in *G* have multiplier effects on GDP will play a central role in the discussion of government stabilization policy that begins in Chapter 11. So it is worth noting here that:

Changes in the volume of government purchases of goods and services will change the equilibrium level of GDP in the same direction, and by a multiplied amount.

This is, more or less, what happened in Kansas starting in 1989. In the "first round," the state government spent money on road building. But in the "second round," the construction workers spent most of their paychecks on unrelated (to road building) items like groceries, paint, and toys for their kids. In the "third" and subsequent rounds, yet more recipients of new income purchased still different goods and services. Pretty soon, the whole state economy was booming.

THE MULTIPLIER EFFECT OF NET EXPORTS

At this point, it will not surprise you to learn that a change in net exports has precisely the same multiplier effect on equilibrium GDP as a change in any of the other components of spending. The reason is hardly mysterious. When foreigners buy U.S. products, they put income into the hands of Americans, just as domestic investment does. As this income is spent and respent, a multiplier process is set in motion, raising GDP.

Although we will have much more to learn about how the U.S. economy is linked to the economies of other countries in Part IV, this simple analysis of the multiplier effect of foreign trade already teaches us an important lesson: *Booms and recessions tend to be transmitted across national borders.*

Why is that? Suppose a boom abroad raises aggregate demand and GDP in foreign countries. With rising incomes, foreigners will buy more American goods—which means that U.S. exports will rise. But a rise in our exports will, via the multiplier, raise GDP in the United States. By this mechanism, rapid economic growth abroad contributes to rapid economic growth here.

Of course, the same mechanism also operates in the downward direction. Suppose some of the countries that trade with us slip into recession. As their GDPs decline, so do their *imports.* But this means that the United States will experience a decline in *exports* which, through the multiplier, will pull down GDP here. Hence, a recession abroad can contribute to recessionary conditions in the United States.

Naturally, what foreign countries do to us, we also do to them. Thus, rapid economic growth in the United States tends to produce boom conditions in the countries from which we buy, and recessions here tend quickly to spill beyond our borders. In summary:

The GDPs of the major economies are linked by trade. A boom in one country tends to raise its imports and hence push up exports and GDP in other countries. Similarly, a recession in one country tends to pull GDP down in other countries.

So, for example, strong economic growth in the United States in 1993 and 1994 helped pull several European countries out of recession, just as recession in the United States in 1990–1991 had hurt Europe.

THE MULTIPLIER IN REVERSE

A good way to check your understanding of the multiplier process is to run it in reverse: What happens if, for example, consumers abruptly decide to spend less? For example, suppose a wave of thriftiness comes over the people of Macroland so that, no matter what their total income, they now want to spend $200 billion *less* than they did previously rather than the $200 billion *more* assumed in Table 9-1.

A decision to spend $200 billion less out of any given level of income is, by definition, a *downward* shift of the total expenditure schedule by $200 billion. This is shown in Figure 9-3, where the $C + I + G + (X - IM)$ schedule falls from $C_0 + I + G + (X - IM)$ to $C_1 + I + G + (X - IM)$. The horizontal distance between these two parallel lines is the $200 billion drop in spending.

There are two ways to calculate the multiplier. First, our oversimplified multiplier formula tells us that the multiplier is:

$$\frac{1}{1 - \text{MPC}} = \frac{1}{1 - 0.75} = \frac{1}{0.25} = 4$$

So a $200 billion drop in spending will lead to a multiplier effect of $800 billion. Alternatively, we can read this conclusion from Figure 9-3. Here the economy's equilibrium point moves down the 45° line from point E_0 to E_1; income drops from $6,000 billion to $5,200 billion—a decline of $800 billion.

Now compare the analysis of a decline in spending summarized in Figure 9-3 with the previous analysis of an increase in spending shown in Figure 9-1 on page 189. You will see that everything is simply turned in the opposite direction. The multiplier works in both directions.

FIGURE 9-3

THE MULTIPLIER IN REVERSE

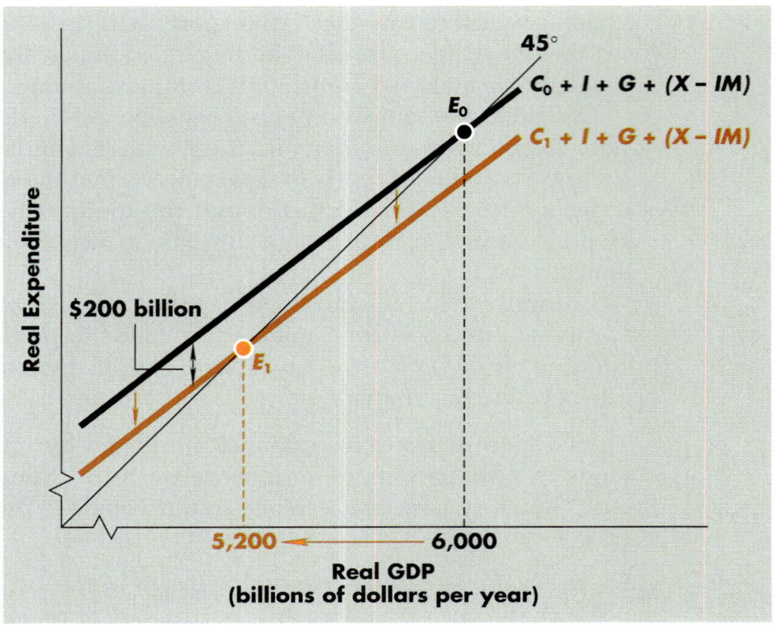

This diagram shows the multiplier effect of an autonomous decline in consumer spending of $200 billion. The decline appears as a downward shift of $200 billion in the expenditure schedule, which falls from $C_0 + I + G + (X - IM)$ to $C_1 + I + G + (X - IM)$. Equilibrium, which is always at the intersection of the expenditure schedule and the 45° line, moves from point E_0 to point E_1, and income falls from $6,000 billion to $5,200 billion.

THE PARADOX OF THRIFT

This last example of multiplier analysis teaches us an important lesson: an increase in the desire to save will lead to a cumulative fall in GDP. And, *because saving depends on income,* the resulting decline in national income will pull saving down. In consequence, saving may fail to rise despite an increase in the public's desire to save.

Let us be a bit more specific about this remarkable result. Before the upsurge in saving, consumers were spending \$3,900 billion out of a total national income of \$6,000 billion, as we can see in Table 8-1 on page 173. How much was being saved? Since taxes in Macroland are assumed to be fixed at \$1,200 billion, disposable income was:

$$\text{DI} = Y - T = \$6{,}000 - \$1{,}200 = \$4{,}800 \text{ billion}$$

Hence, saving was \$900 billion (= \$4,800 − \$3,900).

In Figure 9-3, GDP falls to \$5,200 billion, so disposable income drops to \$4,000. Since investment, government purchases, and net exports are all unchanged, the entire \$800 billion drop in GDP must come out of consumption, which therefore falls by \$800 billion (to \$3,100 billion). Thus, DI is down to \$4,000 billion and C is down to \$3,100 billion, leaving total saving still \$900 billion. The effort to save more has been totally frustrated by the decline in GDP.[4]

The **PARADOX OF THRIFT** is the fact that an effort by a nation to save more may simply reduce national income and fail to raise total saving.

This remarkable result is called the **paradox of thrift,** because it shows that, while saving may pave the road to riches for an individual, if the nation as a whole decides to save more, the result may be a recession and the falling incomes that come with it. The paradox of thrift is important because it is contrary to most people's thinking, and it means that a greater desire to save may be a mixed blessing if it is not accompanied by greater desire to invest.

THE MULTIPLIER AND THE AGGREGATE DEMAND CURVE

At this point, we must recall something mentioned at the start of the chapter: Income-expenditure diagrams such as Figures 9-1 and 9-3 can be drawn up only for a given price level. A different price level leads to a different total expenditure curve. This means that our oversimplified multiplier formula measures *the increase in real GDP demanded that would occur if the price level were fixed.* That is, it measures the *horizontal shift* of the economy's aggregate demand curve.

Figure 9-4 illustrates this conclusion by supposing that the price level that underlies Figure 9-1 is $P = 100$. The top panel simply repeats Figure 9-1 and shows how an increase in investment spending from \$900 to \$1,100 billion leads to an increase in GDP from \$6,000 to \$6,800 billion.

The bottom panel shows two downward-sloping aggregate demand curves. The first, labeled D_0D_0, depicts the situation when investment is \$900 billion. Point E_0 on this curve indicates that, at the given price level ($P = 100$), the equilibrium quantity of GDP demanded is \$6,000 billion. It corresponds exactly to point E_0 in the top panel. The second aggregate demand curve, D_1D_1, depicts the situation after investment has risen to \$1,100 billion. Point E_1 on this curve

---

[4]It is even possible to devise examples in which total saving goes *down* when people attempt to save more. This will happen, for example, if there is *induced investment.*

FIGURE 9-4

TWO VIEWS OF THE MULTIPLIER

The top panel repeats Figure 9-1. The bottom panel shows two aggregate demand curves. Curve D_0D_0, which applies when investment is \$900 billion, shows that equilibrium GDP on the demand side comes at $Y = \$6{,}000$ billion when $P = 100$ (point E_0). Curve D_1D_1, which applies when investment is \$1,100 billion, shows that equilibrium GDP on the demand side comes at $Y = \$6{,}800$ billion when $P = 100$ (point E_1). The horizontal distance between points E_0 and E_1 in the bottom panel indicates the oversimplified multiplier effect.

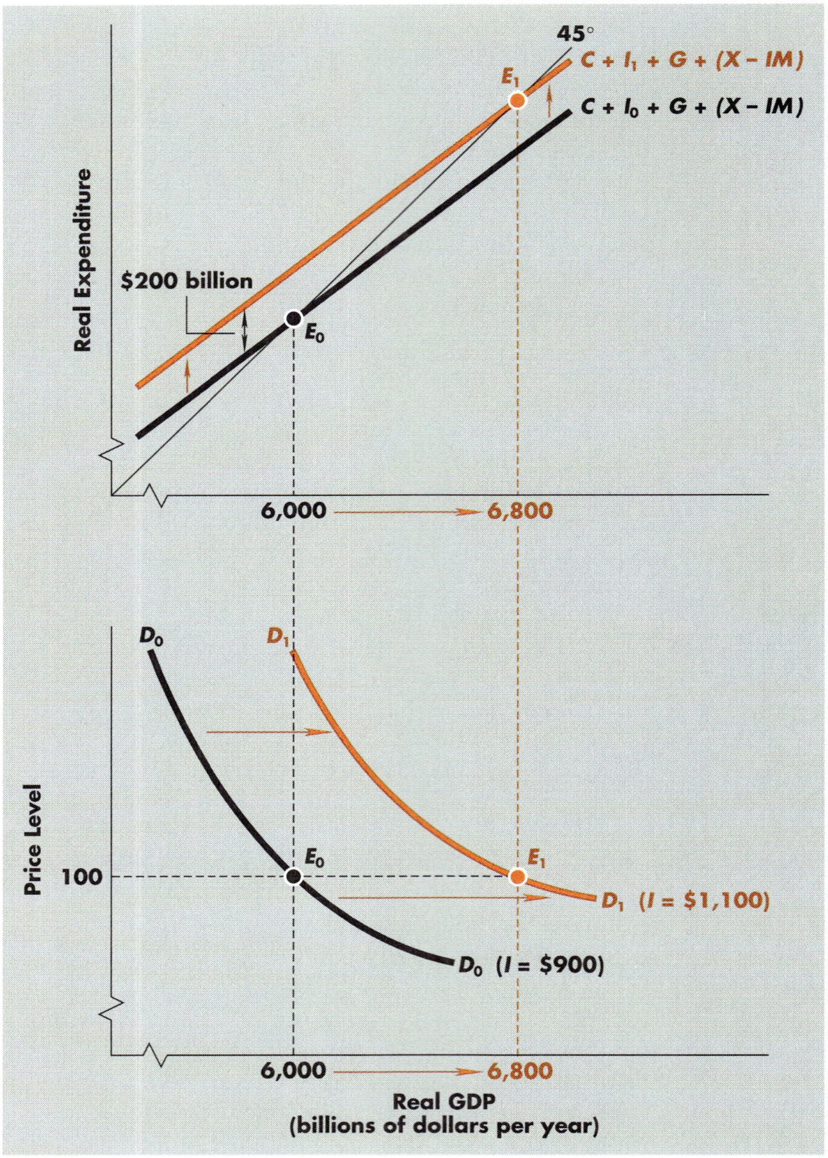

indicates that the equilibrium quantity of GDP demanded when $P = 100$ has risen to \$6,800 billion, which corresponds exactly to point E_1 in the top panel.

As Figure 9-4 shows, the horizontal distance between the two aggregate demand curves is exactly equal to the increase in real GDP shown in the income-expenditure diagram—in this case, \$800 billion. Thus:

An autonomous increase in spending leads to a horizontal shift of the aggregate demand curve by an amount given by the oversimplified multiplier formula.

Thus, everything we have learned about the multiplier applies to *shifts of the economy's aggregate demand curve.* If businesses decide to increase their investment spending, or if the consumption function shifts up, or if the government or foreigners decide to buy more goods, the aggregate demand curve moves horizontally to the right—as indicated in Figure 9-4. If any of these variables move down instead, the aggregate demand curve moves horizontally to the left.

Thus, the economy's aggregate demand curve cannot be expected to stand still for long. Autonomous changes in one or another of the four components of total spending will cause the aggregate demand curve to move around. But to understand the consequences of shifts of aggregate demand, we must bring the aggregate supply curve into the picture. That is the task of the next chapter.

SUMMARY

1. Any autonomous increase in expenditure has a **multiplier** effect on GDP; that is, it increases GDP by more than the original increase in spending.
2. The reason for this multiplier effect is that one person's additional expenditure constitutes a new source of income for another person, and this additional income leads to still more spending, and so on.
3. The multiplier also works in reverse: An autonomous decrease in any component of aggregate demand leads to a multiplied decrease in national income.
4. The multiplier is the same for an **autonomous increase in consumption,** investment, government purchases, or net exports.
5. A simple formula for the multiplier says that its numerical value is $1/(1 - \text{MPC})$. This formula, which is too simple to give accurate results, measures the horizontal shift of the aggregate demand curve.
6. Rapid (or sluggish) economic growth in one country contributes to rapid (or sluggish) growth in other countries because one country's imports are other countries' exports.
7. If the nation as a whole decides to save more, that is, to consume less, the resulting decline in national income may serve to make everyone poorer. This possibility that thriftiness, while a virtue for the individual, may be disastrous for an entire nation, is called the **paradox of thrift.**

KEY TERMS

The multiplier
Induced increase in consumption
Autonomous increase in consumption
Paradox of thrift

QUESTIONS FOR REVIEW

1. Try to remember where you last spent a dollar. Explain how this dollar will lead to a multiplier chain of increased income and spending. (Who received the dollar? What will he or she do with it?)
2. Use both numerical and graphical methods to find the multiplier effect of the following shift in the consumption function in an economy in which investment is always \$220, government purchases are always \$100, and net exports are always \$40. (*Hint:* What is the marginal propensity to consume?)

Income	Consumption before Shift	Consumption after Shift
1,080	880	920
1,140	920	960
1,200	960	1,000
1,260	1,000	1,040
1,320	1,040	1,080
1,380	1,080	1,120
1,440	1,120	1,160
1,500	1,160	1,200

3. Turn back to Review Question 3 in Chapter 8 (page 184). Suppose investment spending rises to \$260, and the price level is fixed. By how much will the equilibrium GDP increase? Derive the answer both numerically and graphically.
4. Explain the paradox of thrift. Why do you think it is called a paradox?
5. (More difficult) Suppose the consumption function is as given in Review Question 8 of Chapter 8 (page 184):

$$C = 300 + 0.75\text{DI}$$

and investment (I) rises to 1,100 while net exports ($X - IM$) remain at -100, government purchases remain at 1,300, and taxes remain at 1,200. Use the equilibrium condition $Y = C + I + G + (X - IM)$ to find the equilibrium level of GDP. (In working out the answer, assume the price level is fixed.) Compare your answer to Table 9-1 and Figure 9-1. Now compare your answer to the answer to Review Question 8 of Chapter 8. What do you learn about the multiplier?
6. (More difficult) Look back at Review Question 9 of Chapter 8 (page 184). What is the multiplier for this economy? If G rises by 100, what happens to Y? What happens to Y if both G and T rise by 100 at the same time?

APPENDIX A THE SIMPLE ALGEBRA OF THE MULTIPLIER

The appendix to Chapter 8 presented a general expression for the equilibrium level of GDP when the price level is fixed, investment (I), government purchases (G), taxes (T), and net exports ($X - IM$) are all constant, and the consumption function is:

$$C = a + b\text{DI} = a + b(Y - T)$$

The answer obtained there (which can be found on page 185) was:

$$Y = \frac{a - bT + I + G + (X - IM)}{1 - b}$$

From this formula, it is easy to derive the oversimplified multiplier formula algebraically and to show that it applies equally well to a change in investment, autonomous consumer spending, government purchases, or net exports. To do so, suppose that any of the symbols in the numerator of the multiplier formula increases by 1 unit. In any of these cases, GDP would rise from the previous formula to:

$$Y = \frac{a - bT + I + G + (X - IM) + 1}{1 - b}$$

By comparing this with the previous expression for Y, we see that a 1-unit change in any component of spending changes equilibrium GDP by:

$$\text{Change in } Y = \frac{a - bT + I + G + (X - IM) + 1}{1 - b} - \frac{a - bT + I + G + (X - IM)}{1 - b}$$

or

$$\text{Change in } Y = \frac{1}{1 - b}$$

Recalling that b is the marginal propensity to consume, we see that this is precisely the oversimplified multiplier formula.

APPENDIX B THE MULTIPLIER WITH VARIABLE IMPORTS

In Chapters 8 and 9, we assumed that net exports were a fixed number. But in fact a nation's imports depend on its GDP. The reason is simple; higher GDP leads to higher incomes, some of which is spent on foreign goods. Thus:

Our imports rise as our GDP rises and fall as our GDP falls.

Similarly, our *exports* are the *imports* of other countries, so it is natural to assume that our

TABLE 9-4 EQUILIBRIUM INCOME WITH VARIABLE IMPORTS (billions of dollars per year)

(1) Gross Domestic Product (Y)	(2) Consumer Expenditures (C)	(3) Investment (I)	(4) Government Purchases (G)	(5) Exports (X)	(6) Imports (IM)	(7) Net Exports (X − IM)	(8) Total Expenditure [C + I + G + (X − IM)]
4,800	3,000	900	1,300	650	570	+80	5,280
5,200	3,300	900	1,300	650	630	+20	5,520
5,600	3,600	900	1,300	650	690	−40	5,760
6,000	3,900	900	1,300	650	750	−100	6,000
6,400	4,200	900	1,300	650	810	−160	6,240
6,800	4,500	900	1,300	650	870	−220	6,480
7,200	4,800	900	1,300	650	930	−280	6,720

exports depend on *their* GDPs, not on our own. Thus:

Our exports are relatively insensitive to our own GDP, but are quite sensitive to the GDPs of other countries.

This appendix derives the implications of these rather elementary observations. In particular, it shows that once we recognize the dependence of a nation's imports on its GDP:

International trade lowers the value of the multiplier.

To see why, we begin with Table 9-4, which adapts the example of Macroland to allow imports to depend on GDP. Columns 2 through 4 are the same as in Table 8-1 on page 173; they show C, I, and G at alternative levels of GDP. Columns 5 and 6 record revised assumptions about the behavior of exports and imports. Exports are fixed at $650 billion regardless of GDP. But imports are assumed to rise by $60 billion for every $400 billion rise in GDP, which is a simple numerical example of the idea that imports depend on GDP. Column 7 subtracts imports from exports to get net exports, $(X - IM)$, and Column 8 adds up the four components of total expenditure, $C + I + G + (X - IM)$. The equilibrium, you can see, occurs at $Y = \$6{,}000$ billion, just as it did in Chapter 8.

Figures 9-5 and 9-6 display the same conclusion graphically. The upper panel of Figure 9-5 shows that exports are fixed at $650 billion regardless of GDP while imports increase as GDP rises, just as in Table 9-4. The difference between exports and imports, or net exports, is positive until GDP reaches around $5,300 billion and negative once GDP surpasses that amount. The bottom panel of Figure 9-5 shows the subtraction explicitly and makes it clear that:

Net exports decline as GDP rises.

Figure 9-6 carries this analysis over to the 45° line diagram. We begin with the familiar $C + I + G + (X - IM)$ line of Chapters 8 and 9 in black. There we simply assumed that net exports were fixed at −$100 billion regardless of GDP. Now that we have amended our model to note that net exports decline as GDP rises, the sum $C + I + G + (X - IM)$ rises more slowly than we previously assumed. This is shown by the orange line. Note that it is less steep than the black line.

Let us now consider what happens if exports rise by $160 billion while imports remain as in Table 9-4. Table 9-5 shows that equilibrium now occurs at a GDP of $Y = \$6{,}400$ billion. Naturally, higher exports have raised domestic GDP. But consider the magnitude. A $160 billion increase in exports (from $650 billion to $810 billion) leads to an increase of $400 billion in GDP (from $6,000 billion to $6,400 billion). So the multiplier is 2.5 (= $400/$160).[5]

[5]EXERCISE: Construct a version of Table 9-4 to show what would happen if imports rose by $160 billion at every level of GDP while exports remained at $650 billion. You should be able to show that the new equilibrium would be $Y = \$5{,}600$.

FIGURE 9-5

THE DEPENDENCE OF NET EXPORTS ON GDP

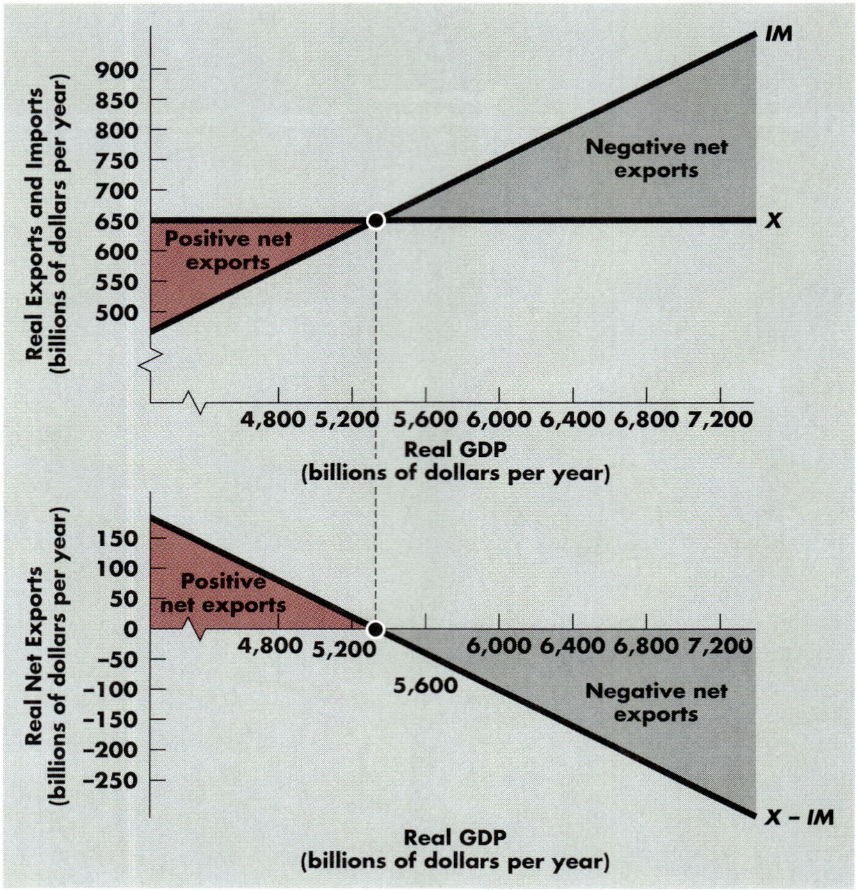

This graph displays the data on exports, imports, and net exports found in Table 9-4. Exports, *X*, are independent of GDP while imports, *IM*, rise as GDP rises (top panel). As a result, net exports, (*X* – *IM*), decline as GDP rises (bottom panel).

FIGURE 9-6

EQUILIBRIUM GDP WITH VARIABLE IMPORTS

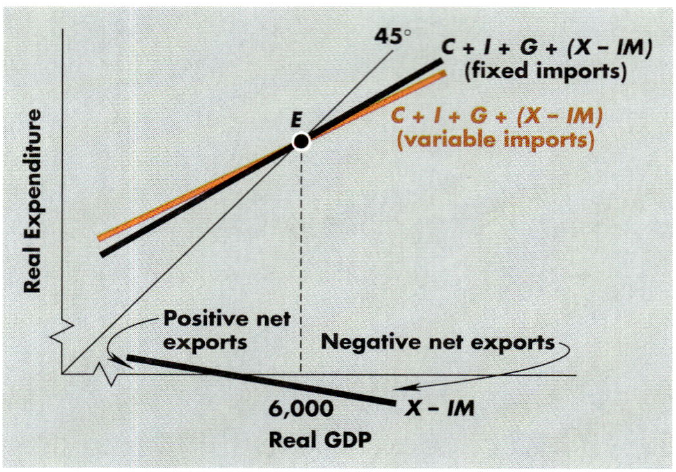

In the presence of variable imports, equilibrium GDP occurs where the orange $C + I + G + (X - IM)$ line, rather than the black one, crosses the 45° line. In the graph, equilibrium is at point *E*, where GDP is $6,000 billion. This matches the equilibrium we found in Chapter 8 (Figure 8-3 on page 175) with fixed imports because we have designed the example to come out that way.

TABLE 9-5 EQUILIBRIUM INCOME AFTER A $160 BILLION RISE IN EXPORTS (billions of dollars per year)

(1) Gross Domestic Product (*Y*)	(2) Consumer Expenditures (*C*)	(3) Investment (*I*)	(4) Government Purchases (*G*)	(5) Exports (*X*)	(6) Imports (*IM*)	(7) Net Exports (*X* − *IM*)	(8) Total Expenditure [*C* + *I* + *G* + (*X* − *IM*)]
4,800	3,000	900	1,300	810	570	+240	5,440
5,200	3,300	900	1,300	810	630	+180	5,680
5,600	3,600	900	1,300	810	690	+120	5,920
6,000	3,900	900	1,300	810	750	+60	6,160
6,400	4,200	900	1,300	810	810	0	6,400
6,800	4,500	900	1,300	810	870	−60	6,640
7,200	4,800	900	1,300	810	930	−120	6,880

This same conclusion is shown graphically in Figure 9-7, where the line $C + I + G + (X_0 - IM)$ represents the original expenditure schedule and the line $C + I + G + (X_1 - IM)$ represents the expenditure schedule after the rise in exports. Equilibrium shifts from point *E* to point *A*, and GDP rises by $400 billion.

Notice that the multiplier in this example is 2.5, whereas in the chapter, with net exports taken to be a fixed number, it was 4. This simple example illustrates a general result: *International trade lowers the numerical value of the multiplier.* Why is this so? Because, in an open economy, any autonomous increase in spending is partly dissipated in purchases of foreign goods, which creates additional income for *foreigners* rather than for domestic citizens.

Figure 9-6 shows this same conclusion graphically. Because net exports decline as GDP rises, the total expenditure line is *flatter* in the presence of variable imports [orange $C + I + G + (X - IM)$ line] than it would be with fixed imports (black

FIGURE 9-7 THE MULTIPLIER WITH VARIABLE IMPORTS

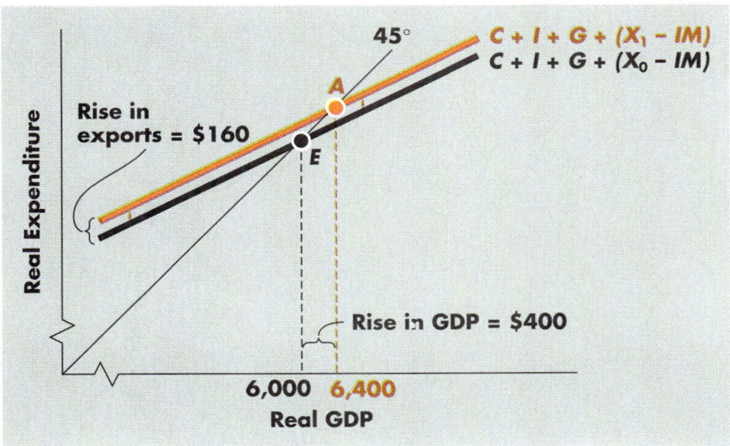

This diagram shows a $160 billion increase in exports as a vertical shift of the total expenditure schedule from $C + I + G + (X_0 - IM)$, to $C + I + G + (X_1 - IM)$. As a result, equilibrium shifts from point *E* to point *A*, and GDP rises from $6,000 billion to $6,400 billion. The multiplier is therefore 2.5 (= $400/$160).

line). As we know from earlier chapters, the *size* of the multiplier depends on the *slope* of the expenditure schedule—steeper expenditure schedules lead to larger multipliers. Since variable imports flatten the expenditure schedule, they lower the multiplier.[6]

Thus, international trade gives us the first of what will eventually be several reasons why the oversimplified multiplier formula overstates the true value of the multiplier.

[6]For those who like formulas, we can amend the oversimplified multiplier formula to allow for international trade. That formula was: Multiplier = $1/(1 - b)$ where b is the marginal propensity to consume. If we define the *marginal propensity to import* as the rise in imports per dollar of GDP (the marginal propensity to import is 0.15 in our example) and symbolize it by the letter m, the formula for the multiplier with foreign trade is: Multiplier $= 1/(1 - b + m)$. This formula clearly shows that a higher value of m leads to a lower multiplier.

SUMMARY

1. Because imports rise as GDP rises while exports are insensitive to (domestic) GDP, net exports decline as GDP rises.
2. If imports depend on GDP, international trade reduces the value of the multiplier.

QUESTIONS FOR REVIEW

1. Suppose exports and imports of a country are given by:

GDP	Exports	Imports
$2,500	$400	$250
3,000	400	300
3,500	400	350
4,000	400	400
4,500	400	450
5,000	400	500

Calculate net exports at each level of GDP.

2. If domestic expenditure (the sum of $C + I + G$ in the economy described in Review Question 1) is as shown below, construct a 45° line diagram and locate the equilibrium level of GDP.

GDP	Domestic Expenditures
$2,500	$3,100
3,000	3,400
3,500	3,700
4,000	4,000
4,500	4,300
5,000	4,600

3. Now raise exports to $650 and find the equilibrium again. How large is the multiplier?

CHAPTER 10

SUPPLY-SIDE EQUILIBRIUM: UNEMPLOYMENT *AND* INFLATION?

We might as well reasonably dispute whether it is the upper or the under blade of a pair of scissors that cuts a piece of paper, as whether value is governed by [demand] or [supply].
Alfred Marshall

In Chapter 8, we learned that the position of the economy's total expenditure schedule governs whether the economy will experience a recessionary or an inflationary gap. If the $C + I + G + (X - IM)$ schedule is "too low," a *recessionary gap* will arise. A $C + I + G + (X - IM)$ schedule that is "too high" leads to an *inflationary gap.* Which sort of gap actually occurs is of considerable importance because a recessionary gap normally spells unemployment while an inflationary gap leads to inflation.

The tools provided in Chapter 8, however, are not sufficient to determine which sort of gap will arise because, as we learned there, the position of the expenditure schedule depends on the price level. And the price level is determined by *both* aggregate demand *and* aggregate supply. Hence, the task of this chapter: to bring the supply side of the economy into the picture.

We begin by explaining how the *aggregate supply curve* is derived from business costs. Next we consider the interaction of aggregate supply and aggregate demand, and how they jointly determine output and the price level. With this apparatus in hand, we return to recessionary and inflationary gaps and study how the economy adjusts to each. Doing this puts us in a position to deal with the crucial question raised in earlier chapters: Does the economy have an efficient self-correcting mechanism? We shall see that the answer is "yes, but." Yes, but it works slowly. Finally, we use aggregate supply–aggregate demand analysis to explain the vexing problem of *stagflation*—the simultaneous occurrence of high unemployment *and* high inflation—that plagued the economy in the 1980s.

DEBATE: TWO SIDES TO THE SUPPLY SIDE

In 1981, President Ronald Reagan brought to Washington a doctrine called *supply-side economics*—a new theory advertised as a replacement for the Keynesian theory we have been studying so far. Reaganite supply-side economics, which was controversial from the start, emphasized tax cuts that allegedly would increase saving and investment—and thus augment the *supply* of capital.

Twelve years later, the American voters repudiated Reaganomics and voted in President Bill Clinton who, ironically, also ran on what might be called a "supply-side" platform. Clintonomics, with its emphasis on upgrading the skills of the American work force through education and training, was starkly different from Reaganomics. But the two programs share one idea in common: that what happens on the *supply* side of the economy greatly affects inflation, unemployment, and economic growth.

This debate rages on as President Clinton and the Republican-controlled Congress battle over budget and tax priorities each year. The president insists on maintaining and expanding key government "investment" programs like job training and education. The Republicans insist on deeper spending cuts to make room for tax cuts. The political impasse over budget priorities actually led to two partial shutdowns of the U.S. government in late 1995. And, as this revision went to press, the budget negotiations of 1997 were off to a rocky start.

It is therefore time for us to consider the origins of the aggregate supply curve and the factors that can make it shift. Only when we have done so will we be ready to analyze the *joint* determination of output *and* the price level—with its consequences for inflationary and recessionary gaps—and to render a judgment on competing supply-side agendas. Read the next two chapters before making up your mind.

THE AGGREGATE SUPPLY CURVE

In earlier chapters we noted that aggregate demand is a schedule, not a fixed number. The quantity of real GDP that will be demanded depends on the price level, as summarized in the economy's *aggregate demand curve.*

Analogously, the concept of *aggregate supply* does not refer to a fixed number, but rather to a schedule (a *supply curve*). The volume of goods and services that profit-seeking enterprises will provide depends on the prices they obtain for their outputs, on wages and other production costs, on the state of technology, and on other things. The relationship between the price level and the quantity of real GDP supplied, *holding all other determinants of quantity supplied constant,* is called the economy's **aggregate supply curve.**

The **AGGREGATE SUPPLY CURVE** shows, for each possible price level, the quantity of goods and services that all the nation's businesses are willing to produce during a specified period of time, holding all other determinants of aggregate quantity supplied constant.

A typical aggregate supply curve is drawn in Figure 10-1. It slopes upward, meaning that as prices rise more output is produced, *other things held constant.* It is not difficult to understand why. Producers in the U.S. economy are motivated mainly by profit. The profit made by producing a unit of output is simply the difference between the price at which it is sold and the unit cost of production:

$$\text{Profit per unit} = \text{Price} - \text{Cost per unit}$$

So, the response of output to a rising price level—which is what the slope of the aggregate supply curve shows—depends on the response of costs.

Many of the prices that firms pay for labor and other inputs are relatively fixed for periods of time—though certainly not forever. Often, workers and firms enter into long-term labor contracts that set money wages up to 3 years in advance. Even where there are no explicit contracts, wage rates typically adjust only once a year. During the interim period, money wages are fixed. Similarly, a variety of material inputs are delivered to firms under long-term contracts at prearranged prices.

Why is it significant that firms often purchase inputs at prices that stay fixed for considerable periods of time? Because firms decide how much to produce by

FIGURE 10-1 AN AGGREGATE SUPPLY CURVE

This graph shows a typical aggregate supply curve. It has a positive slope (that is, it rises as we move to the right), meaning that the quantity of output supplied rises as the price level rises.

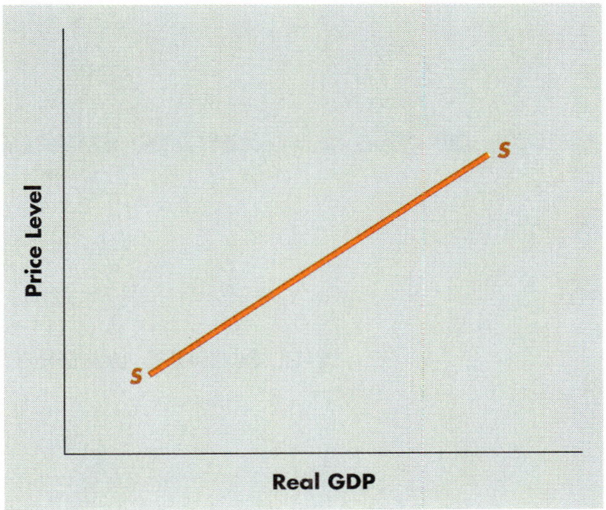

comparing their selling prices with their costs of production; and production costs depend, among other things, on input prices. If the selling prices of the firm's products rise while its wages and other factor costs are fixed, production becomes more profitable, and firms will presumably increase output.

A simple example will illustrate the idea. Suppose a firm uses 1 hour of labor to manufacture a gadget that sells for \$9. If workers earn \$8 per hour, and the firm has no other production costs, its profit per unit is:

$$\begin{aligned}\text{Profit per unit} &= \text{Price} - \text{Cost per unit}\\ &= \$9 - \$8 = \$1\end{aligned}$$

Now what happens if the price of a gadget rises to \$10, but wage rates remain constant? The firm's profit per unit becomes:

$$\begin{aligned}\text{Profit per unit} &= \text{Price} - \text{Cost per unit}\\ &= \$10 - \$8 = \$2\end{aligned}$$

With production more profitable, the firm will likely supply more gadgets.

The same process operates in reverse. If selling prices fall while input costs are relatively fixed, profit margins will be squeezed and production cut back. This behavior is summarized by the upward slope of the aggregate supply curve: Production rises when the price level (henceforth, P) rises, and falls when P falls. In other words:

The aggregate supply curve slopes upward because firms normally can purchase labor and other inputs at prices which are fixed for some period of time. Thus, higher selling prices for output make production more attractive.[1]

---

[1]There are both differences and similarities between the *aggregate* supply curve and the *microeconomic* supply curves studied in Chapter 4. Both are based on the idea that quantity supplied depends on how output prices move relative to input prices. But the aggregate supply curve pertains to the behavior of *the overall price level,* whereas a microeconomic supply curve pertains to the *price of some particular commodity.*

The phrase "for some period of time" alerts us to an important fact: The aggregate supply curve may not stand still for long. If wages or prices of other inputs change, as they surely will during inflationary times, then the aggregate supply curve will shift.

SHIFTS OF THE AGGREGATE SUPPLY CURVE

We have concluded so far that, for given levels of wages and other input prices, there will be an upward-sloping aggregate supply curve relating the price level to aggregate quantity supplied. Now let us consider what happens when these input prices change.

THE MONEY WAGE RATE

The most obvious determinant of the position of the aggregate supply curve is the *money wage rate.* Wages are the major element of cost in the economy, accounting for more than 70 percent of all inputs. Since higher wage rates mean higher costs, they spell lower profits at any given prices. That is why companies like American Airlines and Caterpillar have staged fierce battles with their unions in recent years in an effort to reduce wages.

Returning to our example, consider what would happen to a gadget producer if the money wage rose to $8.75 per hour while the price of a gadget remained $9. Profit per unit would decline from:

$$\$9 - \$8 = \$1$$

to

$$\$9.00 - \$8.75 = \$0.25$$

With profits squeezed, the firm would probably cut back on production.

This is the way firms in our economy typically react to a rise in wages. Therefore, a wage increase leads to a decrease in aggregate quantity supplied at current prices. Graphically, the aggregate supply curve shifts to the left (or inward), as shown in Figure 10-2. In this diagram, firms are willing to supply $6,000 billion in goods and services at a price level of 100 when wages are low (point *A*). But after wages increase these same firms are willing to supply only $5,500 billion at this price level (point *B*). By similar reasoning, the aggregate supply curve will shift to the right (or outward) if wages fall. Thus:

A rise in the money wage rate makes the aggregate supply curve *shift inward,* meaning that the quantity supplied at any price level *declines*. A fall in the money wage rate makes the aggregate supply curve *shift outward,* meaning that the quantity supplied at any price level *increases*.

PRICES OF OTHER INPUTS

In this regard, there is nothing special about wages. An increase in the price of *any* input that firms buy will shift the aggregate supply curve in the same way; that is:

The aggregate supply curve is shifted inward by an increase in the price of any input to the production process, and it is shifted *outward* by any decrease.

While there are many inputs other than labor, the one that has attracted the most attention in recent decades is energy. Increases in the price of energy, such

FIGURE 10-2

A SHIFT OF THE AGGREGATE SUPPLY CURVE

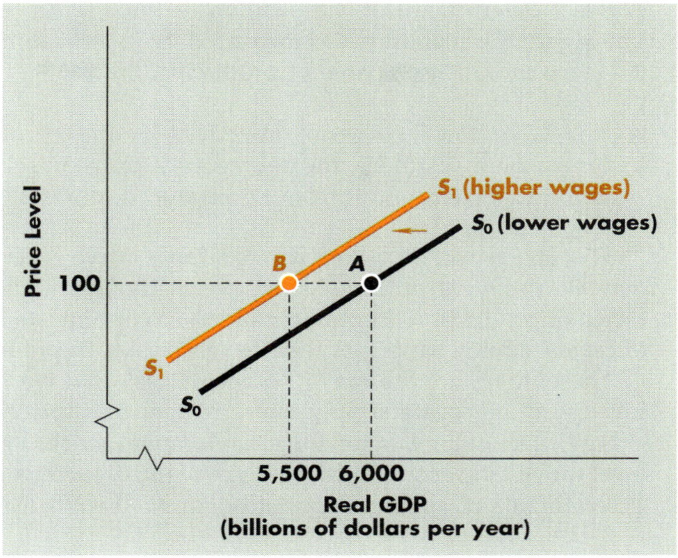

This diagram shows what happens to the economy's aggregate supply curve when money wages rise. Higher wages shift the supply curve inward from S_0S_0 to S_1S_1, leading, for example, to an output level of \$5,500 billion (point *B*), rather than \$6,000 (point *A*), when the price level is 100. The aggregate supply curve will shift inward in the same manner if the price of any other input (such as energy) increases.

as those that took place in the early 1980s and again during the 1990 Gulf war, push the aggregate supply curve inward more or less as shown in Figure 10-2. By the same token, a rise in the price of *any* input we import from abroad would have the effect shown in the figure.

TECHNOLOGY AND PRODUCTIVITY

PRODUCTIVITY is the amount of output produced by a unit of input.

Another factor that determines the position of the aggregate supply curve is the state of technology. Suppose, for example, that a technological breakthrough increases the **productivity** of labor, that is, output per hour of work. If wages do not change, such an improvement in productivity will *decrease* business costs, improve profitability, and encourage more production.

Once again, our gadget company will help us understand how this works. Suppose the price of a gadget stays at \$9 and the hourly wage rate stays at \$8, but gadget workers become much more productive. Specifically, suppose the labor input required to manufacture a gadget falls from 1 hour (which costs \$8) to three-quarters of an hour (which costs \$6). Then profit per unit rises from

$$\$9 - \$8 = \$1$$

to

$$\$9 - \$6 = \$3$$

The lure of higher profits should induce gadget manufacturers to increase production—which is, of course, why manufacturers are constantly striving to raise productivity. In brief, we have concluded that:

Improvements in productivity shift the aggregate supply curve outward.

Figure 10-2 can therefore be viewed as applying to a *decline* in productivity. Since the 1970s, slow growth of productivity has been a persistent problem for the U.S. economy, one that we will examine in depth in Chapter 20.

AVAILABLE SUPPLIES OF LABOR AND CAPITAL

The last determinant of the position of the aggregate supply curve is obvious. The bigger the economy—as measured by its available supplies of labor and capital—the more it is capable of producing. So:

As the labor force grows or improves in quality, and as the capital stock is increased by investment, the aggregate supply curve shifts *outward* to the right, meaning that more output can be produced at any given price level.

This last aspect of the aggregate supply curve is central to the political debate over alternative supply-side strategies. Although neither party excludes the other factor of production, Republicans tend to concentrate on augmenting the supply of *capital* while Democrats tend to emphasize improvements in *labor* quality.

These, then, are the major "other things" that we hold constant when drawing up an aggregate supply curve: wage rates, prices of other inputs (such as energy), technology, labor force, and capital stock. While a change in the price level moves the economy *along a given supply curve,* a change in any of the other determinants of aggregate quantity supplied *shifts the entire supply schedule.*

EQUILIBRIUM OF AGGREGATE DEMAND AND SUPPLY

Chapter 8 taught us that the price level is a crucial determinant of whether equilibrium GDP is below full employment (a "recessionary gap"), precisely at full employment, or above full employment (an "inflationary gap"). We are now in a position to analyze which type of gap, if any, will actually occur in any particular case. By combining the analysis of aggregate supply just completed with the analysis of aggregate demand from the last two chapters, we can determine *simultaneously* the equilibrium level of real GDP (Y) and the equilibrium price level (P).

Figure 10-3 displays the mechanics. Aggregate demand curve *DD* and aggregate supply curve *SS* intersect at point *E,* where real GDP is $6,000 billion and the price level is 100. As can be seen in the graph, at any higher price level, such as 120, aggregate quantity supplied would exceed aggregate quantity demanded. There would be a glut on the market as firms found themselves unable to sell all their output. As inventories piled up, firms would compete more vigorously for the available customers, thereby forcing prices down. Both the price level and production would fall.

At any price level lower than 100, such as 80, quantity demanded would exceed quantity supplied. There would be a shortage of goods on the market. With inventories disappearing and customers knocking on their doors, firms would be encouraged to raise prices. The price level would rise, and so would output. Only when the price level is 100 are the quantities of real GDP demanded and supplied equal. Therefore, only the combination of $P = 100$, $Y = \$6{,}000$ is an equilibrium.

Table 10-1 illustrates the same conclusion in another way, using a tabular analysis similar to that of Chapter 8 (refer back to Table 8-2, page 175). Columns 1 and 2 constitute an aggregate demand schedule corresponding to the aggregate demand curve *DD* in Figure 10-3. Columns 1 and 3 constitute an aggregate supply schedule corresponding exactly to aggregate supply curve *SS* in the figure.

It is clear from the table that equilibrium occurs only at $P = 100$ and $Y = \$6{,}000$. At any other price level, aggregate quantities supplied and demanded

FIGURE 10-3 EQUILIBRIUM OF REAL GDP AND THE PRICE LEVEL

This diagram shows how the equilibrium levels of real GDP and the price level are simultaneously determined by the intersection of the aggregate demand curve (*DD*) and the aggregate supply curve (*SS*). In this example, equilibrium occurs at point *E*, with a real GDP of \$6,000 billion and a price level of 100.

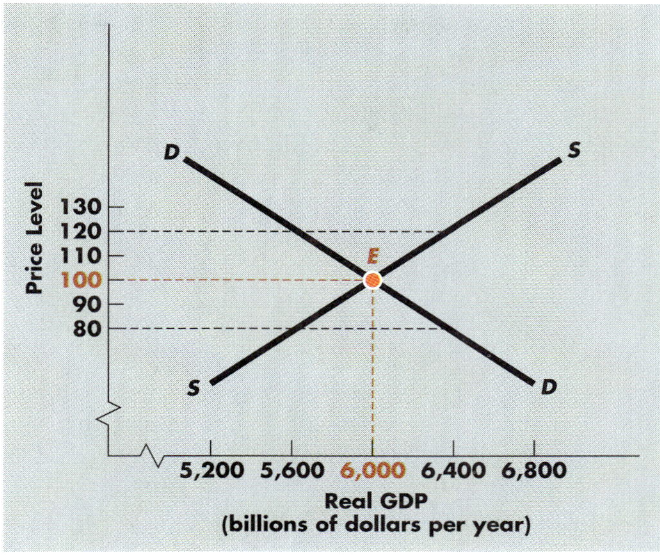

TABLE 10-1 DETERMINATION OF THE EQUILIBRIUM PRICE LEVEL

(1) Price Level	(2) Aggregate Quantity Demanded (billions of dollars)	(3) Aggregate Quantity Supplied (billions of dollars)	(4) Balance of Supply and Demand	(5) Prices Will
80	6,400	5,600	Quantity demanded exceeds quantity supplied	Rise
90	6,200	5,800	Quantity demanded exceeds quantity supplied	Rise
100	6,000	6,000	Quantity demanded equals quantity supplied	Remain the same
110	5,800	6,200	Quantity supplied exceeds quantity demanded	Fall
120	5,600	6,400	Quantity supplied exceeds quantity demanded	Fall

would be unequal, with consequent upward or downward pressure on prices. For example, at a price level of 90, customers demand \$6,200 billion worth of goods and services, but firms wish to provide only \$5,800 billion. The price level is too low and will be forced upward. Conversely, at a price level of, say, 110, quantity supplied (\$6,200 billion) exceeds quantity demanded (\$5,800 billion), implying that the price level must fall.

RECESSIONARY AND INFLATIONARY GAPS REVISITED

Let us now reconsider a question we posed, but could not answer, in Chapter 8: Will equilibrium occur at, below, or beyond full employment?

We could not give a complete answer to this question in Chapter 8 because we had no way to determine the equilibrium price level, and therefore no way to tell which type of gap, if any, would arise. The aggregate supply and demand analysis summarized in Figure 10-3 now gives us what we need. But we find that our answer is the same as it was in Chapter 8—anything can happen.

The reason is that nothing in Figure 10-3 tells us where full employment is; it could be above the $6,000 billion equilibrium level or below it. Depending on the locations of the aggregate demand and aggregate supply curves, then, we can reach equilibrium *above* full employment (an inflationary gap), *at* full employment, or *below* full employment (a recessionary gap). In the short run, with wages and other input costs fixed, that is all there is to it.

All three possibilities are illustrated in Figure 10-4. The three upper panels are familiar from Chapter 8. As we move from left to right, the expenditure schedule rises from $C + I_0 + G + (X - IM)$ to $C + I_1 + G + (X - IM)$ to $C + I_2 + G + (X - IM)$, leading respectively to a recessionary gap, an equilibrium at full employment, and an inflationary gap. In fact, the upper left-hand diagram looks just like Figure 8-6 (page 179), and the upper right-hand diagram duplicates Figure 8-7 (page 180). We emphasized in Chapter 8 that any one of the three cases is possible, depending on the price level and the expenditure schedule.

In the three lower panels, the equilibrium price level is determined at point *E* by the intersection of the aggregate supply curve (*SS*) and the aggregate demand curve (*DD*). But the same three possibilities emerge.

In the lower left-hand panel, aggregate demand is too low to provide jobs for the entire labor force, so there is a recessionary gap equal to distance *EB*, or $1,000 billion. This corresponds precisely to the situation depicted on the income-expenditure diagram immediately above it.

In the lower right-hand panel, aggregate demand is so high that the economy reaches an equilibrium well beyond full employment. There is an inflationary gap equal to *BE*, or $1,000 billion, just as in the diagram immediately above it.

In the lower middle panel, the aggregate demand curve D_1D_1 is at just the right level to produce an equilibrium at full employment. There is neither an inflationary nor a recessionary gap, as in the diagram just above it.

It may seem, therefore, that we have done nothing but restate our previous conclusions. But, in fact, we have done much more. Because now that we have studied the determination of the equilibrium price level, we are able to examine how the economy adjusts to either a recessionary gap or an inflationary gap. Specifically, since wages are fixed in the short run, any one of the three cases depicted in Figure 10-4 can occur. But, in the long run, wages will adjust to labor market conditions. It is to that adjustment that we now turn.

ADJUSTING TO A RECESSIONARY GAP: DEFLATION OR UNEMPLOYMENT?

Suppose the economy starts with a recessionary gap—that is, an equilibrium *below* full employment—as in the lower left-hand panel of Figure 10-4. This might be caused, for example, by inadequate consumer spending or by anemic investment spending. What happens next?

With equilibrium GDP below potential, jobs will be hard to find. The ranks of the unemployed will exceed the number expected to be jobless because of moving, changing occupations, and so on. In the terminology of Chapter 6, there

FIGURE 10-4 RECESSIONARY AND INFLATIONARY GAPS REVISITED

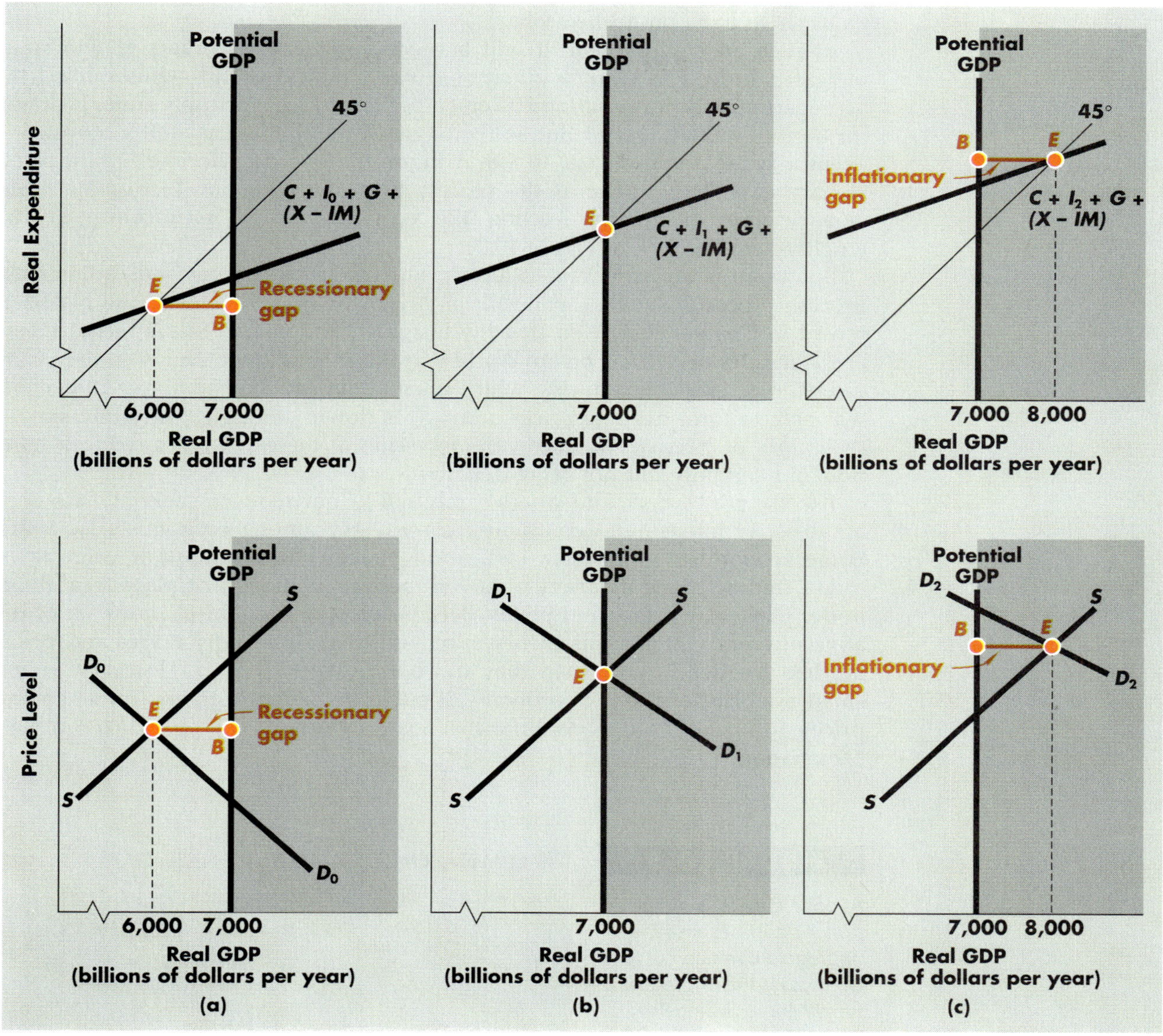

This diagram shows three possible types of equilibrium on two different diagrams. In the top row, income-expenditure diagrams from Chapter 8 are used to depict a recessionary gap, an equilibrium at full employment, and an inflationary gap. In the bottom row, these same three situations are shown on aggregate supply and demand diagrams. In each case, the aggregate supply curve is the same (*SS*), equilibrium occurs at point *E*, and full-employment GDP is $7,000 billion. In Panel (a), the aggregate demand curve D_0D_0 is relatively low, so that equilibrium falls below full employment. There is a recessionary gap measured by the distance *EB*, or $1,000 billion. In Panel (b), the aggregate demand curve D_1D_1 is higher, and equilibrium occurs precisely at full employment. There is no gap of either kind. In Panel (c), the aggregate demand curve D_2D_2 is so high that equilibrium occurs beyond full employment. There is an inflationary gap measured by the distance *BE*, or $1,000 billion.

will be a considerable amount of *cyclical unemployment*. Businesses, on the other hand, will have little trouble finding workers. And their current employees will be eager to hang on to their jobs.

In such an environment, it will be very difficult for workers to win wage increases. Indeed, in extreme situations, wages may even fall—thus shifting the aggregate supply curve *outward*. (Remember, an aggregate supply curve is drawn for a *given* money wage.) But as the aggregate supply curve shifts outward—eventually moving from S_0S_0 to S_1S_1 in Figure 10-5—prices decline and the recessionary gap shrinks. This is the process by which deflation erodes the recessionary gap, eventually leading the economy to an equilibrium at full employment (point F in Figure 10-5).

But there is an important catch. In our modern economy, this adjustment process proceeds slowly—painfully slowly. Our brief review of the historical record in Chapter 5 showed that the history of the United States includes several examples of *deflation* before World War II but none since. Not even the severe recession of 1981–1982, during which unemployment climbed above 10 percent, was able to force average prices and wages down—though it certainly slowed their rates of increase. Similarly, the recession of the early 1990s reduced inflation, but certainly did not bring deflation.

Exactly why wages and prices rarely fall in our modern economy has been a subject of intense and continuing controversy among economists for years. Some economists emphasize institutional factors like minimum wage laws, union contracts, and a variety of government regulations that place legal floors under particular wages and prices. Because most of these institutions are of relatively recent vintage, this theory successfully explains why wages and prices fall less frequently now than they did before World War II. However, only a small minority of the U.S. economy is subject to legal restraints on wage and price cutting. So it seems doubtful that legal restrictions can provide a complete explanation.

FIGURE 10-5 THE ELIMINATION OF A RECESSIONARY GAP

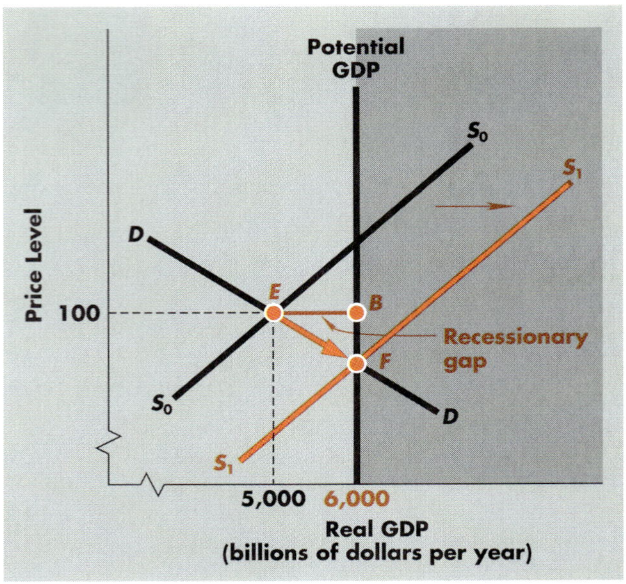

At point E there is a recessionary gap because the aggregate demand curve DD crosses the aggregate supply curve S_0S_0 below the level of potential GDP. As wages fall, the aggregate supply curve gradually shifts outward until it reaches the position indicated by supply curve S_1S_1. Here the economy has attained a full-employment equilibrium at point F. But if wages fall very slowly, the economy gets stuck with a recessionary gap and high unemployment for a long time.

Other observers suggest that workers have a profound psychological resistance to accepting a wage reduction. This theory certainly has the ring of truth. Think how you would react if your boss announced he was cutting your hourly wage rate. You might quit, or you might devote less care to your job. If the boss suspects you will react this way, he may be reluctant to cut your wage. Nowadays, genuine wage reductions are rare enough to be newsworthy. United Airlines was one of the few firms that managed to cut wages; workers accepted an average 15 percent pay cut shortly after a 1994 employee buyout of the company. Many other companies have tried, but failed, to win similar concessions from their workers.

While no one doubts that wage cuts can be bad for morale, the psychological theory has one major drawback. It fails to explain why the psychological resistance to wage cuts apparently started only after World War II. Until a satisfactory answer to this question is provided, many economists will remain skeptical.

A third explanation is based on a fact we emphasized in Chapter 5—that business cycles were less severe in the postwar period than they were in the prewar period. Because workers and firms came to believe that recessions would not turn into depressions, the argument goes, they may have decided to wait out the bad times rather than accept wage or price reductions that they would later regret.

Yet another theory is based on the old adage, "you get what you pay for." The idea is that workers differ in productivity, but that productivities of individual employees are hard to identify. Firms therefore worry that a general wage reduction will result in the loss of their best employees—since these workers have the best opportunities elsewhere in the economy. Rather than take this chance, the argument goes, firms prefer to maintain high wages even in recessions.

There are other theories as well, none of which commands a clear majority of professional opinion. But, regardless of the cause, we may as well accept the fact that, in our modern economy, prices and wages generally fall only sluggishly when demand is weak.

The implications of this rigidity are quite serious, for a recessionary gap cannot cure itself without some deflation. And if wages and prices will not fall, recessionary gaps like *EB* in Figure 10-5 will linger for a long time. That is:

When aggregate demand is low, the economy may get stuck with a recessionary gap for a long time. If wages and prices fall very slowly, the economy will endure a prolonged period of production below potential GDP.

DOES THE ECONOMY HAVE A SELF-CORRECTING MECHANISM?

Now a situation like this would, presumably, not last forever. As the recession lengthened, and perhaps deepened, more and more workers would be unable to find jobs at the prevailing high wages. Eventually, their need to be employed would overwhelm their resistance to wage cuts.

Firms, too, would become increasingly willing to cut prices as the period of weak demand persisted and managers became convinced that the slump was not merely a temporary aberration. Prices and wages did, in fact, fall during the Great Depression of the 1930s. And some fell again in the weak markets of the early 1990s.

However, nowadays political leaders of both parties believe it is folly to wait for falling wages and prices to eliminate a recessionary gap. They agree that *some* government action is both necessary and appropriate under recessionary conditions. But there is still vocal—and highly partisan—debate over how much and what kind of intervention is warranted. One reason for the disagreement is that the *self-correcting mechanism* does operate—if only weakly—to cure recessionary gaps.

AN EXAMPLE FROM RECENT HISTORY: DISINFLATION IN THE 1990s Recent history provides an excellent example. Recovery from the 1990–1991 recession was weak and long delayed, but it did eventually come. The unemployment rate peaked at 7.7 percent in June 1992 and then began a slow descent which brought it all the way down to 5.4 percent by December 1994. Meanwhile the inflation rate was falling from 6.1 percent in 1990 to 3.1 percent in 1991 and down to 2.7 percent in both 1993 and 1994. Qualitatively, this is just the sort of behavior the theoretical model of the self-correcting mechanism predicts. But it sure took a long time! Hence, the practical policy question is: How long can we afford to wait?

ADJUSTING TO AN INFLATIONARY GAP: INFLATION

Let us now consider what happens when the economy starts *above* full employment, that is, with an *inflationary* gap like that shown in Figure 10-6. As we shall see now, the tight labor market produces an inflation that eventually eliminates the gap, though perhaps in a slow and painful way. Let us see how.

When equilibrium GDP is above potential, jobs are plentiful and labor is in great demand. Firms are likely to be having trouble recruiting new workers, or even holding onto their old ones as other firms try to lure them away with higher wages. Such a situation arose in 1995 when the unemployment rate dropped to 5.4 percent. Businesses had to start paying higher wages because many kinds of workers were in short supply. (See the box on the next page.)

Rising wages add to business costs, thus shifting the aggregate supply curve *inward*. As the aggregate supply curve shifts in from S_0S_0 to S_1S_1 in Figure 10-6

FIGURE 10-6 THE ELIMINATION OF AN INFLATIONARY GAP

When the aggregate supply curve is S_0S_0 and the aggregate demand curve is *DD*, the economy will initially reach equilibrium (point *E*) with an inflationary gap. The resulting inflation of wages will push the supply curve inward until it has shifted to the position indicated by curve S_1S_1. Here, with equilibrium at point *F*, the economy is at normal full employment. But, during the adjustment period from *E* to *F*, there will have been inflation.

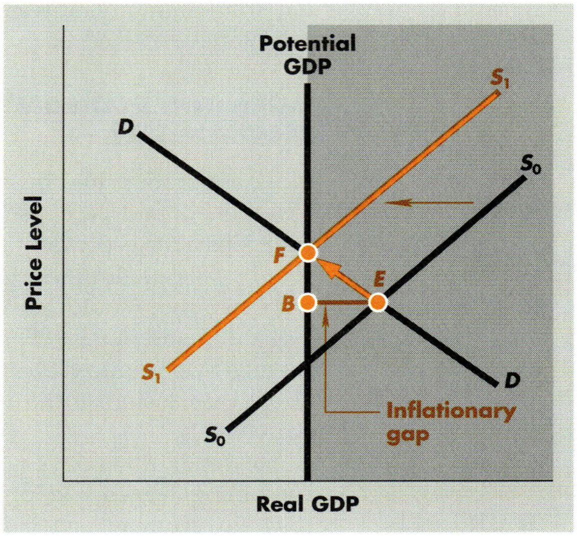

TIGHT LABOR MARKETS IN 1995

When the unemployment rate fell to around 5.5 percent in 1995, jobs became hard to fill in certain parts of the country. The National Federation of Independent Business reported that personnel managers encountered difficulty in filling one out of five corporate job openings. A summary business report prepared by the 12 Federal Reserve banks described the labor market as *tight* and noted wage increases in selected occupations.

Even wages for unskilled workers in retail businesses got a boost. Since 1991, hourly wages for retail help had increased only 3 percent annually. But the low unemployment rate changed things. McDonald's, which normally pays $5.00 per hour, started advertising jobs starting at $6.50 per hour in places like Winston-Salem, North Carolina—a 30 percent increase. The situation was similar for cashiers and clerks in Detroit, where employers had to raise pay rates 10 percent to fill positions.

To firms, it all meant higher labor costs, and, as a result, the aggregate supply curve shifted inward. But for workers accustomed to living under the specter of unemployment, it was the best news in years.

SOURCES: David Hage, "Have Job Prospects Started to Wilt?" *U.S. News and World Report*, May 15, 1995, p. 65; Vivian Brownstein and Joseph Spiers, "The Growing Threat of Inflation," *Fortune*, January 16, 1995, p. 66; and "New Threats to the Expansion," *Fortune*, July 25, 1994, p. 56.

the size of the inflationary gap declines. In other words, inflation eventually erodes the inflationary gap and brings the economy to an equilibrium at full employment (point *F*).

There is a straightforward way of looking at the economics that underlies this process. Inflation arises because buyers are demanding more output than the economy is capable of producing at normal operating rates. To paraphrase an old cliché, there is too much demand chasing too little supply. Such an environment encourages price hikes.

But rising prices eat away at the purchasing power of consumers' wealth, forcing them to cut back on consumption, as explained in Chapter 7. In addition, exports fall and imports rise, as we learned in Chapter 8. Eventually, aggregate quantity demanded is scaled back to the economy's capacity to produce; and, at this point, the self-correcting process stops. That, in essence, is the unhappy process by which the economy cures itself of the excessive aggregate demand. In brief:

If aggregate demand is exceptionally high, the economy may reach a short-run equilibrium above full employment (an *inflationary gap*). When this occurs, the tight situation in the labor market soon forces wages to rise. Since rising wages increase business costs, prices increase; there is inflation. As higher prices cut into consumer purchasing power and net exports, the inflationary gap begins to close.

As the inflationary gap is closing, output falls and prices continue to rise; so the economy experiences *stagflation* until the gap is eliminated. At this point, a long-run equilibrium is established with a higher price level and with GDP equal to potential GDP.

Two caveats about this process should be mentioned. One we have already emphasized: The self-correcting mechanism takes time because wages and prices do not adjust quickly. An inflationary gap sows the seeds of its own destruction, but these seeds germinate slowly. So, once again, policymakers may want to speed up the process.

The other caveat is that the process works *only in the absence of additional forces propelling the aggregate demand curve outward.* But in the last chapter, we encountered several forces that might shift the aggregate demand curve outward.

As you can see by manipulating the aggregate demand–aggregate supply diagram, if aggregate demand is shifting out at the same time that aggregate supply is shifting in, there will certainly be inflation, but the inflationary gap may not shrink. (Try this as an exercise, to make sure you understand how to use the apparatus.) So not all inflations come to a natural end.

DEMAND INFLATION AND STAGFLATION

Simple as it is, this adjustment model teaches us a number of important lessons about inflation in the real world. First, Figure 10-6 reminds us that the real culprit in this particular inflation is excessive aggregate demand—relative to potential GDP. The aggregate demand curve is initially so high that it intersects the aggregate supply curve well beyond full employment. The resulting intense demand for goods and labor pushes prices and wages higher. While aggregate demand in excess of potential GDP is not the only possible cause of inflation, it certainly is the cause in our example.

However, business managers and journalists may blame inflation on rising wages. In a superficial sense, of course, they are right, because higher wages do indeed lead firms to raise their prices. But in a deeper sense they are wrong. Both rising wages and rising prices are symptoms of an underlying malady: too much aggregate demand. Blaming labor for inflation in such a case is a bit like blaming high doctor bills for making you ill.

Second, we see that output falls while prices rise as the economy adjusts from point *E* to point *F* in Figure 10-6. This is our first (but not our last!) explanation of the phenomenon of **stagflation.** Specifically:

STAGFLATION is inflation that occurs while the economy is growing slowly or having a recession.

A period of stagflation is part of the normal aftermath of a period of excessive aggregate demand.

It is easy to understand why stagflation occurs in this case. When aggregate demand is excessive, the economy will temporarily produce beyond its normal capacity. Labor markets tighten and wages rise. Machinery and raw materials may also become scarce and so start rising in price. Faced by higher costs, the natural reaction of business firms is to produce less and to charge a higher price. That is stagflation.

TWO RECENT EXAMPLES

The stagflation that follows a period of excessive aggregate demand is, you will note, a rather benign form of the dreaded disease. After all, while output is falling, it nonetheless remains above potential GDP, and unemployment is low. The U.S. economy has experienced two such episodes in the last decade.

The more notable one came between 1988 and 1990. The long economic expansion of the 1980s brought the unemployment rate down to 5.5 percent by mid-1988 and (briefly) to a 15-year low of 5.0 percent by March 1989. Almost all economists believe that 5.0 percent is below the full-employment unemployment rate, that is, that the U.S. economy had an *inflationary gap* in 1989. As the theory suggests, inflation began to accelerate—from 4.4 percent in 1988 to 4.6 percent in 1989 and 6.1 percent in 1990.

In the meantime, the economy was stagnating. Real GDP growth fell from 3.5 percent during 1988 to 2.4 percent in 1989 and −0.2 percent in 1990. Inflation was eating away at the inflationary gap, which was virtually gone by mid-1990, when the recession started. Yet inflation remained high through the early months of the recession. The U.S. economy was in the *stagflation* phase.

A milder version of this same phenomenon occurred in the first half of 1995. After the unemployment rate fell to 5.4 percent in late 1994, slightly below the full-employment level, the U.S. economy slowed abruptly in the first half of 1995. But inflation during the first half of 1995 ran at a 3.2 percent annual rate, slightly above the 1994 rate of 2.7 percent. In both of these episodes, then, the U.S. economy behaved more or less as our simple model suggests.

Our overall conclusion about the economy's ability to right itself seems to run something like this:

The economy does indeed have a self-correcting mechanism that tends to eliminate either unemployment or inflation. However, this mechanism works slowly and unevenly. In addition, its beneficial effects on either inflation or unemployment are sometimes swamped by strong forces (such as rapid increases or decreases in aggregate demand) pushing in the opposite direction. Thus, the self-correcting mechanism cannot always be relied upon.

STAGFLATION FROM SUPPLY SHIFTS

We have just discussed the type of stagflation that follows in the aftermath of an inflationary boom. However, that is not what happened in the 1970s and early 1980s when unemployment and inflation soared at the same time. What caused this more virulent type of stagflation? Several things, but the principal villain was the rising price of energy.

In 1973, the Organization of Petroleum Exporting Countries (OPEC) quadrupled the price of crude oil. American consumers soon found the prices of gasoline and home heating fuels increasing sharply, and American businesses found that one important cost of doing business—energy prices—rose drastically. OPEC struck again in 1979 to 1980, this time doubling the price of oil. Then the same thing happened a third time, albeit on a smaller scale, when Iraq invaded Kuwait in 1990.

Higher energy prices, we observed earlier, shift the economy's aggregate supply curve *inward* in the manner shown in Figure 10-2 (page 209). If the aggregate supply curve shifts inward, as it surely did in 1973 to 1974, 1979 to 1980, and 1990, production will decline. And in order to reduce demand to the available supply, prices will have to rise. The result is the worst of both worlds: falling production and rising prices.

This conclusion is shown graphically in Figure 10-7, which superimposes an aggregate demand curve, *DD,* on the two aggregate supply curves of Figure 10-2. The economy's equilibrium shifts upward to the left, from point *E* to point *A*. Thus, output falls while prices rise. In brief:

Stagflation is the typical result of adverse supply shifts.

The numbers used in Figure 10-7 are roughly indicative of what happened in the United States after the big "energy shock" of late 1973. Between 1973 (represented by supply curve S_0S_0 and point *E*) and 1975 (represented by supply curve S_1S_1 and point *A*), real GDP fell by about 1 percent, while the price level rose a stunning 19 percent. Thus, inflation soared and the economy weakened. The general lesson to be learned from the U.S. experience with supply shocks is both clear and important:

FIGURE 10-7 STAGFLATION FROM AN ADVERSE SHIFT IN AGGREGATE SUPPLY

This diagram illustrates how stagflation arises if the aggregate supply curve shifts inward to the left (from S_0S_0 to S_1S_1). If the aggregate demand curve does not change, equilibrium moves from point E to point A. Output falls as prices rise, which is what we mean by *stagflation*. The diagram indicates roughly what happened in the United States from 1973 to 1975, when sharply higher energy prices caused severe stagflation.

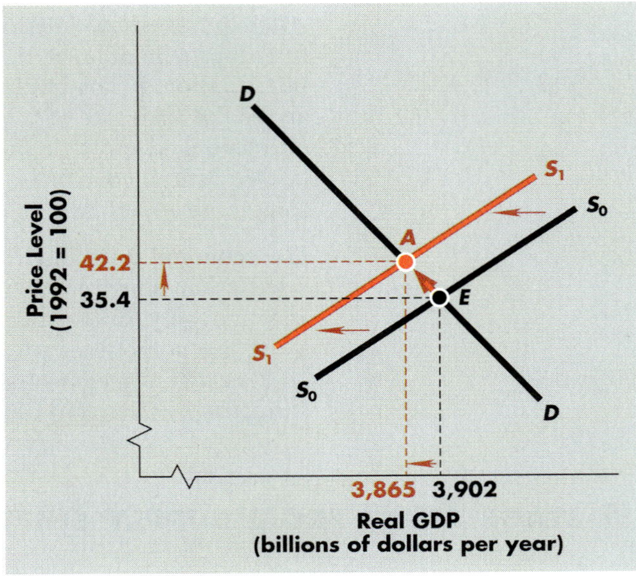

The typical results of an adverse supply shock are a fall in output and an acceleration in inflation. This is one reason why the world economy was plagued by stagflation in the mid-1970s and early 1980s. And it can happen again if another series of supply-reducing events takes place.

Of course, supply shifts can work in the other direction as well. When the world oil market weakened in 1986, oil prices plummeted. And the price of oil tumbled again just after the Persian Gulf war. Both of these favorable supply shocks stimulated U.S. economic growth and curbed inflation. In fact the Consumer Price Index actually fell for a few months in 1986! The aggregate supply curve was shifting outward.

Favorable supply shocks tend to push output up and reduce inflation.

INFLATION AND THE MULTIPLIER

When we introduced the concept of the multiplier in the last chapter, we said that there were several reasons why its actual value is smaller than suggested by the oversimplified multiplier formula. One of these—variable imports—emerged in an appendix to the last chapter. We are now in a position to understand the second:

Inflation reduces the size of the multiplier.

The basic idea is simple. In the last chapter, we described a multiplier process in which one person's spending becomes another person's income, which leads to further spending by the second person, and so on. But this story is confined to the demand side of the economy. Let us therefore consider what is likely to happen on the supply side as the multiplier process unfolds. Will the additional demand be taken care of by firms without raising prices?

If the aggregate supply curve is upward sloping, the answer is no. More goods will be provided only at higher prices. Thus, as the multiplier chain progresses, pulling income and employment up, prices will also be rising. And this, as we know from earlier chapters, will reduce net exports and dampen consumer spending because rising prices erode the purchasing power of consumers' wealth. So the multiplier chain will not proceed as far as it would have in the absence of inflation.

How much inflation results from the rise in demand? How much of the multiplier chain is cut off by inflation? The answers depend on the slope of the economy's aggregate supply curve.

For a concrete example, let us return to the $200 billion increase in investment spending used in the last chapter. There we found (see especially page 198) that $200 billion in additional investment spending eventually leads—through the multiplier process—to *a horizontal shift of $800 billion in the aggregate demand curve.* But to know the actual quantity that will ultimately be produced and the actual price level, we must bring the aggregate supply curve into the picture.

Figure 10-8 does this. Here we show the $800 billion horizontal shift of the aggregate demand curve, from D_0D_0 to D_1D_1, that is derived from the oversimplified multiplier formula (which ignores rising prices). The aggregate supply curve, *SS,* then tells us how this expansion of demand is apportioned between higher output and higher prices. We see that as the economy's equilibrium moves from point E_0 to point E_1, real GDP does not rise by $800 billion. Instead, prices rise, which, as we know, cancels out part of the rise in quantity demanded. So output increases only from $6,000 billion to $6,600 billion—an increase of $600 billion. Thus, in our example, inflation reduces the multiplier from $800/$200 = 4 to $600/$200 = 3. In general:

As long as the aggregate supply curve is upward sloping, any increase in aggregate demand will push up the price level. This, in turn, will drain off some of

FIGURE 10-8 INFLATION AND THE MULTIPLIER

This figure illustrates the complete multiplier analysis, including inflation. The simple multiplier (which ignored changes in the price level) appears as a *horizontal* shift of $800 billion in the aggregate demand curve, meaning that the multiplier would be $800/$200 = 4 if prices did not rise. However, when aggregate demand shifts from D_0D_0 to D_1D_1, the price level increases from 100 to 120. So real GDP increases from $6,000 billion to only $6,600 billion—for a multiplier of $600/$200 = 3.

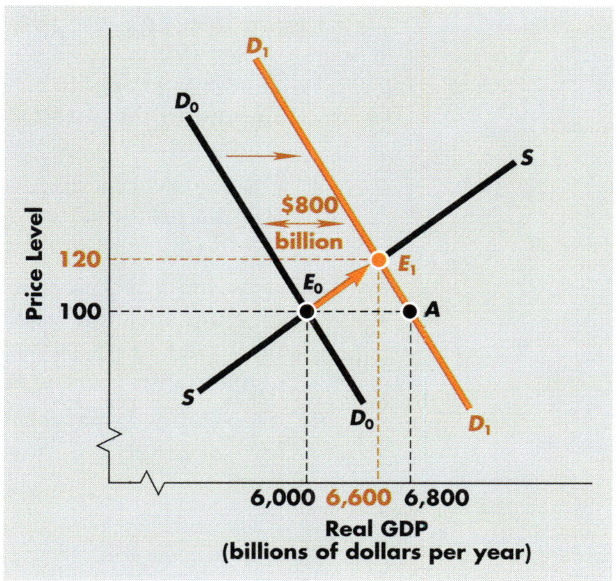

the higher real demand by eroding the purchasing power of consumer wealth and by reducing net exports. Thus, inflation reduces the value of the multiplier below that suggested by the oversimplified formula.

Notice also that the price level in this example has been pushed up (from 100 to 120, or 20 percent) by the rise in investment demand. This, too, is a general result:

As long as the aggregate supply curve is upward sloping, any outward shift of the aggregate demand curve will cause some rise in prices.

The economic behavior behind these results certainly cannot be considered surprising. Firms faced with large increases in quantity demanded at their original prices respond to these changed circumstances in two natural ways: They raise production (so GDP rises), and they raise prices (so the price level rises). But this rise in the price level reduces the purchasing power of the bank accounts and bonds held by consumers, and they too react in the natural way: They cut down on their spending. Such a reaction amounts to a movement *along* aggregate demand curve D_1D_1 in Figure 10-8 from point A to point E_1.

Higher prices thus play their usual dual role in a market economy: They encourage suppliers to produce more, and they encourage demanders to consume less. In this way, equilibrium is reestablished at higher levels of output and higher prices through the process of inflation.

Figure 10-8 also shows us exactly where the oversimplified multiplier formula goes wrong. By ignoring the effects of the higher price level, the oversimplified formula erroneously supposes that the economy moves horizontally from point E_0 to point A. As the diagram clearly shows, output does not actually rise this much. Output *would* rise this much only if the aggregate supply curve were horizontal. (Verify this for yourself by penciling in an imaginary horizontal aggregate supply curve through points E_0 and A in Figure 10-8.) That is, the oversimplified multiplier formula tacitly assumes that the aggregate supply curve is horizontal. Normally, this is an unrealistic assumption, which is one reason why the oversimplified formula exaggerates the size of the multiplier.

In summary, it may be useful to put together what we have learned about multiplier analysis in this chapter and the last:

STEPS IN CALCULATING THE MULTIPLIER

1. Shift the expenditure schedule in the 45° line diagram vertically by the amount of the autonomous shift in spending (as, for example, in Figure 9-1 on page 189).
2. Use the 45° line diagram, or the oversimplified multiplier formula, to calculate the multiplier effect on GDP that *would* occur *if* the price level did not change (again, see Figure 9-1).
3. Now move from the 45° line diagram to an aggregate supply and demand diagram such as Figure 10-8 to see how the price level will react. Enter the multiplier effect calculated in Step 2 as a *horizontal* shift of the aggregate demand curve in the supply-demand diagram.
4. The supply-demand diagram will now show the actual effect on real output as well as the resulting inflation or deflation.[2]

[2]The change in the price level reacts back on the 45° diagram. See Review Question 10 at the end of the chapter.

A ROLE FOR STABILIZATION POLICY

Chapter 8 emphasized the volatility of investment spending, and Chapter 9 noted that changes in investment have multiplier effects on aggregate demand. This chapter took the next step by showing how shifts in the aggregate demand curve cause fluctuations in both real GDP growth and inflation—fluctuations that are widely decried as undesirable. It also suggested that the economy's self-correcting mechanism works, but slowly, thereby leaving room for government stabilization policy to improve the workings of the free market. Can the government really do this? If so, how? These are the questions for the next part of the book.

SUMMARY

1. The economy's **aggregate supply curve** relates the quantity of goods and services that will be supplied to the price level. It normally slopes upward to the right because the costs of labor and other inputs are relatively fixed in the short run, meaning that higher selling prices make input costs relatively "cheaper" and therefore encourage greater production.
2. The position of the aggregate supply curve can be shifted by changes in money wage rates, prices of other inputs, technology, or quantities or qualities of labor and capital.
3. The *equilibrium price level* and the *equilibrium level of real GDP* are jointly determined by the intersection of the economy's aggregate supply and aggregate demand schedules. This intersection may come at full employment, below full employment (a recessionary gap), or above full employment (an inflationary gap).
4. The economy has a self-correcting mechanism that erodes a *recessionary gap*. Specifically, a weak labor market reduces wage increases and, in some cases, may even drive wages down. This shifts the aggregate supply curve outward. But it happens very slowly.
5. If there is an *inflationary gap*, the economy has a similar mechanism that erodes the gap through a process of inflation. Unusually strong job prospects push wages up, which shifts the aggregate supply curve to the left and reduces the inflationary gap.
6. One consequence of this *self-correcting mechanism* is that, if a surge in aggregate demand opens up an inflationary gap, part of the economy's natural adjustment to this event will be a period of stagflation; that is, a period in which prices are rising while output is falling.
7. An inward shift of the aggregate supply curve will cause output to fall while prices rise; that is, it will cause **stagflation.** Among the events that have caused such a shift are abrupt increases in the price of foreign oil.
8. Adverse supply shifts like this plagued our economy when oil prices skyrocketed in 1973 to 1974, 1979 to 1980, and again in 1990, leading to stagflation each time.
9. Among the reasons why the oversimplified multiplier formula is wrong is the fact that it ignores the inflation that is caused by an increase in aggregate demand. Such *inflation decreases the multiplier* by reducing both consumer spending and net exports.

KEY TERMS

Aggregate supply curve
Productivity
Equilibrium of real GDP and the price level
Inflationary gap
Self-correcting mechanism
Stagflation
Recessionary gap
Inflation and the multiplier

QUESTIONS FOR REVIEW

1. In an economy with the following aggregate demand and aggregate supply schedules, find the equilibrium levels of real output and the price level. Graph your solution. If full employment comes at $2,800 billion, is there an inflationary or a recessionary gap?

Aggregate Quantity Demanded (in billions)	Price Level	Aggregate Quantity Supplied (in billions)
3,200	85	2,600
3,100	90	2,750
3,000	95	2,850
2,900	100	2,900
2,800	105	2,925

2. Suppose a worker receives a wage of $18 per hour. Compute the real wage (money wage deflated by the price index) corresponding to each of the following possible price levels: 85, 95, 100, 110, 120. What do you notice about the relationship between the real wage and the price level? Relate this to the slope of the aggregate supply curve.
3. Explain why a decrease in the price of foreign oil shifts the aggregate supply curve outward to the right. What are the consequences of such a shift?
4. Comment on the following statement: "Inflationary and recessionary gaps are nothing to worry about because the economy has a built-in mechanism that cures either type of gap automatically."
5. Give *two* different explanations of how the economy can suffer from stagflation.
6. Why do you think wages tend to be rigid in the downward direction?
7. Add the following aggregate supply and demand schedules to the example in Review Question 3 of Chapter 8 (page 184) to see how inflation affects the multiplier.

   Draw these schedules on a piece of graph paper. Then:

   a. Notice that the difference between Columns 2 and 3 (the aggregate demand schedule at two different levels of investment) is always $200. Discuss how this relates to your answer in the previous chapter.
   b. Find the equilibrium GDP and the equilibrium price level both before and after the increase in investment. What is the value of the multiplier?

(1) Price Level	(2) Aggregate Demand (when investment is $240)	(3) Aggregate Demand (when investment is $260)	(4) Aggregate Supply
90	$3,860	$4,060	$3,660
95	3,830	4,030	3,730
100	3,800	4,000	3,800
105	3,770	3,970	3,870
110	3,740	3,940	3,940
115	3,710	3,910	4,010

8. Explain in words why rising prices reduce the multiplier effect of an autonomous increase in aggregate demand.
9. Use an aggregate supply and demand diagram to show that multiplier effects are smaller when the aggregate supply curve is steeper. Which case gives rise to more inflation—the steep aggregate supply curve or the flat one? What happens to the multiplier if the aggregate supply curve is vertical?
10. (More difficult) Assume that investment spending rises. Draw a set of graphs illustrating the Steps in Calculating the Multiplier listed on page 222. Your aggregate supply and demand diagram from Steps 3 and 4 will show a change in the price level. How would this change in the price level react back on the 45° line diagram you used in Step 1? In view of this, use the 45° line diagram to show that inflation reduces the multiplier.

PART III

FISCAL AND MONETARY POLICY

CHAPTER 11

MANAGING AGGREGATE DEMAND: FISCAL POLICY

Next, let us turn to the problems of our fiscal policy. Here the myths are legion and the truth hard to find.
John F. Kennedy

In the model of the economy constructed in Part II, the government played an entirely passive role. It did a certain amount of spending and collected a fixed amount of taxes, and that was it. We concluded that such an economy has a tendency to move toward an equilibrium with high employment and low inflation, but only a weak one. Furthermore, we hinted that well-designed policies might improve the economy's performance. It is now time to pick up that hint—and to learn some of the difficulties the government must overcome if it is to conduct a successful stabilization policy.

The government's **FISCAL POLICY** is its plan for spending and taxation. It is designed to steer aggregate demand in some desired direction.

Traditionally, the government has used its taxing and spending powers to influence the demand side of the economy. So this chapter begins there, in the domain of **fiscal policy.** The next two chapters take up the government's other main tool for managing aggregate demand: *monetary policy.*

We start by allowing taxes to depend on income—as they do in the real world—and then considering the multipliers for tax policy. As we shall see, this analysis requires no fundamental change in our model of the determination of GDP and the price level. However, it does reduce the size of the multiplier.

As Presidents Reagan, Bush, and Clinton have all realized, the effects of tax policy are not limited to aggregate *demand.* Taxes also affect aggregate *supply.* So the last sections of the chapter examine "supply-side economics."

ISSUE: WILL BALANCING THE BUDGET SLOW THE ECONOMY?

The debate over reducing the federal budget deficit has been vigorous and often highly partisan. At times, it has appeared to be endless. By late 1995, President Clinton and the Republican-controlled Congress had at least agreed on a target: balancing the budget by the year 2002. But not every informed observer believes this is a wise target, or even that balancing the budget is a sensible goal. They fear it will take a toll on economic growth.

According to the President, Congressional leaders, and many economists, the fundamental reason to reduce the deficit is to raise private investment, and thereby to spur long-run economic growth. We will explore in detail the chain of reasoning in Chapter 15. But, roughly, the point is that budget deficits force the government to borrow money, and the resulting increase in demand for credit raises the cost of borrowing. That makes it more expensive for firms to raise funds to build factories and purchase machinery. Note that the growth tonic works on the economy's supply side: the idea is to augment the supply of capital.

But the road from lower deficits to lower interest rates to higher investment to faster growth is a long one. In the meantime, some critics worry, large reductions in government spending might reduce aggregate demand which, as we know, can slow economic growth.

This chapter will explain the logic underlying the concern about aggregate demand. Subsequent chapters will develop the supply-side links and offer some counterarguments. Wait until you finish Chapter 15. Then make up your own mind on this important debate.

INCOME TAXES AND THE CONSUMPTION SCHEDULE

FIXED TAXES are taxes that do not vary with the level of GDP.

VARIABLE TAXES are taxes that do vary with the level of GDP.

To understand how taxes affect equilibrium GDP, we must distinguish between **fixed taxes,** which are the only kind we have considered so far, and **variable taxes,** which are much more important in practice.

Most of the taxes collected by the federal, state, and local governments rise and fall with the level of GDP. In some cases, the reason is obvious: *Personal* and *corporate income tax* collections, for example, depend on how much income there is to be taxed. *Sales tax* receipts depend on GDP because consumer spending is higher when GDP is higher. On the other hand, some types of tax receipts—such as property taxes—do not vary with GDP. We call the first kind of tax *variable taxes* and the second kind *fixed taxes.*

Why is this distinction important? Remember that taxes (T) are the difference between gross domestic product (Y) and disposable income (DI):

$$DI = Y - T$$

Thus, when taxes are increased, disposable income falls—and hence so does consumption—*even if GDP is unchanged.* As a result:

An increase in taxes shifts the consumption schedule in our 45° line diagram downward. Similarly, a reduction in taxes shifts the consumption schedule upward.

But precisely how the consumption schedule shifts depends on the nature of the tax change. If a fixed tax is increased, disposable income falls by the *same* amount regardless of the level of GDP. Hence, the decline in consumer spending is the same. In a word, the C schedule shifts downward in a parallel manner, as shown in Figure 11-1(a).

But many tax policies change disposable income by amounts that depend on the level of income—normally being larger at higher income levels. This is true, for example, whenever Congress alters the bracket rates in the personal income tax code, as it last did in 1993. Since higher tax rates decrease disposable income more when GDP is higher, the C schedule shifts down more sharply at high income levels than at low ones. [See Figure 11-1(b).]

FIGURE 11-1

HOW TAX POLICY SHIFTS THE CONSUMPTION SCHEDULE

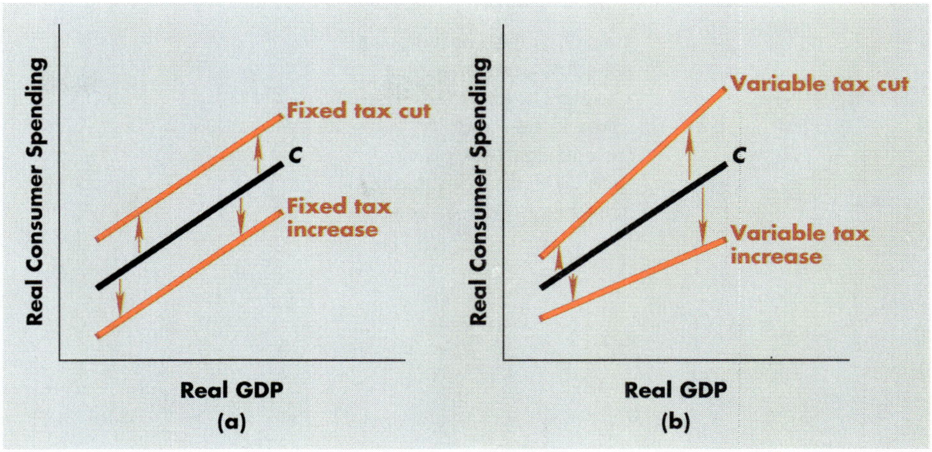

Because consumption depends on disposable income, not GDP, any change in taxes will shift the consumption schedule relating consumption to GDP. Panel (a) shows how the *C* curve shifts for changes in fixed taxes. Panel (b) shows how the *C* curve shifts if the tax cut (or tax increase) is larger at high incomes than at low incomes.

The two parts of Figure 11-1 illustrate the first reason why the distinction between fixed and variable taxes is important. Figure 11-2 illustrates the second. Here we show two consumption lines, C_1 and C_2. C_1 is the consumption schedule used in previous chapters; it is constructed on the assumption that taxes are fixed at $1,200 billion regardless of GDP. C_2 depicts a more realistic case in which tax collections are 20 percent of GDP. You will notice that C_2 is flatter than C_1. This is no accident. In fact:

Variable taxes such as the income tax flatten the consumption schedule in a 45° line diagram.

It is easy to understand why. Table 11-1 shows in Column 1 alternative values of GDP ranging from $4.5 trillion to $7.5 trillion. Column 2 then indicates that taxes are always one-fifth of this amount. Column 3 subtracts Column 2 from Column 1 to arrive at disposable income (*DI*). Column 4 then gives the amount of consumer spending corresponding to each level of *DI*. The schedule relating *C* to *Y*, which we need for our 45° line, is therefore found in Columns 1 and 4.

Notice in Table 11-1 that for each $500 billion increase in GDP, consumer spending rises by $300 billion. Thus, the slope of line C_2 in Figure 11-2 is $300/$500, or 0.60. But, if you look back at any of the tables in Chapter 9, you will find that consumption there rose by $300 billion each time GDP increased $400 billion—making the slope $300/$400, or 0.75. (See the steeper line C_1 in Figure 11-2.)

All of this sounds terribly mechanical, but the economic reasoning behind it is straightforward. When taxes are fixed, as in line C_1, each additional dollar of GDP raises disposable income (*DI*) by $1. Consumer spending then rises by $1 times the marginal propensity to consume (MPC), which is 0.75 in our example. Hence, each additional dollar of GDP leads to 75 cents more spending. But when taxes vary with income, each additional dollar of GDP raises *DI* by less than $1 because the government takes a share in taxes. In our example, taxes are 20 percent of GDP, so each additional $1 of GDP leads to 80 cents more *DI*. With an MPC of 0.75, that means that spending rises 60 cents (75 percent of 80 cents) each time GDP rises by $1. That is why the slope of line C_2 in Figure 11-2 is only 0.60, instead of 0.75.

FIGURE 11-2 THE CONSUMPTION SCHEDULE WITH FIXED AND VARIABLE TAXES

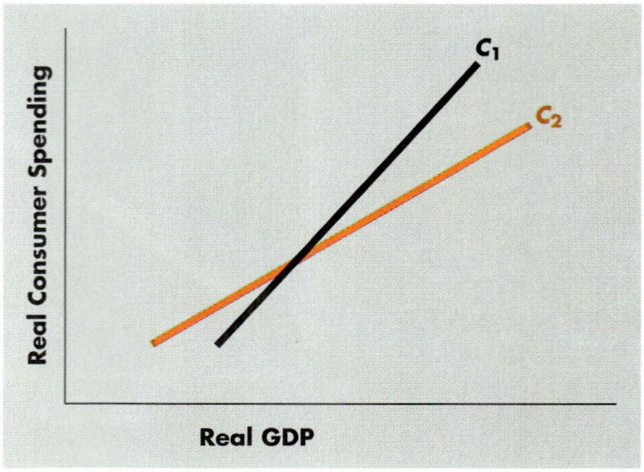

Line C_1 is the consumption schedule used in earlier chapters, when taxes were taken to be fixed. If, instead, tax receipts rise with GDP, the consumption schedule is flatter—see line C_2.

Table 11-2 and Figure 11-3 take the next step by replacing the old consumption schedule with this new one in both the tabular presentation of income determination and the 45° line diagram. We see immediately that the equilibrium level of GDP is at point *E*. Here gross domestic product is \$6,000 billion, consumption is \$3,900 billion, investment is \$900 billion, net exports are −\$100 billion, and government purchases are \$1,300 billion. As we know, full employment may occur above or below $Y = \$6,000$ billion. If below, there is an inflationary gap. Prices probably will start to rise, pulling the expenditure schedule down and reducing equilibrium GDP. If above, there is a recessionary gap, and history suggests that prices will fall only slowly. In the interim, there will be a period of high unemployment.

TABLE 11-1 THE EFFECTS OF AN INCOME TAX ON THE CONSUMPTION SCHEDULE (billions of dollars per year)

(1) Gross Domestic Product	(2) Taxes	(3) Disposable Income (GDP minus taxes)	(4) Consumption
\$4,500	\$ 900	\$3,600	\$3,000
5,000	1,000	4,000	3,300
5,500	1,100	4,400	3,600
6,000	1,200	4,800	3,900
6,500	1,300	5,200	4,200
7,000	1,400	5,600	4,500
7,500	1,500	6,000	4,800

This table shows how an income tax lowers the slope of the consumption schedule (Column 4) in a concrete example. For every \$500 billion increase in GDP, consumption rises by \$300 billion in this example (compare Columns 1 and 4), so the slope of the C_2 line in Figure 11–2 is \$300/\$500, or 0.6. In earlier chapters, the slope of the consumption schedule (line C_1 in Figure 11–2) was \$300/\$400, or 0.75.

TABLE 11-2 TOTAL EXPENDITURE SCHEDULE WITH A 20 PERCENT INCOME TAX (billions of dollars per year)

(1) Gross Domestic Product *Y*	(2) Consumption *C*	(3) Investment *I*	(4) Net Exports (*X* − *IM*)	(5) Government Purchases *G*	(6) Total Expenditures *C* + *I* + *G* + (*X* − *IM*)
$4,500	$3,000	$900	−$100	$1,300	$5,100
5,000	3,300	900	−100	1,300	5,400
5,500	3,600	900	−100	1,300	5,700
6,000	3,900	900	−100	1,300	6,000
6,500	4,200	900	−100	1,300	6,300
7,000	4,500	900	−100	1,300	6,600
7,500	4,800	900	−100	1,300	6,900

This table replaces the previous consumption schedule with a new one that adjusts for the income tax (as shown in Table 11–1) and shows that the equilibrium level of income is still $6,000 billion.

In short, once we adjust the expenditure schedule for variable taxes, the determination of national income proceeds exactly as before. The effects of government spending and taxation, therefore, are fairly straightforward and can be summarized as follows:

Government purchases of goods and services add to total spending directly through the G component of $C + I + G + (X - IM)$. Taxes indirectly reduce total spending by lowering disposable income and thus reduce the C component of $C + I + G + (X - IM)$. On balance, then, the government's actions may raise or lower the equilibrium level of GDP, depending on how much spending and taxing it does.

FIGURE 11-3 INCOME DETERMINATION WITH A VARIABLE INCOME TAX

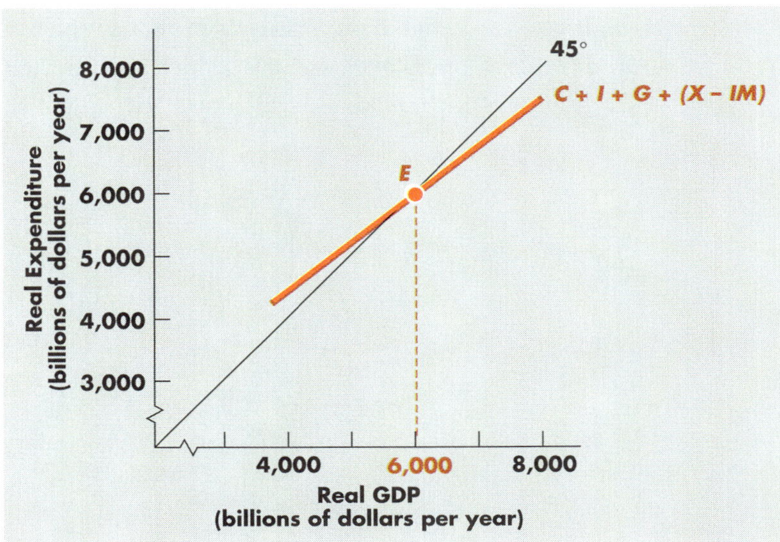

This diagram adds a 20 percent income tax to the model economy portrayed in earlier chapters. Because of this, the $C + I + G + (X - IM)$ schedule is flatter, but otherwise things look just as before. In particular, equilibrium is at point *E*, where the $C + I + G + (X - IM)$ schedule crosses the 45° line. Thus, equilibrium GDP is $6,000 billion.

However, there is more to the story. As we will see now:

The multiplier is smaller in the presence of an income tax.

THE MULTIPLIER REVISITED

We learned in Chapter 9 that the multiplier works through a chain of spending and respending, as one person's expenditure becomes another's income. But, when there is an income tax, some of the additional income leaks out of the circular flow at each stage. Specifically, if the income tax rate is 20 percent, when Generous Motors spends $1 million on salaries, workers actually receive only $800,000 in *after-tax* (that is, disposable) income. If workers spend 75 percent of this amount (because the MPC is 0.75), spending in the next round will be only $600,000. Notice that this is only *60 percent* of the original expenditure, not *75 percent*—just as we observed in the last section.

Thus, the multiplier chain for each original dollar of spending shrinks from

$$1 + 0.75 + (0.75)^2 + (0.75)^3 + \ldots = \frac{1}{1 - 0.75} = \frac{1}{0.25} = 4$$

to

$$1 + 0.6 + (0.6)^2 + (0.6)^3 + \ldots = \frac{1}{1 - 0.6} = \frac{1}{0.4} = 2.5$$

This is clearly a large reduction in the multiplier. We thus have a third reason why the oversimplified multiplier formula of Chapter 9 exaggerates the size of the multiplier: It ignores income taxes.

REASONS WHY THE OVERSIMPLIFIED MULTIPLIER FORMULA IS WRONG

1. It ignores variable imports, which reduce the size of the multiplier.
2. It ignores price-level changes, which reduce the multiplier.
3. It ignores income taxes, which also reduce the size of the multiplier.

The last of these three reasons is very important in practice.

This conclusion about the multiplier is shown graphically in Figure 11-4, where we have drawn our $C + I + G + (X - IM)$ schedules with a slope of 0.6 rather than the 0.75 slope we used in earlier chapters. This new slope reflects an MPC of 0.75 and a tax rate of 20 percent. Figure 11-4 depicts the effect of a $400 billion increase in government purchases of goods and services, which shifts the $C + I + G + (X - IM)$ schedule from $C + I + G_0 + (X - IM)$ to $C + I + G_1 + (X - IM)$. Equilibrium moves from point E_0 to point E_1—an increase of GDP from $Y = \$6{,}000$ billion to $Y = \$7{,}000$ billion. Thus, if we ignore for the moment any increases in the price level (which would further reduce the multiplier), a $400 billion increment in government spending leads to a $1,000 billion increment in GDP. So, when taxes are included in our model, the multiplier is only $1,000/$400 = 2.5, just as we concluded before.

FIGURE 11-4

THE MULTIPLIER IN THE PRESENCE OF AN INCOME TAX

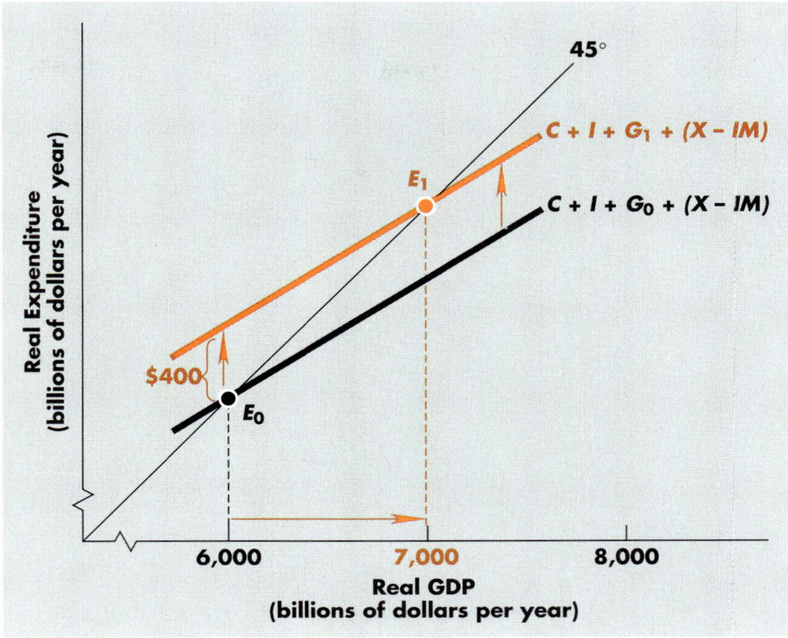

This diagram illustrates that an economy with an income tax (in this case a 20 percent income tax) has a lower multiplier than an economy without one. Specifically, the $C + I + G + (X - IM)$ curve is shifted upward by a $400 billion increase in *G*, and the diagram shows that equilibrium GDP rises by $1,000 billion—from $6,000 billion to $7,000 billion. The multiplier is therefore $1,000/$400 = 2.5, whereas without an income tax it was 4.

MULTIPLIERS FOR TAX POLICY

Because they work indirectly via consumption, multipliers for tax changes are more complicated than multipliers for spending such as *G*. They must be worked out in two steps.

Step 1. Figure out how much any change in the tax law affects consumer spending.

Step 2. Enter this vertical shift of the consumption schedule in the 45° line diagram and see how it affects output.

A reduction in income taxes provides a convenient example of this two-step procedure because we have already done Step 1 in Chapter 7, when we studied how consumer spending would respond to an income tax cut. There, we concluded that, if the tax reduction were viewed as permanent, consumers would increase their spending by an amount equal to the tax cut times the marginal propensity to consume. (If you need review, turn back to pages 146–150.)

To create a simple and familiar numerical example, suppose income taxes fall by $400 billion at each level of GDP—say, from $0.2Y$ (that is, 20 percent of GDP) to $0.2Y$ − $400 billion. Step 1 instructs us to multiply the $400 billion tax cut by the marginal propensity to consume (MPC), which is 0.75, to get $300 billion as the vertical shift of the consumption schedule.

Step 2 then amounts to multiplying this $300 billion increase in consumption by the multiplier—which is 2.5 in our example—giving $750 billion as the rise in GDP. Figure 11-5 verifies that this is so by entering a $300 billion vertical shift

FIGURE 11-5 THE MULTIPLIER FOR A REDUCTION IN FIXED TAXES

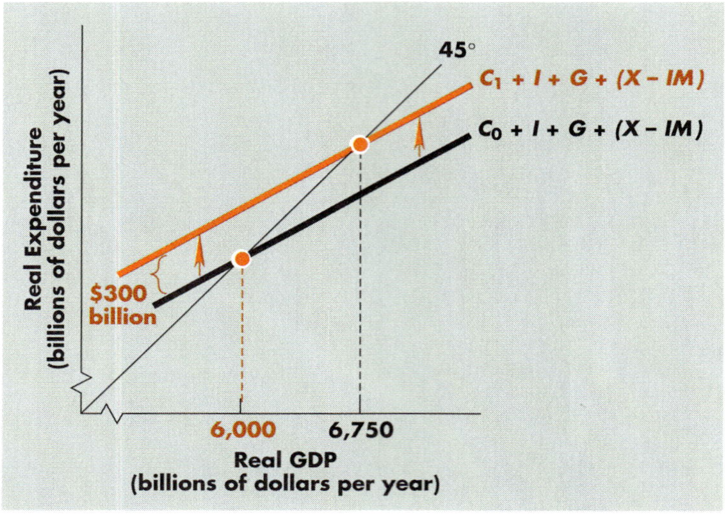

In this example, the $C + I + G + (X - IM)$ schedule is shifted vertically upward by $300 billion, from $C_0 + I + G + (X - IM)$ to $C_1 + I + G + (X - IM)$, by a $400 billion tax cut. Equilibrium GDP therefore increases from $6,000 billion to $6,750 billion. So the multiplier is $750/$400 = 1.875.

of the consumption function into the 45° line diagram and noting that GDP does indeed rise by $750 billion as a result.

Notice something interesting here. The $400 billion tax cut raises GDP by $750 billion. Thus, the multiplier is $700/$400 = 1.875. But the multiplier for the $400 government purchases that we worked out on page 232 and depicted in Figure 11-4 was 2.5. What's going on here? Apparently:

The multiplier for changes in taxes is smaller than the multiplier for changes in government purchases.

The reason is not mysterious. While *G* is a direct component of total expenditure, taxes are not. Taxes work indirectly, by first changing disposable income and then changing *C*. Since some of the change in disposable income affects *saving* rather than *spending*, a $1 tax cut does not pack as much punch as $1 of *G*. That is why we must multiply the $400 billion change in taxes by 0.75 to get the $300 billion shift of the *C* schedule shown in Figure 11-5.

The fact that the multiplier for taxes is smaller than the multiplier for *G* has a surprising implication:

If government purchases (*G*) and taxes (*T*) rise by equal amounts, the government seems to be giving to the public with one hand and taking away an equal amount with the other. But the effects do not cancel out. Instead, the equilibrium level of GDP on the demand side rises. Similarly, if *G* and *T* fall by equal amounts, the equilibrium level of GDP on the demand side falls.

For example, we have seen that a $400 billion increase in *G* raises GDP by $1,000 billion, while a $400 billion hike in *T* lowers GDP by just $750 billion. Thus, if *both G and T* are raised by $400 billion, GDP will go up by $250 billion.

The moral of the story is that fiscal policies that keep the deficit the same do not necessarily keep aggregate demand the same. A cut in government spending balanced by an equal cut in tax revenues can be expected to reduce *Y*—a lesson that policymakers frequently forget.

GOVERNMENT TRANSFER PAYMENTS

Finally, we should mention the last major tool of fiscal policy: *government transfer payments.* A transfer, you will remember, is a payment to an individual that is not compensation for any direct contribution to production. How are transfers treated in our models of income determination—like purchases of goods and services (G) or like taxes (T)?

The answer follows readily from the circular flow diagram back on page 171 or the accounting identity on page 146. The important thing to understand about transfer payments is that they intervene between gross domestic product (Y) and disposable income (DI) in precisely the *opposite* way from income taxes.

Specifically, starting with the wages, interest, rents, and profits that constitute the national income, we *subtract* income taxes to calculate disposable income. We do so because these taxes represent the portion of incomes that are *earned* but never *received* by consumers. But then we must *add* transfer payments because they represent sources of income that are *received* although they were not *earned* in the process of production. Thus:

Transfer payments are basically negative taxes.

So giving consumers \$400 billion in the form of transfer payments is treated in the 45° line diagram as a \$400 billion decrease in taxes. Thus, Figure 11-5, which we devised to illustrate a tax cut, can also be used to illustrate a rise in unemployment benefits, or in Social Security benefits, or any other such transfer payment. Similarly, the analysis of a decrease in transfer payments would proceed exactly like the analysis of an increase in taxes.

PLANNING EXPANSIVE FISCAL POLICY

Now imagine you are a member of Congress trying to decide whether to use fiscal policy to stimulate the economy—and, if so, by how much. Suppose the economy would have a GDP of \$6,000 billion if last year's budget were simply reenacted. Suppose further that your goal is to achieve a fully employed labor force and that staff economists tell you this would require a GDP of approximately \$7,000 billion. Finally, just to keep the calculations manageable, imagine that the price level is fixed. What sort of budget should you vote for?

This chapter has taught us that the government has three ways to raise GDP by \$1,000 billion. Congress can raise government purchases, reduce taxes, or increase transfer payments by enough to close the recessionary gap between actual and potential GDP.

Figure 11-6 illustrates the problem, and its cure through higher government spending, on our 45° line diagram. Figure 11-6(a) shows the equilibrium of the economy if no changes are made in the budget. Except for the full-employment line at $Y = \$7{,}000$ and the corresponding recessionary gap, it looks just like Figure 11-3. With an expenditure multiplier of 2½, you can figure out that an additional \$400 billion of government spending will be needed to push GDP up \$1,000 billion and eliminate the gap ($\$400 \times 2\frac{1}{2} = \$1{,}000$).

So you might vote to raise G from $G_0 = \$1{,}300$ billion to $G_1 = \$1{,}700$ billion, hoping to move the $C + I + G + (X - IM)$ line in Figure 11-6(a) up to the position indicated in Figure 11-6(b), thereby achieving full employment. Or you might prefer to achieve this fiscal stimulus by lowering income taxes instead. Or

FIGURE 11-6 FISCAL POLICY TO ELIMINATE A RECESSIONARY GAP

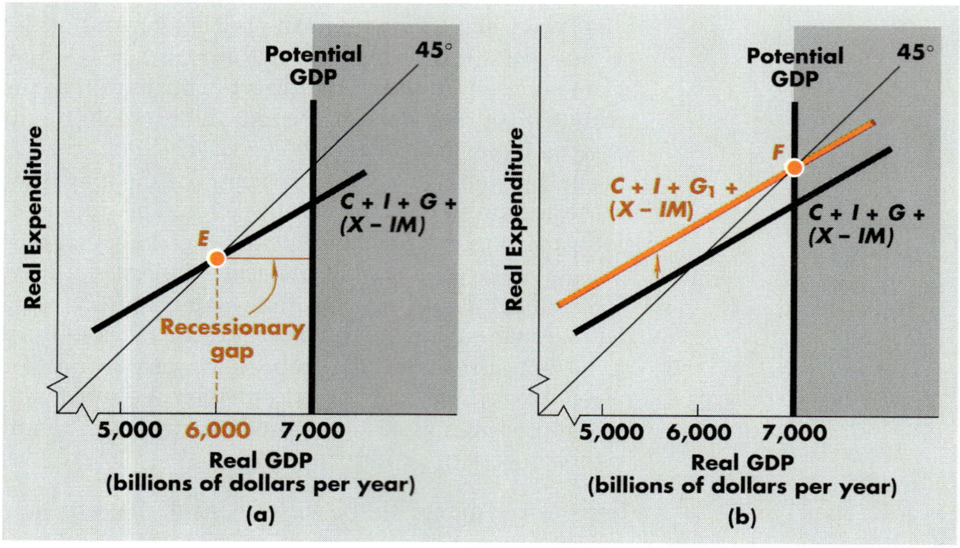

This diagram shows, with more precision than can actually be achieved in practice, how fiscal policy can eliminate a recessionary gap. Panel (a) shows the gap: Equilibrium GDP ($6,000 billion) falls short of potential GDP ($7,000 billion). Panel (b) shows how fiscal policy—by moving the $C + I + G + (X - IM)$ curve up just enough—can wipe out this gap and restore full employment. With a multiplier of 2½, a rise in G of $400 billion or a cut in taxes large enough to shift C up by $400 billion would do the trick.

you might opt for more generous transfer payments. The point is that there are a variety of budgets capable of increasing GDP by $1,000 billion. Figure 11-6 applies equally well to any of them.

PLANNING RESTRICTIVE FISCAL POLICY

The preceding example assumed that the basic problem of fiscal policy is to close a recessionary gap, as was the case at the start of the Clinton administration. Often this is so. But by the end of 1994 many economists believed that the major macroeconomic problem was just the opposite: Aggregate demand exceeded the economy's capacity to produce, leading to an inflationary gap. In such a case, fiscal policy should assume a restrictive stance in order to reduce inflation.

It does not take much imagination to run our previous analysis in reverse. If there is an inflationary gap under a continuation of current budget policies, contractionary fiscal policy tools can eliminate it. By cutting spending, raising taxes, or by some combination of the two, the government can pull the $C + G + I + (X - IM)$ schedule down to a noninflationary position and achieve an equilibrium at full employment.

Notice the difference between this way of eliminating an inflationary gap and the natural self-correcting mechanism that we discussed in the last chapter. There we observed that, if the economy were left to its own devices, a cumulative but self-limiting process of inflation eventually would eliminate the inflationary gap and return the economy to full employment. Here we see that it is not necessary to put the economy through the inflationary wringer. Instead, a restrictive fiscal policy can avoid inflation by limiting aggregate demand to the level the economy can produce at full employment.

But suppose taxes are raised or spending is cut when the economy is approximately at full employment, rather than stuck with an inflationary gap. Then contractionary fiscal policy can cause unemployment. This is the problem that worried President Clinton in 1995, when he argued at first that Republican plans to balance the budget in 7 years were too much, too soon.

THE CHOICE BETWEEN SPENDING POLICY AND TAX POLICY

In principle, fiscal policy can nudge the economy in the desired direction equally well by changing government spending or by changing taxes. For example, if the government wants to expand the economy, it can raise G or lower T. Either policy would shift the total expenditure schedule upward, as depicted in Figure 11-6, thereby raising the equilibrium GDP on the demand side.

In terms of our aggregate demand and supply diagram, either policy shifts the aggregate demand curve outward, from D_0D_0 to D_1D_1 in Figure 11-7. As a result, the economy's equilibrium moves from point E to point A. Both real GDP and the price level rise. As this diagram points out, any combination of higher spending and lower taxes that produces the same aggregate demand curve leads to the same increases in real GDP and prices.

How, then, do policymakers decide whether it is better to raise spending or to cut taxes? The answer depends mainly on how large a public sector they want—a long-running debate in the United States which has become particularly contentious of late.

The small-government point of view is typically advocated by conservatives, who gained the ascendancy in the 1990s. According to this view, the government is much too large; we are foolish to rely on the public sector to do things that private individuals and businesses could do better on their own; and the growth of government interferes too much in our everyday lives, and in so doing circumscribes our freedom. Those who hold this view can argue for *tax cuts* when macroeconomic considerations call for expansionary fiscal policy, and for *reductions in public spending* when restrictive policy is required.

An opposing opinion, expressed most often by liberals, is that there is something amiss when a country as wealthy as the United States has such an impoverished public sector. In this view, America's most pressing needs are not for more fast food and video games, but rather for better schools, more efficient public transportation systems, and cleaner and safer city streets. People on this side of the debate believe that we should *increase* spending when the economy needs

FIGURE 11-7 EXPANSIONARY FISCAL POLICY

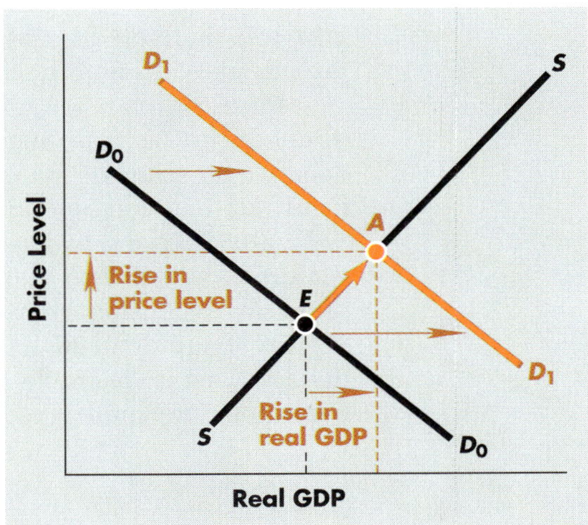

Any of a variety of expansionary fiscal policies will push the aggregate demand curve outward to the right as depicted by the shift from D_0D_0 to D_1D_1 in this aggregate supply and demand diagram. The economy's equilibrium moves upward to the right along aggregate supply curve SS, from point E to point A. Comparing A with E, we note that output is higher but prices are also higher. The expansionary policy has caused some inflation.

stimulus, and pay for these improved public services by *increasing taxes* when the economy needs to be reined in.

Too often the use of fiscal policy for economic stabilization is erroneously associated with a large and growing public sector—that is, with "big government." This need not be the case. Individuals favoring a smaller public sector can advocate an active fiscal policy just as well as those who favor a larger public sector. Advocates of big government budgets should seek to expand demand (when appropriate) through higher government spending and contract demand (when appropriate) through tax increases. By contrast, advocates of small public budgets should seek to expand demand by cutting taxes and reduce demand by cutting expenditures.

SOME HARSH REALITIES

The mechanics outlined so far in this chapter make the fiscal policy planner's job look rather simple. The elementary diagrams suggest, rather misleadingly, that the authorities can drive GDP to any level they please simply by manipulating spending and tax programs. It seems as though they should be able to hit the full-employment bull's eye every time.

But, in fact, a better analogy is shooting through dense fog at an erratically moving target with an inaccurate gun. The target is moving because, in the real world, the investment, net exports, and consumption schedules are constantly shifting due to changes in expectations, new technological breakthroughs, events abroad, and so on. This means that the policies decided upon today, which are to take effect at some future date, may no longer be appropriate by the time that date rolls around. Policy must be based, to some extent, on *forecasting,* and no one has yet discovered a foolproof method of economic forecasting.[1] Because fiscal policy decisions sometimes take a long time to be carried out, poor forecasts may occasionally leave the government fighting the last inflation just when the new recession gets under way.

A second misleading feature of our diagrams is that multipliers are not known with as much precision as our examples suggest. Thus, while the "best guess" may be that a $20 billion cut in government purchases will reduce GDP by $40 billion, the actual outcome may be as little as $20 billion or as much as $60 billion. It is therefore impossible to "fine tune" every wobble out of the economy's growth path; economic science is simply not that precise.

A third complication is that our target—full-employment GDP—may be only dimly visible, as if through a fog. For example, there has recently been a lively debate over whether mainstream economists have overestimated the unemployment rate that corresponds to full employment.

Finally, in trying to decide whether to push the unemployment rate lower, legislators would like to know how large the inflation cost is likely to be. As we know, an expansionary fiscal policy that reduces a recessionary gap by increasing aggregate demand will lower unemployment. But it also tends to be inflationary. This undesirable side effect may make the government hesitant to use fiscal policy to combat recessions.

[1]Some problems and techniques of economic forecasting are considered in Chapter 14.

Is there a way out of this dilemma? Can we carry on the battle against unemployment without aggravating inflation? For almost 20 years, a small but influential minority of economists, journalists, and politicians have argued that we can. They call their approach "supply-side economics." The idea helped sweep Ronald Reagan to smashing electoral victories in 1980 and 1984. By 1992, however, Bill Clinton won the presidency by running against it. Then, just 2 years later, supply-side thinking made something of a comeback when the Republicans swept control of both houses of Congress and began trying to implement their "Contract with America." Just what is supply-side economics?

THE IDEA BEHIND SUPPLY-SIDE TAX CUTS

The central idea of supply-side economics is that certain types of tax cuts can be expected to increase aggregate supply. For example, taxes can be cut in ways that raise the rewards for working, saving, and investing. *If people actually respond to these incentives,* such tax cuts will increase the total supplies of labor and capital in the economy, thereby increasing aggregate supply.

Figure 11-8 illustrates the idea on an aggregate supply and demand diagram. If policy measures can shift the economy's aggregate supply to position S_1S_1, then prices will be lower and output higher than if the aggregate supply curve were S_0S_0. Policymakers will have succeeded in reducing inflation and raising real output (lowering unemployment) at the same time. The trade-off between inflation and unemployment will have been defeated. This is the goal of supply-side economics.

What sorts of policies do supply siders advocate? Here is a small sample of their long list of recommended tax cuts:

1. *Lower personal income tax rates.* Sharp cuts in personal taxes were the cornerstone of President Reagan's economic strategy. Tax rates on individuals were

FIGURE 11-8 THE GOAL OF SUPPLY-SIDE TAX CUTS

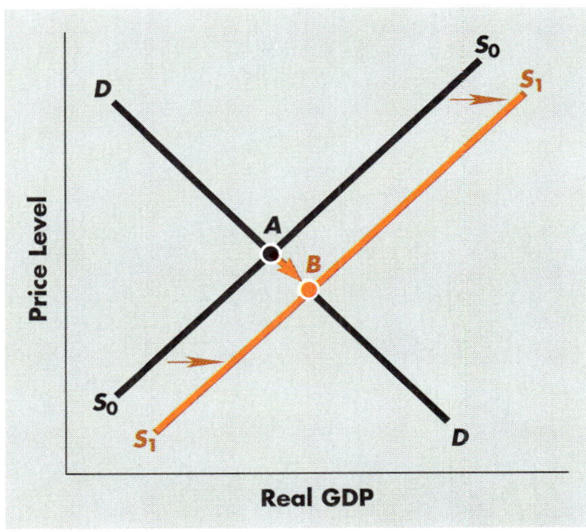

The basic goal of supply-side tax cuts is to shift the economy's aggregate supply curve outward to the right. For example, the aggregate supply curve might be S_1S_1 under a program of supply-side tax cuts, whereas it would only be S_0S_0 without such tax cuts. If aggregate demand is the same in either case, the supply-side tax cuts would lead to the equilibrium point *B* instead of the equilibrium point *A*. Comparing *B* with *A*, we see that the program reduces prices and raises output.

reduced in stages between 1981 and 1984 and then again in 1986. By 1987, the richest Americans were in the 28 percent tax bracket, and most taxpayers were in the 15 percent bracket. Such low tax rates, supply siders argued, augment the supplies of both labor and capital.

2. *Reduce taxes on income from savings.* One extreme form of this proposal would simply exempt from taxation all income from interest and dividends. Since income must be either consumed or saved, this would, in effect, change our present personal income tax into a tax on consumer spending. Several such proposals for radical tax reform were being seriously considered as this edition went to press.
3. *Reduce taxes on capital gains.* When investors sell assets for a profit, that profit is called a *capital gain* on their investments. Supply siders argue that the government can encourage more investment by taxing capital gains at lower rates than ordinary income. This proposal, long favored by many Republicans, was part of the Contract with America in 1994.
4. *Reduce the corporate income tax.* By reducing the tax burden on corporations, it is argued, the government can provide both greater investment incentives (by raising the profitability of investment) and more investable funds (by letting companies keep more of their earnings). This advice was followed in 1981 by making depreciation allowances more generous[2] and in 1986 by lowering the corporate tax rate.

Let us suppose, for the moment, that a successful supply-side tax cut is enacted. Since *both* aggregate demand *and* aggregate supply increase simultaneously, the economy may be able to avoid the painful inflationary consequences of an expansionary fiscal policy that were shown in Figure 11-7 on page 237.

Figure 11-9 illustrates this conclusion. The two aggregate demand curves and the initial aggregate supply curve S_0S_0 are carried over directly from Figure

FIGURE 11-9 A SUCCESSFUL SUPPLY-SIDE TAX REDUCTION

A supply-side tax cut, if successful, shifts *both* aggregate demand *and* supply to the right. Equilibrium is initially at point *E*, where demand curve D_0D_0 intersects supply curve S_0S_0. After the supply-side tax cut, the aggregate demand and supply curves are D_1D_1 and S_1S_1, so equilibrium is at point *C*. Compared to a tax cut that works only on the demand side (point *A*), the supply-side tax cut raises output more and prices less.

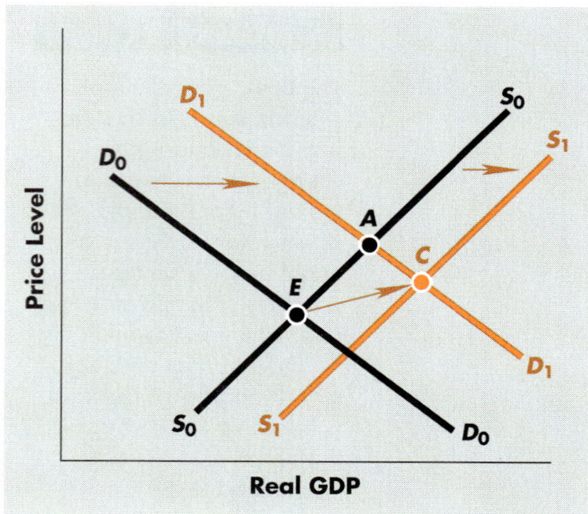

[2]A company investing in a machine or factory may not deduct the entire cost of that asset as a business expense in the year it is purchased. Instead, it must spread the cost over the lifetime of the asset in a series of tax deductions called *depreciation allowances*. Naturally, firms prefer to get these allowances sooner rather than later, because higher depreciation in the early years of an investment means an immediate cut in tax burdens.

11-7. But we have introduced an additional supply curve, S_1S_1, to reflect the successful supply-side tax cut depicted in Figure 11-8. The equilibrium of the economy moves from *E* to *C*, whereas with a conventional demand-side tax cut it would have moved from *E* to *A*. As compared with point *A*, output is higher and prices are lower at point *C*.

A good deal, you say! Indeed it is. The supply-side argument is extremely attractive in principle. The question is: Does it work in practice? Can we actually do what is depicted in Figure 11-9? Let us consider some difficulties.

SOME FLIES IN THE OINTMENT

Critics of supply-side economics rarely question its goals or the basic idea that lower taxes improve incentives. They argue, instead, that supply siders exaggerate the beneficial effects of tax cuts and ignore some undesirable side effects. Here is a brief rundown of some of the main objections to supply-side tax cuts:

1. *Small magnitude of supply-side effects.* The first objection is that supply siders are simply too optimistic: We really do not know how to do what Figure 11-8 shows. While it is easy, for example, to design tax incentives that make saving more *attractive* financially, people may not actually respond to these incentives. In fact, most of the statistical evidence suggests that we should not expect very much from tax incentives for saving. As economist Charles Schultze once quipped: "There's nothing wrong with supply-side economics that division by 10 couldn't cure."
2. *Demand-side effects.* The second objection is that supply siders underestimate the effects of tax cuts on aggregate demand. If you cut personal taxes, for example, individuals *may possibly* work more. But they *will certainly* spend more. If you reduce business taxes and thereby encourage expansion of industrial capacity, business firms will demand more investment goods.

   The joint implication of these two objections is shown in Figure 11-10. Here we depict a small outward shift of the aggregate supply curve (which reflects the first objection) and a large outward shift of the aggregate demand curve

FIGURE 11-10 A MORE PESSIMISTIC VIEW OF SUPPLY-SIDE TAX CUTS

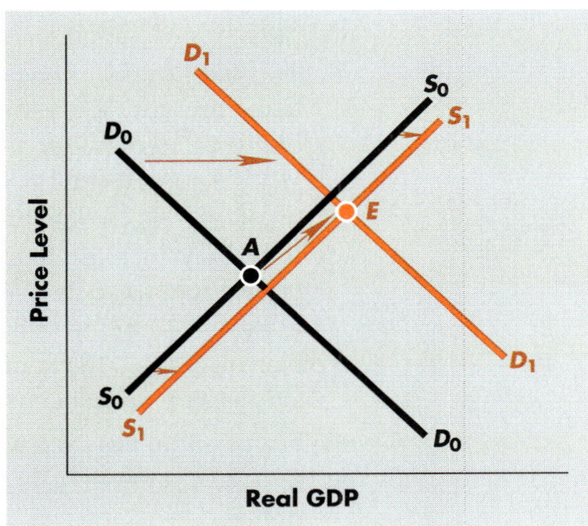

If the effect of supply-side tax initiatives on the aggregate supply curve is actually much smaller than suggested by Figure 11-8, the anti-inflationary impact will be correspondingly smaller. As you can see in this diagram, it is possible that a large shift in the aggregate demand curve could overwhelm the favorable effects of the tax cuts on the price level.

(which reflects the second). The result is that the economy's equilibrium moves from point *A* (the intersection of S_0S_0 and D_0D_0) to point *E* (the intersection of S_1S_1 and D_1D_1). Prices rise as output expands. The outcome differs only a little from the straight "demand-side" fiscal stimulus depicted in Figure 11-7 (page 237).

3. *Problems in timing.* The most promising types of supply-side tax cuts seek to encourage greater business investment. But the benefits from investment do not arrive by overnight mail. It may take years before we see any substantial increases in industrial capacity. Thus, the *expenditures* on investment goods almost certainly come before the *expansion of capacity.* In a word, supply-side tax cuts will have their primary short-run effects on aggregate demand. Effects on aggregate supply come later.
4. *Effect on the distribution of income.* The preceding objections all pertain to the likely effects of supply-side policies on aggregate supply and demand. But there is a different problem that bears mention: Most supply-side initiatives increase income inequality. While raising the incomes of the wealthiest members of our society may not be their primary aim, most supply-side cuts cannot help but concentrate their benefits on the rich simply because it is the rich who own most of the capital.

   Indeed, this tilt toward the rich is almost an inescapable corollary of supply-side logic. The basic aim of supply-side economics is to increase the incentives for working and investing, that is, to increase the gap between the rewards of those who succeed in the economic game (by working hard, investing well, or by just plain luck) and those who fail. It can hardly be surprising, therefore, that supply-side policies tend to increase economic inequality.
5. *Losses of tax revenue.* You can hardly help noticing that most of the policies suggested by supply siders involve cutting one tax or another. Thus, unless some other tax is raised or spending is cut, supply-side tax cuts are bound to raise the government budget deficit. This problem proved to be the Achilles heel of supply-side economics in the United States in the 1980s. It left behind a legacy of budget deficits that have plagued us ever since.

TOWARD ASSESSMENT OF SUPPLY-SIDE ECONOMICS

On balance, most economists have reached the following conclusions about supply-side tax initiatives:

1. The likely effectiveness of supply-side tax cuts depends on what kinds of taxes are cut. Tax reductions aimed at stimulating business investment are likely to pack more punch than tax reductions aimed at getting people to work longer hours or to save more.
2. Such tax cuts probably will increase aggregate supply much more slowly than they increase aggregate demand. Thus, supply-side policies should not be thought of as a substitute for short-run stabilization policy, but rather as a way to promote (slightly) faster economic growth in the long run.
3. Demand-side effects of supply-side tax cuts are likely to overwhelm supply-side effects in the short run.
4. Supply-side tax cuts are likely to widen income inequalities.
5. Supply-side tax cuts are almost certain to lead to bigger, not smaller, budget deficits.

But this list does not close the books on the issue. It does not even tell us whether supply-side tax cuts are a good idea or a bad one. Some people will look over this list and decide that they favor supply-side tax cuts; others, perusing the same facts, will reach the opposite conclusion. We cannot say that either group is "wrong" because, like almost every economic policy, supply-side economics has its pros and cons.

Why, then, did so many economists and politicians react so negatively to supply-side economics as practiced in the early 1980s? The main reason seems to be that the claims made by the most ardent supply siders were clearly excessive. Naturally, these claims were proven wrong. But showing that wild claims are wild does not dispose of the kernel of truth in supply-side economics: Reductions in marginal tax rates do improve economic incentives. Any specific supply-side tax cut must be judged on its individual merits.

CLINTONOMICS AND SUPPLY-SIDE ECONOMICS

During the 1992 presidential campaign, candidate Bill Clinton attacked the Reagan-Bush brand of supply-side economics as "trickle-down economics," and argued that it had failed. He emphasized, in particular, the last two items in our assessment: the effects on income inequality and on the budget deficit. The voters apparently agreed.

Ironically, however, President Clinton also ran on an avowedly supply-side platform—though of a different stripe. His emphasis was on building up the nation's resources of labor, capital, and technology so that our capacity to produce will be higher in the long run. This, of course, is precisely the goal of supply-side economics: to push the aggregate supply curve outward.

But, unlike Presidents Reagan and Bush, President Clinton did not propose to accomplish this mainly by cutting taxes. While some tax cuts were included in the Clinton plan, especially tax credits for investment and R&D, there were more tax *increases* than tax cuts—in order to raise revenue. The real emphasis of Clintonomics was on improving the quality of the American work force through more and better education and training, and on building up the nation's infrastructure.

But programs like these take money, money the federal government did not have because of the huge budget deficit. So the focus of Clintonomics in practice became deficit reduction, not public spending designed to raise aggregate supply. In 1993, at a time when Democrats held majorities in both houses of Congress, the president barely won passage of a large deficit-reduction passage. Then, in November 1994, the Republicans won a resounding electoral victory and the political debate tilted even more toward shrinking both the budget deficit and the size of the federal government. The central political question since 1995 has been how to balance the budget. This focus leaves little room for supply-side initiatives, whether in the form of tax cuts or new spending, although both President Clinton and Republican congressional leaders continue to press for selective tax cuts.

SUMMARY

1. The government's **fiscal policy** is its plan for managing aggregate demand through its spending and taxing programs. It is made jointly by the president and Congress.

2. The government's net effect on aggregate demand—and hence on equilibrium output and prices—depends on whether the expansionary effects of its spending are greater or smaller than the contractionary effects of its taxes.

3. Since consumer spending (C) depends on disposable income (DI), and DI is GDP minus taxes, any change in taxes will shift the consumption schedule on a 45° line diagram. The nature of this shift depends on whether it is **fixed taxes** or **variable taxes** that are changed.
4. Such shifts in the consumption function caused by tax policy are subject to the same multiplier as autonomous shifts in G, I, or $X - IM$.
5. An income tax reduces the size of this common multiplier.
6. The multiplier for changes in taxes is smaller than the multiplier for changes in government purchases.
7. *Government transfer payments* are like negative taxes, not like government purchases of goods and services, because they influence total spending only indirectly through their effect on consumption.
8. If the multipliers were known precisely, it would be possible to plan any of a variety of fiscal policies to eliminate either a recessionary or an inflationary gap. Recessionary gaps can be cured by raising G, cutting taxes, or increasing transfers. Inflationary gaps can be cured by cutting G, raising taxes, or reducing transfers.
9. Active stabilization policy can be carried out either by means that tend to expand the size of government (by raising either G or T when appropriate) or by means that hold back the size of government (by reducing either G or T when appropriate).
10. Expansionary fiscal policy can cure recessions, but it normally exacts a cost in terms of higher inflation. This dilemma has led to a great deal of interest in *"supply-side" tax cuts* designed to stimulate aggregate supply.
11. Supply-side tax cuts aim to push the economy's aggregate supply curve outward to the right. If successful, they can expand the economy and reduce inflation at the same time—a highly desirable outcome.
12. But critics point out at least five serious problems with supply-side tax cuts: They also stimulate aggregate demand; the beneficial effects on aggregate supply may be small; the demand-side effects occur before the supply-side effects; they make the income distribution more unequal; and large tax cuts lead to large budget deficits.

KEY TERMS

Fiscal policy
Fixed taxes
Variable taxes
Government transfer payments
Effect of income taxes on the multiplier
Supply-side tax cuts

QUESTIONS FOR REVIEW

1. America's defense budget has fallen since the end of the Cold War. How would GDP in the United States be affected if the reduced defense spending were used to:
   a. Reduce the budget deficit, so that government purchases fell?
   b. Free funds for other public purposes, so that government purchases remained the same?
2. Consider an economy in which tax collections are always $800 and in which the four components of aggregate demand are as follows:

GDP	Taxes	*DI*	*C*	*I*	*G*	(*X* − *IM*)
$1360	$800	$560	$420	$200	$800	$30
1480	800	680	510	200	800	30
1600	800	800	600	200	800	30
1720	800	920	690	200	800	30
1840	800	1040	780	200	800	30

Find the equilibrium of this economy graphically. What is the marginal propensity to consume? What is the multiplier? What would happen to equilibrium GDP if government purchases were reduced by $60 and the price level were unchanged?

3. Now consider a related economy in which investment is also $200, government purchases are also $800, net exports are also $30, and the price level is also fixed. But taxes now vary with income, and as a result the consumption schedule looks like the following:

GDP	Taxes	*DI*	*C*
$1360	$720	$640	$510
1480	760	720	570
1600	800	800	630
1720	840	880	690
1840	880	960	750

Find the equilibrium graphically. What is the marginal propensity to consume? What is the tax rate? Use your diagram to show the effect of a decrease of \$60 in government purchases. What is the multiplier? Compare this answer to your answer to Review Question 2 above. What do you conclude?

4. Explain why G has the same multiplier as I, but taxes have a different multiplier.
5. Return to the hypothetical economy in Review Question 2 and suppose that *both* taxes and government purchases are increased by \$120. Find the new equilibrium under the assumption that consumer spending continues to be exactly three-quarters of disposable income (as it is in Review Question 2).
6. If the government today decides that aggregate demand is excessive and is causing inflation, what options are open to it? What if it decides that aggregate demand is too weak instead?
7. Suppose that you are in charge of the fiscal policy of the economy in Review Question 2. There is an inflationary gap and you want to reduce income by \$120. What specific actions can you take to achieve this goal?
8. Now put yourself in charge of the economy in Review Question 3, and suppose that full employment comes at a GDP of \$1,840. How can you push income up to that level?
9. Which of the proposed supply-side tax cuts appeals to you most? Draw up a list of arguments for and against enacting such a cut right now.
10. (More difficult) Advocates of lower taxes on capital gains argue that this type of tax cut will raise aggregate supply by spurring business investment. But, of course, any increase in investment spending will also raise aggregate demand. Compare the effects on aggregate supply, aggregate demand, and tax revenue of three different ways to cut the capital gains tax:
    a. Reduce capital gains taxes on *all* investments, including those that were made before tax rates were cut.
    b. Reduce capital gains taxes only on investments made after tax rates are cut.
    c. Reduce capital gains taxes only on certain types of investments, such as corporate stocks and bonds.

    Which of the three seems most desirable to you? Why?

APPENDIX

ALGEBRAIC TREATMENT OF FISCAL POLICY AND AGGREGATE DEMAND

In this appendix, we explain the simple algebra behind the fiscal policy multipliers discussed in the chapter. In so doing, we deal only with a simplified case in which prices do not change. While it is possible to work out the corresponding algebra for the more realistic aggregate demand–aggregate supply analysis with variable prices, the analysis is rather complicated and is best left to more advanced courses.

We start with the example used in the chapter (especially on pages 231 and 233). The government spends \$1,300 billion on goods and services ($G = 1{,}300$) and levies an income tax equal to 20 percent of GDP. So, if the symbol T denotes tax receipts:

$$T = 0.20Y$$

Since the consumption function we have been working with is:

$$C = 300 + 0.75DI$$

where DI is disposable income, and since disposable income and GDP are related by the accounting identity:

$$DI = Y - T$$

it follows that the C schedule used in the 45° line diagram is described by the algebraic equation:

$$\begin{aligned} C &= 300 + 0.75(Y - T) \\ &= 300 + 0.75(Y - 0.20Y) \\ &= 300 + 0.75(0.80Y) \\ &= 300 + 0.60Y \end{aligned}$$

We can now apply the equilibrium condition:

$$Y = C + I + G + (X - IM)$$

Since investment in this example is $I = 900$ and net exports are -100, substituting for C, I, G, and $(X - IM)$ into this equation gives:

$$\begin{aligned} Y &= 300 + 0.60Y + 900 + 1{,}300 - 100 \\ 0.40Y &= 2{,}400 \\ Y &= 6{,}000 \end{aligned}$$

This is all there is to finding equilibrium GDP in an economy with a government.

To find the multiplier for government spending, increase G by 1 and solve the problem again:

$$\begin{aligned} Y &= C + I + G + (X - IM) \\ Y &= 300 + 0.60Y + 900 + 1{,}301 - 100 \\ 0.40Y &= 2{,}401 \\ Y &= 6{,}002.5 \end{aligned}$$

So the multiplier is 6,002.5 − 6,000 = 2.5, as stated in the text.

To find the multiplier for an increase in fixed taxes, change the tax schedule to:

$$T = 0.20Y + 1$$

Disposable income is then:

$$\begin{aligned} DI &= Y - T = Y - (0.20Y + 1) \\ &= 0.80Y - 1 \end{aligned}$$

so the consumption function is:

$$\begin{aligned} C &= 300 + 0.75DI \\ &= 300 + 0.75(0.80Y - 1) \\ &= 299.25 + 0.60Y \end{aligned}$$

Solving for equilibrium GDP as usual gives:

$$\begin{aligned} Y &= C + I + G + (X - IM) \\ Y &= 299.25 + 0.60Y + 900 + 1{,}300 - 100 \\ 0.40Y &= 2{,}399.25 \\ Y &= 5{,}998.125 \end{aligned}$$

So a \$1 increase in fixed taxes lowers Y by \$1.875. The tax multiplier is −1.875.

Now let us proceed to a more general solution, using symbols rather than specific numbers. The equations of the model are as follows:

$$Y = C + I + G + (X - IM) \quad (1)$$

is the usual equilibrium condition;

$$C = a + bDI \quad (2)$$

is the same consumption function we have used in the appendixes of Chapters 8 and 9;

$$DI = Y - T \quad (3)$$

is the accounting identity relating disposable income to GDP;

$$T = T_0 + tY \quad (4)$$

is the tax function, where T_0 represents fixed taxes (which are zero in our numerical example) and t represents the tax rate (which is 0.20 in the example). Finally, I, G, and $(X - IM)$ are just fixed numbers.

We begin the solution by substituting (3) and (4) into (2) to derive the consumption schedule relating C to Y:

$$\begin{aligned} C &= a + bDI \\ C &= a + b(Y - T) \\ C &= a + b(Y - T_0 - tY) \\ C &= a - bT_0 + b(1 - t)Y \quad (5) \end{aligned}$$

You will notice that a change in fixed taxes (T_0) shifts the *intercept* of the C schedule while a change in the tax rate (t) changes its *slope*, as explained in the chapter (pages 228–232).

Next substitute Equation (5) into Equation (1) to find equilibrium GDP:

$$\begin{aligned} Y &= C + I + G + (X - IM) \\ Y &= a - bT_0 + b(1 - t)Y + I + G + (X - IM) \\ [1 - b(1 - t)]Y &= a - bT_0 + I + G + (X - IM) \end{aligned}$$

or

$$Y = \frac{a - bT_0 + I + G + (X - IM)}{1 - b(1 - t)} \quad (6)$$

Equation (6) shows us that the multiplier for G, I, a, or $(X - IM)$ is:

$$\text{Multiplier} = \frac{1}{1 - b(1 - t)}$$

To see that this is in fact the multiplier, raise any of G, I, a, or $(X - IM)$ by 1 unit. In each case, Equation (6) would be changed to read:

$$Y = \frac{a - bT_0 + I + G + (X - IM) + 1}{1 - b(1 - t)}$$

Subtracting Equation (6) from this expression gives the change in Y stemming from a 1-unit change in G or I or a:

$$\text{Change in } Y = \frac{1}{1 - b(1 - t)}$$

We noted in Chapter 9 (page 193) that if there were no income tax ($t = 0$), a realistic value for b (the marginal propensity to consume) would yield a multiplier of 10, which is much bigger than the true multiplier. Now that we have added taxes to the model, our multiplier formula produces much more realistic numbers. Approximate values for these parameters for the U.S. economy are $b = 0.90$ and $t = \frac{1}{3}$. The multiplier formula then gives:

$$\text{Multiplier} = \frac{1}{1 - 0.90(1 - \frac{1}{3})}$$
$$= \frac{1}{1 - \frac{3}{5}} = \frac{1}{\frac{2}{5}}$$
$$= 2.50$$

which is not far from its actual estimated value, nearly 2.

Finally, we can see from Equation (6) that the multiplier for a change in fixed taxes (T_0) is:

$$\text{Tax multiplier} = \frac{-b}{1 - b(1 - t)}$$

For the example considered in the text and earlier in this appendix, $b = 0.75$ and $t = 0.20$, so the formula gives:

$$\frac{-0.75}{1 - 0.75(1 - 0.20)} = \frac{-0.75}{1 - 0.75(0.80)}$$
$$\frac{-0.75}{1 - 0.60} = \frac{-0.75}{0.40} = -1.875$$

According to these figures, each $1 *increase* in T_0 *reduces* Y by $1.875.

QUESTIONS FOR REVIEW

1. Consider an economy described by the following set of equations:

$$C = 120 + 0.80DI$$
$$I = 320$$
$$G = 480$$
$$(X - IM) = -80$$
$$T = 200 + 0.25Y$$

Find the equilibrium level of GDP. Then find the multipliers for government purchases and for fixed taxes. If full employment comes at $Y = 1{,}800$, what are some policies that would get GDP there?

2. This is a variant of the previous problem that approaches things the way a fiscal policy planner might. In an economy whose consumption function and tax function are as given in Review Question 1, with investment fixed at 320 and net exports fixed at −80, find the value of G that would make GDP equal to 1,800.

3. You are given the following information about an economy.

$$C = 0.90DI$$
$$I = 100$$
$$G = 540$$
$$(X - IM) = -40$$
$$T = (\tfrac{1}{3})Y$$

a. Find equilibrium GDP and the budget deficit.
b. Suppose the government, unhappy with the budget deficit, decides to cut government spending by precisely the amount of the deficit you found in Review Question 3(a). What actually happens to GDP and the budget deficit, and why?

4. (More difficult) In the economy considered in Review Question 3, suppose the government, seeing that it has not wiped out the deficit, keeps cutting G until it succeeds in balancing the budget. What levels of GDP will then prevail?

CHAPTER 12

Money and the Banking System

[Money] is a machine for doing quickly and commodiously what would be done, though less quickly and commodiously, without it.
John Stuart Mill

The circular flow diagrams of earlier chapters had a "financial system" in the upper left-hand corner. Savings flowed into this system and investment flowed out. Something obviously goes on inside the financial system to channel the savings into investment, and it is time we learned just what this something is.

There is another, equally important, reason for studying the financial system. *Fiscal policy* is not the only lever the government has on the economy's aggregate demand curve; it also exercises significant control over aggregate demand by manipulating *monetary policy.* If we are to understand monetary policy (the subject of Chapters 13 and 14), we must first acquire some understanding of the financial system.

The present chapter has three major objectives. It first seeks to explain the nature of money: what it is, what purposes it serves, and how it is measured. Once this is done, we turn our attention to the banking system, explaining its historical origins, the nature of banking as a business, and why this industry is so heavily regulated. Finally, we learn how banks create money—a subject that is of great importance because you cannot hope to understand monetary policy until you first understand how money is created.

At the end of the chapter, we will see why government authorities must exercise control over the supply of money in a modern economy. This leads naturally into next chapter's discussion of *central banking,* that is, the techniques used to implement monetary policy.

ISSUE: TO REGULATE OR TO DEREGULATE? THAT IS THE QUESTION

The pendulum of bank regulation has swung back and forth over the last 2 decades. In the late 1970s and early 1980s, the United States eased several restrictions on interest rates and permissible activities for banks. Then, after a number of banks and a much larger number of savings institutions went bankrupt in the

1980s, Congress and the bank regulatory agencies cracked down with stiffer regulation and closer scrutiny. In the last few years, the pendulum has swung back toward deregulation again. Restrictions on banking across state lines were lifted in 1994 and regulators have expanded the list of activities permissible for banks.

How much bank regulation is enough? To make an informed judgment on this issue, we must first ask a more basic question: Why were banks so heavily regulated in the first place?

Banking is certainly not heavily monopolized. While there are financial giants such as Citibank (New York) and Bank of America (California), the industry is populated by literally thousands of small banks located in cities and towns throughout the country. There are over 10,000 commercial banks and several thousand savings institutions nationwide. So why did government regulations formerly tell banks, to some degree, how much they could accept in deposits, how much interest they could pay on these deposits, what types of investments they could make, and so on?

A first reason is that the major "output" of the banking industry—the nation's supply of money—is an important determinant of aggregate demand, as we will see in Chapter 13. Bank managers presumably do what is best for their stockholders. That, at any rate, is their job. But as we shall see, what is best for bank stockholders may not be best for the whole economy. For this reason, the government does not allow bankers to determine the level of the nation's money supply by profit considerations alone.

A second reason for the extensive regulation of banks is concern for the safety of depositors. In a free-enterprise system, new businesses are born and die every day; and no one other than the people immediately involved takes much notice of these goings-on. When a firm goes bankrupt, stockholders lose money and employees may lose their jobs. (The latter may not even happen if new management takes over the assets of the bankrupt firm.) But, except for the case of very large firms, that is about it.

A **RUN ON A BANK** occurs when many depositors withdraw cash from their accounts all at once.

But banking is different. If banks were treated like other firms, depositors would lose money whenever one went bankrupt. That is bad enough by itself, but the real danger comes in the case of a **run on a bank.** When depositors get jittery about the security of their money, they may all rush to cash in their accounts. For reasons we will learn in this chapter, most banks could not survive such a "run" and would be forced into insolvency.

Worse yet, this disease is highly contagious. If Mr. Smith hears that his neighbor has just lost her life savings because the Main Street National Bank went broke, he is quite likely to rush to his own bank to make a hefty withdrawal. In fact, that is precisely what happened to a number of savings banks in the 1980s.

Without modern forms of bank regulation, therefore, one bank failure might lead to another. Indeed, bank failures have been common throughout most of American history. (See Figure 12-1.) But, since the 1930s, bank failures generally have not been precipitated by runs because the government has taken steps to ensure that such an infectious disease, if it occurs, will not spread. It has done this in several ways that we will mention in this chapter.

BARTER VERSUS MONETARY EXCHANGE

Money is so much a part of our daily existence that we take it for granted and fail to appreciate all that it accomplishes. But money is in no sense "natural."

BARTER is a system of exchange in which people directly trade one good for another, without using money as an intermediate step.

Like the wheel, it had to be invented. The most obvious way to trade commodities is not by using money, but by **barter**—a system in which people exchange one good directly for another. And the best way to appreciate what monetary exchange accomplishes is to imagine a world without it.

Under a system of direct barter, if Farmer Jones grows corn and has a craving for peanuts, he has to find a peanut farmer, say, Farmer Smith, with a taste for corn. If he finds such a person (this was called the *double coincidence of wants* by the classical economists), they make the trade. If this sounds easy, try to imagine how busy Farmer Jones would be if he had to repeat the sequence for every commodity he consumed in a week. For the most part, the desired double coincidences of wants are more likely to turn out to be double wants of coincidence. Jones gets no peanuts and Smith gets no corn. Worse yet, with so much time spent looking for trading partners, Jones would have far less time to grow corn. In brief:

Money greases the wheels of exchange, and thus makes the whole economy more productive.

Under a monetary system, Farmer Jones gives up his corn for money. He does so not because he wants the money per se, but because of what that money can buy. Money makes his shopping tasks much easier, allowing him simply to locate a peanut farmer who wants money. And what peanut farmer does not? For these reasons, monetary exchange replaced barter at a very early stage of human civilization, and only extreme circumstances, like massive wars and runaway inflations, have been able to bring barter (temporarily) back.

FIGURE 12-1 BANK FAILURES IN THE UNITED STATES, 1915–1996

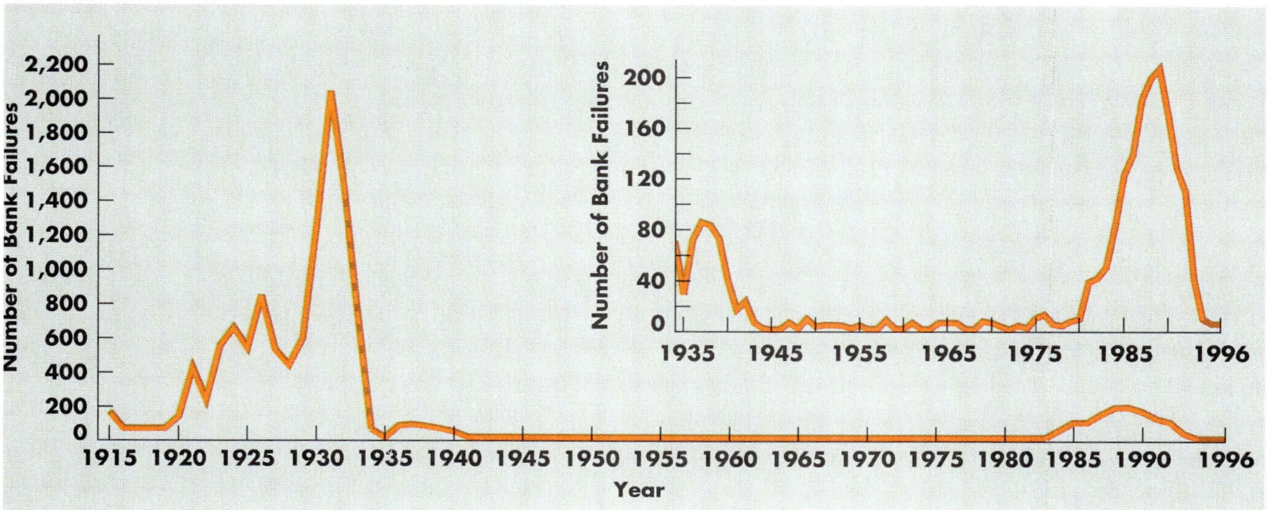

This chart shows the number of commercial banks that failed each year from 1915 through 1996. Notice the sharp drop in the number of failures from 1932 to 1934 and the spurt in the 1980s. In general, however, failures clearly are much less common in the postwar period than they were in earlier years.

SOURCE: Federal Deposit Insurance Corporation.

THE CONCEPTUAL DEFINITION OF MONEY

MONEY is the standard object used in exchanging goods and services. In short, money is the **MEDIUM OF EXCHANGE.**

The **UNIT OF ACCOUNT** is the standard unit for quoting prices.

A **STORE OF VALUE** is an item used to store wealth from one point in time to another.

Monetary exchange is the alternative to barter. In a system of monetary exchange, people trade **money** for goods when they purchase something and trade goods for money when they sell something; but they do not trade goods directly for other goods. This defines money's principal role as the **medium of exchange.** But once it has become accepted as the medium of exchange, whatever serves as money is bound to take on other functions as well. For one, it will inevitably become the **unit of account,** that is, the standard unit for quoting prices. Thus, if inhabitants of an idyllic tropical island use coconuts as money, they would be foolish to quote prices in terms of sea shells.

Money may also come to be used as a **store of value.** If Farmer Jones' corn sales bring in more value than he wants to spend right away, he may find it convenient to store the difference temporarily in the form of money. This is because he knows that money can be "sold" easily for goods and services at a later date, whereas land, gold, and other stores of value might not be. Of course, if money pays no interest and inflation is substantial, he may decide to forgo the convenience of money and store his wealth in some other form rather than see its purchasing power eroded. So this role of money is far from inevitable.

Since money may not always serve as a store of value, and since there are stores of value other than money, it is best not to include the store-of-value function as part of our conceptual definition of money. Instead, we simply label as "money" whatever serves as the medium of exchange.

WHAT SERVES AS MONEY?

Anthropologists and historians will testify that a bewildering variety of objects have served as money in different times and places. Cattle, stones, candy bars, cigarettes, woodpecker scalps, porpoise teeth, and giraffe tails are a few of the more colorful examples.

A **COMMODITY MONEY** is an object in use as a medium of exchange, but which also has a substantial value in alternative (nonmonetary) uses.

In primitive or less organized societies, the commodities that served as money generally had value in themselves. If not used as money, cattle could be slaughtered for food, cigarettes could be smoked, and so on. But such **commodity money** generally runs into several severe difficulties. To be useful as a medium of exchange, the commodity must be divisible. This makes cattle a poor choice. It must also be of uniform, or at least readily identifiable, quality so that inferior substitutes are easy to recognize. This may be why woodpecker scalps never achieved great popularity. The medium of exchange must also be storable and durable, which presents a serious problem for candy-bar money. Finally, because commodity money needs to be carried and stored, it is helpful if the item is compact, that is, has high value per unit of volume and weight.

All of these traits make it sensible that gold and silver have circulated as money since the first coins were struck about 2,500 years ago. As they have high value in nonmonetary uses, a lot of purchasing power can be carried without too much weight. Pieces of gold are also storable, divisible (with a little trouble), and of identifiable quality (with a little more trouble).

The same characteristics suggest that paper would make an ideal money. The Chinese invented paper money in the 11th century, and Marco Polo brought the idea to Europe. Since we can print any number on it that we please, we can make paper money as divisible as we like and also make it possible to carry a large value in a lightweight and compact form. Paper is easy to store and, with a little cleverness, we can make counterfeiting hard (though never impossible).

Paper cannot, however, serve as commodity money because its value per square inch in alternative uses is so small. A paper currency that is repudiated by its issuer can, perhaps, be used as wallpaper or to wrap fish, but these uses will surely represent only a small fraction of the paper's value as money.[1] Contrary to the popular expression, such a currency literally *is* worth the paper it is printed on—which is to say that it is not worth much. Thus, paper money is always **fiat money.**

FIAT MONEY is money that is decreed as such by the government. It is of little value as a commodity, but it maintains its value as a medium of exchange because people have faith that the issuer will stand behind the pieces of printed paper and limit their production.

Money in the contemporary United States is almost entirely fiat money. Look at a dollar bill. Next to George Washington's picture it states: "This note is legal tender for all debts, public and private." Nowhere on the certificate is there a promise, stated or implied, that the U.S. government will exchange it for anything else. A dollar bill is convertible into, say, 4 quarters or 10 dimes—but not into gold, chocolate, or any other commodity.

Why do people hold these pieces of paper? Only because they know that others are willing to accept them for things of intrinsic value—food, rent, shoes, and so on. If this confidence ever evaporated, these dollar bills would cease serving as a medium of exchange and, given that they make ugly wallpaper, would become virtually worthless.

But don't panic. This is not likely to occur. Our current monetary system has evolved over hundreds of years during which *commodity* money was first replaced by *full-bodied paper money*—paper certificates that were backed by gold or silver of equal value held in the issuer's vaults. Then the full-bodied paper money was replaced by certificates that were only partially backed by gold and silver. Finally, we arrived at our present system, in which paper money has no "backing" whatsoever. Like a hesitant swimmer who first dips her toes, then her

---

[1]The first paper money issued by the federal government, the Continental dollar, was essentially repudiated. (Actually, the new government of the United States redeemed the Continentals for 1 cent on the dollar in the 1790s.) This gave rise to the derisive expression, "It's not worth a Continental."

legs, then her whole body into a cold swimming pool, we have "tested the water" at each step of the way—and found it to our liking. It is unlikely that we will ever take a step back in the other direction.

HOW THE QUANTITY OF MONEY IS MEASURED

Since the amount of money in circulation is of profound importance for the determination of national product and the price level, it is important that the government know how much money there is. So we must devise some *measure* of the money supply.

Our conceptual definition of money describes it as the medium of exchange. But this raises difficult questions about just what items to include and exclude when we count up the money supply—questions that have long made the statistical definition of money a subject of dispute. In fact, the U.S. government has several official definitions of the money supply, two of which we will meet shortly.

Some components are obvious. All of our coins and paper money, the small change of our economic system, clearly should count as money. But we cannot stop there if we want to include the main vehicle for making payments in our society, for the lion's share of our nation's payments are made neither in metal nor in paper money, but by check.

Checking deposits are actually no more than bookkeeping entries in bank ledgers. Many people think of checks simply as a convenient way to give coins or dollar bills to someone else. But that is not so. In fact, the volume of money held in the form of checkable deposits far exceeds the volume of currency. For example, when you pay the grocer $50 by check, dollar bills rarely change hands. Instead, that check normally travels back to your bank, where $50 is deducted from the bookkeeping entry that records your account and added to the bookkeeping entry for your grocer's account. (If you and the grocer hold accounts at different banks, more books get involved; but still no coins or bills are likely to be moved.)

Since so many transactions are made by check, it seems imperative that checkable deposits be included in any useful definition of the money supply. Unfortunately, this is not an easy task nowadays because of the wide variety of ways to transfer money by check. Traditional checking accounts in commercial banks are the most familiar. But many people can also write checks on their savings accounts, on their deposits at credit unions, on their mutual funds, their accounts with stockbrokers, and so on.

The narrowly defined money supply, usually abbreviated **M1,** is the sum of all coins and paper money in circulation, plus certain checkable deposit balances at banks and savings institutions.[2]

One popular definition of the money supply draws the line early and includes only coins, paper money, travelers' checks, conventional checking accounts, and certain other checkable deposits in banks and savings institutions. In the official U.S. statistics, this narrowly defined concept of money is called **M1.** The left-hand side of Figure 12-2 shows the composition of M1 as of February 1997.

But there are other types of accounts that allow withdrawals by check and which therefore are candidates for inclusion in the money supply. Most notably, *money market deposit accounts* allow only a few checks per month but pay market-determined interest rates. Consumers have found these accounts extremely

[2]This includes travelers' checks and NOW (negotiable order of withdrawal) accounts.

FIGURE 12-2 TWO DEFINITIONS OF THE MONEY SUPPLY (FEBRUARY 1997)

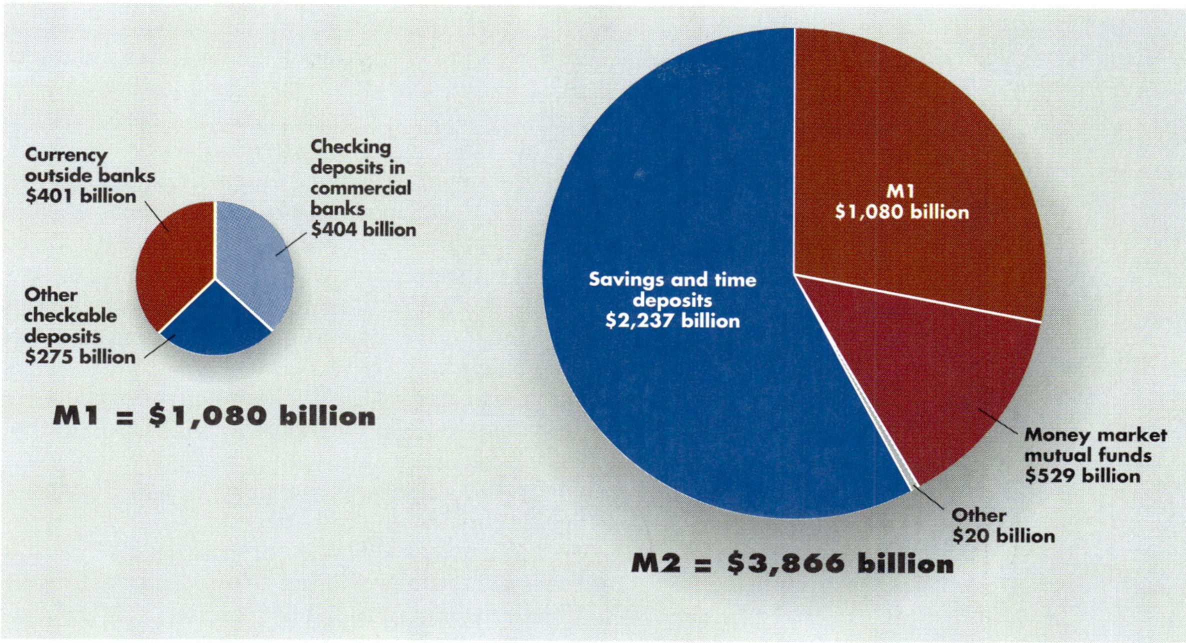

SOURCE: Federal Reserve.

attractive vehicles for short-term investment, and balances in them now exceed all the checkable deposits included in M1.

In addition, many mutual fund organizations and brokerage houses offer *money market mutual funds.* These funds sell shares and use the proceeds to purchase a variety of short-term securities. But the important point, for our purposes, is that owners of shares in money market mutual funds can make withdrawals by writing a check. So depositors can—and sometimes do—use their holdings of fund shares just like checking accounts.

Finally, although you cannot write a check on a *savings account,* most economists feel that modern banking procedures have blurred the distinction between checking balances and savings balances. For example, most banks these days offer convenient electronic transfers of funds from one account to another, either by telephone or by pushing a button on an automated teller. Consequently, savings balances can become checkable almost instantly. For this reason, savings accounts are included—along with money market deposit accounts, money market mutual fund shares, and a few other small items—in the broader definition of the money supply known as **M2.**

The broadly defined money supply, usually abbreviated **M2,** is the sum of all coins and paper money in circulation, plus all types of checking account balances, plus most forms of savings account balances, plus shares in money market mutual funds, and a few other minor items.

The composition of M2 as of February 1997 is shown on the right-hand side of Figure 12-2. You can see that savings deposits predominate, dwarfing everything that is included in M1. Figure 12-2 illustrates two points that are worth remembering. First, our money supply comes not only from banks, but also from savings institutions, brokerage houses, and mutual fund organizations. Second, however, banks still play a predominant role.

Some economists do not want to stop counting at M2; they prefer still broader definitions of money (M3, and so on) which include more types of bank deposits and other closely related assets. The inescapable problem, however, is that there is no obvious place to stop, no clear line of demarcation between those assets that *are* money and those that are merely *close substitutes* for money—so-called **near moneys.**

NEAR MONEYS are liquid assets that are close substitutes for money.

An asset's **LIQUIDITY** refers to the ease with which it can be converted into cash.

If we define an asset's **liquidity** as the ease with which it can be converted into cash, there is a range of assets of varying degrees of liquidity. Everything in M1 is completely "liquid," the money market fund shares and passbook savings accounts included in M2 are a bit less so, and so on, until we encounter such things as short-term government bonds, which, while still quite liquid, would not normally be included in the money supply. Any number of different *Ms* can be defined—and have been—by drawing the line in different places.

And there are still more complexities. For example, credit cards clearly serve as a medium of exchange. So should they be included in the money supply? Yes, you say. But how much money does your credit card represent? Is it the amount you currently owe on the card, which may well be zero? Or is it your entire line of credit, even though you may never use it all? Neither seems a sensible choice, which is one reason why economists have so far ignored credit cards in the definition of money. And soon Americans may start using electronic money instead of cash. Money will be transferred via computer hookups or by so-called *smart cards* with memory chips. (See the box on the next page.)

There are further definitional issues that we have not mentioned. But an introductory course in economics is not the place to get bogged down in complex definitional issues. So we will simply adhere to the convention that *"money" consists only of coins, paper money, and checkable deposits.*

Now that we have defined money and seen how it can be measured, we turn our attention to the principal creators of money—the banks.

HOW BANKING BEGAN

When Adam and Eve left the Garden of Eden, they did not encounter a branch of Citibank. Banking had to be invented, and some time passed before it came to be practiced as it is today. With a little imagination, we can see how the first banks must have begun.

When money was made of gold, it was most inconvenient for consumers and merchants to carry it around and weigh and assay it for purity every time a transaction was made. So the practice developed of leaving one's gold in the safe storage facilities of a goldsmith and carrying in its place a receipt stating that John Doe did indeed own 5 ounces of gold. When people began trading goods and services for the goldsmiths' receipts, rather than for the gold itself, the receipts became an early form of paper money.

At this stage, paper money was fully backed by gold. But gradually the goldsmiths began to notice that the amount of gold they were actually required to pay out in a day was but a small fraction of the total gold they had stored in their warehouses. Then one day some enterprising goldsmith hit upon a momentous idea that must have made him fabulously wealthy.

His thinking probably ran something like this. "I have 2,000 ounces of gold stored away in my vault, for which I collect storage fees from my customers. But I am never called upon to pay out more than 100 ounces on a single day. What harm could it do if I lent out, say, half the gold I now have? I'll still have more than enough to pay off any depositors that come in for a withdrawal, so no one will ever know the difference. And I could earn 30 additional ounces of gold each year in interest on the loans I make (at 3 percent interest on 1,000 ounces).

IS THERE A SMART CARD IN YOUR FUTURE?

In the mid-1990s, several banks and other companies began test marketing new forms of high-tech electronic currency or "e-cash." One proposed form uses encrypted electronic messages to send balances from one computer to another, possibly bypassing banks entirely.

But the most commonly discussed form of e-cash, at least so far, is the so-called *stored-value card.* It works as follows. Soon you may be able to buy a "smart card" (which looks much like a credit card) with an embedded memory chip on which your initial payment is recorded. At this point, your conventional money is transformed into electronic currency. Thereafter, you can use the cash stored on the card to make purchases simply by inserting your card into specially designed slots in vending machines and stores. When the stored value on your card gets depleted, you can replenish it at an ATM.

Electronic currency raises several novel issues. For one thing, the federal government has long held a monopoly over currency issue; e-cash may erode that monopoly. For another, consumers and businesses may have privacy and safety concerns: Will their electronic transactions be safe from system errors and computer snoopers and hackers? Law enforcement agencies are also worried that large, untraceable electronic transfers of funds may be a draw to criminals and tax evaders.

While futurists confidently predict that these new products represent the money of the future, skeptics note that we have heard such claims before—and they have never come true. Only time will tell if the new technologies will catch on.

With this profit, I could lower my service charges to depositors and so attract still more deposits. I think I'll do it."

FRACTIONAL RESERVE BANKING is a system under which bankers keep as reserves only a fraction of the funds they hold on deposit.

With this resolution, the modern system of **fractional reserve banking** was born. This system has three features that are crucially important to this chapter.

1. *Bank profitability.* By getting deposits at zero interest and lending some of them out at positive interest rates, goldsmiths made a profit. The history of banking as a profit-making industry was begun and has continued to this date. *Banks, like other enterprises, are in business to earn profits.*

2. *Bank discretion over the money supply.* When goldsmiths decided to keep only fractions of their total deposits on reserve and lend out the balance, they acquired the ability to *create money.* As long as they kept 100 percent reserves, each gold certificate represented exactly 1 ounce of gold. So whether people decided to carry their gold or leave it with their goldsmith did not affect the money supply, which was set by the volume of gold.

   With the advent of fractional reserve banking, however, new paper certificates were added whenever goldsmiths lent out some of the gold they held on deposit. The loans, in effect, created new money. In this way, the total amount of money came to depend on the amount of gold that each goldsmith felt compelled to keep in his vault. For any given volume of gold on deposit, the lower the reserves the goldsmiths kept, the more loans they could make, and therefore the more money there would be. While we no longer use gold to back our money, this principle remains true today. *Bankers' business decisions influence the supply of money.*

3. *Exposure to runs.* A goldsmith who kept 100 percent reserves never had to worry about a run on his vault. Even if all his depositors showed up at the door at once, he could always convert their paper receipts back into gold. But as soon as the first goldsmith decided to get by with only fractional reserves, the possibility of a run on the vault became a real concern. If that first goldsmith who lent out half his gold had found 51 percent of his customers at his door one unlucky day, he would have had a lot of explaining

to do. Similar problems have worried bankers for centuries. *The danger of runs on the bank has induced bankers to keep prudent reserves and to lend out money carefully.*

PRINCIPLES OF BANK MANAGEMENT: PROFITS VERSUS SAFETY

Bankers have a reputation for conservatism in politics, dress, and business affairs. From what has been said so far, the economic rationale for this conservatism should be clear. Checking deposits are pure fiat money. Years ago, these deposits were "backed" by nothing more than the bank's promise to convert them into currency on demand. If people lost trust in a bank, the bank was doomed.

Thus, it has always been imperative for bankers to acquire a reputation for prudence. This they did in two principal ways. First, they had to maintain a sufficiently generous level of reserves to minimize their vulnerability to runs. Second, they had to be somewhat cautious in making loans and investments, since any large losses on their loans would undermine the confidence of depositors.

It is important to realize that banking under a system of fractional reserves is an inherently risky business that is rendered safe only by cautious and prudent management. America's continuing history of bank failures bears sober testimony to the fact that many bankers have been neither cautious nor prudent. Why? Because this is not a recipe for high profits. Bank profits are maximized by keeping reserves as low as possible, by making at least some risky investments, and by granting loans to borrowers of questionable credit standing who will pay high interest rates.

The art of bank management is to strike the appropriate balance between the lure of profits and the need for safety. If a banker errs by being too stodgy, his bank will earn inadequate profits. If he errs by taking unwarranted risks, his bank may not survive at all. Many banks have perished in the latter way in recent years, especially in the savings and loan industry. (See the box on the next page.)

BANK REGULATION

Governments in virtually every society have decided that the balance between profits and safety likely to be preferred by profit-minded bankers may not be where society wants it struck. So they have thrown up a web of regulations designed to insure the safety of depositors and to control the supply of money.

DEPOSIT INSURANCE is a system that guarantees that depositors will not lose money even if their bank goes bankrupt.

The principal innovation guaranteeing the safety of bank deposits is **deposit insurance.** Today most bank deposits are insured against loss by the *Federal Deposit Insurance Corporation (FDIC)*—an agency of the U.S. government. If your bank belongs to the FDIC (and almost all do), your account is insured for up to \$100,000 regardless of what happens to the bank. Thus, while bank failures may spell disaster for the bank's stockholders, they do not give many depositors cause for concern. Deposit insurance eliminates the motive for customers to rush to their bank just because they hear some bad news about the bank's finances. Many observers give this innovation much of the credit for the pronounced decline in bank failures after 1933, the year the FDIC was established. (Refer back to Figure 12-1 on page 251.)

In addition to insuring depositors against loss, the government takes steps to see that banks do not get into financial trouble. For one thing, various regulatory authorities conduct periodic *bank examinations* in order to keep tabs on the

THE SAVINGS AND LOAN CRISIS: OVER AT LAST

At last, it's over! The Resolution Trust Corporation (RTC), the agency Congress created to clean up the debris left by the collapse of America's savings and loan industry, closed its doors at the end of 1995, having merged or sold off the assets of approximately 750 thrift institutions. The final bill to the American taxpayer has been estimated at about $150 billion.

How did this mess happen? Like many debacles, it took both bad luck and bad policy. The bad luck started in the 1970s and early 1980s, when interest rates skyrocketed. S&Ls found themselves stuck with old mortgages carrying low interest rates while paying high current interest rates to depositors—a losing proposition.

The bad policy came in two waves. First came the financial deregulation of the 1980s, which eased supervision just as thrifts were allowed to expand their lending beyond their traditional domain of home mortgages. The result was ill-advised investments, imprudent risk-taking, and an outrageous amount of fraud. With their institutions teetering on the brink, many S&L executives decided to "bet the bank" on risky ventures that, they hoped, would pay off. After all, if the investments went sour, depositors would be protected by deposit insurance.

Then came the second mistake: procrastination in Washington. The broad outlines of the S&L problem were apparent by the mid-1980s, but Congress and the Reagan administration temporized rather than face up to the costs of closing the moribund thrifts. Politicians feared (correctly!) that taxpayers would be angry when they received the huge bill for deposit insurance. Only in 1989, when the problem had reached crisis dimensions, did President Bush persuade Congress to bite the bullet and create the RTC to finish the job.

The lesson of the thrift debacle was a painful one, not likely to be forgotten soon. It led, among other things, to tighter regulations, stiffer penalties for fraud, and higher premiums for deposit insurance (which were just reduced in 1995)—all designed to make sure it never happens again.

financial conditions and business practices of the banks under their purview. Bank supervision was tightened in 1992 by legislation which permits the authorities to intervene early in the affairs of financially troubled banks. There are also laws and regulations that *limit the kinds and quantities of assets in which banks may invest.* For example, banks are permitted to own only limited amounts of common stock. Both of these forms of regulation are clearly aimed at maintaining bank safety.

A final type of regulation also has some bearing on safety but is motivated primarily by the government's desire to control the money supply. We have seen that the amount of money any bank will issue depends on the amount of reserves it elects to keep. For this reason, most banks are subject by law to minimum **required reserves.** While banks may (and sometimes do) keep reserves in excess of these legal minimums, they may not keep less. It is this regulation that places an upper limit on the money supply. The rest of this chapter is concerned with the details of this mechanism.

REQUIRED RESERVES are the minimum amount of reserves (in cash or the equivalent) required by law. Normally, required reserves are proportional to the volume of deposits.

HOW BANKERS KEEP BOOKS

Before we can fully understand the mechanics of modern banking and the process by which money is "created," we must acquire at least a nodding

POLICY DEBATE ABOLISH THE COMMUNITY REINVESTMENT ACT?

Not all bank regulation is aimed at the safety of depositors. Some regulation is designed to protect borrowers from discriminatory practices by banks. One particularly controversial law is the Community Reinvestment Act (CRA), which was designed to combat "redlining"—the practice of delineating certain geographical areas, often minority neighborhoods, in which banks did not lend.

Bankers complain that CRA regulations bury them in paperwork and force them to make unprofitable loans. Such lending amounts to government-enforced allocation of credit, critics contend. Community advocacy groups counter that access to credit, which is inadequate in low-income and moderate-income areas, is crucial for economic success. A strong CRA keeps the pressure on banks to do better, they argue.

Because the statute is terse and somewhat vague, much depends on how bank regulators interpret it. So in 1993 President Clinton ordered the regulatory agencies to rewrite the CRA rules in ways that would focus more on *results* and less on *paperwork*. The lengthy and contentious rule-making process took more than 2 years. Then, after the 1994 elections, Republicans in Congress introduced several legislative proposals that would essentially repeal the CRA, thereby relieving banks of the regulatory burden and letting the market work. President Clinton threatened to veto any such legislation, and the idea died in Congress in 1995.

But the controversy continues. Should the government pursue what some people consider an affirmative action policy for bank lending? Or should such matters be left to the market? What do you think?

acquaintance with the way bankers keep their books. The first thing to know is how to distinguish assets from liabilities.

An **ASSET** of an individual or business firm is an item of value that the individual or firm owns.

A **LIABILITY** of an individual or business firm is an item of value that the individual or firm owes. Many liabilities are known as *debts*.

An **asset** of a bank is something of value that the bank *owns*. This "thing" may be a physical object, such as the bank building or a computer, or it may be just a piece of paper, such as an IOU of a customer to whom the bank has made a loan. A **liability** of a bank is something of value that the bank *owes*. Most bank liabilities take the form of bookkeeping entries. For example, if you have an account in the Main Street Bank, your bank balance is a liability of the bank. (It is, of course, an asset to you.)

There is an easy test to see whether some piece of paper or bookkeeping entry is a bank's *asset* or *liability*. Ask yourself whether, if this paper were converted into cash, the bank would receive the cash (if so, it is an asset) or pay it out (if so, it is a liability). This test makes it clear that loans to customers are bank assets (when loans are repaid, the bank collects), while customers' deposits are bank liabilities (when deposits are cashed in, the bank must pay). Of course, things are just the opposite to the bank's customers: The loans are liabilities and the deposits are assets.

A **BALANCE SHEET** is an accounting statement listing the values of all the assets on the left-hand side and the values of all the liabilities *and net worth* on the right-hand side.

When accountants draw up a complete list of all the bank's assets and liabilities, the resulting document is called the bank's **balance sheet.** Typically, the value of all the bank's assets exceeds the value of all its liabilities. (On the rare occasions when this is not so, the bank is in serious trouble.) In what sense, then, do balance sheets "balance"?

NET WORTH is the value of all assets minus the value of all liabilities.

They balance because accountants have invented the concept of **net worth** to balance the books. Specifically, they define the net worth of a bank to be the difference between the value of all its assets and the value of all its liabilities. Thus, by definition, when accountants add net worth to liabilities, the sum they get must be the same as the value of the bank's assets. In short:

$$\text{Assets} = \text{Liabilities} + \text{Net Worth}$$

Table 12-1 illustrates this with the balance sheet of a fictitious bank, Bank-a-mythica, whose finances are extremely simple. On December 31, 1996, it had only

TABLE 12-1 BALANCE SHEET OF BANK-A-MYTHICA, DECEMBER 31, 1996

Assets		Liabilities and Net Worth	
Assets		**Liabilities**	
Reserves	$1,000,000	Checking deposits	$5,000,000
Loans outstanding	4,500,000		
Total	$5,500,000	**Net Worth**	
		Stockholders' equity	500,000
Addendum: Bank Reserves			
Actual reserves	$1,000,000	Total	$5,500,000
Required reserves	1,000,000		
Excess reserves	0		

two kinds of assets (listed on the left-hand side of the balance sheet)—$1.0 million in cash, which it held as reserves, and $4.5 million in outstanding loans to its customers, that is, in customers' IOUs. And it had only one type of liability (listed on the right-hand side)—$5.0 million in checking deposits. The difference between total assets ($5.5 million) and total liabilities ($5.0 million) was the bank's net worth ($500,000), shown on the right-hand side of the balance sheet.

THE LIMITS TO MONEY CREATION BY A SINGLE BANK

Let us now turn to the process of deposit creation. Many bankers will deny that they have any ability to "create" money. The phrase itself has a suspiciously hocus-pocus sound to it. But they are not quite right. For although any individual bank's ability to create money is severely limited, the banking system as a whole can achieve much more than the sum of its parts. Through the modern alchemy of *deposit creation*, it can turn one dollar into many dollars. But to understand this important process, we had better proceed in steps, beginning with the case of a single bank, our hypothetical Bank-a-mythica.

According to the balance sheet in Table 12-1, Bank-a-mythica is holding cash reserves of $1 million, equal to 20 percent of its $5 million in deposits. Assume that this is the minimum reserve ratio prescribed by law and that the bank strives to keep its reserves down to the legal minimum; that is, it strives to keep its **excess reserves** down to zero.

EXCESS RESERVES are any reserves held in excess of the legal minimum.

Now let us suppose that on January 2, 1997, an eccentric widower comes into Bank-a-mythica and deposits $100,000 in cash in his checking account. The bank now has $100,000 more in cash reserves, and $100,000 more in checking deposits. But since deposits are up by $100,000, *required* reserves are up by only $20,000, leaving $80,000 in *excess* reserves. Table 12-2 illustrates the effects of this transaction on Bank-a-mythica's balance sheet. Tables such as this, which show *changes* in balance sheets rather than the balance sheets themselves, will help us follow the money-creation process.[3]

[3]Notice that in all such tables, which are called *T accounts*, the two sides of the ledger must balance. This is because changes in assets and changes in liabilities must be equal if the balance sheet is to balance both before and after the transaction.

TABLE 12-2 CHANGES IN BANK-A-MYTHICA'S BALANCE SHEET, JANUARY 2, 1997

Assets		Liabilities	
Reserves	+$100,000	Checking deposits	+$100,000
Addendum: Changes in Reserves			
Actual reserves	+$100,000		
Required reserves	+ $20,000		
Excess reserves	+ $80,000		

Bank-a-mythica receives a $100,000 cash deposit. It now holds excess reserves of $80,000, since required reserves rise by only $20,000 (20 percent of $100,000).

Bank-a-mythica is unlikely to be happy with the situation illustrated in Table 12-2, for it is holding $80,000 in excess reserves on which it earns no interest. So as soon as possible it will lend out the extra $80,000—let us say to Hard-Pressed Construction Company. This loan leads to the balance sheet changes shown in Table 12-3: Bank-a-mythica's loans rise by $80,000 while its holdings of cash reserves fall by $80,000.

By combining Tables 12-2 and 12-3, we arrive at Table 12-4, which summarizes all the bank's transactions for the week. Reserves are up $20,000, loans are up $80,000, and, now that the bank has had a chance to adjust to the inflow of deposits, it no longer holds excess reserves.

Looking at Table 12-4 and keeping in mind our specific definition of money, it appears at first that the chairman of Bank-a-mythica is right when he claims not to have engaged in the nefarious practice of "money creation." All that happened was that, in exchange for the $100,000 in cash it received, the bank issued the widower a checking balance of $100,000. This does not change M1; it merely converts one form of money into another.

But wait. What happened to the $100,000 in cash that the eccentric man brought to the bank? The table shows that $20,000 was retained by Bank-a-mythica in its vault. Since this currency is no longer in circulation, it no longer counts in the official money supply. (Notice that Figure 12-2 included only "currency

TABLE 12-3 CHANGES IN BANK-A-MYTHICA'S BALANCE SHEET, JANUARY 3–6, 1997

Assets		Liabilities
Loans outstanding	+$80,000	No change
Reserves	−$80,000	
Addendum: Changes in Reserves		
Actual reserves	−$80,000	
Required reserves	No change	
Excess reserves	−$80,000	

Bank-a-mythica gets rid of its excess reserves by making a loan of $80,000 to Hard-Pressed Construction Company.

TABLE 12-4 CHANGES IN BANK-A-MYTHICA'S BALANCE SHEET, JANUARY 2–6, 1997

Assets		Liabilities	
Reserves	+$20,000	Checking deposits	+$100,000
Loans outstanding	+$80,000		
Addendum: Changes in Reserves			
Actual reserves	+$20,000		
Required reserves	+$20,000		
Excess reserves	No change		

When it receives $100,000 in cash deposits, Bank-a-mythica keeps only the required $20,000 in reserves and lends out the remaining $80,000 to Hard-Pressed Construction Company. Its excess reserves return to zero.

outside banks.") But the other $80,000, which the bank lent out, is still in circulation. It is held by Hard-Pressed Construction, which probably will redeposit it in some other bank. But even before this happens, the original $100,000 in cash has supported a rise in the money supply: there is now $100,000 in checking deposits and $80,000 in cash in circulation, making a total of $180,000. The money creation process has begun.

MULTIPLE MONEY CREATION BY A SERIES OF BANKS

Let us now trace the $80,000 in cash and see how the process of money creation gathers momentum. Suppose that Hard-Pressed Construction Company, which banks across town at the First National Bank, deposits the $80,000 into its bank account. First National's reserves increase by $80,000. But because deposits are up by $80,000, *required* reserves rise by only 20 percent of this amount or $16,000. If the management of First National Bank behaves like that of Bank-a-mythica, the $64,000 of excess reserves will be lent out.

Table 12-5 shows the effects of these events on First National Bank's balance sheet. (The preliminary steps corresponding to Tables 12-2 and 12-3 are not

TABLE 12-5 CHANGES IN FIRST NATIONAL BANK'S BALANCE SHEET

Assets		Liabilities	
Reserves	+$16,000	Checking deposits	+$80,000
Loans outstanding	+$64,000		
Addendum: Changes in Reserves			
Actual reserves	+$16,000		
Required reserves	+$16,000		
Excess reserves	No change		

Hard-Pressed deposits its $80,000 in First National Bank, which sets aside the required $16,000 in reserves (20 percent of $80,000) and lends $64,000 to Al's Auto Shop.

shown separately.) At this stage in the chain, the original $100,000 in cash has led to $180,000 in deposits—$100,000 at Bank-a-mythica and $80,000 at First National Bank—and $64,000 in cash, which is still in circulation (in the hands of the recipient of First National's loan—Al's Auto Shop). Thus, from the original $100,000, a total of $244,000 has been added to the money supply ($180,000 in checking deposits plus $64,000 in cash).

But, to coin a phrase, the bucks do not stop here. Al's Auto Shop will presumably deposit the proceeds from its loan into its own account at Second National Bank, leading eventually to the balance sheet adjustments shown in Table 12-6 when Second National makes an additional loan rather than hold on to excess reserves. You can see how the money creation process continues.

Figure 12-3 is a graphical summary of the balance sheet changes of the first five banks in the chain (from Bank-a-mythica through the Fourth National Bank), on the assumptions that each bank holds exactly the 20 percent required reserves and that each loan recipient redeposits the proceeds in the next bank. But the chain does not end there. The Main Street Movie Theatre, which received a $32,768 loan from the Fourth National Bank, then deposits these funds into the Fifth National Bank. Fifth National has to keep only 20 percent of this deposit, or $6,553.60, on reserve and will lend out the balance. And so the chain continues.

Where does it all end? The running sums in Figure 12-3 show what eventually happens to the entire banking system. The initial deposit of $100,000 in cash is ultimately absorbed in bank reserves (Column 1), leading to a total of $500,000 in new deposits (Column 2) and $400,000 in new loans (Column 3). The money supply rises by $400,000 because the nonbank public eventually holds $100,000 *less* in currency and $500,000 *more* in checking deposits.

So there really is some hocus-pocus. Somehow, an initial deposit of $100,000 leads to $500,000 in new bank deposits—a multiple expansion of $5 for every original dollar—and a net increase of $400,000 in the money supply. We had better understand why this is so. But first let us verify that the calculations in Figure 12-3 are correct.

If you look carefully at the numbers, you will see that each column forms a *geometric progression;* specifically, each entry is equal to exactly 80 percent of the entry before it. Recall that in our discussion of the multiplier in Chapter 9, we learned how to sum an infinite geometric progression, which is just what each of these chains eventually will be. In particular, if the common ratio is R, the sum of an infinite geometric progression is:

TABLE 12-6 CHANGES IN SECOND NATIONAL BANK'S BALANCE SHEET

Assets		Liabilities	
Reserves	+$12,800	Checking deposits	+$64,000
Loans outstanding	+$51,200		
Addendum: Changes in Reserves			
Actual reserves	+$12,800		
Required reserves	+$12,800		
Excess reserves	No change		

When Al deposits his $64,000 in Second National Bank, that bank retains $12,800 as required reserves (20 percent of $64,000) and lends out the remaining $51,200.

FIGURE 12-3

THE CHAIN OF MULTIPLE DEPOSIT CREATION

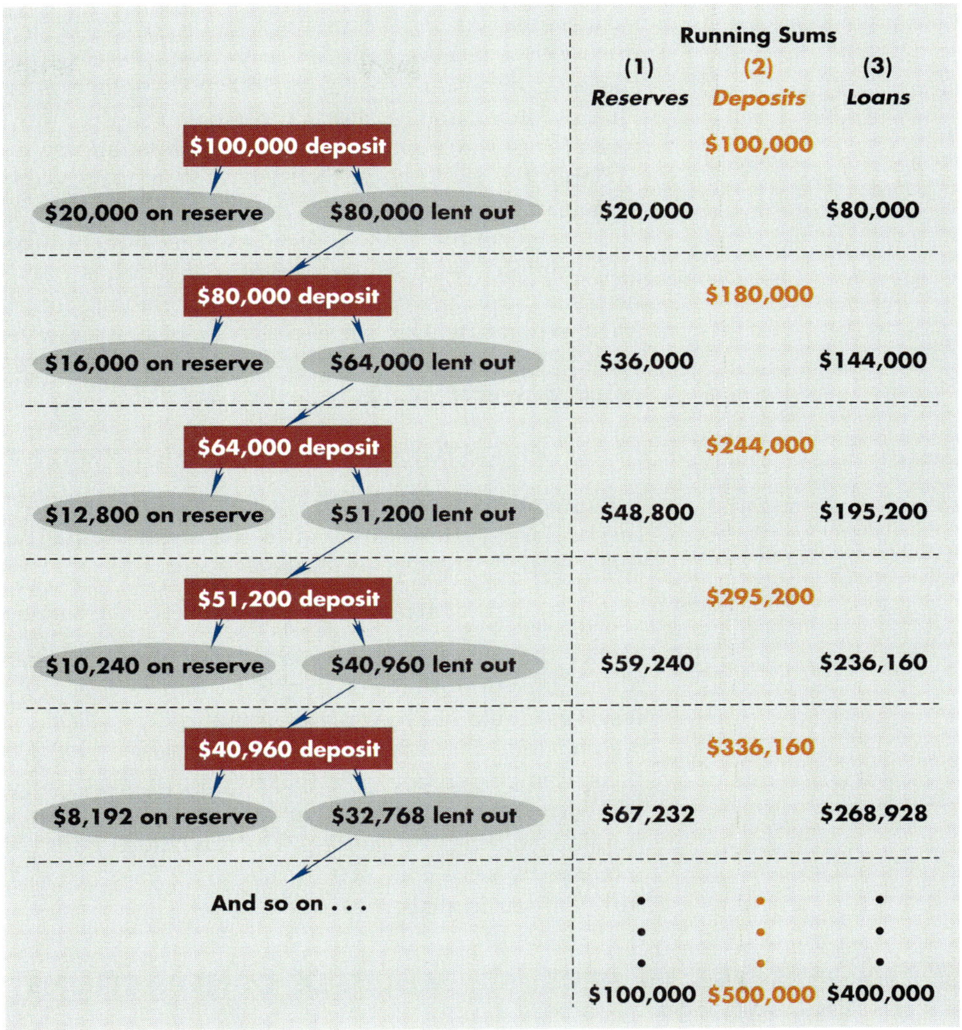

This diagram indicates how the deposit creation process spreads through the banking system. Each bank that receives a deposit keeps 20 percent of the deposit as reserves and lends out the other 80 percent—which becomes a deposit to the next bank in the chain. And so the chain continues. The numbers on the right-hand side of the diagram indicate the running sums of reserves, deposits, and loans caused by the initial $100,000 deposit.

SOURCE: This schematic diagram was suggested to us by Dr. Ivan K. Cohen, whom we thank.

$$1 + R + R^2 + R^3 + \ldots = \frac{1}{1 - R}$$

By applying this formula to the chain of checking deposits in Figure 12-3, we get:

$$\begin{aligned}
&\$100{,}000 + \$80{,}000 + \$64{,}000 + \$51{,}200 + \ldots \\
&= \$100{,}000 \times (1 + 0.80 + 0.64 + 0.512 + \ldots) \\
&= \$100{,}000 \times (1 + 0.80 + 0.80^2 + 0.80^3 + \ldots) \\
&= \$100{,}000 \times \frac{1}{1 - 0.80} = \frac{\$100{,}000}{0.20} = \$500{,}000
\end{aligned}$$

Proceeding similarly, we can verify that the new loans sum to $400,000 and that the new required reserves sum to $100,000. (Check these as exercises.) So the numbers in Figure 12-3 are correct. Let us, therefore, think through the logic behind them.

The chain of deposit creation can end only when there are no more *excess* reserves to be loaned out; that is, when the entire \$100,000 in cash is tied up in *required* reserves. That explains why the last entry in Column 1 must be \$100,000. But, with a reserve ratio of 20 percent, excess reserves disappear only when checking deposits expand by \$500,000—which is the last entry in Column 2. Finally, since balance sheets must balance, the sum of all newly created assets (reserves plus loans) must equal the sum of all newly created liabilities (\$500,000 in deposits). That leaves \$400,000 for new loans—which is the last entry in Column 3.

More generally, if the reserve ratio is some number m (rather than the 1/5 in our example), each dollar of deposits requires only a fraction m of a dollar in reserves. So R, the common ratio in the above formula, is $1 - m$, and deposits must expand by $1/m$ for each dollar of new reserves that are injected into the system. This suggests the general formula for multiple deposit creation when the required reserve ratio is some number m.

OVERSIMPLIFIED DEPOSIT MULTIPLIER FORMULA

If the required reserve ratio is some fraction, m, each \$1 of reserves injected into the banking system can lead to the creation of \$$1/m$ in new deposits. That is, the so-called "deposit multiplier" is given by:

$$\text{Change in deposits} = (\tfrac{1}{m}) \times \text{Change in reserves}$$

Notice that this formula correctly describes what happens in our example. The initial deposit of \$100,000 in cash at Bank-a-mythica constitutes \$100,000 in new reserves (Table 12-2). Applying a multiplier of $1/m = 1/0.20 = 5$ to this \$100,000, we conclude that bank deposits will rise by \$500,000—which is just what happens. Remember, however, that the expansion process started when some eccentric widower took \$100,000 in cash and deposited it in his bank account. So the public's holdings of *money*—which includes both checking deposits *and cash*—increase by only \$400,000 in this case: There is \$500,000 *more* in deposits, but \$100,000 *less* in cash.

THE PROCESS IN REVERSE: MULTIPLE CONTRACTIONS OF THE MONEY SUPPLY

Let us now briefly consider how this deposit creation mechanism operates in reverse—as a system of deposit *destruction*. In particular, suppose that our eccentric widower came back to Bank-a-mythica to withdraw \$100,000 from his checking account and return it to his mattress, where it rightfully belongs. Bank-a-mythica's *required* reserves would fall by \$20,000 as a result of this transaction (20 percent of \$100,000), but its *actual* reserves would fall by \$100,000. The bank would be \$80,000 short, as indicated in Table 12-7(a).

How does it react to this discrepancy? As some of its outstanding loans are routinely paid off, the bank will cease granting new ones until it has accumulated the necessary \$80,000 in required reserves. The data for Bank-a-mythica's contraction are shown in Table 12-7(b), assuming that borrowers pay off their loans in cash.[4]

[4]In reality, they would probably pay with checks drawn on other banks. Bank-a-mythica would then cash these checks to acquire the reserves.

TABLE 12-7 CHANGES IN THE BALANCE SHEET OF BANK-A-MYTHICA

(a)

Assets		Liabilities	
Reserves	−$100,000	Checking deposits	−$100,000
Addendum: Changes in Reserves			
Actual reserves	−$100,000		
Required reserves	−$20,000		
Excess reserves	−$80,000		

(b)

Assets		Liabilities
Reserves	+$80,000	No change
Loans outstanding	−$80,000	
Addendum: Changes in Reserves		
Actual reserves	+$80,000	
Required reserves	No change	
Excess reserves	+$80,000	

When Bank-a-mythica loses a $100,000 deposit, it must reduce its loans by $80,000 to replenish its reserves.

But where did the borrowers get this money? Probably by making withdrawals from other banks. In this case, let us assume it all came from First National Bank, which loses an $80,000 deposit and $80,000 in reserves. It finds itself short some $64,000 in reserves [see Table 12-8(a)] and therefore must reduce its loan commitments by $64,000 [see Table 12-8(b)]. This, of course, causes some other bank to suffer a loss of reserves and deposits of $64,000, and the whole process repeats just as it did in the case of deposit expansion.

After the entire banking system had become involved, the picture would be just as shown in Figure 12-3, except that all the numbers would have *minus* signs in front of them. Deposits would shrink by $500,000, loans would fall by $400,000, bank reserves would be reduced by $100,000, and the money supply would fall by $400,000. As suggested by our deposit multiplier formula with $m = 0.20$, the decline in the bank deposits is $1/0.20 = 5$ times as large as the decline in excess reserves.

TABLE 12-8 CHANGES IN THE BALANCE SHEET OF THE FIRST NATIONAL BANK

(a)

Assets		Liabilities	
Reserves	−$80,000	Checking deposits	−$80,000
Addendum: Changes in Reserves			
Actual reserves	−$80,000		
Required reserves	−$16,000		
Excess reserves	−$64,000		

(b)

Assets		Liabilities
Reserves	+$64,000	No change
Loans outstanding	−$64,000	
Addendum: Changes in Reserves		
Actual reserves	+$64,000	
Required reserves	No change	
Excess reserves	+$64,000	

First National Bank's loss of the $80,000 deposit forces it to cut back its loans by $64,000.

One of the authors of this book was a student in Cambridge, Massachusetts, during the height of the radical student movement of the late 1960s. One day a circular appeared urging citizens to withdraw all funds from their checking accounts on a prescribed date, hold them in cash for a week, and then redeposit them. This act, the circular argued, would surely wreak havoc upon the capitalist system. Obviously, some of these radicals were well-schooled in modern money mechanics, for the argument was basically correct. The tremendous multiple contraction of the banking system and consequent multiple expansion that a successful campaign of this sort could have caused might have seriously disrupted the local financial system. But history records that the appeal met with little success. Checking-account withdrawals are not the stuff of which revolutions are made.

WHY THE DEPOSIT CREATION FORMULA IS OVERSIMPLIFIED

So far, our discussion of the process of money creation has made it all seem rather mechanical. If all proceeds according to formula, each $1 in new excess reserves will lead to a $1/*m* increase in new deposits. But in reality things are not this simple. Just as in the case of the expenditure multiplier, the oversimplified formula for deposit creation is accurate only under very particular circumstances. These circumstances require that:

1. Every recipient of cash must redeposit the cash into another bank rather than hold it.
2. Every bank must hold reserves no larger than the legal minimum.

The "chain" diagram in Figure 12-3 shows clearly what happens if either of these assumptions is violated.

Suppose first that the business firms and individuals who receive bank loans decide to redeposit only a fraction of the proceeds into their bank accounts. Then, for example, the first $80,000 loan would lead to a deposit of less than $80,000—and similarly down the chain. The whole chain of deposit creation would therefore be reduced. Thus:

If individuals and business firms decide to hold more cash, the multiple expansion of bank deposits will be curtailed because fewer dollars of cash will be available to be used as reserves to support new checking deposits. Consequently, the money supply will be smaller.

The basic idea here is simple. Each $1 of cash held by a bank can support several dollars (specifically, $1/*m*) of money. But $1 of cash held by an individual is exactly $1 of money; it supports no bank deposits. Hence, any time cash leaves the banking system, the money supply will decline. And any time cash enters the banking system, the money supply will rise.

Next, suppose that bank managers become more conservative, or that the outlook for loan repayments worsens because of a recession. Then banks might decide to keep more reserves than the legal requirement and lend out less than the amounts assumed in Figure 12-3. If this happens, banks further down the chain receive smaller deposits and, once again, the chain of deposit creation is curtailed. Thus:

If banks wish to keep excess reserves, the multiple expansion of bank deposits will be restricted. A given amount of cash will support a smaller supply of money than would be the case if banks held no excess reserves.

THE NEED FOR MONETARY POLICY

If we pursue this point a bit further, we will see why government regulation of the money supply is so important for economic stability. We have just suggested that banks will wish to keep excess reserves when they do not foresee profitable and secure opportunities to make loans. This is most likely to happen during the downswing and around the bottom of a business contraction. At such times, the propensity of banks to hold excess reserves can turn the deposit creation process into one of deposit destruction. Thus:

During a recession, profit-oriented banks would be prone to reduce the money supply by increasing their excess reserves—if the government did not intervene. As we will learn in subsequent chapters, the money supply is an important influence on aggregate demand, so such a contraction of the money supply would aggravate the recession.

This is precisely what happened—with a vengeance—during the Great Depression of the 1930s. Although total bank reserves grew, the money supply contracted violently because banks preferred to hold excess reserves rather than make loans that might not be repaid.

On the other hand, banks will want to squeeze the maximum possible money supply out of any given amount of cash reserves by keeping their reserves at the bare minimum when the demand for bank loans is buoyant, profits are high, and secure investment opportunities abound. This reduced incentive to hold excess reserves in prosperous times means that:

During an economic boom, the behavior of profit-oriented banks is likely to make the money supply expand, adding undesirable momentum to the booming economy and paving the way for a burst of inflation. The authorities must intervene to prevent this.

Regulation of the money supply, then, is necessary because profit-oriented bankers might otherwise provide the economy with a gyrating money supply that dances to the tune of the business cycle. Precisely how the authorities keep the money supply under control is the subject of the next chapter.

SUMMARY

1. It is more efficient to exchange goods and services by using **money** as a **medium of exchange** than by **bartering** them directly.
2. In addition to being the medium of exchange, whatever serves as money is likely to become the standard **unit of account** and a popular **store of value.**
3. Throughout history, all sorts of things have served as money. **Commodity money** gave way to full-bodied paper money (certificates backed 100 percent by some commodity, like gold), which in turn gave way to partially backed paper money. Nowadays our paper money has no commodity backing whatsoever; it is pure **fiat money.**
4. One popular definition of the U.S. money supply is **M1,** which includes coins, paper money, and several types of checking deposits. However, many economists prefer the **M2** definition, which adds to M1 other types of checkable accounts and most savings deposits. Much of M2 is held outside of banks.
5. Under our modern system of **fractional reserve banking,** banks keep cash reserves equal to only a fraction of their total deposit liabilities. This is the key to their profitability, since the remaining funds can be loaned out at interest. But it also leaves them potentially vulnerable to **runs.**

6. Because of this vulnerability, bank managers are generally conservative in their investment strategy. They also keep a prudent level of reserves. Even so, the government keeps a watchful eye over banking practices.
7. Before 1933, bank failures were common; but they declined sharply when **deposit insurance** was instituted.
8. Because it holds only fractional reserves, even a single bank can create money. But its ability to do so is severely limited because the funds it lends out probably will be deposited in another bank.
9. As a whole, the banking system can create several dollars of deposits for each dollar of reserves it receives. Under certain assumptions, the ratio of new deposits to new reserves will be $\$1/m$, where m is the required reserve ratio.
10. The same process works in reverse, as a system of money destruction, when cash is withdrawn from the banking system.
11. Because banks and individuals may want to hold more cash when the economy is shaky, the money supply would probably contract under such circumstances if the government did not intervene. Similarly, the money supply would probably expand rapidly in boom times if it were unregulated.

KEY TERMS

Run on a bank
Barter
Money
Medium of exchange
Unit of account
Store of value
Commodity money
Fiat money
M1
M2
Near moneys
Liquidity
Fractional reserve banking
Deposit insurance
Federal Deposit Insurance Corporation (FDIC)
Required reserves
Asset
Liability
Balance sheet
Net worth
Deposit creation
Excess reserves

QUESTIONS FOR REVIEW

1. If ours were a barter economy, how would you pay your tuition bill? What if your college did not want the goods or services you offered in payment?
2. How is "money" defined, both conceptually and in practice? Does the U.S. money supply consist of commodity money, full-bodied paper money, or fiat money?
3. What is fractional reserve banking, and why is it the key to bank profits? (*Hint:* What opportunities to make profits would banks have if reserve requirements were 100 percent?) Why does fractional reserve banking give bankers discretion over how large the money supply will be? Why does it make banks potentially vulnerable to runs?
4. During the 1980s and early 1990s, there was a rash of bank failures. Explain why these failures did not lead to runs on banks.
5. Suppose that no banks keep excess reserves and no individuals or firms hold on to cash. If someone suddenly discovers $12 million in buried treasure, explain what will happen to the money supply if the required reserve ratio is 10 percent.
6. How would your answer to Review Question 5 differ if the reserve ratio were 25 percent? If the reserve ratio were 100 percent?
7. Each year during Christmas shopping season, consumers and stores wish to increase their holdings of cash. Explain how this could lead to a multiple contraction of the money supply. (As a matter of fact, the authorities prevent this contraction from occurring by methods explained in the next chapter.)
8. Excess reserves make a bank less vulnerable to runs. Why, then, don't bankers like to hold excess reserves? What circumstances might persuade them that it would be advisable to hold excess reserves?
9. Use tables such as Tables 12-2 and 12-3 to illustrate what happens to bank balance sheets when each of the following transactions occurs:
   a. You withdraw $50 from your checking account to buy concert tickets.

b. Sam finds a $50 bill on the sidewalk and deposits it into his checking account.
c. Mary Q. Contrary withdraws $1,000 in cash from her account at Hometown Bank, carries it to the city, and deposits it into her account at Big City Bank.

10. For each of the transactions listed in Review Question 9, what will be the ultimate effect on the money supply if the required reserve ratio is 1/8 (12.5 percent)? Assume that the oversimplified deposit multiplier formula applies.

11. If the government takes over a failed bank with liabilities (mostly deposits) of $2.0 billion, pays off the depositors, and sells the assets for $1.5 billion, where does the missing $500 million come from? Why?

CHAPTER 13

MONETARY POLICY AND THE NATIONAL ECONOMY

Victorians heard with grave attention that the Bank Rate had been raised. They did not know what it meant. But they knew that it was an act of extreme wisdom.
J. K. Galbraith

Now that we understand the rudiments of the banking system, we are ready to bring money and interest rates into our model of income determination and the price level. In earlier chapters, we took investment (*I*) to be a fixed number. But this is a poor assumption. Not only is investment highly variable, it also depends on interest rates. And interest rates are, in turn, heavily influenced by *monetary policy*. The main task of this chapter is to explain how monetary policy affects interest rates, and thereby investment and aggregate demand.

We begin by learning about the operations of America's *central bank,* the *Federal Reserve System*. The "Fed," as it is called, is a very special kind of bank. Its customers are banks rather than individuals, and it performs some of the same services for them as your bank performs for you. Although it makes enormous profits, that is not its goal. Instead, the Fed tries to manage the money supply and interest rates in what it perceives to be the national interest. Just how the Fed does its job, and why its performance has fallen short of perfection, are the first subjects of this chapter.

Next, we integrate money and interest rates into our model of the macroeconomy. The mechanisms through which monetary policy affects aggregate demand are spelled out and analyzed in detail, and we learn an additional reason why the aggregate demand curve slopes downward. By the end of the chapter, we will have constructed a complete macroeconomic model, which we will use in the next few chapters to investigate a variety of important policy issues.

MONEY AND INCOME: THE IMPORTANT DIFFERENCE

But first we must get some terminology straight. The words *money* and *income* are used almost interchangeably in common parlance. This is a pitfall we must learn to avoid.

Money is a snapshot concept. It is the answer to questions like: "How much money do you have right now?" or "How much money did you have at 3:32 p.m. on Friday, November 5th?" To answer questions like these, you would add up the cash you are (or were) carrying and whatever checkable balances you have (or had), and answer something like: "I have $126.33," or "On Friday, November 5th, at 3:32 p.m., I had $31.43."

Income, by contrast, is more like a motion picture; it comes to you only over a period of time. If you are asked "What is your income?" you must respond by saying "$200 *per week*," or "$800 *per month*," or "$10,000 *per year*," or something like that. Notice that there is a unit of time attached to each of these responses. If you just say "My income is $452," without indicating whether it is per week or per month or per year, no one will understand what you mean.

That the two concepts are very different is easy to see. A typical American family has an *income* of perhaps $38,000 per year, but its holdings of *money* at any point in time (using the M1 definition) may be under $2,000. Similarly, at the national level, nominal GDP in 1995 was just over $7,200 billion, while the money stock (M1) in the middle of the year was only about $1,150 billion.

While money and income are very different, they are certainly related. This chapter is precisely about that relationship. Specifically, we will look at how the stock of *money* in existence at any moment of time influences the rate at which people will be earning *income,* that is, how money affects the GDP.

THE FEDERAL RESERVE SYSTEM: ORIGINS AND STRUCTURE

A **CENTRAL BANK** is a bank for banks. America's central bank is the *Federal Reserve System.*

When the *Federal Reserve System* was established in 1914, the United States joined the company of most of the other advanced industrial nations. Up until then, the United States, distrustful of centralization of economic power, was almost the only important nation without a **central bank.** Britain's central bank, the Bank of England, for example, dates from 1694.

The impetus for the establishment of a central bank in the United States came not from the power of economic logic but from some painful experiences with economic reality. Four severe banking panics between 1873 and 1907, in which many banks failed, convinced legislators and bankers alike that a central bank that would regulate credit conditions was not a luxury but a necessity. The 1907 crisis led to a study of the shortcomings of the banking system and, eventually, to the establishment of the Federal Reserve System.

Although the basic idea of central banking came from Europe, some changes were made when it was imported, making the Federal Reserve System a uniquely American institution. Owing to the vastness of our country, the extraordinarily large number of commercial banks, and our tradition of dual state-federal regulations, it was decided that the United States should have not one central bank but 12.

Technically, each of the Federal Reserve banks is a corporation; its stockholders are the banks that belong to it. But your bank, if it is a member of the system, does not enjoy the privileges normally accorded to stockholders: it receives only a token share of the Federal Reserve's immense profits (the bulk is turned over to the U.S. Treasury), and it has virtually no say in the decisions of the corporation. The private banks are more like customers of the Fed than like owners.

Who, then, controls the Fed? Most of the power resides in the seven-member Board of Governors of the Federal Reserve System in Washington, and especially in its chairman, who is now Alan Greenspan, an economist. Members of the board are appointed by the president of the United States, with the advice and consent of the Senate, for 14-year terms. The president also designates one of the members to serve a 4-year term as chairman of the board, and thus to be the most powerful central banker in the world, for the Federal Reserve is *independent* of the rest of the government. As long as it stays within the statutory authority delineated by Congress, it alone has responsibility for determining the nation's monetary policy. The power of appointment, however, gives the president considerable long-run influence over Federal Reserve policy.

Closely allied with the Board of Governors is the powerful *Federal Open Market Committee (FOMC),* which meets eight times a year in Washington. For reasons to be explained shortly, the decisions of the FOMC largely determine short-term interest rates and the size of the U.S. money supply. This 12-member committee consists of the seven governors of the Federal Reserve System, the president of the Federal Reserve Bank of New York, and, on a rotating basis, four of the other 11 district bank presidents.[1]

THE INDEPENDENCE OF THE FED

The institutional independence of the Federal Reserve System is looked upon as a source of pride by some and as an antidemocratic embarrassment by others.

Proponents of Federal Reserve independence argue that it enables monetary policy decisions to be made on objective, technical criteria and keeps monetary control out of the "political thicket." Without this independence, they argue, politicians might try to force the Fed to expand the money supply too rapidly, thereby contributing to chronic inflation and undermining faith in America's financial system. They point to international evidence showing that countries with more independent central banks have lower inflation. (See the box on page 277.)

Opponents of this view counter that there is something profoundly undemocratic about letting a group of unelected bankers and economists make decisions that affect the well-being of every American. Monetary policy, they argue, should be formulated by the elected representatives of the people, just like fiscal policy. Those who argue for political control over the Fed can point to historical instances in which monetary and fiscal policy were at loggerheads—with the Fed undermining or even overwhelming the effects of fiscal policy decisions.

There is plenty of middle ground between the two extremes. One far less drastic proposal would shift the term of the Fed chairman to make it start shortly after that of the president of the United States. As things stand today, a newly elected president must retain the chairman that his predecessor appointed, whether or not he agrees with his policies. A second suggestion would let either the president or the Federal Reserve Board appoint the presidents of the 12 district banks. As things stand now, they are chosen by their own boards of directors. A third proposal would take FOMC voting rights away from the bank presidents, who are not presidential appointees.

A much weaker reform would simply require the Fed to announce its ultimate targets for unemployment and inflation and explain how it expects its

---

[1]Alan Blinder was the vice chairman of the Federal Reserve Board and a member of the Federal Open Market Committee when this was written.

YOU ARE THERE — THE FOMC MEETS

Meetings of the Federal Open Market Committee are serious and formal affairs. All 19 members—7 governors and 12 reserve bank presidents—sit around a mammoth table in the Fed's cavernous but austere board room. A limited number of top Fed staffers join them at and around the table, for access to FOMC meetings is strictly controlled.

At precisely 9 a.m.—for punctuality is a high virtue at the Fed—the doors are closed and the chairman calls the meeting to order. No press is allowed and, unlike most important Washington meetings, nothing will leak. Secrecy is another high virtue at the Fed.

After hearing a few routine staff reports, the chairman calls on each of the members in turn to give their views of the current economic situation. Although he knows them all well, he addresses each member formally as "Governor X" or "President Y." District bank presidents offer insights into their local economies, and all members comment on the outlook for the national economy. Disagreements are raised, but voices are not. There are no interruptions while people talk. Strikingly, in this most political of cities, politics is almost never mentioned.

Once he has heard from all the others, the chairman offers his own views of the economic situation. Then he usually recommends a course of action. Members of the committee, in their turn, comment on the chairman's proposal. Most agree, though some note differences of opinion. After hearing all this, the chairman announces what he perceives to be the committee's consensus and asks the secretary to call the roll. Only the 12 voting members answer, saying "yes" or "no." Negative votes are rare, for the FOMC tries to operate by consensus and a dissent is considered a loud objection.

The meeting adjourns, and at about 2:15 p.m. a Fed spokesman announces the decision to the public. Within minutes, financial markets around the world react.

monetary policy actions to promote these goals. In one version of this proposal, the Fed would have to adopt the goals of the administration or Congress. But a more moderate version would simply make the Fed announce its own goals and subject them to public scrutiny.

How people react to these and other reform proposals that would affect the Fed's independence depends partly on how they perceive the office. Are Federal Reserve governors like judges and therefore, at least in principle, best thought of as nonpartisan and independent technocrats? The 14-year term of office certainly suggests an analogy to the judiciary, but the board's role most assuredly involves policy-making, not just interpreting the law. Or are the governors more like members of the cabinet, that is, policy-making officials who should properly serve only at the pleasure of the president? Since neither analogy fits precisely, the issue is a vexing one.

POLICY DEBATE **HOW INDEPENDENT SHOULD THE CENTRAL BANK BE?**

The debate over central bank independence is somewhat "academic" in the United States, since the Fed's independence is widely respected and not under any serious threat. But the issue is a live one in many other countries.

Nations vary a great deal in how much independence they grant their central banks. At one extreme, the German Bundesbank and the Swiss National Bank are often cited as the world's most independent central banks, with the Fed not far behind. But in the United Kingdom, monetary policy is still set by the chancellor of the exchequer (their equivalent of the secretary of the treasury), not by the Bank of England.

In recent years, a number of countries have moved toward greater central bank independence and no major country has moved in the other direction. Why? The main reason seems to be the desire to fight inflation. As the accompanying chart shows, countries with more independent central banks turn in better inflation performance, on average.

Under the terms of the Maastricht Treaty, which commits members of the European Union to move toward a single currency, each country must have an independent central bank. France has already made the switch, but Britain has not. And making such a change in a 300-year-old institution is sure to be controversial.

In Latin America, several formerly high-inflation countries have found that giving their central banks more independence helped them reduce inflation dramatically.

Some of the formerly socialist countries in Europe, finding themselves saddled with high inflation and "unsound" currencies, are either thinking or moving along the same lines. This group includes Russia, where inflation is severe and the issue is a political hot potato. (Russia's parliament rejected a tough-minded central banker several times in 1995 before accepting a second nominee.)

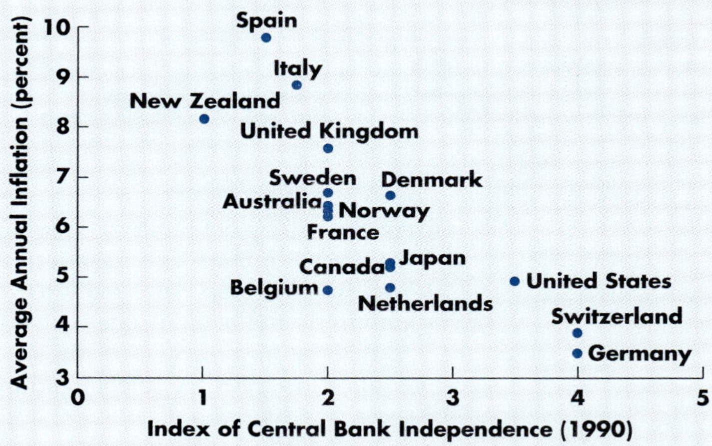

CONTROLLING THE MONEY SUPPLY: OPEN-MARKET OPERATIONS

OPEN-MARKET OPERATIONS refer to the Fed's purchase or sale of government securities through transactions in the open market.

When it wants to change the money supply and interest rates, the Fed normally relies on what are called **open-market operations.** Open-market operations have the effect of giving the banks more reserves or taking reserves away from them, thereby triggering a multiple expansion or contraction of the money supply as described in the last chapter.

How does this work? Suppose the Federal Open Market Committee decides that the money supply is too low. It can issue instructions that the money supply be expanded through operations in the open market. Specifically, this means that the Federal Reserve System *purchases* U.S. government securities (generally short-term securities called *Treasury bills*) from any individual or bank that wishes to sell, thus putting more reserves in the hands of the banks.

An example will illustrate the mechanics. Suppose the order is to purchase \$100 million worth of securities in the open market and that commercial banks are the sellers. *The Fed makes payment by giving the banks \$100 million in new*

TABLE 13-1 EFFECTS OF AN OPEN-MARKET PURCHASE OF SECURITIES ON THE BALANCE SHEETS OF BANKS AND THE FED

Banks			**Federal Reserve System**		
Assets		**Liabilities**	**Assets**		**Liabilities**
Reserves	+ $100 million		U.S. government securities	+ $100 million	Bank reserves + $100 million
U.S. government securities	− $100 million				
		Banks get reserves			
Addendum: Changes in Reserves		Fed gets securities			
Actual reserves	+ $100 million				
Required reserves	No Change				
Excess reserves	+ $100 million				

When the Fed buys $100 million worth of securities from banks, it adds this amount to the bookkeeping entries that represent the banks' accounts at the Fed (called *bank reserves*). Since deposits have not increased at all, required reserves are unchanged by this transaction. But actual reserves are increased by $100 million, so there are $100 million in excess reserves. This will trigger a multiple expansion of the banking system.

reserves. So, if they held only the required amount of reserves initially, the banks now have $100 million in excess reserves, as shown in Table 13-1.

When the Fed buys $100 million worth of securities from the banks, it adds this amount to the bookkeeping entries that represent the banks' accounts at the Fed (called "bank reserves" in the table). Since deposits have not increased at all, required reserves are unchanged by this transaction. But actual reserves are increased by $100 million, so there are $100 million in excess reserves. This will trigger a multiple expansion of the banking system.

Where does the Fed get the money that it gives to the banks in return for the securities? It could pay in cash, but normally does not. Instead, it manufactures the funds out of thin air or, more literally, by punching the keyboard of a computer terminal. Specifically, the Fed pays the banks for the securities by adding the appropriate sums to the accounts that the banks maintain at the Fed. Balances held in these accounts constitute bank reserves, just like cash in bank vaults.

While this process of creating bookkeeping entries at the Federal Reserve is commonly referred to as "printing money," the Fed does not literally run the printing presses. Instead, it simply exchanges its IOUs for an existing asset (a government security). But unlike your IOUs, the Fed's IOUs constitute legal bank reserves, and thus can support a multiple expansion of the money supply in the same way that cash does. The banks, not the Fed, actually increase the money supply; but the Fed's actions give the banks the wherewithal to do it.

Once excess reserves are created, multiple expansion of the banking system proceeds in the usual way. It is not hard for the Fed to estimate the ultimate increase in the money supply that will result from its actions. As we saw in the last chapter, each dollar of excess reserves can support $1/m$ dollars of checking deposits, if m is the required reserve ratio. In our example, $m = 0.20$; so $100 million in new reserves can support $100/0.2 = $500 million in new money.

But *estimating* the ultimate monetary expansion is a far cry from *knowing it* with certainty. As we know from the previous chapter, the simple deposit multiplier formula is predicated on the assumptions that people will want to hold no more cash, and that banks will want to hold no more excess reserves, as the monetary expansion proceeds. In practice, these assumptions are unlikely to be literally true. So, to predict the eventual effect of its action on the money supply correctly, the Fed must estimate both the amount that firms and individuals will want to add to their currency holdings and the amount that banks will want to add to their excess reserves. Neither of these can be estimated with utter precision. In summary:

When the Federal Reserve System wants to increase the money supply, it purchases U.S. government securities in the open market. It pays for these securities by creating new bank reserves, and these additional reserves lead to a multiple expansion of the money supply. However, because of fluctuations in people's desires to hold cash and banks' desires to hold excess reserves, the Fed cannot predict the consequences of these actions with perfect accuracy. Thus, over short periods, control over the money supply must of necessity be imperfect.

The procedures followed when the FOMC wants to *contract* the money supply are just the opposite of those we have just explained. In brief, it orders a *sale* of government securities in the open market. This takes reserves *away* from banks, since banks pay for the securities by drawing down their deposits at the Fed. A multiple *contraction* of the banking system ensues. The principles are exactly the same as when the process operates in reverse—and so are the uncertainties.

OPEN-MARKET OPERATIONS, BOND PRICES, AND INTEREST RATES

When it offers more government bonds for sale on the open market, the Federal Reserve normally depresses the price of bonds. This is illustrated by Figure 13-1, which shows a rightward shift of the (vertical) supply curve of bonds—from S_0S_0 to S_1S_1—with an unchanged demand curve, DD. The price of bonds falls from P_0 to P_1 as equilibrium in the bond market shifts from point A to point B.

Falling bond prices translate directly into rising interest rates. Why is that? Most bonds pay a fixed number of dollars of interest per year. For concreteness, consider a bond that pays $90 each year. If the bond sells for $1,000, bondholders earn a 9 percent return on their investment since $90 is 9 percent of $1,000. We say that *the interest rate on the bond is 9 percent*. Now suppose the price of the bond falls to $900. The annual interest payment is still $90, so bondholders now earn 10 percent on their money ($90 is 10 percent of $900). *The effective interest rate on the bond has risen to 10 percent*. This relationship between bond prices and interest rates is completely general:

When bond prices fall, interest rates must rise because the purchaser of a bond spends less money than before to earn a given number of dollars of interest per year. Similarly, when bond prices rise, interest rates must fall.

In fact, the relationship amounts to nothing more than two ways of saying the same thing. Higher interest rates *mean* lower bond prices; lower interest rates *mean* higher bond prices.[2]

[2]For further discussion and examples, see Review Question 6 at the end of the chapter.

FIGURE 13-1 OPEN-MARKET SALES AND BOND PRICES

If the Fed offers bonds for sale in the open market, the supply curve of bonds shifts rightward from S_0S_0 to S_1S_1. In consequence, equilibrium in the bond market shifts from point *A* to point *B*. The price of bonds declines from P_0 to P_1. By the same reasoning, an open-market purchase drives bond prices up.

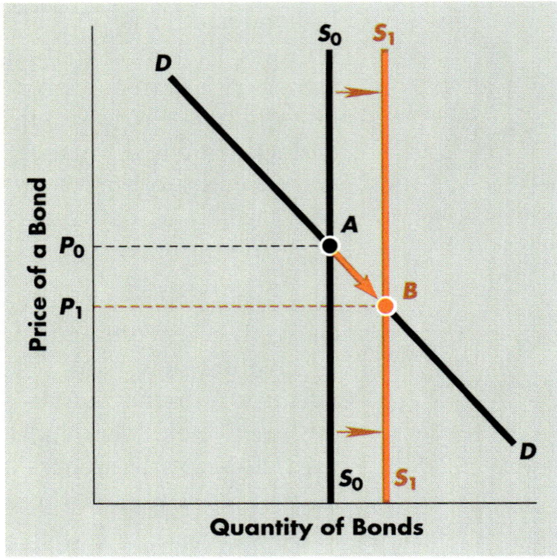

We thus see that the Fed, through its open-market operations, exercises direct influence over interest rates. Specifically:

An open-market purchase of bonds by the Fed not only raises the money supply but also drives up bond prices and pushes interest rates down. Conversely, an open-market sale of bonds, which reduces the money supply, lowers bond prices and raises interest rates.

CONTROLLING THE MONEY SUPPLY: LENDING TO BANKS

When the Federal Reserve System was first established, its founders did not intend it to pursue an active monetary policy to stabilize the economy. Indeed, the basic ideas of stabilization policy were foreign at the time. Instead, the Fed's founders viewed it as a means of preventing the supplies of money and credit from drying up during economic contractions, as had happened so often in the pre-1914 period.

One of the principal ways in which the Fed was to provide such insurance against financial panics was to act as a "lender of last resort." When risky business prospects made commercial banks hesitant to extend new loans, or when banks were in trouble, the Fed would step in by lending money to the banks, thus inducing the banks to lend more money to their customers. The Fed last performed this role in dramatic fashion in October 1987, when the stock market crash stunned the financial world. Its prompt actions helped avert a financial panic.

When the Fed extends borrowing privileges to a bank in need of reserves, that bank receives a credit in its deposit account at the Fed (see Table 13-2). This addition to bank reserves may lead to an expansion of the money supply; or it may eliminate a reserve deficiency and thereby prevent a multiple contraction of the banking system. In either case, the Fed eases monetary conditions by lending to banks.

TABLE 13-2 BALANCE SHEET CHANGES FOR BORROWING FROM THE FED

Bank				Federal Reserve System			
Assets		**Liabilities**		**Assets**		**Liabilities**	
Reserves	+ $5 million	Loan from Fed	+ $5 million	Loan to bank	+ $5 million	Bank reserves	+ $5 million
Addendum: Changes in Reserves							
Actual reserves	+ $5 million						
Required reserves	No Change						
Excess reserves	+ $5 million						

Bank borrows $5 million and the proceeds are credited to its reserve account

When the Fed lends $5 million to a bank, it simply adds this amount to the bookkeeping entry that represents that bank's account at the Fed. Once again, actual reserves increase while required reserves do not change (because bank deposits do not change). Hence, this loan would be expected to initiate a multiple expansion of the banking system.

The **DISCOUNT RATE** is the interest rate the Fed charges on loans that it makes to banks.

In principle, Federal Reserve officials can influence the amount banks borrow by manipulating the *rate of interest charged on these loans.* For historical reasons, this is called the **discount rate** in the United States. In foreign countries, it is often known as the *bank rate.* If the Fed wants banks to have more reserves, it can reduce the interest rate that it charges on loans, thereby tempting banks to borrow more. Alternatively, it can soak up reserves by raising its rate and persuading the banks to reduce their borrowings.

Such *active* use of the discount rate to regulate the money supply is practiced in a number of foreign countries, where the bank rate is the centerpiece of monetary policy. But it is extremely rare in the United States, where the Fed lends infrequently and in small amounts. Instead, it relies on open-market operations in conducting its monetary policy. The discount rate is normally adjusted *passively* to keep it in line with market interest rates.

When it changes its discount rate, the Fed cannot know for sure how banks will react. Sometimes they may respond vigorously to a cut in the rate, borrowing a great deal from the Fed and lending a correspondingly large amount to their customers. At other times they may essentially ignore the change in the discount rate. The link between the lending rate and the money supply is apt to be quite loose.

CONTROLLING THE MONEY SUPPLY: RESERVE REQUIREMENTS

The Fed has one final method of controlling the money supply: varying the minimum required reserve ratio. To see how this works, imagine that banks hold reserves that just match their required minimums. Excess reserves are zero.

If the Federal Reserve Board decides that the money supply needs to be increased, it can lower the required reserve ratio, thereby transforming some of what were previously *required* reserves into *excess* reserves. Although no new money is created directly by this action, we know from the previous chapter that it will set in motion the wheels of a multiple expansion of the banking system. Similarly, raising the required reserve ratio will set off a multiple contraction of bank deposits. In point of fact, however, the Fed no longer uses the reserve ratio as a weapon of monetary control. Current law and regulations provide for a basic reserve ratio of 10 percent against transactions deposits—a figure that has not been changed since 1992.

THE MONEY SUPPLY MECHANISM

This completes our discussion of the Fed's three methods of controlling the money supply—open-market operations, lending policy, and reserve requirements—and the limitations of each. One point, however, merits further emphasis. We have noted that the Fed's control of the money supply is imperfect because banks can and do vary their holdings of excess reserves. Since reserves earn no interest, banks will hold substantial *excess* reserves only when they feel that funds cannot be put to profitable uses. This may happen if shaky business conditions make loans to customers look unusually risky or if interest rates are very low. Conversely, banks will work hard to keep reserves to the legal minimum when loans to customers look safe and when interest rates are high. Thus:

As interest rates rise, banks normally find it more profitable to expand their volume of loans and deposits, thus increasing the supply of money. However, the Fed can shift the relationship between the money supply and interest rates by employing any of its principal weapons of monetary control: open-market operations, changes in reserve requirements, or changes in lending policy to banks.

FIGURE 13-2 THE SUPPLY SCHEDULE FOR MONEY

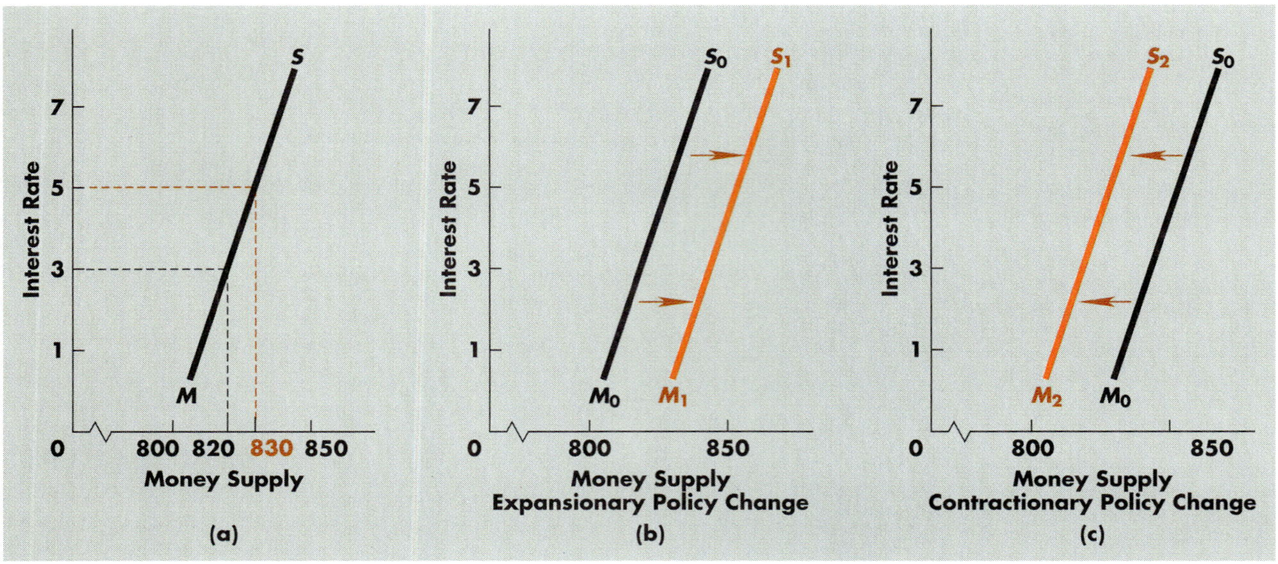

Panel (a) shows a typical supply schedule for money. It is rising as we move toward the right, meaning that banks will supply more money when interest rates are higher. Panel (b) illustrates what happens to the money supply schedule when the Fed purchases securities in the open market, or lowers required reserves, or provides banks with more loans. The supply schedule shifts outward. Panel (c) depicts the effect of using these same policy instruments in the opposite (contractionary) direction. The supply schedule shifts inward.

These ideas are depicted graphically in Figure 13-2. Figure 13-2(a) shows a typical money supply schedule labeled *MS*, illustrating the fact that banks will supply more money as interest rates rise.[3] Notice that the sensitivity of the money supply to interest rates is rather weak in the diagram—a large rise in the rate of interest (from 3 percent to 5 percent) induces only a small increase in the supply of money (from $820 billion to $830 billion). The drawing is deliberately constructed that way because that is what the statistical evidence shows.

The curve in Figure 13-2(a) shows the money supply schedule corresponding to some specific monetary policy. Figure 13-2(b) portrays how the money supply schedule responds to an *expansionary change in monetary policy* such as an open-market purchase of government bonds. The money supply schedule shifts outward from M_0S_0 to M_1S_1, as indicated by the arrows. After banks have adjusted to the change, there is more money at any given interest rate.

Figure 13-2(c) shows what happens in the reverse case—a *contractionary monetary policy* such as an open-market sale of securities. The money supply shifts inward from M_0S_0 to M_2S_2.

As we have emphasized, the diagrams make things look rather more precise than they actually are. Since the Fed's control over the money supply schedule is imperfect in the short run, the actual *MS* schedule is obscured by a bit of fog. In what follows, we portray all the graphs as clean straight lines only for pedagogical simplicity. The Fed wishes things were so simple in the real world!

THE DEMAND FOR MONEY

Just as we must know something about both the supply of and the demand for wheat before we can predict how much will be sold and at what price, it is necessary to know something about the *demand for money* if we are to understand the amount of money actually in existence and the prevailing interest rate.

The definition of *money* given in the previous chapter suggests the most important reason why people hold money balances: The medium of exchange is needed to carry out purchases and sales of goods and services. More dollars are needed to conduct the nation's business if more purchases and sales are made or if each transaction takes place at a higher price. Since nominal gross domestic product (GDP) is normally considered to be the best measure of the money volume of goods and services traded in the economy, it seems safe to assume that the demand for money will rise as nominal GDP rises. And, indeed, an impressive amount of statistical evidence supports this supposition.

But nominal GDP is not the only factor affecting the demand for money; interest rates matter, too. At first, that may seem surprising because many forms of money pay either no interest or a fixed interest rate. Why, then, are interest rates relevant? They are relevant because money is only one of a variety of forms in which individuals can hold their wealth. Holders of money *give up* the opportunity to hold one of these other assets, such as government bonds, in order to gain the convenience of money. In so doing, they *give up* the interest that they could have earned on one of these alternative assets.

This is another example of the concept of *opportunity cost*.[4] On the surface, it seems virtually costless to hold money. But, *compared with the next best alternative,*

[3]There are many interest rates in the economy. However, they all tend to move up and down together. Hence, for present purposes, we can speak of "the" rate of interest.

[4]If you need to review this concept, see Chapter 3.

FIGURE 13-3 THE DEMAND SCHEDULE FOR MONEY

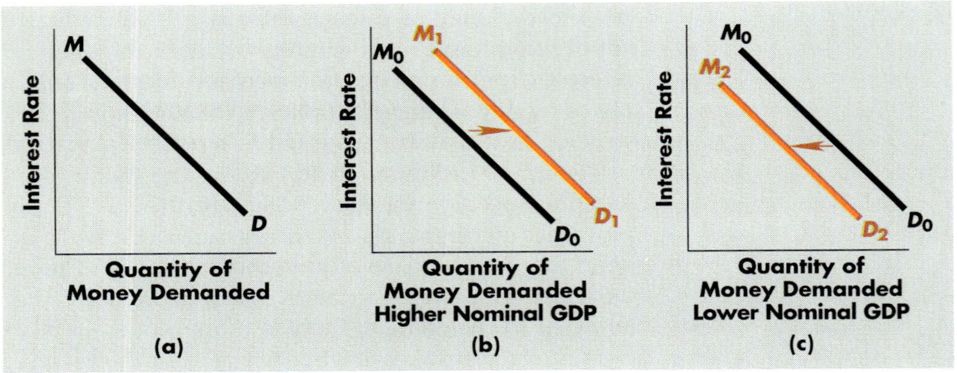

The downward-sloping line *MD* in Panel (a) is a typical demand curve for money. It slopes down because money is a less attractive asset when interest rates on alternative assets are higher. However, such a curve can be drawn only for a particular level of nominal GDP. A rise in nominal GDP will shift the money-demand curve outward, as shown in Panel (b). Conversely, a fall in nominal GDP will shift the curve inward, as in Panel (c).

this action is not costless at all. For example, if the best alternative to holding \$100 in cash is to put those funds into a government bond that pays 7 percent interest, then the opportunity cost of holding that cash is \$7 per year (7 percent of \$100).

Money holdings should therefore be lower when the rate of interest is higher. Why? Because, while people hold money to facilitate making transactions, this benefit comes at a cost. For example, holders of cash give up the potential interest they could earn by investing the funds in, say, government bonds. It is natural, therefore, to assume that higher interest rates induce households and firms to economize more on their holdings of money balances. In a word, the demand to hold money should *decline* as the interest rate *rises*. Once again, careful analysis of the data shows this to be true. To summarize:

People and business firms hold money primarily to finance their transactions. Therefore, the quantity of money demanded *increases* as nominal output rises. However, the quantity of money demanded *decreases* as the rate of interest rises because the rate of interest is the opportunity cost of holding money balances.

It is possible to portray the demand for money by a graphical device, as shown in the three panels of Figure 13-3. In Panel (a), we show a downward-sloping demand schedule for money (the curve labeled *MD*)—the quantity of money demanded decreases as the rate of interest rises. But since the quantity of money demanded also depends on nominal GDP, we must hold nominal GDP constant in drawing such a curve. Changes in this variable will shift the *MD* curve in the manner indicated in the other two panels because at higher levels of nominal GDP, demand for money is greater, and at lower levels of nominal GDP, demand for money is smaller.

EQUILIBRIUM IN THE MONEY MARKET

As is usual in supply and demand analysis, it is useful to put both sides of the market together on a single graph. Figure 13-4 combines the money supply schedule of Figure 13-2(a) (labeled *MS*) with the money demand schedule of Figure 13-3(a) (labeled *MD*). Point *E* is the equilibrium of the money market. The diagram thus shows that *given* nominal GDP (which locates the *MD* curve) and *given* the Federal Reserve's monetary policy (which locates the *MS* curve), the money market is in equilibrium at an interest rate of 5 percent and a money stock

FIGURE 13-4 EQUILIBRIUM IN THE MONEY MARKET

Equilibrium in the market for money is determined by the intersection of demand curve *MD* and supply curve *MS*. At point *E*, the interest rate is 5 percent, and the money supply is $830 billion. At no other interest rate would the demand for and the supply of money be in balance.

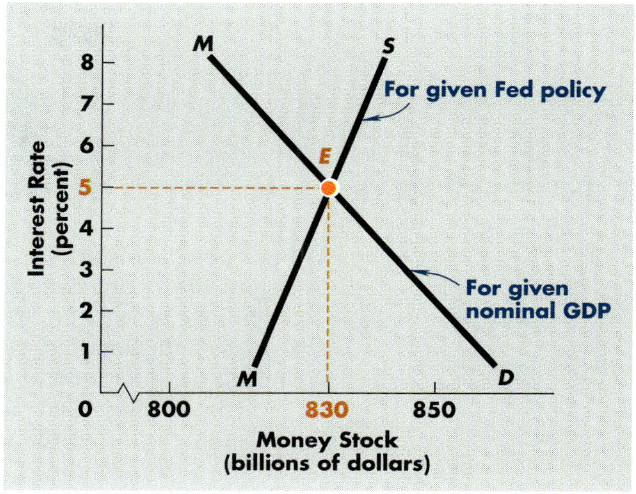

of $830 billion. At any interest rate above 5 percent, the quantity of money supplied would exceed the quantity demanded and the interest rate—which is the price for renting money—would therefore decline. At any interest rate below 5 percent, more money would be demanded than supplied, and so the interest rate would rise. This is familiar ground.

MONETARY POLICY refers to actions that the Federal Reserve System takes in order to change the equilibrium of the money market; that is, to alter the money supply, move interest rates, or both.

Since the Fed can shift the *MS* curve, it can alter this equilibrium through its **monetary policy.** Purchasing government securities in the open market will provide additional excess reserves to the banking system, thus encouraging banks to increase their loans and deposits. As money becomes more plentiful, interest rates drop.

Our supply-demand analysis of the money market shows this in Figure 13-5(a). By shifting the money supply schedule outward from M_0S_0 to M_1S_1, the Fed moves the market equilibrium from point *E* to point *A*—thus forcing the

FIGURE 13-5 THE EFFECTS OF MONETARY POLICY ON THE MONEY MARKET

The two parts of this figure show the effects of monetary policy on the money supply (*M*) and the rate of interest (*r*). In Panel (a), expansionary monetary policies shift the supply schedule from M_0S_0 to M_1S_1 and push the equilibrium from point *E* to point *A; M* rises while *r* falls. In Panel (b), contractionary policies pull the supply schedule in from M_0S_0 to M_2S_2, causing equilibrium to move up from point *E* to point *B; M* falls as *r* rises.

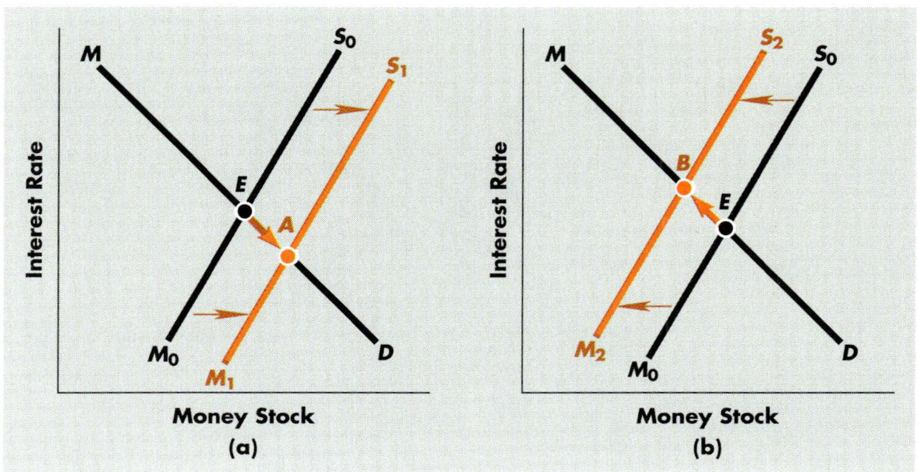

interest rate down. Contractionary monetary policy actions, such as selling securities in the open market, have the opposite effect. They push interest rates up, as Figure 13-5(b) shows. Thus:

Monetary policies that expand the money supply normally lower interest rates. Monetary policies that reduce the money supply normally raise interest rates.

INTEREST RATES AND TOTAL EXPENDITURE

We are now ready to see precisely how the Federal Reserve's monetary policy decisions affect unemployment, inflation, and the overall state of the economy. To begin, we go back to the analysis of Chapters 7 through 11, where we learned that aggregate demand is the sum of consumption spending (*C*), investment spending (*I*), government purchases of goods and services (*G*), and net exports (*X* − *IM*). We know that *fiscal policy* controls *G* directly and exerts influence over both *C* and *I* through the tax laws. We now want to find out how *monetary policy* affects total spending.

Most economists agree that, of the four components of aggregate demand, investment and net exports are the most sensitive to monetary policy. We will study the effects of monetary and fiscal policy on net exports in detail in Chapter 19, after we have learned about international exchange rates. For now, we will assume that net exports (*X* − *IM*) are fixed and focus on investment (*I*).

Business investment in new factories and machinery is sensitive to interest rates for reasons that have been explained in earlier chapters.[5] Since the rate of interest that must be paid on borrowings is one element of the cost of making an

FIGURE 13-6 THE EFFECT OF INTEREST RATES ON AGGREGATE DEMAND

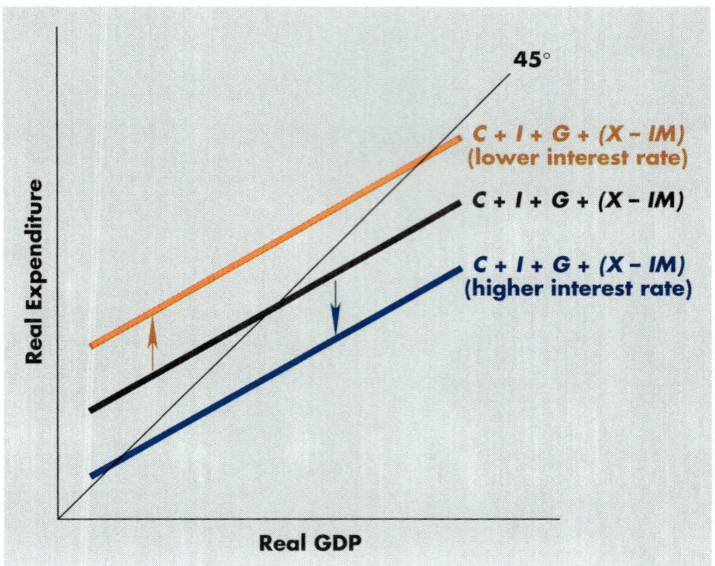

Because interest rates are an important determinant of investment spending, *I*, the *C* + *I* + *G* + (*X* − *IM*) schedule shifts whenever the rate of interest changes. Specifically, as shown here, lower interest rates shift the curve upward and higher interest rates shift it downward.

[5]See, for example, Chapter 8, page 168.

investment, business executives will find investment prospects less attractive as interest rates rise. Therefore, they will spend less. For similar reasons, *investment in housing* by individuals may also be deterred by high interest rates. Since the interest cost of a home mortgage is the major component of the total cost of owning a home, fewer families will want to buy a new home when interest rates are high than when interest rates are low. We conclude that:

Higher interest rates lead to lower investment spending. But investment (I) is a component of total spending, $C + I + G + (X - IM)$. Therefore, when interest rates rise, total spending falls. In terms of the 45° line diagram of previous chapters, a higher interest rate leads to a lower expenditure schedule. Conversely, a lower interest rate leads to a higher expenditure schedule. (See Figure 13-6.)

MONETARY POLICY AND AGGREGATE DEMAND

The effect of interest rates on spending provides a mechanism through which monetary policy affects aggregate demand. We know from our analysis of the money market that monetary policy can have a profound effect on the rate of interest. Let us, therefore, outline how monetary policy works.

Suppose the Federal Reserve, seeing the economy stuck with unemployment and a recessionary gap, raises the money supply. It would normally do this by purchasing government securities in the open market, but the specific weapon that the Fed uses is not terribly important for present purposes. What matters is that the money supply schedule shifts outward as in Figure 13-7.

With the demand schedule for money (temporarily) fixed, such a shift in the supply curve for money has the effect that an increase in supply always has in a free market—it lowers the price, as Figure 13-7 shows. In this case, the price of renting money is the rate of interest, r, so r falls.

Next, for reasons we have just outlined, investment spending (I) rises in response to the lower interest rates. But, as we learned in Chapter 9, such an

FIGURE 13-7 THE EFFECT OF EXPANSIONARY MONETARY POLICY ON THE MONEY SUPPLY AND RATE OF INTEREST

An expansionary monetary policy pushes the money supply schedule outward from M_0S_0 to M_1S_1, causing equilibrium in the money market to shift from point E_0 to point E_1. The money supply rises from $830 billion to $880 billion, while the interest rate falls from 5 percent to 3 percent.

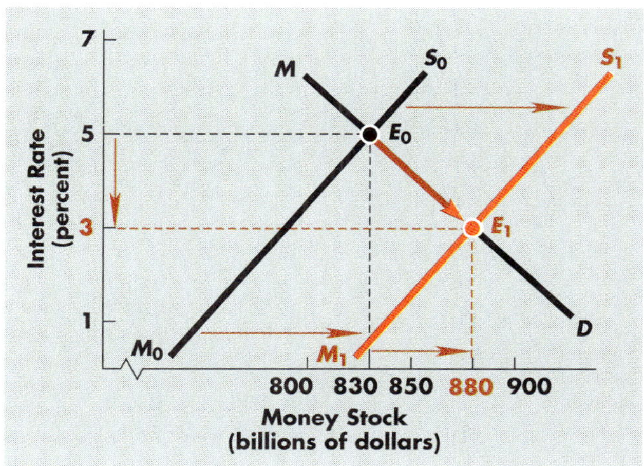

autonomous rise in investment kicks off a multiplier chain of increases in output and employment. Thus, finally, we have completed the links from the money supply to the level of aggregate demand. In brief, monetary policy works as follows:

A higher money supply leads to lower interest rates, and these lower interest rates encourage investment, which has multiplier effects on aggregate demand.

The process operates equally well in reverse. By contracting the money supply, the Fed can force interest rates up, causing investment spending to fall and pulling down aggregate demand via the multiplier mechanism. This, in outline form, is how monetary policy operates in the Keynesian model. Since the chain of causation is fairly long, the following schematic diagram may help clarify it.

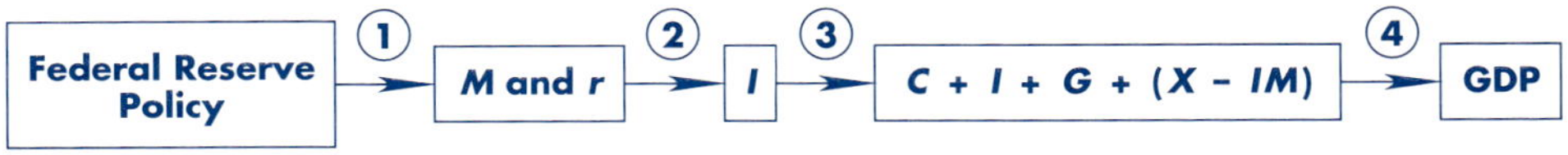

In this causal chain, Link 1 indicates that the actions of the Federal Reserve affect money and interest rates. Link 2 stands for the effect of interest rates on investment. Link 3 simply notes that investment is one component of total spending. And Link 4 is the multiplier, relating an autonomous change in investment to the ultimate change in aggregate demand.

Let us next review what we know about each of these links and fill in some illustrative numbers. In the process, we will see what economists must study if they are to estimate the effects of monetary policy.

Link 1 is the subject of this chapter and of Figure 13-7. Given the initial level of real GDP and prices, the demand schedule for money is shown by curve *MD*. The Fed's expansionary action shifts the supply schedule out from M_0S_0 to M_1S_1, resulting in an increase in the money stock from $830 billion to $880 billion in this example, and a decline in the interest rate from 5 percent to 3 percent. Thus, the first thing an economist must know is how sensitive interest rates are to changes in the supply of money.

Link 2 translates the drop in the interest rate into an increase in investment spending (*I*), which we take to be $200 billion in this example. To estimate this effect in practice, economists must study the sensitivity of investment to interest rates.

Link 3 instructs us to enter this $200 billion rise in *I* as an autonomous shift in the $C + I + G + (X - IM)$ schedule of a 45° line diagram. Figure 13-8 carries out this step. The expenditure schedule rises from $C + I_0 + G + (X - IM)$ to $C + I_1 + G + (X - IM)$.

Finally, Link 4 applies multiplier analysis to this vertical shift in the expenditure schedule in order to predict the eventual increase in real GDP demanded. We have been using a multiplier of 2.5 in our examples, so multiplying $200 billion by 2.5 gives the final effect on aggregate demand—a rise of $500 billion. This is shown in Figure 13-8 as a shift in equilibrium from E_0 (where GDP is $6,000 billion) to E_1 (where GDP is $6,500 billion). Of course, the size of the multiplier itself must also be estimated. To summarize:

The effect of monetary policy on aggregate demand depends on the sensitivity of interest rates to the money supply, on the responsiveness of investment spending to the rate of interest, and on the size of the multiplier.

FIGURE 13-8 THE EFFECT OF EXPANSIONARY MONETARY POLICY ON AGGREGATE DEMAND

Expansionary monetary policies, which lower the rate of interest, will cause the $C + I + G + (X - IM)$ schedule to shift upward from $C + I_0 + G + (X - IM)$ to $C + I_1 + G + (X - IM)$, as shown here. In this example, since the multiplier is 2.5, a $200 billion rise in investment leads, via the multiplier process, to a $500 billion rise in GDP.

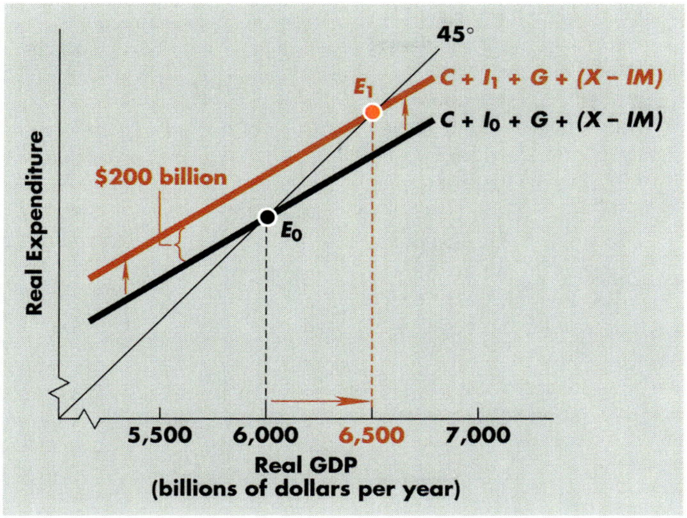

MONEY AND THE PRICE LEVEL IN THE KEYNESIAN MODEL

The analysis up to this point leaves one important question unanswered: What happens to the price level? To find the answer, we must simply remember once again that prices and output are determined jointly by aggregate demand *and* aggregate supply. Our analysis of monetary policy so far has shown us how an increase in the money supply shifts the aggregate demand curve, that is, increases the *aggregate quantity demanded at any given price level*. But to learn what happens to the price level and to real output, we must consider *aggregate supply* as well.

Specifically, in considering shifts in aggregate demand caused by *fiscal* policy in Chapter 11, we noted that an upsurge in total spending normally induces firms to increase output somewhat *and* to raise prices somewhat. This is just what an aggregate supply curve shows. Whether prices or real output respond more depends on the slope of the aggregate demand curve.

Since this analysis of output and price responses applies equally well to monetary policy or, for that matter, to anything else that raises aggregate demand, we conclude that:

Expansionary monetary policy causes some inflation under normal circumstances. But how much inflation it causes depends on the slope of the aggregate supply curve.

The effect of a rise in the money supply on the price level is depicted graphically on an aggregate supply and demand diagram in Figure 13-9. In the example we have been using, the Fed's actions raise the money supply by $50 billion, and this increases aggregate demand (through the multiplier) by $500 billion. We enter this as a horizontal shift of $500 billion in the aggregate demand curve of Figure 13-9, from D_0D_0 to D_1D_1. The diagram shows that this expansionary monetary policy raises the economy's equilibrium from point E to point B—the price

FIGURE 13-9 THE INFLATIONARY EFFECTS OF EXPANSIONARY MONETARY POLICY

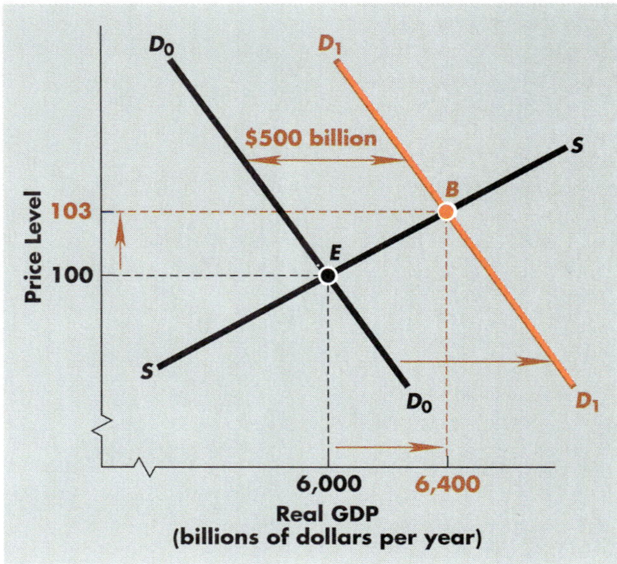

Raising the money supply normally causes inflation. When expansionary monetary policy causes the aggregate demand curve to shift outward from D_0D_0 to D_1D_1, the economy's equilibrium shifts from point *E* to point *B*. Real output expands (in this case by $400 billion), but prices also rise (in this case by 3 percent).

level therefore rises from 100 to 103, or 3 percent. The diagram also shows that real GDP rises by only $400 billion, which is less than the $500 billion stimulus to aggregate demand. The reason, as we know from earlier chapters, is that rising prices stifle real aggregate demand.

By taking account of the effect of an increase in the money supply on the price level, we have completed our story about the role of monetary policy in the Keynesian model. We can thus expand our schematic diagram of monetary policy as follows:

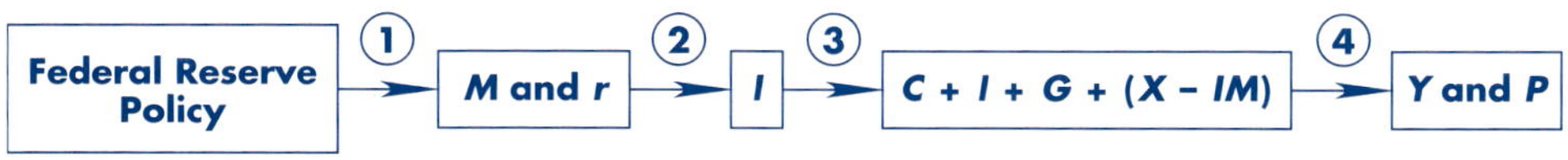

The last link now recognizes that *both* output *and* prices normally are affected by changes in the money supply.

APPLICATION: WHY THE AGGREGATE DEMAND CURVE SLOPES DOWNWARD

This analysis of the effect of money on the price level puts us in a better position to understand why higher prices reduce aggregate quantity demanded; that is, why the aggregate demand curve slopes downward. In earlier chapters, we explained this phenomenon in two ways. First, we observed that rising prices reduce the purchasing power of certain assets held by consumers, especially money and government bonds, and that this in turn retards consumption spending. Second, we noted that higher domestic prices depress exports and stimulate imports.

There is nothing wrong with this analysis. But higher prices have another important effect on aggregate demand, through a channel that we are now in a position to understand.

Money is demanded primarily to conduct transactions and, as we have noted in this chapter, a rise in the *average money cost* of each transaction—that is, a rise in the price level—will increase the quantity of money demanded by pushing up nominal GDP. This means that when expansionary policy of any kind raises the price level, more money will be demanded at any given interest rate.

But, if the supply of money is *not* increased, an increase in the quantity of money demanded at any given interest rate must force the cost of borrowing money—the rate of interest—to rise. As we know, increases in interest rates reduce investment and, hence, reduce aggregate demand. This, then, is the main reason why the economy's aggregate demand curve has a negative slope, meaning that aggregate quantity demanded is lower when prices are higher. In sum:

At higher price levels, the quantity of money demanded is greater. Given a fixed supply schedule, therefore, a higher price level must lead to a higher interest rate. Since high interest rates discourage investment, aggregate quantity demanded is lower when the price level is higher. That is, the aggregate demand curve slopes downward to the right.

FROM MODELS TO POLICY DEBATES

You will no doubt be relieved to hear that we have now provided just about all the technical apparatus we need to analyze stabilization policy. To be sure, you will encounter many graphs in the next few chapters. But most of them are repeats of diagrams with which you are already familiar. Our attention now turns from *building* a theory to *using* that theory to understand important policy issues.

The next three chapters take up a trio of important and controversial policy debates that surface regularly in the newspapers: the debate over the efficacy of monetary policy (Chapter 14), the continuing debate over the government budget deficit (Chapter 15), and the controversy over the trade-off between inflation and unemployment (Chapter 16).

SUMMARY

1. A **central bank** is a bank for banks.
2. The *Federal Reserve System* is America's central bank. There are 12 Federal Reserve banks, but most of the power is held by the Board of Governors in Washington and by the *Federal Open Market Committee.*
3. The Federal Reserve is independent of the rest of the government. There is controversy over whether this *independence* is a good idea, and a number of reforms have been suggested that would make the Fed more accountable to the president or to Congress.
4. The Fed has three major weapons for control of the money supply: **open-market operations,** reserve requirements, and its lending policy to banks. But only open-market operations are used frequently.
5. The Fed raises the money supply by purchasing government securities in the open market. When it pays banks for such purchases, the Fed provides banks with new reserves, which in turn lead to a larger money supply. Conversely, open-market sales of securities take reserves from banks and lead to a smaller money supply.
6. When the Fed buys bonds, bond prices rise and interest rates fall. When the Fed sells bonds, bond prices fall and interest rates rise.
7. The Fed can also increase the money supply by allowing banks to borrow more reserves, perhaps by reducing the interest rate it charges on such loans, or by reducing reserve requirements.

8. None of these weapons, however, gives the Fed perfect control over the money supply in the short run, because it cannot predict perfectly how far the process of deposit creation or destruction will go.
9. The *money supply schedule* shows that more money is supplied at higher interest rates because, as interest rates rise, banks find it more profitable to expand their loans and deposits. This schedule can be shifted by Federal Reserve policy.
10. The *money demand schedule* shows that less money is demanded at higher interest rates because interest is the opportunity cost of holding money. This schedule shifts when output or the price level changes, that is, when nominal GDP changes.
11. The *equilibrium* money stock (M) and the equilibrium rate of interest (r) are determined by the intersection of the money supply and money demand schedules.
12. Federal Reserve policy can shift this equilibrium. Expansionary policies cause M to rise and r to fall. Contractionary policies reduce M and increase r.
13. Investment spending (I), including business investment and investment in new homes, is sensitive to interest rates (r). Specifically, I is lower when r is higher.
14. This explains how **monetary policy** works in the Keynesian model. Raising the money supply (M) leads to lower r; the lower interest rates stimulate investment spending; and this investment stimulus, via the multiplier, then raises aggregate demand.
15. However, prices are likely to rise as output rises. The amount of inflation caused by increasing the money supply depends on the slope of the aggregate supply curve. There will be much inflation if the supply curve is steep, but little inflation if it is flat.
16. The main reason *why the aggregate demand curve slopes downward* is that higher prices increase the demand to hold money in order to finance transactions. Given the money supply, this pushes interest rates up; and this, in turn, discourages investment.

KEY TERMS

Central bank
Federal Reserve System
Federal Open Market Committee (FOMC)
Independence of the Fed
Open-market operations
Bond prices and interest rates
Contraction and expansion of the money supply
Federal Reserve lending to banks
Reserve requirements
Supply of money
Demand for money
Opportunity cost
Equilibrium in the money market
Discount rate
Monetary policy
Why the aggregate demand curve slopes downward

QUESTIONS FOR REVIEW

1. Why does a modern industrial economy need a central bank?
2. The chapter listed several current proposals for changing the structure of the Fed. Which, if any, of these provisions would you favor? Explain why.
3. Suppose there is $120 billion of cash, and that half of it is held in bank vaults as *required* reserves (that is, banks hold no *excess* reserves). How large will the money supply be if the required reserve ratio is 10 percent? 12-1/2 percent? 16-2/3 percent?
4. Show the balance sheet changes that would take place if the Federal Reserve Bank of San Francisco purchased an office building from the Bank of America for a price of $100 million. Compare this to the effect of an open-market purchase of securities shown in Table 13-1. What do you conclude?
5. Suppose that the Fed purchases $8 million worth of government bonds from Donald Trump, who banks at Citibank in New York. Show the effects on the balance sheets of the Fed, Citibank, and Donald Trump. (*Hint:* What will Trump do with the $8 million check he receives from the Fed?) Does it make any difference if the Fed buys bonds from a bank or from an individual?
6. Treasury bills have a fixed face value and pay interest by selling "at a discount." For example, if a 1-year bill with a $1,000 face value sells today for $950, it will pay $1,000 − $950 = $50 in interest over its life. The interest rate on the bill is therefore $50/$950 = 0.0526, or 5.26 percent.

a. Suppose the price of the Treasury bill falls to \$940. What happens to the interest rate?
b. Suppose, instead, that the price rises to \$960. What is the interest rate now?
c. (More difficult) Now generalize this example. Let P be the price of the bill and r be the interest rate. Develop an algebraic formula expressing r in terms of P. (*Hint:* The interest earned is \$1,000 – P. What is the percentage interest rate?) Show that this formula illustrates the point made in the text (page 279): Higher bond prices mean lower interest rates.

7. Explain why the quantity of money supplied normally is higher and the quantity of money demanded normally is lower at higher interest rates.
8. Starting in February 1994, the Fed decided that interest rates were too low and took steps to drive them up—a process it continued for about a year. How did the Fed push interest rates up? Illustrate on a diagram.
9. Explain why both business investments and purchases of new homes decline when interest rates rise.
10. Explain what a \$50 billion increase in the money supply will do to real GDP under the following assumptions:
    a. Each \$10 billion increase in the money supply reduces the rate of interest by 0.5 percentage point.
    b. Each 1 percentage point decline in interest rates stimulates \$30 billion worth of new investment.
    c. The expenditure multiplier is 2.
    d. The aggregate supply curve is so flat that prices do not rise noticeably when demand increases.
11. Explain how your answer to Review Question 10 would differ if each of the assumptions were changed. Specifically, what sorts of changes in the assumptions would make monetary policy very weak?
12. Use graphs like Figures 13-4 and 13-6 to explain why the aggregate demand curve has a negative slope.
13. The federal government is now in the process of lowering its budget deficit by reducing spending. If the Federal Reserve wants to maintain the same level of aggregate demand in the face of large-scale deficit reduction, what should it do? What would you expect to happen to interest rates?
14. (More difficult) Consider an economy in which government purchases, taxes, and net exports are all zero, the consumption function is:

$$C = 300 + 0.75Y$$

and investment spending (I) depends on the rate of interest (r) in the following way:

$$I = 1{,}000 - 100r$$

Find the equilibrium GDP if the Fed makes the rate of interest (a) 2 percent ($r = 0.02$), (b) 5 percent, (c) 10 percent.

CHAPTER 14

THE DEBATE OVER MONETARY POLICY

The love of money is the root of all evil.
New Testament

Lack of money is the root of all evil.
George Bernard Shaw

Up to now our discussion of stabilization policy has been almost entirely objective and technical. In seeking to understand how the national economy works and how government policies affect it, we have mostly ignored the intense economic and political controversies that surround the actual conduct of stabilization policy. Chapters 14 through 16 are about precisely these issues.

We begin the chapter by explaining an alternative theory of how money affects the economy, known as *monetarism.* Although the monetarist and Keynesian views seem to contradict one another, we will see that the conflict is more apparent than real. In fact, the disagreement is akin to hearing a Briton say, "Yes," and a Frenchman say, "Oui." The uninitiated hear two different languages, but knowledgeable listeners understand that they mean the same thing.

However, while monetarist and Keynesian *theories* are not very different, there *are* significant differences among economists over the appropriate design and execution of monetary *policy.* These differences occupy the rest of the chapter. We will learn about the continuing debates over the nature of aggregate supply, over the relative virtues of monetary versus fiscal policy, and over whether the Federal Reserve should try to control the money stock or interest rates. As we shall see, the resolution of these issues is crucial for the proper conduct of monetary policy and, indeed, to the decision of whether the government should try to conduct any stabilization policy at all. Finally, since economists' abilities to forecast the future are critical for the success or failure of stabilization efforts, we devote some time to the techniques and accuracy of economic forecasting.

ISSUE: SHOULD WE FORSAKE STABILIZATION POLICY?

We have suggested several times in this book that well-timed changes in fiscal or monetary policy can mitigate economic fluctuations. And we have devoted many pages, including most of Chapters 11 and 13, to explaining how this can be done. While full examination of the complexities of such stabilization policy requires more advanced discussion, the basic principles are simple enough to be grasped by beginning students—as we hope you have done.

But some economists argue that these lessons are best forgotten. In practice, they claim, attempts at macroeconomic stabilization are likely to do more harm than good. Policymakers are therefore best advised to follow fixed rules rather than use their best judgment on a case-by-case basis.

Nothing we have said so far leads to this conclusion. But we have not yet told the whole story. By the end of the chapter you will have encountered several arguments in favor of rules, and hence be in a better position to make up your own mind on this important debate.

VELOCITY AND THE QUANTITY THEORY OF MONEY

We saw in the last chapter how money influences real output and the price level in the Keynesian model. But there is another way to look at these matters, using a model that is much older than the Keynesian model. This model is known as the *quantity theory of money*, and it is easy to understand once we have introduced one new concept—*velocity*.

We learned in Chapter 12 that because barter is so cumbersome, virtually all economic transactions in advanced economies are conducted by the use of money. This means that if there are, say, $5,000 billion worth of transactions in the economy during a particular year, and there is an average money stock of $1,000 billion during that year, then each dollar of money is used an average of five times during the year.

VELOCITY indicates the number of times per year that an "average dollar" is spent on goods and services. It is the ratio of nominal GDP to the number of dollars in the money stock. That is:

$$\text{Velocity} = \frac{\text{Nominal GDP}}{\text{Money stock}}$$

The number 5 in this example is called the *velocity of circulation*, or just **velocity** for short, because it indicates the *speed* at which money circulates. For example, a particular dollar bill might be used to buy a haircut in January; the barber might use it to buy a sweater in March; the storekeeper might then use it to pay for gasoline in May; the gas station owner could pay it out to the house painter in October; and the painter might spend it on a Christmas present in December. This would mean that the dollar was used five times during the year. If it were used only four times during the year, its velocity would be 4, and so on. Similarly, a $20 bill circulating with a velocity of 8 would be the monetary instrument used to finance $160 worth of transactions in that year.

No one has data on all the transactions in the economy. To make velocity an operational concept, economists must settle on a workable definition of transactions that they can actually measure. The most popular choice is nominal gross domestic product, even though it ignores many transactions that use money—such as sales of existing assets. If we accept nominal GDP as a measure of the money value of transactions, we are led to a concrete definition of velocity as the ratio of nominal GDP to the number of dollars in the money stock. Since nominal GDP is the product of real GDP times the price level, we can write this definition in symbols as:

The **EQUATION OF EXCHANGE** states that the money value of GDP transactions must be equal to the product of the average stock of money times velocity. That is:

$$M \times V = P \times Y$$

$$\text{Velocity} = \frac{\text{Value of transactions}}{\text{Money stock}} = \frac{\text{Nominal GDP}}{M} = \frac{P \times Y}{M}$$

By multiplying both sides of the equation by M, we arrive at an identity called the **equation of exchange** that relates the money supply and nominal GDP:

$$\text{Money supply} \times \text{Velocity} = \text{Nominal GDP}$$

Alternatively, stated in symbols, we have:

$$M \times V = P \times Y$$

Here we have an obvious link between the stock of money, M, and the nominal value of the nation's output. But it is only a matter of arithmetic, not of economics. For example, it does not imply that the Fed can raise nominal GDP by increasing M. Why not? Because V might simultaneously fall by enough to prevent $M \times V$ from rising. In other words, if there were more dollar bills in circulation than before, but each bill changed hands more slowly, total spending might not rise. Thus, we need an auxiliary assumption to change the arithmetic into an economic theory:

The quantity theory of money transforms the equation of exchange from an accounting identity into an economic model by assuming that changes in velocity are so minor that velocity can be taken to be virtually constant.

You can see that if V never changed, the equation of exchange would be a marvelously simple model of the determination of nominal GDP—far simpler than the Keynesian model. To see this, it is convenient to rewrite the equation of exchange in growth-rate form:

$$\%\Delta M + \%\Delta V = \%\Delta P + \%\Delta Y$$

If V was constant (so its percentage change was always zero), this equation would say, for example, that if the Federal Reserve wanted to make nominal GDP grow by 8.7 percent per year, it need only raise the money supply by 8.7 percent per year. In such a simple world, economists could use the equation of exchange to *predict* nominal GDP growth simply by predicting the growth rate of money. And policymakers could *control* nominal GDP growth simply by controlling growth of the money supply.

In the real world things are not so simple because velocity is not a fixed number. But this does not necessarily destroy the usefulness of the quantity theory. We explained in Chapter 1 why all economic models make assumptions that are at least mildly unrealistic—without such assumptions they would not be models at all, just tedious descriptions of reality. The question is really whether the assumption of constant velocity is a useful abstraction from annoying detail or a gross distortion of facts.

Figure 14-1 sheds some light on this question by showing the behavior of velocity since 1929. You will note that there are two different measures of velocity, labeled V_1 and V_2. Why? Recall from Chapter 12 that there are several ways to measure money, the most popular of which are M1 and M2. Since velocity (V) is simply nominal GDP divided by the money stock (M), we get a different measure of V for each measure of M. Figure 14-1 shows the velocities of both M1 and M2.

Several features are apparent. You will undoubtedly notice the difference in the behavior of V_1 versus V_2. There is a clear downward trend in V_1 from 1929 until 1946, a pronounced upward trend until 1981, and quite erratic behavior with some downward trend in recent years. Clearly, *the velocity of M1 is not constant over long periods of time. The velocity of M2 is much closer to constant,* but it has risen noticeably in recent years. Furthermore, closer examination of monthly or quarterly data on either V_1 or V_2 reveals some rather substantial fluctuations of velocity. Such fluctuations have led most economists to conclude that *velocity is not constant in the short run.* And predictions of nominal GDP growth based on

FIGURE 14-1 VELOCITY OF CIRCULATION, 1929–1996

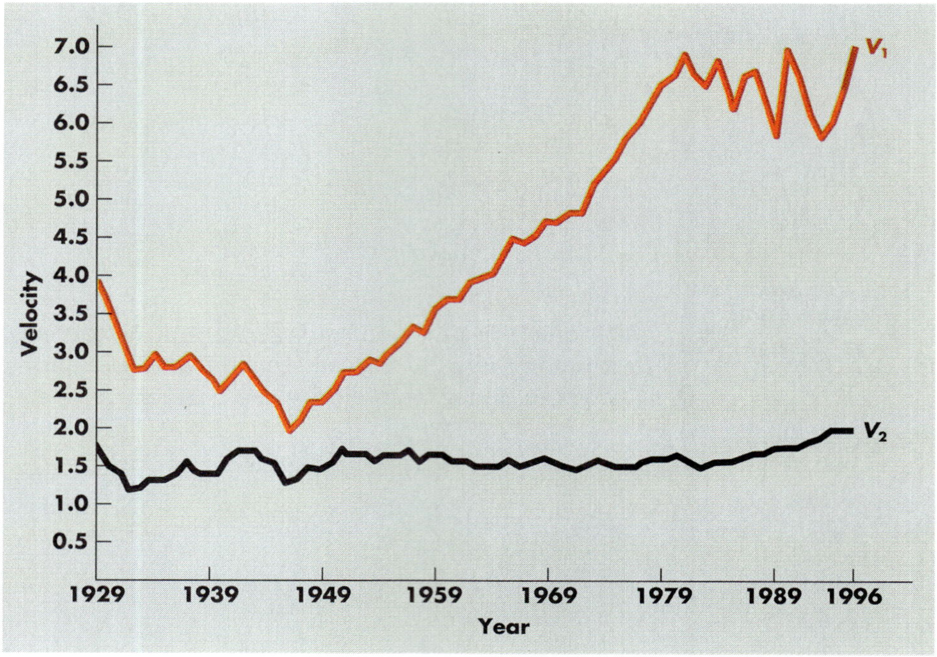

During a period of American history of over 65 years, the velocity of M1 fell from almost 4 in 1930 to 2 in 1946, and then rose to almost 7 in 1981. Since then, it has gyrated dramatically. Clearly, then, M1 velocity has not been constant over long periods of time. The velocity of M2 looks much more stable, but it too has displayed some marked gyrations.

SOURCE: Constructed by the authors; data from Bureau of Economic Analysis, Federal Reserve Board, and Professor Robert Rasche.

assuming constant velocity have not fared very well, regardless of how M is measured. It seems, then, that the strict quantity theory of money is not an adequate model of aggregate demand.

THE DETERMINANTS OF VELOCITY

Since it is abundantly clear that velocity is a variable, not a constant, the equation of exchange is useful as a model of GDP determination only if we can explain movements in velocity. What factors decide whether V_1 or V_2 will be 4 or 5 or 6; that is, whether a dollar will be used to buy goods and services four or five or six times a year?

Perhaps the principal factor is the *frequency with which paychecks are received.* The idea can best be explained through a numerical example. Consider a worker who earns $24,000 a year, paid to her in 12 monthly paychecks of $2,000 each. Suppose she spends the whole $2,000 over the course of each month and maintains a minimum balance in the checking account of $500. Each payday her bank balance will jump to $2,500 and then gradually decline as she makes withdrawals to purchase goods and services. Finally, on the day before her next paycheck arrives, her checking balance will be just $500. Over the course of a typical month, then, her average checking account balance will be $1,500 (halfway between $2,500 and $500).

Now suppose her employer switches to a twice-a-month payroll. Her paychecks come twice as often, but are reduced to $1,000 each. There is no reason for her rate of spending to change, but her average *cash balance* will change. For now her checking balance will rise only to $1,500 on payday (the $500 minimum balance plus the $1,000 paycheck), and it will still be drawn down gradually to

$500. Her average cash balance will therefore decline to $1,000 (halfway between $1,500 and $500). Why is this so? Because, with the next paycheck coming sooner than before, it is not necessary to keep as much cash in the bank in order to carry out a given quantity of transactions.

But what does this have to do with velocity? Notice that when she was on a monthly payroll, this worker's personal velocity was:

$$V = \frac{\text{Annual income}}{\text{Average cash balance}} = \frac{\$24{,}000}{\$1{,}500} = 16$$

When she switched to a semimonthly payroll, velocity rose to:

$$V = \frac{\text{Annual income}}{\text{Average cash balance}} = \frac{\$24{,}000}{\$1{,}000} = 24$$

The general lesson to be learned is that:

More frequent wage payments mean that people can conduct their transactions with lower average cash balances. Since they will want to hold less cash, money will circulate faster. In other words, velocity will rise.

A second factor influencing velocity is the nature and *efficiency of the payments mechanism,* including how quickly checks clear banks, the use of credit cards, and other methods of transferring funds. It is easy to see how this works.

Our example assumed that the worker holds her entire paycheck in her checking account until she uses it to make a purchase. But, given that ordinary checking accounts pay little or no interest, this may not be sensible behavior. If it is possible to convert interest-bearing assets into money on short notice and at low cost, a rational individual might use her paycheck to purchase such assets and then use credit cards for most purchases, making periodic transfers to her checking account as necessary. For the same amount of total transactions, then, she would require lower money balances. This means that money would circulate faster: Velocity would rise.

The incentive to limit cash holdings depends on the ease and speed with which it is possible to exchange money for other assets. This is what we mean by the "efficiency of the payments mechanism." As computerization has speeded up the bookkeeping procedures of banks, as financial innovations have made it possible to transfer funds rapidly between checking accounts and other assets, and as credit cards have come to be used instead of cash, the need to hold money balances has declined. By definition, then, velocity has risen.

In practice, changes in the payments mechanism have posed severe practical problems for analysts interested in predicting velocity. A host of financial innovations, beginning in the 1970s and continuing to this day (some of which were mentioned in Chapter 12's discussion of the definitions of money), have made forecasting velocity a hazardous occupation. In fact, many economists believe the task is impossible and should not even be attempted.

A third determinant of velocity is the *rate of interest*. The basic motive for economizing on money holdings is that most money (at least M1) pays little or no interest, while many alternative stores of value pay higher rates. The higher these alternative rates of interest, the greater the incentive to economize on holding money. Therefore, as interest rates rise, people want to hold less money. So the existing stock of money circulates faster, and velocity rises.

It is this factor that most directly undercuts the usefulness of the quantity theory of money as a guide for monetary policy. For in the last chapter we learned that expansionary monetary policy, which increases M, normally also decreases the interest rate. But if interest rates fall, other things being equal, velocity (V) will also fall. Thus, *when the Fed raises the money supply* (M), *the product* $M \times V$ *may go up by a smaller percentage than does* M *itself.*

One component of the interest rate is worth singling out for special attention: *the expected rate of inflation.* We explained in Chapter 6 why an "inflation premium" equal to the expected inflation rate often gets built into market interest rates.[1] Thus, in many instances, high inflation is the principal cause of high nominal interest rates. High rates of inflation, which erode the purchasing power of money, therefore lead both individuals and businesses to hold as little money as they can get by on—actions that increase velocity. To summarize this discussion of the determinants of velocity:

Velocity is not a strict constant but depends on such things as the frequency of payments, the efficiency of the financial system, the rate of interest, and the rate of inflation. Only by studying these determinants of velocity can we hope to predict the growth rate of nominal GDP from knowledge of the growth rate of the money supply.

MONETARISM: THE QUANTITY THEORY MODERNIZED

A group of economists called *monetarists* tries to do precisely this. Monetarists recognize that velocity changes, but they believe that such changes are fairly *predictable*—certainly in the long run and perhaps even in the short run. So they conclude that the best way to study economic activity is to start with the equation of exchange in growth-rate form:

$$\%\Delta M + \%\Delta V = \%\Delta P + \%\Delta Y$$

From here, careful study of the determinants of money growth (which we provided in the previous two chapters) and of changes in velocity (which we just completed) can be used to *predict* the growth rate of nominal GDP. Similarly, given an understanding of movements in V, control over M gives the Fed *control* over nominal GDP.

MONETARISM is a mode of analysis that uses the equation of exchange to organize and analyze macroeconomic data.

These are the central tenets of **monetarism.** When something happens in the economy, monetarists ask two questions:

1. What does this event do to the growth rate of money?
2. What does this event do to velocity?

From the answers, they assert that they can predict how the growth rate of nominal GDP will be affected.

By comparing the monetarist approach with the Keynesian approach that we described in the previous chapter, we can put both theories into perspective and understand the limitations of each. As we mentioned earlier, they differ more in style than in substance. Keynesians divide economic knowledge into four neat compartments—marked C, I, G, and $(X - IM)$—and unite them all with the equi-

---

[1]If you need review, turn back to pages 128–129.

librium condition that $Y = C + I + G + (X - IM)$. In Keynesian analysis, money affects the economy by first affecting interest rates.

Monetarists, on the other hand, organize their knowledge into two alternative boxes—labeled M and V—and then use a simple identity that says $M \times V = P \times Y$ to bring this knowledge to bear in predicting aggregate demand. In the monetarist model, the role of money in the national economy is not necessarily limited to working through interest rates.

The bit of arithmetic that multiplies M and V to get $P \times Y$ is neither more nor less profound than the one that adds up C, I, G and $(X - IM)$ to get Y. And certainly both are correct. The only substantive difference is that the monetarist equation leads to a prediction of *nominal* GDP while the Keynesian equation leads to a prediction of *real* GDP.

Why, then, do we not simply mesh the two theories—using the monetarist approach to study nominal GDP and the Keynesian approach to study real GDP? It seems that by doing so we could use the separate analyses of real and nominal GDP to obtain a prediction of the future behavior of the price level, which, of course, is the ratio of nominal GDP to real GDP.

The reason that this appealing procedure will not work helps point out the major limitation of each theory. *Taken by itself, either theory is incomplete.* Each gives us a picture of the *demand* side of the economy without saying anything about the *supply* side. To try to predict both the price level and real output solely from these demand-oriented models would be like trying to predict the price of peanuts by studying only the behavior of consumers and ignoring that of farmers. It just will not work. In terms of our earlier aggregate supply and demand analysis:

Both the monetarist and Keynesian analyses are ways of studying the *aggregate demand curve.* In neither case is it possible to learn anything about both output and the price level without also studying the *aggregate supply curve.*

Economists thus are forced to choose between two alternative ways of predicting aggregate demand. Those who choose the monetarist route will use velocity and the money supply to study aggregate demand in nominal terms. But then they must turn to the supply side to estimate how any predicted change in nominal demand gets apportioned between changes in production and changes in prices. The schematic diagram on page 290, with its emphasis on interest rates, plays little role in the monetarist analysis of how monetary policy affects the economy.

On the other hand, an economist working with the Keynesian approach will start by using the schematic diagram on page 290 to predict how monetary policy affects aggregate demand in real terms, that is, real GDP. But then he will have to turn to the aggregate supply curve to estimate the inflationary consequences of this real demand.

Which approach works better? There is no generally correct answer for all economies in all periods of time. When velocity behaved predictably in the 1960s and early 1970s, monetarism won many converts—in the United States and around the world. But, since then, velocity has behaved so erratically here and in many other countries that most economists have abandoned monetarism. Among the major industrial nations, only Germany still pays much attention to monetarist principles—and even there, erratic fluctuations in velocity have given the central bank fits.

FISCAL POLICY, INTEREST RATES, AND VELOCITY

We have now almost reconciled the Keynesian and monetarist views of how the economy operates. Because G is a part of $C + I + G + (X - IM)$, Keynesian analysis lends itself naturally to the study of fiscal policy. But we learned in the previous chapter that Keynesian economics also provides a powerful and important role for monetary policy: An increase in the money supply reduces interest rates, which, in turn, stimulates the demand for investment.

Monetarist analysis provides an obvious and direct route by which monetary policy influences both output and prices. But can the monetarist approach also handle fiscal policy? It can, because fiscal policy has an important effect on the rate of interest. Let us see how this works.

What happens to real output and the price level following, say, a rise in government purchases of goods and services? We learned in Chapter 11 that both real GDP (Y) and the price level (P) rise, and so nominal GDP certainly rises. But Chapter 13's analysis of the demand for money taught us that rising nominal GDP pushes the demand curve for money outward to the right. With no change in the supply curve for money, the rate of interest must rise. So *expansionary fiscal policy raises interest rates.*

If the government uses its spending and taxing weapons in the opposite direction, the same process works in reverse. Falling output and (possibly) falling prices shift the demand curve for money inward to the left. With a fixed supply curve for money, equilibrium in the money market leads to a lower interest rate. Thus:

Monetary policy is not the only type of policy that affects interest rates. Fiscal policy also affects interest rates. Specifically, increases in government spending or tax cuts normally push interest rates up, whereas restrictive fiscal policies normally pull interest rates down.

The fact that fiscal policy affects interest rates gives it a role in the monetarist model despite the fact that the equation of exchange, $M \times V = P \times Y$, does not include either government spending or taxation among its variables. Any fiscal policy that a Keynesian would call "expansionary"—higher spending, lower taxes, and so on—pushes up the rate of interest. And rising interest rates push up velocity because people want to hold less money when the interest they can earn on alternative assets increases. So it is through the V term in $M \times V$ that fiscal policy does its work in the monetarist framework. The equation of exchange then implies that nominal GDP must rise when, say, government spending increases—even if M is fixed—because velocity is higher.

Conversely, restrictive fiscal policies like tax increases and expenditure cuts reduce the quantity of money demanded and lower interest rates. The consequent drop in velocity reduces income through the equation of exchange, because the money supply circulates more slowly.

The translation, then, is complete. The Keynesian story about how fiscal policy works can be phrased in the monetarist dialect. And the monetarist tale about monetary policy can be told with a Keynesian accent. Furthermore, both modes of analysis help only to explain the mysteries of aggregate *demand* and must be supplemented by an analysis of aggregate *supply* to be complete. We must conclude, then, that:

The differences between Keynesians and monetarists have been grossly exaggerated by the news media. Indeed, when it comes to matters of basic economic theory, there are hardly any differences at all.

The fact that changes in fiscal policy move interest rates up and down has two other important consequences that merit some discussion.

APPLICATION: THE MULTIPLIER FORMULA REVISITED

We have just noted that expansionary fiscal policy raises interest rates. And we know that higher interest rates deter private investment spending. So when the government raises the G component of $C + I + G + (X - IM)$, one notable side effect will be to reduce the I component. Consequently, total spending will rise by less than simple multiplier analysis might suggest. The fact that a surge in government demand (G) discourages some private demand (I) provides another reason why the oversimplified multiplier formula, $1/(1 - \text{MPC})$, exaggerates the size of the multiplier:

Because a rise in G (or, for that matter, an autonomous rise in any component of total expenditure) pushes interest rates higher, and hence deters some investment spending, the increase in the sum $C + I + G + (X - IM)$ is smaller than what the oversimplified multiplier formula predicts.

Combining this observation with our previous analysis of the multiplier, we now have the following complete list of:

REASONS WHY THE OVERSIMPLIFIED MULTIPLIER FORMULA IS WRONG

1. It ignores variable imports, which reduce the size of the multiplier.
2. It ignores price-level changes, which reduce the size of the multiplier.
3. It ignores the income tax, which reduces the size of the multiplier.
4. It ignores the rising interest rates that accompany any autonomous increase in spending, which also reduce the size of the multiplier.

Notice that all four of these adjustments point in the same direction. No wonder the actual multiplier (estimated to be below 2 for the U.S. economy) is so much less than the oversimplified formula suggests.

APPLICATION: DEFICIT REDUCTION AND INVESTMENT

We will discuss the government budget deficit in greater detail in the next chapter. But one major argument for reducing the deficit is that lower deficits should lead to higher levels of private investment spending. It is now simple to understand why. The government reduces its budget deficit by engaging in contractionary fiscal policies—lower spending or higher taxes. But we have just seen that any such measure should reduce real interest rates. These lower real interest rates should spur investment spending.

DEBATE: SHOULD STABILIZATION POLICY RELY ON FISCAL OR MONETARY POLICY?

We have seen that the Keynesian and monetarist approaches are more like two different languages than two different theories. However, it is well-known that language influences attitudes in many subtle ways. For example, the Keynesian language biases things subtly toward thinking first about fiscal policy simply because G is a part of $C + I + G + (X - IM)$ while M works indirectly.

Monetarists, on the other hand, think first about the equation of exchange, $M \times V = P \times Y$, which makes the effect of money on aggregate demand apparent and direct.

Years ago, economists engaged in a spirited debate in which extreme monetarists claimed that fiscal policy was futile, while extreme Keynesians argued that monetary policy was useless. But substantial evidence accumulated against both extreme positions, and these arguments are rarely heard today.

Instead of arguing over which type of policy is more powerful, economists nowadays debate which type of medicine—fiscal or monetary—cures the patient more quickly. Up to now, we have ignored questions of timing and pretended that the authorities instantly noticed the need for stabilization policy, decided upon a course of action, and administered the appropriate medicine. In reality, each of these steps takes time.

First, delays in data collection mean that the latest macroeconomic data pertain to the economy of a few months ago. Second, one of the prices of democracy is that the government often takes a distressingly long time to decide what should be done, to muster the necessary political support, and to put its decisions into effect. Finally, our $7 trillion economy is a bit like a sleeping elephant that reacts rather sluggishly to moderate fiscal and monetary prods. As it turns out, these *lags in stabilization policy,* as they are called, play a pivotal role in the choice between fiscal and monetary policy. Here's why.

The main policy tool for manipulating consumer spending (C) is the personal income tax, and Chapter 7 documented why the fiscal policy planner can feel fairly confident that each $1 of tax reduction will lead to about 90 to 95 cents of additional spending *eventually.* But not all of this will happen at once.

First, consumers must learn about the tax change. Then they may need to be convinced that the change is permanent. Finally, there is the simple force of habit: Households need time to adjust their spending habits when circumstances change. For all these reasons, consumers may increase their spending by only 30 to 50 cents for each $1 of additional income within the first few months after a tax cut. Only gradually will they raise their spending up to about 90 to 95 cents for each additional dollar of income.

Lags are much longer for investment (I), which provides the main vehicle by which monetary policy affects aggregate demand. Planning for capacity expansion in a large corporation is a long, drawn-out process. Ideas must be submitted and approved, plans must be drawn up, funding acquired, orders for machinery or contracts for new construction placed. And most of this occurs *before* any appreciable amount of money is spent. Economists have found that much of the response of investment to changes in interest rates or tax provisions is delayed for several *years.*

The fact that C responds more quickly than I has important implications for the choice among alternative stabilization policies. The reason is that the most common varieties of fiscal policy either affect aggregate demand directly—G is a component of $C + I + G + (X - IM)$—or work through consumption with a relatively short lag, while monetary policy has its major effects on investment. Therefore:

Conventional types of fiscal policy actions, such as changes in G or in personal taxes, probably affect aggregate demand much more promptly than do monetary policy actions.

This important fact was once used to argue that fiscal policy should bear the major burden of economic stabilization. But such a conclusion is a bit hasty, for

"Daddy's not mad at you, dear—Daddy's mad at the Fed."

the lags we have just described—which are beyond the control of policymakers—are not the only ones affecting the timing of stabilization policy. Further lags stem from the behavior of the policymakers themselves! We are referring here to the delays that occur while the policymakers study the state of the economy, contemplate what steps they should take, and finally put their decisions into effect. And here monetary policy has a huge advantage; that is:

Policy lags are normally much shorter for monetary policy than for fiscal policy.

The reasons are apparent. The Federal Open Market Committee (FOMC) meets eight times a year—and more often if necessary. So monetary policy decisions are made frequently. And once the Fed decides on a course of action, it is normally executed immediately by buying or selling bonds on the open market.

In contrast, federal budgeting procedures operate on an annual budget cycle. Except in rare circumstances, *major* fiscal policy initiatives can occur only at the time of the annual budget. In principle, tax laws can be changed at any time; but the wheels of Congress grind slowly and are often gummed up by partisan politics. So it may take many months for Congress to change fiscal policy. Even President Clinton's first budget, which passed Congress in record time in 1993, took almost 6 months from introduction to enactment. And in 1995, Congress failed to pass any budget before the government's fiscal year began, leading to two partial shutdowns of the federal government. In sum, one has to be very optimistic to suppose that the government can take important fiscal policy actions on short notice.

So where does the combined effect of expenditure lags and policy lags leave us? With nothing conclusive, we are afraid—at least in principle. In practice, however, most observers of contemporary America find it unrealistic to imagine using fiscal policy rationally for stabilization purposes until both partisanship and the budget deficit are sharply reduced. For now, but not necessarily forever, monetary policy appears to be the only game in town.

DEBATE: SHOULD THE FED CONTROL THE MONEY SUPPLY OR CONTROL INTEREST RATES?

Once we recognize that monetary policy must bear the current burden of stabilization policy, other questions arise. One major controversy, which raged for decades, was over how the Federal Reserve should conduct monetary policy. Some economists argued that the Fed should use its open-market operations to control the rate of interest (r) while others, especially monetarists, insisted that the Fed should concentrate on controlling some measure of the money supply (M). To understand the nature of this debate, we must first understand why the Fed cannot control both M and r at the same time.

Figure 14-2 will help us see why. It shows an initial equilibrium in the money market at point E, where money demand curve M_0D_0 crosses money supply curve MS. Here the interest rate is $r = 5$ percent and the money stock is $M =$ \$830 billion. Let us assume that these are the Fed's targets for M and r; it wants to keep the money supply and interest rates just where they are.

If the demand curve for money holds still, this is possible. But suppose the demand for money is not so obliging. Suppose, instead, that the demand curve shifts outward to the position indicated by M_1D_1 in Figure 14-2. We learned in the last chapter that this might happen because output increases or because prices rise. Or it might happen simply because people decide to hold more

FIGURE 14-2

THE FEDERAL RESERVE'S POLICY DILEMMA

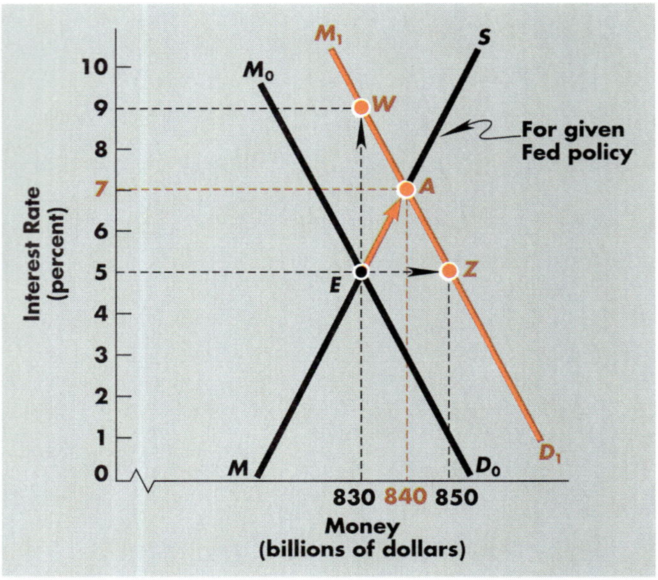

This diagram illustrates the dilemma facing the Fed when the demand schedule for money shifts. In this case, we suppose that it increases from M_0D_0 to M_1D_1. If the equilibrium at point *E* satisfied its goals both for the money supply ($830 billion) and for the rate of interest (5 percent), either one or both of these goals will have to be abandoned after the demand schedule shifts. Points *W*, *A*, and *Z* illustrate three of the many choices. At *W*, the Fed is keeping the money supply at $830 billion through contractionary policies, but at a cost of skyrocketing interest rates. At *Z*, the Fed is holding interest rates at 5 percent, but the required expansionary monetary policies raise the money supply to $850 billion. At *A*, the Fed is not adjusting its policy and is accepting an increase in both the money supply and the rate of interest.

money. Whatever the reason, the Fed can no longer achieve both of its previous targets.

If the Fed takes no action, the outward shift in the demand curve will push up both the quantity of money (*M*) and the rate of interest (*r*). Figure 14-2 shows this graphically as the move from point *E* to point *A*. If the demand curve for money shifts outward from M_0D_0 to M_1D_1, and there is no change in monetary policy (so the supply schedule does not move), the money stock rises to $840 billion and the interest rate rises to 7 percent.

But suppose, first, that the Fed is targeting the money supply and is therefore unwilling to let *M* rise. In that case, it must use contractionary open-market operations to prevent *M* from rising. But, in so doing, it will push *r* up even higher—as Figure 14-2 shows. After the demand curve for money shifts out, point *E* is unattainable. The Fed must choose from among the points on M_1D_1, and point *W* is the point on this curve that keeps the money supply at $830 billion. By pushing the supply curve inward so that it passes through point *W*, the Fed can hold *M* at $830 billion. But the interest rate will skyrocket to 9 percent.

Alternatively, if the Fed is pursuing an interest rate target, it might decide that a rise in *r* is to be avoided. In this case, the Fed would be forced to engage in expansionary open-market operations to prevent the outward shift of the demand curve for money from pushing *r* up. In terms of Figure 14-2, the interest rate can be held at 5 percent by shifting the supply curve outward to pass through point *Z*. But to do this, the Fed will have to let the money supply rise to $850 billion. To summarize this discussion:

When the demand curve for money shifts outward, the Fed must tolerate a rise in interest rates, a rise in the money stock, or both. It simply does not have the weapons to control *both* the supply of money *and* the interest rate. If it tries to keep *M* steady, then *r* will rise sharply. Conversely, if it tries to stabilize *r*, then *M* will shoot up.

TWO IMPERFECT ALTERNATIVES

For years, economists have debated how the Fed should deal with its inability to control both the money supply and the rate of interest. Should it adhere rigidly to its target growth path for the money supply, regardless of the consequences for interest rates? Should it hold interest rates steady even if that causes wild gyrations in the money stock? Or is some middle ground more appropriate? Let us explore the issues before considering what has actually been done.

The main problem with rigid targets for the *supply* of money is that the *demand* for money does not cooperate by growing smoothly and predictably from month to month; instead it dances about quite a bit in the short run. This confronts the recommendation to control the money supply with two problems:

1. It is almost impossible to achieve. Since the volume of money in existence depends on *both* the demand *and* supply curves, keeping *M* on target in the face of significant fluctuations in demand for money would require exceptional dexterity on the part of the Fed.
2. For reasons just explained, rigid adherence to money-stock targets might lead to wide fluctuations in interest rates, which could create an unsettled atmosphere for business decisions.

By the same token, even more powerful objections can be raised against exclusive concentration on interest rate movements. Since increases in nominal GDP shift the demand schedule for money outward (as in Figure 14-2), a central bank determined to keep interest rates from rising would have to expand the money supply in response. Conversely, when GDP sagged, it would have to contract the money supply to keep rates from falling. Thus, interest rate *pegging* would make the money supply expand in boom times and contract in recessions—with potentially grave consequences for the stability of the economy. Ironically, this is precisely the sort of monetary behavior the Federal Reserve System was designed to prevent. Hence, if the Fed is to control interest rates, it had better formulate flexible targets, not fixed ones.

WHAT HAS THE FED ACTUALLY DONE?

In the early part of the postwar period, the predominant Keynesian view held that the interest rate target was much the more important of the two. The rationale was that gyrating interest rates would cause abrupt and unsettling changes in investment spending, which in turn would make the whole economy fluctuate. Stabilizing interest rates was therefore believed to be the best way to stabilize GDP. If doing so required fluctuations in the money supply, so be it. Consequently, the Fed focused on interest rates and paid little attention to the money supply.

In the 1960s, this prevailing view came under attack by Professor Milton Friedman and other monetarists. They argued that the Fed's obsession with stabilizing interest rates actually *destabilized* the economy by making the money supply fluctuate too much. The monetarist prescription was simple: The Fed should stop worrying about fluctuations in interest rates and make the money supply grow at a constant rate from month to month and year to year.

Monetarism made important inroads at the Fed during the inflationary 1970s. Early in the decade, the central bank began to keep much closer tabs on the money stock than it previously had. More important, a major change in the conduct of monetary policy was announced by then-Chairman Paul Volcker in

October 1979. Henceforth, he asserted, the Fed would stick more closely to its target for money-stock growth regardless of the implications for interest rates. Interest rates would go wherever the law of supply and demand took them.

According to our analysis, this change in policy should have led to wider fluctuations in interest rates. And it did. Unfortunately, the Fed ran into some bad luck. The ensuing 3 years were marked by unusually severe gyrations in the demand for money, so the ups and downs of interest rates were far more extreme than anyone had expected. Figure 14-3 gives an indication of just how volatile interest rates were between late 1979 and late 1982. Naturally, this erratic performance provoked some heavy criticism of the Fed.

Then, in October 1982, Chairman Volcker announced that the Fed was temporarily abandoning its attempts to stick to a target growth path for the money supply. Although he did not say so, his announcement presumably meant that the Fed started once again to pay more attention to interest rate targets. As you can see in Figure 14-3, interest rates became much more stable after the change in policy. Most observers think this was no coincidence.

After 1982, the Fed gradually distanced itself from the position that the money supply should grow at a constant rate. Finally, in 1993, Chairman Alan Greenspan officially confirmed what was already widely known: that the Fed was no longer using the various *M*s to guide policy. He strongly hinted that the Fed was targeting interest rates, especially *real* interest rates, instead—a hint that has been repeated many times since then. In truth, the Fed had little choice. The demand curve for money behaved so erratically and so unpredictably in the 1980s and 1990s that stabilizing the money stock was probably impossible and certainly undesirable. Whether this situation will continue is anyone's guess. But as of this writing, the Fed has shown no inclination to return to the *M*s.

DEBATE: THE SHAPE OF THE AGGREGATE SUPPLY CURVE

Another lively debate over stabilization policy revolves around the shape of the economy's aggregate supply curve. Many economists think of the aggregate supply curve as quite flat—as in Figure 14-4(a)—so that large increases in output

FIGURE 14-3 THE BEHAVIOR OF INTEREST RATES, 1979–1985

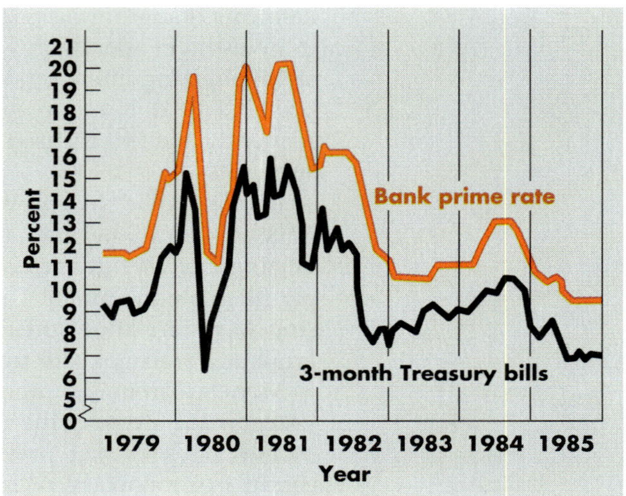

This chart traces interest rate movements from 1979 through 1985. Notice the extreme volatility of rates during the period from late 1979 to mid-1982—the period in which the Fed was concentrating more on stabilizing the money supply. After mid-1982, interest rates became much less volatile.

FIGURE 14-4

ALTERNATIVE VIEWS OF THE AGGREGATE SUPPLY CURVE

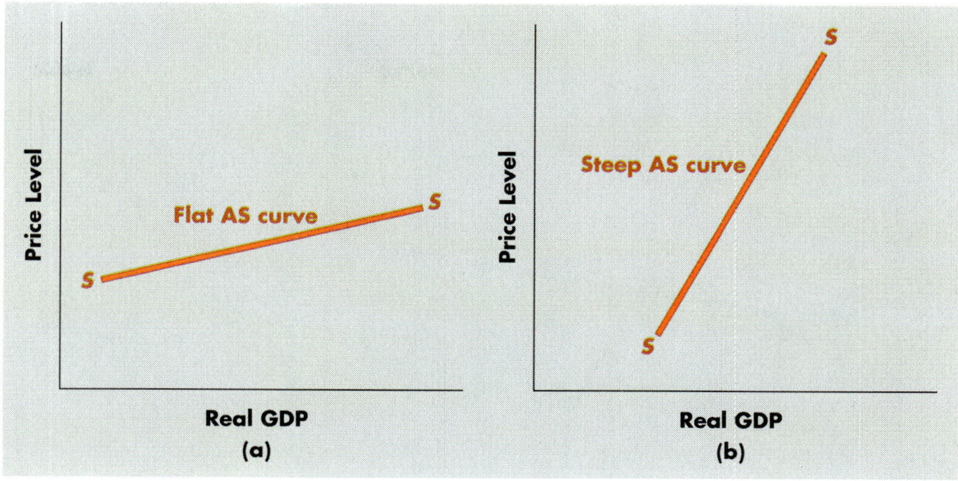

Some economists think of the economy's aggregate supply schedule as very flat, as in Panel (a). Others think of it as quite steep, as in Panel (b).

can be achieved with little inflation. But other economists envision the supply curve as steep, as in Figure 14-4(b), so that prices are very responsive to changes in output. The differences for public policy are substantial.

If the aggregate supply curve is flat, expansionary fiscal or monetary policy that raises the aggregate demand curve can buy large gains in real GDP at low cost in terms of inflation. In Figure 14-5(a), stimulation of demand pushes the aggregate demand curve outward from D_0D_0 to D_1D_1, thereby moving the economy's equilibrium from point *E* to point *A*. There is a substantial rise in output ($400 billion) with only a pinch of inflation (1 percent).

Conversely, when the supply curve is flat, a restrictive stabilization policy is not a very effective way to bring inflation down; instead, it serves mainly to reduce real output, as Figure 14-5(b) shows. Here, a leftward shift of the aggregate demand curve moves equilibrium from point *E* to point *B*, lowering real GDP by $400 billion but cutting the price level by merely 1 percent.

Things are quite different if the aggregate supply curve is steep. In that case, expansionary fiscal or monetary policies will cause a good deal of inflation without adding much to real GDP. [See Figure 14-6(a) on page 311, where expansionary policies shift equilibrium from *E* to *A*.] Similarly, contractionary policies are effective ways of bringing down the price level without much sacrifice of output, as shown by the shift from *E* to *B* in Figure 14-6(b).

The resolution of this debate is of fundamental importance for the proper conduct of stabilization policy. If the supply curve is flat, stabilization policy is much more effective at combating recession than inflation. If the supply curve is steep, precisely the reverse is true.

But why does the argument persist? Why cannot economists determine the shape of the aggregate supply curve and stop arguing? The answer is that supply conditions in the real world are far more complicated than our simple diagrams suggest. Some industries may have flat supply curves while others have steep ones. For reasons explained in Chapter 10, supply curves shift over time. And, unlike many laboratory scientists, economists cannot perform the controlled experiments that would reveal the shape of the aggregate supply curve directly. Instead, they must use statistical inference to make educated guesses.

FIGURE 14-5 STABILIZATION POLICY WITH A FLAT AGGREGATE SUPPLY CURVE

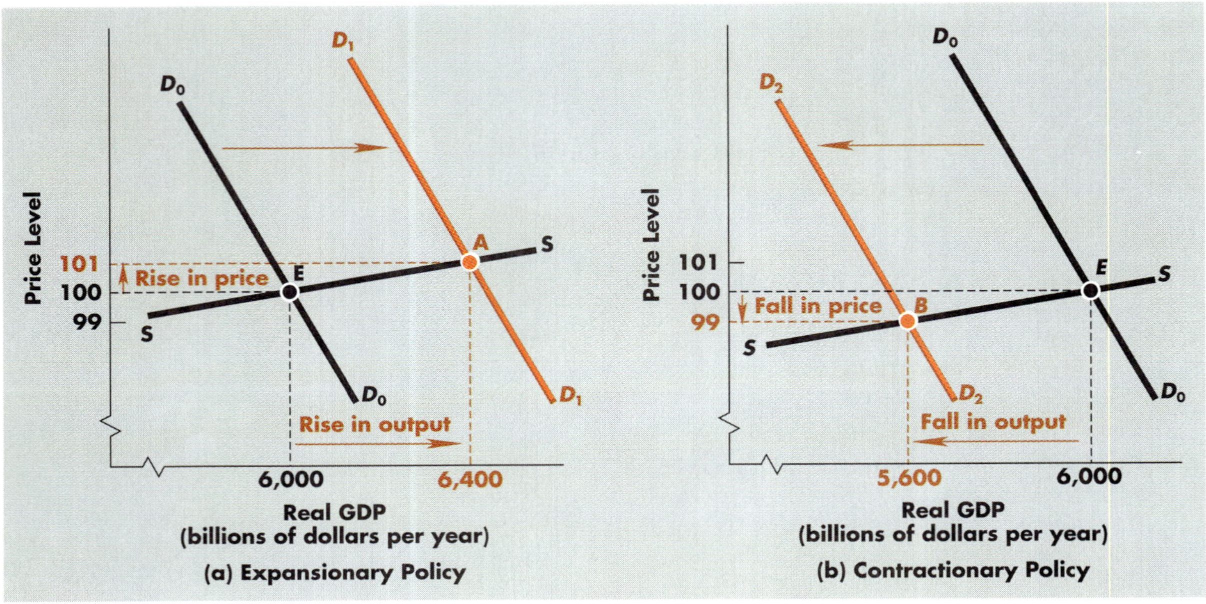

These two diagrams show that stabilization policy is much more effective as an antirecession policy than as an anti-inflation policy when the aggregate supply curve is flat. In Panel (a), monetary or fiscal policies push the aggregate demand curve outward from D_0D_0 to D_1D_1, causing equilibrium to shift from point *E* to point *A*. You can see that output rises substantially (from $6,000 billion to $6,400 billion), while prices rise only slightly (from 100 to 101, or 1 percent). So the policy is quite successful. In Panel (b), contractionary policies are used to combat inflation by pushing the aggregate demand curve inward from D_0D_0 to D_2D_2. Prices do fall slightly (from 100 to 99) as equilibrium shifts from point *E* to point *B*, but real output falls much more dramatically (from $6,000 billion to $5,600 billion); so the policy has had little success.

Although empirical research is proceeding, our understanding of aggregate supply remains much less settled than our understanding of aggregate demand. Nevertheless, many economists believe that the outline of a consensus view has emerged. This view holds that the steepness of the aggregate supply schedule depends on the time period under consideration.

In the very short run, the aggregate supply curve is quite flat, so Figure 14-5 applies. Over short time periods, therefore, fluctuations in aggregate demand have large effects on output but only minor effects on prices. In the long run, however, the aggregate supply curve becomes quite steep, perhaps even vertical. In that case, Figure 14-6 applies, so that changes in demand affect mainly prices, not output.[2] The implication is that:

Any change in aggregate demand will have most of its effect on *output* in the short run but on *prices* in the long run.

Not all economists accept this middle-of-the-road view, but many do.

---

[2]The reasoning behind the view that the aggregate supply curve is flat in the short run but steep in the long run will be developed in Chapter 16.

FIGURE 14-6 STABILIZATION POLICY WITH A STEEP AGGREGATE SUPPLY CURVE

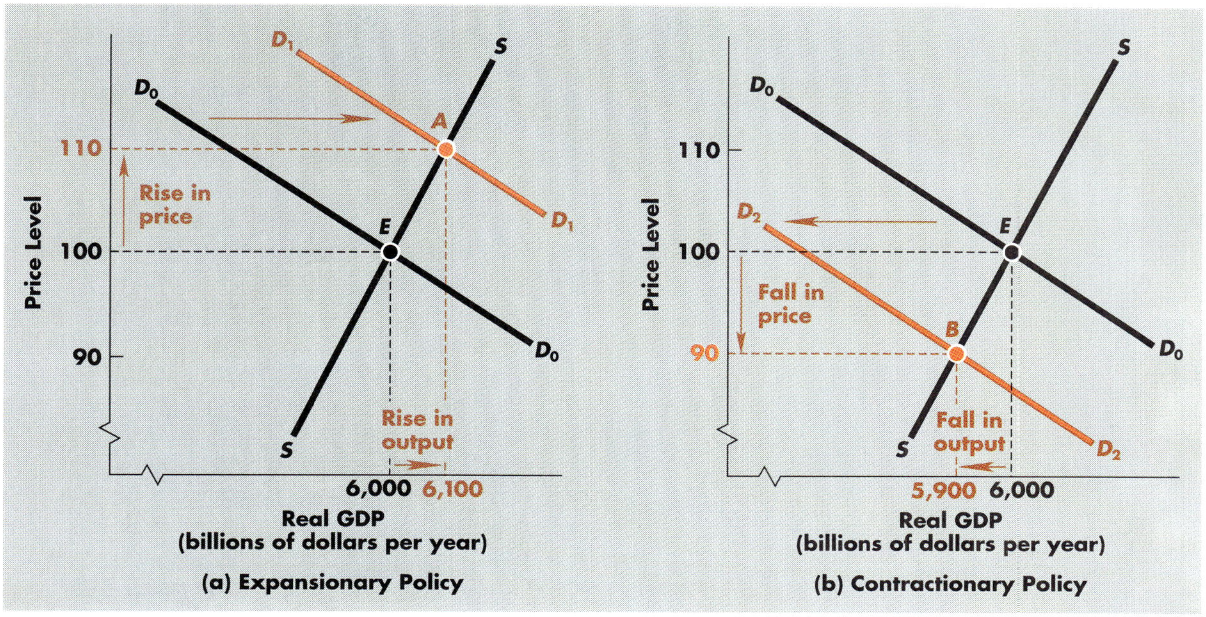

These two diagrams show that stabilization policy is much more effective at fighting inflation than at fighting recession when the aggregate supply curve is steep. In Panel (a), expansionary policies that push aggregate demand outward from D_0D_0 to D_1D_1 raise output by only $100 billion but push up prices by 10 percent as equilibrium moves from point *E* to point *A*. So demand management is not a good way to end a recession. In Panel (b), contractionary policies that pull aggregate demand inward to D_2D_2 are successful in that they lower prices markedly (from 100 to 90, or about 10 percent) but reduce output only slightly (from $6,000 billion to $5,900 billion).

DEBATE: SHOULD THE GOVERNMENT INTERVENE?

We have yet to consider what may be the most fundamental and controversial debate of all—the issue posed as a puzzle at the beginning of the chapter. Is it likely that the government can conduct a successful stabilization policy? Or are its well-intentioned efforts likely to be harmful, so that it would be better to adhere to fixed rules?

This controversy has raged for several decades, and there is no end in sight. It is partly a political or philosophical debate because economists, like other people, come with both liberal and conservative stripes. Liberal economists tend to be more intervention-minded and hence look more favorably on discretionary stabilization policy. Conservative economists are more inclined to keep the government's hands off the economy and hence are more attracted to fixed rules. Such political differences are not surprising. But more than ideology propels the debate. We need to understand the economic issues.

Critics of stabilization policy point to the lags and uncertainties that surround the operation of both fiscal and monetary policies—lags and uncertainties that we have stressed repeatedly in this and earlier chapters. Will the Fed's actions have the desired effects on the money supply? What will these actions do to interest rates and spending? Can fiscal policy actions be taken promptly? How large is the expenditure multiplier? The list could go on and on.

They look at this formidable catalogue of difficulties, add a dash of skepticism about our ability to forecast the future state of the economy (see below), and worry that stabilization policy may do more harm than good. These skeptics advise both the fiscal and monetary authorities to pursue a passive policy rather than an active one—adhering to fixed rules that, while incapable of ironing out every bump in the economy's growth path, will at least keep it roughly on track in the long run.

Advocates of active stabilization policy admit that perfection is unattainable. But they are much *more optimistic* about the prospects for success. And they are much *less optimistic* about how smoothly the economy would function in the absence of demand management. They therefore advocate discretionary increases in government spending (or decreases in taxes) and lower interest rates when the economy has a recessionary gap. Such policies, they believe, will help keep the economy closer to its full-employment growth path.

Naturally, each side can point to evidence that buttresses its own view. Activists look back with pride at the tax cut of 1964 and the sustained period of economic growth that it helped usher in. They also point to the tax cut of 1975, which was enacted at just about the trough of a severe recession, the Federal Reserve's switch to easy money in 1982, and the Fed's expert steering of the economy from 1992 to 1995. Advocates of rules remind us of the government's refusal to curb what was obviously a situation of runaway demand during the 1966–1968 Vietnam buildup, its overexpansion of the economy in 1972, the monetary overkill that helped bring on the sharp recession of 1981–1982, and the inadequate antirecession policies of the early 1990s.

The historical record of fiscal and monetary policy is far from glorious. It shows that while the authorities have sometimes taken appropriate and timely action to stabilize the economy, there are also many cases in which they either took inappropriate steps or did nothing at all. The question of whether the government should adopt passive rules or attempt an activist stabilization policy therefore merits a closer look. As we shall see, the lags in the effects of policy that we discussed earlier in this chapter play a pivotal role in the debate.

LAGS AND THE RULES-VERSUS-DISCRETION DEBATE

The reason why lags lead to a fundamental difficulty for stabilization policy—a difficulty so formidable that it has led some economists to conclude that attempts to stabilize economic activity are likely to do more harm than good—can be explained best by referring to Figure 14-7. Here we chart the behavior of both actual and potential GDP over the course of a business cycle in a hypothetical economy with no stabilization policy. At point *A*, the economy begins to slip into a recession and does not recover to full employment until point *D*. Then, between points *D* and *E*, it overshoots and is in an inflationary boom.

The case for stabilization policy runs like this. Policymakers recognize that the recession is a serious problem at point *B* and take appropriate actions. These actions have their major effects around point *C* and therefore curb both the depth and the length of the recession.

But suppose the lags are really longer and less predictable than this. Suppose, for example, that actions do not come until point *C* and that stimulative policies do not have their major effects until after point *D*. Then policy will be of little

FIGURE 14-7 A TYPICAL BUSINESS CYCLE

This is a stylized representation of the relationship between actual and potential GDP during a typical business cycle. The imaginary economy slips into a recession at point *A*, bottoms out around point *B*, and is in a recovery period until point *D*. After point *D*, it enters an inflationary boom that lasts until point *E*.

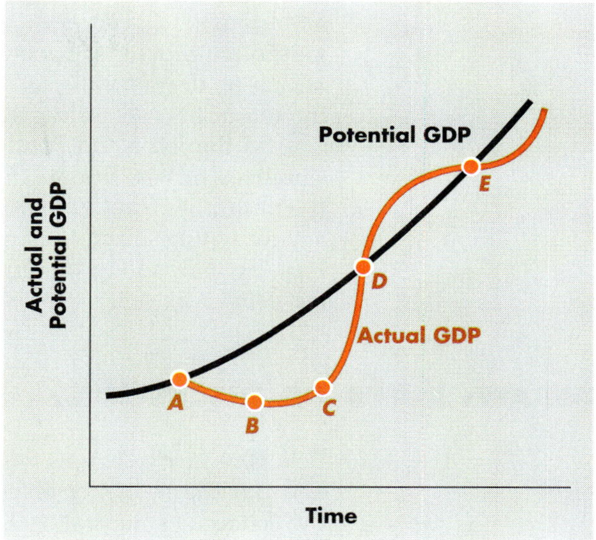

help during the recession and will actually do harm by overstimulating the economy during the ensuing boom. Thus:

In the presence of long lags, attempts at stabilizing the economy can actually succeed in destabilizing it.

Because of this, some economists argue that we are better off letting the economy alone and relying on its natural self-corrective forces to cure recessions and inflations. Instead of embarking on periodic programs of monetary and fiscal stimulus or restraint, they advise policymakers to stick to fixed rules, that is, to rigid formulas that ignore current economic events.

AUTOMATIC STABILIZERS

An **AUTOMATIC STABILIZER** is any arrangement that automatically serves to support aggregate demand when it would otherwise sag and to hold down aggregate demand when it would otherwise surge ahead. In this way, an automatic stabilizer reduces the sensitivity of the economy to shifts in demand.

We have already mentioned the monetarist policy rule: The Fed should keep the money supply growing at a constant rate. For fiscal policy, proponents of rules often recommend that the government resist temptations to manage aggregate demand actively and rely instead on **automatic stabilizers**—features of the economy that reduce its sensitivity to shocks.

Examples of automatic stabilizers are not hard to find in the federal budget. The personal income tax is the most obvious example. The tax acts as a shock absorber because it makes disposable income, and thus consumer spending, less sensitive to fluctuations in GDP. When GDP rises, disposable income (*DI*) rises less because part of the increase in GDP is siphoned off by the U.S. Treasury. This helps limit the upward fluctuation in consumption spending. And when GDP falls, *DI* falls less sharply because part of the loss is absorbed by the Treasury rather than by consumers. So consumption does not drop as much as it otherwise might. Thus, as we noted in Chapter 11, income taxes lower the value of the multiplier. In truth, the much-maligned personal income tax is one of several features of our modern economy that helps ensure against a repeat performance of the Great Depression.

There are many other automatic stabilizers in our economy. For example, Chapter 6 discussed the U.S. system of unemployment insurance. This serves as an automatic stabilizer in a similar way. When GDP drops and people lose their jobs, unemployment benefits prevent the disposable incomes of the jobless from falling as dramatically as their earnings. As a result, unemployed workers can maintain their spending, and consumption fluctuates less than employment.

And the list could continue. The basic principle is the same: Each automatic stabilizer serves, in one way or another, as a shock absorber, thereby lowering the multiplier. And each does so without the need for any decision maker to take action. Unlike discretionary policy changes, automatic stabilizers are not bothered by either long or unpredictable lags because, in a word, they work *automatically.*

DEBATE: RULES OR DISCRETION?

Believers in fixed rules assert that we should forget about discretionary policy and put the economy on automatic pilot—relying on automatic stabilizers and the economy's natural, self-correcting mechanisms. Are they right? As usual, the answer depends on many factors.

HOW FAST DOES THE ECONOMY'S SELF-CORRECTING MECHANISM WORK?

We emphasized in Chapter 10 that the economy has a self-correcting mechanism. If the economy can cure recessions and inflations quickly by itself, then the case for intervention is weak. For if such problems typically last only a short time, then lags in discretionary stabilization policy mean that the medicine will often have its major effects only after the disease is over. In terms of Figure 14-7, this would be a case where point *D* comes very close to point *A*.

While extreme advocates of rules argue that this is what indeed happens, most economists agree that the economy's self-correcting mechanism is slow and not terribly reliable, even when supplemented by the automatic stabilizers. On this count, then, a point is scored for discretionary policy.

HOW LONG ARE THE LAGS IN STABILIZATION POLICY?

We explained earlier why long and unpredictable lags in the formulation or operation of stabilization make it unlikely that policy can do much good. Short, reliable lags point in the opposite direction. Thus, advocates of fixed rules emphasize the length of lags while proponents of discretion discount them.

Who is right? It all depends on the circumstances. Sometimes fiscal policy actions are taken promptly, and the economy receives much of the stimulus from expansionary policy within a year after slipping into a recession. While far from perfect, such timely actions certainly would be felt soon enough to do some good. But, as we have seen, very slow fiscal responses may actually be destabilizing. Since history offers examples of each type, no general conclusion can be drawn.

HOW ACCURATE ARE ECONOMIC FORECASTS?

One way to cut down the policy-making lag enormously is to have good economic forecasts. If we could see a recession coming a full year ahead of time (which we certainly *cannot* do), even a rather sluggish policy response would still be timely. In terms of Figure 14-7, this would be a case where the recession is predicted well before point *A*.

It therefore behooves us to take a look at the techniques that economists in universities, government agencies, and private businesses have developed over the years to assist them in predicting what the economy will do. There are a variety of techniques, none of them foolproof.

TECHNIQUES OF ECONOMIC FORECASTING

THE USE OF ECONOMETRIC MODELS

An **ECONOMETRIC MODEL** is a set of mathematical equations that embody the economist's model of the economy.

Among the most widely publicized forecasts are those generated by the use of **econometric models** of the economy. Put simply, an econometric model is merely a mathematical version of the models of macroeconomic activity that we have described in Parts II and III. The difference is that the basic notions are cast in equations rather than in diagrams. For example, our consumption function could have been expressed by the formula:

$$C = a + bDI$$

where C is consumer spending and DI is disposable income, instead of by a graph.[3]

The builder of an econometric model takes equations like these and uses actual data to estimate the sizes of a and b. For example, statistical analysis may lead to the conclusion that the correct magnitude of a in the previous formula is approximately 300 and that the most reasonable value of b is 0.75. Then the consumption function formula is:

$$C = 300 + 0.75DI$$

that is, consumer spending is $300 billion plus 75 percent of disposable income. The economist can complete the model by adding a definition of disposable income as GDP minus tax receipts:

$$DI = Y - T$$

and appending the fact that GDP is the sum of C, I, G and $(X - IM)$:

$$Y = C + I + G + (X - IM)$$

This simple model has a total of three equations. If we hypothesize that government purchases, tax receipts, net exports, and investment are all unaffected by the relationships in the model, then these three equations are just enough to determine the values of the three remaining variables: C, DI, and Y. These last three variables are called the model's *endogenous variables*, meaning that their values are determined *inside* the model. The remaining variables—G, T, I, and $(X - IM)$—are called the model's *exogenous variables* because they must be provided from *outside* the model. Given an econometric model, it takes only algebra to turn forecasts of the exogenous variables into corresponding forecasts of the endogenous variables.

Models actually used to forecast the behavior of the U.S. economy have hundreds of variables and equations. Because of their complexity, the only practical

[3]This is nothing but the formula for a straight line with a slope of b and an intercept of a.

way to solve them for forecasts of all the endogenous variables is to use a high-speed computer. But making the forecasts accurate is another thing entirely because of the "GIGO" (garbage in, garbage out) problem: If you feed garbage into a computer, that's exactly what will come out at the end. In the forecasting context, this "garbage" can be either inaccurate forecasts of the exogenous variables or bad equations. This is why model builders are constantly seeking to improve their equations. But they have yet to achieve perfection.

And, even if they did, their forecasts would still not be infallible because there is a certain amount of unavoidable randomness in macroeconomic behavior. After all, we are dealing with the behavior of literally millions of individuals and business firms, and events essentially outside our control can sometimes exert a profound influence on our economy. (Example: The Gulf war in 1990 made both inflation and unemployment higher than forecasters expected.) So forecasts of the exogenous variables are bound to be wide of the mark at times. Furthermore, econometric models are basically complicated statistical summaries of the past. No one can really be sure that the future will be like the past. But this is what we assume whenever we forecast with an econometric model.

LEADING INDICATORS

A **LEADING INDICATOR** is a variable that, experience has shown, normally turns down before recessions start and turns up before expansions begin.

A second forecasting method exploits observed historical timing relationships through the use of certain **leading indicators** that have in the past given advance warning of economic events.

For example, the stock market is a leading indicator because stock market downturns normally begin several months before downturns in industrial production. *Why* does this happen? Does the decline in the stock market cause economic downturns by reducing consumer spending? Or are both the stock market and industrial production just reacting to some other influence, with the stock market's reaction coming sooner? Certainly these are fascinating questions. But the answers may not be crucial to a forecaster *if* the stock market continues to be as good a leading indicator of industrial production in the future as it has been in the past. In that event, she can make use of the observed relationship between stock prices and industrial production for forecasting even if she does not entirely understand it.

As it turns out, however, excessive reliance on any single leading indicator produces an unimpressive forecasting record. An obvious solution is to look at many indicators. But when we do this, we often receive conflicting signals. If one indicator is rising rapidly while another is falling, what are we to do?

One way to resolve this conflict is to combine several leading indicators into one. For example, every month the news media report the latest reading on the Conference Board's composite index of 11 leading indicators. One frequently cited rule of thumb holds that three consecutive monthly declines in this index indicate that a recession is on the way. Unfortunately, history shows that this rule signals many downturns that never come. (The most recent example was in 1995.)

SURVEY DATA

A third method of forecasting utilizes periodic surveys of the intentions of business and consumers. These surveys are conducted by government agencies, by business groups like the Conference Board and the National Association of Purchasing Managers, and by the Survey Research Center of the University of Michigan. Their findings are published in the financial press and are widely used by economists in industry, government, and academia. Some economists have found them useful in forecasting, say, consumer spending and industrial production.

JUDGMENTAL FORECASTS

This term is used to describe the forecasts of those opportunistic (and undoubtedly prudent!) forecasters who refuse to rely on any one method, but look instead at every available scrap of evidence. They study the outputs of the econometric models; they watch the leading indicators; and they scrutinize the findings of surveys. At times, it seems, they even gaze at the stars. Somehow, judgmental forecasters distill all this information in their heads and arrive at a forecast of GDP and other key variables. How do they go about it? An outside observer can never really tell, since the very nature of judgmental forecasting precludes the existence of a formula that can be written down or precisely described.

Official forecasts of the Federal Reserve, the Council of Economic Advisers, and the Congressional Budget Office are all judgmental. So are virtually all forecasts made by private business economists.

THE ACCURACY OF ECONOMIC FORECASTS

Which method wins the prize for the most accurate forecasts? First, no technique is clearly superior all the time. If it were, no one would use any other method. Second, because econometric forecasters use surveys, lead-lag patterns, and judgment in forming their predictions of exogenous variables, and since judgmental forecasters watch the models and surveys closely, a clean comparison is impossible. However, it seems that the most accurate forecasts have been derived by judgmental adjustment of forecasts from econometric models.

How accurate are economic forecasts? That depends both on the variable being forecast (consumption, for example, is easier than investment) and on the time period (for example, recession years are particularly difficult times for forecasters). To give a rough idea of magnitudes, forecasts of either the inflation rate or the real GDP growth rate for the year ahead typically err by plus or minus 3/4 to 1 percentage point. But, in a bad year for forecasters, errors of 2 or 3 percentage points are common.

Is this record good enough? That depends on how the forecasts are used. It is certainly not good enough to support so-called *fine tuning,* that is, attempts to keep the economy always within a hair's breadth of full employment. But it probably is good enough if our interest in using discretionary stabilization policy is to close persistent and sizable gaps between actual and potential GDP.

OTHER DIMENSIONS OF THE RULES-VERSUS-DISCRETION DEBATE

While lags and forecasting play major roles in the debate between advocates of rules and advocates of discretionary policy, these are not the only battlegrounds.

THE SIZE OF GOVERNMENT

One bogus argument that is nonetheless sometimes heard is that active fiscal policy must inevitably lead to a growing public sector. Since proponents of fixed rules tend also to oppose big government, they view this as undesirable. Of course, others think that a larger public sector is just what society needs.

This argument, however, is completely beside the point because, as we pointed out in Chapter 11 (page 238): *One's opinion about the proper size of government should have nothing to do with one's view on stabilization policy.* For example, President Ronald Reagan was as conservative as they come and devoted to *shrinking* the size of the public sector. But his tax-cutting initiatives in the early 1980s constituted an extremely *activist* policy to spur the economy. Furthermore, most stabilization policy these days is *monetary* policy, which neither increases nor decreases the size of government.

UNCERTAINTIES CAUSED BY GOVERNMENT POLICY

Advocates of rules are on stronger ground when they argue that frequent changes in tax laws, government spending programs, or monetary conditions make it difficult for firms and consumers to formulate and carry out rational plans. They argue that the authorities can provide a more stable environment for the private sector by adhering to fixed rules, which are known to businesses and consumers.

No one disputes that a more stable environment is better for private planning. But supporters of discretionary policy emphasize that stability in the economy is more important than stability in the government budget (or in Federal Reserve operations). The goal of stabilization policy is to help *prevent* gyrations in the pace of economic activity by *causing* timely gyrations in the government budget (or in monetary policy). Which atmosphere is better for business, they ask, one in which fiscal and monetary rules keep things peaceful on Capitol Hill and at the Federal Reserve while recessions and inflations rack the economy, or one in which policy instruments are changed abruptly on occasion but the economy grows more steadily? They think that the answer is self-evident.

A POLITICAL BUSINESS CYCLE?

A final argument used by advocates of rules is political rather than economic in nature. Fiscal policy, they note, is decided upon by elected politicians: the president and members of Congress. When elections are on the horizon (and for members of the House of Representatives they *always* are), politicians may be as concerned with keeping their jobs as with doing what is right for the economy. This leaves fiscal policy subject to all sorts of "political manipulations," meaning that lawmakers may take inappropriate actions to attain short-run political goals. A system of purely automatic stabilization, its proponents argue, would eliminate this peril by replacing the rule of men by the rule of law.

It is certainly *possible* that politicians could deliberately *cause* economic instability to help their own reelection. And some observers of these "political business cycles" have claimed that several American presidents have taken full advantage of the opportunity. Furthermore, even if there is no insidious intent, politicians may take the wrong actions for perfectly honorable reasons. Decisions in the political arena are never clear-cut, and it certainly is easy to find examples of grievous errors in the history of U.S. fiscal policy.

So, taken as a whole, the political argument against discretionary fiscal policy seems to have a great deal of merit. But what are we to do about it? It is unrealistic to believe that fiscal decisions could or should be made by a group of objective and nonpartisan technicians. Tax and budget policies require inherently political decisions which, in a democracy, should be made by elected officials.

This fact may seem worrisome in view of the possibilities for political chicanery. But it should not bother us any more (or any less!) than similar maneuvering in other areas of policy-making. After all, the same problem besets international relations, national defense, formulation and enforcement of the law, and so on. Politicians make all these decisions for us, subject only to sporadic accountability at elections. Is there really any reason why fiscal decisions should be different?

But monetary policy is different. Because Congress was concerned that elected officials have short time horizons, and might therefore pursue monetary policies that are too inflationary, it long ago gave the unelected technocrats at the Federal Reserve System day-to-day decision-making authority over monetary policy. There is political influence over monetary policy, but it is quite indirect: The Fed must report to Congress, and the president has the power to appoint Federal Reserve governors to his liking.

CONCLUSION: WHAT SHOULD BE DONE?

So where do we come out on the question posed at the start of this chapter? On balance, is it better to pursue the best discretionary policy we can, knowing full well that perfection cannot be achieved? Or is it wiser to rely on fixed rules and automatic stabilizers?

In weighing the pros and cons, your basic view of the economy is crucial. Some economists believe that the economy, if left unmanaged, would generate a series of ups and downs that are hard to predict, but that it would correct each of them by itself in a relatively short period of time. They conclude that, because of long lags and poor forecasts, our ability to anticipate whether the economy will need stimulus or restraint by the time policy actions have their effects is quite limited. And so they advocate fixed rules.

Other economists liken the economy to a giant glacier with a great deal of inertia. This means that, if we observe an inflationary or recessionary gap today, it is likely still to be there a year or two from now because the self-correcting mechanism works so slowly. In such a world, accurate forecasting is not imperative, even if policy lags are long. If we base policy on a forecast of a 2 percent gap between actual and potential GDP a year from now, and the gap turns out to be only 1 percent, we still will have done the right thing despite the inaccurate forecast. So holders of this view of the economy tend to support discretionary policy.

There is certainly no consensus on this issue, either among economists or among politicians. After all, the question touches upon political ideology as well as economics. And liberals have always looked to government to solve social problems, while conservatives have consistently pointed out that many efforts of government fail despite the best intentions. A prudent view of the matter might be that:

The case for active discretionary policy is strong when the economy has a serious deficiency or excess of aggregate demand. However, advocates of fixed rules are right that it is unwise to try to iron out every little wiggle in the growth path of GDP.

But one thing seems certain: The rules-versus-discretion debate seems likely to go on for quite some time.

SUMMARY

1. Monetarist and Keynesian analyses are two different ways of studying the determination of aggregate demand. Neither is a complete theory of the behavior of the economy until aggregate supply is brought into the picture.
2. **Velocity** (V) is the ratio of nominal GDP to the stock of money (M). It indicates how quickly money circulates.
3. One important determinant of velocity is the rate of interest (r). At higher interest rates, people find it less attractive to hold money because money pays no or little interest. Thus, when r rises, money circulates faster, and V rises.
4. **Monetarism** is a type of analysis that focuses attention on velocity and the money supply (M). Though monetarists realize that V is not constant, they believe that it is predictable enough to make it a useful tool for policy analysis and forecasting.
5. Because it raises output and prices, and hence increases the demand for money, expansionary fiscal policy pushes interest rates higher. This is how a monetarist explains the effect of fiscal policy. Because higher r leads to higher velocity, it leads to a higher product $M \times V$ even if M is unchanged.
6. Because fiscal policy actions affect aggregate demand either directly through G or indirectly through C, the expenditure lags between fiscal actions and their effects on aggregate demand are probably fairly short. By contrast, monetary policy operates mainly on investment, I, which responds slowly to changes in interest rates.
7. However, the policy-making lag normally is much longer for fiscal policy than for monetary policy. Hence, when the two lags are combined, it is not clear which type of policy acts more quickly.
8. Because it cannot control the demand curve for money, the Federal Reserve cannot control *both* M and r. If the demand for money changes, the Fed must decide whether it wants to hold M steady, hold r steady, or adopt some compromise position.
9. Monetarists emphasize the importance of stabilizing the growth path of the money supply while Keynesians put more emphasis on keeping interest rates on target.
10. In practice, the Fed has changed its views on this issue several times. For decades, it attached primary importance to interest rates. Between 1979 and 1982, it stressed its commitment to stable growth of the money supply. But lately the focus is clearly on interest rates again.
11. When the aggregate supply curve is very flat, increases in aggregate demand will add much to the nation's real output and add little to the price level. Under those circumstances, stabilization policy works well as an antirecession device, but has little power to combat inflation.
12. When the aggregate supply curve is steep, increases in aggregate demand increase real output rather little and succeed mostly in pushing up prices. In such a case, stabilization policy can do much to fight inflation but is not a very effective way to cure unemployment.
13. The aggregate supply curve is likely to be relatively flat in the short run but relatively steep in the long run. Hence, stabilization policy affects mainly output in the short run, but mainly prices in the long run.
14. When there are long and unpredictable *lags in the operation of fiscal and monetary policy*, attempts to stabilize economic activity may actually destabilize it.
15. The U.S. economy has a number of **automatic stabilizers** which make it less vulnerable to shocks than it would otherwise be. Among these are the personal income tax and unemployment benefits.
16. Economic forecasts are made by **econometric models,** by exploiting **leading indicators,** and by judgment. Each method seems to play a role in arriving at good forecasts. But no method is foolproof, and economic forecasts are not as accurate as we would like.
17. Some economists believe that our imperfect knowledge of the channels through which stabilization policy works, and the long lags involved, make it unlikely that discretionary stabilization policy can succeed.
18. Other economists recognize these difficulties but do not believe they are quite as serious. They also place much less faith in the economy's ability to cure recessions and inflations on its own. They therefore think that *discretionary policy* is not only advisable, but essential.
19. Stabilizing the economy by fiscal policy need *not* imply a tendency toward "big government."

KEY TERMS

Quantity theory of money
Velocity
Equation of exchange
Effect of interest rate on velocity
Monetarism
Effect of fiscal policy on interest rates
Lags in stabilization policy
Controlling M versus controlling r
Automatic stabilizers
Econometric models
Leading indicators
Judgmental forecasts
Rules versus discretionary policy

QUESTIONS FOR REVIEW

1. How much money (including cash and checking account balances) do you typically have at any particular moment? Divide this into your total income over the past 12 months to obtain your own personal velocity. Are you typical of the nation as a whole?

2. Just below, you will find data on nominal gross domestic product and the money supply (M1 definition) for selected years. Compute velocity in each year. Can you see any trend?

Year	Money Supply (M1) (billions of dollars) (end of year)	Nominal GDP (billions of dollars)
1974	274	1,497
1984	552	3,902
1994	1,149	6,931

3. Use the concept of opportunity cost to explain why velocity is higher at higher interest rates.

4. How does monetarism differ from the quantity theory of money? How does it differ from Keynesian analysis?

5. Given the behavior of velocity shown in Figure 14-1, would it make more sense for the Federal Reserve to formulate targets for M1 or M2?

6. Distinguish between the expenditure lag and the policy lag in stabilization policy. Does monetary or fiscal policy have the shorter expenditure lag? What about the policy lag?

7. Explain why their contrasting views on the shape of the aggregate supply curve lead some economists to argue much more strongly for stabilization policies to fight unemployment and others to argue much more strongly for stabilization policies to fight inflation.

8. Use a supply and demand diagram similar to Figure 14-2 (page 306) to show the choices open to the Fed following an unexpected decline in the demand for money. If the Fed is following a monetarist policy rule, what will happen to the rate of interest?

9. Explain why lags make it possible for policy actions intended to stabilize the economy actually to destabilize it.

10. Which of the following events would strengthen the argument for the use of discretionary policy, and which would strengthen the argument for rules?
    a. Structural changes make the economy's self-correcting mechanism work more quickly and reliably than before.
    b. New statistical methods are found that improve the accuracy of economic forecasts.
    c. A Democratic president is elected when there is an overwhelmingly Republican Congress. Congress and the president differ sharply on what should be done about the national economy.

11. (More difficult) Use the following hypothetical econometric model of the U.S. economy to obtain a forecast of the GDP:

$$C = 300 + 0.75DI$$
$$DI = Y - T$$
$$Y = C + I + G + (X - IM)$$

T, I, G, and $(X - IM)$ are the exogenous variables, and their forecasted values are $T = 1{,}200$, $I = 900$, $G = 1{,}300$, $(X - M) = -100$.

12. (More difficult) Answer the same question for an economy described by:

$$C = 48 + 0.9DI$$
$$DI = Y - T$$
$$T = 10 + (\tfrac{1}{3})Y$$
$$Y = C + I + G + (X - IM)$$

with forecasts $I = 200$, $G = 850$, $(X - IM) = 0$.

13. Many observers think that from 1993 to 1995 the Federal Reserve succeeded in using deft applications of monetary policy to "fine tune" the U.S. economy into the full-employment zone without worsening inflation. Use the data on money supply, interest rates, real GDP, unemployment, and the price level given on the inside back cover of this book to evaluate this claim. Ask your instructor what has happened since.

CHAPTER 15

Budget Deficits and the National Debt: Fact and Fiction

Blessed are the young, for they shall inherit the national debt.
Herbert Hoover

There is a belief that runs deep in the American character that there is something inherently wrong with government budget deficits. Opinion polls consistently show that the public wants smaller deficits. Yet for more than a decade our political process failed to produce them. Then, after the 1992 election, things began to change. President Clinton made deficit reduction the centerpiece of his economic policy, pushing a large, multiyear package of tax hikes and expenditure cuts through a reluctant Congress in 1993. But that, apparently, just whetted political appetites, for the Republican party rode to a smashing victory in the 1994 midterm elections partly by arguing that the president had not gone nearly far enough! We had to balance the budget. Since then, the drive for a balanced budget has been at the top of the national political agenda.

What is the economic substance in this debate? What kinds of problems do large deficits pose for the economy, both now and in the future? Should we strive to balance the budget? And if so, by what means? These are the questions for this chapter.

We begin by explaining why the principles of stabilization policy that we have been learning in this part of the book do not imply that the budget should always be balanced. (Neither, however, do they lead to the conclusion that massive deficits should be the norm.) Next we look at the facts: We discuss the size of the national debt, how it grew so large, and why some economists claim that the federal budget deficit is mismeasured.

With the facts established, we examine the alleged ill effects of deficits. We shall see that many popular arguments against deficits are based on faulty reasoning. But others are not. In particular, we devote special attention to two potentially severe costs of deficit spending: It can be inflationary, and it can "crowd out" private investment spending.

A PUZZLE: ARE SMALLER DEFICITS GOOD OR BAD FOR GROWTH?

The speed at which Congress should reduce or eliminate the budget deficit has been and continues to be hotly debated. One group of economists and politicians argues that the sooner we balance the budget, the better. But another group urges moderation, warning that it can be dangerous to cut the deficit too quickly.

The average person is bound to be confused by this debate. The first group argues for speed on the grounds that a lower deficit is the way to spur economic growth, while the second group urges caution on the grounds that too much deficit reduction too soon might slow the economy down! Surely, both cannot be right. Or can they? Although it sounds paradoxical, we will see in this chapter that there are elements of truth in both claims.

SHOULD THE BUDGET BE BALANCED?

Let us begin by reviewing the basic principles of fiscal policy that we have learned so far (especially in Chapter 11) and what they say about the goal of balancing the budget.

In brief, these principles tell us that the focus of fiscal policy should not be on *balancing the budget*, but rather on *balancing aggregate supply and aggregate demand*. They point to the desirability of budget *deficits* when private demand, $C + I + (X - IM)$, is too weak and budget *surpluses* when private demand is too strong. The budget should be balanced, according to these principles, only when $C + I + G + (X - IM)$ under a balanced-budget policy approximately equals full-employment levels of output. This may sometimes occur, but it will not necessarily be the norm.

The reason why a balanced budget is not always advisable should be clear from our earlier discussion of stabilization policy. Consider the fiscal policy that the government would follow if its goal were to balance the budget continuously. If private spending sagged for some reason, the multiplier would pull GDP down. Since personal and corporate tax receipts fall sharply when GDP declines, the budget would automatically start swinging into the red. To bring the budget back to balance, the government would then be forced either to lower spending or raise taxes—exactly the opposite of the appropriate policy response. Thus:

Attempts to balance the budget—as done, say, during the Great Depression—will prolong and deepen recessions.

"The 'Twilight Zone' will not be seen tonight, so that we may bring you the following special on the federal budget."

Budget balancing can also lead to inappropriate fiscal policy under boom conditions. If rising tax receipts induce a budget-balancing government to spend more or cut taxes, fiscal policy will "boom the boom"—with unfortunate inflationary consequences. Fortunately, believers in budget balancing usually are not alarmed by surpluses.

Actually, the issue is even more complicated than we have indicated so far. As we learned in Chapter 13, fiscal policy is not the only way the government affects aggregate demand. The government also influences aggregate demand through its monetary policy. For this reason:

The appropriate fiscal policy depends, among other things, on the stance of monetary policy. While a balanced budget may be appropriate under one monetary policy, a deficit or a surplus may be appropriate under another monetary policy.

An example will illustrate the point. Suppose Congress and the president believe that the aggregate supply and demand curves will intersect approximately at full employment if the budget is balanced. Then a balanced budget would seem to be the appropriate fiscal policy.

Now suppose monetary policy turns contractionary, pulling the aggregate demand curve inward to the left as shown in Figure 15-1 and creating a recessionary gap. If the fiscal authorities wish to restore real GDP to its original level, they must shift the aggregate demand curve back to its original position, D_0D_0. To do so, they must either raise spending or cut taxes, thereby opening up a budget deficit. Thus, the tightening of monetary policy changes the appropriate fiscal policy from a balanced budget to a deficit.

By the same token, a given target for aggregate demand implies that any change in fiscal policy will alter the appropriate monetary policy. For example, suppose Figure 15-1 indicates the effects of reducing the budget deficit by cutting government spending. Then, if the authorities do not want real GDP to fall, monetary policy must become sufficiently more expansionary to restore the aggregate demand curve to D_0D_0. Indeed, it is precisely this change in the mix of policy—a smaller budget deficit balanced by easier money—that both the Clinton administration and the Republican Congress are seeking.

So we should not expect a balanced budget to be the norm. How, then, can we tell whether any particular deficit is too large or too small? That is a good question, but a complicated one. Before attempting an answer, we should get some facts straight.

DEFICITS AND DEBT: SOME TERMINOLOGY

First, some critical terminology. The title of this chapter contains two terms that seem similar but have different meanings: *budget deficits* and the *national debt*. We must learn to distinguish between the two.

FIGURE 15-1 THE INTERACTION OF MONETARY AND FISCAL POLICY

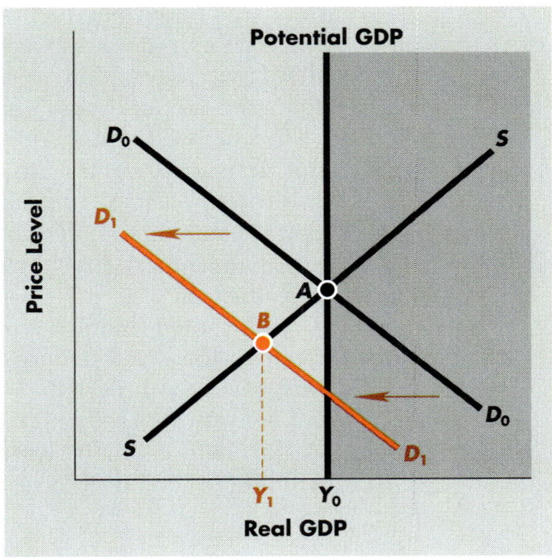

Both monetary and fiscal policy affect the aggregate demand curve. If monetary policy turns contractionary, the aggregate demand curve shifts inward from D_0D_0 to D_1D_1 thereby lowering real GDP from Y_0 to Y_1. If Y_0 represented full employment with a balanced budget, then Y_1 represents an economy with a recessionary gap. Expansionary fiscal policy can push the aggregate demand curve back to D_0D_0, but only by opening up a deficit in the government budget.

The **BUDGET DEFICIT** is the amount by which the government's expenditures exceed its receipts during a specified period of time, usually 1 year.

The **NATIONAL DEBT** is the federal government's total indebtedness at a moment in time. It is the result of previous deficits.

The **budget deficit** is the amount by which the government's expenditures exceed its receipts during some specified period of time, usually 1 year. For example, during fiscal year 1996, the government raised about $1,453 billion in taxes but spent almost $1,560 billion, leaving a deficit of about $107 billion.[1]

The **national debt,** also called the *public debt,* is the total value of the government's indebtedness at a moment in time. Thus, for example, the national debt at the end of fiscal year 1996 was about $5,182 trillion.

These two concepts—debt and deficits—are closely related because the government accumulates *debt* by running *deficits* or reduces its debt by running surpluses. The relationship between the debt and the deficit can be explained by a simple analogy. As you run water into a bathtub ("run a deficit"), the accumulated volume of water in the tub ("the debt") rises. Alternatively, if you let water out of the tub ("run a surplus"), the level of the water ("the debt") falls. Analogously, budget deficits raise the national debt while budget surpluses lower it. But, of course, getting rid of the deficit (shutting off the flow of water) will not get rid of the accumulated debt (drain the tub).

Having made this distinction, let us look first at the size and nature of the accumulated public debt, and then at the annual budget deficit.

SOME FACTS ABOUT THE NATIONAL DEBT

How large a public debt do we have? How did we get it? Who owns it? Is it really growing rapidly?

To begin with the simplest question, the public debt is enormous. At the end of 1996 it amounted to about $19,520 for every man, woman, and child in America. But more than one-third of this outstanding debt was owned by agencies of the U.S. government—in other words, one branch of the government owed it to another. If we deduct this portion, the net national debt was just about $3.7 trillion, or around $13,900 per person.

Furthermore, when we compare the debt with the gross domestic product—the volume of goods and services our economy produces in a year—it does not seem so large after all. With a GDP more than $7.5 trillion in late 1996, the net debt was under one-half of the nation's yearly income. By contrast, many families who own homes owe *several years'* worth of income to the bank that granted them mortgages. Many U.S. corporations also owe their bondholders much more than one-half of a year's sales.

But before these analogies make you feel too comfortable, we should point out that simple analogies between public and private debt are almost always misleading. A family with a large mortgage debt also owns a home with a value that presumably exceeds the mortgage. A solvent business firm has assets (factories, machinery, inventories, and so forth) that far exceed its outstanding bonds in value.

Is the same thing true of the U.S. government? No one knows for sure. How much is the White House worth? Or the national parks? And what about military bases, both here and abroad? Simply because these government assets are *not* sold on markets, no one really knows their value. However, recent federal government estimates concluded that its assets were worth "only" about $2.3 trillion at the end of 1994—a number far less than the national debt.

[1]*Reminder:* The fiscal year of the U.S. government ends on September 30. Thus, fiscal year 1996 ran from October 1, 1995, to September 30, 1996.

FIGURE 15-2 THE U.S. NATIONAL DEBT RELATIVE TO GDP, 1915–1996

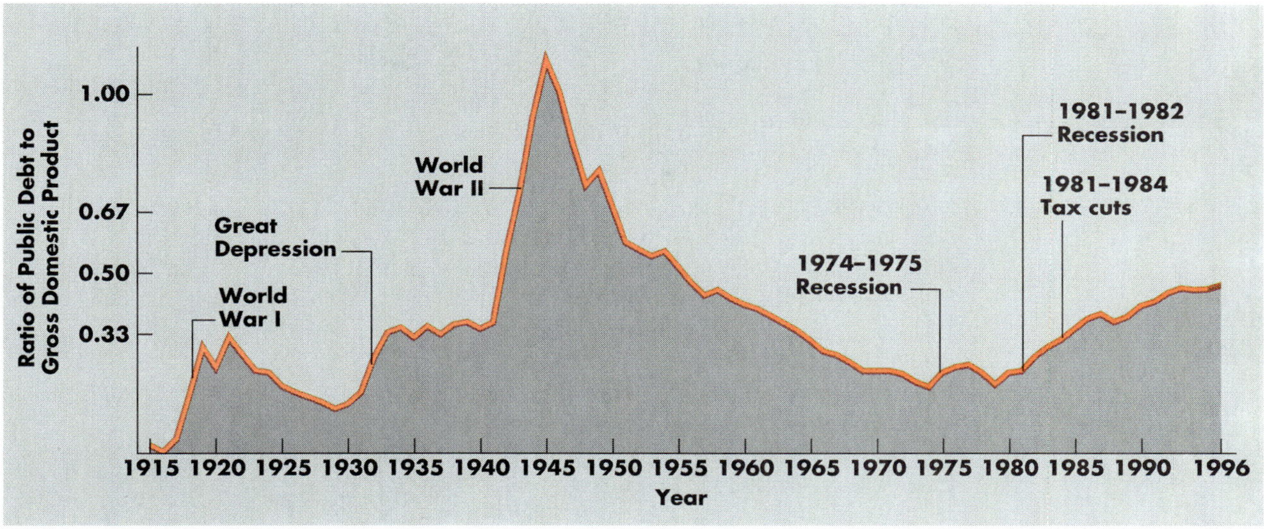

This graph charts the behavior of the public debt in the United States, after (a) subtracting out the portion of the debt that is held by government agencies and (b) dividing by nominal GDP. We can see that the debt grew relative to GDP during the two world wars, during the Great Depression, during the 1974–1975 recession, and from 1981 to the early 1990s. Other than that, the debt generally has fallen relative to GDP.

SOURCE: Constructed by the authors from data in *Historical Statistics of the United States* and *Economic Report of the President.*

Figure 15-2 charts the path of the national debt from 1915 to 1996, expressing each year's national debt as a fraction of that year's nominal GDP. Looking at the debt relative to GDP is important for two reasons. First, we must remember that everything grows in a growing economy. Private debt and business debt have grown rapidly since 1915; it would have been surprising indeed if the public debt did not grow while GDP expanded so enormously. In fact, federal debt grew more slowly than private debt for most of the period from World War II until about 1980.

Second, the debt is measured in dollars and, as long as there is any inflation, the amount of purchasing power that each dollar represents declines each year. Dividing the debt by nominal GDP, as done in Figure 15-2, adjusts for both real growth and inflation, and so puts the debt numbers in better perspective.

The diagram shows us how and when the U.S. government acquired all this debt. Notice the sharp increases in the ratio of debt to GDP during World War I, the Great Depression, and especially World War II. Thereafter, you see an unmistakable downward trend until the recession of 1974–1975. In 1945, the national debt was the equivalent of 13 months' national income. By 1974, this figure had been whittled down to just 2 months' worth.

Thus, until the 1980s, most of the debt was acquired either during wars or recessions. As we shall see later, the *cause* of the debt is quite germane to the question of whether or not the debt is a burden. So it is important to remember that:

Until about 1983, almost all of the U.S. national debt stemmed from financing wars and from the losses of tax revenues that accompany recessions.

But then things changed. From the early 1980s until 1993, the national debt grew faster than nominal GDP, reversing the pattern that had prevailed since

1945. And this happened with no wars and only one recession. By 1995, the debt exceeded 5 months' GDP—nearly triple its value in 1974. This disturbing development is a major reason why economists are alarmed by continued large budget deficits.

INTERPRETING THE BUDGET DEFICIT

We have observed that the federal government's annual budget deficits have been extremely large since the Reagan administration. As Figure 15-3 shows, the budget deficit ballooned from $40 billion to the $80 billion range in fiscal years 1979 through 1981 and to $208 billion by fiscal year 1983—setting a record which was subsequently eclipsed several times. The budget for fiscal year 1996, which ended just after this edition went to press, is expected to show a deficit of $145 billion. These are enormous, even mind-boggling, numbers. But what do they mean? How are they to be interpreted?

THE STRUCTURAL DEFICIT

First, it is important to understand that the same fiscal program can lead to a large or small deficit, depending on the state of the economy. Failure to appreciate this point has led many people to assume that a larger deficit always signifies a more expansionary fiscal policy. But that is not always true.

Think, for example, about what happens to the budget during a recession. As GDP falls, the government's most important sources of tax revenue—income taxes, corporate taxes, and payroll taxes—all shrink because firms and people pay lower taxes when they earn less. Similarly, some types of government spending, notably transfer payments like unemployment benefits, rise when GDP falls because more people are out of work.

FIGURE 15-3

OFFICIAL BUDGET DEFICITS, 1979–1996 (FISCAL YEARS)

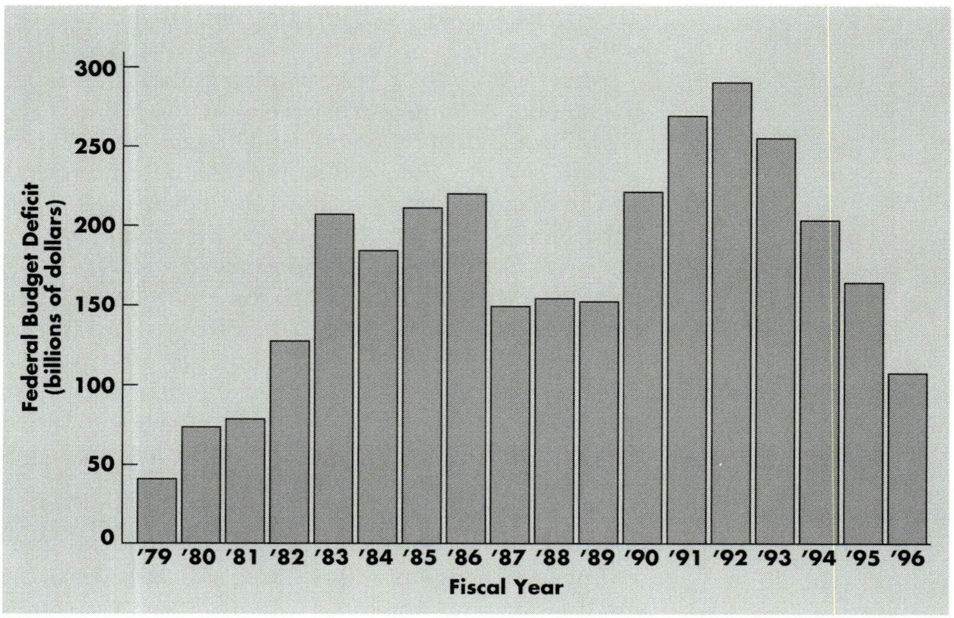

The budget deficit almost tripled between fiscal year 1981 and fiscal year 1983 and did not change much between then and fiscal 1986. After dipping for a few years in the late 1980s, it then soared to a peak of $290 billion in fiscal 1992. Since then it has declined.

SOURCE: *Economic Report of the President.*

Remember that the deficit is the difference between government expenditures, which are either purchases or transfer payments, and tax receipts:

$$\text{Deficit} = G + \text{Transfers} - \text{Taxes}$$

Since a falling GDP means higher expenditures and lower tax receipts:

The deficit rises in a recession and falls in a boom, even with no change in fiscal policy.

Figure 15-4 depicts the relationship between GDP and the budget deficit. The government's fiscal program is summarized by the blue and orange lines. The horizontal blue line labeled *G* indicates that federal purchases of goods and services are approximately unaffected by GDP. The rising orange line labeled "Taxes minus Transfers" indicates that taxes rise and transfer payments fall as GDP rises. Notice that the same fiscal policy (that is, the same two lines) can lead to a large deficit if GDP is Y_1, a small deficit if GDP is Y_2, a balanced budget if GDP is Y_3, or even a surplus if GDP is as high as Y_4. Clearly, the deficit itself is not a good measure of the government's fiscal policy.

For this reason, many economists pay less attention to the *actual* deficit or surplus and more attention to what is called the **structural budget deficit or surplus.** This is a hypothetical measure that replaces both the spending and taxes in the *actual* budget by estimates of how much the government *would be* spending and receiving, given current tax rates and expenditure rules, if the economy were operating at some fixed, high-employment level. For example, if the high-employment benchmark in Figure 15-4 was Y_2, while actual GDP was only Y_1, the actual deficit would be *AB* while the structural deficit would be only *CD*.

The **STRUCTURAL BUDGET DEFICIT** is the hypothetical deficit we *would have* under current fiscal policies if the economy were operating near full employment.

Because it is based on the spending and taxing the government would be doing at some fixed level of GDP, rather than on actual expenditures and receipts, the structural deficit is insensitive to the state of the economy. It changes only when policy changes. That is why most economists view it as a better measure of the thrust of fiscal policy than the actual deficit.

This new concept helps us understand the changing nature of the large budget deficits of the 1980s. Table 15-1 displays both the actual deficit and the

FIGURE 15-4

THE EFFECT OF THE ECONOMY ON THE BUDGET

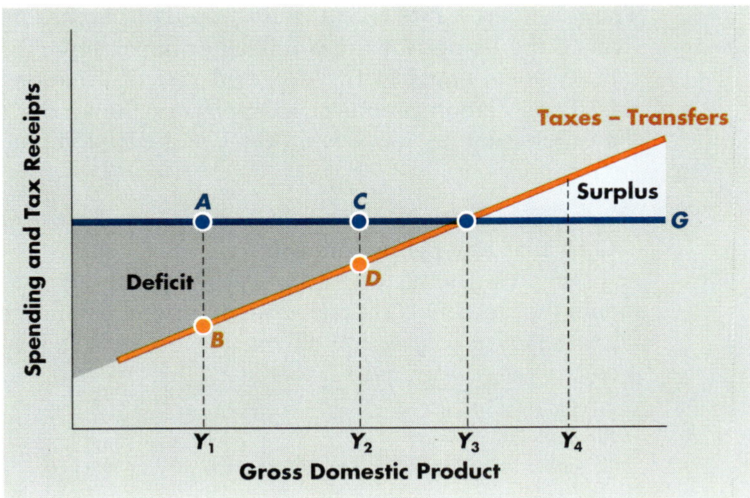

Since government purchases (*G*) do not depend on GDP, but taxes and transfer payments do, the deficit shrinks as GDP rises—even for a fixed fiscal policy. In this figure, the deficit is *AB* if GDP is Y_1, but only *CD* if GDP is Y_2. At still higher levels of GDP, the same policies could produce a balanced budget (at Y_3) or even a surplus (at Y_4).

TABLE 15-1 UNEMPLOYMENT AND THE DEFICIT

Fiscal Year	Official Deficit (billions of dollars)	+	Adjustment to High Employment (billions of dollars)	=	Structural Deficit (billions of dollars)
1981	−79		+25		−54
1983	−208		+83		−125
1985	−212		+20		−192
1987	−150		+21		−129
1989	−153		+4		−149
1991	−269		+79		−190
1993	−255		+33		−222
1995	−164		−28		−192
1996	−107		−47		−154

SOURCE: Congressional Budget Office.

structural deficit for every other year since 1981. Because of recessions in 1983 and 1991, the difference between the two budgets was particularly large in those years. But it was negligible in 1989, when the economy was at full employment.

Two interesting facts stand out when we compare the numbers in the first and last columns. First, even though the official deficit was smaller in fiscal 1995 than in fiscal 1983, the structural deficit was actually larger in 1995—despite years of budget "stringency." Second, the structural deficit rose steadily from 1987 to 1993. It was this trend toward larger structural deficits that most alarmed keen students of the federal budget.

INFLATION ACCOUNTING FOR INTEREST PAYMENTS[2]

The next major problem is one of measurement rather than interpretation. Government accountants treat every dollar of interest payments as part of the government's spending. At first blush, that seems like the right thing to do, but it ignores the fundamental distinction between real and nominal interest rates that we emphasized in Chapter 6. To review the analysis:

The real interest rate tells us the amount of purchasing power the borrower turns over to the lender for the privilege of borrowing. To this we must add an *inflation premium,* equal to the expected rate of inflation, to get the *nominal interest rate.* The inflation premium compensates the lender for the expected erosion of the purchasing power of her money and is best thought of as repayment of principal.[3]

The last sentence has important implications for the government budget—implications that few people understand.

From an economic point of view, the portion of the government's interest payments that merely compensates lenders for inflation should be counted as early *repayment of principal,* not as *interest,* because it simply returns to lenders the

[2]This section contains difficult material which may be skipped in shorter courses.

[3]If you need review, see pages 128–129.

INFLATION ACCOUNTING means adjusting standard accounting procedures for the fact that inflation lowers the purchasing power of money.

purchasing power of their original funds. Only the *real* interest that the government pays should be treated as an expenditure item in the budget. Breaking up interest payments in this way is called **inflation accounting.** Since so few people understand inflation accounting, it is worth taking the time to illustrate the idea with an analogy and a simple example.

Imagine that you lend a roommate, who is enrolled in a chemistry course, a bar of radium that you happen to own. Your roommate uses the radioactive bar (carefully!) in experiments for a year, and then returns it to you. Has your loan been repaid in full? Certainly not. Because of radioactive decay, what you get back is smaller than what you originally loaned. To pay you back in full, your roommate would have to give you enough additional radium to replace the portion that eroded during the year.

The analogy to interest rates on loans is straightforward: Inflation erodes the purchasing power of money just as radioactive decay erodes radium. So, in figuring out how many dollars constitute repayment of principal, we must take inflation into account. Let's illustrate this by a concrete example: comparing a loan made at zero inflation (no decay) with a loan made at 10 percent inflation (rapid decay).

First, suppose the government borrows $1,000 for a year when the inflation rate is zero, paying 2 percent interest. At the end of the year it must pay back $1,000 in principal and $20 in interest, for a total of $1,020. Of this, only $20—the interest payment—counts as expenditure in the budget. The repayment of principal is not counted as spending. The loan transaction is summarized simply in Column 1 of Table 15-2.

Now let us see how inflation (radioactive decay of money) complicates the accountant's job. Suppose the same transaction takes place when the rate of inflation is 10 percent. To compensate the lender for 10 percent inflation, the government must return $1.10 for each dollar originally borrowed. If the real interest rate is still 2 percent, the government must return 2 percent more than this, or 1.02 × $1.10 = $1.122 per dollar borrowed. Thus, each dollar of lending earns 12.2 cents in interest, meaning that the nominal interest rate is 12.2 percent.

So suppose the government borrows $1,000 at the start of the year and repays $1,122 at year's end. Conventional accounting procedures will treat $1,000 as

TABLE 15-2 ACCOUNTING FOR A $1,000 LOAN AT A 2 PERCENT REAL INTEREST RATE

Item	(1) At Zero Inflation	(2) At 10% Inflation: Conventional Accounting	(3) At 10% Inflation: Inflation Accounting
Interest (included in budget)	$ 20	$ 122	$ 22
plus			
Principal (excluded from budget)	1,000	1,000	1,100
equals			
Total payment	$1,020	$1,122	$1,122
Addendum:			
Purchasing power of principal repayment	$1,000	$ 909	$1,000

repayment of principal (and hence not as an expenditure) and $122 as interest (which *is* an expenditure). This conventional accounting treatment is indicated in Column 2 of Table 15-2.

But these numbers are misleading since $1,000 at the end of the year is not full repayment of principal because inflation has eroded the real value of money. In fact, it is worth just $909 in beginning-of-the-year money. The correct inflation accounting treatment recognizes that it takes $1,100 at the end of the year to buy what $1,000 bought at the beginning of the year. So $1,100 is treated as repayment of principal, leaving only $22 ($1,122 − $1,100) to be treated as interest. The correct inflation accounting for the loan is shown in Column 3 of Table 15-2.

In general, the proper economic treatment of a loan in an inflationary environment must recognize that more dollars (in our example, $1,100) must be returned to the lender in order to give back the purchasing power of the original loan ($1,000). Only the excess of the nominal interest payment ($122) over the compensation for inflation ($100) should be counted as interest. Because conventional accounting does not recognize the difference between nominal and real interest:

Inflation distorts the government budget deficit under conventional accounting procedures by exaggerating interest expenses.

Our example suggests how this error can be corrected:

To correct the deficit for inflation, we must subtract the inflation premium from the interest paid on the national debt, thereby counting only *real* interest payments.

Table 15-3 shows that making the inflation adjustment to interest payments would have reduced reported deficits by about $60 billion to $90 billion in recent years, a sizable adjustment.

OTHER MEASUREMENT ISSUES

There are other complicated issues in measuring and interpreting the federal budget deficit. We conclude this section by mentioning just two.

TABLE 15-3 INFLATION ACCOUNTING AND THE DEFICIT

Fiscal Year	Official Deficit (billions of dollars)	+	Inflation Adjustment for Interest Paid (billions of dollars)	=	Inflation-Adjusted Deficit (billions of dollars)
1981	−79		+73		−62
1983	−208		+33		−175
1985	−212		+44		−168
1987	−150		+46		−104
1989	−153		+82		−71
1991	−269		+91		−178
1993	−255		+65		−190
1995	−164		+80		−84
1996	−107		+67		−40

SOURCE: Congressional Budget Office and authors' estimates.

1. *State and local budget surpluses.* Part of the reason for the federal deficit is that the federal government gives a good deal of money (around $200 billion in recent years) to state and local governments in the form of *grants-in-aid* each year. These funds help state and local governments run small annual surpluses in most years. Thus, the *combined* deficit of all levels of government is smaller than the *federal* deficit.
2. *Capital expenditures.* Some federal spending goes to purchase capital of various sorts—government buildings, military equipment, and so on. There is nothing unusual about borrowing to purchase assets. Private businesses and individuals do it all the time. For this reason, many people have suggested that the federal government compile a separate capital budget, just as most state and local governments now do.

CONCLUSION: WHAT HAPPENED AFTER 1981?

Table 15-4 puts our two major adjustments—for inflation accounting and for unemployment—together and compares the official deficits recorded since 1981 (Column 1) with the corresponding figures for the structural, inflation-corrected deficit (Column 4). The difference between the two columns is startling in some years. For example, in 1981 the economy was weak and inflation was high; the apparently substantial budget deficit of 1981 was actually a surplus on a structural, inflation-corrected basis! But since 1983 even the structural, inflation-corrected budget has been in substantial deficit.

Table 15-4 tells the following story about the recent evolution of the budget deficit. On a structural, inflation-corrected basis, the federal budget swung from a small surplus to a large deficit in the first half of the 1980s—largely due to tax cuts. Some progress was made toward reducing the deficit in the late 1980s, but the problem worsened after 1989 as government spending grew faster than tax receipts. Thus, the recent heightened concern with the deficit seems entirely appropriate.

TABLE 15-4 ACTUAL AND ADJUSTED BUDGET DEFICITS

Fiscal Year	(1) Official Deficit (billions of dollars)	+	(2) Adjustment for Inflation (billions of dollars)	+	(3) Adjustment to High Employment (billions of dollars)	=	(4) Adjusted Deficit (−) or Surplus (+) (billions of dollars)
1981	−79		+73		+25		+19
1983	−208		+33		+83		−92
1985	−212		+44		+20		−148
1987	−150		+46		+21		−83
1989	−153		+82		+4		−67
1991	−269		+91		+79		−99
1993	−255		+65		+33		−157
1995	−164		+80		−28		−112
1996	−107		+67		−47		−87

SOURCE: Congressional Budget Office and authors' estimates.

BOGUS ARGUMENTS ABOUT THE BURDEN OF THE DEBT

Having gained some perspective on the facts, let us now turn to some of the arguments advanced by those who claim that budget deficits place an intolerable burden on future generations.

Argument 1: Our children and grandchildren will be burdened by heavy interest payments. Higher taxes will be necessary to make these payments.

Answer: It is certainly true that a higher debt will necessitate higher interest payments and, other things being equal, this will force our children and grandchildren to pay higher taxes. But think who will receive the higher interest payments as income: our children and grandchildren! Thus, one group of future Americans will be making interest payments to another group of future Americans. So we conclude that:

As long as the national debt is owned by domestic citizens, as the bulk of the U.S. debt is, future interest payments transfer money from one group of Americans to another. These transfers may or may not be desirable, but they hardly constitute a burden on the nation as a whole.

However, this argument *is* valid—and worrisome—for the 22 percent of our debt that is held by foreigners. Paying interest on this portion of the debt will burden future Americans in a concrete way: In the 21st century, a portion of America's GDP will have to be sent abroad to pay interest on the debts we incurred in the 1980s and 1990s. For this reason, many thoughtful observers are more concerned about the amount America is borrowing from abroad than they are about the total budget deficit.[4]

Another valid element of the argument is that the taxes that will have to be raised to pay interest even to U.S. citizens may reduce the efficiency of the economy.

Argument 2: Repaying the enormous debt will ruin the nation.

Answer: A first answer to this merely rephrases the answer to the previous argument: Most of America's debt is owed to Americans. But there is an even more fundamental point. *Unlike a private family, the nation need never pay off its debt.* Instead, each time the principal is due, the U.S. Treasury can simply "roll it over" by floating more debt. Indeed, this is precisely what the Treasury does.

Is this a bit of chicanery? How can the U.S. government get away with making loans that it never intends to pay back? The answer lies in the fallacy of comparing the U.S. government to a family or an individual. People cannot borrow in perpetuity because they will not live that long. Sensible lenders will not extend long-term credit to very old people because their heirs cannot be forced to pay up. But the U.S. government will never "die"; at least, we hope not! So this problem does not arise. In this respect, the government is in much the same position as a large corporation. AT&T never worries about paying off its debt. It too rolls it over by floating new debt all the time.

Argument 3: Like any family or any business firm, a nation has a limited capacity to borrow. If it exceeds this limit, it is in danger of being unable to pay its creditors. It may go bankrupt with calamitous consequences for everyone.

---

[4]We will discuss the linkages between the federal budget deficit and foreign borrowing in greater detail in Chapter 19.

Answer: This is another example of a false analogy. What is claimed about private debtors is certainly true. But the U.S. government need never fear defaulting on its debt. Why? First, because it has enormous power to raise revenues by taxation. If you had such power, you would never have to fear bankruptcy either.

But there is a more fundamental point—one that distinguishes the U.S. debt from that of most other nations. *The American national debt is an obligation to pay U.S. dollars:* Each debt certificate obligates the Treasury to pay the holder so many U.S. dollars on a prescribed date. But the U.S. government is the source of these dollars. It prints them! *No nation need ever fear defaulting on debts that call for repayment in its own currency.* If worse comes to worst, it can always print whatever money it needs to pay off its creditors. This option is not open to countries whose debts call for payment in U.S. dollars, as Mexico learned in a particularly painful way in 1995.

It does not, of course, follow that acquiring more debt through budget deficits is necessarily a good idea for the U.S. government. Sometimes it is a very bad idea. As we know, printing money to pay the debt will expand aggregate demand and cause inflation. In addition, as we will learn in Chapter 19, printing more dollars will make the international value of the dollar fall. We may not relish either of these outcomes. The point is not that budget deficits are either good or bad; they can be either under the appropriate circumstances. Rather, the point is that worrying about a possible default on the national debt is unnecessary and even foolish. There are other things to worry about.

Having cleared the air of these fallacious arguments, we are now in a position to explore some genuine problems that may arise when the government spends more than it takes in through taxation.

BUDGET DEFICITS AND INFLATION

One indictment of deficit spending that certainly *does* have validity under some circumstances is the charge that it is inflationary. Why? Because when government policy pushes up aggregate demand, firms may find themselves unwilling or unable to produce the higher quantities that are being demanded at the going prices. Prices will therefore have to rise.

Figure 15-5 is an aggregate supply and demand diagram that shows this analysis graphically. Initially, equilibrium is at point *A*—where demand curve D_0D_0 and supply curve *SS* intersect. Output is $7,000 billion, and the price index is at 100. The diagram indicates that the economy is operating at full employment since the aggregate demand and supply curves intersect precisely at potential GDP.

Now suppose the government raises its spending or cuts taxes enough to shift the aggregate demand schedule upward from D_0D_0 to D_1D_1. Equilibrium shifts from point *A* to point *B*, thereby raising the equilibrium price level to 106, or 6 percent. But that is not the end of the story because there is an inflationary gap at point *B*. We know from previous chapters that inflation will continue until the aggregate supply curve shifts far enough upward to the left so that it passes through point *C*, at which point the inflationary gap is gone. In the long run, then, deficit spending will have raised the price level 12 percent in this example.

Although Figure 15-5 is entirely hypothetical, it illustrates how the Vietnam war caused inflation in the United States in the late 1960s. The U.S. economy was roughly at full employment in 1965 when government spending on the war

FIGURE 15-5 THE INFLATIONARY EFFECTS OF DEFICIT SPENDING

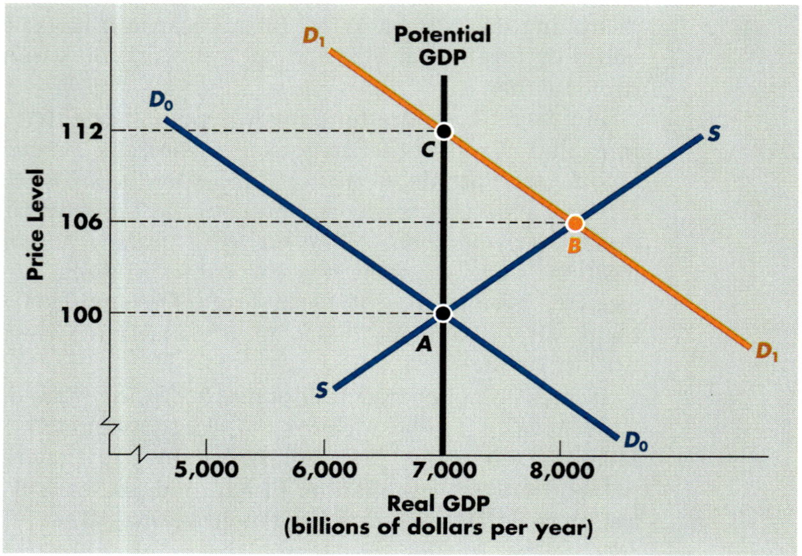

In this diagram, expansionary fiscal policy pushes the aggregate demand curve out from D_0D_0 to D_1D_1, causing equilibrium to move from *A* (where there is full employment) to *B* (where there is an inflationary gap). The demand shift, by itself, pushes the price level up. Then the economy's self-correcting mechanism takes over: Wages rise, shifting the aggregate supply curve to the left until it passes through point *C*. In total, the price level rises from 100 to 112; that is, there is a 12 percent inflation.

soared, thereby shifting the aggregate demand curve outward and opening up an inflationary gap. Inflation rose from 2.5 percent in 1965 to 5.0 percent in 1969.

Thus, the cries that budget deficits are "inflationary" have the ring of truth. How much truth, however, depends on several factors. One is the slope of the aggregate supply curve; Figure 15-5 clearly shows that a steep supply curve leads to more inflation than a flat one. A second factor is the degree of resource utilization. Deficit spending is more inflationary in a fully employed economy (like Figure 15-5) than in an economy with lots of slack. Finally, it is important to remember that the Federal Reserve's monetary policy can always cancel out the potential inflationary effects of deficit spending by pulling the aggregate demand curve back to its original position.

THE MONETIZATION ISSUE

But will the Federal Reserve always behave this way? This question brings up another reason why some people worry about the inflationary consequences of budget deficits. They fear that the Federal Reserve may have to "monetize" part of the deficit, by which they mean that the Fed may feel compelled to purchase some of the newly issued government debt. Let us explain, first, why the Fed might make such purchases, and second, why these purchases are called **monetizing the deficit.**

The central bank is said to **MONETIZE THE DEFICIT** when it purchases the bonds that the government issues.

Deficit spending, we have just noted, normally drives up both real GDP and the price level. As we have emphasized before, such an economic expansion shifts the demand curve for money outward to the right—as depicted in Figure 15-6. The figure shows that, if the Federal Reserve takes no actions to shift the money supply curve, interest rates will rise.

Suppose now that the Fed does not want interest rates to rise. What can it do? To prevent the incipient rise in *r*, it must engage in *expansionary monetary policies* that shift the supply curve for money outward to the right—as indicated in Figure 15-7. Because expansionary monetary policies normally take the form of

FIGURE 15-6 FISCAL EXPANSION AND INTEREST RATES

If expansionary fiscal policy pushes real GDP and the price level higher, the demand curve for money will shift outward from M_0D_0 to M_1D_1. Equilibrium in the money market shifts from point *A* to point *B*, so interest rates rise.

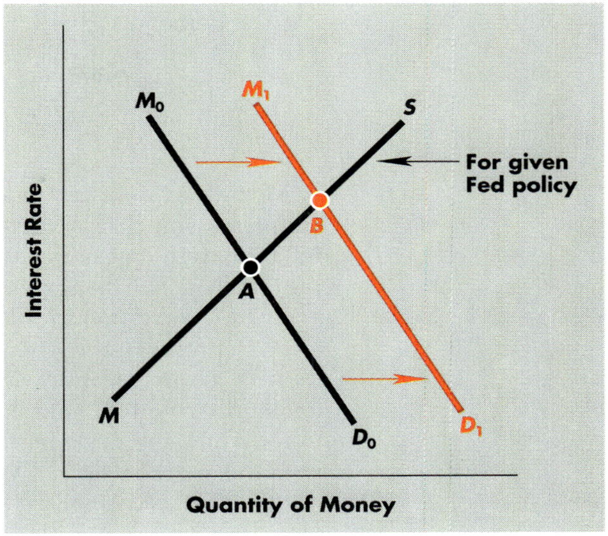

open-market purchases of government bonds, this means that deficit spending might induce the Federal Reserve to buy more government debt.

But why is this called *monetizing* the deficit? The reason is simple. As we learned in Chapter 13, open-market purchases of bonds by the Fed give banks more reserves, which leads, eventually, to an increase in the money supply. This is also shown in Figure 15-7: The outward shift of the money supply schedule from M_0S_0 to M_1S_1 leads to an increase in the quantity of money. By this indirect route, then, larger budget deficits may lead to an expansion of the money supply. To summarize:

FIGURE 15-7 MONETIZATION AND INTEREST RATES

If the Federal Reserve does not want a fiscal expansion to raise interest rates, it must increase the money supply. In this diagram, the fiscal expansion shifts the demand curve for money from M_0D_0 to M_1D_1, precisely as it did in Figure 15-6. To keep the rate of interest constant, the Fed will have to shift the money supply curve outward from M_0S_0 to M_1S_1. Points *A* and *C* correspond to the same rate of interest.

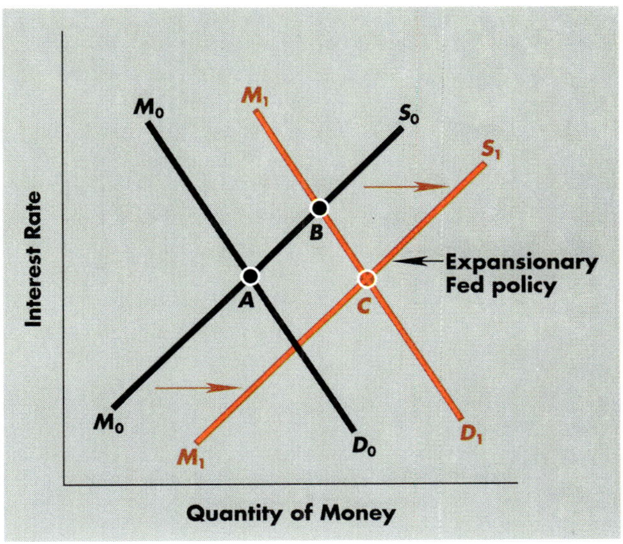

If the Federal Reserve takes no countervailing actions, an expansionary fiscal policy that increases the budget deficit will raise real GDP and prices, thereby shifting the demand curve for money outward and driving up interest rates. If the Fed does not want interest rates to rise, it can engage in expansionary open-market operations, that is, purchase more government debt. If the Fed does this, the money supply will increase. In this case, we say that part of the deficit is *monetized.*

Monetized deficits are more inflationary than nonmonetized deficits for the simple reason that expansionary monetary and fiscal policy *together* are more inflationary than expansionary fiscal policy *alone.* Figure 15-8 illustrates this simple conclusion. The aggregate supply curve and aggregate demand curves D_0D_0 and D_1D_1 correspond to those in Figure 15-5 (page 336). The shift from D_0D_0 to D_1D_1 represents the effect of expansionary fiscal policy (raising the budget deficit). If, in addition, the Fed monetizes part of the deficit, the aggregate demand curve will shift out still further—perhaps to the position indicated by D_2D_2. Thus, the price level will rise even more (compare points *B* and *C*).

Is this a real worry? Does the Fed actually monetize any substantial portion of the deficit? Normally it does not. The clearest evidence is the fact that the Fed managed to reduce inflation during the 1980s and 1990s even though the government was running unprecedented deficits. Nonetheless, many economists and business leaders are concerned about the long-run dangers of monetization when deficits are large and chronic. The reason is simple arithmetic. When budget deficits are extremely large, even a small percentage of monetization can lead to substantial increases in bank reserves and the money supply.

This last point has been amply illustrated by the experiences of a number of countries. While monetization of deficits has not been much of a problem for the United States, it has been a major source of inflation in a variety of Latin American countries. And it was recently the root cause of a ruinous hyperinflation in Russia.

FIGURE 15-8 MONETIZED DEFICIT SPENDING

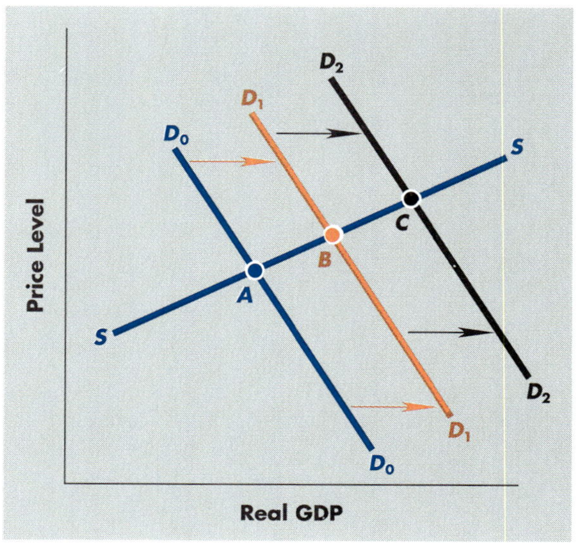

Expansionary fiscal policies that raise the budget deficit push the aggregate demand curve outward from D_0D_0 to D_1D_1. If the Fed monetizes some of the deficit, then expansionary monetary policy pushes the aggregate demand curve out even further—to D_2D_2. Monetized deficits (point *C*) are therefore more inflationary than deficits that are not monetized (point *B*).

DEFICITS, INTEREST RATES, AND CROWDING OUT

So far we have been looking for possible burdens of the national debt on the *demand* side of the economy. But the real case for cutting the deficit probably comes on the *supply* side. In a word, large budget deficits discourage investment and therefore retard the growth of our nation's capital stock. The mechanism is easy to understand.

We have just seen that budget deficits tend to raise interest rates unless the Fed engages in substantial monetization. But the rate of interest (r) is a major determinant of investment spending (I). In particular, higher r leads to lower I. And if we spend less on I today, we will have a smaller capital stock tomorrow. This, according to most economists, is the true sense in which a large national debt may burden future generations:

Because of the large national debt, we may bequeath less physical capital to future generations. If they inherit less plant and equipment, these generations will be burdened by a lower productive capacity—a lower potential GDP.

CROWDING OUT occurs when deficit spending by the government forces private investment spending to contract.

Phrasing this point another way explains why it is often called the **crowding-out effect.** Consider what happens in financial markets when the government engages in deficit spending. When it spends more than it takes in through tax revenues, the government must borrow the balance. It does this by issuing bonds, which compete with corporate bonds and other financial instruments for the available supply of funds. If some savers decide to buy government bonds, the funds remaining to invest in private bonds must be smaller. Thus, some private borrowers will get "crowded out" of the financial markets as the government claims an increasing share of the economy's total saving.

Some critics of deficits have taken this lesson to its illogical extreme and argued that each $1 of deficit spending by government crowds out exactly $1 of private spending, so that expansionary fiscal policy has no net effect on total demand. In their view, when G rises, I falls by the same amount, so that the total of $C + I + G + (X - IM)$ is unchanged.

Under normal circumstances, this would not be expected to occur. Why? First, moderate budget deficits push up interest rates only slightly. Second, the sensitivity of private spending to interest rates is modest. Even at the higher interest rates that government deficits cause, most corporations will continue to borrow to finance their investments.

CROWDING IN occurs when government spending, by raising real GDP, induces increases in private investment spending.

Furthermore, there is a counterforce that might be called the **crowding-in effect.** Deficit spending in time of economic slack presumably quickens the pace of economic activity; that, at least, is its purpose. As the economy expands, businesses find it both necessary and profitable to add to their capacity in order to meet the greater demands of consumers. Because of this *induced investment,* as we called it in earlier chapters, any increase in G tends to *increase* investment rather than *decrease* it as predicted by the crowding-out hypothesis.

The strength of the crowding-in effect depends on how much additional real GDP is stimulated by government spending (that is, on the size of the multiplier) and on how sensitive investment spending is to the improved profit opportunities that accompany rapid growth. It is even conceivable that the crowding-in effect can dominate the crowding-out effect in the short run, so that I rises on balance when G rises.

But how can this be true in view of the crowding-out argument? Certainly, if government is borrowing more *and the total volume of private saving is fixed,* then

POLICY DEBATE

A BALANCED-BUDGET AMENDMENT TO THE CONSTITUTION?

Since 1995, both President Clinton and the Republican-dominated Congress have agreed that the federal government should move gradually toward a balanced budget. But in 1995 and again in 1997, the two sides clashed sharply over a proposed constitutional amendment that would have required a balanced budget, with most Republicans in favor and the president and most Democrats opposed. (The amendment failed in the Senate by a single vote on both occasions.)

What's the difference? Why do many people who favor a balanced budget nonetheless oppose a constitutional amendment to require one? There are many reasons.

Let's start with stabilization policy. Establishing a balanced budget as a long-run norm is one thing. But a constitutional mandate to balance the budget every year is quite another—and might destabilize the economy. To understand why, remember that tax receipts decline and unemployment benefits rise automatically whenever economic activity weakens. No explicit government actions are necessary; it all happens before the government even recognizes that there is a problem. Such automatic stabilizers cushion the decline in GDP, but they also increase the deficit.

If there were a constitutional amendment requiring a balanced budget, however, this process would not be allowed to run its course. Instead, as tax receipts fell, the government would be forced to raise taxes or cut spending even as the economy sagged—precisely the wrong fiscal policy.

Constitutional experts also raise legal questions about the amendment. For example, views on the advisability of balanced budgets have changed over the years, and likely will change again. Will we amend the Constitution as economic theories change? And who will enforce the amendment if the president and Congress fail to balance the budget? Do we want judges making fiscal policy?

A final objection, ironically, illuminates the main argument in favor of the amendment. Critics point out that merely passing a balanced-budget amendment will not reduce the deficit by even $1; Congress must still pass the spending cuts or tax increases needed to do the job. But that, proponents of the amendment argue, is precisely why the amendment is needed: to force Congress to

private industry must be borrowing less. That's just arithmetic. The fallacy in the strict crowding-out argument comes in supposing that the economy's flow of saving is really fixed. If government deficits succeed in raising output, there will be more income and therefore more saving. In that way, *both* government *and* industry can borrow more.

Which effect dominates, crowding out or crowding in? Crowding out stems from the increases in interest rates caused by deficits, while crowding in derives from the faster real economic growth that deficits sometimes produce. In the short run, the crowding-in effect—which derives from the outward shift of the aggregate demand curve—is often the more powerful, especially when the economy has a great deal of slack. In the long run, however, the supply side dominates because the economy's self-correcting mechanism forces actual GDP toward potential GDP. Here the crowding-out effect takes over: With higher interest rates, the capital stock grows more slowly, and hence so does potential GDP.

Let us summarize what we have learned about the crowding-out controversy.

"Would you mind explaining again how high interest rates and the national deficit affect my allowance?"

SUMMARY

1. The basic argument of the crowding-out hypothesis is sound: *Unless there is enough additional saving,* more government borrowing will force out some private borrowers who are discouraged by the high interest rates. This will reduce investment spending and cancel out some of the expansionary effects of higher government spending.

2. This force is rarely strong enough to cancel out the *entire* expansionary thrust of government spending, however. Some net stimulus to the economy remains.
3. If deficit spending induces substantial growth in GDP, then there will be more saving. There might even be so much more that private industry can borrow *more* than before, despite the increase in government borrowing.
4. The crowding-out effect is likely to dominate in the long run or when the economy is operating near full employment. The crowding-in effect is likely to dominate in the short run, especially when there is a great deal of slack.

THE TRUE BURDEN OF THE NATIONAL DEBT

This analysis of crowding out versus crowding in helps us to understand whether or not budget deficits impose a burden on future generations:

When government budget deficits take place in a high-employment economy, the crowding-out effect will probably dominate. So deficits will exact a burden by leaving a smaller capital stock to future generations. However, deficits in a slack economy may well lead to *more* investment rather than *less*. In this case, where the crowding-in effect dominates, the new debt is a blessing rather than a burden.

Which case applies to the U.S. national debt? To answer this, let us go back to the historical facts and recall how we accumulated debt prior to the 1980s. The first cause was the financing of wars, especially World War II. Since this debt was contracted in a fully employed economy, it undoubtedly constituted a burden in the formal sense. After all, the bombs, ships, and planes that it financed were used up in the war, not invested and bequeathed as capital to future generations.

Yet today's Americans may not feel terribly burdened by the decisions of the people in power in the 1940s, for consider the alternatives. We could have financed the entire war by taxation and thus placed the burden on consumption rather than on investment. But that would truly have been ruinous, and probably impossible, given the colossal wartime expenditures. Or we could have printed money. But that would have unleashed an inflation that nobody wanted. Or the government could have just spent much less money and perhaps not have won the war, leaving future generations a far more severe burden. Compared to these alternatives, opting for massive deficit spending in the 1940s looks like a sound decision.

A second major contributor to the national debt prior to 1983 was a series of recessions. But these are precisely the circumstances under which increasing the debt might prove to be a blessing rather than a burden. So, it is only quite recently that we have had the type of deficits to which the valid burden-of-the-debt argument applies—deficits acquired in a fully employed, peacetime economy.

This sharp departure from historical norms is what makes recent budget deficits so worrisome. The tax cuts of 1981 to 1984 blew a large hole in the government budget. And the recession of 1981–1982 ballooned the deficit even further. By the late 1980s, the U.S. economy had recovered to full employment, but a structural deficit of around $150 billion per year remained. This was something that had never happened before. Then, in the early 1990s, the structural deficit ratcheted up again—to above $200 billion per year. Such large structural deficits pose a real threat of crowding out and constitute a serious potential burden on future generations.

Let us now summarize our evaluation of the burden of the national debt and thereby clarify one of the **Ideas for Beyond the Final Exam** introduced in Chapter 1.

THE BURDEN OF THE NATIONAL DEBT

First, the arguments that a large national debt may lead the nation into bankruptcy, or unduly burden future generations who have to make onerous payments of interest and principal, are mostly bogus.

Second, the national debt *will* be a burden if it is sold to foreigners or contracted in a fully employed, peacetime economy. In the latter case, it will reduce the nation's capital stock.

Third, there are circumstances in which budget deficits are appropriate for stabilization-policy reasons.

Fourth, until the 1980s, the actual public debt of the U.S. government was mostly contracted as a result of wars and recessions—precisely the circumstances under which the valid burden-of-the-debt argument does not apply. However, the large deficits of recent years are not mainly attributable to recessions, and are therefore worrisome.

DEFICIT REDUCTION AND GROWTH: PUZZLE RESOLVED

We are now in a position to answer the question posed at the start of this chapter: How can some economists argue that we should reduce the budget deficit as a way to speed economic growth, while others claim that reducing the deficit too quickly will imperil economic growth? The answer comes from distinguishing carefully between the short-run and long-run effects of smaller budget deficits.

In the short run, reducing the deficit means pursuing a contractionary fiscal policy: either cutting spending or raising taxes. Unless monetary policy turns sufficiently expansionary, we know from earlier chapters that such a fiscal contraction will pull the aggregate demand curve inward—thereby reducing both real GDP and the price level as shown in Figure 15-9. A sufficiently strong dose of contractionary fiscal medicine might even cause a recession. Those who warn of the dangers of overzealous deficit reduction are thinking about the short run.

In the long run, as we have seen in this chapter, smaller budget deficits lead to lower real interest rates and hence to higher levels of private investment. That makes the nation's capital stock grow faster, thereby boosting the growth rate of potential GDP and shifting the aggregate supply curve outward at a faster pace. (See Figure 15-10.) This is the main argument in favor of deficit reduction, and it focuses squarely on the long run.

Which view is correct? Paradoxically, both are! In the short run, aggregate demand factors dominate economic performance and deficit reduction is therefore a contractionary force—unless it is offset by monetary policy. But, in the long run, output gravitates toward potential GDP no matter what is happening to aggregate demand, so aggregate supply rules the roost. And because smaller deficits spur investment spending, they increase the economy's potential growth rate.

FIGURE 15-9 THE SHORT-RUN EFFECT OF DEFICIT REDUCTION

Higher taxes or lower government spending shift the aggregate demand curve downward from D_0D_0 to D_1D_1, moving equilibrium from point *A* to point *B*. Both real GDP and the price level wind up lower than they would have been without the deficit reduction program.

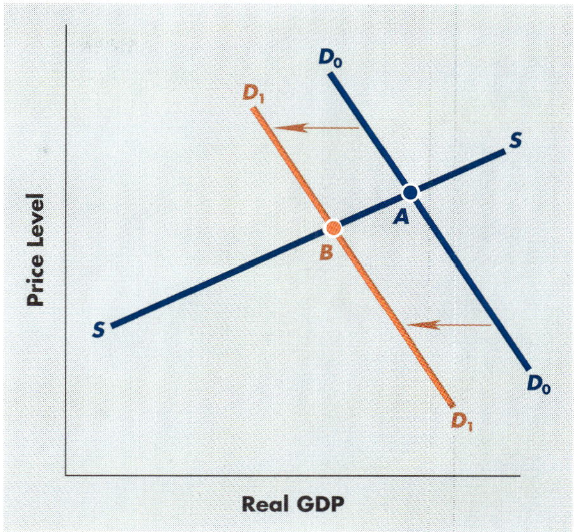

FIGURE 15-10 THE LONG-RUN EFFECT OF DEFICIT REDUCTION

By lowering real interest rates, smaller budget deficits lead to more investment, which makes potential GDP grow faster (to Y_1 rather than to Y_0). But this process takes a long time. In the long run, the self-correcting mechanism pushes the economy toward the point where the aggregate demand curve (*DD*) crosses the vertical line representing potential GDP. Hence, as the figure shows, deficit reduction spurs growth in the long run—and is also anti-inflationary. (Compare points *A* and *B*.)

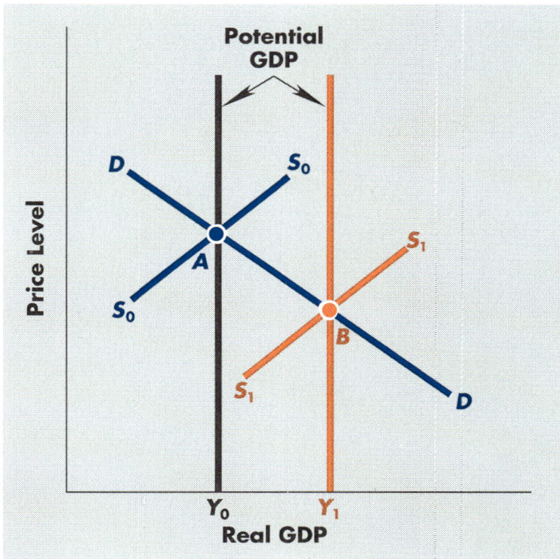

CONCLUSION: THE ECONOMICS AND POLITICS OF THE BUDGET DEFICIT

Given what we have learned in this chapter about the theory and facts of budget deficits, we can now address some of the issues that have been debated in the political arena for over a decade.

1. *How did we get such a large deficit?* Triple-digit deficits began in 1982. At first, the most important cause was the deep recession, not President Reagan's budget policies. As we saw in Table 15-1 (page 330), the structural deficit was

AMERICA SPEAKS: HOW TO REDUCE THE BUDGET DEFICIT

We Americans, it seems, have public opinion polls on everything. Why not a poll on how to balance the federal budget? Such a poll was conducted for the House Budget Committee in 1995. The results were, to say the least, novel.

The more merchandise-minded respondents suggested selling off seized assets through a giant home-shopping network. The more down-home types, about 80 percent to be exact, endorsed a national garage sale to unload some of the government's nonessential, nonrecreational national assets. A few thought we should sell advertising space on postage stamps.

Some slightly less imaginative ideas were also offered. The politically courageous suggested raising taxes and placing curbs on Social Security benefits. A freeze on spending, with annual increases for Social Security and Medicare capped at 2 percent, was another proposal. Almost two-thirds of Americans thought it would be a good idea to post a big scoreboard in front of the Capitol. The scoreboard would continually flash the deficit, along with timely data on how pending legislation would impact the budget.

But, as a possible sign of the times, almost 70 percent of the people who completed the poll thought members of Congress would find some way to make the scoreboard flash misleading numbers.

SOURCE: Steven Thomma, "Citizens Offer Congress Offbeat Ways to Balance the Budget," Knight Ridder Washington Bureau, January 17, 1995.

far smaller than the actual deficit in, say, 1983. But within a few years, the economy improved and the tax cuts became fully effective, leaving an enormous structural deficit.

By the late 1980s, the economy was at or beyond full employment, so deliberate fiscal policy actions (and inactions) accounted for virtually all of the deficit. Then the budget deteriorated further as the government's interest bill mounted (because of past deficits) and spending on items like health care soared. Whether the blame for failing to address the deficit problem earlier rests with Presidents Reagan and Bush or with the Democratic Congress is a matter of politics, not economics. But the fact is that little was done to solve the problem until President Clinton's large deficit-reduction package was enacted in 1993.

2. *Is the deficit really a problem?* Once again, the answer to the question was different in 1981 to 1983 from what it has been since. In 1981 and 1982, the economy went through a deep recession. And in 1983, the first year of the recovery, unemployment was still far above its full-employment level. Under these circumstances, crowding out would not be expected to be a serious problem and actions to close the deficit would have threatened the recovery. According to the basic principles of fiscal policy, a large deficit was probably appropriate.

But things were much different by the late 1980s. Crowding out became a more serious issue as the economy neared full employment. So budget deficits should have fallen. But the actual deficit did not fall, and the structural deficit actually rose. For about a decade now, we have had persistently large structural deficits regardless of whether the economy is strong (as in 1994 to 1995) or weak (as in 1990 to 1991). So worries about the burden of the national debt, once mostly myths, have become all too realistic.

3. *What can be done about the deficit?* There is no magic bullet when it comes to deficit reduction. It is a matter of simple arithmetic that you close a budget deficit either by raising taxes or by reducing spending. The Clinton plan enacted in 1993 had some of each. The 1996 budget packages that President Clinton and the Republican Congress struggled over relied exclusively on spending cuts. But either taxing more or spending less is a contractionary fiscal policy that reduces aggregate demand.

Is that a problem? Not necessarily, if fiscal and monetary policies are well-coordinated. If fiscal policy turns contractionary to reduce the deficit, monetary policy can turn expansionary to counteract the effects on aggregate demand. In this way, we can hope to shrink the deficit without shrinking the economy. Such a change in the "policy mix" should also bring down interest rates, since both tighter budgets and easier money tend to push interest rates down. This, indeed, was the central hope of both Clintonomics in 1993 and the Republican plan in 1995. And it appears to be working. Interest rates fell dramatically in 1993, rose due to the Fed's tighter monetary policy in 1994, but then fell sharply again in late 1994 and 1995. Investment spending has been extremely strong in recent years.

SUMMARY

1. Rigid adherence to budget balancing would make the economy less stable by reducing aggregate demand (via tax increases and reductions in government spending) when private spending is low and raising aggregate demand when private spending is high.
2. Since both monetary and fiscal policy influence aggregate demand, the appropriate **budget deficit** or surplus depends on monetary policy. Similarly, the appropriate monetary policy depends on budget policy.
3. The **national debt** has grown dramatically relative to GDP since the early 1980s, reversing the previous postwar trend.
4. One major reason for the large budget deficits of the early 1980s and early 1990s was the fact that the economy operated well below full employment. In those years, the **structural deficit,** which uses estimates of what the government's receipts and outlays would be at full employment, was much smaller than the official deficit.
5. Inflation exaggerates the deficit because all *nominal interest payments* are counted as expenditures. Under **inflation accounting,** only *real interest payments* would count as expenditures, and the deficit would be seen to be much smaller.
6. If we correct the official deficit for inflation and adjust it to high levels of employment, we find that deficits in the structural, inflation-corrected budget began only around 1983. Before that, there were balanced budgets or surpluses.
7. Arguments that the public debt will burden future generations, who will have to make huge payments of interest and principal, are mostly based on false analogies. In fact, most of these payments are simply transfers from one group of Americans to another. However, taxes must be raised to pay the interest, and there is a legitimate worry about the portion of the national debt that is owned by foreigners.
8. The bogus argument that a large national debt can bankrupt a country like the United States ignores the fact that our national debt consists of obligations to pay U.S. dollars—a currency the government can raise by taxation or create by printing money.
9. Under many circumstances, budget deficits are inflationary because they expand aggregate demand. They are even more inflationary if they are **monetized,** that is, if the Federal Reserve buys some of the newly issued government debt in the open market.
10. Unless the deficit is substantially monetized, deficit spending forces interest rates higher and discourages private investment spending. This is called the **crowding-out effect.** If there is a great deal of crowding out, then deficits really do impose a *burden on future generations* by leaving them a smaller capital stock to work with.
11. But there is also a **crowding-in effect** from higher government spending (G). If expansionary fiscal policy succeeds in raising real output (Y), more investment will be induced by the higher Y.
12. Whether crowding out or crowding in dominates largely depends on the time horizon. In the short run, and especially when unemployment is high, crowding in is probably the stronger force; so higher G does not cause lower investment. But, in the long run, the economy will be near full employment, and the proponents of the crowding-out hypothesis will be proven right: High government spending mainly displaces private investment.
13. Whether or not deficits are a burden therefore depends on how and why the government ran these deficits in the first place. If the government runs

deficits to fight recessions, it is possible that more investment is crowded in by the increases in income that these deficits make possible than is crowded out by the increases in interest rates. Deficits contracted to carry on wars certainly impair the future capital stock, though they may not be considered a burden for noneconomic reasons. Since these two cases account for most of the debt the U.S. government contracted until the mid-1980s, that debt cannot reasonably be considered a serious burden. However, recent deficits are more worrisome on this score. This is one of the **Ideas for Beyond the Final Exam.**

KEY TERMS

Budget deficit
National debt
Real versus nominal interest rates
Inflation accounting
Structural deficit or surplus
Monetization of deficits
Crowding out
Crowding in
Burden of the national debt
Mix of monetary and fiscal policy

QUESTIONS FOR REVIEW

1. Explain the difference between the budget deficit and the national debt. If we reduce the deficit, will the debt stop growing?
2. Explain how the U.S. government has managed to accumulate a debt of over $5 trillion. To whom does it owe this debt? Can the debt be considered a burden on future generations?
3. Comment on the following: "Deficit spending paves the road to ruin. If we keep it up, the whole nation will go bankrupt. Even if things do not go this far, what right have we to burden our children and grandchildren with these debts while we live high on the hog?"
4. Calculate the budget deficit and the inflation-corrected deficit for an economy with the following data:

   Government expenditures other than interest = 1,400
   Tax receipts = 1,500
   Interest payments = 240
   Interest rate = 6 percent
   Inflation rate = 3 percent
   National debt at start of year = 4,000
   (*Note:* 6 percent interest on a $4,000 debt is $240.)
5. Explain in words why the structural budget might show a surplus while the actual budget is in deficit. Illustrate this with a diagram like Figure 15-4.
6. If the Federal Reserve begins to increase the money supply more slowly than before, what will happen to the government budget deficit? (*Hint:* What will happen to tax receipts and interest expenses?) If the government wants to offset the effects of the Fed's actions on aggregate demand, what might it do? How will this affect the deficit?
7. Newspaper reports frequently suggest that the administration (regardless of who is president) is pressuring the Fed to lower interest rates. In view of your answer to Review Question 6, why do you think that might be?
8. Given the current state of the economy, do you think the Fed should monetize more of the deficit? (*Note:* There is no one correct answer to this question. It is a good question to discuss in class.)
9. Explain the difference between crowding out and crowding in. Given the current state of the economy, which effect would you expect to dominate right now?

CHAPTER 16

THE TRADE-OFF BETWEEN INFLATION AND UNEMPLOYMENT

We must seek to reduce inflation at a lower cost in lost output and unemployment.
Jimmy Carter

In the late 1980s, unemployment fell to extremely low levels in the United States. Soon thereafter, inflation rose. Then, during and after the 1990–1991 recession, unemployment rose, and inflation soon declined. From 1994 to 1996, inflation was fairly stable while unemployment hovered close to commonly accepted estimates of the "full-employment" rate—between 5.5 and 6.0 percent. Most economists believe that this conjunction of events was no coincidence. Rather, they insist, the extremely low unemployment rates of 1988 to 1990 led to higher inflation.* And the period of high unemployment in 1991 to 1993 was the price we paid to reduce inflation. Although some optimists claim that it is possible to reduce inflation without suffering from unemployment, the United States clearly paid a sizable price for the disinflation of the early 1990s. Was this price inevitable, or could we have avoided it? That is the question for this chapter.

You may recall from Chapter 1 that the existence of an agonizing trade-off between inflation and unemployment is one of the **Ideas for Beyond the Final Exam.** The importance of this trade-off can hardly be overestimated. It is probably the area of macroeconomics where confusion is most widespread. And because this confusion can have disastrous consequences for the conduct of stabilization policy, the trade-off merits the comprehensive examination that we give it in this chapter.

We begin the chapter by reviewing briefly what we have already learned about inflation. Then we contrast the differing empirical implications of inflation that emanates from rapid growth of aggregate demand versus that which comes from slow growth in aggregate supply. We next examine how people's expectations about inflation affect the nature of the trade-off, and consider some special things that can happen if these expectations are "rational"—a term that we will define precisely. Finally, we discuss some political and economic aspects of the trade-off between inflation and unemployment and look into some suggested remedies.

*Fears that this might happen again prompted the Federal Reserve to raise interest rates in the spring of 1997.

DEMAND-SIDE INFLATION VERSUS SUPPLY-SIDE INFLATION: A REVIEW

Since this chapter is the capstone of Part III, we begin by reviewing some of what we have learned about inflation in earlier chapters.

One major cause of inflation, though certainly not the only one, is *excessive growth of aggregate demand.* We know that any autonomous increase in spending—whether by consumers, investors, the government, or foreigners—will have a multiplier effect on aggregate demand. So each additional $1 of C or I or G or $(X - IM)$ will lead to more than $1 of additional demand. We also know that firms normally find it profitable to supply the additional output only at higher prices. Hence, a stimulus to aggregate demand will normally pull up *both* real output *and* prices.

Figure 16-1, which is familiar from earlier chapters, reviews this conclusion. Initially, the economy is at point A, where aggregate demand curve D_0D_0 intersects aggregate supply curve SS. Then something happens to increase demand, and the aggregate demand curve shifts horizontally to D_1D_1. The new equilibrium is at point B, where both prices and output are higher than they were at A.

The slope of the aggregate supply curve measures the amount of inflation that accompanies any specified rise in output and therefore embodies the trade-off between unemployment and inflation. We observed in Chapter 14 that this trade-off looks rather different in the short and long runs because the aggregate supply curve is fairly flat in the short run but quite steep (perhaps even vertical) in the long run. Thus, a stimulus to demand mostly raises output (lowers unemployment) in the short run but mostly raises prices in the long run.

But we have learned in this book (especially in Chapter 10) that inflation need not always emanate from the demand side. Restrictions in the growth of aggregate supply—caused, for example, by an increase in the price of foreign oil—can shift the economy's aggregate supply curve inward. This is illustrated in Figure 16-2, where the aggregate supply curve shifts from S_0S_0 to S_1S_1, and the economy's equilibrium consequently moves from point A to point B. Prices rise as output falls. We have *stagflation.*

FIGURE 16-1 INFLATION FROM THE DEMAND SIDE

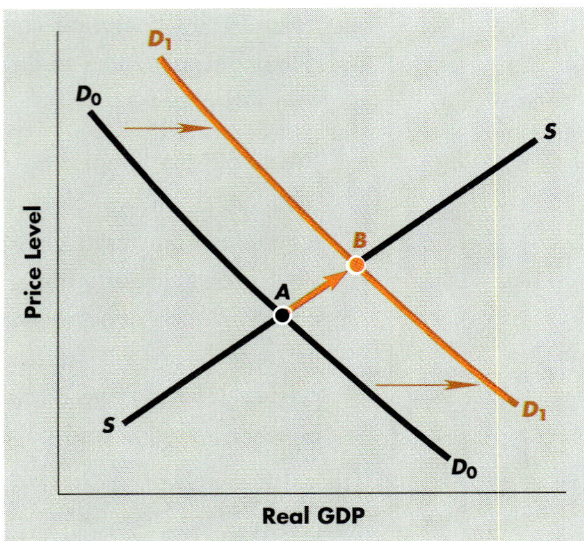

An increase in aggregate demand, whether it comes from consumers, investors, foreigners, or the government, shifts the aggregate demand curve outward from D_0D_0 to D_1D_1. The economy's equilibrium moves from point A to point B. Since point B corresponds to a higher price level than does point A, there is inflation (that is, a rising price level) as the economy moves from A to B.

FIGURE 16-2 INFLATION FROM THE SUPPLY SIDE

A decrease in aggregate supply—which can be caused by such factors as an autonomous increase in wages or an increase in the price of foreign oil—can cause inflation. When the aggregate supply curve shifts to the left, from S_0S_0 to S_1S_1, the equilibrium point moves from *A* to *B*. Comparing *B* with *A*, we see that the price level is higher, which means there must have been *inflation* (rising prices) in the interim. Notice also that adverse supply shifts make real output decline while prices are rising; that is, they produce *stagflation*.

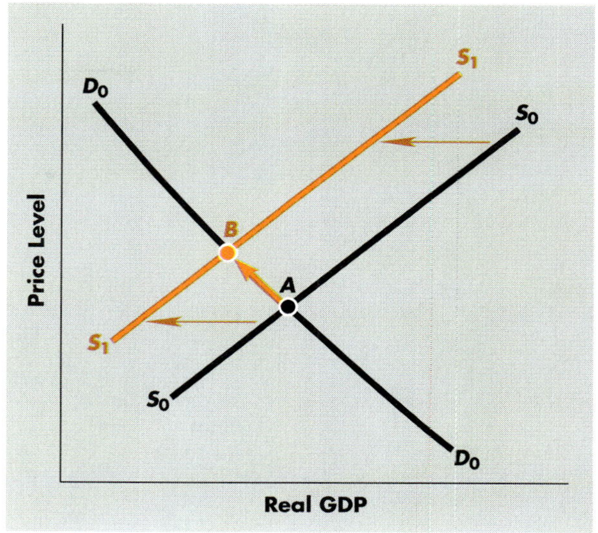

Thus, while inflation can be initiated from either the *demand* side or the *supply* side of the economy, there is a crucial difference. Demand-side inflation is normally accompanied by rising real GDP (see Figure 16-1), while supply-side inflation may well be accompanied by falling GDP (see Figure 16-2). This is a crucial distinction, as we shall see in this chapter.

APPLYING THE MODEL TO A GROWING ECONOMY

You may have noticed that our simple model of aggregate supply and demand determines an equilibrium *price level* and an equilibrium *level of real GDP.* But, in the real world, neither the price level nor real GDP remains constant for long. Instead, both normally rise from year to year.

This is illustrated in Figure 16-3, which is a scatter diagram of the U.S. price level and the level of real GDP for every year from 1972 to 1996. The points are labeled to show the clear upward march of the economy through time—toward higher prices and higher levels of output.

It is certainly no mystery why this occurs. The normal state of affairs is for *both* the aggregate demand curve *and* the aggregate supply curve to shift to the right each year. Aggregate supply grows because there are more workers and more capital each year, and because technology improves. Aggregate demand grows because a growing population generates more demand for both consumer and investment goods, because the government increases its spending, and because the Federal Reserve increases the money supply. We can think of each point in Figure 16-3 as the intersection of an aggregate supply curve and an aggregate demand curve for that particular year. To help you visualize this, the curves for 1980 and 1988 are sketched in the diagram.

Figure 16-4 illustrates how our theoretical model of aggregate supply and aggregate demand applies to a growing economy. We have chosen the numbers

FIGURE 16-3 THE PRICE LEVEL AND REAL OUTPUT IN THE UNITED STATES, 1972–1996

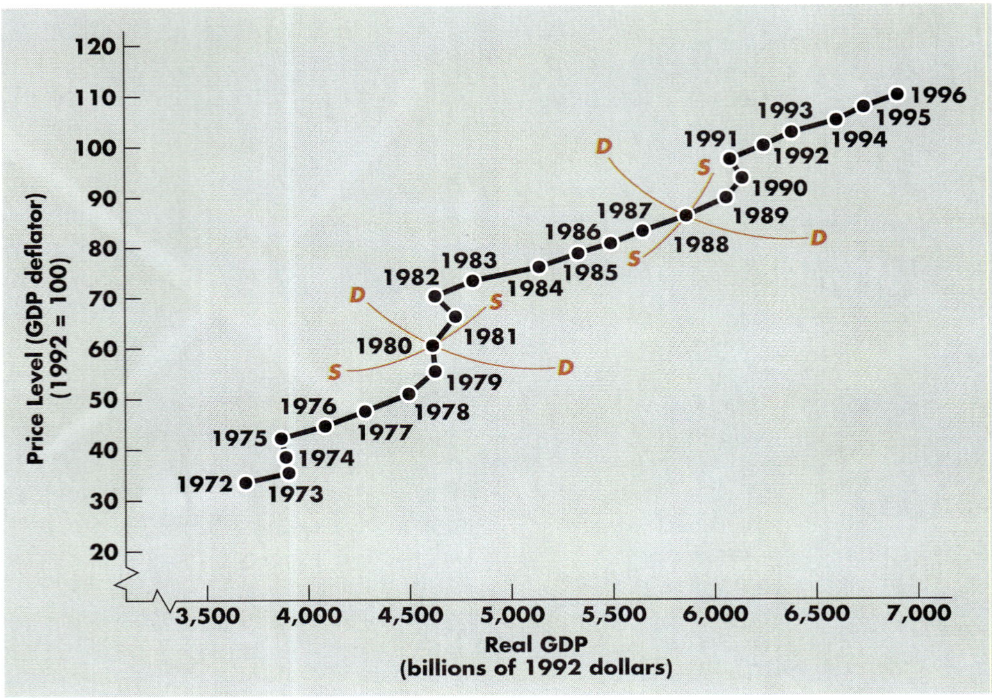

This scatter diagram shows, for each year from 1972 to 1996, the price level (GDP deflator) and real GDP for the United States. Clearly the normal state of affairs is for both prices and output to rise from one year to the next.

SOURCE: U.S. Department of Commerce, Bureau of Economic Analysis.

FIGURE 16-4 AGGREGATE SUPPLY AND DEMAND ANALYSIS OF A GROWING ECONOMY

This diagram illustrates how aggregate supply and demand analysis can be applied to a real-world economy, in which both the supply curve and the demand curve shift outward from one year to the next. Here, demand curve D_0D_0 and supply curve S_0S_0 represent the U.S. economy in 1995. Equilibrium was at point *A*, with a price level of 100 and real GDP of \$6,000 billion (in 1995 dollars). Demand curve D_1D_1 and supply curve S_1S_1 represent 1996. During the year, the price index rose by 3 percent and output increased by \$180 billion (or 3 percent).

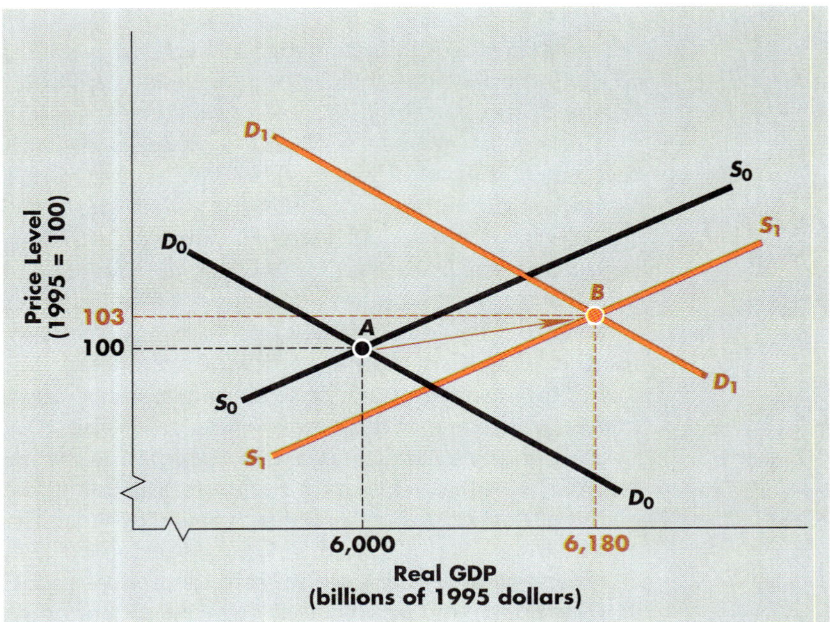

so that curves D_0D_0 and S_0S_0 roughly represent the year 1995, and the curves D_1D_1 and S_1S_1 roughly represent 1996, except that we use nice round numbers to make the computations simple. Thus, the equilibrium in 1995 was at point *A*, with a real GDP of $6,000 billion (in 1995 dollars) and a price level of 100, while the equilibrium a year later was at point *B*, with real GDP at $6,180 billion and the price level at 103. The orange arrow in the diagram shows how equilibrium moved from 1995 to 1996. It points upward and to the right, meaning that both prices and output increased. In this case, both increased 3 percent.

DEMAND-SIDE INFLATION AND THE PHILLIPS CURVE

Let us now use our theoretical model to rerun history. Suppose that between 1995 and 1996 aggregate demand grew *faster* than it actually did. What difference would this have made for the performance of the national economy? Figure 16-5 provides the answers. Here the demand curve D_0D_0 and both supply curves are exactly as they were in the previous diagram, but the demand curve D_2D_2 is farther to the right than the demand curve D_1D_1 in Figure 16-4. Equilibrium is at point *A* in 1995 and point *C* in 1996. Comparing point *C* in Figure 16-5 with point *B* in Figure 16-4, we see that output would have increased more over the year ($300 billion versus $180 billion) and prices would also have increased more (to 104 instead of 103); that is, there would have been more *inflation*. This is generally what happens when the growth rate of aggregate demand speeds up.

For any given rate of growth of the aggregate supply curve, a faster rate of growth of the aggregate demand curve will lead to more inflation and faster growth of real output.

FIGURE 16-5

THE EFFECTS OF FASTER GROWTH OF AGGREGATE DEMAND

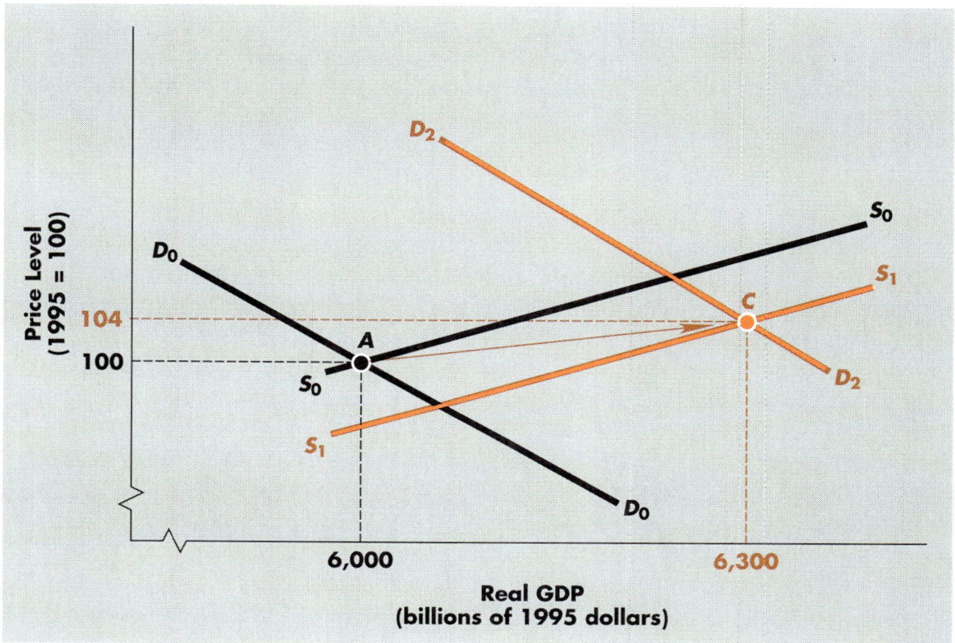

In this hypothetical example, we imagine that because either private citizens spent more or the government pursued more expansionary policies, aggregate demand grew faster between 1995 and 1996 than it did in Figure 16-4. The consequence is that, in this diagram, the price level rises 4 percent from 1995 to 1996 compared with 3 percent in Figure 16-4. Growth of real output is also greater: $300 billion here versus only $180 billion in the previous figure.

FIGURE 16-6 THE EFFECTS OF SLOWER GROWTH OF AGGREGATE DEMAND

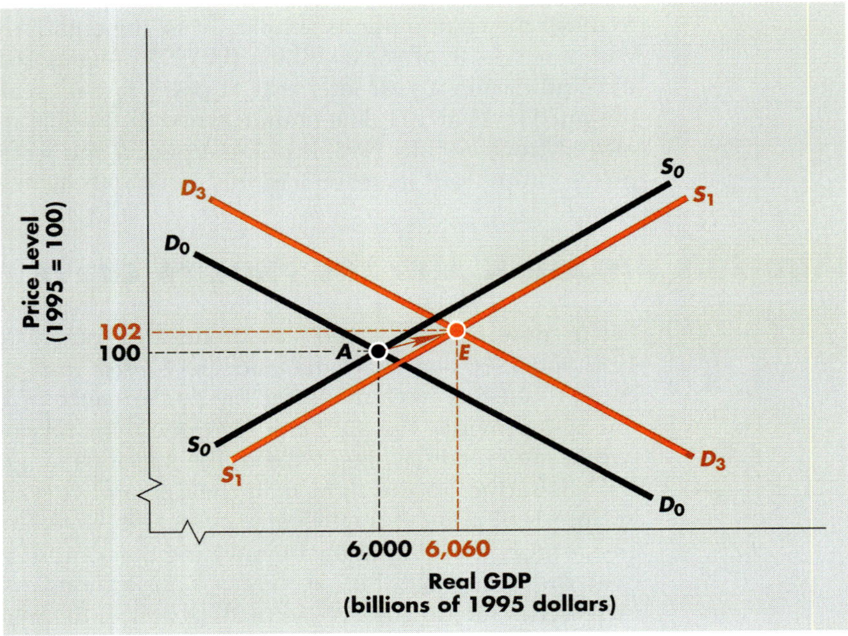

Here, the aggregate demand curve is assumed to shift outward less than it did in Figure 16-4. Consequently, the movement from equilibrium point *A* to equilibrium point *E* from 1995 to 1996 entails a smaller rise in the price level and a smaller increase in real output than actually occurred.

Figure 16-6 illustrates the opposite case. Here we imagine that the aggregate demand curve shifted out *less* than in Figure 16-4. That is, demand curve D_3D_3 in Figure 16-6 is to the left of demand curve D_1D_1 in Figure 16-4. The consequence, we see, is that the shift of the economy's equilibrium from 1995 to 1996 (from point *A* to point *E*) would have entailed *less inflation* and *slower growth of real output* than actually took place. This again is generally the case.

For any given rate of growth of the aggregate supply curve, a slower rate of growth of the aggregate demand curve will lead to less inflation and slower growth of real output.

If we put these two findings together, we have a clear prediction from our theory:

If fluctuations in the economy's real growth rate from year to year are caused primarily by variations in the rate at which aggregate demand increases, then the data should show the most rapid inflation occurring when output grows most rapidly and the slowest inflation occurring when output grows most slowly.

Does the theory fit the facts? We will put it to the test in a moment, but first let us translate it into a prediction about the relationship between inflation and *unemployment*. Faster growth of real output naturally means faster growth in the number of jobs and, hence, *lower unemployment*. Conversely, slower growth of real output means slower growth in the number of jobs and, hence, *higher unemployment*. So we conclude that, if business fluctuations emanate from the demand side, unemployment and inflation should move inversely: Unemployment should be low when inflation is high, and inflation should be low when unemployment is high.

FIGURE 16-7 ORIGINS OF THE PHILLIPS CURVE

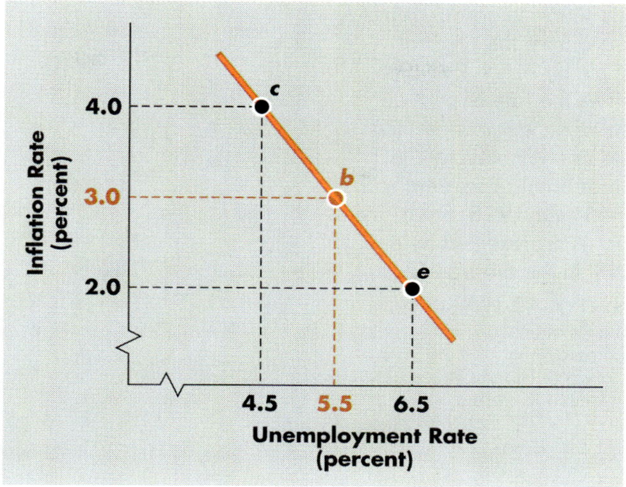

The three previous diagrams indicated three different rates of growth of real GDP between 1995 and 1996 and three different inflation rates. Since each different real growth rate corresponds to a different rate of unemployment, we can put the information contained in the three preceding diagrams together in a scatter diagram to show the relationship between inflation and unemployment. Points *b, c,* and *e* in this figure correspond to points *B, C,* and *E* in Figures 16-4, 16-5, and 16-6, respectively. The inflation numbers are read directly from the previous three graphs. The unemployment numbers are indicative of the fact that faster growth (Figure 16-5) is associated with lower unemployment (point *c*), while slower growth (Figure 16-6) is associated with higher unemployment (point *e*). Scatter diagrams like this one are called "Phillips curves," after their inventor, A. W. Phillips.

Figure 16-7 illustrates this idea. The unemployment rate in the United States in 1996 averaged approximately 5.4 percent, and the inflation rate from 1995 to 1996 was about 3 percent. This is point *b* in Figure 16-7, which corresponds to equilibrium point *B* in Figure 16-4. The faster growth rate of demand depicted by point *C* in Figure 16-5 would have led to higher inflation and lower unemployment. For the sake of a concrete example, we suppose that unemployment would have been 4.5 percent and inflation would have been 4 percent; this is point *c* in Figure 16-7. Point *E* in Figure 16-6 summarized the results of slower growth of aggregate demand: Unemployment would have been higher and inflation lower. In Figure 16-7, this is represented by point *e,* with an unemployment rate of 6.5 percent and an inflation rate of 2 percent. This figure shows graphically the principal empirical implication of our theoretical model:

If fluctuations in economic activity are primarily caused by variations in the rate at which the aggregate demand curve shifts outward from year to year, then the data should show an inverse relationship between unemployment and inflation, as in Figure 16-7.

Now we are ready to look at real data. Do we actually observe such an inverse relationship between inflation and unemployment? Almost 40 years ago, economist A. W. Phillips plotted data on unemployment and the rate of change of *wages* (not prices) for several extended periods of British history on a series of scatter diagrams, one of which is reproduced as Figure 16-8. He then sketched in a curve that seemed to "fit" the data well. This type of curve, which is now called a **Phillips curve,** shows that wage inflation normally is high when unemployment is low and is low when unemployment is high. So far, so good.

A **PHILLIPS CURVE** is a graph depicting the rate of unemployment on the horizontal axis and either the rate of inflation or the rate of change of money wages on the vertical axis. Phillips curves are normally downward sloping, indicating that higher inflation rates are associated with lower unemployment rates.

Phillips curves have also been constructed for *price* inflation, and one of these for the postwar United States is shown in Figure 16-9. The curve appears to fit the data well, though not perfectly. As viewed through the eyes of our theory, these facts suggest that economic fluctuations in Great Britain between 1861 and 1913 and in the United States between 1954 and 1969 probably were accounted for primarily by changes in the growth of aggregate demand. The simple model of demand-side inflation really does seem to describe what happened.

FIGURE 16-8 THE ORIGINAL PHILLIPS CURVE

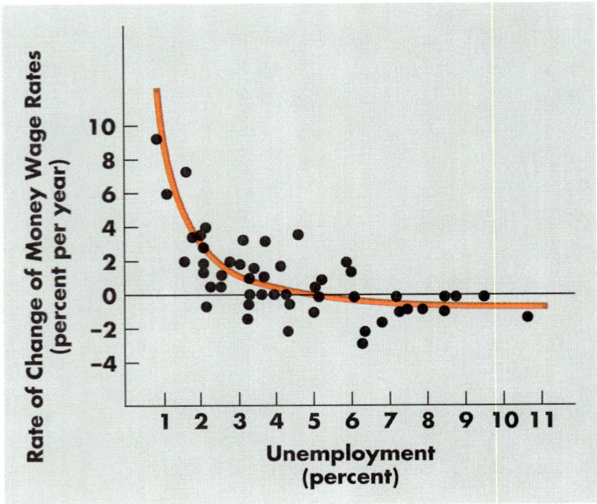

This scatter diagram, reproduced from the original article by A. W. Phillips, shows the rate of change of money wages and the rate of unemployment in Great Britain between 1861 and 1913. Each year is represented by a point in the diagram.

SOURCE: A. W. Phillips, "The Relation between Unemployment and the Rate of Change of Money Wages in the United Kingdom, 1861–1957," *Economica,* New Series, vol. 25 (November 1958).

During the 1960s and early 1970s, economists often thought of the Phillips curve as a "menu" of choices available to policymakers. In this view, policymakers could opt for low unemployment and high inflation—as in 1969. Or they might prefer higher unemployment coupled with lower inflation—as, for example, in 1961. The Phillips curve, it was thought, described the *quantitative* trade-off between inflation and unemployment. And, for a number of years, it worked rather well.

Then something happened. The economy in the 1970s and early 1980s behaved far worse than the Phillips curve shown in Figure 16-9 led economists to expect. In particular, given the unemployment rates in each of those years, inflation was astonishingly high by historical standards. This is shown in Figure

FIGURE 16-9 A PHILLIPS CURVE FOR THE UNITED STATES

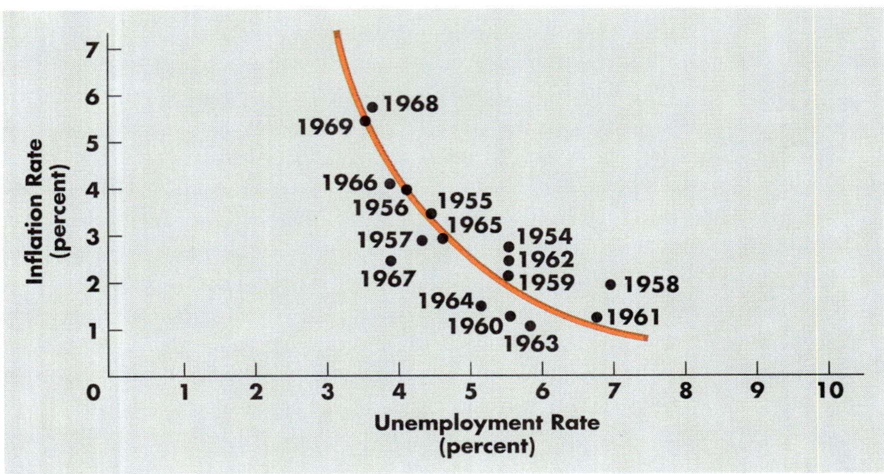

This Phillips curve relates *price* inflation (rather than wage inflation) to the unemployment rate in the United States for the years 1954 to 1969. Though it misses badly in a few instances (for example, 1958), it generally "fits" the data well.

FIGURE 16-10

A PHILLIPS CURVE FOR THE UNITED STATES?

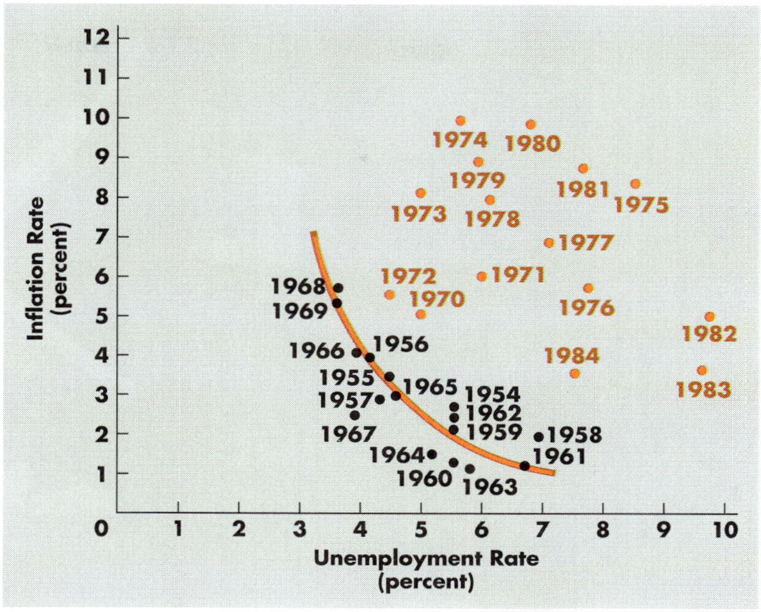

This scatter diagram adds the points for 1970 to 1984 to the scatter diagram shown in Figure 16-9. It is clear that inflation in each of those years was higher than the Phillips curve would have led us to predict.

16-10, which simply adds to Figure 16-9 the points for 1970 to 1984. Clearly something had gone wrong with the old view of the Phillips curve as a menu for policy choices. But what?

SUPPLY-SIDE INFLATION AND THE COLLAPSE OF THE PHILLIPS CURVE

There are two major answers to this question, and a full explanation contains elements of each. We begin with the simpler answer, which is that much of the inflation of the period from 1972 to 1982 did not emanate from the demand side. Instead, the 1970s and early 1980s were full of adverse "supply shocks"—events like the crop failures of 1972 to 1973 and the oil price increases of 1973 to 1974 and 1979 to 1980. These events pushed the economy's aggregate supply curve inward to the left. What kind of Phillips curve will be generated when economic fluctuations come from the supply side?

To find out, let us take the events of 1979 and 1980 as an example. In Figure 16-11, aggregate demand curve D_0D_0 and aggregate supply curve S_0S_0 represent the economic situation in 1979. Equilibrium was at point *A*, with a price level of 55 and real output of $4,624 billion. By 1980, the aggregate demand curve had shifted out to the position indicated by D_1D_1, and, under normal conditions, the aggregate supply curve would have shifted out as well. But 1979 to 1980 was anything but normal. The Iranian revolution led to a long shutdown of Iran's oil fields and a doubling of the price of oil.

Thus, instead of shifting *outward* as it normally does from one year to the next, the aggregate supply curve shifted *inward* from 1979 to 1980, to S_1S_1. The equilibrium for 1980 (point *B* in the figure) therefore wound up to the left of the equilibrium point for 1979. Real output declined slightly and prices—led by energy costs—rose rapidly.

FIGURE 16-11 STAGFLATION FROM A SUPPLY SHOCK

Instead of shifting outward as it normally does, the aggregate supply curve shifted inward—from S_0S_0 to S_1S_1—between 1979 and 1980. Coupled with fairly slow growth of the aggregate demand curve—from D_0D_0 in 1979 to D_1D_1 in 1980—equilibrium moved from point A to point B. There was a slight decline of real output, and prices rose rapidly.

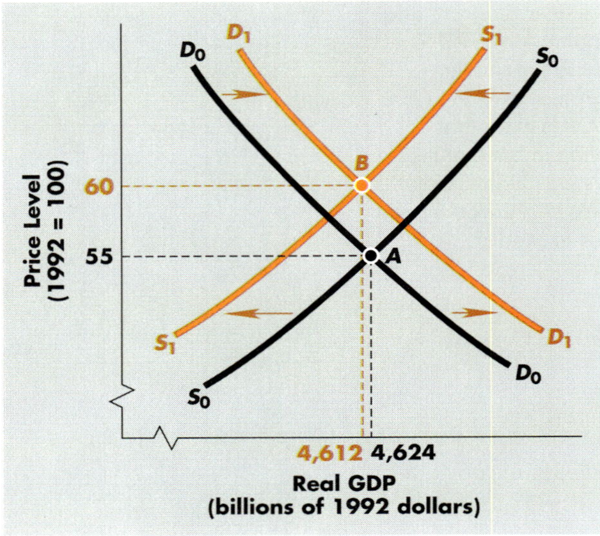

Now, in a growing population with more people looking for jobs each year, a stagnant economy that is not generating new jobs suffers a rise in the unemployment rate. This is precisely what happened in the United States; the unemployment rate averaged 5.8 percent in 1979 and 7.1 percent in 1980. Thus, inflation and unemployment increased at the same time: The Phillips curve basically shifted upward. A general conclusion is that:

If fluctuations in economic activity emanate from the supply side, higher rates of inflation will be associated with higher rates of unemployment, and lower rates of inflation will be associated with lower rates of unemployment.

The major supply shocks of the 1970s stand out clearly in Figure 16-10. (Remember these are *real* data, not textbook examples.) Food prices boomed in 1972 to 1974 and again in 1978. Energy prices soared in 1973 to 1974 and again in 1979 to 1980. Clearly, the inflation and unemployment data generated by the U.S. economy in 1972 to 1974, and again in 1978 to 1980, are consistent with our model of supply-side inflation. It was supply shocks, many economists believe, that made the Phillips curve shift.

WHAT THE PHILLIPS CURVE IS NOT

But there is another view of what went wrong in the 1970s. This one holds that policymakers misinterpreted the Phillips curve and tried to pick unsustainable combinations of inflation and unemployment.

Specifically, the Phillips curve is a *statistical relationship* between inflation and unemployment that we expect to emerge *if changes in the growth of aggregate demand are the predominant factor accounting for economic fluctuations*. But the curve was widely misinterpreted as depicting a number of *alternative equilibrium points* that the economy could achieve and from which policymakers could choose.

We can understand the flaw in this reasoning by quickly reviewing an earlier lesson. We know from Chapter 10 that the economy has a *self-correcting mecha-*

FIGURE 16-12 THE ELIMINATION OF A RECESSIONARY GAP

When the aggregate supply curve is S_0S_0 and the aggregate demand curve is *DD,* the economy will reach an equilibrium with a recessionary gap (point *A*). The resulting deflation of wages will cause the aggregate supply curve to shift outward (downward) from S_0S_0 to S_1S_1 and eventually to S_2S_2. Here, with equilibrium at point *C,* the recessionary gap is gone and the economy is back at normal full employment.

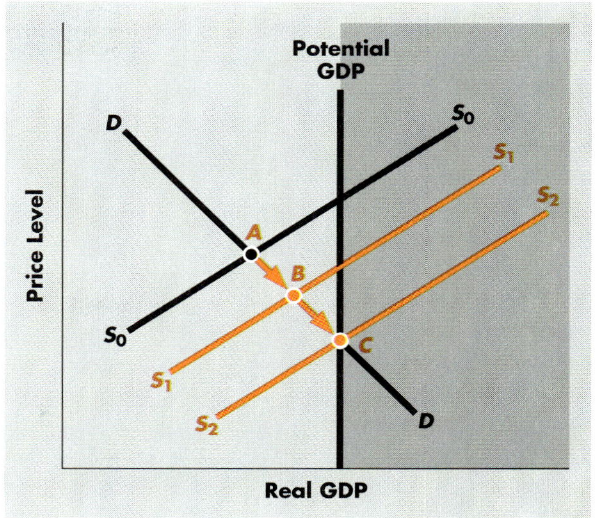

nism that will cure both inflations and recessions *eventually* even if the government does nothing. Why is this relevant here? Because it tells us that many combinations of output and prices cannot be maintained indefinitely. Some will "self-destruct." For example, if the economy finds itself far away from the normal full-employment level of unemployment, forces will be set in motion that tend to erode the inflationary or recessionary gap.

Figure 16-12 depicts the case of a recessionary gap where aggregate supply curve S_0S_0 intersects aggregate demand curve *DD* at point *A*. With equilibrium output well below potential GDP, there is unused industrial capacity and unsold output. So firms will not raise prices much. At the same time, the availability of unemployed workers eager for jobs limits the rate at which labor can push up wage rates. But wages are the main component of business costs, so when wages decline (relative to what they would have been without a recession) so do costs. And lower costs stimulate greater production. Figure 16-12 illustrates this idea as an outward shift of the aggregate supply curve—from S_0S_0 to S_1S_1.

As the figure shows, the outward shift of the aggregate supply curve brought on by the recession pushes equilibrium output up as the economy moves from point *A* to point *B*. Thus, the size of the recessionary gap begins to shrink. This process continues until the aggregate supply curve reaches the position indicated by S_2S_2 in Figure 16-12. Here wages have fallen enough to eliminate the recessionary gap, and the economy has reached a full-employment equilibrium at point *C*.[1]

We can relate this to our discussion of the origins of the Phillips curve with the help of Figure 16-13, which is a hypothetical Phillips curve. Point *a* in Figure 16-13 corresponds to point *A* in Figure 16-12: It shows the initial recessionary gap with unemployment (assumed to be 7.0 percent) above full employment, which we assume to occur at 5.5 percent.

[1]This simple analysis assumes that the aggregate demand curve does not move during the adjustment period. If it is shifting to the right, the recessionary gap will disappear even faster, but inflation will not slow down as much. EXERCISE: Construct the diagram for this case by adding a shift in the aggregate demand curve to Figure 16-12.

FIGURE 16-13 THE VERTICAL LONG-RUN PHILLIPS CURVE

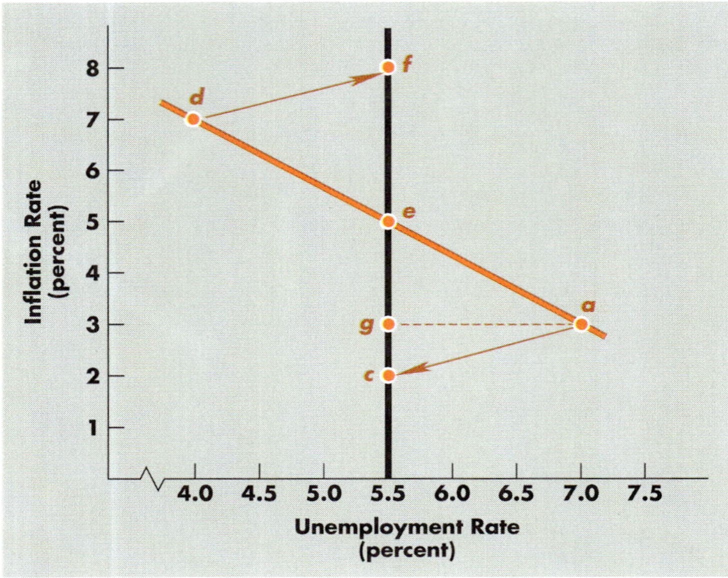

In the long run, points like *a*, where unemployment is above the normal "full-employment" unemployment rate, are unsustainable. The economy's natural self-correcting mechanism (which was described in Figure 16-12) will erode the recessionary gap by reducing both inflation and unemployment. In the diagram, this will force the economy toward a point like *c*. The long-run choices, therefore, are among points like *c* and *f*, which constitute what is called the vertical (long-run) Phillips curve, not among points like *d* and *a* on the downward-sloping (short-run) Phillips curve.

But we have just seen that point *A* in Figure 16-12—and therefore also point *a* in Figure 16-13—is not sustainable. The economy tends to rid itself of the recessionary gap through the disinflation process we have just described. The adjustment path from *A* to *C* depicted in Figure 16-12 would appear on our Phillips curve diagram as a movement toward less inflation and less unemployment—something like the orange arrow from point *a* to point *c* in Figure 16-13.

Similarly, points representing inflationary gaps—such as point *d* in Figure 16-13—are not sustainable. They are also gradually eliminated by the self-correcting mechanism that we studied in Chapter 10. Wages are forced up by the abnormally low unemployment, and this in turn pushes prices higher. Higher prices deter investment spending by forcing up interest rates and deter consumer spending by lowering the purchasing power of consumer wealth. The inflationary process continues until the amount people want to spend is brought into balance with the amount firms want to supply at normal full employment. During such an adjustment period, unemployment and inflation are both rising—as indicated by the orange arrow from point *d* to point *f* in Figure 16-13.

Putting these two conclusions together, we see that:

On a Phillips curve diagram, neither points corresponding to an inflationary gap (like *d* in Figure 16-13) nor points corresponding to a recessionary gap (like *a* in Figure 16-13) can be maintained indefinitely. Inflationary gaps lead to rising unemployment and rising inflation. Recessionary gaps lead to falling inflation and falling unemployment.

All the points that are sustainable in the long run (such as *c*, *e*, and *f* in Figure 16-13) correspond to the same rate of unemployment, which is therefore called the **natural rate of unemployment.** The natural rate corresponds to what we have so far been calling the "full-employment" unemployment rate.

The economy's self-correcting mechanism always tends to push the unemployment rate back toward a specific rate of unemployment that we call the **NATURAL RATE OF UNEMPLOYMENT.**

The **VERTICAL (LONG-RUN) PHILLIPS CURVE** shows the menu of inflation/unemployment choices available to society in the long run. It is a vertical straight line at the natural rate of unemployment.

Thus, the Phillips curve connecting points *d, e,* and *a* is not a menu of policy choices. While we can move from a point like *e* to a point like *d* by stimulating aggregate demand sufficiently, the economy will not stay at point *d*. Unemployment cannot be kept this low indefinitely. Instead, policymakers must choose from among points like *c, e,* and *f,* all of which correspond to the same "natural" rate of unemployment. For obvious reasons, the line connecting these points has been dubbed the **vertical (long-run) Phillips curve.** It is this vertical Phillips curve, connecting points like *e* and *f,* that represents the true long-run menu of policy choices. We thus conclude:

THE TRADE-OFF BETWEEN INFLATION AND UNEMPLOYMENT

In the short run, it is possible to "ride up the Phillips curve" toward lower levels of unemployment by stimulating aggregate demand. (See, for example, point *d* in Figure 16-13.) Conversely, by restricting the growth of demand, it is possible to "ride down the Phillips curve" toward lower rates of inflation (like point *a* in Figure 16-13). Thus, there is a *trade-off between unemployment and inflation* in the short run. Stimulating demand will improve the unemployment picture but worsen inflation; restricting demand will lower inflation but aggravate the unemployment problem.

However, *there is no such trade-off in the long run.* The economy's self-correcting mechanism ensures that unemployment eventually returns to the "natural rate," no matter what happens to aggregate demand. In the long run, faster growth of demand leads only to higher inflation, not to lower unemployment; and slower growth of demand leads only to lower inflation, not to higher unemployment.

FIGHTING UNEMPLOYMENT WITH FISCAL AND MONETARY POLICY

Now let us apply this analysis to a concrete policy problem, one that has troubled Presidents Reagan, Bush, and Clinton, and many others before them. How, if at all, should the government's ability to manage aggregate demand through fiscal and monetary policy be used to combat unemployment?

Since unemployment in the United States has been low since late 1994, we must go back to early 1993 for a real-world example. When President Clinton took office in January 1993, the inflation rate was about 3 percent and the unemployment rate was about 7 percent—a starting point just like point *a* in Figure 16-13. The president considered 7 percent unemployment intolerably high. What were his options? Should he have adopted a policy of boosting the growth of aggregate demand by expansionary fiscal and/or monetary policies?

Suppose first that nothing was done. The economy's self-correcting mechanism would have gradually eroded the recessionary gap that existed at point *a*. Both unemployment and inflation would have declined gradually as the economy moved along the orange arrow from point *a* to point *c* in Figure 16-13. Eventually, the diagram shows, the economy would have returned to its natural rate of unemployment (5.5 percent) and inflation would have fallen—from 3 percent to 2 percent in the diagram.

This eventual outcome is quite satisfactory—lower unemployment *and* lower inflation. But it may take an agonizingly long time to get there. Suppose now that the president was impatient and wanted to see unemployment decline much faster. A large dose of expansionary fiscal and monetary policy could have pushed the economy up the short-run Phillips curve from point *a* toward point *e* in Figure 16-13. The faster economic growth and lower unemployment would have made the president (and the voters) happy. But it would also have left us with higher inflation, roughly 5 percent in the example.

This, then, is the range of choices: Wait patiently while the economy's self-correcting mechanism pulls unemployment down to the natural rate—leading to a long-run equilibrium like point *c* in Figure 16-13. Or rush the process along with expansionary stabilization policy—and wind up with the same unemployment rate but higher inflation. In what sense, then, do policymakers face a *trade-off* between inflation and unemployment? The answer is:

The cost of reducing unemployment more rapidly by expansionary fiscal and monetary policies is a permanently higher inflation rate.

WHAT SHOULD BE DONE?

Should the government pay the inflationary costs of fighting unemployment? When the transitory benefit (lower unemployment for a while) is balanced against the permanent cost (higher inflation), have we made a good bargain?

The United States opted for an intermediate strategy in 1993 to 1994. The Federal Reserve had embarked on an expansionary monetary policy to reduce unemployment well before President Clinton was elected, and it maintained this policy into early 1994. So two forces were acting simultaneously: The self-correcting mechanism was pulling the economy toward point *c* in Figure 16-13, and the Fed's expansionary policy was pushing it toward point *e*. The net result was an intermediate path (shown as the dotted line) leading to a point like *g*. By the end of 1994, the unemployment rate was down to about 5.5 percent and inflation remained around 3 percent.

How do policymakers make such decisions? Our analysis highlights three critical issues on which the answer depends.

THE COSTS OF INFLATION AND UNEMPLOYMENT

We spent an entire chapter (Chapter 6) examining the social costs of inflation and unemployment. Most of the benefits of lower unemployment, we concluded, are easily translated into dollars and cents. Basically, we need only estimate the real GDP that is gained each year. However, the costs of the permanently higher inflation rate are harder to measure. Thus, there is considerable controversy over the costs and benefits of using demand management to fight unemployment.

Some economists and public figures believe that inflation is extremely costly. They may therefore deem it unwise to accept the inflationary consequences of reducing unemployment faster. As just noted, U.S. policymakers apparently disagreed with that view in 1993.

THE SLOPE OF THE (SHORT-RUN) PHILLIPS CURVE

The shape of the short-run Phillips curve is also critical. Look back at Figure 16-13, and now suppose that the Phillips curve connecting points *a* and *e* was much steeper than shown. Then the inflationary costs of using expansionary policy to reduce unemployment would be more substantial. On the other hand, if the short-run Phillips curve was much flatter than shown in Figure 16-13, unemployment could be reduced with little inflationary cost.

THE EFFICIENCY OF THE ECONOMY'S SELF-CORRECTING MECHANISM

We have emphasized that, once a recessionary gap has opened up, it is the economy's natural self-correcting mechanism that closes it—if there is no policy response. The obvious question here is: How long do we have to wait? If the self-correcting mechanism—which works through reductions in the rate of wage inflation—is slow and halting, high unemployment will last a long time. So the costs of waiting will be enormous. But if wage inflation responds promptly, the costs of waiting will be small.

This is another issue that is surrounded by controversy. Most economists believe that the weight of the evidence points to extremely sluggish wage behavior. The rate of wage inflation appears to respond only slowly to economic slack. In terms of our Figure 16-13, this means that the economy will traverse the path from *a* to *c* at an agonizingly slow pace, so that a long period of weak economic activity will be necessary if there is to be any appreciable effect on inflation.

But a significant minority opinion finds this assessment far too pessimistic. Economists in this group argue that the costs of reducing inflation are not nearly so severe and that the key to a successful anti-inflation policy is its effects on people's *expectations*. To understand this argument, we must first examine why expectations are relevant to the Phillips-curve trade-off.

INFLATIONARY EXPECTATIONS AND THE PHILLIPS CURVE

Recall from Chapter 10 that the main reason why the economy's aggregate supply curve slopes upward—that is, why output increases as the price level rises—is that businesses typically purchase labor and other inputs under long-term contracts that fix the cost of the input in *money* terms. (The money wage rate is the clearest example.) If such contracts are in force when prices of goods go up, then *real* wages fall. Labor therefore becomes cheaper in real terms, which persuades businesses to expand employment and output. Buying cheaply and selling dearly is, after all, the route to higher profits.

Table 16-1 illustrates how this works in a concrete example. We suppose that workers and firms agree today that the money wage to be paid a year from now will be $10 per hour. The table then shows the real wage corresponding to each

TABLE 16-1 MONEY AND REAL WAGES UNDER UNEXPECTED INFLATION

Inflation Rate (percent)	Price Level 1 Year from Now	Money Wage 1 Year from Now (dollars per hour)	Real Wage 1 Year from Now (dollars per hour)
0	100	10.00	10.00
2	102	10.00	9.80
4	104	10.00	9.62
6	106	10.00	9.43

Note: Each real-wage figure is obtained by dividing the $10 nominal wage by the corresponding price level a year later and multiplying by 100. Thus, for example, when the inflation rate is 4 percent, the real wage at the end of the year is ($10.00/104) × 100 = $9.62.

alternative rate of inflation. Clearly, the higher the inflation rate, the higher the price level at the end of the year and the lower the real wage.

Lower real wages provide an incentive for the firm to increase output, as we have just noted. But lower real wages also impose losses of purchasing power on workers. Thus, there is a sense in which workers are "cheated" by inflation if they sign a contract specifying a fixed money wage in an inflationary environment.

Many economists doubt that workers will sign such contracts *if they can see inflation coming*. Would it not be wiser, these economists ask, to insist on being compensated for inflation in advance? After all, firms should be willing to offer higher money wages if they expect inflation, because they realize that higher money wages need not imply higher *real* wages. Table 16-2 illustrates how this can be done. For example, if 4 percent inflation is expected, the contract could stipulate that the wage rate be increased to $10.40 (which is 4 percent more than $10) at the end of the year. That would keep the real wage at $10, the same as it would be under zero inflation. The other money wage figures in Table 16-2 are derived similarly.

If workers and firms behave this way, and if they forecast inflation accurately, then the real wage will not decline as the price level rises. Instead, prices and wages will go up together, leaving the real wage unchanged. Workers will not lose from inflation, and firms will not gain. (In the table, the expected future real wage is $10 per hour regardless of the expected rate of inflation.) But then there would be no reason for firms to raise production when the price level rises. In a word, the aggregate supply curve would become *vertical*. In general:

If workers can see inflation coming, and if they receive compensation for it, inflation does not erode *real* wages. The economy's aggregate supply curve will then not slope upward. It will, instead, be a vertical line at the level of output corresponding to potential GDP.

Such a curve is shown in Panel (a) of Figure 16-14. Since we derived the Phillips curve from the aggregate supply curve earlier in the chapter, it follows that even the *short-run* Phillips curve would be vertical under these circumstances [see Panel (b) of Figure 16-14].[2]

If this analysis is correct, it has profound implications for the costs and benefits of inflation fighting. To see this, refer once again to Figure 16-13 on page 358, but now use the graph to depict the strategy of fighting inflation by caus-

TABLE 16-2 MONEY AND REAL WAGES UNDER EXPECTED INFLATION

Expected Inflation Rate (percent)	Expected Price Level 1 Year from Now	Money Wage 1 Year from Now (dollars per hour)	Expected Real Wage 1 Year from Now (dollars per hour)
0	100	10.00	10.00
2	102	10.20	10.00
4	104	10.40	10.00
6	106	10.60	10.00

[2]See Review Question 7 at the end of the chapter.

FIGURE 16-14 A VERTICAL AGGREGATE SUPPLY CURVE AND THE CORRESPONDING VERTICAL PHILLIPS CURVE

If workers foresee inflation, and if they also receive full compensation for it in advance, then inflation will no longer erode real wages. In that case, firms will have no incentive to raise production as prices rise, and the aggregate supply curve will be vertical as in Panel (a). Since we derived the short-run Phillips curve from the aggregate supply curve, the short-run Phillips curve will also become vertical [Panel (b)].

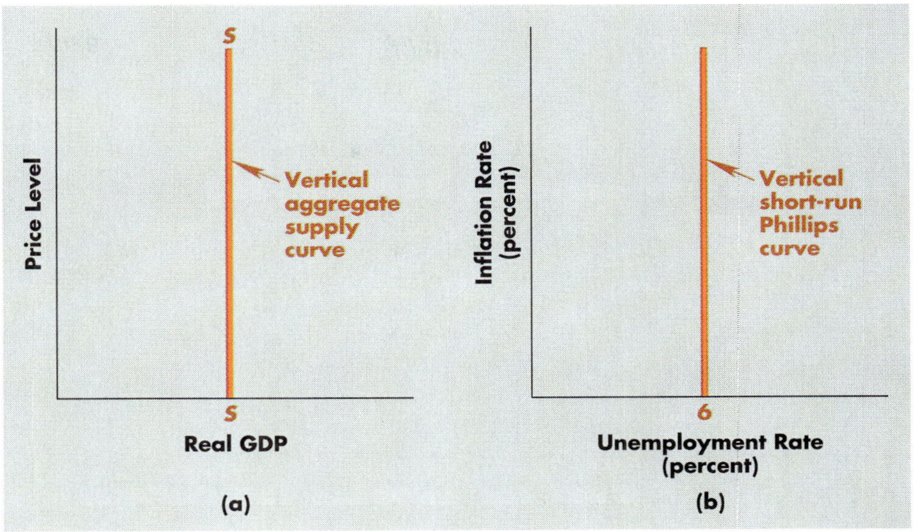

ing a recession. Suppose we start at point *e*, with 5 percent inflation. In order to move to point *c* (representing 2 percent inflation), the economy must take a long and unpleasant detour through point *a*. Specifically, contractionary policies must push the economy down the Phillips curve toward point *a* before the self-correcting mechanism takes over and moves the economy from *a* to *c*. In other words, we must endure a recession to reduce inflation.

But what if even the *short-run* Phillips curve were *vertical* rather than downward sloping? Then this unpleasant recessionary detour would not be necessary. It would be possible for inflation to fall without unemployment rising. The economy could jump directly from point *e* to point *c*.

Is this analysis correct? Can we really slay the inflationary dragon so painlessly? Not necessarily, for our discussion of expectations so far has made at least one unrealistic assumption: that inflation can be predicted accurately. Under this assumption, as Table 16-2 shows, real wages are unaffected by inflation—leaving the aggregate supply curve vertical, even in the short run.

But forecasts of inflation are often inaccurate. Suppose workers underestimate inflation. For example, suppose they expect 4 percent inflation but actually get 6 percent. Then real wages will decline by 2 percent. More generally, real wages will fall if workers underestimate inflation *at all*. The effect of inflation on real wages will be somewhere in between those shown in Tables 16-1 and 16-2.[3] So firms will retain some incentive to raise production as the price level rises. The aggregate supply curve will remain upward sloping. We thus conclude that:

The short-run aggregate supply curve is *vertical* when inflation is predicted accurately, but *upward sloping* when inflation is underestimated. Thus, only an *unexpectedly* high inflation will raise output, because only unexpected inflation

[3]To make sure you understand why, construct a version of Table 16-2 based on the assumption that workers expect 4 percent inflation (and hence set next year's wage at $10.40 per hour), regardless of what the actual rate of inflation is. If you do this correctly, your table will show that higher inflation leads to lower real wages, as in Table 16-1.

reduces real wages. (To see this, compare Tables 16-1 and 16-2.) Similarly, only an *unexpected* decline in inflation will lead to a recession.

Since people often fail to anticipate changes in inflation correctly, this seems to leave our earlier analysis of the Phillips curve almost intact. And, indeed, most economists nowadays believe that the Phillips curve is downward sloping in the short run but vertical in the long run.

THE THEORY OF RATIONAL EXPECTATIONS

However, a vocal minority of economists—led by 1995 Nobel Prize winner Robert Lucas of the University of Chicago—disagrees. This group, believers in the hypothesis of *rational expectations,* insists that the Phillips curve is vertical even in the short run. To explain their point of view, we must first explain what rational expectations are. Then we will be in a position to understand why rational expectations have such radical implications for the trade-off between inflation and unemployment.

WHAT ARE RATIONAL EXPECTATIONS?

In many economic contexts, people must formulate expectations about what the future will bring. For example, those who invest in the stock market need to forecast the future prices of the stocks they buy and sell. And we have just discussed why workers and businesses may want to forecast future prices before agreeing on a money wage. **Rational expectations** is a controversial hypothesis about how such forecasts are made.

RATIONAL EXPECTATIONS are forecasts which, while not necessarily correct, are the best that can be made given the available data. Rational expectations, therefore, cannot err systematically. If expectations are rational, forecasting errors are pure random numbers.

As used by economists, a forecast (an "expectation") of a future variable is considered rational if the forecaster makes *optimal* use of all relevant information that is *available.* Let us elaborate on the italicized words in this definition, using as an example a hypothetical stock market investor who has rational expectations.

First, proponents of rational expectations recognize that *information is limited.* An investor interested in buying General Motors stock would like to know how much profit the company will make in the coming years. Armed with such information, she could predict the future price of GM stock more accurately. But that information is simply not available. Her forecast of the future price of GM stock is not "irrational" just because she does not know GM's future profits. On the other hand, if GM stock normally goes down on Fridays and up on Mondays, she should be aware of this fact.

Next we have the word *optimal.* As used by economists, this means using proper statistical inference to process all the relevant information that is available before making a forecast. In a word, to have rational expectations, your forecasts do not have to be correct; but they cannot have systematic errors that could be avoided by applying better statistical methods. This requirement, while exacting, is not quite as outlandish as it may seem. A good billiards player makes expert use of the laws of physics even without understanding the theory. Similarly, an experienced stock market investor may make good use of information even without formal training in statistics.

RATIONAL EXPECTATIONS AND THE TRADE-OFF

Let us now see how the hypothesis of rational expectations has been used to deny that there is any trade-off between inflation and unemployment—even in the short run.

Although they recognize that inflation cannot always be predicted accurately, rational expectationists insist that workers will not make *systematic* errors. The preceding argument about expectations tacitly assumed that workers normally *underestimate* inflation when it is rising and *overestimate* inflation when it is falling. Advocates of rational expectations claim that this is unrealistic. Workers, they argue, will always make the best possible forecast of inflation, using all the latest data and the best available economic models. Such forecasts will sometimes be too high and sometimes be too low; but they will not err systematically in one direction or the other. Consequently:

If expectations are rational, the difference between the *actual* rate of inflation and the *expected* rate of inflation (the forecasting error) must be a purely random number.

Now recall that the argument in the previous section concluded that employment is affected by inflation only to the extent that inflation *differs* from what was expected. But, under rational expectations, no *predictable* change in inflation can make the *expected* rate of inflation deviate from the *actual* rate of inflation. Hence, according to the rational expectations hypothesis, unemployment will always remain at the natural rate—except for random, and therefore totally unpredictable, gyrations due to forecasting errors. Thus:

If expectations are rational, the inflation rate can be reduced without the need for a period of high unemployment because the short-run Phillips curve is vertical.

According to the rational expectations view, the government's ability to manipulate aggregate demand gives it no ability to control real output and unemployment because the aggregate supply curve is vertical—even in the short run. [To see why, experiment by moving an aggregate demand curve when the aggregate supply curve is vertical, as in Figure 16-14(a).] Any *predictable* change in aggregate demand will lead to a change in the *expected* rate of inflation, and hence will leave real wages unaffected.

The government therefore can influence output only by making *unexpected* changes in aggregate demand. But, according to the rational expectations hypothesis, this is not easy to do because people understand what policymakers are up to. If the monetary and fiscal authorities typically react to high inflation by reducing aggregate demand, people will soon come to anticipate this reaction. And anticipated reductions in aggregate demand do not cause *unexpected* changes in inflation.

AN EVALUATION

Proponents of rational expectations are optimistic that inflation can be reduced without losses of output, even in the short run. Are they right?

As a piece of pure logic, the rational expectations argument is impeccable. Controversy arises, however, over how best to apply the idea in practice. While the theory has attracted some adherents, the evidence to date leads most economists to reject the extreme rational expectationist position in favor of the view that there is a trade-off between inflation and unemployment in the short run. There are several reasons for this.

1. Many contracts for labor and other raw materials cover such long periods of time that the expectations on which they were based, while rational at the time, may appear quite irrational from today's point of view. For example,

when 3-year labor contracts were drawn up in 1980, inflation was above 10 percent. It might therefore have been rational to expect the 1984 price level to be 30 percent above the 1981 price level and to have set 1984 wages accordingly. By late 1982, such an expectation would have been plainly irrational. But it might already have been written into contracts. If so, real wages would have wound up much higher than intended, giving firms a powerful incentive to reduce employment—even though no one behaved irrationally.

2. Many people believe that inflationary expectations do not adapt as quickly to changes in the economic environment as the rational expectations hypothesis assumes. If, for example, the government embarks on an anti-inflation policy, workers may continue to expect high inflation for quite a while. Thus, they may continue to insist on rapid money wage increases. Then, if inflation actually slows down, real wages will rise faster than anyone expected, and unemployment will result. Such behavior may not be strictly *rational*. But, to many observers, it seems realistic.
3. Some observers question whether wage agreements typically compensate workers for *expected* inflation *in advance,* as assumed by the rational expectations theory. More typically, they argue, wages catch up to *actual* inflation *after the fact*. If so, real wages will be eroded by inflation, as in the conventional view.
4. The facts have not been kind to the rational expectations point of view. The theory suggests that unemployment should hover around the natural rate most of the time, with random gyrations in one direction or the other. Yet this does not seem to be the case. The theory also predicts that preannounced (and thus expected) anti-inflation programs should be relatively painless. Yet, in practice, inflation fighting looks to be very costly. Finally, many direct tests of the rationality of expectations have cast doubt on the hypothesis. For example, survey data on people's expectations rarely meet the exacting requirements of rationality.

But all these problems with rational expectations should not obscure a basic truth. In the long run, the rational expectations viewpoint should be more or less appropriate since people will not hold incorrect expectations indefinitely. As Abraham Lincoln said, you cannot fool all of the people all of the time.

WHY ECONOMISTS (AND POLITICIANS) DISAGREE

This chapter has now taught us some of the reasons why economists often disagree about the proper conduct of national economic policy. And it also helps us understand some of the related political debates.

Should the government take stern actions to reduce inflation? You will say *yes* if you believe that (1) inflation is more costly than unemployment, (2) the short-run Phillips curve is steep, (3) expectations react quickly, and (4) the economy's self-correcting mechanism works smoothly and rapidly. These views on the economy tend to be held by monetarists and rational expectationists and by the (generally conservative) politicians who listen to them.

But you will say *no* if you believe that (1) unemployment is more costly than inflation, (2) the short-run Phillips curve is flat, (3) expectations react sluggishly, and (4) the self-correcting mechanism is slow and unreliable. These views are held by many Keynesian economists, so it is not surprising that the (generally liberal) politicians who follow their advice often oppose the use of recession to fight inflation.

The tables turn, however, when the question is whether to use demand management to bring a recession to a rapid end. The Keynesian view of the world—that unemployment is costly, that the short-run Phillips curve is flat, that expectations adjust slowly, and that the self-correcting mechanism is unreliable—leads to the conclusion that the benefits of fighting unemployment are high while the costs are low. And so Keynesians are eager to fight recessions. The monetarist and rational expectationist positions on these four issues are precisely the reverse, and so are the policy conclusions.

THE DILEMMA OF DEMAND MANAGEMENT

So we have seen that the makers of monetary and fiscal policy face an agonizing trade-off. If they stimulate aggregate demand to reduce unemployment, they will aggravate inflation. If they restrict aggregate demand to fight inflation, they will cause higher unemployment.

But wait. Early in the chapter we learned that when inflation comes from the supply side, inflation and unemployment are *positively* associated: We suffer from more of both or enjoy less of each. Does this mean that monetary and fiscal policymakers can escape the trade-off between inflation and unemployment? Certainly not.

THE TRADE-OFF BETWEEN INFLATION AND UNEMPLOYMENT

Adverse shifts in the aggregate supply curve can cause both inflation and unemployment to rise together, and thus can destroy the statistical Phillips curve relationship. Nevertheless, anything that monetary and fiscal policy can do will make unemployment and inflation move in *opposite* directions because monetary and fiscal policy give the government control only over the *aggregate demand* curve, not over the *aggregate supply* curve. Thus, no matter what the source of inflation, and no matter what happens to the Phillips curve, the monetary and fiscal policy authorities must still face up to the disagreeable trade-off between inflation and unemployment. This is a principle that many policymakers have failed to recognize, and one of the **Ideas** that we hope you will remember well **Beyond the Final Exam.**

Naturally, the unpleasant nature of this trade-off has led both economists and public officials to search for a way out of the dilemma. The rest of this chapter—including the Policy Debate box on the next page—considers some of these ideas, none of which are panaceas.

ATTEMPTS TO REDUCE THE NATURAL RATE OF UNEMPLOYMENT

One highly desirable approach—if only we knew how to do it—would be to reduce the natural rate of unemployment. Then we could enjoy lower unemployment without higher inflation. The question is: How?

The most promising approaches have to do with education, training, and job placement. The data clearly show that more educated workers are unemployed

POLICY DEBATE: SHOULD THE FED CONCENTRATE ONLY ON REDUCING INFLATION?

One disarmingly simple way to sidestep the dilemma of demand management is to eliminate one of the two traditional goals. In particular, some economists and politicians have proposed that the Federal Reserve be directed to concentrate on price stability and forget about trying to stabilize output and employment. The argument runs something like this.

1. Price stability is of overriding importance to the smooth functioning of a market economy.
2. The short-run trade-off between inflation and unemployment impedes the Fed's efforts to reduce inflation. (In more extreme versions of the argument, this step denies the existence of any short-run trade-off.)
3. The Fed has failed in its efforts to stabilize output and employment and, in the process, it has lost ground in the war against inflation.

Let us briefly examine each step of the argument.

The first proposition is a matter of intense debate, as we have emphasized in this and earlier chapters. Someone who believes that inflation is a terrible problem and unemployment a minor one might very well want the Fed to concentrate on reducing inflation. But other people hold the opposite view.

The second proposition is undoubtedly true. Concerns about the unemployment consequences of its actions surely have tempered the Fed's inflation-fighting zeal on many occasions.

The third proposition is again debatable. As we have learned in previous chapters, there have been episodes in which the Fed's stabilization policy has been stunningly successful (such as 1993 to 1995) and episodes in which it has been a miserable failure (such as the 1930s and 1972 to 1973). Lately, however, most observers give the Fed good marks.

In 1995, legislation was introduced that would direct the Fed to make price stability its primary goal. But the bill has yet to reach the floor of either house of Congress.

less frequently than less educated ones. Vocational training and retraining programs, if successful, help unemployed workers with obsolete skills acquire abilities that are currently in demand. By so doing, they both raise employment and help alleviate upward pressures on wage rates in jobs where qualified workers are in short supply.

Government job placement services play a similar role. Such programs try to improve the match of workers to jobs by funneling information from prospective employers to prospective employees.

These ideas sound promising and sensible. But there are two big problems. First, training and placement programs often look better on paper than they do in practice, where they have achieved only modest success. Too often, people are trained for jobs that do not exist by the time they finish their training—if indeed they ever existed.

The second problem is that the high cost of these programs restricts the number of workers that can be accommodated, even when they work. For this reason, publicly supported job training is done on a very small scale in the United States—much less, say, than in most European countries. Such small expenditures can hardly be expected to make a significant dent in the natural rate of unemployment. Here job placement and counseling may have an important edge because the cost per unemployed worker is far less than the cost of retraining.

The Clinton administration has vigorously promoted initiatives in both retraining and placement; the expressed goal is to transform the unemployment system into a reemployment system. But, so far, Congress has been reluctant to go along.

WAGE–PRICE CONTROLS

WAGE–PRICE CONTROLS are legal restrictions on the ability of industry and labor to raise wages and prices.

To many people, the most natural way to control inflation is to impose mandatory **wage–price controls.** After all, if we do not like something, why not just outlaw it? Then the government could concentrate on fighting unemployment without worrying about the trade-off.

Economists generally oppose controls for reasons we learned back in Chapter 4. When price ceilings are effective, they force prices below equilibrium levels, thereby causing shortages. With prices no longer serving as rationing devices, something else must take their place. One possibility is long lines of buyers waiting their turn, as was typical in the former Soviet bloc. Another is government ration coupons, a device used successfully in the United States during World War II.

But neither of these measures is likely to be popular with the electorate in peacetime. And both are likely to spawn black markets, which erode respect for law and order at the same time they undermine the effects of controls. As critics are fond of pointing out, controls give perfectly law-abiding citizens incentives to break the law in an effort to circumvent the controls.

Wage–price controls were last used in the United States in the early 1970s under President Nixon, and have acquired a bad name. But some foreign countries like Argentina and Israel have used controls successfully to engineer dramatic reductions of inflation.

INDEXING

INDEXING refers to provisions in a law or a contract whereby monetary payments are automatically adjusted whenever a specified price index changes. Wage rates, pensions, interest payments on bonds, income taxes, and many other things can be indexed in this way, and have been. Sometimes such contractual provisions are called *escalator clauses.*

Indexing—which refers to provisions in a law or contract whereby monetary payments are automatically adjusted whenever a specific price index changes—presents a very different approach to the inflation–unemployment dilemma. Instead of trying *to lower the inflation rate,* the primary purpose of indexing is *to reduce the social costs of inflation.*

The most familiar example of indexing in the United States is an *escalator clause* in a wage agreement. An escalator clause provides for an automatic increase in money wages—without the need for new contract negotiations—any time the price level rises by more than a specified amount. In this way, workers are partly protected from inflation. Nowadays, with inflation low and stable, less than half of all workers employed by large, unionized firms, and very few nonunion workers, are covered by escalator clauses.

Interest payments on bonds or savings accounts can also be indexed, and the United States government began doing so with a small fraction of its bonds in January 1997.[4] The most extensive indexing to be found in the United States today, however, is in government transfer payments. Social Security benefits, for instance, are indexed so that retirees are not victimized by inflation.

Some economists believe that the United States should follow the example of several foreign countries and adopt a much more widespread system of indexing. Why? Because, they argue, it would take most of the sting out of inflation. To see how, let us review some of the social costs of inflation that we enumerated in Chapter 6.

One important cost is the capricious redistribution of income caused by unexpected inflation. We saw that borrowers and lenders normally incorporate an *inflation premium* equal to the *expected rate of inflation* into the nominal interest

[4]Some other countries, with much higher inflation than ours, do extensive indexing of interest rates. Brazil and Israel are notable examples.

rate. Then, if inflation turns out to be higher than expected, the borrower has to pay the lender only the agreed-upon nominal interest rate, including the premium for *expected* inflation; he does not have to compensate the lender for the (higher) *actual* inflation. Thus, the borrower enjoys a windfall gain and the lender loses out. The opposite happens if inflation turns out to be lower than expected.

But if interest rates on loans were indexed, none of this would occur. Borrowers and lenders would agree on a fixed *real* rate of interest, and then the borrower would compensate the lender for whatever *actual inflation* occurred. No one would have to guess what the inflation rate would be.[5]

A second social cost we mentioned in Chapter 6 stems from the fact that our tax system levies taxes on nominal interest and nominal capital gains. As we learned, this flaw in the tax system leads to extremely high effective tax rates in an inflationary environment. But indexing could fix this problem easily. We need only rewrite the tax code so that only *real* interest payments and *real* capital gains are taxed.

A final problem noted in Chapter 6 is that uncertainty over future price levels makes it difficult to enter into long-term contracts—wage agreements, rental agreements, construction agreements, and so on. One way out of this problem is to write indexed contracts, which specify all future payments in real terms.

In the face of all these benefits, why do many economists oppose indexing? Probably the major reason is the fear that indexing will lead to an acceleration of inflation. With the costs of inflation reduced so markedly, they argue, what will persuade governments to pay the price of fighting inflation? What will stop them from inflating more and more? They fear that the answer to these questions is: Nothing. Voters who stand to lose nothing from inflation are unlikely to pressure their legislators into stopping it. Opponents of indexing worry that a mild inflationary disease could turn into a ravaging epidemic in a highly indexed economy.

[5]For example, an indexed loan with a 2 percent real interest rate would require a 5 percent nominal interest payment if inflation were 3 percent, a 7 percent nominal interest payment if inflation were 5 percent, and so on.

SUMMARY

1. Inflation can be caused either by rapid growth of aggregate demand or by sluggish growth of aggregate supply.

2. When fluctuations in economic activity emanate from the demand side, prices will rise rapidly when real output grows rapidly. Since rapid growth means more jobs, unemployment and inflation will be inversely related.

3. This inverse relationship between unemployment and inflation is called the **Phillips curve.** U.S. data for the 1950s and 1960s display a Phillips-curve relation, but data for the 1970s and 1980s do not.

4. The Phillips curve is not a menu of *long-run* policy choices for the economy because the *self-correcting mechanism* guarantees that neither an inflationary gap nor a recessionary gap can last indefinitely.

5. Because of the self-correcting mechanism, the economy's true long-run choices lie along a **vertical long-run Phillips curve,** which shows that the so-called **natural rate of unemployment** is the only unemployment rate that can persist indefinitely.

6. In the short run, the economy can move up or down its short-run Phillips curve. *Temporary* reductions in unemployment can be achieved at the cost of higher inflation. Similarly, *temporary* increases in unemployment can be used to fight inflation.

7. Whether it is advisable to use unemployment to fight inflation depends on four principal factors: the relative social costs of inflation versus unemployment, the efficiency of the economy's self-correcting mechanism, the shape of the short-run Phillips curve, and how quickly inflationary expectations adjust.

8. If workers expect inflation to occur, and if they demand (and receive) compensation for inflation, output will be independent of the price level. Both the aggregate supply curve and the short-run Phillips curve are vertical in this case.
9. However, errors in predicting inflation will still change real wages and therefore the quantity of output that firms wish to supply. Thus, *unpredicted* movements in the price level will lead to a normal, upward-sloping aggregate supply curve.
10. According to the hypothesis of **rational expectations,** errors in predicting inflation are purely random. This means that, except for some random (and uncontrollable) gyrations, the aggregate supply curve is vertical even in the short run.
11. Many economists reject the rational expectations view of the world. Some deny that expectations are "rational" and believe instead that people tend, for example, to underpredict inflation when it is rising. Others point out that contracts signed years ago cannot possibly embody expectations that are "rational" in terms of what we know today.
12. When fluctuations in economic activity are caused by shifts of the aggregate supply curve, output will grow slowly (causing unemployment to rise) when inflation speeds up. Hence, the rates of unemployment and inflation will be positively related. Many observers feel that this sort of *stagflation* is why the Phillips curve collapsed in the 1970s.
13. Even if inflation is initiated by supply-side problems, so that inflation and unemployment occur together, the monetary and fiscal authorities still face this trade-off: Anything they do to improve unemployment is likely to worsen inflation, and anything they do to reduce inflation is likely to aggravate unemployment. The reason is that monetary and fiscal policy mainly influence the aggregate demand curve, not the aggregate supply curve. This is one of our **Ideas for Beyond the Final Exam.**
14. Policies that improve the functioning of the labor market—including retraining programs and employment services—can in principle lower the natural rate of unemployment. To date, however, the U.S. government has had only modest success with these measures.
15. **Wage–price controls** reduce inflation quite directly. But legal limits on wage and price increases seriously interfere with the workings of a market economy.
16. **Indexing** is another way to approach the trade-off problem. Instead of trying to improve the trade-off, it concentrates on reducing the social costs of inflation—perhaps eliminating them altogether. Opponents of indexing worry, however, that the economy's resistance to inflation may be lowered by indexing.

KEY TERMS

Demand-side inflation
Supply-side inflation
Phillips curve
Stagflation caused by supply shocks
Self-correcting mechanism
Natural rate of unemployment
Vertical (long-run) Phillips curve
Trade-off between unemployment and inflation in the short run and in the long run
Rational expectations
Wage–price controls
Indexing (escalator clauses)
Real versus nominal interest rates

QUESTIONS FOR REVIEW

1. Seeing that inflation and unemployment sometimes rise together, some observers deny that policymakers face a trade-off between inflation and unemployment. Are they correct?
2. "There is no sense in trying to shorten recessions through fiscal and monetary policy because the effects of these policies on the unemployment rate are sure to be temporary." Comment on both the truth of this statement and its relevance for policy formulation.
3. Why is it said that decisions on fiscal and monetary policy are, at least in part, political decisions that cannot be made on "objective" economic criteria?
4. What is a "Phillips curve"? Why did it seem to work so much better in the 1954 to 1969 period than it did in the 1970s?
5. Explain why expectations about inflation affect the wages that result from labor-management bargaining.
6. What is meant by "rational" expectations? Why does the hypothesis of rational expectations have such stunning implications for economic policy? Would believers in rational expectations want to shorten a recession by expanding aggregate demand? Would they want to fight inflation by reducing aggregate demand?

7. Show that, if the economy's aggregate supply curve is vertical, fluctuations in the growth of aggregate demand produce only fluctuations in inflation with no effect on output. Relate this to your answer to the previous question.
8. Long-term government bonds now pay approximately 6 percent *nominal* interest. Would you prefer to trade yours in for an indexed bond that paid a 3 percent *real* rate of interest? What if the real interest rate offered were 2 percent? What if it were 1 percent? What do your answers to these questions reveal about your personal attitudes toward inflation?
9. In the late 1980s, the unemployment rate in the United States hovered in the 5.0 to 5.5 percent range, and the inflation rate rose. In the mid-1990s, unemployment fluctuated between 5.5 percent and 6.0 percent, and inflation was stable. What do these facts suggest about the numerical value of the natural rate of unemployment?
10. It is said that the Federal Reserve Board typically cares more about inflation and less about unemployment than the administration. If this is true, why might President Clinton have been worried about what Fed Chairman Alan Greenspan would do in early 1995, when inflation increased for a few months?
11. The year 1996 opened with the unemployment rate under 6 percent, real GDP growing moderately, inflation about 3 percent, and the federal budget deficit around $145 billion.
    a. Make an argument for engaging in contractionary monetary or fiscal policies under these circumstances.
    b. Make an argument for engaging in expansionary monetary or fiscal policies under these circumstances.
    c. Which argument do you find more persuasive?

PART IV

The United States in the World Economy

CHAPTER 17

INTERNATIONAL TRADE AND COMPARATIVE ADVANTAGE

No nation was ever ruined by trade.
Benjamin Franklin

International trade is vital to the health of any nation, and so it is essential to our study of economics. The world's major economies have always been linked in various ways. But dramatic improvements in transportation, telecommunications, and international relations in recent decades have drawn the industrial nations of the world ever closer together.

Economic events in other countries affect our economy for both macroeconomic and microeconomic reasons. For example, we learned in Parts II and III that the level of net exports is one important determinant of a nation's output and employment. But we have not delved very deeply into the factors that determine a nation's exports and imports. Chapters 18 and 19 will take up these *macroeconomic* linkages in greater detail.

But, first, this chapter studies some of the reasons why international trade is important to a nation's *microeconomic* well-being. The central principle here is the *law of comparative advantage,* which plays a major role in determining the patterns of world trade. We will also learn how the prices of internationally traded goods are determined by supply and demand in a free world market. Finally, we will examine the effects of government interferences with foreign trade through quotas, tariffs, and other devices designed to protect domestic industries from foreign competition.

A PUZZLE: HOW CAN AMERICANS COMPETE WITH "CHEAP FOREIGN LABOR"?

Why do Americans (like the citizens of other nations) often want their government to limit or prevent import competition? One major reason is the common belief that imports take bread out of the mouths of American workers. According to this view, "cheap foreign labor" steals jobs from Americans and puts pressure on U.S. businesses to lower wages.

Unfortunately, the facts are not consistent with this story. For one thing, wages in industrialized countries that export to the United States have risen spectacularly during the past 25 years. Table 17-1 shows that wages in seven leading

TABLE 17-1

LABOR COSTS IN INDUSTRIALIZED COUNTRIES

	1970	1995
	(percentage of U.S. labor costs)	
France	41	112
United Kingdom	35	80
Italy	42	96
Japan	24	138
Netherlands	51	141
Sweden	70	124
(West) Germany	56	185

Data are compensation estimates per hour and relate to production workers in the manufacturing sector.

SOURCE: U.S. Bureau of Labor Statistics.

countries rose from an average of only 46 percent of American wages in 1970 to 113 percent by 1994. By 1994, labor costs in Sweden, the Netherlands, western Germany, and Japan exceeded our own, and costs in France were about equal. Yet American imports of Toyotas from Japan, Volkswagens from Germany, and Volvos from Sweden grew as wages in those countries rose relative to American wages.

By comparison, when European and Japanese wages were far below those in the United States in the 1950s, American industry had no trouble marketing our products abroad. In fact, the main problem then was to bring our imports up to the level at which they roughly balanced our bountiful exports. Ironically, our position in the international marketplace deteriorated as wage levels in Europe and Japan began to rise closer to our own.

Clearly, then, cheap foreign labor must not be a major obstacle to U.S. sales abroad—as a "common-sense" view of the matter suggests. In this chapter we will see what is wrong with that view.

WHY TRADE?

The earth's resources are not equally distributed across the planet. While the United States can produce its own coal and wheat, it is almost *entirely* dependent on the rest of the world for such items as rubber and coffee. Similarly, Saudi Arabia has little land that is suitable for farming, but sits atop a huge pool of oil. Because of the seemingly whimsical distribution of vital resources, every nation must trade with others to acquire what it lacks.

Even if countries had all the resources they needed, other differences in natural endowments—such as climate, terrain, and so on—would lead them to engage in trade. Americans *could,* with great difficulty, grow their own banana trees and coffee shrubs in hothouses. But these crops are much more efficiently grown in Honduras and Brazil, where the climates are appropriate.

The skills of a nation's labor force also play a role. If New Zealand has a large group of efficient farmers and few workers with industrial experience while the opposite is true in Japan, it makes sense for New Zealand to specialize in agriculture and let Japan concentrate on manufacturing.

Finally, a small country that tried to produce every product would end up with many industries too small to utilize mass-production techniques and other methods that confer cost advantages on large-scale operations. For example, some countries operate their own international airlines for reasons that can only be political, not economic. Inevitably, small nations that insist on competing in industries that are economical only when their scale of operation is large find that these enterprises can survive only with the aid of large government subsidies.

To summarize, the main reason why nations trade with one another is to exploit the many advantages of **specialization.**

SPECIALIZATION means that a country devotes its energies and resources to only a small proportion of the world's productive activities.

International trade is essential for the prosperity of trading nations because:

1. Every country lacks some vital resources that it can get only by trading with others.
2. Each country's climate, labor force, and other endowments make it a relatively efficient producer of some goods and an inefficient producer of other goods.
3. Specialization permits larger outputs and can therefore offer economies of large-scale production.

MUTUAL GAINS FROM TRADE

Many people believe that a nation can gain from trade only at the expense of another. Centuries ago, writers on international trade pointed out that nothing new is produced by the mere act of trading. They therefore incorrectly argued that, if one country gains from a swap, the other country must necessarily lose. One of the consequences of this mistaken belief was and is a policy prescription calling for each country to try to disadvantage its trading partners—on the grounds that one nation's gain must be another's loss.

Yet, as Adam Smith emphasized, and as we learned in Chapter 3, both parties *must* expect to gain something from any *voluntary exchange*. Otherwise why would they agree to trade?

But how can mere exchange of goods leave *both* parties better off? The answer is that while trade does not increase the total output of goods, it does allow each party to acquire items better suited to its tastes. Suppose Scott has four cookies and nothing to drink, while William has two glasses of milk and nothing to eat. A trade of two of Scott's cookies for one of William's glasses of milk does not increase the total supply of either milk or cookies, but it almost certainly improves the welfare of both boys.

By exactly the same logic, both the United States and Mexico must be better off if Mexico voluntarily ships tomatoes to the United States in return for chemicals. In general:

MUTUAL GAINS FROM VOLUNTARY EXCHANGE

Both parties must expect to gain from any *voluntary exchange*. Trade brings about mutual gains by redistributing products so that both parties end up holding more preferred combinations of goods than they held before. This principle, which is one of our **Ideas for Beyond the Final Exam,** applies to nations just as it does to individuals.

INTERNATIONAL VERSUS INTRANATIONAL TRADE

The 50 states of the United States may be the most eloquent testimony to the gains from specialization and free trade. Florida specializes in growing oranges, Iowa in growing corn, Pennsylvania makes steel, and Michigan builds cars. All these states trade freely with one another and enjoy great material prosperity. Try to imagine how much lower your standard of living would be if you could consume only items produced in your own state.

The essential logic of international trade is no different from that underlying trade among different states; the basic reasons for trade are equally applicable *within* a country or *among* countries. Why, then, do we study international trade as a special subject? There are at least three reasons.

POLITICAL FACTORS IN INTERNATIONAL TRADE

First, domestic trade takes place under a single national government, while foreign trade always involves at least two governments. But a nation's government is normally much less concerned about the welfare of citizens of other countries than it is about its own citizens. So, for example, the Constitution of the United States prohibits tariffs on trade among states but does not prohibit the United States from imposing tariffs on imports from abroad. One major issue in the economic analysis of international trade is the use and misuse of impediments to free international trade.

THE MANY CURRENCIES INVOLVED IN INTERNATIONAL TRADE

Second, all trade within the borders of the United States is carried out in U.S. dollars. But trade across national borders must involve at least two currencies. Rates of exchange between different currencies can and do change. In 1985, it took about 250 Japanese yen to buy a dollar; now it takes only about 105. Variability in exchange rates brings with it a host of complications and policy problems that are discussed in Chapters 18 and 19.

IMPEDIMENTS TO MOBILITY OF LABOR AND CAPITAL

Third, it is much easier for labor and capital to move about within a country than to move from one country to another. If jobs are plentiful in Michigan but scarce in West Virginia, workers can move freely to follow the job opportunities. Of course, there are personal costs, including the financial cost of moving and the psychological cost of leaving friends and familiar surroundings. But such relocations are not inhibited by immigration quotas, by laws restricting the employment of foreigners, nor by the need to learn new languages.

There are also greater impediments to the transfer of capital across national boundaries than to its movement within a country. For example, many countries have rules limiting foreign ownership; even the United States limits foreign ownership of broadcast outlets and airlines. Foreign investment is also subject to special political risks, such as the danger of outright expropriation after a change in government. For example, in 1994 U.S. citizens had more than 1,300 unresolved expropriation claims against the government of Nicaragua.

But even if nothing as extreme as expropriation occurs, capital invested abroad faces significant risks from changes in exchange rates. An investment valued at 250 million yen will be worth \$1.0 million to American investors if the dollar is worth 250 yen, but \$2.5 million if the dollar is worth just 100 yen.

THE LAW OF COMPARATIVE ADVANTAGE

The gains from international specialization and trade are clear when one country is better at producing one item while its trading partner is better at producing another. For example, no one finds it surprising that Brazil sells coffee to the United States while America exports aircraft to Brazil. We know that coffee can be produced using less labor and other inputs in Brazil than in the United States. And America can produce passenger aircraft at a lower resource cost than can Brazil.

One country is said to have an **ABSOLUTE ADVANTAGE** over another in the production of a particular good if it can produce that good using smaller quantities of resources than can the other country.

We say that in such a situation Brazil has an **absolute advantage** in coffee production, and the United States has an absolute advantage in aircraft production. And, in such cases, it is obvious that both countries can gain by producing the item in which they have an absolute advantage and then trading with one another.

What is much less obvious—and is in fact one of the great ideas of economics—is that two countries can generally gain from trade *even if one of them is more efficient than the other in producing everything*. A simple parable will help explain why.

Some lawyers are better typists than their secretaries. Should such a lawyer fire her secretary and do her own typing? Not likely. Even though the lawyer may type better than the secretary, good judgment tells her to concentrate on the practice of law and leave the typing to a lower-paid secretary. Why? Because the *opportunity cost* of an hour devoted to typing is an hour less spent practicing law, which is a far more lucrative activity.

One country is said to have a **COMPARATIVE ADVANTAGE** over another in the production of a particular good relative to other goods if it produces that good less inefficiently as compared with the other country.

This is an example of the principle of **comparative advantage** at work. The lawyer specializes in arguing cases despite her absolute advantage in typing because she has a still greater absolute advantage as an attorney. She suffers some direct loss by not doing her own typing. But that loss is more than compensated for by the income she earns selling her legal services to clients.

Precisely the same principle applies to nations, and it underlies the economic analysis of patterns of international trade. The principle, called the *law of comparative advantage*, was discovered by David Ricardo, one of the giants in the history of economic analysis (see the box on the next page). It is one of our **Ideas for Beyond the Final Exam.**

THE LAW OF COMPARATIVE ADVANTAGE

Even if one country is at an absolute disadvantage relative to another country in the production of *every* good, it is said to have a *comparative advantage* in making the good at which it is *least inefficient* (compared with the other country).

Ricardo discovered that two countries can still gain by trading even if one country is more efficient than another in the production of every commodity—that is, has an absolute advantage in every commodity.

In determining the most efficient patterns of production, it is comparative advantage, not absolute advantage, that matters. Thus, a country can gain by importing a good even if that good can be produced at home more efficiently than it can be produced abroad. Such imports make sense if they enable the country to specialize in producing goods at which it is even more efficient.

DAVID RICARDO (1772–1823)

David Ricardo was born 4 years before publication of Adam Smith's *Wealth of Nations*. Descended from a wealthy Jewish family of Portuguese origins, he had about 20 brothers and sisters. Ricardo's formal education ended at the age of 13, and so he was largely self-educated. He began his career by working in his father's stock brokerage firm. At age 21, Ricardo married a Quaker woman and decided to become a Unitarian, a sect then considered "little better than atheist." By Jewish custom, Ricardo's father broke with him, though apparently they remained friendly.

Ricardo then decided to go into the brokerage business on his own and was enormously successful. During the Napoleonic Wars he regularly scored business coups over leading British and foreign financiers, including the Rothschilds. After gaining a huge profit on government securities that he had bought just before the Battle of Waterloo, Ricardo decided to retire from business when he was just over 40 years old.

He purchased a country estate, Gatcomb (now owned by the royal family), where a brilliant group of intellectuals met regularly. Particularly remarkable for the period was the number of women included in the circle, among them Maria Edgeworth, the novelist (who wrote extravagant praise of Ricardo's mind), and Jane Marcet, an author of textbooks, one of which was probably the first textbook in economics. Ricardo's close friends included the economists T. R. Malthus and James Mill, father of John Stuart Mill, the noted philosopher-economist. Malthus remained a close friend of Ricardo even though they disagreed on many subjects and continued their arguments in personal correspondence and in their published works.

James Mill persuaded Ricardo to go into Parliament. As was then customary, Ricardo purchased his seat by buying a piece of land that entitled its owner to a seat in Parliament. There he proved to be a noteworthy advocate of many causes that were against his personal interests.

James Mill also helped persuade Ricardo to write his masterpiece, *The Principles of Political Economy and Taxation*, which may have been the first book of pure economic theory. It was noteworthy that Ricardo, the most practical of practical men, had little patience with empirical economics and preferred instead to rest his analysis explicitly and exclusively on theory. His book made considerable contributions to the analysis of pricing, wage determination, and the effects of various types of taxes, among many other subjects. It also gave us the law of comparative advantage.

Ricardo died in 1823 at the age of 51. He seems to have been a wholly admirable person—honest, charming, witty, conscientious, brilliant—altogether too good to be true.

THE ARITHMETIC OF COMPARATIVE ADVANTAGE

TABLE 17-2

ALTERNATIVE OUTPUTS FROM ONE YEAR OF LABOR INPUT

	In the United States	In Japan
Computers	50	10
Televisions	50	40

Let's see precisely how this works using a hypothetical example that gives a somewhat exaggerated impression of the trading positions of the United States and Japan a few years ago. We imagine that labor is the only input used to produce microcomputers and television sets in the two countries. Suppose further that America has an absolute advantage in both goods, as indicated in Table 17-2. In this example, a year's worth of labor can produce either 50 computers or 50 TV sets in the United States, but only 10 computers or 40 televisions in Japan. So America is the more efficient producer of both goods. Nonetheless, as our lawyer-secretary example suggests, it pays for the United States to specialize and trade with Japan.

To demonstrate this conclusion, we begin by noting that America has a comparative advantage in computers while Japan has a comparative advantage in TVs. Specifically, the numbers in Table 17-2 show that the United States can produce 50 televisions with a year's labor while Japan can produce only 40; so the

TABLE 17-3 EXAMPLE OF THE GAINS FROM TRADE

	United States	Japan	Total
Computers (thousands)	+25	−10	+15
Televisions (thousands)	−25	+40	+15

United States is 25 percent more efficient than Japan in producing TV sets. However, America is five times as efficient as Japan in producing computers: It can produce 50 per year of labor rather than 10. Because America's competitive edge is far greater in computers than in televisions, we say that the United States has a *comparative advantage* in computers.

From the Japanese perspective, these same numbers indicate that Japan is only slightly less efficient than America in TV production but drastically less efficient in computer production. So Japan's comparative advantage is in the television industry. According to Ricardo's law of comparative advantage, then, the two countries can gain if the United States specializes in producing computers, Japan specializes in producing TVs, and the two countries trade. Let us verify that this is true.

Suppose Japan transfers 1,000 years of labor out of the computer industry and into TV manufacturing. According to the figures in Table 17-2, its computer output falls by 10,000 units while its TV output rises by 40,000 units. (See the middle column of Table 17-3.) Suppose, at the same time, the United States transfers 500 years of labor out of television manufacturing (thereby losing 25,000 TVs) and into computer making (thereby gaining 25,000 computers). Table 17-3 shows us that these transfers of resources in the two countries increase the world's production of both outputs. Together, the two countries now have 15,000 additional TVs and 15,000 additional computers—surely a nice outcome.

Was there some sleight of hand here? How did both the United States and Japan gain both computers and TVs? The explanation is that the process we have just described involves more than just a swap of a fixed bundle of commodities. It is also a *change in the production arrangements,* with some of Japan's inefficient computer production taken over by more efficient American makers, and with some of America's TV production taken over by Japanese television companies who are *less* inefficient at making TVs than Japanese computer manufacturers are at making computers. The underlying principle is both simple and fundamental:

When every country does what it can do best, all countries can benefit because more of every commodity can be produced without increasing the amounts of labor used.

THE GRAPHICS OF COMPARATIVE ADVANTAGE

The gains from trade can also be displayed graphically, and doing so helps us understand whether they are large or small.

The lines *US* and *JN* in Figure 17-1 are closely related to the production possibilities frontiers of the two countries, but differ in that they pretend that each

FIGURE 17-1 PER-CAPITA PRODUCTION POSSIBILITIES FRONTIERS FOR TWO COUNTRIES

Because America can produce more of every commodity using the same quantity of labor as does Japan, its per-capita production possibilities frontier, *US*, is higher than Japan's, *JN*. But the United States has a comparative advantage in computers, in which it is 5 times as productive as Japan. (It can produce 50 million computers, point *S*, compared with Japan's 10 million, point *N*.) On the other hand, America is only 25 percent more productive in TVs (point *U*) than Japan (point *J*). Thus, Japan has a comparative advantage in producing televisions.

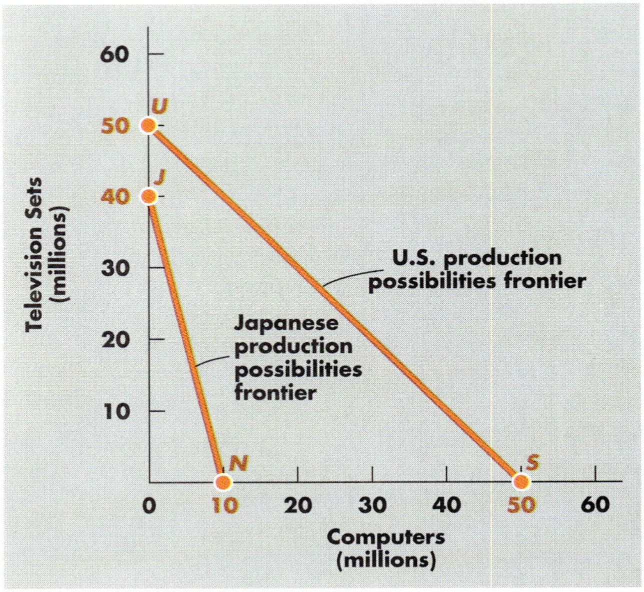

country has the same amount of labor available—in this case, 1 million person-years.[1] For example, Table 17-2 tells us that, for each 1 million person-years of labor, the United States can produce 50 million TVs and no computers (point *U* in Figure 17-1), 50 million computers and no TVs (point *S*), or any combination between (the line *US*). Similar reasoning leads to line *JN* for Japan.

America's actual production possibilities frontier would be even higher, relative to Japan's, than shown in Figure 17-1 because the U.S. population is larger. But Figure 17-1 is more useful to us because it highlights the differences in efficiency that determine both absolute and comparative advantage. Let us see how.

The fact that line *US* lies *above* line *JN* means that the United States can manufacture more televisions and more computers than Japan with the same amount of labor. This reflects our assumption that America has an *absolute* advantage in both commodities.

America's comparative advantage in computer production and Japan's comparative advantage in TV production are shown in a different way—by the relative *slopes* of the two lines. Look back to Table 17-2, which shows that the United States can acquire a computer on its own by giving up a TV. Thus, the opportunity cost of a computer in the United States is one television set. This opportunity cost is depicted graphically by the slope of the U.S. production possibilities frontier in Figure 17-1, which is $OU/OS = 50/50 = 1$.

Table 17-2 also tells us that the opportunity cost of a computer in Japan is four TVs. And this is depicted in Figure 17-1 by the slope of Japan's production possibilities frontier, which is $OJ/ON = 40/10 = 4$.

A country's absolute advantage in production over another country is shown by its having a higher per-capita production possibilities frontier. The difference in

[1]To review the concept of the production possibilities frontier, see Chapter 3.

the comparative advantages of the two countries is shown by the difference in the slopes of their frontiers.

Because opportunity costs differ in the two countries, gains are possible if the two countries specialize and trade with one another. Specifically, it is cheaper, in terms of real resources forgone, for *either* country to acquire its computers in the United States. By a similar line of reasoning, the opportunity cost of TVs is higher in the United States than in Japan, so it makes sense for both countries to acquire their televisions in Japan.[2]

Notice that if the slopes of the two production possibilities frontiers, *JN* and *US*, were equal, then opportunity costs would be the same in each country. In that case, there would be no potential gains from trade. Gains from trade arise from *differences* across countries, not from similarities. This is an important point on which people are often confused. It is often argued that two very different countries—say, the United States and Mexico—cannot gain much by trading with one another. In fact:

Two very similar countries may gain little from trade. Large gains from trade are most likely when countries are very different.

How the gains from trade are divided between the two countries depends on the prices that emerge from world trade, which is the subject of the next section. But we already know enough to see that world trade must, in our example, leave a computer costing more than one TV and less than four. Why? Because, if a computer brought less than one TV (its opportunity cost in the United States) on the world market, America would produce its own TVs rather than buying them from Japan. And if a computer cost more than four TVs (its opportunity cost in Japan), Japan would prefer to produce its own computers rather than buy them from the United States.

We conclude, therefore, that if both countries are to trade, the rate of exchange between TVs and computers must be somewhere between 4 to 1 and 1 to 1. To illustrate the gains from trade in a concrete example, suppose the world price ratio settles at 2 to 1; that is, one computer costs the same as two televisions. How much, precisely, do the United States and Japan gain from world trade?

Figure 17-2 is designed to help us see the answer. Production possibilities frontiers *US* in Panel (b) and *JN* in Panel (a) are the same as in Figure 17-1. But America can do better than line *US*. Specifically, with a world price ratio of 2 to 1, the United States can buy a TV by giving up only one-half of a computer, rather than one (which is the opportunity cost of TVs in America). Hence, if the United States produces only computers [point *S* in Figure 17-2(b)] and buys its TVs from Japan, America's *consumption possibilities* will be as indicated by the blue line that begins at point *S* and has a slope of 2—indicating that each computer it sells brings America two television sets. Since trade allows the United States to choose a point on *AS* rather than on *US*, trade opens up consumption possibilities that were simply not available before.

The story is similar for Japan. If the Japanese produce only televisions [point *J* in Figure 17-2(a)], they can acquire a computer from the United States for every two TVs they give up as they move along the blue line *JP* (whose slope is 2). This is better than they can do on their own, since a sacrifice of two TVs in Japan yields only one-half of a computer. Hence, world trade enlarges Japan's consumption possibilities from *JN* to *JP*.

---

[2]As an exercise, provide this line of reasoning.

FIGURE 17-2 THE GAINS FROM TRADE

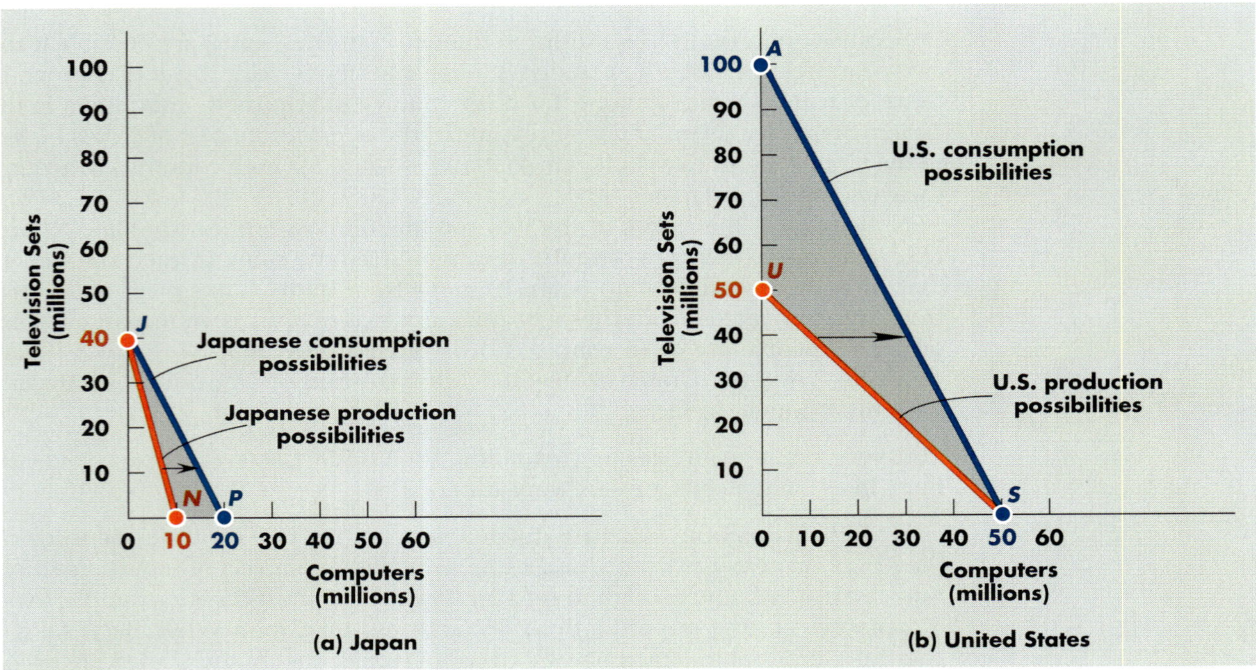

In this diagram, we suppose that trade opens up between the United States and Japan and that the world price of computers is twice the world price of TVs. Now America's consumption possibilities are all the points on line *AS* (which starts at *S* and has a slope of 2), rather than just the points on its own production possibilities frontier, *US*. Similarly, Japan can choose any point on line *JP* (which begins at *J* and has a slope of 2), rather than just points on *JN*. Thus, both nations gain from trade.

Figure 17-2 shows graphically that gains from trade arise to the extent that world prices (2 to 1 in our example) differ from domestic opportunity costs (4 to 1 and 1 to 1 in our example). So it is a matter of some importance to understand how prices in international trade are established. This we shall do shortly.

COMPARATIVE ADVANTAGE AND COMPETITION OF "CHEAP FOREIGN LABOR"

But first let us observe that the principle of comparative advantage takes us a long way toward uncovering the fallacy in the "cheap foreign labor" argument described earlier in the chapter. Given the assumed productive efficiency of American labor, and the inefficiency of Japanese labor, we would expect wages to be much higher in the United States. And, indeed, they were until recent years.

In these circumstances, one might expect American workers to be apprehensive about an agreement to permit open trade between the two countries—"How can we hope to meet the unfair competition of those underpaid Japanese workers?" And Japanese laborers might also be concerned—"How can we hope to meet the competition of those Americans, who are so efficient in producing everything?"

The principle of comparative advantage shows us that both fears are unjustified. As we have just seen, when trade is opened up between Japan and the

United States, *workers in both countries will be able to earn higher real wages than before* because of the increased productivity that comes about through specialization.

As Figure 17-2 shows, once trade opens up, Japan can end up with more TVs and more computers than it had before. So the living standards of its workers can rise even though they have been left vulnerable to the competition of the superefficient Americans. The United States also can end up with more TVs and with more computers; so the living standards of its workers can rise even though they have been exposed to the competition of cheap Japanese labor. These higher standards of living are, of course, a reflection of the higher real wages earned by workers in both countries.

The lesson to be learned here is elementary: Nothing helps raise standards of living more than does a greater abundance of goods.

SUPPLY-DEMAND EQUILIBRIUM AND PRICING IN WORLD TRADE

How the gains from trade are shared depends on the prices that emerge from world trade. As usual, price determination in a free market depends on supply and demand.

When applied to international trade, however, the supply-demand model runs into several new complications. First, it involves at least two demand curves: that of the exporting country and that of the importing country. Second, it may also involve two supply curves, since the importing country may produce part of its own consumption. Third, equilibrium does not take place at the intersection point of *either* pair of supply-demand curves. Why? Because if there is any trade, the exporting country's quantity supplied must be *greater* than its quantity demanded, while the quantity supplied by the importing country must be *less* than its quantity demanded.

These complications are illustrated in Figure 17-3, where we show the supply and demand curves of a country that exports wheat in Panel (a) and of a country that imports wheat in Panel (b). For simplicity, we assume that these countries do not deal in wheat with anyone else.

Where will the two-country wheat market reach equilibrium? If there is free trade, the equilibrium price must satisfy two requirements:

1. The price of wheat must be the same in both countries.
2. The quantity of wheat exported must equal the quantity of wheat imported.

In Figure 17-3, this happens at a price of \$2.50 per bushel. At that price, the distance *AB* between what the exporting country produces and what it consumes equals the distance *CD* between what the importing country consumes and what it produces. This means that, at a price of \$2.50 per bushel, the amount the exporting country wants to sell is exactly equal to the amount the importing country wants to buy.

At any price above \$2.50, producers in both countries will want to sell more and consumers in both countries will want to buy less. For example, if the price rises to \$3.25 per bushel, the exporter's quantity supplied will rise from *B* to *F*, and the exporter's quantity demanded will fall from *A* to *E*, as shown in Figure 17-3(a). As a result, there will be more available for export—*EF* rather than *AB*. For exactly the same reason, the price increase will cause higher production and lower sales in the importing country, leading to a reduction in imports from *CD* to *GH* in Panel (b).

FIGURE 17-3 SUPPLY-DEMAND EQUILIBRIUM IN THE INTERNATIONAL WHEAT TRADE

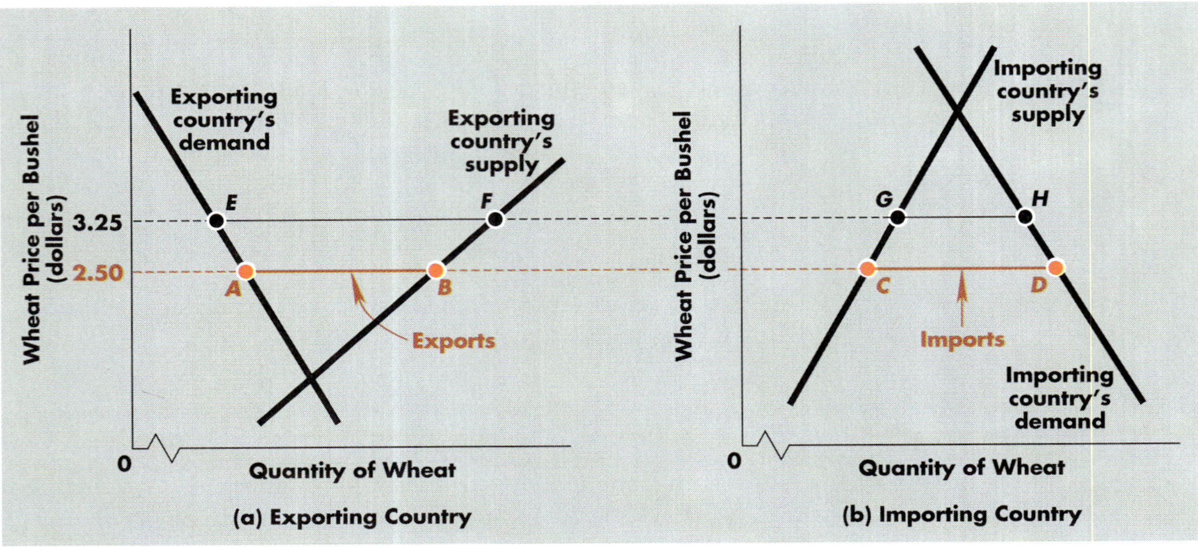

Equilibrium requires that exports, *AB* (which is the exporting nation's quantity supplied, *B*, minus the exporter's quantity demanded, *A*), exactly balance imports, *CD*, by the importing country. At $2.50 per bushel of wheat, there is equilibrium. But at a higher price, say, $3.25, there is disequilibrium because export supply, *EF*, exceeds import demand, *GH*.

But this means that the higher price, $3.25 per bushel, cannot be sustained in a free and competitive international market. With export supply *EF* far greater than import demand *GH*, there must be downward pressure on price and a move back toward the $2.50 equilibrium price. Similar reasoning shows that prices below $2.50 also cannot be sustained. Thus:

In international trade, the equilibrium price is the one that makes the exporting country want to export exactly the amount that the importing country wants to import. Equilibrium will thus occur at a price at which the horizontal distance *AB* in Figure 17-3(a) (the excess of the exporter's quantity supplied over its quantity demanded) is equal to the horizontal distance *CD* in Figure 17-3(b) (the excess of the importer's quantity demanded over its quantity supplied). At this price, the *world's* quantity demanded is equal to the *world's* quantity supplied.

TARIFFS, QUOTAS, AND OTHER INTERFERENCES WITH TRADE

Despite the mutual gains from international trade, nations often interfere with the operation of free international markets. In fact, until the rise of the free-trade movement about 200 years ago (with such economists as Adam Smith and David Ricardo as its vanguard), it was taken for granted that one of the essential tasks of government was to impede trade—presumably in the national interest.

There were many who argued then (and many who still argue today) that the proper aim of government policy was to promote exports and discourage imports, for that would increase the amount foreigners owed the nation. According to this view, a nation's wealth consists of the amount of gold or other monies at its command.

Obviously, there are limits to which such a policy can be pursued. A country *must* import vital foodstuffs or critical raw materials that it cannot supply for itself. Moreover, it is mathematically impossible for *every* country to sell more than it buys, for one country's exports *must* be some other country's imports. If everyone competes in this game and cuts imports to the bone, then obviously exports must go the same way. The result will be that everyone is deprived of the mutual gains from trade—which is precisely what happens in a trade war.

After the protectionist 1930s, the United States moved away from policies designed to impede imports and gradually assumed a leading role in promoting free trade. Over the last 50 years, tariffs and other trade barriers have been reduced dramatically. In recent years, the United States has led the world to complete the Uruguay Round of tariff reductions, and has joined Canada and Mexico in the North American Free Trade Agreement (NAFTA). The latter caused a political firestorm in the United States in 1993 and 1994, with critic Ross Perot predicting a "giant sucking sound" as American workers lost their jobs to competition from "cheap Mexican labor." (Does that sound familiar?)

Modern governments use three main devices when seeking to control trade: tariffs, quotas, and export subsidies.

A **TARIFF** is a tax on imports.

A **tariff** is simply a tax on imports. An importer of wheat, for example, may be charged $1 for each bushel brought into the country. The United States is generally a low-tariff country, with only a few notable exceptions such as the 25 percent tariff on light trucks. However, many other countries rely on heavy tariffs to protect their industries. Tariff rates of 100 percent or more are not uncommon.

A **QUOTA** specifies the maximum amount of a good that is permitted into the country from abroad per unit of time.

A **quota** is a legal limit on the amount of a good that may be imported. For example, the government might allow no more than 25 million bushels of wheat to be imported in a year. In some cases, governments ban the importation of certain goods outright—a quota of zero. The United States now imposes quotas on a smattering of goods, including textiles, meat, and sugar. (See the box on the next page.) But most imports are free of quotas.

An **EXPORT SUBSIDY** is a payment by the government to exporters to permit them to reduce the selling prices of their goods so they can compete more effectively in foreign markets.

An **export subsidy** is a payment by the government to an exporter. By reducing the exporter's costs, such subsidies permit exporters to lower their selling prices and to compete more effectively in world trade. While export subsidies are minor in the United States, they are used extensively by some foreign governments to assist their industries—a practice that provokes bitter complaints from American manufacturers about "unfair competition." For example, years of heavy government subsidies helped the European Airbus consortium take a sizable share of the world market for commercial aircraft away from American manufacturers.

HOW TARIFFS AND QUOTAS WORK

Both tariffs and quotas restrict supplies coming from abroad and drive up prices. A tariff works by raising prices and hence cutting the demand for imports, while the sequence associated with a quota is just the reverse—a restriction in supply forces prices up.

The supply and demand curves in Figure 17-4 illustrate how tariffs and quotas work. Just as in Figure 17-3, the equilibrium price of wheat under free trade is $2.50 per bushel (in both countries). At this price, the exporting country produces 125 million bushels [point *B* in Panel (a)] and consumes 80 million (point *A*); so its exports are 45 million bushels—the distance *AB*. Similarly, the importing country consumes 95 million bushels [point *D* in Panel (b)] and produces

HOW SWEET IT IS: THE U.S. SUGAR QUOTA

The United States has restricted sugar imports since 1934. But the current program, which many economists feel is the most egregious of all our agricultural subsidies, dates only from 1990. It is called a "tariff-rate quota," which most economists view as a fancy name for grotesque protectionism.

Each year a small amount of imported sugar is allowed to enter the United States under a negligible tariff. Beyond that, however, the U.S. government posts a tariff so high that no one wants to pay it in order to import sugar. (Lately, the high tariff has been 15 cents per pound, which is generally above the world price of raw sugar.) In consequence, our domestic price of sugar is roughly twice the world price.

This high price is, of course, a great boon to American producers of sugar and sugar-substitutes like corn syrup. But it costs U.S. consumers of sugar, and manufacturers of candy and soft drinks, between $1 billion and $2 billion per year. And it has also led to some bizarre attempts to evade the quota—like importing sugar as an ingredient in chocolate and Kool-Aid, and then removing the sugar content in the United States.

only 50 million (Panel *C*), so that its imports are also 45 million bushels—the distance *CD*.

Now suppose the government of the importing nation imposes an import quota of (no more than) 30 million bushels. The free-trade equilibrium is no longer possible. Instead, the market must equilibrate at a point where both exports and imports are 30 million bushels. As Figure 17-4 indicates, this requires different prices in the two countries.

Imports in Panel (b) will be 30 million—the distance *QT*—only when the price of wheat in the importing nation is $3.25 per bushel, because only at this price will quantity demanded exceed domestic quantity supplied by 30 million bushels. Similarly, exports in Panel (a) will be 30 million bushels—the distance *RS*—only when the price in the exporting country is $2.00 per bushel. At this price, quantity supplied exceeds domestic quantity demanded by 30 million bushels in the exporting country. Thus, the quota *raises* the price in the importing country to $3.25 and *lowers* the price in the exporting country to $2.00. In general:

An import quota on a product normally will reduce the volume of that product traded, raise the price in the importing country, and reduce the price in the exporting country.

The same restriction of trade can be accomplished through a tariff. In our example, a quota of 30 million bushels led to a price that was $1.25 higher in the importing country than in the exporting country ($3.25 versus $2.00). Suppose that, instead of a quota, the importing nation posts a $1.25 per bushel tariff. International trade equilibrium then must satisfy the following two requirements:

1. The price that consumers in the importing country pay for wheat must exceed the price that suppliers in the exporting country receive by $1.25 (the amount of the tariff).
2. The quantity of wheat exported must equal the quantity of wheat imported.

FIGURE 17-4 QUOTAS AND TARIFFS IN INTERNATIONAL TRADE

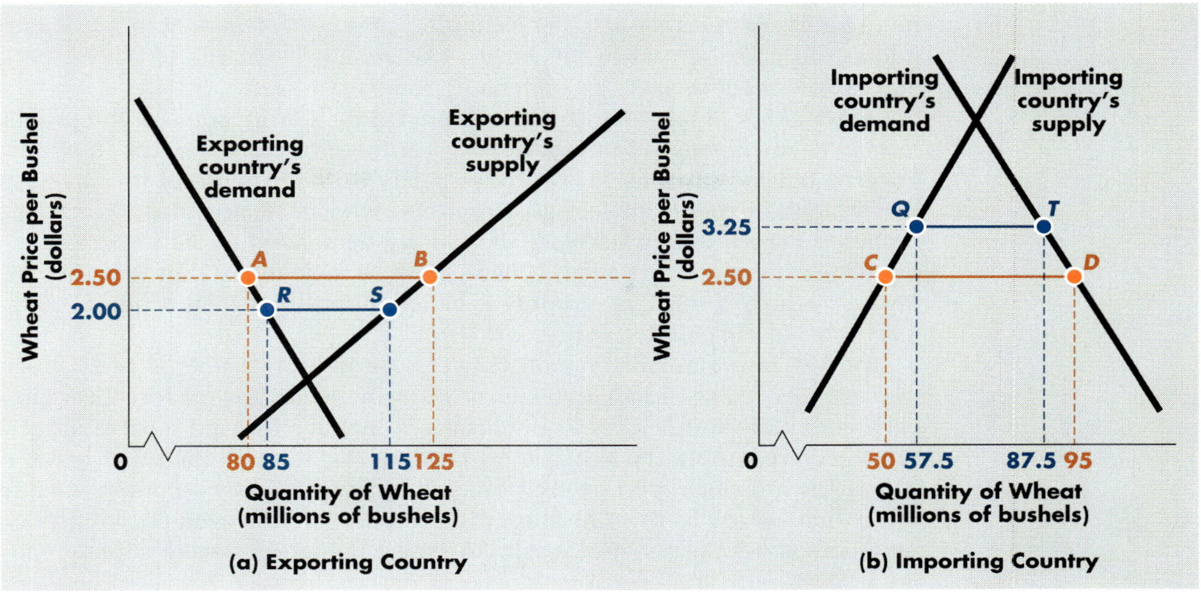

Under free trade, the equilibrium price of wheat is $2.50 per bushel. The exporting country, in Panel (a), sends *AB*, or 45 million bushels, to the importing country (distance *CD*). If a quota of 30 million bushels is imposed by the importing country, these two distances must shrink to 30 million bushels. The solution is shown by distance *RS* for exports and distance *QT* for imports. Exports and imports are equal, as must be the case, but the quota forces prices to be unequal in the two countries. Wheat sells for $3.25 per bushel in the importing country but only $2.00 per bushel in the exporting country. A tariff achieves the same result differently. It *requires* that the prices in the two countries be $1.25 apart. And this, as the graph shows, dictates that exports and imports will be equal at 30 million bushels.

By consulting the graphs in Figure 17-4, you can see exactly where these two requirements are satisfied. If the exporter produces at *S* and consumes at *R*, while the importer produces at *Q* and consumes at *T*, then exports and imports are equal (at 30 million bushels), and the two domestic prices differ by exactly $1.25. (They are $3.25 and $2.00.) What we have just discovered is a general result of international trade theory:

Any restriction of imports that is accomplished by a quota normally can also be accomplished by a tariff.

In this case, the tariff corresponding to an import quota of 30 million bushels is $1.25 per bushel.

TARIFFS VERSUS QUOTAS

But while tariffs and quotas can accomplish the same reduction in international trade and lead to the same domestic prices in the two countries, there *are* some important differences between the two types of restrictions.

First, under a quota, profits from the price increases in the importing country usually go into the pockets of the foreign and domestic sellers of the product.

Because supplies are limited by quotas, customers in the importing country must pay more for the product. So the suppliers, whether foreign or domestic, receive more for every unit they sell. For example, it has been estimated that U.S. import quotas on Japanese cars in the early 1980s raised the profits of both American and Japanese automakers by billions of dollars per year.

On the other hand, when trade is restricted by a tariff, some of the profits go instead as tax revenues to the *government* of the importing country. In effect, the government increases its tax revenues partly at the expense of its citizens and partly at the expense of foreign exporters, who must accept a reduced price because of the resulting decrease in quantity demanded in the importing country. (Domestic producers again benefit, because they are exempt from the tariff.) In this respect, a tariff is certainly a better proposition than a quota from the viewpoint of the country that enacts it.

Another important distinction between the two measures is their different implications for productive efficiency. A tariff handicaps all foreign suppliers equally. It still awards sales to the firms and nations that are most efficient and can therefore supply the goods most cheaply. A quota, on the other hand, necessarily awards its import licenses more or less capriciously—perhaps on a first-come, first-served basis or in proportion to past sales or even on political criteria. There is not the slightest reason to expect the most efficient suppliers to get the import permits.

The U.S. quota on Japanese cars in the 1980s illustrates all of these effects. Japanese automakers responded to the limit on the number of cars by shipping bigger models equipped with more "optional" equipment. The "stripped-down" Japanese car became a thing of the past. And the newer, smaller Japanese automakers—like Subaru and Mitsubishi—found it difficult at first to compete in the U.S. market because their quotas were so much smaller than those of Toyota, Nissan, and Honda.

If a country must inhibit imports, there are two important reasons for it to give preference to tariffs over quotas: (1) Some of the resulting financial gains from tariffs go to the government of the importing country rather than to foreign and domestic producers; and (2) unlike quotas, tariffs offer special benefits to more efficient exporters.

WHY INHIBIT TRADE?

To state that tariffs are a better way to inhibit international trade than quotas leaves open a far more basic question: Why limit trade in the first place? It has been estimated that trade restrictions cost American consumers about $70 billion per year in the form of higher prices. Why should they be asked to pay these higher prices?

Two answers are commonly given. One holds that a country should restrict trade to get more advantageous prices for its own goods. The other argues that particular industries need protection from foreign competition. Let us examine each in turn.

GAINING A PRICE ADVANTAGE

A tariff forces foreign exporters to sell more cheaply by restricting their market. If they do not cut their prices, they will be left with unsold goods. Suppose, as in Figure 17-4(b), that a $1.25 tariff on wheat raises the price of a bushel in the importing country from \$2.50 to \$3.25 per bushel. This rise in price drives down imports from an amount represented by the length of the orange line *CD* to the smaller amount represented by the blue line *QT*. And to the exporting country, this means an equal reduction in exports [see the change from *AB* to *RS* in Figure 17-4(a)].

As a result, the price at which the exporting country can sell its wheat is driven down (from \$2.50 to \$2.00 in the example) while producers in the importing country—being exempt from the tariff—can charge \$3.25 per bushel. In effect, such a tariff amounts to government intervention to rig prices in favor of domestic producers.

However, this technique works only as long as foreigners accept tariff exploitation passively. They rarely do. Instead, they retaliate, usually by imposing tariffs or quotas of their own on their imports from the country that first began the tariff game. This can easily lead to a trade war in which no one gains in terms of more favorable prices and everyone loses in terms of the resulting reductions in overall trade. Something like this happened to the world economy in the 1930s and helped prolong the worldwide depression.

Tariffs or quotas can benefit particular domestic industries in a country that is able to impose them without fear of retaliation. But when every country uses them, everyone is likely to lose in the long run.

PROTECTING PARTICULAR INDUSTRIES

The second, and probably more frequent, reason why countries restrict trade is to protect particular industries from foreign competition. If foreigners can produce steel or watches or shoes more cheaply, domestic businesses and unions in these industries are quick to demand protection; and their governments are often reluctant to deny it to them. It is here that the cheap foreign labor argument is most likely to be invoked.

Protective tariffs and quotas are explicitly designed to rescue firms whose relative inefficiency does not permit them to compete with foreign exporters in an open, world market. But it is precisely the harsh competition from abroad that gives consumers the benefits of international specialization. In our numerical example of comparative advantage, one can well imagine the complaints from Japanese computer makers as the opening of trade led to increased importation of U.S. computers. At the same time, American TV manufacturers would probably have expressed outrage over the flood of imported TVs from Japan. Yet it is Japanese specialization in televisions and U.S. specialization in computers that enables citizens of both countries to enjoy higher standards of living. If governments interfere with this process, consumers in both countries will lose out.

Industries threatened by foreign competition often argue that some form of protection against imports is needed to prevent loss of jobs. This argument is frequently made, for example, by the U.S. apparel industry since nearly two-thirds of all clothing purchased by Americans is imported. But we know from basic macroeconomics that there are better ways to stimulate employment, such as raising aggregate demand.

A program that limits foreign competition will be more effective at preserving employment *in the particular protected industry*. But it will typically do so at a high cost to consumers and to the economy. Table 17-4 gives some estimates of the costs to American consumers of using tariffs and quotas to save jobs in selected industries. In every case, the costs far exceed the wages of the workers in the protected industries—ranging as high as \$600,000 per job for the sugar quota.

TABLE 17-4 ESTIMATED COSTS OF PROTECTIONISM TO CONSUMERS

Industry	Cost per Job Saved
Apparel	$139,000
Costume jewelry	97,000
Shipping	415,000
Sugar	600,000
Textiles	202,000
Women's footwear	102,000

SOURCE: Gary C. Hufbauer and Kimberly Ann Elliott, *Measuring the Costs of Protectionism in the United States* (Washington, D.C.: Institute for International Economics, January 1994), Table 1.3, pp. 12–13.

Nevertheless, complaints over proposals to reduce a tariff or a quota are justified unless something is done to ease the cost to individual workers of switching to the lines of production that trade makes profitable.

The argument for free trade between countries cannot be considered airtight if there is no adequate program to assist those few citizens in each country who are harmed whenever patterns of production change drastically—as would happen, for example, if tariff and quota barriers were suddenly reduced.

Owners of television factories in the United States and of computer factories in Japan may see heavy investments suddenly rendered unprofitable. So would workers whose investments in acquiring special skills and training are no longer marketable. Nor are the costs to displaced workers only monetary. They may have to move to new locations as well as to new industries, uprooting their families, losing old friends and neighbors, and so on. That the *majority* of citizens undoubtedly gain from free trade is no consolation to those who are its victims.

To mitigate this problem, the United States follows two basic approaches. First, provisions in the trade laws offer temporary protection from sudden surges of imports, on the grounds that unexpected changes in trade patterns do not give people enough time to adjust.

TRADE ADJUSTMENT ASSISTANCE provides special unemployment benefits, loans, retraining programs, and other aid to workers and firms that are harmed by foreign competition.

Second, the government has set up **trade adjustment assistance** programs to help workers and businesses who lose their jobs or their markets because of increases in imports. Firms may be eligible for technical assistance, government loans or loan guarantees, and permission to delay tax payments. Workers may qualify for retraining programs, longer periods of unemployment compensation, and funds to defray moving costs. Each form of assistance is designed to ease the burden on the victims of free trade so that the rest of us can enjoy its considerable benefits.

OTHER ARGUMENTS FOR PROTECTION

NATIONAL DEFENSE AND OTHER NONECONOMIC CONSIDERATIONS

Sometimes a tariff or other interference with trade may be justified on noneconomic grounds. If a country considers itself vulnerable to military attack, it may be perfectly rational to keep alive industries whose outputs can be obtained more cheaply abroad but whose supplies might be cut off in an emergency. The argument is valid, but there is a danger: Industries with the most peripheral relationship to defense are likely to invoke this argument on their behalf. For instance, for years the U.S. watchmaking industry claimed protection for itself on the grounds that its skilled craftsmen would be invaluable in wartime.

Similarly, the United States has occasionally banned either exports to or imports from nations such as Cuba, Iran, and Iraq on political grounds. Such actions often have important economic effects, creating either bonanzas or disasters for particular American industries. But they are justified by politics, not by economics. Noneconomic reasons also explain quotas on importation of whaling products and on the furs of other endangered species.

THE INFANT-INDUSTRY ARGUMENT

Another common argument for protectionism is the so-called *infant-industry argument.* Promising new industries, it is alleged, often need breathing room to flourish and grow. If we expose these infants to the rigors of international competition too soon, the argument goes, they may never develop to the point where they can survive on their own in the international marketplace.

The argument, while valid in certain instances, is less defensible than it seems at first. It makes sense to protect an infant industry only if the prospective future gains are sufficient to repay the social losses incurred while it is being protected. But if the industry is likely to be so profitable in the future, why doesn't private capital rush in to take advantage of the prospective net profits? The annals of business are full of cases in which a new product or a new firm lost money at first but profited handsomely later.

The infant-industry argument for protection stands up to scrutiny only where funds are not available to a particular industry for some reason, despite its glowing profit prospects. And even then it may make more sense to provide a government loan to the infant industry than to provide trade protection.

It is hard to think of examples where the infant-industry argument applies. But even if such a case were found, one would have to be careful that the industry not remain in diapers forever. There are too many cases in which new industries were awarded protection when they were being established and, somehow, the time to withdraw that protection never arrived. One must beware of infant industries that never grow up.

STRATEGIC TRADE POLICY

A stronger argument for (temporary) protection is beginning to have substantial influence on U.S. trade policy. Advocates of this argument, including some top officials in the Clinton administration, agree that free trade for all is the best system. But they point out that we live in an imperfect world in which many nations refuse to play by the rules of the free-trade game. And they fear that a nation that pursues free trade in a protectionist world is likely to lose out. It therefore makes sense, they argue, to *threaten* to protect your markets unless other nations agree to open theirs. (See the article on the next page by columnist William Safire.)

The United States has followed this strategy in trade negotiations with several countries in recent years. The most prominent case came in 1995, when the U.S. government threatened to impose 100 percent tariffs on imported Japanese luxury cars unless Japan agreed to open up its domestic markets for automobiles

CAN PROTECTIONISM SAVE FREE TRADE?

In this 1983 column, William Safire shook off his longstanding attachment to free trade and argued eloquently for retaliation against protectionist nations.

WASHINGTON—Free trade is economic motherhood. Protectionism is economic evil incarnate. . . . Never should government interfere in the efficiency of international competition.

Since childhood, these have been the tenets of my faith. If it meant that certain businesses in this country went belly-up, so be it. . . . If it meant that Americans would be thrown out of work by overseas companies paying coolie wages, that was tough. . . .

The thing to keep in mind, I was taught, was the Big Picture and the Long Run. America, the great exporter, had far more to gain than to lose from free trade; attempts to protect inefficient industries here would ultimately cost more American jobs.

While playing with my David Ricardo doll and learning nursery rhymes about comparative advantage, I was listening to another laissez-fairy tale: Government's role in the world of business should be limited to keeping business honest and competitive. In God we antitrusted. Let businesses operate in the free marketplace.

Now American businesses are no longer competing with foreign companies. They are competing with foreign governments who help their local businesses. That means the world arena no longer offers a free marketplace; instead, most other governments are pushing a policy that can be called *helpfulism.*

Helpfulism works like this: A government like Japan decides to get behind its baseball-bat industry. It pumps in capital, knocks off marginal operators, finds subtle ways to discourage imports of Louisville Sluggers, and selects target areas for export blitzes. Pretty soon, the favored Japanese companies are driving foreign competitors batty.

How do we compete with helpfulism? One way is to complain that it is unfair; that draws a horselaugh. Another way is to demand a "Reagan Round" of trade negotiations under GATT, the Gentlemen's Agreement To Talk, which is equally laughable. Yet another way is to join the helpfuls by subsidizing our exports and permitting our companies to try monopolistic tricks abroad not permitted at home. But all that makes us feel guilty, with good reason.

The other way to deal with helpfulism is through—here comes the dreadful word—*protection.* Or, if you prefer a euphemism, *retaliation.* Or if that is still too severe, *reciprocity.* Whatever its name, it is a way of saying to the cutthroat cartelists we sweetly call our trading partners: "You have bent the rules out of shape. Change your practices to conform to the agreed-upon rules, or we will export a taste of your own medicine."

A little balance, then, from the free trade theorists. The demand for what the Pentagon used to call "protective reaction" is not demagoguery, not shortsighted, not self-defeating. On the contrary, the overseas pirates of protectionism and exemplars of helpfulism need to be taught the basic lesson in trade, which is: tit for tat.

SOURCE: William Safire, "Smoot-Hawley Lives," *The New York Times,* March 17, 1983.

and auto parts. A dangerous trade war was narrowly averted when an agreement was reached at the 11th hour.

The strategic argument for protection is a hard one for economists to deal with. While it accepts the superiority of free trade, it argues that threatening protectionism is the best way to establish free trade. Such a strategy might work, but it clearly involves great risks. If threats that America will turn protectionist induce other countries to scrap existing protectionist policies, then the gamble will have succeeded. But, if the gamble fails, protectionism increases.

CAN CHEAP IMPORTS BE BAD FOR A COUNTRY?

DUMPING means selling goods in a foreign market at lower prices than those charged in the home market.

One of the most curious features of the protectionist position is the fear of low prices charged by foreign sellers. Countries that subsidize exports are accused of **dumping**—of getting rid of their goods at unconscionably low prices. For example, Japan and Korea have frequently been accused of dumping a variety of goods on the U.S. market.

Economists find this argument strange. As a nation of consumers, we should be indignant when foreigners charge us *high* prices, not *low* ones. That is the common-sense rule that guides every consumer's daily life. Only from the topsy-turvy viewpoint of an industry seeking protection from competition are low prices seen as being against the public interest.

Ultimately, it must be in the best interest of a country to get its imports as cheaply as possible. It would be ideal for the United States if the rest of the world were willing to provide its exports to us free or virtually so. We could then live in luxury at the expense of the rest of the world.

But, of course, what benefits the United States as a whole does not necessarily benefit every single American. If quotas on, say, sugar imports were dropped, American consumers and industries that purchase sugar would gain from lower prices. But owners of sugar fields and their employees would suffer serious losses in the form of lower profits, lower wages, and lost jobs—losses they would fight hard to prevent. For this reason, politics often leads to the adoption of protectionist measures that would likely be rejected on strictly economic criteria.

CONCLUSION: A LAST LOOK AT THE "CHEAP FOREIGN LABOR" ARGUMENT

The preceding discussion reveals the fundamental fallacy in the argument that American workers have to fear cheap foreign labor. If workers in other countries are willing to supply their products to us with little compensation, this must ultimately *raise* the standard of living of the average American worker. As long as the government's monetary and fiscal policies succeed in maintaining high levels of employment at home, how can we possibly lose by getting the products of the world at bargain prices?

There are, however, some important qualifications. First, our macroeconomic policy may not be effective. If workers who are displaced by foreign competition cannot find jobs in other industries, then American workers will indeed suffer from international trade. But that is a shortcoming of the government's monetary and fiscal policies, not of its international trade policies.

Second, we have noted that an abrupt stiffening of foreign competition *can* hurt U.S. workers by not giving them an adequate chance to adapt gradually to the new conditions. The more rapid the change, the more painful it will be. If it occurs fairly gradually, workers can retrain and move on to the industries that now require their services. If the change is even more gradual, people who retire or leave the threatened industry for other reasons simply need not be replaced. But competition that inflicts its damage overnight is certain to impose real costs upon the affected workers, costs that are no less painful for being temporary. That is why our trade laws make provisions for people and industries damaged by import surges.

UNFAIR FOREIGN COMPETITION

Satire and ridicule are often more persuasive than logic and statistics. Exasperated by the spread of protectionism under the prevailing Mercantilist philosophy, French economist Frédéric Bastiat decided to take the protectionist argument to its illogical conclusion. The fictitious petition of the French candlemakers to the Chamber of Deputies, written in 1845 and excerpted below, has become a classic in the battle for free trade.

> We are subject to the intolerable competition of a foreign rival, who enjoys, it would seem, such superior facilities for the production of light, that he is enabled to inundate our national market at so exceedingly reduced a price, that, the moment he makes his appearance, he draws off all custom for us; and thus an important branch of French industry, with all its innumerable ramifications, is suddenly reduced to a state of complete stagnation. This rival is no other than the sun.
>
> Our petition is, that it would please your honorable body to pass a law whereby shall be directed the shutting up of all windows, dormers, skylights, shutters, curtains, in a word, all openings, holes, chinks, and fissures through which the light of the sun is used to penetrate our dwellings, to the prejudice of the profitable manufactures which we flatter ourselves we have been enabled to bestow upon the country. . . .
>
> We foresee your objections, gentlemen; but there is not one that you can oppose to us . . . which is not equally opposed to your own practice and the principle which guides your policy. . . . Labor and nature concur in different proportions, according to country and climate, in every article of production. . . . If a Lisbon orange can be sold at half the price of a Parisian one, it is because a natural and gratuitous heat does for the one what the other only obtains from an artificial and consequently expensive one. . . .
>
> Does it not argue the greatest inconsistency to check as you do the importation of coal, iron, cheese, and goods of foreign manufacture, merely because and even in proportion as their price approaches *zero*, while at the same time you freely admit, and without limitation, the light of the sun, whose price is during the whole day at *zero*?

SOURCE: F. Bastiat, *Economic Sophisms* (New York: G. P. Putnam's Sons, 1922).

But these are, after all, only qualifications to an overwhelming argument. They call for intelligent monetary and fiscal policies and for transitional assistance to unemployed workers, not for abandonment of free trade. In general, the nation as a whole need not fear competition from cheap foreign labor.

In the long run, labor will be "cheap" only where it is not very productive. Wages will be high in countries with high labor productivity—which holds down costs and permits exporters to compete effectively despite high wages. It is thus misleading to say that the United States held its own in the international marketplace until recently *despite* high wages. Rather it is much more illuminating to point out that the high wages of American workers were a result of high worker productivity, which gave the United States a heavy competitive edge.

We note that in this matter it is *absolute* advantage, not *comparative* advantage, that counts. The country that is most efficient in every output can pay its workers more in every industry.

SUMMARY

1. Countries trade because differences in their natural resources and other inputs create discrepancies in the efficiency with which they can produce different goods, and because **specialization** may offer them greater economies of large-scale production.
2. Voluntary trade will generally be advantageous to both parties in an exchange. This is one of our **Ideas for Beyond the Final Exam.**

3. International trade is more complicated than trade within a nation because of political factors, different national currencies, and impediments to the movement of labor and capital across national borders.
4. Two countries will gain from trade with one another if each exports goods in which it has a **comparative advantage.** Even a country that is generally inefficient will benefit by exporting the goods in whose production it is *least inefficient.* This is another of the **Ideas for Beyond the Final Exam.**
5. When countries specialize and trade, each can enjoy consumption possibilities that exceed its production possibilities.
6. The prices of goods traded between countries are determined by supply and demand, but one must consider explicitly the demand curve and the supply curve of *each* country involved. Thus, in international trade, the equilibrium price must be where the excess of the exporter's quantity supplied over its domestic quantity demanded is equal to the excess of the importer's quantity demanded over its quantity supplied.
7. The *"cheap foreign labor" argument* ignores the principle of comparative advantage, which shows that real wages can rise in both the importing and exporting countries as a result of specialization.
8. **Tariffs** and **quotas** are designed to protect a country's industries from foreign competition. Such protection may sometimes be advantageous to that country, but not if foreign countries adopt tariffs and quotas of their own as a means of retaliation.
9. While the same restriction of trade can be accomplished by either a tariff or a quota, tariffs offer at least two advantages to the country that imposes them: (1) Some of the gains go to the government rather than to foreign producers, and (2) there is greater incentive for efficient production.
10. When a nation shifts from protection to free trade, some industries and their workers will lose out. Equity then demands that these people and firms be compensated in some way. The U.S. government offers protection from import surges and various forms of **trade adjustment assistance** to do this.
11. Several arguments for protectionism can, under the right circumstances, have validity. These include the national defense argument, the *infant-industry argument,* and the use of trade restrictions for *strategic* purposes. But each of these arguments is frequently abused.
12. **Dumping** will hurt certain domestic producers; but it always benefits domestic consumers.

KEY TERMS

Imports
Exports
Specialization
Mutual gains from trade
Absolute advantage
Comparative advantage
"Cheap foreign labor" argument
Tariff
Quota
Export subsidy
Trade adjustment assistance
Infant-industry argument
Strategic trade protection
Dumping

QUESTIONS FOR REVIEW

1. You have a dozen shirts and your roommate has six pairs of shoes worth roughly the same amount of money. You decide to swap six shirts for three pairs of shoes. In financial terms, neither of you gains anything. Explain why you are nevertheless both likely to be better off.
2. In the 18th century, some writers argued that one person in a trade could be made better off only by gaining at the expense of the other. Explain the fallacy in the argument.
3. Country A has a cold climate with a short growing season, but a highly skilled labor force. What sorts of products do you think it is likely to produce? What are the characteristics of the countries with which you would expect it to trade?
4. Upon removal of a quota on sugar, many U.S. sugar farms go bankrupt. Discuss the pros and cons of removing the quota in the short and long runs.
5. Country A's government believes that it is always best to export more than it imports. As a consequence, it exports more to Country B every year than it imports from Country B. After 100 years of this arrangement, both countries are destroyed in an earthquake. What were the advantages and disadvantages of the surplus to Country A? To Country B?
6. The following table describes the number of yards of cloth and barrels of wine that can be produced with a week's worth of labor in England and Portugal. Assume that no other inputs are needed.

	In England	In Portugal
Cloth (yards)	8	12
Wine (barrels)	2	6

a. If there is no trade, what is the price of wine in terms of cloth in England?
b. If there is no trade, what is the price of wine relative to cloth in Portugal?
c. Suppose each country has 1 million weeks of labor available per year. Draw the production possibilities frontier for each country.
d. Which country has an absolute advantage in the production of which good(s)? Which country has a comparative advantage in the production of which good(s)?
e. If the countries start trading with each other, which country will specialize and export which good?
f. What can be said about the price at which trade will take place?

7. Suppose that the United States and Mexico are the only two countries in the world, and that labor is the only productive input. In the United States, a worker can produce 12 bushels of wheat *or* 2 barrels of oil in a day. In Mexico, a worker can produce 2 bushels of wheat *or* 4 barrels of oil per day.
   a. What will be the price ratio between the two commodities (that is, the price of oil in terms of wheat) in each country if there is no trade?
   b. If free trade is allowed and there are no transportation costs, what commodity would the United States import? What about Mexico?
   c. In what range would the price ratio have to fall under free trade? Why?
   d. Picking one possible post-trade price ratio, show clearly how it is possible for both countries to benefit from free trade.

8. The table below presents the demand and supply curves for microcomputers in Japan and the United States.

Price per Computer (thousands of dollars)	Quantity Demanded in United States (thousands)	Quantity Supplied in United States (thousands)	Quantity Demanded in Japan (thousands)	Quantity Supplied in Japan (thousands)
1	90	30	50	50
2	80	35	40	55
3	70	40	30	60
4	60	45	20	65
5	50	50	10	70
6	40	55	0	75

   a. Draw the demand and supply curves for the United States on one diagram and those for Japan on another one.
   b. If there is no trade between the United States and Japan, what are the equilibrium price and quantity in the computer market in the United States? In Japan?
   c. Now suppose trade is opened up between the two countries. What will be the equilibrium price in the world market for computers? What has happened to the price of computers in the United States? In Japan?
   d. Which country will export computers? How many?
   e. When trade opens, what happens to the quantity of computers produced, and therefore employment, in the computer industry in the United States? In Japan? Who benefits and who loses *initially* from free trade?

9. Under current trade law, the president of the United States must report periodically to Congress on countries engaging in unfair trade practices that inhibit U.S. exports. How would you define an "unfair" trade practice? Suppose Country X exports much more to the United States than it imports, year after year. Does that constitute evidence that Country X's trade practices are unfair? What would constitute such evidence?

10. Suppose the United States finds Country X guilty of unfair trade practices and penalizes it with import quotas. So U.S. imports from Country X fall. Suppose, further, that Country X does not alter its trade practices in any way. Is the United States better or worse off? What about Country X?

CHAPTER 18

THE INTERNATIONAL MONETARY SYSTEM: ORDER OR DISORDER?

Cecily, you will read your Political Economy in my absence. The chapter on the Fall of the Rupee you may omit. It is somewhat too sensational.
Miss Prism in Oscar Wilde, *The Importance of Being Earnest*

The last chapter discussed the reasons for international trade and the benefits that accrue to all nations when countries specialize in producing goods in which they have a comparative advantage. But when goods cross national borders, *money* must generally move in the opposite direction. When the United States buys coffee from Brazil, we must send money to the Brazilians. When Japan purchases petroleum from Saudi Arabia, it must send money to the Saudis, and so on. This chapter is about the system that has been set up to handle these international movements of money—the *international monetary system.*

We begin by investigating a system in which rates of exchange among national currencies are determined in free markets by the laws of supply and demand. We shall see that the main macroeconomic variables that we have been studying—output, the price level, and the rate of interest—each play a role in the determination of a country's exchange rate. This discussion sets the stage for Chapter 19, where we will learn how movements of the exchange rate, in turn, affect the national economy.

Next, we turn to the opposite polar form—an international monetary system in which exchange rates are fixed by government authority, rather than by the market. The United States does not now fix its exchange rate, but other countries do. And studying such a system will help us understand why some people believe that the world should move toward greater fixity in exchange rates.

PUZZLE: WHATEVER HAPPENED TO MEXICO?

For much of 1994, Mexico was considered an economic success story: a model of how a developing country can turn its economy around by pursuing sound economic policies. The Mexican government had balanced its budget, opened its economy to world trade, and brought inflation down from over 100 percent per year to under 5 percent. Furthermore, it was guaranteeing the soundness of its currency by pledging to keep the value of the peso fixed in terms of U.S. dollars. With the North American Free Trade Agreement (NAFTA) bringing new opportunities to Mexico's now-vibrant export industries, rapid growth seemed assured.

Then, around Christmas of 1994, the bottom fell out. With a suddenness that was both stunning and vicious, massive amounts of money started flowing out of Mexico. Interest rates soared, and the stock market collapsed. The value of the peso, which had been fixed at about 29 cents, tumbled to 19 cents within a few weeks and to about 14 cents within a few months. Soon inflation, which had been down to about 4 percent, was soaring (for a few months) at annual rates around 100 percent. And Mexico plunged into a severe recession.

What went wrong? What forced the Mexican government to abandon its fixed exchange rate policy? And why did that decision have such dire consequences? We will learn some of the answers in the pages to come. But first we need to understand what determines exchange rates.

WHAT ARE EXCHANGE RATES?

We noted in the previous chapter that international trade is more complicated than domestic trade. There are no national borders to be crossed when, say, California lettuce is shipped to Massachusetts. The consumer in Boston pays with *dollars,* just the currency that the farmer in Modesto wants. But if that same farmer ships his lettuce to Japan, consumers there will have only Japanese *yen* with which to pay, rather than the dollars the farmer in California wants. Thus, if international trade is to take place, there must be a way to transform one currency into another. The rates at which such transformations are made are called **exchange rates.**

The **EXCHANGE RATE** states the price, in terms of one currency, at which another currency can be bought.

There is an exchange rate between every pair of currencies. For example, $1 is currently the equivalent of about 5 French francs. The exchange rate between the franc and the dollar, then, may be expressed as roughly "5 francs to the dollar" (meaning that it costs 5 francs to buy a dollar) or about "20 cents to the franc" (meaning that it costs 20 cents to buy a franc).

There have been some dramatic changes in the international value of the dollar over time. In a nutshell, the dollar soared in the period from mid-1980 to early 1985, fell against most major currencies from early 1985 until early 1988, and has generally fluctuated without any pronounced trend since. This chapter seeks to explain such currency movements.

A nation's currency is said to **APPRECIATE** when exchange rates change so that a unit of its own currency can buy more units of foreign currency.

The currency is said to **DEPRECIATE** when exchange rates change so that a unit of its currency can buy fewer units of foreign currency.

Under our present system, currency rates change frequently. When other currencies become more expensive in terms of dollars, we say that they have **appreciated** relative to the dollar. Alternatively, we can look at this same event as the dollar buying less foreign currency, meaning that the dollar has **depreciated** relative to another currency.

What is a depreciation to one country must be an appreciation to the other.

For example, if the cost of a German mark rises from 50 cents to 60 cents, the cost of a U.S. dollar in terms of marks simultaneously falls from 2.00 marks to 1.67 marks. The Germans have had a currency *appreciation* while we have had a currency *depreciation.*

Notice also that, when many currencies are changing in value, the dollar may be appreciating with respect to one currency but depreciating with respect to another. Table 18-1 gives an indication of exchange rates prevailing in July 1980, February 1985, and April 1996, showing how many dollars or cents it cost at each of those times to buy each unit of foreign currency. You will note that, between

TABLE 18-1

EXCHANGE RATES WITH THE U.S. DOLLAR (dollars per unit of foreign currency)

Country	Currency Unit	Symbol	July 1980	Cost in Dollars February 1985	April 1997
Australia	dollar	$	$1.16	$0.74	$0.77
Canada	dollar	$	0.87	0.74	0.71
France	franc	FF	0.25	0.10	0.17
Germany	mark	DM	0.57	0.30	0.58
Italy	lira	L	0.0012	0.00049	0.00059
Japan	yen	¥	0.0045	0.0038	0.0079
Mexico	new peso	$	44.0[a]	5.0[a]	0.13
Sweden	krona	Kr	0.24	0.11	0.13
Switzerland	franc	S.Fr.	0.62	0.36	0.68
United Kingdom	pound	£	2.37	1.10	1.62

[a]On January 1, 1993, the peso was redefined so that 1,000 old pesos were equal to 1 new peso. Hence, the numbers 44 and 5 listed for July 1980 and February 1985 were actually 0.044 and 0.005 on the old basis.

SOURCE: International Financial Statistics and *The Wall Street Journal.*

February 1985 and April 1996, the dollar *depreciated* sharply relative to the Japanese yen and most European currencies. For example, the British pound rose from $1.10 to $1.51. Yet during that same period the dollar *appreciated* dramatically relative to the Mexican peso; it bought about 0.2 pesos in 1985 but over 7.1 in 1996.[1]

A **DEVALUATION** is a reduction in the official value of a currency.

A **REVALUATION** is an increase in the official value of a currency.

While this is the terminology used to describe movements of exchange rates in free markets, another set of terms is used to describe decreases and increases in currency values when those values are set by government decree. When an officially set exchange rate is altered so that a unit of a nation's currency can buy *fewer* units of foreign currency, we say there has been a **devaluation** of that currency. When the exchange rate is altered so that the currency can buy *more* units of foreign currency, we say there has been a **revaluation.**

EXCHANGE RATE DETERMINATION IN A FREE MARKET

FLOATING EXCHANGE RATES are rates determined in free markets by the law of supply and demand.

Why is it that a German mark now costs about 66 cents and not 60 cents or 75 cents? In a world of **floating exchange rates,** with no government interferences, the answer would be straightforward. Exchange rates would be determined by the forces of supply and demand, just like the prices of apples, computers, and haircuts.

In a leap of abstraction, imagine that the United States and Germany are the only countries on earth, so there is only one exchange rate to be determined. Figure 18-1 depicts the determination of this exchange rate at the point (denoted *E* in the figure) where demand curve *DD* crosses supply curve *SS*. At this price (70 cents per mark), the number of marks demanded is equal to the number of marks supplied.

[1]In fact, the dollar bought about 200 pesos in February 1985, but that is because the old peso was replaced by a new peso in January 1993, which moved the decimal point three places.

FIGURE 18-1 DETERMINATION OF EXCHANGE RATES IN A FREE MARKET

Like any price, an exchange rate in a free market will be determined by the intersection of the demand and supply curves. Point *E* depicts this point for the exchange rate between the U.S. dollar and the German mark, which settles at 70 cents per mark in this example.

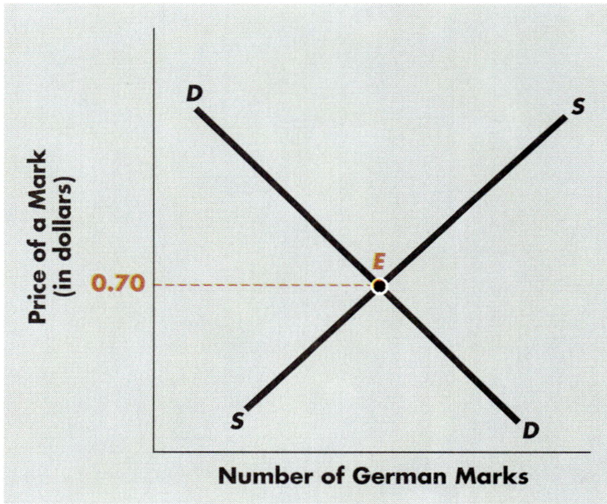

In a free market, exchange rates are determined by the law of supply and demand. If the rate were below the equilibrium level, the quantity of marks demanded would exceed the quantity of marks supplied, and the price of a mark would be bid up. If the rate were above the equilibrium level, quantity supplied would exceed quantity demanded, and the price of a mark would fall. Only at the equilibrium exchange rate is there no tendency for the rate to change.

As usual, supply and demand determine price. But in this case, we must ask: Where do the supply and demand come from? Why does anyone demand a German mark? The answer has three parts:

1. *International trade in goods and services.* This was the subject of the last chapter. If, for example, Jane Doe, an American, wants to buy a German automobile, she will first have to buy marks with which to pay the dealer in Munich.[2] So Jane's demand for a German *car* leads to a demand for German *marks.* In general, *demand for a country's exports leads to a demand for its currency.*[3]
2. *International trade in financial instruments like stocks and bonds.* For example, if American investors want to purchase German stocks, they will first have to acquire the marks that the sellers will insist upon. In this way, demand for German financial assets leads to demand for German marks. Thus, *demand for a country's financial assets leads to a demand for its currency.*
3. *Purchases of physical assets like factories and machinery overseas.* If IBM wants to buy out a small German computer manufacturer, the owners will no doubt want to receive marks. So IBM will first have to acquire German currency. In general, *direct foreign investment leads to a demand for a country's currency.*

---

[2]Actually, she will not do this because banks generally handle foreign exchange transactions for consumers. An American bank probably will buy the marks for her. But the effect is exactly the same as if Jane had done it herself.

[3]See Review Question 2 at the end of the chapter (page 421).

Now, where does the supply come from? To answer this, just turn all of these transactions around. Germans wanting to buy U.S. goods and services, or invest in U.S. financial markets, or make direct investments in America will have to offer their marks for sale in the foreign-exchange market (which is similar to the stock market) to acquire the needed dollars. To summarize:

The *demand* for a country's currency is derived from the demands of foreigners for its export goods and services and for its assets—including financial assets, like stocks and bonds, and real assets, like factories and machinery. The *supply* of a country's currency arises from its imports, and from foreign investment by its own citizens.

To appreciate the usefulness of even this simple supply and demand analysis, think about how the exchange rate between the dollar and the mark would change if there were an economic boom in the United States. One important effect of such a boom would be to stimulate American demand for German products, such as machine tools, cameras, and beer. In terms of the supply-demand diagram shown in Figure 18-2, the increased desires of Americans for German goods would shift the demand curve for German marks out from D_1D_1 (the black line in the figure) to D_2D_2 (the blue line). Equilibrium would shift from point *E* to point *A*, and the exchange rate would rise from 70 cents per mark to 75 cents per mark. The increased demand for marks by U.S. citizens causes the mark to *appreciate* relative to the dollar.

EXERCISE:

Test your understanding of the supply and demand analysis of exchange rates by showing why each of the following events would lead to an appreciation of the mark (a depreciation of the dollar) in a free market:

1. A recession in Germany cuts German purchases of American goods.
2. American investors are attracted by prospects for profit on the German stock market.

FIGURE 18-2 THE EFFECT OF AN ECONOMIC BOOM ON THE EXCHANGE RATE

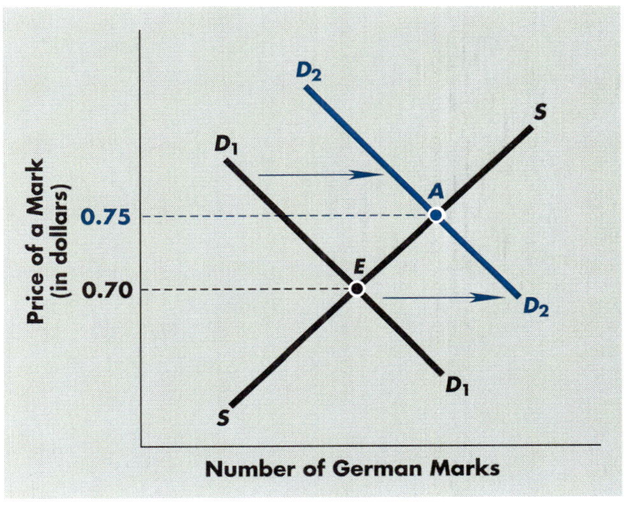

If the U.S. economy suddenly booms, Americans will spend more on imports from Germany. Thus, the demand curve for German marks will rise from D_1D_1 to D_2D_2 as Americans seek to acquire the marks they need. The diagram shows that this will cause the mark to appreciate, from 70 cents to 75 cents, as equilibrium shifts from point *E* to point *A*. Looked at from the U.S. perspective, the dollar will depreciate.

3. Interest rates on government bonds rise in Germany but are stable in the United States. (*Hint:* Which country's citizens will be attracted by high interest rates in the other country?)

To say that supply and demand determine exchange rates in a free market is at once to say everything and to say nothing. If we are to understand the reasons why some currencies appreciate while others depreciate, we must look into the factors that move the supply and demand curves. Economists believe that the principal determinants of exchange rate movements are rather different in the long, medium, and short runs. So we turn in the next three sections to the analysis of exchange rate movements over these three "runs," beginning with the long run.

THE PURCHASING-POWER PARITY THEORY: THE LONG RUN

As long as there is free trade across national borders, exchange rates should eventually adjust so that the same product costs the same whether measured in dollars in the United States, marks in Germany, yen in Japan, and so on—except for differences in transportation costs and the like. This simple statement forms the basis of the major theory of exchange rate determination in the long run.

The *purchasing-power parity theory of exchange rate determination* holds that the exchange rate between any two national currencies adjusts to reflect differences in the price levels in the two countries.

An example will bring out the basic truth in this theory and also suggest some of its limitations. Suppose that German and American steel are identical and that these two nations are the only producers of steel for the world market. Suppose further that steel is the only tradable good that either country produces.

Question: If American steel costs $210 per ton and German steel costs 300 marks per ton, what must be the exchange rate between the dollar and the mark?

Answer: Since 300 marks or $210 each buys a ton of steel, they must be of equal value. Hence, each mark must be worth 70 cents. Why? Any higher price for a mark, like 80 cents, would mean that steel would cost $240 per ton (300 marks at 80 cents each) in Germany but only $210 per ton in the United States. In that case, all foreign customers would shop for their steel in the United States—which would increase the demand for dollars and decrease the demand for marks. Similarly, any exchange rate below 70 cents per mark would send all the steel business to Germany, driving the value of the mark up toward its purchasing-power parity level.

EXERCISE:
Show why an exchange rate of 60 cents per mark is too low.

The purchasing-power parity theory is used to make long-run predictions about the effects of inflation on exchange rates. To continue our example, suppose that over a 10-year period, prices in the United States rise by 50 percent while prices in Germany rise by 110 percent. The purchasing-power parity theory predicts that the mark will depreciate relative to the dollar. It also predicts the amount of the depreciation. After the inflation, American steel costs $315 per ton (50 percent more than $210), while German steel costs 630 marks per ton (110 percent more than 300 marks). For these two prices to be equivalent, 630 marks must be worth $315, or 1 mark must be worth 50 cents. The mark, therefore, must have fallen from 70 cents to 50 cents.

According to the purchasing-power parity theory, differences in domestic inflation rates are a major cause of adjustments in exchange rates. If one country has higher inflation than another, then its exchange rate should be depreciating.

For many years, the theory seemed to work tolerably well. While precise numerical predictions based on purchasing-power parity calculations were never very accurate (see the box on the next page), nations with higher inflation did at least experience depreciating currencies. But in the 1980s, even this broke down. For example, while the U.S. inflation rate was higher than both Germany's and Japan's, the dollar nonetheless rose sharply relative to both the mark and the yen from 1980 to 1985. Clearly, the theory was missing something. What?

Many things. But perhaps the principal failing of the purchasing-power parity theory is that it focuses too much on trade in goods and services. Financial assets like stocks and bonds are also traded actively across national borders—and in vastly greater dollar volumes than trade in goods and services. If investors decide that, say, U.S. assets are a better bet than German assets, the dollar will rise even if our inflation rate is well above Germany's. For this and other reasons:

Most economists believe that other factors are much more important than relative price levels for exchange rate determination in the short run. But in the long run, purchasing-power parity plays an important role.

ECONOMIC ACTIVITY AND EXCHANGE RATES: THE MEDIUM RUN

Since consumer spending increases when income rises and decreases when income falls, the same is likely to happen to spending on imported goods. For this reason:

A country's imports will rise quickly when its economy is booming and slowly when its economy is stagnating.

We have already illustrated this point with Figure 18-2. There we saw that a boom in the United States would shift the demand curve for marks outward as Americans bought more German goods. And that, in turn, would lead to an appreciation of the mark (depreciation of the dollar) as Americans sold dollars to buy marks. However, if Germany were booming at the same time, German citizens would be buying more American exports, which would shift the supply curve of marks outward. On balance, the value of the dollar might or might not fall. What matters is whether exports are growing faster than imports. The general lesson is that:

Holding other things equal, a country whose aggregate demand grows faster than the rest of the world's normally finds its imports growing faster than its exports. Thus, its demand curve for foreign currency shifts outward more rapidly than its supply curve, causing its currency to depreciate.

This is one reason why it is unwise to interpret a "strong currency" as an indication of a "strong economy." A nation that grows more rapidly than its trading partners may find itself with a depreciating currency.

PURCHASING-POWER PARITY AND THE BIG MAC

Since 1986, *The Economist* magazine has been using a well-known international commodity—the Big Mac—to assess the purchasing-power parity theory of exchange rates, or as the magazine puts it, "to make exchange-rate theory more digestible." The famous burger is now available in 79 countries. The 1995 survey included 32 of them, and it showed that the theory does not always work terribly well.

Here's how the survey works. In the spring of 1995, the average price of a Big Mac in the United States was \$2.32, including sales tax. In Japan, the same commodity cost ¥391. For those two amounts to be equal, a dollar would have had to be worth about ¥391/\$2.32 = ¥169. But the actual value of the dollar at the time was just ¥84, meaning that the Big Mac indicates an overvalued yen relative to the dollar. (In fact, the dollar rose about 28 percent against the yen in the year following the survey.)

The same calculation using the British pound yields much the same conclusion. By the Big Mac standard, the pound was overvalued by 21 percent. At £1.74 per burger, the implied purchasing-power parity value of the pound was \$2.32/£1.74 = \$1.33, versus a market value of \$1.61.

True Big Mac aficionados will find the following data helpful, especially if they are planning international travel. The cheapest Big Macs can be found in China; the 9 yuan price was a mouthwatering dollar equivalent of \$1.05. The Hong Kong version is almost as good, weighing in at just \$1.23. The priciest Big Macs in the world were to be found in Switzerland and Denmark, at the local equivalents of \$5.20 and \$4.92, respectively.

SOURCE: "Big MacCurrencies," *The Economist,* April 15, 1995, p. 74.

THE HAMBURGER STANDARD

	Big Mac Prices				
	In Local Currency	**In Dollars**	**Implied PPP[a] of the Dollar**	**Actual \$ Exchange Rate 7/4/97**	**Local Currency Under (−)/Over (+) Valuation, %**
United States[b]	\$2.42	2.42	—	—	—
Britain	£1.81	2.95	1.34[c]	1.63[c]	+22
China	Yuan9.70	1.16	4.01	8.33	−52
Denmark	DKr25.75	3.95	10.6	6.52	+63
France	FFr17.5	3.04	7.23	5.76	+26
Hong Kong	HK\$9.90	1.28	4.09	7.75	−47
Italy	Lire4,600	2.73	1,901	1,683	+13
Japan	¥294	2.34	121	126	−3
Mexico	Peso14.9	1.89	6.16	7.90	−22
Switzerland	SFr5.90	4.02	2.44	1.47	+66

[a]Purchasing-power parity: local price divided by price in the United States.
[b]Average of New York, Chicago, San Francisco, and Atlanta.
[c]Dollars per pound.

SOURCE: McDonald's; reported in "Big MacCurrencies," *The Economist,* April 12, 1997, p. 71.

INTEREST RATES AND EXCHANGE RATES: THE SHORT RUN

While economic activity is important for exchange rate determination in the medium run, "other things" often are not equal in the short run. Specifically, one factor that often seems to call the tune in determining exchange rate movements in the short run is *interest rate differentials.* A multi-trillion dollar pool of so-called *hot money*—owned by banks, mutual funds, multinational corporations, and wealthy individuals of all nations—travels rapidly around the globe in search of the highest interest rates.

Thus, suppose that British government bonds are paying a 6 percent rate of interest when yields on equally safe American government securities rise to 8 percent. British investors will be attracted by the high interest rates in the United States and will offer pounds for sale in order to buy dollars, planning to use those dollars to buy American securities. At the same time, American investors will find investing in the United States more attractive than ever, so fewer pounds will be demanded by Americans.

When the demand schedule falls and the supply curve rises, the effect on price is predictable: The pound will depreciate, as Figure 18-3 shows. In the figure, the supply curve of pounds shifts outward from S_1S_1 to S_2S_2 when British investors seek to sell pounds in order to purchase U.S. securities. At the same time, American investors wish to buy fewer pounds because they no longer wish to invest in British securities. Thus, the demand curve shifts inward from D_1D_1 to D_2D_2. The result, in our example, is a depreciation of the pound from \$1.60 to \$1.40. In general:

Holding other things equal, countries that offer investors higher rates of return are able to attract more capital than are countries that offer lower rates. Thus, a rise in interest rates often will lead to an appreciation of the currency, and a drop in interest rates will lead to a depreciation.

FIGURE 18-3 THE EFFECT OF A RISE IN U.S. INTEREST RATES

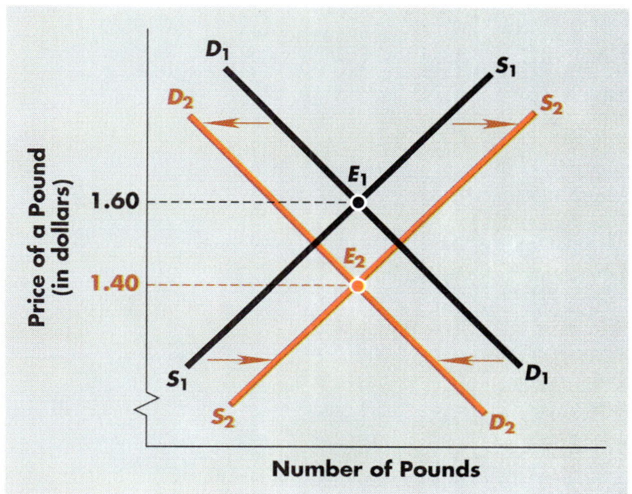

When the United States raises its interest rates, more British investors will want to buy American bonds, and so the supply curve of pounds will shift outward from S_1S_1 to S_2S_2. At the same time, fewer Americans will seek to buy British bonds, so the demand curve for pounds will shift inward from D_1D_1 to D_2D_2. The combined effect of these two shifts is to move the market equilibrium from point E_1 to point E_2. The British pound depreciates, and the dollar appreciates.

Most experts in international finance agree that this factor is the major determinant of exchange rates in the short run. It has certainly played a predominant role in the stunning movements of the U.S. dollar since the 1980s. In the early 1980s, American interest rates rose well above comparable interest rates abroad. In consequence, foreign capital was attracted here, American capital stayed at home, and the dollar soared. Something quite similar happened to the German mark in the early 1990s.

MARKET DETERMINATION OF EXCHANGE RATES: SUMMARY

We can summarize this discussion of exchange rate determination in free markets as follows:

1. Currency values generally will be *appreciating* in countries whose inflation rates are lower than the rest of the world's because buyers in foreign countries will demand their goods and thus drive up their currencies.
2. Exchange rates would also be expected to rise in countries where aggregate demand is growing more slowly than average, because these countries will be importing rather little.
3. We expect to find appreciating currencies in countries which offer high rates of return to investors because these countries will attract capital from all over the world.

Reversing each of these, we expect that currencies will be *depreciating* in countries with relatively high inflation rates, or rapid demand growth, or low interest rates.

FIXED EXCHANGE RATES AND THE BALANCE OF PAYMENTS

FIXED EXCHANGE RATES are rates set by government decisions and maintained by government actions.

The **BALANCE OF PAYMENTS DEFICIT** is the amount by which the quantity supplied of a country's currency (per year) exceeds the quantity demanded. Balance of payments deficits arise whenever the exchange rate is pegged at an artificially high level.

Some exchange rates today are truly floating, determined by the forces of supply and demand without government interference. But many are not. Furthermore, some people claim that exchange rate fluctuations are so troublesome that the world would be better off with fixed exchange rates. For these reasons, we turn our attention next to a system of **fixed exchange rates,** or rates that are set by government. Naturally, under such a system the exchange rate, being fixed, is not closely watched. Instead, international financial specialists focus on a country's *balance of payments*—a term we must now define.

To understand what the balance of payments is, look at Figure 18-4, which depicts a situation that might represent, say, Mexico just before the peso tumbled in the winter of 1994 to 1995—an *overvalued* currency. While the supply and demand curves for pesos indicate an equilibrium exchange rate of 15 cents to the peso (point *E*), the Mexican government is keeping the rate at 30 cents. Notice that, at 30 cents per peso, more people are supplying pesos than are demanding them. In the example, suppliers are selling 100 billion pesos per year, but purchasers want only 60 billion.

This gap between the 100 billion pesos that some people sell and the 60 billion that others buy is what we mean by Mexico's **balance of payments deficit**—40 billion pesos per year in this case. It is shown by the horizontal distance between points *A* and *B* in Figure 18-4.

FIGURE 18-4 A BALANCE OF PAYMENTS DEFICIT

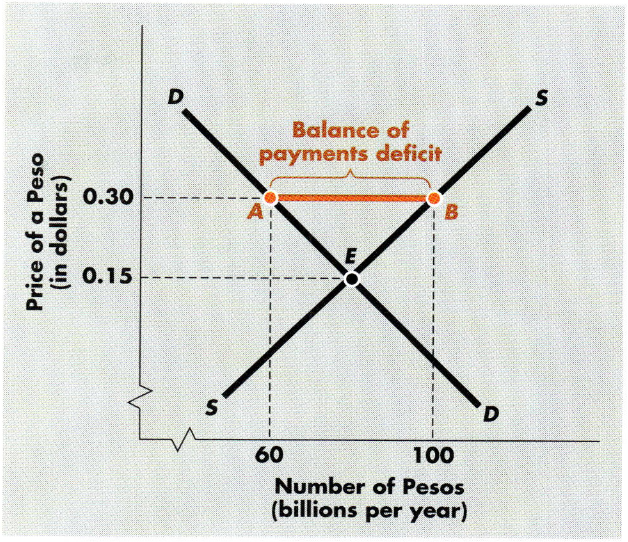

At a fixed exchange rate of 30 cents per peso, which is well above the equilibrium level of 15 cents per peso, Mexico's currency is overvalued in this example. As a consequence, more pesos will be supplied (point *B*) than are demanded (point *A*). The difference—distance *AB*, or 40 billion pesos per year—represents Mexico's balance of payments deficit.

How can market forces be flouted in this way? Since sales and purchases on any market must be equal, as a simple piece of arithmetic, the excess of quantity supplied over quantity demanded of Mexican currency (40 billion pesos per year in this example) must be bought by the Mexican government. To buy up these pesos, it must give up some of the foreign currency that it holds as *reserves.* Thus, the Bank of Mexico would be losing about $12 billion in reserves per year as the cost of keeping the peso at 30 cents.

Naturally, this cannot go on forever; the reserves eventually will run out. And this is the fatal flaw in a system of fixed exchange rates. Once speculators become convinced that the exchange rate can be held for only a short while longer, they will sell the overvalued currency in massive amounts rather than hold on to money whose value they expect to fall.

That is precisely what happened to Mexico in the winter of 1994 to 1995. The supply curve of pesos shifted outward drastically, as shown in Figure 18-5, causing a sharp rise in the balance of payments deficit—from 40 billion to 90 billion pesos in the example. (The numbers are fictitious.) Lacking sufficient reserves, the Mexican government had no choice but to let the peso fall to its equilibrium level, and this probably amounted to an even larger devaluation than would have been required before the speculative "run" on the peso.

The **BALANCE OF PAYMENTS SURPLUS** is the amount by which the quantity demanded of a country's currency (per year) exceeds the quantity supplied. Balance of payments surpluses arise whenever the exchange rate is pegged at an artificially low level.

For an example of the reverse case, a severely *undervalued* currency, let us go back in history to the case of West Germany in 1973. Figure 18-6 depicts demand and supply curves for marks that intersect at an equilibrium price of 50 cents per mark (point *E* in the diagram). Yet, in the example, we suppose that the German authorities are holding the rate at 33 cents. At this rate, the quantity of marks demanded (50 billion) greatly exceeds the quantity supplied (40 billion). The difference is Germany's **balance of payments surplus,** and is shown by the horizontal distance *AB*.

Germany can keep the rate at 33 cents only by providing the marks that foreigners want to buy: 10 billion marks per year in this example. In return, it receives U.S. dollars, British pounds, French francs, gold, and so on. All of this

FIGURE 18-5 A SPECULATIVE RUN ON THE PESO

When speculators become convinced that a devaluation of the peso is in the offing, they will rush to sell pesos. Their actions shift the supply curve outward from S_1S_1 to S_2S_2 and, in the process, widen the Mexican balance of payments deficit from *AB* to *AC*.

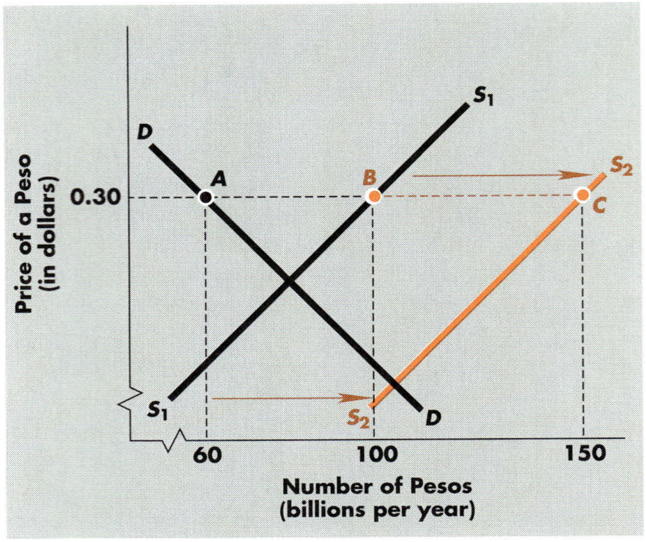

serves to increase Germany's reserves of foreign currencies. But notice the important difference between this case and the overvalued U.S. dollar.

The accumulation of reserves rarely will *force* a central bank to revalue in the way that depletion of reserves can force a devaluation.

This asymmetry was a clear weakness of the system of fixed exchange rates that prevailed between 1944 and 1971. In principle, an imbalance in exchange rates could be cured either by a *devaluation* by the country with a balance of payments deficit or by an upward *revaluation* by the country with a balance of

FIGURE 18-6 A BALANCE OF PAYMENTS SURPLUS

In this example, Germany's currency is undervalued at 33 cents per mark since the equilibrium exchange rate is 50 cents per mark. Consequently, more marks are being demanded (point *B*) than are being supplied (point *A*). The gap between quantity demanded and quantity supplied—distance *AB*, or 10 billion marks per year—measures Germany's balance of payments surplus.

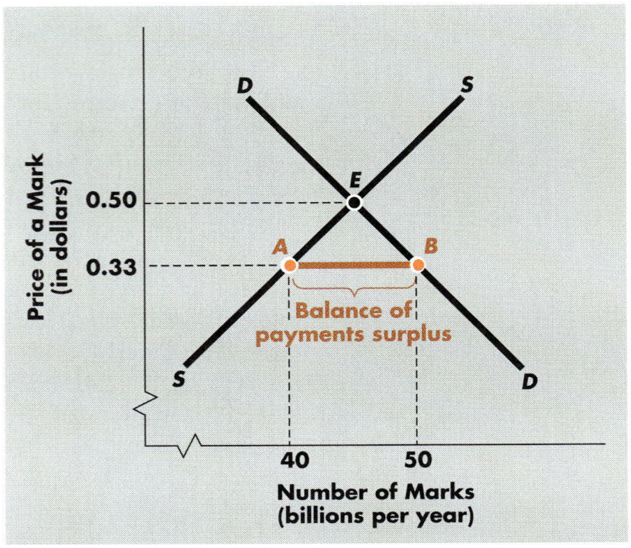

payments surplus. In practice, though, it was almost always the deficit countries that were forced to act.

Why did the surplus countries refuse to revalue? One reason was a stubborn refusal to recognize some basic economic realities. They viewed the disequilibrium as the problem of the deficit countries and believed that the deficit countries, therefore, should take the corrective steps. This, of course, is nonsense in a worldwide system of fixed exchange rates. Some currencies are overvalued *because* some other currencies are undervalued. In fact, the two statements mean exactly the same thing.

The other reason why exporters in Germany, Japan, and other surplus countries resisted upward revaluations is that such actions would have made their products more expensive to foreigners and thus cut into their sales. And these exporters had the political clout to make their views stick. Meanwhile, since the values of the mark and the yen on world markets were artificially held down, German and Japanese consumers were put in the unenviable position of having to pay more for imported goods than they need have paid. Rather than buy these excessively expensive foreign goods, they watched domestically produced goods go overseas in return for pieces of paper (dollars, francs, pounds, and so on).

DEFINING THE BALANCE OF PAYMENTS IN PRACTICE

The preceding discussion makes it look simple to measure a nation's balance of payments position: You just count up the private demand for and supply of its currency and subtract quantity supplied from quantity demanded. Conceptually, that is all there is to it. But in practice the difficulties are great because we never observe directly the number of dollars demanded and supplied.

If we look at actual market transactions, we will see that the number of, say, U.S. dollars actually *purchased* and the number of U.S. dollars actually *sold* are identical. Unless someone has made a bookkeeping error, this must always be so. How, then, can we recognize a balance of payments surplus or deficit? Easy, you say. Just look at the transactions of the central bank, whose purchases or sales must make up the difference between private demand and private supply. If the Federal Reserve is buying dollars, its purchases measure our balance of payments deficit. If it is selling, its sales represent our balance of payments surplus.

Thus, the suggestion is to measure the balance of payments by *excluding official transactions among governments*. This is roughly how the balance of payments surplus or deficit is defined today although, for a variety of complicated reasons, the U.S. government decided long ago to stop publishing any official statistic called "the balance of payments deficit." Instead, it lists all foreign transactions and invites readers to define the balance of payments any way they wish. Many experts focus on the surplus or deficit in what is called the *current account*. This account includes all exports and imports of goods and services, all cross-border payments of interest and dividends, and all cross-border gifts from and to individuals or governments. For more than a decade now, the United States has run large current account deficits.

But this hardly represents our "balance of payments," as it leaves out all purchases and sales of assets. Purchases of U.S. assets by foreigners bring us foreign currency, and U.S. purchases of foreign assets cost us foreign currency. Netting the capital flows in each direction gives us our surplus or deficit on *capital account*. In recent years, this element of our balance of payments has registered persistently large surpluses, as the United States borrowed large amounts of money from abroad.

The balance of payments can balance in one of two ways. If the government does not intervene to fix the exchange rate, all private transactions—current account plus capital account—must add up to zero (dollars purchased = dollars sold). But if, instead, the exchange rate is fixed, as shown in Figures 18-4 and 18-6, the two accounts need not balance one another. Government purchases or sales of foreign currency make up the surplus or deficit in the overall balance of payments.

A BIT OF HISTORY: THE GOLD STANDARD

It is hard to find examples of strictly fixed exchange rates in the historical record. About the only time exchange rates were truly fixed was under the old *gold standard,* at least when it was practiced in its ideal form.[4]

Under the gold standard, fixed exchange rates were maintained by an automatic equilibrating mechanism that went something like this: All currencies were defined in terms of gold; indeed, some were actually made of gold. When a nation had a deficit in its balance of payments, this meant, essentially, that more gold was flowing *out* than was flowing *in.* Since the domestic money supply was based on gold, losing gold to foreigners meant that the quantity of money fell *automatically.* This raised interest rates and attracted foreign capital. At the same time, the restrictive "monetary policy" pulled down output and prices, thus discouraging imports and encouraging exports. The balance of payments problem quickly rectified itself. This meant, however, that:

Under the gold standard, no nation had control of its domestic monetary policy, and therefore no nation could control its domestic economy very well.

At least in principle, the effects on surplus countries were perfectly symmetrical under the gold standard. A balance of payments surplus led to gold inflows, and thus to an increase in the domestic money supply, whether the surplus country liked the idea or not. This raised prices and output, thereby increasing imports and decreasing exports. And it also lowered interest rates, thereby encouraging outflows of capital. Because of these automatic adjustments, nations rarely reached the point at which devaluations or revaluations were necessary. Exchange rates were fixed as long as countries abided by the rules of the gold standard game.

In addition to the loss of control over domestic monetary conditions, the gold standard posed one other serious difficulty.

A fundamental problem with the gold standard was that the world's commerce was at the mercy of gold discoveries.

Discoveries of gold meant higher prices in the long run and higher real economic activity in the short run, through the standard monetary-policy mechanisms that we studied in the previous part of this book. And when the supply of gold did not keep pace with growth of the world economy, prices had to fall in the long run and employment had to fall in the short run.

---

[4]As a matter of fact, while the gold standard lasted (on and off) for hundreds of years, it was rarely practiced in its ideal form. Except for a brief period of fixed exchange rates in the late 19th and early 20th centuries, there were periodic adjustments of exchange rates even under the gold standard.

THE BRETTON WOODS SYSTEM AND THE INTERNATIONAL MONETARY FUND

The gold standard faltered many times and finally collapsed amid the financial chaos of the Great Depression of the 1930s and World War II. Without it, the world struggled through a serious breakdown in international trade.

Then, as World War II drew to a close, with much of Europe in ruins and with the United States holding the lion's share of the free world's reserves, officials of the industrial nations met at Bretton Woods, New Hampshire, in 1944. Their goal was to establish a stable monetary environment that would facilitate world trade. Since the dollar was the only "strong" currency at that time, it was natural to turn to the dollar as the basis of the new international economic order. And that is just what they did.

The Bretton Woods agreements reestablished a system of fixed exchange rates based not on the old gold standard but on the free convertibility of the U.S. dollar into gold. The United States agreed to buy or sell gold to maintain the $35 per ounce price that had been established by President Franklin Roosevelt in 1933. The other signatory nations, which had almost no gold in any case, agreed to buy and sell *dollars* to maintain their exchange rates at agreed-upon levels. Thus, all currencies were indirectly on a modified "gold standard." A holder of French francs, for example, could exchange these for dollars at (roughly) 5 francs per dollar and then exchange these into gold at $35 per ounce. In this way, the value of the franc was fixed at 175 francs per ounce of gold (5 francs per dollar times 35 dollars per ounce). The new system was dubbed the *Bretton Woods system*.

The *International Monetary Fund (IMF)* was set up to police and manage this new system. Using funds that had been contributed by member countries, the IMF was empowered to make loans to countries that were running low on reserves. A change in exchange rates was to be permitted only in the case of a "fundamental disequilibrium" in a nation's balance of payments—for it was believed that only relatively fixed exchange rates could provide the stable climate needed to restore world trade.

Of course, the Bretton Woods conferees did not define clearly what a "fundamental disequilibrium" was, nor could they have. As the system evolved, it came to mean a chronic *deficit* in the balance of payments of sizable proportions. Such nations would then *devalue* their currencies relative to the dollar. So the system was not really one of fixed exchange rates but rather one where rates were "fixed until further notice."

The Bretton Woods system had many of the flaws that we mentioned in our discussion of the pure system of fixed exchange rates. First, since devaluations were permitted only after a long run of balance of payments deficits, these devaluations (a) could be clearly foreseen and (b) normally had to be large. Speculators then saw opportunities for profit and would "attack" weak currencies with waves of selling.

This problem led many economists to question whether the system of fixed exchange rates was really providing the stable climate for world trade that had been intended. Was a system where rates were constant for long periods and then altered by large amounts really more conducive to international trade than one where overvalued currencies would gradually depreciate, as they would under a system of floating rates?

The second problem arose from the custom that deficit nations were expected to devalue when forced to, while surplus nations could resist upward revaluations. Since the U.S. dollar defined the monetary value of gold (at $35 per ounce),

America was the one nation in the world that had no way to devalue its currency relative to gold, no matter how "fundamental" the disequilibrium became. The only way exchange rates between the dollar and foreign currencies could change was if the surplus nations revalued their currencies upward relative to the dollar. They did not do this frequently enough, so the United States, with its chronically overvalued currency, ran persistent balance of payments deficits in the 1960s.

ADJUSTMENT MECHANISMS UNDER FIXED EXCHANGE RATES

Under the Bretton Woods system of fixed exchange rates, devaluation was viewed as a last resort, to be used only after other methods of adjusting to payments imbalances had failed. What were these other methods?

We have already encountered most of them in our discussion of exchange rate determination in free markets (see pages 401–408). Any factor that increases the demand for, say, U.S. dollars or that reduces the supply will push the value of the dollar upward if it is free to adjust. If, however, the exchange rate is pegged, it is the balance of payments deficit rather than the exchange rate that will adjust. Specifically, the U.S. balance of payments deficit will shrink if either the demand for dollars increases or the supply decreases.

The two panels of Figure 18-7 illustrate this adjustment. In each case, the United States has a payments deficit, since the official exchange rate (3 marks) exceeds the equilibrium rate (2 marks). The deficit starts at *AB* in each diagram. Then either the demand curve moves outward as in Panel (a), or the supply curve moves inward as in Panel (b). With the exchange rate held at 3 marks to the dollar, the balance of payments deficit shrinks—to *CB* in Panel (a) or to *AC* in Panel (b).

Referring back to our earlier discussions of the factors that underlie the demand and supply curves, then, we see that one way a deficit nation can improve its balance of payments is to *reduce its aggregate demand,* thus discouraging imports and cutting down its demand for foreign currency. Another is to *slow its rate of inflation,* thus encouraging exports and discouraging imports. Finally, it can *raise its interest rates* in order to attract more foreign capital.

In other words, deficit nations were expected to follow restrictive monetary and fiscal policies *voluntarily* just as they would have done *automatically* under the old gold standard. However, just as under the gold standard, this medicine was often unpalatable—as it was to the United States in the 1960s.

A surplus nation could, of course, have taken the opposite measures: pursuing expansive monetary and fiscal policies to increase economic growth and lower interest rates. By increasing the supply of the country's currency and reducing the demand for it, such actions would have reduced the balance of payments surplus. But often surplus countries did not relish the inflation that accompanies expansionary policies; and so, once again, they left the burden of adjustment to the deficit nations. The general point about fixed exchange rates is that:

Under a system of fixed exchange rates, the government of a country loses some control over its domestic economy. There may be times when balance of payments considerations force it to contract its economy in order to cut down its demand for foreign currency, even though domestic needs are calling for expansion. Conversely, there may be times when the domestic economy needs to be reined in, but balance of payments considerations suggest expansion.

FIGURE 18-7 ADJUSTING TO BALANCE OF PAYMENTS DEFICITS

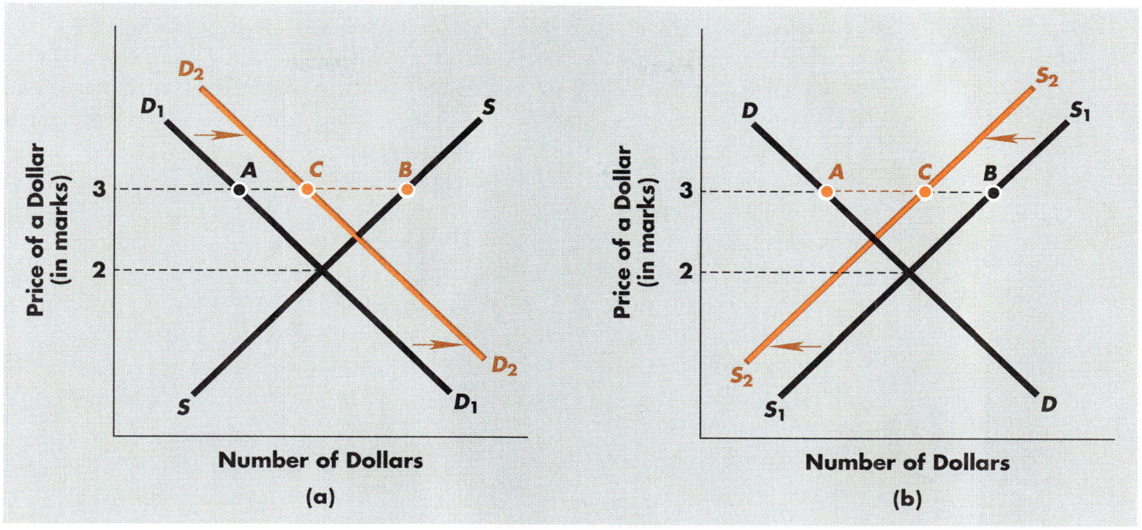

The two panels of this diagram illustrate alternative ways to cut America's balance of payments deficit while maintaining the exchange rate at 3 marks per dollar. Panel (a) might represent a reduction in our inflation rate, which would increase world demand for U.S. export products. Or it could represent a rise in American interest rates, which would attract foreign capital. Panel (b) might represent a reduction in domestic incomes, which would diminish American appetites for foreign goods. In either case, whether demand rises or supply falls, the balance of payments deficit is reduced: from *AB* to *CB* in Panel (a) and from *AB* to *AC* in Panel (b).

While we used the historical example of the dollar-mark exchange rate in Figure 18-7, this discussion also helps us understand what the government of Mexico would have needed to do in late 1994 to defend its exchange rate. But Mexico was in an election year and beset by political instability. So the authorities did not want to risk the recession that more restrictive monetary and fiscal policies probably would have brought on. Instead of taking that bitter medicine, they hoped for the best. But they did not get it.

Back to history. The Bretton Woods system worked fairly well for a number of years, but it finally broke down over its inability to devalue the U.S. dollar. By August 1971, the depletion of America's reserves and the accumulation of foreign debts resulting from America's chronic balance of payments deficits forced President Richard Nixon to end fixed exchange rates, which he did by announcing that the United States would no longer peg the value of the dollar by buying and selling gold. After some futile attempts by the major trading nations to reestablish fixed rates in 1971 and 1972, the Bretton Woods system ended in 1973.

Most observers agree, however, that fixed exchange rates could not have survived the tumultuous events of the next decade in any case. The worldwide inflationary boom of 1972, the supply-side inflations of 1972 to 1974 and 1979 to 1980, and the great worldwide recessions of 1974 to 1976 and the early 1980s led to dramatically different inflation rates in the major countries. For example, between 1975 and 1985, inflation averaged 4 percent per year in Germany, 7 percent in the United States, 11 percent in Great Britain, and 15 percent in Italy. As the purchasing-power parity theory reminds us, large differences in inflation rates call for *major* changes in currency values. The Bretton Woods system was ill-suited to handle such major changes.

WHY TRY TO FIX EXCHANGE RATES?

In view of these and other severe problems with fixed exchange rates, why did the international financial community work so hard to maintain them for so many years? And why do some people today want to return to fixed exchange rates? The answer is that floating exchange rates, determined in free markets by supply and demand, also pose problems.

Chief among these is the possibility that freely floating rates might prove to be highly variable rates, which add an unwanted element of risk to foreign trade. For example, if the exchange rate is 20 cents to the French franc, then a 2,000-franc Parisian dress will cost $400. But should the franc appreciate to 25 cents, that same dress would cost $500. An American department store thinking of buying the dress may need to place its order far in advance and will want to know the cost *in dollars*. It may be worried about the possibility that the value of the franc will rise, so that the dress will cost more than $400. And such worries might inhibit trade.

There are two answers to this concern. First, we might hope that freely floating rates would prove to be fairly stable in practice. Prices of most ordinary goods and services, for example, are determined by supply and demand in free markets and do not fluctuate unduly. Unfortunately, experience since 1973 has dashed this hope. Exchange rates have been extremely volatile—much more volatile than advocates of floating rates anticipated. This volatility is a major reason why some observers want to move back toward fixed exchange rates.

A second possibility is that speculators might relieve business firms of exchange rate risks—for a fee, of course. Consider the department store example. If French francs cost 20 cents today, the department store manager can assure herself of paying exactly $400 for the dress several months from now by arranging for a speculator to deliver francs to her at 20 cents per franc on the day she needs them. If the franc appreciates in the interim, it is the speculator, not the department store, that will take the financial beating. And, of course, if the franc depreciates, the speculator will pocket the profits. Thus, speculators play an important role in a system of floating exchange rates.

"Then it's agreed. Until the dollar firms up, we let the clamshell float."

SOURCE: Drawing by Ed Fisher © 1971, The New Yorker Magazine, Inc.

The widespread fears that speculative activity in free markets will lead to wild gyrations in prices, while occasionally valid, are often unfounded. The reason is simple. To make profits, international currency speculators must buy a currency when its value is low (thus helping to support the currency by pushing up its demand curve) and sell it when its value is high (thus holding down the price by adding to the supply curve).

This means that, to be successful, speculators must come into the market as *buyers* when demand is weak (or when supply is strong), and come in as *sellers* when demand is strong (or supply is scant). In doing so, they will help limit price fluctuations. Looked at the other way around, speculators can destabilize prices only if they are systematically willing to lose money.[5]

Notice the stark contrast to the system of fixed exchange rates in which speculation often leads to wild "runs" on currencies that are on the verge of devaluation. Speculative activity, which may well be destabilizing under fixed rates, is more likely to be stabilizing under floating rates.

[5]See Review Question 11 at the end of the chapter.

We do not mean to imply that speculation makes floating rates trouble-free. At the very least, speculators will demand a fee for their services—a fee that adds to the costs of trading across national borders. In addition, not all exchange rate risks can be eliminated through speculation. For example, few contracts on foreign currencies nowadays last more than, say, a year or two. Thus, a business cannot easily protect itself from exchange rate changes over periods of many years. Finally, speculative markets can and do get carried away from time to time, moving currency rates in ways that are hard to understand and that governments find frustrating.

Yet, despite all these problems, international trade has flourished under floating exchange rates. Apparently, exchange rate risk is not as burdensome as some people feared.

THE CURRENT MIXED SYSTEM

Our current international financial system—where some currencies are still pegged in the old Bretton Woods manner, many are floating freely, and others are floating subject to government interferences—has evolved gradually since the United States severed the dollar's link to gold. Though it continues to change and adapt, at least three features have been evident.

The first is the decline in the notion that exchange rates should be fixed for long periods of time. The demand by many countries that the world quickly return to fixed exchange rates had largely subsided by the mid-1970s. Even where rates are still pegged, devaluations and revaluations are now much more frequent—and smaller—than they were in the Bretton Woods era. Most currency rates change slightly on a day-to-day basis, and market forces generally determine the basic trends, up or down. Even advocates of greater fixity in exchange rates generally propose that governments keep rates within certain *ranges,* rather than literally fix them.

Second, however, central banks do not hesitate to intervene to moderate exchange movements whenever they feel that such actions are appropriate. Typically, these interventions are aimed at ironing out what are deemed to be transitory fluctuations. But there are times in which central banks oppose basic trends in exchange rates. For example, the Federal Reserve and other central banks sold dollars aggressively in 1985 to push the dollar down, and they bought dollars in 1994 and 1995 to arrest the rise of the mark and, especially, the yen. While the world has relatively few truly fixed exchange rates, most of the major currencies are floating less than freely. The terms *dirty float* or *managed float* have been coined to describe this mongrel system.

The third unmistakable feature of the present international monetary system is the virtual elimination of any role for gold. The trend away from gold actually began before 1971, and by now gold plays essentially no role in the world's financial system. Instead, there is a *free market* in gold in which dentists, jewelers, industrial users, speculators, and ordinary citizens who think of gold as a good store of value can buy or sell as they wish. The price of gold is determined each day by the law of supply and demand.

THE VOLATILE DOLLAR

We mentioned earlier that floating exchange rates have not been stable exchange rates. No currency illustrates this better than the U.S. dollar. (See Figure 18-8.)

FIGURE 18-8 THE UPS AND DOWNS OF THE DOLLAR

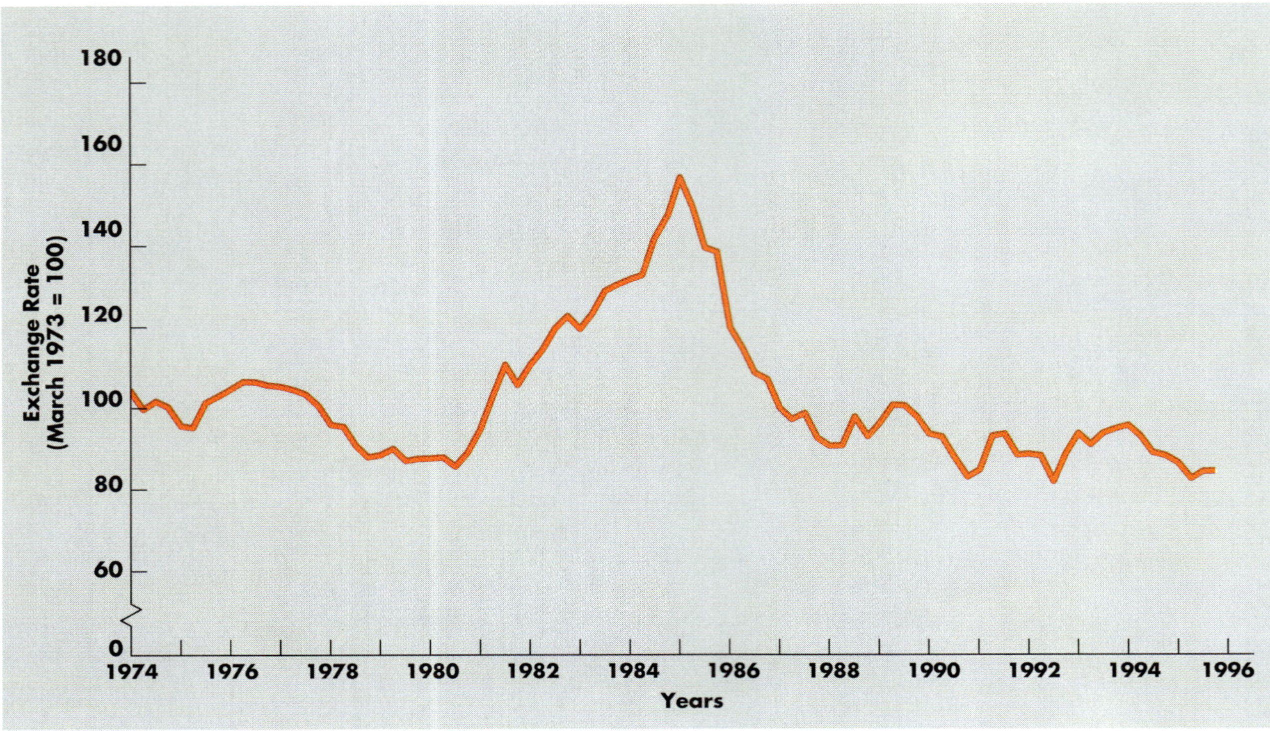

This graph charts the behavior of the international value of the dollar relative to a basket of ten major foreign currencies since 1974. (The index is based on March 1973 = 100.) The net change in the value of the dollar over the entire period is small, but the ups and downs have been pronounced. The stunning climb of the dollar from its 1980 low to its 1985 high stands out on the graph, as does the pronounced decline from 1985 to 1988.

SOURCE: Federal Reserve System.

In 1977 and 1978, the international value of the dollar plummeted until a concerted effort by central banks to buy dollars stopped the fall. The dollar then stabilized for almost 2 years before rising like a rocket for a period of almost 5 years. As Table 18-1 (page 401) showed, in July 1980 a U.S. dollar bought less than 2 German marks, about 4 French francs, and about 830 Italian lira. By the time it peaked in February 1985, the mighty dollar could buy more than 3 German marks, about 10 French francs, and over 2,000 Italian lira. Such major currency changes had dramatic effects on world trade.

The rising dollar was a blessing to Americans who traveled abroad or who bought foreign goods because foreign prices, when translated to dollars by the exchange rate, looked cheap to Americans.[6] But the arithmetic worked just the other way for U.S. firms seeking to sell their goods abroad; foreign buyers found everything American very expensive.[7] It was no surprise, therefore, that as the dollar climbed our exports fell, our imports rose, and many of our leading manufacturing industries were decimated by foreign competition. An expensive currency, Americans came to learn, is a mixed blessing.

[6]EXAMPLE: How much does a 600-franc hotel room in Paris cost in dollars when the franc is worth 20 cents? 16 cents? 10 cents?

[7]EXAMPLE: How much does a $55 American camera cost a German consumer when the mark is worth 55 cents? 44 cents? 33.33 cents?

From early 1985 until early 1988, the value of the dollar fell even faster than it had risen. The cheaper dollar curbed American appetites for imports and alleviated the plight of our export industries, many of which boomed. However, rising prices for imported goods and foreign vacations were a source of consternation to many American consumers.

Since 1988, the overall value of the dollar has not changed much—on average. But there have been quite a few appreciations and depreciations sharp enough to gain the attention of the world's financial markets and central banks. The international currency markets are anything but boring.

THE EUROPEAN EXCHANGE RATE MECHANISM

As noted earlier, floating exchange rates are no magical cure-all. One particular problem confronts the members of the European Union (EU). These countries have pledged to create a unified market like the United States. As part of that pledge, they need eventually to establish a single currency for all member countries. That, of course, precludes floating rates.

The *European Exchange Rate Mechanism (ERM)* was designed as an important step along the road to fixed exchange rates within Europe, and thence to a common currency. Under the ERM, the values of the major European currencies are supposed to remain fixed within relatively narrow bands, while EU currencies as a group rise or fall *relative to the rest of the world.* The German mark has clearly become the dominant currency in this group—so much so that many observers now see Europe as a "mark area."

The ERM has had a tumultuous history thus far in the 1990s. Problems first arose in 1990 when the reunification of Germany required a variety of major economic adjustments—including, perhaps, a change in the value of the mark. Germany found itself in somewhat the same position as the United States under Bretton Woods: Since the mark could not easily be realigned within the ERM, the burden of adjustment fell on other countries.

In 1992, the system began to break down, causing great currency turmoil throughout Europe. The United Kingdom and Italy left the ERM and several other countries realigned their currencies vis-à-vis the mark. But, despite tremendous pressure, the French franc maintained its fixed parity with the mark and the ERM weathered the storm—albeit smaller and more fragile than before.

The calm lasted less than a year. In 1993, speculators became convinced that several European currencies would have to be devalued relative to the mark; and they began selling these currencies to buy marks. Europe's central banks resisted for a while, but eventually succumbed to market forces. Currency bands were widened enough to give the weaker currencies room to float downward, and with that added flexibility the storm passed with the ERM intact. Since then, the system has held together, albeit without the pound and the lira, despite periodic attacks by speculators.

But many observers have come to question how and when the next step—to a common currency—will take place. The EU countries are committed to this goal under the Treaty of Maastricht, and 1999 is the target date. But as of 1996 there were many clouds on the horizon. The United Kingdom and Italy were still out of the system. Almost none of the countries met the fiscal requirements of the Maastricht treaty. And public opinion in many countries opposed the move to a common currency. On balance, prospects for a single currency by 1999 looked shaky.

SUMMARY

1. **Exchange rates** state the value of one currency in terms of another and thus influence the patterns of world trade in important ways.
2. If governments do not interfere by buying or selling their currencies, exchange rates will be determined in free markets by the usual laws of supply and demand. Such a system is called **floating exchange rates.**
3. Demand for a nation's currency is derived from foreigners' desires to purchase that country's goods and services or to invest in its assets. Any change that increases the demand for a nation's currency will cause its exchange rate to **appreciate** under floating rates.
4. Supply of a nation's currency is derived from the desire of that country's citizens to purchase foreign goods and services or to invest in foreign assets. Any change that increases the supply of a nation's currency will cause its exchange rate to **depreciate** under floating rates.
5. In the long run, purchasing-power parity plays a major role in exchange rate movements. The *purchasing-power parity theory* states that relative price levels in any two countries determine the exchange rate between their currencies. Therefore, countries with relatively low inflation rates normally will have appreciating currencies.
6. Over shorter periods, purchasing-power parity has little influence over exchange rate movements. The pace of economic activity and the level of interest rates exert greater influence. In particular, short-term capital movements are typically the dominant factor.
7. Exchange rates can be fixed at nonequilibrium levels by governments that are willing and able to mop up any excess of quantity supplied over quantity demanded, or provide any excess of quantity demanded over quantity supplied. In the first case, the country is suffering from a **balance of payments deficit** because of its overvalued currency. In the second, an undervalued currency has given it a **balance of payments surplus.**
8. In the early part of this century, the world was on a particular system of **fixed exchange rates** called the *gold standard,* in which the value of every nation's currency was fixed in terms of gold. But this created problems because nations could not control their own money supplies and because the world could not control its total supply of gold.
9. After World War II, the gold standard was replaced by the *Bretton Woods system* under which rates were again fixed—or rather fixed until further notice. This system made the U.S. dollar the basis of international currency values.
10. The Bretton Woods system served the world well and helped restore world trade, but it ran into trouble when the dollar became chronically overvalued since the system provided no way to remedy this situation.
11. Since 1971, the world has moved toward a system of relatively free exchange rates, though there are plenty of exceptions. We now have a thoroughly mixed system of *"dirty"* or *"managed" floating* which continues to evolve and adapt.
12. Floating rates are not without their problems. For example, importers and exporters justifiably worry about fluctuations in exchange rates. Though these problems seem manageable, some people would like to see a return to fixed exchange rates.
13. Under floating exchange rates, investors who speculate on international currency values provide a valuable service by assuming the risks of those who do not wish to speculate. Normally, speculators stabilize rather than destabilize exchange rates, because that is how they make profits.
14. The U.S. dollar rose dramatically in value from 1980 to 1985, making our imports cheaper and our exports more expensive. Then, from 1985 to 1988, the dollar tumbled, which had precisely the reverse effects.
15. The European Union seeks eventually to establish a single currency for all member nations. As a step in that direction, the European Exchange Rate Mechanism was set up to fix exchange rates among member countries.

KEY TERMS

International monetary system
Exchange rate
Appreciation
Depreciation
Devaluation
Revaluation
Supply of and demand for foreign exchange
Floating exchange rates
Purchasing-power parity theory
Fixed exchange rates

Balance of payments deficit and surplus
Current account
Capital account
Gold standard
Bretton Woods system
International Monetary Fund (IMF)
"Dirty" or "managed" float
European Exchange Rate Mechanism (ERM)

QUESTIONS FOR REVIEW

1. What items do you own or routinely consume that are produced abroad? From what countries do these come? Suppose Americans decided to buy more of these things? How would that affect the exchange rates between the dollar and these currencies?

2. If the dollar depreciates relative to the Japanese yen, will the Sony television you have wanted become more or less expensive? What effect do you imagine this will have on American demands for Sonys? Does the American demand curve for yen, therefore, slope upward or downward? Explain.

3. During the first half of the 1980s, inflation in (West) Germany was consistently lower than that in the United States. What, then, does the purchasing-power parity theory predict should have happened to the exchange rate between the mark and the dollar between 1980 and 1985? (Look at Table 18-1 to see what actually happened.)

4. Use supply and demand diagrams to analyze the effect on the exchange rate between the dollar and the yen if:
   a. Japan opens its domestic markets to more foreign competition.
   b. Investors come to fear that values on the Tokyo stock market will decline.
   c. The Federal Reserve lowers interest rates in America.
   d. The U.S. government, to help settle the problems of the Middle East, gives huge amounts of foreign aid to Israel and her Arab neighbors.
   e. Both Japan and the United States recover from recessions, but the Japanese recovery is slower.
   f. Prospects for inflation in the United States worsen.

5. How are the problems of a country faced with a balance of payments deficit similar to those posed by a government regulation that holds the price of milk above the equilibrium level? (*Hint:* Think of each in terms of a supply-demand diagram.)

6. For each of the transactions listed below, indicate how it would affect the U.S. balance of payments if exchange rates were fixed.
   a. You spent the summer traveling in Europe.
   b. Your uncle in Canada sent you $20 as a birthday present.
   c. You bought a new Honda.
   d. You sold some stock you own on the Tokyo Stock Exchange.

7. Suppose each of the transactions listed in Review Question 6 was done by many Americans. Indicate how each would affect the international value of the dollar if exchange rates were floating.

8. Under the old gold standard, what do you think happened to world prices when there was a huge gold strike in California in 1849? What do you think happened when the world went without any important new gold strikes for 20 years or so?

9. Explain why the members of the Bretton Woods conference in 1944 wanted to establish a system of fixed exchange rates. What was the flaw that led to the ultimate breakdown of the system in 1971?

10. Suppose you want to reserve a hotel room in London for the coming summer but are worried that the value of the pound may rise between now and then, making the rooms too expensive for your budget. Explain how a speculator could relieve you of this worry. (Don't actually try it. Speculators deal only in very large sums!)

11. We learned on page 416 that successful speculators buy a currency when demand is weak and sell it when demand is strong. Use supply and demand diagrams for two different periods (one with weak demand, the other with strong demand) to show why this will limit price fluctuations.

12. In early 1995, market forces were pushing up the international value of the Japanese yen. Why do you think the government of Japan was unhappy about this currency appreciation? What could the Bank of Japan (Japan's central bank) have done to try to prevent it? How could the Federal Reserve have helped? Why might the central banks have failed in this attempt?

CHAPTER 19

MACROECONOMICS IN A WORLD ECONOMY

No man is an island,
entire of itself.
John Donne

America is not an isolated economy immune from foreign influences. Today, more than ever before, the nations of the world are locked together in an uneasy economic union. Fluctuations in foreign GDP growth, foreign inflation, and foreign interest rates profoundly affect the U.S. economy. Economic events that originate in our country reverberate around the globe. Without a deeper understanding of these international linkages, we cannot hope to understand many of the most important economic developments of our time.

What we have learned so far about the macroeconomics of international trade in goods and services was correct, but limited. In particular, it ignored such crucial influences as exchange rates and international financial movements. Changes in exchange rates alter the prices of one country's goods in terms of the currency of another. In the previous chapter, we learned how major macroeconomic variables such as GDP, prices, and interest rates affect exchange rates. In this chapter, we complete the circle by studying how changes in the exchange rate affect the domestic economy. Then we bring international capital flows into the picture and learn how monetary and fiscal policy work in an **open economy.**

An **OPEN ECONOMY** is one that trades with other nations in goods and services, and perhaps also in financial assets.

ISSUE: DEFICIT REDUCTION AND THE DOLLAR

When the movement to balance the federal budget caught political fire in 1995, a lively side-debate arose over how lower deficits would affect the value of the dollar. Many politicians and business people argued that deficit reduction would strengthen the dollar. In their view, decisive action to cut government spending would bolster confidence in the United States, thereby increasing the international demand for dollars and making the dollar appreciate.

Most economists, however, took the opposite position, arguing that lower deficits should lead to a lower dollar. As evidence, they pointed to the events of the early 1980s, when soaring U.S. budget deficits led to a stunning appreciation of the dollar. Shouldn't the opposite happen, they asked, if the budget deficit is cut? In this chapter, we will learn the reasoning behind the economists' position.

INTERNATIONAL TRADE AND AGGREGATE DEMAND: A QUICK REVIEW

We know from earlier chapters (especially Chapters 8 and 9) that a country's net exports, $(X - IM)$, are one component of its aggregate demand, $C + I + G + (X - IM)$. For this reason, an autonomous increase in exports or decrease in imports has a multiplier effect on the economy, just like an increase in consumption, investment, or government purchases.[1] Figure 19-1 depicts this conclusion on an aggregate demand and supply diagram. A rise in net exports shifts the aggregate demand curve outward to the right, thereby raising both GDP and the price level.

But what can make net exports rise? One factor we mentioned in Chapter 8 was a rise in foreign incomes. If foreigners become richer, they are likely to spend more on a wide variety of products, some of which will be American exports. Thus, Figure 19-1 illustrates the effect on the U.S. economy of a boom in foreign countries. Similarly, a recession abroad would reduce U.S. exports and shift the U.S. aggregate demand curve inward. Thus, as we learned in Chapter 9:

Booms or recessions in one country tend to be transmitted to other countries through international trade in goods and services.

One other important determinant of net exports was mentioned in Chapter 8, but not discussed in depth: the relative prices of foreign and domestic goods. The idea is a simple application of the law of demand: If the prices of the goods of Country X rise, then people everywhere will tend to buy fewer of them—and

FIGURE 19-1 THE EFFECTS OF HIGHER NET EXPORTS

If real exports rise or real imports fall, the economy's aggregate demand curve shifts outward, from D_0D_0 to D_1D_1. Real GDP and the price level both rise as the equilibrium moves from point *A* to point *B*.

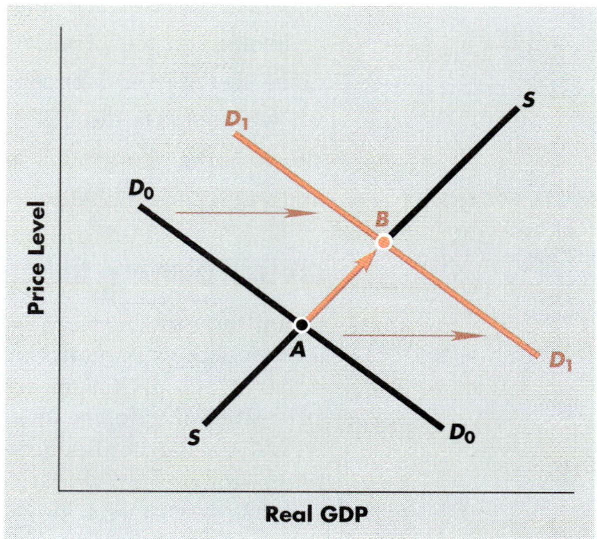

[1]An appendix to Chapter 9 showed that international trade lowers the numerical value of the multiplier. Nonetheless, autonomous changes in C, I, G, or $(X - IM)$ all have the same multiplier.

more of the goods of Country Y. As we shall see now, this simple idea holds the key to understanding how exchange rates affect international trade.

RELATIVE PRICES, EXPORTS, AND IMPORTS

First assume—just for this short section—that exchange rates are *fixed*. What happens if the prices of American goods fall while, say, Japanese prices are constant? With U.S. products now less expensive *relative to Japanese products*, both Japanese and American consumers will probably buy more American goods and fewer Japanese goods. So America's exports will rise and imports will fall, adding to aggregate demand in this country—as shown in Figure 19-1. Conversely, a rise in American prices (relative to Japanese prices) will *decrease* our net exports and aggregate demand. Thus:

For given foreign prices, a fall in the prices of a country's exports will lead to an increase in that country's net exports, and hence to a rise in its real GDP. Analogously, a rise in the prices of a country's exports will decrease that country's net exports and GDP.

Precisely the same logic applies to changes in Japanese prices. If Japanese prices rise, Americans will export more and import less. So $X - IM$ will rise, boosting GDP in the United States. Figure 19-1 applies to this case without change. By similar reasoning, falling Japanese prices decrease U.S. net exports and depress our economy. Thus:

Price increases abroad raise a country's net exports and hence its GDP. Price decreases abroad have the opposite effects.

THE EFFECTS OF CHANGES IN EXCHANGE RATES

From here it is a simple matter to figure out how changes in *exchange rates* affect a country's net exports, for currency appreciations or depreciations change international relative prices.

Recall that the basic role of an exchange rate is to convert one country's prices into the currency of another. Table 19-1 uses two examples of U.S.-Japanese trade to remind us of this role. Suppose the dollar depreciates from 120 yen to 100 yen.

TABLE 19-1 EXCHANGE RATES AND HOME-CURRENCY PRICES

	¥60,000 Japanese TV Set		$2,000 U.S. Home Computer	
Exchange Rate	**Price in Japan**	**Price in United States**	**Price in United States**	**Price in Japan**
$1 = 120 yen	¥60,000	$500	$2,000	¥240,000
$1 = 100 yen	¥60,000	$600	$2,000	¥200,000

Then, from the viewpoint of American consumers, a television set that costs ¥60,000 in Japan goes up in price from $500 (that is, 60,000/120) to $600. To Americans, it is just as if Japanese manufacturers had raised TV prices by 20 percent. Naturally, Americans react by purchasing fewer Japanese products. So American imports go down.

Now consider the implications for Japanese consumers interested in buying American personal computers that cost $2,000. When the dollar falls from 120 yen to 100 yen, they see the price of these computers falling from ¥240,000 (that is, 2,000 × 120) to ¥200,000. To them, it is just as if American producers had offered a 16.7 percent markdown. Under such circumstances, we expect U.S. sales to the Japanese to rise. So U.S. exports should increase. Putting these two findings together, we conclude that:

A currency depreciation should raise net exports and therefore increase aggregate demand. Conversely, a currency appreciation should reduce net exports and therefore decrease aggregate demand.

The aggregate supply and demand diagram in Figure 19-2 illustrates this conclusion. If the currency depreciates, net exports rise and the aggregate demand curve shifts outward from D_0D_0 to D_1D_1. Both prices and output rise as the economy's equilibrium moves from E_0 to E_1. If the currency appreciates, everything operates in reverse: Net exports fall, the aggregate demand curve shifts inward to D_2D_2, and both prices and output decline.

This simple analysis already helps us understand why the U.S. trade deficit grew so large in the 1980s. We saw in Figure 18-8 (page 418) that the international value of the dollar soared in the first half of the 1980s. According to the reasoning we have just completed, such a stunning appreciation of the dollar should have raised U.S. imports and damaged U.S. exports. That is precisely what happened. In constant dollars, American imports soared by 60 percent

FIGURE 19-2 THE EFFECTS OF EXCHANGE RATE CHANGES ON AGGREGATE DEMAND

A depreciation of the exchange rate raises net exports and hence shifts the aggregate demand curve outward to the right, from D_0D_0 to D_1D_1 in the diagram. An appreciation of the currency shifts the aggregate demand curve inward to the left, to D_2D_2. Thus, depreciations are expansionary and appreciations are contractionary.

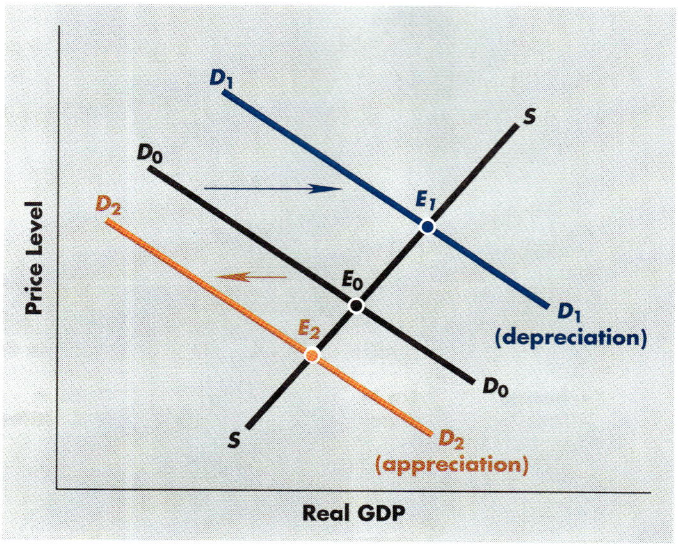

between 1981 and 1986, while American exports rose a scant 8 percent. The result is that a $6 billion net export *surplus* in 1981 turned into a $164 billion *deficit* by 1986.

AGGREGATE SUPPLY IN AN OPEN ECONOMY

So we have concluded that a currency depreciation increases aggregate demand while a currency appreciation decreases it. To complete our model of macroeconomics in an open economy, we must now turn to the implications of international trade for *aggregate supply.*

Part of the story is familiar. As we know from previous chapters, the United States, like all economies, purchases some of its productive inputs from abroad. Oil is only the most prominent example. We also rely on foreign suppliers for metals like titanium, raw agricultural products like coffee beans, and thousands of other items used by American industry. When the dollar depreciates, these imported inputs become more costly in terms of U.S. dollars—just as if foreign prices had risen.

The consequence is clear: With imported inputs more expensive, American firms will be forced to charge higher prices at any given level of output. Graphically, this means that *the aggregate supply curve will shift inward* (to the left).

When the dollar depreciates, the prices of imported inputs rise. The U.S. aggregate supply curve therefore shifts inward, pushing up the prices of American-made goods and services. By exactly analogous reasoning, an appreciation of the dollar makes imported inputs cheaper and shifts the U.S. aggregate supply curve *outward,* thus pushing American prices down. (See Figure 19-3.)

Beyond this, a depreciating dollar has further inflationary effects that do not show up on the aggregate demand and supply diagram. Most obviously, prices

FIGURE 19-3

THE EFFECTS OF EXCHANGE RATE CHANGES ON AGGREGATE SUPPLY

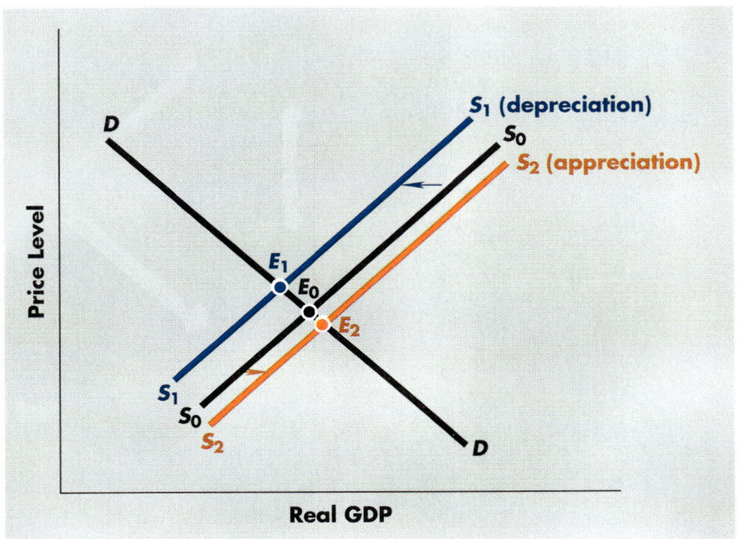

A depreciation of the currency pushes the aggregate supply curve inward, from S_0S_0 to S_1S_1 in the diagram, and is therefore inflationary. A currency appreciation has a deflationary effect because it pushes the aggregate supply curve outward, from S_0S_0 to S_2S_2.

of imported goods are included in American price indexes like the Consumer Price Index (CPI). So when dollar prices of Japanese cars, French wine, and Swiss watches increase, the CPI goes up *even if no American prices rise.* For this and other reasons, the inflationary impact of a dollar depreciation is even greater than that indicated by Figure 19-3.[2]

THE MACROECONOMIC EFFECTS OF EXCHANGE RATES

Let us now put aggregate demand and aggregate supply together and study the macroeconomic effects of changes in exchange rates.

First suppose that the international value of the dollar falls. Referring back to Figures 19-2 and 19-3, we see that this will shift the aggregate demand curve *outward* and the aggregate supply curve *inward*. The result, as Figure 19-4 shows, is that the U.S. price level certainly rises. Whether real GDP rises or falls depends on whether the supply or demand shift is the dominant influence. The evidence strongly suggests that aggregate *demand* shifts are usually more important, so we expect GDP to rise. Hence:

A currency depreciation is inflationary and probably also expansionary.

What is the intuitive explanation for this result? When the dollar falls, foreign goods become more expensive to Americans. That is directly inflationary. At the same time, aggregate demand in the United States is stimulated by rising net exports. As long as the expansion of demand outweighs the adverse shift of the aggregate supply curve brought on by the depreciation, real GDP should rise.

Now let's reverse things. Suppose the dollar *appreciates*. In this case, net exports *fall* so the aggregate demand curve shifts *inward*. At the same time,

FIGURE 19-4 THE EFFECTS OF A CURRENCY DEPRECIATION

If the currency depreciates, aggregate demand increases because net exports are stimulated, and aggregate supply decreases because imported inputs become more expensive. Prices rise as equilibrium moves from point *E* to point *A*. If the demand shift is the more important influence, output increases, too.

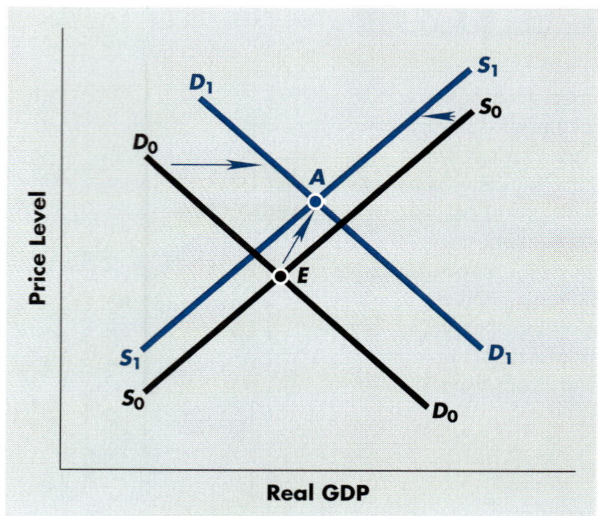

[2]The diagram should be interpreted as showing the effects of currency depreciations and appreciations on the prices of *domestically produced* goods.

FIGURE 19-5 THE EFFECTS OF A CURRENCY APPRECIATION

If the currency appreciates, aggregate demand declines because net exports fall, and aggregate supply increases because imported inputs become cheaper. Prices fall as equilibrium moves from point *E* to point *B*. If the demand shift is the more important influence, output also falls.

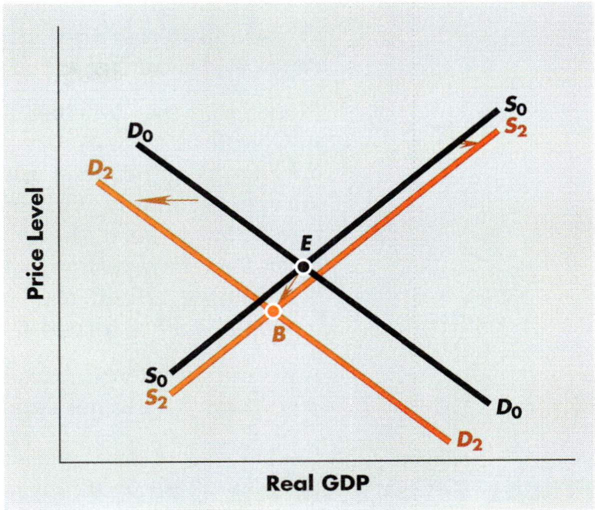

imported inputs become cheaper, so the aggregate supply curve shifts *outward*. (See Figure 19-5.) Once again, we can be sure of the movement of the price level: It falls. Output also falls if the demand shift is more important than the supply shift, as is likely. Thus:

A currency appreciation is certainly disinflationary and is probably contractionary.

In the rest of the chapter, we shall assume that the effect of the exchange rate on aggregate *demand* dominates its effect on aggregate *supply*, because that is what the evidence suggests.

INTEREST RATES AND INTERNATIONAL CAPITAL FLOWS

There is one important piece left in our international economic puzzle. We have analyzed international trade in goods and services rather fully, but we have ignored international movements of *capital*.

For some nations, this omission is of little consequence because they are rarely involved in international capital flows. But things are quite different for the United States because the dollar is the world's major international currency. The vast majority of international financial flows involve either buying or selling assets whose values are stated in U.S. dollars. Fortunately, given what we have just learned about the effects of exchange rates, it is easy to add international capital flows to our analysis.

Recall from the previous chapter that interest rate differentials and capital flows are typically the most important determinants of exchange rate movements in the short run. Specifically, suppose interest rates in the United States rise while foreign interest rates remain unchanged. We learned in the last chapter that this will attract capital to the United States and cause the dollar to appreciate. This chapter has just taught us that an appreciating dollar will, in turn, reduce net exports, prices, and output in the United States—as indicated in Figure 19-5. Thus:

A rise in interest rates tends to contract the economy by appreciating the currency and reducing net exports.

Notice that this conclusion has a familiar ring. While studying monetary policy in Chapter 13, we observed that higher interest rates deter investment spending and hence reduce the I component of $C + I + G + (X - IM)$. Now, in studying an open economy with international capital flows, we see that higher interest rates also reduce the $X - IM$ component. Thus, *international capital flows strengthen the negative effects of interest rates on aggregate demand.*

If interest rates in the United States fall, or if those abroad rise, everything we have just said is turned in the opposite direction. The conclusion is:[3]

A decline in interest rates tends to expand the economy by depreciating the currency and raising net exports.

FISCAL POLICY IN AN OPEN ECONOMY

Now we are ready to use our model to analyze how fiscal and monetary policy work when the exchange rate is floating and capital is internationally mobile. Doing so will teach us how international economic relations modify the effects of stabilization policies that we learned in earlier chapters. Fortunately, no new theoretical apparatus is necessary; we only need remember what we have learned in the chapter up to this point. Specifically:

- A rise in the domestic interest rate leads to capital inflows and makes the exchange rate appreciate. A fall in the domestic interest rate leads to capital outflows and makes the exchange rate depreciate.
- A currency appreciation reduces aggregate demand and raises aggregate supply (see Figure 19-5). A currency depreciation raises aggregate demand and reduces aggregate supply (see Figure 19-4).

A **CLOSED ECONOMY** is one that does not trade with other nations in either goods or assets.

With this in mind, suppose the government cuts taxes or raises spending. Aggregate demand increases, which pushes up both real GDP and the price level in the usual manner. This is shown as the shift from D_0D_0 to the blue line D_1D_1 in Figure 19-6. In a **closed economy,** that is the end of the story. But in an *open economy* with international capital flows, we must add in the macroeconomic effects that work through the exchange rate. We do this by answering two questions.

First, what will happen to the exchange rate? We know from earlier chapters that a fiscal expansion pushes up interest rates—a fact that is sure to be noticed in international financial markets. At higher interest rates, American securities become more attractive to foreign investors, who go to the foreign exchange markets to buy dollars for use in purchasing American securities. This buying pressure drives up the value of the dollar. Thus:

A fiscal expansion normally makes the exchange rate appreciate.

Second, what are the effects of a higher dollar? As we know, when the dollar rises in value, American goods become more expensive abroad and foreign

[3]EXERCISE: Provide the reasoning behind this conclusion.

FIGURE 19-6 A FISCAL EXPANSION IN AN OPEN ECONOMY

A fiscal expansion pushes the aggregate demand curve outward, from D_0D_0 to D_1D_1 in the diagram. But it also raises interest rates, which attracts international capital and appreciates the currency. The currency appreciation, in turn, reduces aggregate demand and raises aggregate supply—as shown by the orange curves S_2S_2 and D_2D_2. The result is that equilibrium occurs at point *C* rather than at point *B*. Output and prices both rise less than they would in a closed economy.

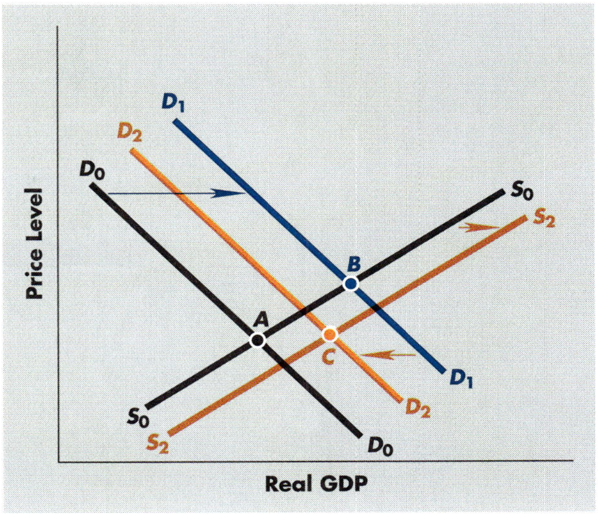

goods become cheaper here. So exports fall and imports rise, driving down the $X - IM$ component of aggregate demand. The fiscal expansion thus winds up increasing both America's *capital account surplus* (by attracting foreign capital) and its *current account deficit* (by reducing net exports). In fact, the two must rise by equal amounts because, under floating exchange rates, it is always true that:[4]

Current account surplus + Capital account surplus = 0

Since a fiscal expansion leads in this way to a trade deficit, many economists believe that the U.S. trade deficit of the 1980s was a side effect of the large tax cuts made early in the decade. We will come back to that issue shortly.

But first note that the induced rise in the dollar will shift the aggregate supply curve *outward* and the aggregate demand curve *inward*, as we saw in Figure 19-5. Figure 19-6 adds these two shifts (in orange) to the effect of the original fiscal expansion (in blue). The final equilibrium in an open economy is point *C*, whereas in a closed economy it would be point *B*. By comparing points *B* and *C*, we can see how international linkages change the picture of fiscal policy that we painted earlier in the book.

There are two main differences. First, a higher exchange rate offsets part of the inflationary effect of a fiscal expansion by making imports cheaper. Second, a higher exchange rate reduces the expansionary effect on real GDP by reducing $X - IM$. Here we have a new kind of "crowding out," different from the one we studied in Chapter 15. There we learned that an increase in *G* will crowd out some private investment spending by raising interest rates. Here a rise in *G*, by raising both interest rates and the exchange rate, crowds out *net exports*. But the effect is the same: The fiscal multiplier is reduced. Thus, we conclude that:

International capital flows reduce the power of fiscal policy.

---

[4]If you need review, turn back to Chapter 18, pages 411–412.

TABLE 19-2

PERCENTAGE SHARES OF REAL GDP
IN THE UNITED STATES: 1981 AND 1986

Year	C	I	G	X − IM
1981	64.5%	14.6%	20.1%	0.1%
1986	67.6%	14.8%	20.7%	−3.0%
Change	+3.1	+0.2	+0.6	−3.1

Note: Totals do not add up due to rounding and deflation.

Table 19-2 suggests that this new international variety of crowding out was much more important than the traditional type of crowding out in the early 1980s. Between 1981 and 1986, the share of investment in GDP actually *increased* slightly (from 14.6 percent to 14.8 percent) despite the rise in the shares of both consumer spending and government purchases. Only the share of net exports, $X - IM$, fell—from 0.1 percent to −3.0 percent.

This was an important lesson that American economists learned in the 1980s. In 1980, many economists worried that large government budget deficits would crowd out private investment. By the end of the decade, most were more concerned that deficits were crowding out net exports. Similarly, nowadays most economists believe that the benefits of a large deficit-reduction program, such as the one Congress and the president debated in 1995 and 1996, should be split between higher investment and a smaller trade deficit.

MONETARY POLICY IN AN OPEN ECONOMY

Now let us consider how monetary policy works in an open economy with floating exchange rates and international capital mobility. To remain consistent with the history of the 1980s, we consider a tightening, rather than a loosening, of monetary policy.

As we know from earlier chapters, contractionary monetary policy reduces aggregate demand, which lowers both real GDP and prices. This is shown in Figure 19-7 by the shift from D_0D_0 to the blue line D_1D_1, and it looks like the exact opposite of a fiscal expansion. Without international capital flows, that would be the end of the story.

But, in the presence of internationally mobile capital, we must think through the consequences for interest rates and exchange rates. We know from previous chapters that a monetary contraction raises interest rates, just like a fiscal expansion. Hence, tighter money attracts foreign capital into the United States in search of higher rates of return. The exchange rate therefore rises. The appreciating dollar encourages imports and discourages exports; so $X - IM$ falls. America therefore winds up with capital flowing in and an increase in its trade deficit. This time, as you will notice from Figure 19-7:

International capital flows increase the power of monetary policy.

Why do capital flows *strengthen* monetary policy but *weaken* fiscal policy? The answer lies in their effects on interest rates. The main international repercussion of either a fiscal *expansion* or a monetary *contraction* is to raise interest rates and

FIGURE 19-7 A MONETARY CONTRACTION IN AN OPEN ECONOMY

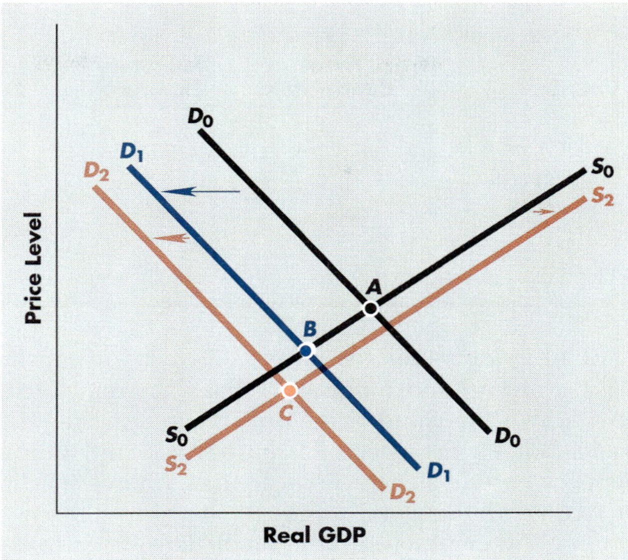

A monetary contraction pulls the aggregate demand curve inward, from D_0D_0 to D_1D_1, just like a fiscal contraction. But it raises, rather than lowers, interest rates, which leads to international capital inflows and a currency appreciation. The appreciation decreases net exports and therefore reduces aggregate demand—which shifts inward from D_1D_1 to D_2D_2. But it also reduces foreign prices and raises aggregate supply—as indicated by the shift from S_0S_0 to S_2S_2. The result is that output and prices both fall more in an open economy (point *C*) than they would in a closed economy (point *B*).

the exchange rate, thereby crowding out net exports. But that means that the initial effects of a fiscal expansion on aggregate demand are *weakened* while the initial effects of a monetary contraction are *strengthened*.

INTERNATIONAL ASPECTS OF DEFICIT REDUCTION

This completes our theoretical analysis of the macroeconomics of open economies. Now let us put the theory through its paces by applying it to the prospective changes in U.S. macroeconomic policy over the balance of this decade. Doing so will help us answer the question posed at the beginning of the chapter: Should deficit reduction be expected to strengthen or weaken the dollar?

The multiyear budget program debated in 1995 and 1996 called for fiscal policy to become tighter and tighter over the rest of this century and into the next, as the budget deficit fell from about 2.5 percent of GDP to zero. This movement toward a balanced budget was to have been accomplished mainly by reducing government expenditures.

The first column of Table 19-3 indicates what the theory predicts a fiscal contraction should do: It should lower real interest rates, make the dollar depreciate, reduce real GDP, and be less disinflationary than normal because of the falling dollar. This information is recorded by entering + signs for increases and − signs for decreases.

Now let us consider the monetary policy that may accompany the fiscal contraction. Since reducing the budget deficit reduces aggregate demand, the Federal Reserve would be expected to restore the missing demand by lowering interest rates. According to the analysis in this chapter, such a monetary expansion should lower real interest rates, make the dollar depreciate, raise real GDP, and be a bit more inflationary than usual because of the falling dollar. All this is recorded in Column 2.

TABLE 19-3 EXPECTED EFFECTS OF POLICY

Variable	(1) Fiscal Contraction	(2) Monetary Expansion	(3) Combination
Real interest rate	–	–	–
Exchange rate	–	–	–
Net exports	+	+	+
Real GDP	–	+	?
Inflation	–	+	?

Column 3 puts the two pieces together. We conclude that a policy mix of fiscal contraction and monetary expansion should reduce interest rates strongly, push down the value of the dollar, and act as a strong stimulus to our foreign trade. But its net effects on output and inflation are uncertain; the balance depends on whether the fiscal contraction overwhelms the monetary expansion, or vice versa.

Only time will tell if these predictions come true. But we can "test" the theory by looking back 10 to 15 years to an historical episode in which essentially the same experiment was run in the opposite direction. In broad outline, the early 1980s witnessed a dramatic change in the policy mix toward *tighter* money and much *looser* fiscal policy, as the Federal Reserve's anti-inflation policy collided with the large tax cuts ushered in by President Ronald Reagan. So the predictions for the early 1980s are precisely the opposite of what Table 19-3 shows higher real interest rates, an appreciating dollar, declining net exports, and uncertain effects on real GDP and inflation.

What really happened? We have already observed that the international value of the dollar soared and American foreign trade was clobbered, just as the theory predicts.

But what about interest rates? Figure 19-8 shows an estimate of the real interest rate on long-term U.S. government bonds from 1978 to 1990. (The historic norm for this rate is between 2 and 3 percent.) The real rate of interest rose dramatically between the 1980 election and the time the Reagan economic program was enacted into law (September 1981). It then fell during the 1982 recession, but rose again to very high levels in mid-1984. Again, this is in accord with the theory: Except for a brief recessionary interlude, the policy changes raised real interest rates.

What about real GDP? The U.S. economy suffered through a severe recession in 1981 to 1982 and then rebounded strongly. To appraise the effects of Reaganomics on real output, we must consider a longer period of time. If we look at the period from 1981 to 1989 as a whole, the average annual growth rate of real GDP was 3.2 percent—just a bit below the average growth rate of the previous 20 years. So the conclusion seems to be that the monetary contraction and fiscal expansion combined to have little net effect on the growth rate of aggregate demand.

If this is so, that would leave only the supply shifts caused by the appreciating dollar (see Figures 19-6 and 19-7). The rising dollar certainly helped slow inflation in the early 1980s by holding down the prices of imported inputs. In addition, the fact that the deep recession came early in President Reagan's term of office meant that the economy had a recessionary gap throughout the period

FIGURE 19-8 REAL INTEREST RATES IN THE UNITED STATES, 1978–1990

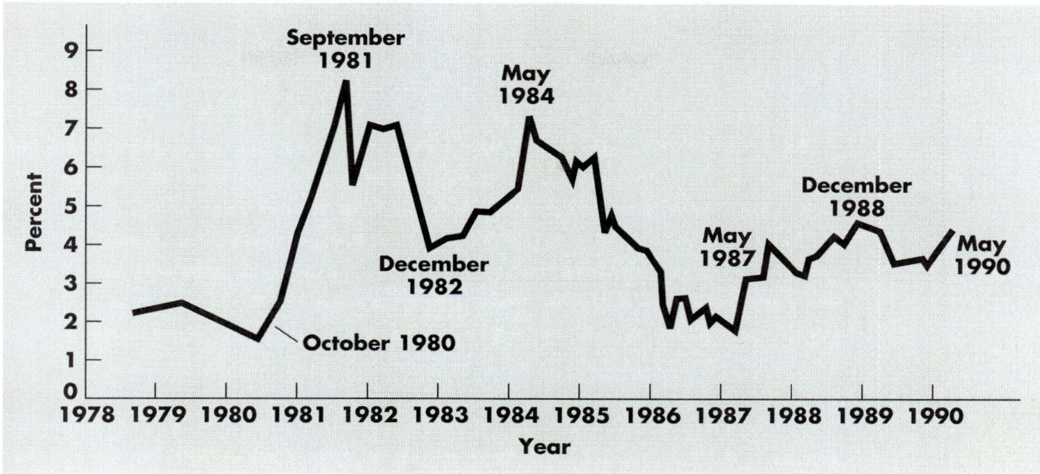

This figure charts the behavior of the real interest rate on 10-year U.S. government bonds on the basis of a survey of inflationary expectations. It rises steeply in 1980 to 1981.

SOURCE: Richard B. Hoey.

from 1981 to 1986. Finally, as we saw in earlier chapters, energy prices were falling rapidly. Each of these factors played a role in the rapid disinflation.

On balance, then, the theory did quite well in predicting the effects of tight money and rising budget deficits in the 1980s. If it works as well in the future, deficit reduction and looser monetary policy will lead to lower interest rates, a weaker dollar, and strong U.S. trade performance.

THE LINK BETWEEN THE BUDGET DEFICIT AND THE TRADE DEFICIT

Let us now consider the link between the budget deficit and the trade deficit in more detail. To do so, we need only recall two simple pieces of arithmetic.

The first begins with the familiar equilibrium condition for GDP in an open economy:

$$Y = C + I + G + (X - IM)$$

Since GDP can either be spent, saved, or taxed away:[5]

$$Y = C + S + T$$

Equating these two expressions for Y gives:

$$C + I + G + (X - IM) = C + S + T$$

Finally, subtracting C from both sides, and bringing terms involving the government to the left-hand side and terms involving the private sector to the right

[5]If you do not see why, recall that GDP equals disposable income (DI) plus taxes (T), $Y = DI + T$, and that disposable income can either be consumed or saved, $DI = C + S$. These two definitions together imply that $Y = C + S + T$.

leads to an accounting relationship between the budget deficit and the trade deficit:

$$G - T = (S - I) - (X - IM)$$

In words, the government budget deficit, $G - T$, must be equal to the surplus of savings over investment plus the trade deficit, $-(X - IM)$.

This result may seem mechanical and not particularly interesting, but our second piece of arithmetic will bring out both the common sense behind this equation and its importance for understanding recent events.

As we have noted, under floating exchange rates any deficit or surplus in the current account must be balanced by an equal and opposite surplus or deficit in the capital account. Thus, the current account *deficit*, which is $-(X - IM)$ in the previous equation, can be replaced by the capital account *surplus* to get:

$$G - T = (S - I) + \text{Net capital inflows}$$

This last equation makes an obvious point. If the U.S. government runs a budget deficit ($G - T$), that deficit must be financed either by an excess of saving over investment by American businesses and individuals ($S - I$), or by borrowing from foreigners.

But what is the economic mechanism that makes the trade deficit follow the government budget deficit? There is no mystery. To attract the necessary foreign capital, America must offer higher interest rates. As capital flows into the United States in response to the higher rates, the value of the dollar rises. And the more costly dollar leads to a larger trade deficit. Thus, the adjustments of interest rates and exchange rates that we have been discussing close the loop between a larger budget deficit and a larger trade deficit.

Applying the same logic in the opposite direction, smaller budget deficits in coming years are expected to lead to lower interest rates, a lower value of the dollar, and smaller trade deficits.

IS THE TRADE DEFICIT A PROBLEM?

The preceding explanation suggests that America's large trade deficits over the last 15 years are a symptom of a deeper trouble: The nation as a whole—including our government—has spent more than it has produced and has been forced to borrow the difference from foreigners. The trade deficit is just the mirror image of the required capital inflows.

Those who worry about trade deficits point out that these capital inflows create debts on which interest and principal payments will have to be made in the future. In this view, Americans have been mortgaging their future to finance higher consumer spending.

But there is another, quite different, interpretation of the trade deficit. Suppose foreign investors in the 1980s began to see the United States as a much more attractive place to invest their capital. Then capital would have flowed here not because Americans needed to borrow it, but because foreigners were eager to lend it. In that case, the trade deficit would still be the mirror image of the capital inflows; however, it would now signify America's economic strength, not its weakness.

The policy implications of these two views differ dramatically. The first view suggests that we should strive to reduce the trade deficit and, thereby, our need for foreign borrowing. The second view suggests that we should welcome the capital inflows and, therefore, not worry about the trade deficit. Which view is right?

The answer is in dispute. However, most economists in the 1980s ascribed to the first view—that the trade deficit was a problem, not a prize. At least two pieces of evidence persuaded them. First, real interest rates in the 1980s were generally high, not low. This suggested that America was being forced to pay high interest rates to attract the capital it needed, not that foreigners had suddenly decided that America was the place to invest.

Second, as we saw in Table 19-2 (page 432), it was mainly the *consumption* share of GDP, not the *investment* share, that rose between 1981 and 1986. This suggests that America was borrowing to finance a consumption binge, not an investment boom.

ON CURING THE TRADE DEFICIT

We now understand how the United States acquired massive trade and budget deficits in the 1980s and became the world's most indebted nation. And we have explained why many economists think the trade deficit is a problem. Next comes the hard question: What can be done about it? How can we cure our foreign trade problem and end our addiction to foreign borrowing?

The answer, of course, is highly controversial. Both economists and politicians disagree over the appropriate course of action. The best we can do here is outline some alternatives.

CHANGE THE MIX OF FISCAL AND MONETARY POLICY

The fundamental equation:

$$G - T = (S - I) - (X - IM)$$

suggests a *reduction in the budget deficit* as one good way to reduce the trade deficit. According to the analysis in this chapter, a reduction in G or an increase in T would lead to lower real interest rates in the United States, a depreciating dollar, and, eventually, a shrinking trade deficit.

This is the route that American economists urged for years and that the American government has been pursuing in the 1990s. And, as a matter of fact, the dollar has come down considerably since the mid-1980s, and so has our trade deficit (as a share of GDP), although it remains large. Partisan political bickering stood in the way of deficit reduction until President Clinton pushed through a comprehensive deficit-reduction plan in 1993. And the bipartisan support for balancing the budget promises an even tougher fiscal policy.

When the government curtails its spending or raises taxes to reduce its budget deficit, aggregate demand falls. If we do not want deficit reduction to cause an economic contraction in the United States, we must therefore compensate for it by monetary stimulus. Like contractionary fiscal policy, expansionary monetary policy lowers interest rates, depreciates the dollar, and should therefore help reduce the trade deficit.

MORE RAPID ECONOMIC GROWTH ABROAD

If foreign economies grew faster, residents of these countries would buy more American goods. That would raise American exports and reduce our trade deficit. Since the mid-1980s, the United States has been urging our major trading partners to stimulate their economies and to open their markets more to American goods—with some modest success. In the late 1980s, foreign countries rightly asked why they should tailor their economic policies to America's needs. But since the early 1990s, with the European and Japanese economies often producing well below capacity, domestic needs in those countries have also called for more expansionary policies.

RAISE DOMESTIC SAVINGS OR REDUCE DOMESTIC INVESTMENT

Our fundamental equation calls attention to two other routes to a smaller trade deficit: higher savings or lower investment.

U.S. personal saving rates have been near all-time lows in recent years. If Americans would save more, we could finance more of our government budget deficit at home and therefore would not need to borrow so much abroad. This, too, would lead to a cheaper dollar and a smaller trade deficit. The only trouble is that no one has yet found a reliable way to induce Americans to save more. A variety of tax incentives for saving has been tried, and more are suggested every year. But there is not much evidence that these incentives have worked. We seem to be a nation of consumers.

If the other cures for our trade deficit fail to work in time, the trade deficit may cure itself in a particularly unpleasant way: by dramatically reducing U.S. domestic investment. Let us see how this might work. As our trade deficits and foreign borrowing persist, foreigners wind up holding more and more U.S. dollar assets. At some point, their willingness to acquire yet more dollar assets will begin to wear thin, and they will begin demanding much higher interest rates. At best, higher interest rates lead to lower investment in the United States. At worst, foreigners cease lending to the United States, interest rates skyrocket, and we experience a severe recession. A recession, of course, would reduce our trade deficit substantially by curbing our appetite for imports. But it is a painful cure.

PROTECTIONISM

We have saved the worst remedy for last. One seemingly obvious way to cure our trade deficit is to limit imports by imposing stiff tariffs, strict quotas, and other protectionist devices. We discussed protectionism, and the reasons why almost all economists oppose it, in Chapter 17. Despite the economic arguments against it, protectionism has an undeniable political allure. It seems, superficially, to "save American jobs." And it conveniently shifts the blame for our trade problems onto foreigners.

In addition to depriving us and other countries of the benefits of comparative advantage, protectionism might not even succeed in reducing our trade deficit. One reason is that other nations may retaliate. If we erect trade barriers to reduce our imports, IM will fall. But if foreign countries erect corresponding barriers to our exports, X will fall, too. On balance, our *net* exports, $X - IM$, may or may not improve. However, world trade will surely suffer. This is a game that may have no winners, only losers.

Even if other nations do not retaliate, tariffs and quotas may not improve our trade deficit much. Why? If they succeed in reducing American spending on imports, tariffs and quotas will thereby reduce the supply of dollars on the world

SAVING PATTERNS AND TRADE DEFICITS: THE ARITHMETIC OF U.S.-JAPANESE ECONOMIC RELATIONS

The huge U.S. trade deficit with Japan has been a significant source of friction between the two countries for years and has led to frequent calls for protectionist measures here. Our fundamental equation,

$$G - T = (S - I) - (X - IM)$$

teaches us that part of the problem traces to different saving habits in the two countries. The Japanese are among the biggest savers in the world. So $S - I$ is a large, positive number in Japan. Furthermore, unlike the U.S. government, the Japanese government has often (though not recently) had a budget surplus. It therefore follows that, in order to balance the international books, Japan must generate a large trade *surplus.*

The contrast between the United States and Japan in this regard is marked. While the Japanese people and government together are big net *savers*, the American people and government together are big net *borrowers*. In an integrated world financial system, it is therefore natural that the Japanese should be lending to us. In short, Japan should have capital *outflows* and we should have capital *inflows*—which is just what has been happening. Remembering that:

Current account surplus +
Capital account surplus = 0

the implication is that Japan should have a current account *surplus,* and we should have a current account *deficit.*

Once again this is only natural. In fact, the United States has had a trade deficit with Japan for a long time—even when our overall trade position and Japan's were nearly balanced. Being an island nation almost devoid of natural resources, Japan must run huge trade deficits in primary products. Much of this trade is with developing countries. To offset this trade deficit in primary products, Japan needs a surplus in trade in manufactured goods. And who are likely to be the leading customers for these goods? The biggest consumers on earth, of course—the Americans.

So it is natural for the United States to run a bilateral deficit in trading goods with Japan. However, that does not imply that an annual deficit of $50 billion or more is appropriate, nor that the Japanese are blameless. In fact, Japan has long been among the most protectionist of all the advanced, industrial nations. Only a little of this protectionism takes the form of high tariffs or stiff quotas. Most is more subtle, coming instead through a variety of bureaucratic regulations that make importing difficult.

So one possible solution to the U.S.-Japan trade problem is to persuade Japan to open its markets more. And the Clinton administration has devoted considerable time and energy toward this end. But no one really thinks that, even in a completely free market, we could sell in Japan nearly as much as they sell here.

Macroeconomic policy might be a more effective tool. Look once again at the fundamental equation:

$$G - T = (S - I) - (X - IM)$$

If Japan stimulated its economy by more expansionary fiscal policy, $G - T$ would rise and $(X - IM)$ would fall. If, at the same time, the United States reduced its budget deficit, $G - T$ would fall here and $(X - IM)$ would rise. In all likelihood, our bilateral trade deficit with Japan would narrow. That is precisely the "deal" that the two countries are working on now.

market. That would push the value of the dollar up. A rising dollar, of course, would hurt U.S. exports and encourage more imports. The fundamental equation,

$$G - T = (S - I) - (X - IM)$$

reminds us that protectionism can raise $X - IM$ only if it reduces the budget deficit, raises saving, or reduces investment.[6]

CONCLUSION: WE ARE NOT ALONE

We do indeed live in a world economy. The major trading nations of the world are linked by exports and imports, by capital flows, and by exchange rates. What happens to national income, prices, and interest rates in one country affects other nations.

Thus, policymakers in Europe, Asia, and South America keep a watchful eye on developments in the U.S. economy. If the U.S. economy expands, these other countries have better markets for their exports. If we pursue policies that make the dollar depreciate, they find their currencies appreciating. If interest rates rise in the United States, they see capital flowing out of their countries into ours. Some observers think that, as the "big guy on the block," America bears a special responsibility for the health of the world economy.

But we are not the *only* big guys on the block. Japan also has a giant economy which profoundly affects the rest of the world. And, once fully unified, the European Union will give western Europe the biggest economy of all. What happens in Europe, Japan, and elsewhere often has important effects on the U.S. economy.

That the major economies of the world are linked suggests the need for greater policy coordination among nations. But since the national interests of particular countries often differ, countries are understandably reluctant to surrender any of their sovereignty. Hence, international policy coordination remains an elusive goal. Economically speaking, we all live in one world. Politically, however, we live in a world of separate nation-states.

---

[6]Here tariffs, which raise revenue for the government, have a clear advantage over quotas, which do not.

SUMMARY

1. The nations of the world are linked together economically because national income, prices, and interest rates in one country affect those in another. They are thus **open economies.**
2. Because one country's *imports* are another country's *exports,* rapid (or sluggish) economic growth in one country contributes to rapid (or sluggish) growth in other countries.
3. A country's *net exports* depend on whether its prices are high or low relative to those of other countries. Since exchange rates translate one country's prices into the currencies of other countries, the *exchange rate* is a key determinant of net exports.
4. If the currency depreciates, net exports rise and aggregate demand increases, thereby raising both real GDP and the price level. A depreciating currency also reduces aggregate supply by making imported inputs more costly.
5. If the currency appreciates, net exports fall and aggregate demand, real GDP, and the price level all decrease. But an appreciating currency also increases aggregate supply by making imported inputs cheaper.
6. *International capital flows* respond strongly to interest rate differentials among countries. Hence, higher domestic interest rates lead to currency *appreciations,* and lower interest rates lead to *depreciations.*
7. Contractionary monetary policies raise interest rates and therefore make the currency appreciate. Both the higher interest rates and the stronger currency

reduce aggregate demand. Hence, international capital flows make monetary policy more powerful than it would be in a *closed economy*.

8. Expansionary fiscal policies also raise interest rates and make the currency appreciate. But, in this case, the international repercussions cancel out part of the demand-expanding effects of the policies. Hence, international capital flows make fiscal policy less powerful than it would be in a closed economy.
9. Since Reaganomics in the early 1980s combined tight money with highly expansionary fiscal policy, it raised interest rates, pushed the dollar up, and caused a large trade deficit in the United States. Conversely, deficit reduction and easier money in the 1990s are expected to reduce interest rates, the value of the dollar, and the trade deficits.
10. *Budget deficits and trade deficits* are linked by the fundamental equation $G - T = (S - I) - (X - IM)$. This also implies that the budget deficit equals the sum of $S - I$ + *Capital inflows*.
11. It follows from this equation that the U.S. trade deficit must be cured by some combination of lower budget deficits, higher savings, and lower investment.
12. Protectionist policies might not cure the U.S. trade deficit because (a) they will make the dollar appreciate and (b) they may provoke foreign retaliation.

KEY TERMS

Exports
Imports
Net exports
Closed economy
Open economy
Exchange rate
Appreciation
Depreciation
Trade deficit
International capital flows
Budget deficits and trade deficits
$G - T = (S - I) - (X - IM)$

QUESTIONS FOR REVIEW

1. For years, the U.S. government has been trying to get Japan to expand its economy faster. Explain how more rapid growth in Japan would affect the U.S. economy.
2. If inflation is higher in Germany than in France, and the exchange rate between the two countries is fixed, what is likely to happen to the balance of trade between the two countries?
3. Explain why a currency depreciation leads to an improvement in a country's trade balance.
4. Explain why American fiscal policy is less powerful and American monetary policy is more powerful than indicated in the closed-economy model of the previous part of this book.
5. Use an aggregate supply-demand diagram to analyze the effects of a currency appreciation.
6. Explain why $G - T = (S - I) - (X - IM)$.
7. Given what you now know, do you think it was a good idea for the United States to adopt a policy mix of tight money and large government budget deficits in the early 1980s? Why or why not?
8. What, in your view, is the best way for America to reduce its trade deficit?
9. During 1994 and early 1995, the international value of the yen rose sharply. This development worried the Japanese authorities. Why?
10. (More difficult) Suppose consumption and investment are described by:

$$C = 50 + 0.75DI$$
$$I = 400 + 0.2Y - 50r$$

Here DI is disposable income, Y is GDP, and r, the interest rate, is measured in percentage points. (For example, a 5 percent interest rate is $r = 5$.) Exports and imports are as follows:

$$X = 200$$
$$IM = -150 + 0.2Y$$

Government purchases are $G = 800$, and taxes are 20 percent of income.

The price level is fixed and the central bank uses its monetary policy to peg the interest rate at $r = 8$.

a. Find equilibrium GDP, the budget deficit or surplus, and the trade deficit or surplus.
b. Suppose the currency depreciates and, as a result, exports and imports change to:

$$X = 250$$
$$IM = -200 + 0.2Y$$

Now find equilibrium GDP, the budget deficit or surplus, and the trade deficit or surplus.

CHAPTER 20

PRODUCTIVITY AND GROWTH IN THE WEALTH OF NATIONS

The enormous wealth of Britain is attributable [primarily] to . . . the wonderful skill of her entrepreneurs . . . and the superiority of her workmen in rapid and masterly execution. . . . The English laborer . . . gives his work more care, attention and diligence, than the workmen of most other nations.

Jean Baptiste Say, 1819

Japan commercially, I regret to say, does not bear the best reputation for executing business. Inferior goods, irregularity and indifferent shipments have caused no end of worry . . . you are a very satisfied easy-going race . . . the habits of national heritage.

From a report of an Australian expert for the Japanese government, 1915

This chapter introduces a major topic of growing importance for all Americans: the role of productivity in the well-being of nations. We are conscious as never before of competition from other industrial economies. Our prosperity depends increasingly on that of other countries, and theirs, in turn, depends vitally on ours. This chapter compares for a number of countries the growth in living standards and *productivity* (output per hour of work) over many decades. The chapter is divided into two parts. The first focuses on the wealthier, industrialized nations and the second deals with the poorer, less developed countries (LDCs).

PART 1: GROWTH IN THE UNITED STATES AND OTHER INDUSTRIAL COUNTRIES

Human history in the last two centuries has been unlike anything ever experienced before. In the world's industrial countries, the quantity and quality of food, clothing, and comforts have reached levels that were never before dreamed possible. The change has been so revolutionary that it is difficult to grasp. This chapter helps us envision how great the accomplishment has been. It also suggests that the transformation was made possible by productivity growth: the fact that the hourly production of a person in the United States today is perhaps 20 times as high as it was in 1800. Just two figures will suggest the magnitude of the achievement. In 1800 about 90 percent of America's labor force had to work on farms, but all that farm labor barely managed to produce enough food to feed the country adequately. Today less than 3 percent of U.S. workers earn their livings on farms. Yet those few farm workers provide an outpouring of surpluses which the U.S. government constantly struggles to contain.

LIFE IN THE "GOOD OLD DAYS"

The United States, and the 13 colonies before it, has always been a privileged land with relatively high levels of nutrition. In the 18th century, an average white, native-born male who reached the age of 10 could expect to live to

Late 19th-century sod house in the Dakotas.

somewhere between age 50 and 55. By contrast, an English *nobleman* at that time could expect to live only to something between age 39 and 46.

Nevertheless, in the mid-19th century, low farm productivity, an almost complete lack of refrigeration, and limited transport of goods bound a large part of even the U.S. population to a minimal and nutritionally inferior variety of foods. Such uninspiring staples as lard, cornmeal, and salt pork were mainstays in the diet, particularly outside the population centers. Travelers' accounts of meals often mentioned the universal one-pot stew, the main meal of the day for the family. According to one study, "There were, of course, a few people who knew what it was to . . . eat a meal that consisted of more than one course; but there were very, very few such people, and they were all very rich."[1]

But, most Americans rightly felt they lived in a land of unprecedented abundance, for that one-pot stew was usually there. For many centuries most Europeans had devoted nearly half their food budgets to breadstuffs. For example, in 1790 in France, "The price of bread [for a family of five], even in normal times . . . was half . . . the daily wage of common labor."[2] Often the bread took the form of gruel—a sort of cooked breakfast cereal—served in a single bowl with a single spoon, both passed around the table to the entire family. In bad years, even gruel was unavailable. Famine and widespread death by starvation continued to threaten Europe until the beginning of the 19th century, and earlier it had constituted a normal fact of existence. Food shortages were but one manifestation of the unimaginably poor living conditions in all the major cities of Europe.

Even in 19th-century America, though, living conditions were far from ideal. Most rural homes that travelers saw were tiny and crudely built, with no glass windows, no lighting except the fireplace, no indoor plumbing, and scanty homemade furniture. The housing of relatively well-off Americans was still primitive by modern standards. Bathtubs, for example, were rare. No homes

---

[1]Ruth Schwartz Cowan, *More Work for Mother: The Ironies of Household Technology from the Open Hearth to the Microwave* (New York: Basic Books, 1983), p. 38.

[2]Robert Palmer, *The Age of Democratic Revolution*, vol. 2 (Princeton, N.J.: Princeton University Press, 1964), p. 49.

had electricity and few had gas. Fewer still had hot running water, and not even 2 percent had indoor toilets and cold running water. Boston, with a population of nearly 200,000 in 1860, had only 31,000 sinks, 4,000 bathtubs, and 10,000 water closets. Outdoor privies were the norm and baths, for the great majority, a luxury.

Like the common man, the rich have also gained much in terms of health and personal comfort in the course of two or three centuries. By the early 1900s, life expectancy at birth for a member of the British nobility had reached 65 years. Home heating technology illustrates the dramatic improvements in "creature comforts." It was not until early in the 18th century that heating technology made any improvements on the open fireplace. Until then the bitter cold of winter was a serious threat to both the poor and the highest nobility. Princess Palatine, the German sister-in-law of King Louis XIV, reported that in February 1695, "in the Hall of Mirrors at Versailles at the King's table the wine and water froze in the glasses."[3]

Though living conditions were vastly improved from earlier centuries, by today's standards, life in the United States just 100 years ago was hard and primitive.

THE MAGNITUDE OF PRODUCTIVITY GROWTH

Today, of course, things are vastly different. Recent surveys indicate that only 1.1 percent of American housing units lack complete plumbing—defined as hot and cold piped water, a flush toilet, and a bathtub or shower for the exclusive use of that housing unit. Less than 5 percent are occupied by more than one person per room. Of the new, privately owned, one-family houses built in 1993, 58 percent had three or more bedrooms, 49 percent had 2.5 or more bathrooms, and 79 percent had central air conditioning. Furthermore, in that year over 98 percent of all households owned a television (with an average of 2.2 sets per home), virtually 100 percent were equipped with electric refrigerators, 76 percent owned electric washing machines, 79 percent owned microwave ovens, and 55 percent had two or more vehicles.[4]

The revolution in manner of living was made possible by an unprecedented rate of growth in human efficiency in producing output.

LABOR PRODUCTIVITY refers to the amount of output a worker turns out in an hour (or a week or a year) of labor. It can be measured as total national output (GDP) in a given year divided by the total number of hours of work performed for pay in the country during that year. That is, labor productivity is defined as GDP per hour of labor.

PRODUCTIVITY AND OUTPUT PER CAPITA

There are two basic concepts for the long-run growth story: *labor productivity* and *output per capita (per person)*. They are, respectively, the indicators of the production and the consumption side of economic growth.

Labor productivity refers to the amount of output turned out by a *given* amount of labor [*gross domestic product (GDP) per labor hour*]. An increase in productivity means that a human being has become a more effective instrument of production. This can be the result of harder work, better training, more or better equipment, innovative technology, or a variety of other causes.

---

[3]Fernand Braudel, *The Structures of Everyday Life: The Limits of the Possible,* vol. 1, *Civilization and Capitalism, 15th–18th Century* (New York: Harper & Row, 1979).

[4]U.S. Bureau of the Census, *Statistical Abstract of the United States, 1995,* 115th ed. (Washington, D.C.: U.S. Government Printing Office, 1995).

The *standard of living*, on the other hand, is more naturally measured by *GDP per capita*, that is, by total output (GDP) divided by the number of persons among whom it will be distributed. The more output there is for each person, the better off in economic terms the average person must be.

We usually measure a nation's prosperity not in terms of its total output but in terms of its output *per person*. For instance, India has a GDP more than seven times as large as Sweden's. But with a population more than 100 times as large as Sweden's, India remains a poor country while Sweden is highly prosperous. The point is that:

If the objective of growth is the material welfare of the *individuals* who make up a country, then the proper measure of the success of a program of economic development is how much it adds to output per person—total output *divided by total population*.

To make the appropriate comparison of well-being in Sweden and India, we note that per-capita GDP in Sweden is over $18,000 a year, whereas in India, even after a generous adjustment to correct for lower prices in that country, the figure is about $1,360 a year.[5]

The fantastic magnitude of the increases in both labor productivity and output per capita since 1800 is best appreciated by contrasting it with the dismal average record of many previous centuries. It is estimated that in Europe, even by the time of the American Civil War, neither labor productivity nor GDP per capita had yet come back up to the levels that had been achieved in ancient Rome! Thus, on the average, *productivity and GDP per capita did not grow at all for over 1,600 years!* Even for those wealthy enough to buy them, the number of important new consumer goods introduced in all those centuries was remarkably small. Firearms, glass windowpanes, eyeglasses, mechanical clocks, tobacco, and printed books constitute almost the entire list of major new consumer products invented between the fall of the Roman Empire and the beginning of the 19th century.

In contrast, the period since the 1830s has been characterized by an endless explosion of innovations. The railroad and the steamship revolutionized transportation. Steel-making technology changed drastically. The chemical and electronics industries were born and produced hundreds of new consumer products. The range of personal and household goods that we now take for granted—TV sets, dishwashers, cameras, automobiles, personal computers, and many, many others—appeared in an accelerating stream and became commonplace. This has reached a point where today our one unchanging expectation for the future is that it will be characterized by constant change.

Figure 20-1 shows, for five countries, the impressive growth of labor productivity over the past century.[6] For example, it indicates that between 1870 and

---

[5]These comparisons are based on per-capita GDP figures, expressed in U.S. dollars and converted from the national currencies using purchasing-power-parity exchange rates. The source is the Central Intelligence Agency, *The World Factbook 1995* (Washington, D.C.: CIA, 1995). For an explanation of purchasing-power-parity rates, see footnote 6 below.

[6]Throughout this chapter, as we compare output per capita or output per work hour (productivity) in different countries, we run into a problem. U.S. output is measured in dollars and other countries' outputs in their own currencies. It is *not* legitimate to compare them by finding out the amounts of different foreign currencies that your bank will give you for a dollar, because those exchange rates change from day to day, but relative productivity levels do not. Instead we try to measure the outputs of different countries in money (usually dollars) of constant purchasing power. For example,

FIGURE 20-1

LABOR PRODUCTIVITY, 1870–1992

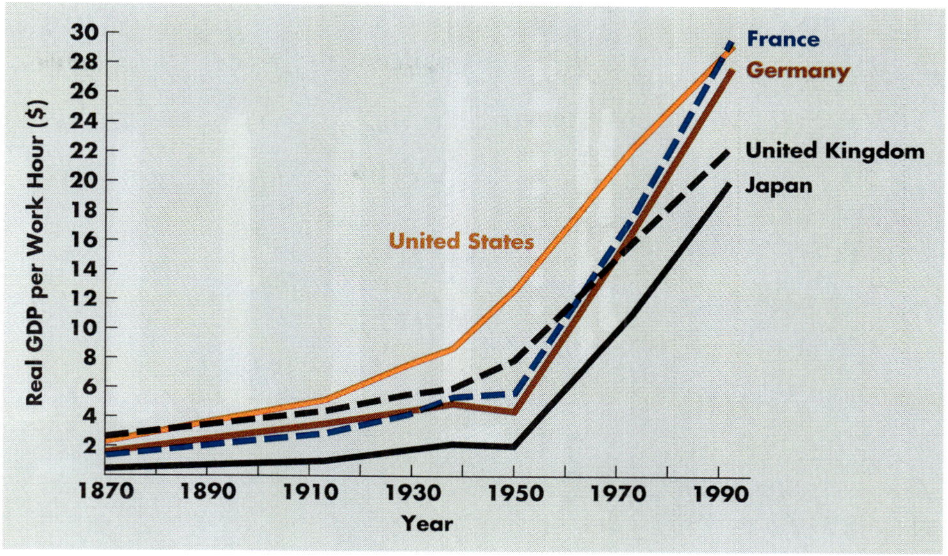

The productivity growth shown here for five industrial countries is typical of today's leading industrial economies. The explosive pattern of increase is unprecedented.

SOURCE: Angus Maddison, *Monitoring the World Economy, 1820–1992* (Paris: Development Centre of the Organisation for Economic Cooperation and Development, 1995).

1992 Japanese productivity has risen about 4,300 percent; French and German productivity levels went up 2,100 percent and 1,600 percent, respectively; productivity in the United States increased about 1,200 percent; and British productivity jumped 800 percent!

To see the implications of this dramatic rise in productivity for living standards (as measured by output per capita) we must first note what has happened to labor time spent by the typical worker. In the industrialized, free-market countries, the average number of hours worked per year has fallen by half. This is partly the result of a fall in work hours per day—typically from about 12 hours in 1900 down to some 7.5 hours per day by 1979—and partly the result of a decline from six working days to five. But most surprising is the almost total absence of any vacations for most of the population before the 20th century. The two-week or four-week vacation is another luxury made possible by the rise in productivity.

Increases in output per person (or average income per head) have also been spectacular. Over the 174-year period from 1820 to 1994, output per capita went up almost 2,700 percent in Japan, about 1,600 percent in Germany and the United States, about 1,400 percent in Italy and France, and more than 800 percent in Great Britain.[7] In the United States, for example, average income measured in

---

we ask how many yen does it cost to buy the same bundle of goods in Japan that one can buy for, say, $100 in the United States. This figure is referred to as a *purchasing-power-parity* exchange rate. Such numbers are used in all the international comparisons in this chapter.

[7] It is important to notice that all of these numbers have been corrected to eliminate the effects of inflation. Thus, it is true, of course, that because of the subsequent inflation, a dollar in the mid-1800s could purchase much more bread or many more shoes than it can today, so that a $12 weekly salary then is not as low, in purchasing power, as it may seem. But the statistics reported here have been corrected to eliminate this source of confusion, using GDP price indexes. See the appendix to Chapter 6 for further explantion.

FIGURE 20-2 IMPROVEMENT IN LIVING STANDARDS, 1820 VERSUS 1994

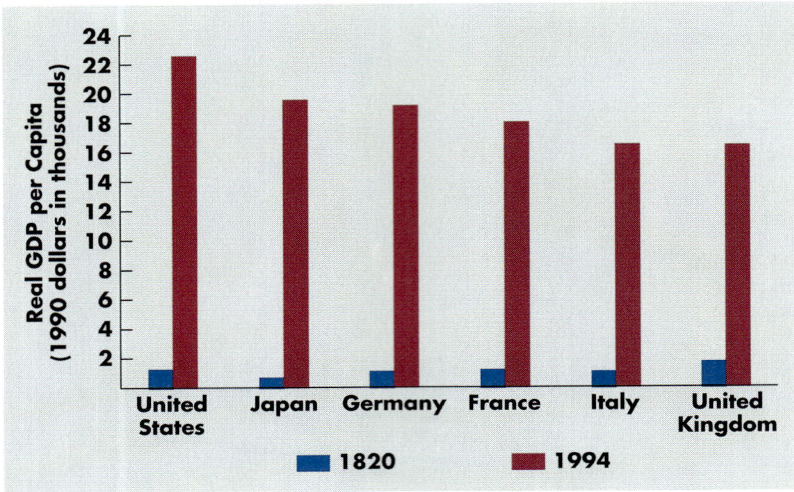

The graph shows how much higher GDP per capita is today than it was in 1820 in each of the six countries shown. The pattern is typical for free-market, industrialized countries. The numbers are in dollars adjusted to have roughly the same purchasing power in all countries and at both dates listed.

SOURCE: Angus Maddison, *Monitoring the World Economy, 1820–1992* (Paris: Development Centre of the Organisation for Economic Co-operation and Development, 1995).

dollars of constant purchasing power was only about one-seventeenth as large in 1820 as it is today.

To imagine what it is like to live on an income so small, one must think of *Egypt, Bolivia, or the Philippines,* whose per-capita incomes today have been calculated to be on a par with that of an average American in the 19th century! Figure 20-2 translates the productivity growth since the beginning of the 20th century into the resulting and extraordinary rise in living standards—in national output per capita.

Obviously, the economic well-being of an average American, and of an average resident of the other countries in Figures 20-1 and 20-2, has increased dramatically. *It is noteworthy that, according to the World Bank's latest estimates, though other countries are catching up, the United States still leads the world in per-capita GDP.*

Since 1800, productivity in the United States has increased at an average annual rate of slightly less than 2 percent. An apparently small change in this figure would have enormous consequences over a long period. Had productivity grown at an average rate of only 1 percent per year instead, an average American today would command about 6.6 times as large a quantity of goods and services as his forebears did in 1800. Actually, though it is hard to believe, real per-capita income has risen about 30-fold in this period. And if productivity had grown over the entire interval at an annual rate of 3 percent, average living standards would be an incredible 275 times as high as they were in 1800.

Productivity growth can make an enormous difference in a nation's standing in the hierarchy of the world's economies. Keeping its annual productivity growth just one-half of 1 percent ahead of Great Britain for about a century transformed the United States from a minor, developing country into a superpower, while Great Britain declined from the world's preeminent power into a second-rate economy. Japan's 3 percent average annual productivity growth rate since 1870 also transformed it from one of the world's poorest countries into a nation with one of the highest GDP figures in the world.

THE OVERWHELMING IMPORTANCE OF PRODUCTIVITY GROWTH IN THE LONG RUN

As we pointed out in our list of **Ideas for Beyond the Final Exam,** only rising productivity can raise standards of living in the long run.

Over long periods of time, small differences in rates of productivity growth compound like interest in a bank account and can make an enormous difference to a society's prosperity. Nothing contributes more to reduction of poverty, to increases in leisure, and to the country's ability to finance education, public health, environmental improvement, and the arts.

THE SECOND MAJOR DEVELOPMENT: CONVERGENCE

Not only has each of the industrial countries grown in productivity and income per capita, but these countries have also become more similar to one another both in terms of labor productivity and GDP per capita. In other words, among the industrial countries, those which were furthest behind in 1870 have been catching up with those that were ahead. For example, in 1870 the productivity level of the leading country (Australia) was about seven times as high as that of the least productive country (Japan). In 1992 that ratio was only about 1.5. That is, about three-quarters of the difference between the most productive and the least productive countries was eliminated during the 122-year period.

Such a dramatic narrowing of productivity gaps among the industrial countries means that everyone else must be catching up with the leader, and that leader, ever since World War I, has been the United States. This is illustrated in Figure 20-3, which shows what happened to the *relative* labor productivity levels of four leading industrialized countries over the period 1950 to 1992. Specifically, it shows GDP per work-hour in each of those countries *as a percentage of the U.S. level.* (The U.S. figure is, therefore, always 100 percent.) It indicates that, in 1950, per-capita GDP for the average of the countries shown was about 28 percent of that of the United States. By 1992 the average was about 89 percent of the U.S. level. Figure 20-3 also shows that productivity in *each* of these countries has been moving closer to the United States in this 42-year period, with France caught up and Germany not far behind.[8]

These and other data indicate that levels of labor productivity are converging among the leading industrialized countries.[9]

Figure 20-3 also indicates that, as productivity levels in the other countries have come closer to those in the United States, the speed at which they have approached has slowed. Note also that, despite the impression given in the press, Japan is still the lowest in this group, and that Germany is falling behind France (and several other countries).

[8]To interpret the graph, remember that if the curve representing some country reaches precisely the curve for the United States, it means that this country's productivity per worker is equal to that of the United States.

[9]Note that this conclusion has been challenged, at least for the years before World War II, on the grounds that the sample of countries studied happens to include those that have been converging toward the United States because they are the success stories for which statistics are available. Thus, the critics point out, Argentina is omitted from the sample of countries, even though in 1870 many observers would have predicted a brilliant economic future for that country.

FIGURE 20-3

LABOR PRODUCTIVITY LEVELS AS A PERCENT OF U.S. LEVEL, 1950–1992

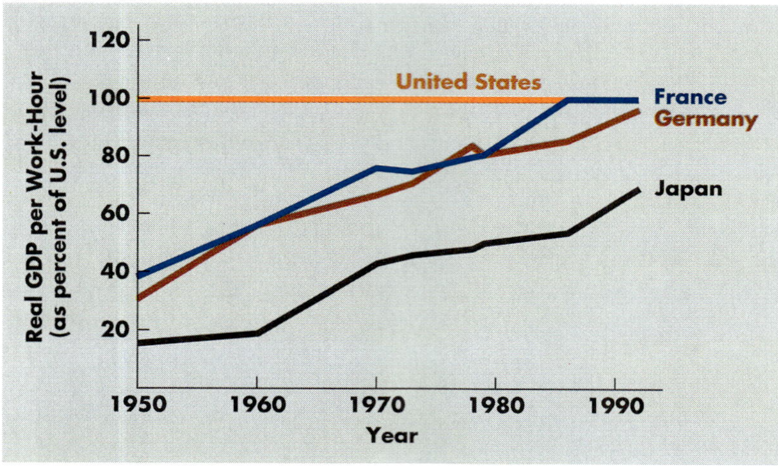

The graph shows that real GDP per worker in each of the countries approached the (growing) U.S. level during the period 1950 to 1992. However, as productivity in those countries got closer to our own, the catch-up process seemed to slow. You may also be surprised to see that in 1992 Japan was still at the bottom of the group and that France was ahead of Germany (and has caught up to the U.S. level).

SOURCE: Angus Maddison, *Monitoring the World Economy, 1820–1992* (Paris: Development Centre of the Organization for Economic Cooperation and Development, 1995).

WHY INTERNATIONAL EQUALIZATION?

Why are these countries growing more alike in productivity and average standards of living? No one has the entire answer, but a good part of the story is probably the speed with which new technology spreads around the world. Better communications permit innovative techniques to move from one country to another far more quickly than in the past. Better and more widespread education permits countries to learn technical details from one another and to train their labor forces rapidly to make use of them. At the beginning of the 18th century when the Newcomen steam engine (the predecessor of Watt's steam engine) was invented in England, it took half a century for the engine to spread to western European countries and to the American colonies. In contrast, the innovations in transistor and semiconductor technology since World War II have, on average, taken about two and one-half years to spread among countries.

All industrial countries benefit from the process of shared information; each learns from the innovations that occur in all the others. The British, the French, and the Germans benefit from American computer technology while the United States and others benefit from Japanese advances in robotics.

But there is one crucial asymmetry. Countries that are behind have a great deal to learn from countries that are ahead, but the leaders have less to learn from those that have lagged behind. This is generally believed to be a prime explanation of the convergence in living standards.

Lagging countries have more to learn from leaders than leaders can learn from laggards. This fact, and the growing speed with which innovations are spread, help explain why the world's industrial economies are growing more equal.

ARE ALL COUNTRIES PARTICIPATING IN EQUALIZATION?

So far we have seen that the world's industrialized countries are growing increasingly similar to one another in terms of productivity and living standards. But we have yet to consider the world's poorest nations—usually referred to as *less developed countries, or LDCs.* (See Part 2 of this chapter.) Have most of those countries also benefited from the spread of innovation and closed the gap between themselves and the world's economic leaders?

Unfortunately, among the LDCs, where equalization is most desperately needed, the picture is very mixed. Some countries, such as Taiwan and South Korea, have achieved spectacular successes. But, as a group, the LDCs have grown less equal among themselves and have fallen further behind the United States. On average, GDP per capita grew about 3 percent per year in the industrialized countries in the period after World War II. But in the LDCs it rose only about 1 and 1/2 percent a year on average.

While the leading economies in the world are becoming more equal in terms of productivity and living standards, a number of the poorest countries are falling further behind and are holding back the average performance of the LDCs. Later in the chapter we will discuss the reasons cited for the poor performance of many LDCs.

THE U.S. PRODUCTIVITY SLOWDOWN: IS AMERICAN ECONOMIC LEADERSHIP DOOMED?

Since the mid-1960s there has been a sharp decline in the growth rate of productivity in the United States. From 1950 to 1973, productivity per work-hour grew at an estimated average rate of 2.7 percent per year, which is probably somewhat faster than it had ever grown before over so long a period. Then, between 1973 and 1992 productivity growth fell sharply from its earlier postwar rate, back 1.1 percent per year.

Some observers have concluded that the U.S. economy, and particularly its manufacturing sector, are in terrible trouble and that the United States may lose its leadership in both productivity and living standards. But these fears are, at the very least, exaggerated for several reasons.

First, it is important to note that throughout most of this period the *level* of U.S. productivity continued to improve. In almost every year it was higher than the last. The *rate of improvement* simply slowed from a gallop to a walk, and finally to a crawl. Second, the United States is still by far the world's largest economy in terms of total production, wealth, and factors such as spending on research and development.

Third, some analysts question whether the U.S. productivity slowdown is as serious as it appears. They argue that the United States is not alone in suffering a slowdown in productivity growth. The problem has affected virtually every industrial country. Figure 20-4 compares productivity growth rates for five industrial countries from 1950 to 1973 with those from 1973 to 1992—the years when the slowdown occurred. We find that the U.S. growth rate fell 58 percent, but the growth rates of Japan, the United Kingdom, France, and Germany also fell nearly as much. Compared with the others, the U.S. decline does not seem so far out of line.

In addition, very-long-run data on U.S. productivity growth exhibit no long-term downward trend. Productivity plunged during the Great Depression of the 1930s then leaped upward with the end of World War II. But this catch-up period also came to an end, and the growth rate fell from its postwar high. From this view, then, the deceleration after the 1970s, rather than being entirely a drop below its historical norms, was partly a return toward normalcy from a period of extraordinary growth, which (in retrospect!) seems to have been predictably

FIGURE 20-4 FALL IN PRODUCTIVITY GROWTH RATES, 1950–1973 VERSUS 1973–1992

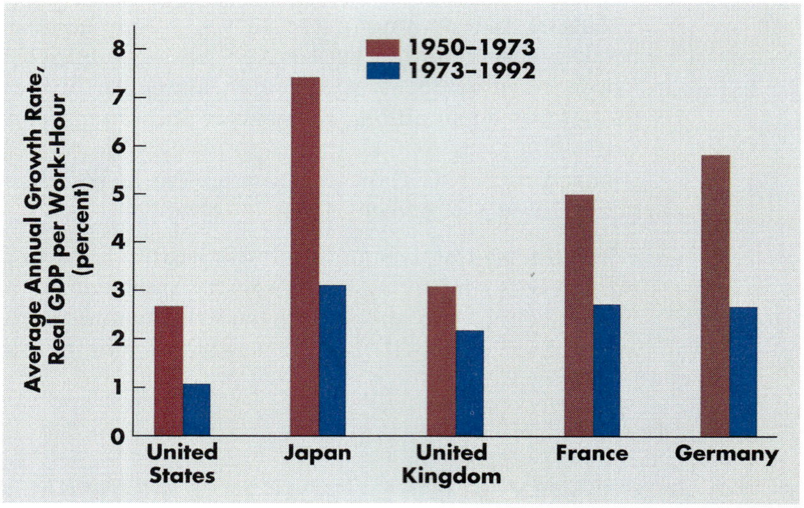

This graph confirms that productivity growth *did* decline in the period widely publicized as the "U.S. productivity slowdown." However, at the same time, it also fell throughout the industrial world and not just in the United States.

SOURCE: Angus Maddison, *Monitoring the World Economy, 1820–1992* (Paris: Development Centre of the Organization for Economic Cooperation and Development, 1995).

temporary. The data do indicate that since 1973 the growth rate of the U.S. productivity (an average annual rate of 1.1 percent) continues below the historical figure (about 2 percent). However, per-capita income has done better than productivity. The average annual growth rate of U.S. GDP per capita between 1954 and 1977 (2.1 percent) was, indeed, significantly higher than it has been since (1.6 percent).[10] However, this more recent figure is *exactly* the same as the average growth rate in the earlier 84-year period between 1869 and 1953 (again, 1.6 percent).

During the recent decline in the growth rate of *overall* U.S. productivity, some sectors—such as construction, mining, and the service industry—have had poor recent records. However, the main focus of public concern has been *manufacturing;* Americans seem to believe that this sector of our economy is most vulnerable to foreign competition because of its poor productivity performance. Yet the record shows something quite different: *U.S. manufacturing productivity has experienced no trend toward a declining growth rate.* This is shown in Figure 20-5 which reports the growth rate of labor productivity in American manufacturing over the entire period since World War II. No downward trend is apparent. Moreover, we see that the growth rates of manufacturing productivity in Japan and Germany are no longer far out of line with those of the United States.

THE U.S. PRODUCTIVITY GROWTH LAG BEHIND OTHER INDUSTRIAL COUNTRIES

What about the second disturbing fact about U.S. productivity growth—that it has recently been so much lower than that of other industrial countries? There is a simple and plausible explanation. It is the equalization of productivity in the world's industrial countries—the convergence phenomenon we just studied. If the forces making for equalization did in fact dominate the growth paths of those countries, it is necessarily true that productivity in the lagging countries *had* to

[10]"What's Happening to Americans' Income?" *The Southwest Economy*, Federal Reserve Bank of Dallas, Issue 2 (1995), pp. 3–6.

FIGURE 20-5 GROWTH RATES IN MANUFACTURING PRODUCTIVITY, 1950–1994

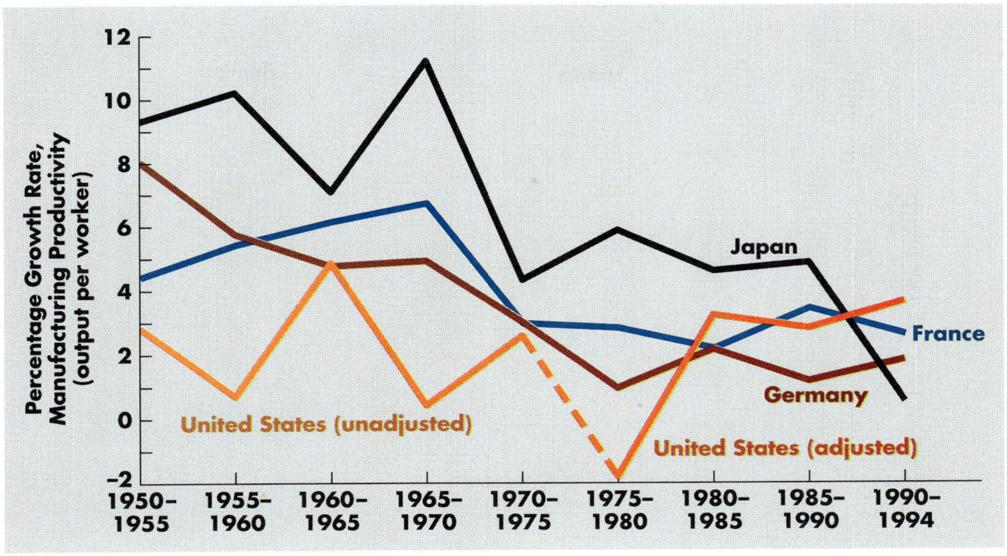

In the important manufacturing sector of the economy, the graph shows that U.S. productivity has shown no sign of a declining trend. Moreover, the growth rates in other leading economies are now coming closer to the American level.

Note: U.S. data for 1950–1976 are based on 1982 price weights; data for 1977–1994 are based on 1987 price weights.

SOURCE: U.S. Department of Labor, Bureau of Labor Statistics, *BLS News: International Comparisons of Manufacturing Productivity and Unit Labor Cost Trends, 1994* (Washington, D.C.: U.S. Department of Labor, September 8, 1995); and various BLS news releases.

grow more quickly than that in the countries at the head of the line. Otherwise, they could never have grown more equal.

Viewed in this way, there is little to be alarmed about in the relatively slow growth rate of U.S. productivity compared with that of other countries. Indeed, if the higher growth rates of other countries are attributable in good part to their having much to copy from the United States as a productivity leader, we should not be surprised if the rapid growth rates of those countries were to slow as they approach the high American levels. There are, as a matter of fact, signs that this is beginning to happen.

PRODUCTIVITY AND THE DEINDUSTRIALIZATION THESIS

Let us now turn to the popular notion that lagging productivity growth is turning the United States into a service economy, the "deindustrialization thesis." The trends are said to portend a future in which the United States suffers chronic and apparently incurable problems in its trade with other countries because its manufactured products are not competitive with those of foreign countries. As a result, it is argued, the United States will either be forced to bear heavy unemployment or to see its labor force driven into low-paying, service-sector jobs, thus transforming the nation into a "service economy" in which people earn their livings by flipping hamburgers and washing dishes. The "deindustrialization"

FIGURE 20-6 GROWTH IN THE SHARE OF SERVICE-SECTOR JOBS, 1967–1994

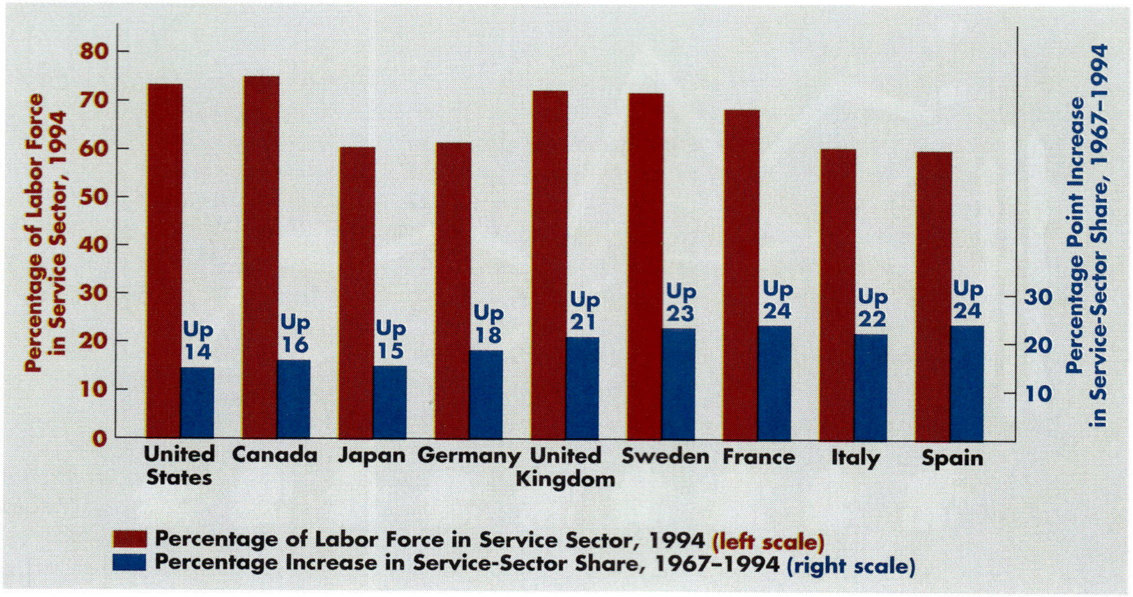

The brown bars show how much of the labor force works in the service sector in the corresponding industrial countries. The blue bars indicate how much shares have increased in percentage points since 1967. The graph demonstrates that the United States is hardly the only country in which the proportion of labor employed in the services has been rising. Indeed, the shares of service-sector jobs have grown far more rapidly in many other countries.

SOURCE: Organization for Economic Cooperation and Development, *Labour Force Statistics, 1970–1990,* Paris: OECD, 1992; and *Quarterly Labour Force Statistics,* Number 1, 1995.

story, oversimplified, asserts that slow productivity growth in manufacturing allows other countries to steal our industrial markets away.

At first glance, the data seem to confirm this. Between 1967 and 1994 the share of the U.S. labor force engaged in industry fell about 12 percentage points, while that in the services rose by about 14 percentage points, just as the deindustrialization thesis asserts. (The difference between these two numbers is accounted for by a 2-percentage-point fall in the share of labor in agriculture.) But, as shown by the blue bars in Figure 20-6, the story breaks down when we seek to identify the countries that have supposedly stolen our industrial markets. The data, for nine leading industrial countries, show that *every* country in the sample has increased the share of its labor force in the services *by a greater percentage than ours.* Which country, then, was "industrialized" by the "deindustrialization" of the United States? Or are all industrial nations becoming service economies and, if so, why?

It turns out that there is a straightforward answer in which productivity plays a key role; but it is very different from the deindustrialization parable. The simple explanation is that throughout the industrial world productivity in manufacturing has grown considerably faster than it has in most services. For example, productivity has grown far faster in automobile manufacturing than in selling real estate. This means that, though manufacturing outputs have grown, less and less of each nation's labor force has been needed to produce them, just as had happened previously in agriculture. So a declining share of each nation's

FIGURE 20-7

SHARES OF WORLD INDUSTRIAL EMPLOYMENT, 1962–1993

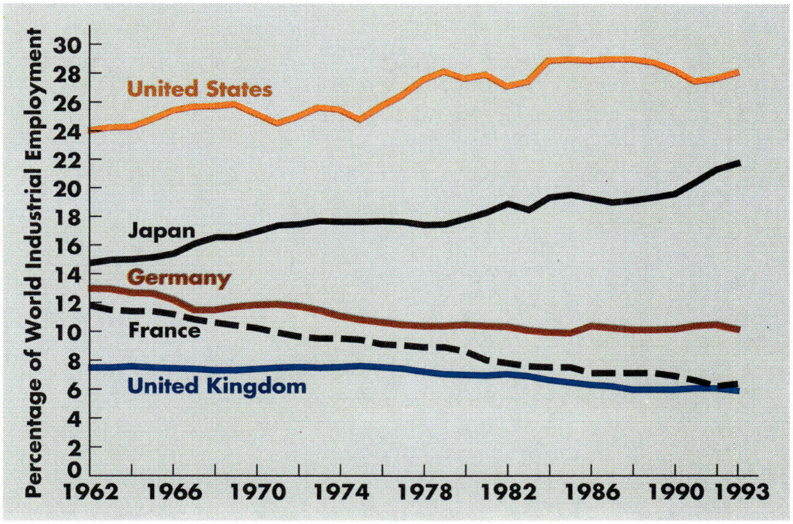

The graph shows that over the 31 years for which the data are available, Japan has steadily gained a larger share of the world's industrial jobs. But the U.S. share also rose significantly, at the expense of France, Germany, and the United Kingdom.

Note: World industrial employment here encompasses the 25 member countries of the OECD, which includes the bulk of the free-market, industrial economies of the world.

SOURCE: Organization for Economic Cooperation and Development, *Indicators of Industrial Activity*, various issues; and *Labour Force Statistics*, various issues.

jobs has been provided in the manufacturing sector just as, in earlier decades, a falling portion of the nation's jobs was provided by agriculture.

Thus, the growing share of service workers in U.S. employment is not attributable to lack of competitiveness of U.S. manufacturers. On the contrary, between 1962 and 1993 the U.S. share of the total industrial employment of the world's 25 most industrialized economies actually *increased* about 4 percentage points. (See Figure 20-7, which shows the nearly parallel growth of the U.S. and Japanese shares of world industrial jobs.) That is hardly a picture of faltering competitiveness in our manufacturing sector.

UNEMPLOYMENT AND PRODUCTIVITY GROWTH

Popular discussions of productivity growth often warn that rapid increases in labor productivity are not as beneficial as they are cracked up to be. We are told that each gain in productivity reduces the demand for labor because it means that fewer work-hours are needed to produce a given output. As a result, according to this view, productivity growth allegedly creates unemployment. Second, and perhaps somewhat inconsistently, it is argued that if an economy's productivity growth lags behind that of other countries, it will lose jobs to foreign workers, its industry will suffer, and its exports will fall. However, the data do not support either of these conclusions, at least for the long run.

If the specter of growing long-run unemployment were a reality, we would expect that the enormous increases in output per labor hour in the United States, Great Britain, and Germany since 1870 would have had devastating effects on the demand for labor in these countries. After all, with productivity rising almost 13-fold in the United States during the last century, output per capita could have been kept about constant if employment were cut to one-thirteenth of its initial share of the U.S. population. Even with a 50 percent fall in the number of hours an average person works per year, we might expect unemployment of perhaps five-sixths of the U.S. labor force by now.

In fact, nothing of the sort has happened. Unemployment rates for Great Britain, the United States, and Germany going back to the 1870s indicate that over this long period there was no upsurge in unemployment. Before 1914, unemployment in the three countries averaged about 4 percent of the labor force, while in the 1952 to 1973 period it averaged a bit more than 3 percent. Even though there has been a rise in unemployment throughout the industrial world recently, much of it is attributable to short-term influences and reorientation of public policy away from government intervention to reduce unemployment.

How have we maintained employment in the face of rising productivity? The answer, of course, is that output per capita has not remained constant. The demand for consumer goods and services, schools, hospitals, and factories has expanded explosively as productivity growth increased the purchasing power in the hands of the American public. That has sufficed to prevent any long-term increase in unemployment.

THE REAL COSTS OF LAGGING PRODUCTIVITY: LAGGING WAGES AND LIVING STANDARDS

As we have just seen, lagging productivity does not lead to a long-term rise in unemployment. For example, Great Britain, the most noted laggard in productivity growth among industrialized countries, has not suffered from unemployment problems markedly more serious than other countries'. In addition, its exports of goods and services have increased and its share of employment in manufacturing has pretty well kept up with other countries. These observations may make one wonder how Britain was able to score these apparent successes despite its comparatively poor productivity performance.

The secret, which also shows the true price Britain has paid, is found in its lagging real wages. In the 19th century, British workers were the best paid in Europe. According to one estimate, which admittedly is not very reliable, around 1860 an English worker's wages permitted the purchase of about 2 and 1/2 times as many goods and services as a German worker's. Yet by the end of the 1980s, the purchasing power of a German worker's wages was almost twice as great as that of a British worker's wages. In other words, in a little more than a century the relative position of workers in the two countries had almost been reversed.

How do lagging British wages relate to its productivity lag? The answer is straightforward. If Britain cannot compete on world markets by virtue of growing efficiency (productivity), it still can sell its products by providing cheap British labor. Of course, Britain does not volunteer to adopt low real wages; rather, market forces make it happen automatically, because inefficiently produced goods cannot be sold on the international marketplace unless those goods are produced by cheaper inputs. Hence, the invisible hand forces British wages to lag. Labor simply cannot extract higher wages from an economy that has little to offer.

A country with lagging productivity is likely to be condemned to become an exporter of cheap labor. That is the only way it can keep its industry viable, maintain its exports, and preserve domestic jobs. This is the real danger that the United States faces if its productivity performance is unsatisfactory for any substantial period of time.

The costs of failure in this arena are very high. Above all, lagging productivity growth must slow or bring to an end the rising living standards and rising real wages which have so long been a prime accomplishment of the U.S. economy. If there is no rise in output per worker, then it will be impossible to keep increasing the quantity of goods and services provided to each consumer. Indeed, something of the sort has already happened. Since about the beginning of the 1970s, the growth in the purchasing power of an average American worker's hourly wage has fallen far behind its previous pace.

While U.S. productivity growth continues, as we have seen since the 1970s it has been below its historical rate.

REQUIREMENTS FOR INCREASED GROWTH

What can be done to increase the growth rate of production in an economy? Unfortunately, no one has a handy list of sure-fire recipes.

Growth can be attributed to a number of factors that no one knows how to explain: (1) *inventiveness,* which produces the new technology and other innovations that have contributed so much to economic expansion; (2) *entrepreneurship,* the leadership that recognizes no obstacles and undertakes the daring industrial ventures needed to move the economy ahead; and (3) *the work ethic* that leads a work force to high levels of productivity. No one really knows what features of economic organization and social psychology actually lead a community to adopt these goals, as Great Britain is said to have done at the beginning of the 19th century, as the United States is reputed to have done in the first half of the 20th century, and as some east Asia countries are apparently doing today. We do know, however, that growth requires two things that people can influence directly: a large expenditure on *capital equipment* and the devotion of considerable effort to *research and development* from which innovations are derived.

The *composition* of aggregate demand is a major determinant of the rate of economic growth. If a larger fraction of total spending goes toward investment rather than toward consumption, government purchases, or net exports, the capital stock will grow faster and the aggregate supply schedule will shift more quickly to the right.

Figure 20-8 shows, for a set of 20 countries on 4 continents, how investment in one period (in this case, 1973) is related to subsequent growth (from 1973 to

FIGURE 20-8

GROWTH AND INVESTMENT, 20 COUNTRIES

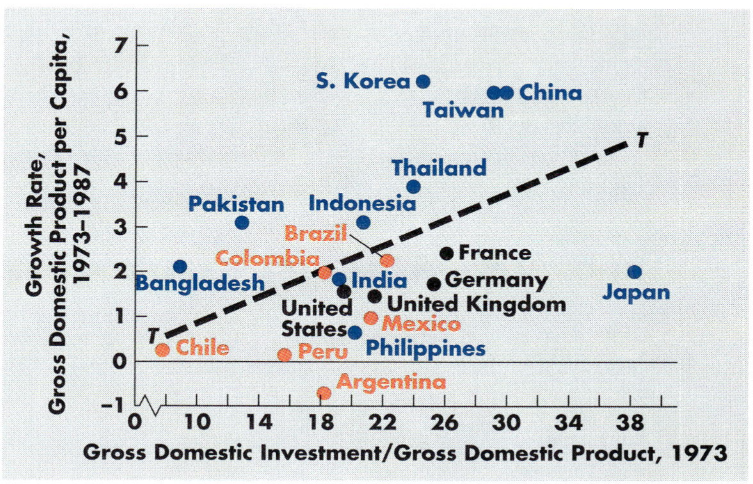

The graph shows, for 20 countries, how investment in 1973 was related to subsequent growth in per-capita GDP (1973 to 1987). The positive slope of the "trend line," *TT,* means that higher investment rates are associated with more rapid growth rates.

SOURCE: Angus Maddison, *The World Economy in the 20th Century* (Paris: Organization for Economic Cooperation and Development, 1989).

1987) in per-capita output. The graph confirms that the share of an economy's output devoted to investment does not, *by itself*, determine future growth. But higher investment rates clearly *are* associated with more rapid subsequent growth.

GROWTH WITHOUT SACRIFICING CONSUMPTION: SOMETHING FOR NOTHING?

We learned in Chapter 3 that the decision to invest involves a trade-off. By choosing to devote resources to future needs rather than current consumption, a society can achieve economic growth. In other words, through saving, the public gives up some consumption, which is the price it must pay for the accumulation of plant, equipment, and infrastructure. But while a substantial proportion of growth is embodied in these increased quantities of plant, equipment, and infrastructure, a very large proportion of the economy's growth is *disembodied*. That is, it is attributable to better ideas—to improved methods of finding and using the same quantities of resources. Everyone knows that this has in fact occurred. From the invention of the steam engine to that of the modern computer, our economy has benefited from a stream of inventions—some sensational, some more routine—which together have increased enormously the productivity of the nation's resources.

Embodied growth has two serious costs that disembodied growth avoids. First, embodied growth necessarily speeds up the use of society's depletable resources: its iron ore, its petroleum supplies, and its stocks of other minerals and fuels. Second, the greater the quantity of resources used in the productive process, the greater the quantity of wastes that must ultimately result.

So far, we have enjoyed substantial success in our efforts to achieve growth in output without commensurate increases in our use of resources. One statistical analysis, for example, attributes only about half of the growth in the United States to increased use of physical inputs. The remainder must be ascribed to improvements in technology as well as to increased education and skill of the labor force.[11]

One final remark on disembodied growth is in order. Economists are fond of pointing out that there is no such thing as a free lunch. Except in rare instances, improvements in technology are not "manna from heaven." They result, instead, from the work of scientists and technicians in government and industrial laboratories, from the labor of inventors in their basements or garages, and from the effort of management specialists studying the organization of factories and assembly lines. This means that labor (along with other resources) is diverted from other activities into the production of knowledge. *In a fully employed economy, the opportunity costs of investing in the discovery of new knowledge are the forgone consumption and physical investment of goods that would otherwise have been produced.* So even here, we cannot quite get something for nothing.

ON GROWTH IN POPULATION: IS LESS REALLY MORE?

We have just discussed some of the ways in which growth can be stimulated. There are also influences that impede growth. Many observers believe that

[11]Edward F. Denison, *Accounting for United States Economic Growth 1929–1969* (Washington, D.C.: The Brookings Institution, 1974).

expansion in population is one of the main obstacles to growth in per-capita income. Even though an expanding population means a rising labor force, there are reasons why output cannot keep up. Indeed, as we will see, there are reasons to believe that continuation of the rate of population growth of the past century is literally impossible.

The problem was first brought to the public's attention in 1798, when the Reverend Thomas R. Malthus (who was to become England's first professor of political economy) published *An Essay on the Principle of Population*. This book, which had a profound effect on attitudes toward population, argued that sexual drives and other influences induce people to reproduce themselves as rapidly as their means permit. Unfortunately, he said, when the number of humans increases, the production of food and other consumption goods generally cannot keep up.

The problem is the noted *law of diminishing returns* to additional labor using a fixed supply of land. This states that if we use more and more labor to cultivate a fixed stock of land, we will eventually reach a point at which each additional laborer will contribute less additional output than the previous laborer. Ultimately, as the labor force increases, output per worker will decline.

Malthus and his followers concluded that the tendency of humankind to reproduce itself must constantly exert pressure on the economy to keep living standards from rising. Wages will gravitate toward some minimal subsistence level—the lowest income on which people are willing to marry and raise a family. If wages are above subsistence, the population can and will grow. Thus, a wage that is above subsistence will set forces into motion that will drive wages down toward subsistence because of diminishing returns.

Sometimes, according to Malthus, the population will grow beyond the capability of the economy to support it. Then the number of people will be brought back into line by means that are far more unpleasant than a decrease in wages—by starvation and disease or by wars that produce the required number of casualties.

Later, in the 19th century and the first half of the 20th century, the gloomy Malthusian vision seemed to lose credibility. New technology and improved agricultural practices generally enabled the output of food and other agricultural products to increase faster than the population (at least in the wealthier, industrialized nations). In addition, it turned out that as living standards rose, people became less anxious to reproduce, and so the expansion of population slowed substantially. Figure 20-9 illustrates this trend in the United States for more than a century and a half. All in all, it began to look as though population growth constituted no significant threat—it was something with which human technological skills and ingenuity could cope.

More recently, however, there has been renewed concern over population. With improvements in medicine—notably, improved hygiene in hospitals, the use of such public-health measures as swamp drainage, insecticide spraying, inexpensive vaccination programs, and the discovery of antibiotics—death rates have plunged in the developing countries, especially for infants. At the same time, birth-control programs in most of these countries have, at least until quite recently, not been very successful. As a result, the populations of developing countries have continued to expand dramatically, eating up a good proportion of any output increases obtained through their governments' economic development programs. It has been widely concluded that significant improvement in living standards in the developing areas is impossible without substantial reductions in their population growth. But the "neo-Malthusians" go further than this, arguing that a rapid approach to birthrates so low that populations cease

FIGURE 20-9 AMERICAN BIRTHRATES, 1820–1995

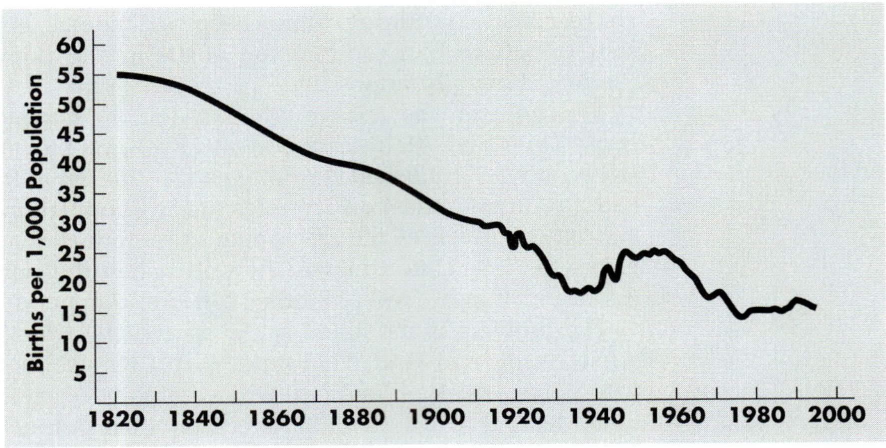

This chart shows that birthrates in the United States have generally been declining since 1820.

SOURCE: U.S. Bureau of the Census, *Historical Statistics of the United States, Colonial Times to 1970, Part I* (Washington, D.C.: U.S. Government Printing Office, 1975); and U.S. Bureau of the Census, *Statistical Abstract of the United States* (Washington, D.C.: U.S. Government Printing Office, various editions).

expanding—that is, to *zero population growth*—is virtually a matter of life and death even for the most prosperous nations. It is illuminating to consider the logic of their argument.

THE CROWDED PLANET: EXPONENTIAL POPULATION GROWTH

Malthus used an argument that has caught many imaginations ever since:

> Population, when unchecked, increases in a geometrical ratio. Subsistence increases only in an arithmetical ratio. A slight acquaintance with numbers will shew the immensity of the first power in comparison of the second.[12]

EXPONENTIAL GROWTH is growth at a constant percentage rate.

In modern discussions, such a "geometric" growth pattern is referred to as **exponential growth,** "compounded growth," or "snowballing." Exponential growth is growth at a constant *percentage rate.* For example, at a 10 percent growth rate, a population of 100 persons will increase by 10 persons a year; but a population of a million persons will increase by 100,000 persons a year. The bigger the population, the more it will add annually. And each year's growth implies still faster growth in the following year. It is like a snowball rolling downhill, accumulating more snow the bigger it gets, thus expanding faster and faster all the time.

If the population doubles (grows 100 percent) in 35 years, it will quadruple (grow another 100 percent) in 70 years, increase 8-fold in 105 years, 16-fold in 140 years, and so on indefinitely. The doubling sequence 2, 4, 8, 16, 32, 64, and so on, is the basic pattern of exponential growth. Figure 20-10 shows how astronomical such a growth sequence is. Projecting the world's population 175 years into the future on the assumption that population will grow exponentially at about its current rate, the graph shows that by the year 2165 the population will exceed 90 billion—nearly 20 times as many people as there are today.

It turns out that in describing the consequences of exponential growth, Malthus was conservative. He did not begin to spell out the wonders and the

[12]Thomas R. Malthus, *An Essay on the Principle of Population* (New York: W. W. Norton, 1976).

FIGURE 20-10 PROJECTED GROWTH OF THE WORLD'S POPULATION IN 175 YEARS AT CURRENT RATE OF GROWTH

This figure shows the sensational acceleration of population growth *if* population expands exponentially.

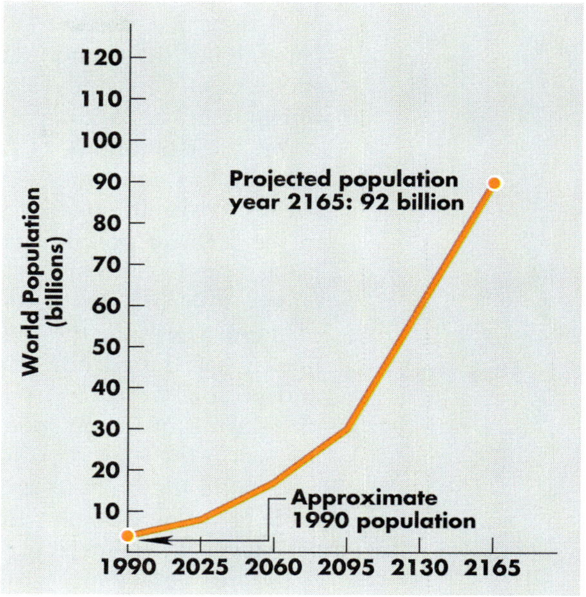

horrors that his premise implied. Consider some calculations by one leading authority on population (who derived his conclusions simply by carrying through the arithmetic of exponential growth rates):

- If population were to grow at today's rates for another 600–700 years, every square foot of the surface of the earth would contain a human being;
- If it were to expand at the same rate for 1,200 years, the combined weight of the human population would exceed that of the earth itself;
- If that growth rate were to go on for 6,000 years (a very short period of time in terms of biological history), the globe would constitute a sphere whose diameter was growing with the speed of light.[13]

And none of this is conjecture. It is *sure* to come about *if* the present (exponential) rate of growth of the earth's population continues unabated.

Of course, none of this can really happen. Our finite earth just does not have room for that sort of expansion. If the number of humans continues to swell until it presses upon the earth's capacity, the process will ultimately be brought to a halt in a Malthusian apocalypse. Disease, famine, and war must finally put a stop to the expansion process. But there is a better alternative. People can choose to stop raising large families. And it can be done. Even in the developing nations, as we will see later in this chapter, the birthrate has recently been declining.

IS MORE GROWTH REALLY BETTER?

Many have questioned the desirability of faster economic growth as an end in itself, at least in the wealthier industrialized countries. Yet faster growth does

[13]Ansley J. Coale, "Man and His Environment," *Science*, vol. 179 (October 9, 1970), pp. 132–136. Copyright 1970 by the American Association for the Advancement of Science.

mean more wealth, and to most people the desirability of wealth is beyond question. "I've been rich and I've been poor—and I can tell you, rich is better," a noted stage personality is said to have told an interviewer. Most people seem to have the same attitude about the economy as a whole. To those who hold this belief, a healthy economy is one that is capable of turning out vast quantities of shoes, food, cars, and TV sets. An economy whose capacity to provide all these things is not expanding is said to have succumbed to the disease of *stagnation*.

Yet the desirability of further economic growth for a society that is already wealthy has been questioned on reasonable grounds. It is pointed out that the sheer increase in quantity of products has imposed an enormous cost on society in the form of pollution, crowding, and proliferation of wastes that need disposal; some economists claim it has had unfortunate psychological and social effects. It is said that industry has transformed the satisfying and creative tasks of the artisan into the mechanical and dehumanizing routine of the assembly line. It has dotted our roadsides with junkyards, filled our air with pollution, and poisoned our food with dangerous chemicals. The question is whether the outpouring of frozen foods, talking dolls, CD players, and headache remedies are worth the high costs to society.

Despite the costs of growth in terms of human and environmental damage, there is strong evidence that if the economy's total output were kept at its present level, the community would pay a high price over and above the loss of additional goods and services.

First, it is not easy to carry out a decision to prevent further economic growth. Mandatory controls are abhorrent to most Americans. We cannot *order* people to stop inventing means to expand productivity. Nor does it make any sense to order every firm and industry to freeze its output level, since changing tastes and needs require some industries to expand their outputs at the same time that others are contracting. But who is to decide which should grow and which should contract, and how shall such decisions be made?

Second, without continued growth it will be no easy matter to finance effective programs to improve the quality of life—programs such as environmental protection. To improve the purity of our air and water and to clean up urban neighborhoods, tens of billions of dollars must be made available every year. Continued growth can permit the required resources to be provided without any reduction in consumer goods. But without such growth, we may actually be forced to cut back on our programs to protect the environment. Society could thus end up with fewer goods and a worse environment.

Finally, zero economic growth may seriously hamper efforts to eliminate poverty both within our economy and throughout the world. Much of the earth's population today lives in a state of extreme want. And though wealthier nations have been reluctant to provide more than token amounts of help to the less developed countries, less wealth means there would be even less to share. So the best hope for improved living standards in the impoverished countries of Africa, Asia, and Latin America lies in continued increases in output.

PART 2: PROBLEMS OF THE LESS DEVELOPED COUNTRIES

A substantial proportion of the world's population lives in areas whose average per-capita GDP is $4,000 or less per year, evaluated (as well as is possible) in current U.S. prices. And Table 20-1 shows that there are countries in which annual per-capita GDP is less than $1,000. Even after adjustment for differences

TABLE 20-1

1995 PER-CAPITA GDP IN DEVELOPED AND LESS DEVELOPED COUNTRIES[a]

	Per-Capita GDP
Developed Countries	
United States	27,500
United Kingdom	19,500
Sweden	20,100
Less Developed Countries	
Bolivia	2,530
China	2,900
Egypt	2,760
Ethiopia	400
Haiti[b]	1,000
India	1,500
Tanzania	800

[a]Measured in U.S. dollars, using PPP exchange rates. See text footnote 6 for an explanation.

SOURCE: Central Intelligence Agency, *The World Factbook 1996* (http://www.odci.gov/cia/publications/nsolo/factbook).

in measurement of GDP in the United States and these extremely poor countries, their annual per-capita GDP figures are still under $1,500.

To us, residents of an economy that offers an average GDP more than 15 times as high as this, such a figure is not only likely to seem incredible, it is all but incomprehensible. Yet these figures do *not* represent the living standards of a small group of outcasts from their own societies. Rather, they are *typical* of many people living in Asia, Africa, and Latin America.

What is life like in such circumstances? No brief description can really bridge the gulf between us and them, but it can provide a glimpse of a way of life few of us want to share.

Inhabitants of many of the LDCs live with their large families in one-room shanties or apartments; their water supplies are scanty, polluted, and often miles from home; their only source of energy is that of human and beast; in good years sparse harvests are wrung from miserable soil, with starvation threatened perhaps every five years when the rains do not come and the crops fail. Low production permits no food reserves, and the old, the infirm, and the very young are likely to perish in famine years.

The life of a man in an LDC is hard enough, with its poor nutrition, lack of work equipment, and frequency of debilitating diseases. But his life is luxurious compared with that of a woman in these countries. She is usually married by the age of 14, bears 8 or 10 children with minimal medical assistance, and by 35 is often beset by chronic disease and aged far beyond her years. If (as is true of some 80 percent of the population) she inhabits a rural area, she may have to walk miles every day to fetch water for the family. She sews the family's clothes and cooks its meals. There is not enough money for pre-ground flour, so part of

TABLE 20-2 INFANT MORTALITY AND LIFE EXPECTANCY IN DEVELOPED AND LESS DEVELOPED COUNTRIES, 1995

	Infant Mortality (deaths per 1,000 live births)	Life Expectancy at Birth (years)	
		Males	Females
Developed Countries			
United States	8.0	72	79
Germany	5.8	73	79
Sweden	4.8	76	81
Less Developed Countries			
Bolivia	71.0	59	62
China	44.0	67	70
Egypt	62.0	62	65
Ethiopia	120.0	48	52
Haiti	74.0	55	58
India	74.0	60	60
Tanzania	92.0	47	50

SOURCE: Population Reference Bureau, Inc., *World Population Data Sheet, 1995.*

a woman's daily work is to pound the grain by hand for food for the family—perhaps an additional two hours of hard labor. She also tends the gardens that produce food for the family, although, except in Moslem countries where women are sequestered, she is also expected to put in a full day in the fields during the six months of the agricultural season.

Another duty of the woman in an LDC is to bring produce, wood, or whatever she has to trade to market a couple of times a week, and she must often walk as many as 10 miles each way with bundles as heavy as she can carry on her back or on her head. She has no respite in the raising of her children, since they are likely not to have a school to attend when they are well or a hospital to go to when they are sick. It is no wonder that she ages so much faster than a woman in our society.

Table 20-2 gives the percentage of infant deaths for each 1,000 live births and the average life expectancy of a newborn child in a sample of countries ranging from the most underdeveloped to the most affluent. The contrasts are dramatic. In Ethiopia, 120 babies die of every 1,000 that are born, while the comparable figure in Sweden is under 5. In many countries people survive only until their 40s or 50s, while in Sweden the average life expectancy is 76 years for men and 81 years for women. There is little question about the quality of life in less developed lands.

RECENT TRENDS

Despite population increases, some LDCs, particularly in the Far East, have succeeded in breaking out of the stagnation trap. In those successful economies, if growth were to continue as it was in the 1970s, an average family could look forward to a doubling of its living standards in less than 30 years. Or put another way, in earlier decades standards of living were increasing faster than they did in the United States in the 19th century!

While in the 1970s such good news applied to a number of LDCs in several parts of the world, the 1980s were not so favorable. Many of the LDCs had drastic debt problems. In addition, their per-capita incomes tended to fall behind those of the developed countries. Largely because their population growth has been faster, the percentage growth rates in per-capita incomes have been lower in the LDCs. But even if the *percentage* increases in their per-capita incomes had been similar, *absolute* incomes would have continued to rise more quickly in the richer lands. For example, where per-capita income is $100 a year, a 2.5 percent growth rate translates into a $2.50 annual improvement. However, where per-capita income is $5,000 a year, the same 2.5 percent rate of growth adds $125 a year to the income of the average person.

A few numbers will indicate how discouraging the relative performance of the LDCs as a group has been. A study of some 70 countries by a group of noted economists showed how much the disparity between the LDCs and the other two groups has been increasing.[14] The average annual growth rates of real GDP were 3.1 percent (compounded) for the industrial countries, 3.0 percent for the middle-income countries, and only 1.5 percent for the LDCs. With average growth rates half as big as those for the more affluent economies, the LDCs as a group fell further behind the rest of the world for much of the period since World War II.

IMPEDIMENTS TO DEVELOPMENT IN THE LDCs

No one has produced a definitive list of causes of the poverty of the LDCs, just as no one can pretend to have produced a foolproof prescription for its cure. Yet there is general agreement on the main conditions contributing to the economic problems of LDCs. These include a dearth of physical capital, rapid growth of populations, lack of education, unemployment, and social and political impediments to business activity. Let us consider each of these.

SCARCITY OF PHYSICAL CAPITAL

The LDCs are obviously handicapped by their lack of modern factories and machinery. In addition, they lack infrastructure—good roads, railroads, port facilities, and so on. But capital is not easy to acquire. If it is to be provided by the populations of the LDCs themselves, they must save the required resources—that is, as we noted earlier, they must give up consumption in order to free the resources needed to build plants, equipment, and roads. That is comparatively easy in a rich community, where substantial saving still leaves the public well off in terms of current consumption. But in an LDC, where malnutrition is a constant threat, the bulk of the inhabitants cannot save except at enormous sacrifice

[14]Robert Summers, Irving B. Kravis, and Alan Heston, "Changes in World Income Distribution," *Journal of Policy Modeling*, vol. 6 (May 1986), pp. 237–269.

to their families. Moreover, in many of the LDCs, tradition imputes little virtue to investment in business, so that even the wealthy are not terribly anxious to put their savings into productive equipment. Thus:

Because poverty makes saving difficult and traditions often do not encourage investment, the LDCs' growth rates of domestically financed capital are lower than those in the developed countries.

One way to help matters is to obtain the funds for investment from abroad. In recent decades a considerable share of the resources going to the LDCs has come from foreign aid programs. While some such resources have been squandered, informed observers generally agree that the waste has not been spectacularly great. They conclude that these capital transfers from the rich countries to the poor are a step in the right direction.

Capital can also be transferred to an LDC when a private firm invests money to build a factory or to explore for oil. This increases the firm's profits and benefits the LDC. In earlier days, it sometimes gave an unacceptable degree of political influence to the foreign firms, particularly when the LDC was a colony of an industrial country. In recent years this difficulty may have become more rare. Nowadays, it is more often the outside firm that is afraid of the government of the LDC rather than vice versa. Foreign proprietors frequently fear rigid governmental controls. Another fear is outright expropriation—where the LDC's government simply takes over the foreign firm's property, with or even without compensation, because of the hostile attitudes that local residents may hold toward large foreign companies.

POPULATION GROWTH

Population growth is often described as the primary villain in the LDCs. We have already noted that their populations grow far more rapidly than those in the wealthier countries. And although growth rates have recently been declining in many of the less developed countries, overall, the population of the LDCs is expanding at a rate that will double in less than 30 years, requiring a doubling of housing, schools, hospitals, and so on—a heavy real cost for an LDC.

Table 20-3 tells the story. For the LDCs shown, the average annual growth rate of population is 10 times the average rate of the industrialized countries. Clearly, the more closely the growth in population approximates the growth in national income, the more slowly standards of living will rise, since there will be that many more persons among whom the additional product must be divided.

As we noted earlier, the growth in population has been stimulated by improvements in medical care, which have reduced death rates spectacularly. Today, in some areas, death rates (ratio of deaths to population) are only one-quarter or one-fifth as high as birthrates. In the past it was not unusual for half of a nation's children to die before the age of 20. In many countries today this is true of only some 4 percent of the population.

Not all LDCs suffer from serious population problems such as those that plague India, Indonesia, and Egypt. In fact, many countries in Africa and Latin America have populations so small that they are denied economies of larger-scale communication and transportation. The economy of a sparsely settled country whose electric power and telecommunication lines must traverse great unpopulated areas is under a costly handicap.

Governments in a number of LDCs have been struggling to find workable ways to cut population growth. Programs set up to distribute contraceptives and propaganda against large families have achieved modest success; but in some

TABLE 20-3

NATURAL INCREASE IN POPULATION
(BIRTHRATE MINUS DEATH RATE)
IN DEVELOPED AND LESS DEVELOPED COUNTRIES, 1995

	Births Minus Deaths (as percentage of population)
Developed Countries	
United States	0.7
Germany	−0.1
Sweden	0.1
Less Developed Countries	
Bolivia	2.6
China	1.1
Egypt	2.3
Ethiopia	3.1
Haiti	2.3
India	1.9
Tanzania	3.0

SOURCE: Population Reference Bureau, Inc., *World Population Data Sheet, 1995.*

countries with particularly severe population problems the governments have been dissatisfied with the results of these voluntary efforts and have opted instead for compulsory sterilization. This has aroused the anger of the public and in some cases has led to the downfall of the governments.

EDUCATIONAL AND TECHNICAL TRAINING

Everyone knows that educational levels in the LDCs are much lower than those in wealthier countries. There are fewer graduates of elementary schools, far fewer graduates of high schools, and enormously fewer college graduates. The percentage of the population that is literate is much lower than that in industrialized nations. The issue is how much of a handicap this constitutes for economic growth.

The evidence is that general education, as distinguished from technical (trade) schooling, makes considerably less difference for economic growth than is often believed. For example, the number of jobs that clearly require secondary (high school) education rarely exceeds 10 percent of the labor force. Various studies that have investigated whether there is a statistical relationship between the economic growth of an economy and its typical educational level have found only weak correlations between the two.

This is not meant to imply that education is worthless. On the contrary, it obviously offers many inherent benefits, which need not be discussed here. But it does suggest that if a government invests in education *purely as a means to stimulate economic growth,* only a very limited outlay on *general* education beyond the achievement of literacy may be justifiable.

Matters are quite different when we turn to technical training. There is apparently a high payoff to the training of electricians, machinists, draftsmen, construction workers, and the like. While the number of persons involved need not be very high in proportion to the population, the role played by such specialists is crucial. One of the main inhibitions to adequate training in these areas is that in many countries such skills are held in low esteem and considered inferior to training in the liberal arts. Consequently, technical education is often handicapped by low budgets, low teacher salaries—which discourage good people from entering the field—and the prejudice of potential students against such fields.

Training in improved farming methods also has a great deal to contribute. As one leading observer, the late Nobel Prize-winner Sir W. Arthur Lewis, remarked, ". . . no impact can be made on mass [LDC] living standards without revolutionizing agricultural performance."[15] There seem to be no easy ways to provide the necessary education to farmers who cannot spare the time to attend schools. Religious beliefs often lead parents to object to schooling of their children, particularly of girls; truly literate and knowledgeable teachers are often almost impossible to find in any substantial numbers; and children who do complete schooling often leave the farms for the cities.

UNEMPLOYMENT

Growth in the LDCs has been accompanied by increased unemployment as population has shifted from agriculture to the cities. Increased schooling has stimulated this migration, as has unionization, which has often produced a huge gap between urban and rural wages. Government investment policies have also favored construction of schools, hospitals, and other facilities in the cities, and as a result, large numbers of migrants have entered the cities to swell the ranks of the unemployed. The unemployment rate among young, urban workers has been particularly high; indeed, rates as high as 50 percent are not unheard of.

These figures are compounded by the phenomenon of *disguised unemployment*. For example, ten persons may do a job for which only six are needed. The statistics would show no unemployment among the ten workers, even though four of them really contribute nothing to output. Some observers believe that this is such a widespread problem in rural areas that even a substantial reverse migration of the urban unemployed back to the farms would add very little to production, at least in some of the LDCs.

An important consequence of all this is that in many LDCs unemployment may not be accompanied by any substantial reduction in output, in contrast to the situation in industrialized economies. But unemployment in the LDCs is a serious social problem.

SOCIAL IMPEDIMENTS TO ENTREPRENEURSHIP

As we noted earlier in this chapter, one of the magic ingredients of economic growth is *entrepreneurship*. It is clear that the LDCs need entrepreneurs if their economies are to grow rapidly. But in many of these economies there are serious inhibitions to entrepreneurship. Traditional social values often accord relatively low status to business activity. Indeed, those traditional values even prevent businesses from seeking ways to attract and please their customers and their

---

[15] W. Arthur Lewis, *Development Economics: An Outline* (Morristown, N.J.: General Learning Press, 1974), p. 25.

work forces. In addition, high positions in business in many LDCs are often determined by family connections and inheritance, not by ability.

In the LDCs, growth will be inhibited until customs can be modified to increase the social status of economic activity, to make it respectable for private business people and managers of public enterprises to do their best to attract business and increase productivity, and to assign responsibility on the basis of ability rather than family connections.

GOVERNMENT INHIBITION OF BUSINESS ACTIVITY

In addition to social impediments to business, the political situation in the LDCs often is detrimental to business success. Business is not helped by unstable governments or by the uncertainty that accompanies such an environment, especially if there is a high likelihood of revolution or internal warfare. Foreign investment will be discouraged where there is fear of expropriation or of unstable currencies that may fall in value and wipe out hard-earned profits. And indigenous business people may live in fear of nationalization or even imprisonment—possibilities that are not likely to encourage investment.

In the normal course of events, governments in the LDCs are often inclined to interfere with business activity in a variety of ways that seem relatively innocuous—but whose effects can be deadly. Price controls are often imposed at levels that make the controlled activity totally unprofitable and cause it to wither. Licenses and other direct controls are frequently administered by incompetent bureaucrats who tie up business activity in red tape. As a matter of prestige of the currency, exchange rates are often set so high that exports from the LDC cannot compete on the world market. The governments sometimes expropriate and seek to operate foreign firms before they have trained native personnel to run them. In short:

Poorly conceived economic policies can impede business activity and hence economic growth in the LDCs. But, then, it must be admitted that the LDCs have no monopoly on foolish economic policies!

HELP FROM INDUSTRIALIZED ECONOMIES

We have just seen that the two primary needs of the LDCs are technical skills and capital resources. Happily, these are precisely the things that the more prosperous nations are in a position to offer. We have the trained teachers, classrooms, laboratories, and equipment necessary to provide an education of the highest quality to students from the LDCs. However, there is a danger here that has received a great deal of attention, the so-called *brain drain*. This refers to the temptation for students from LDCs to try to stay in the countries where they have studied and enjoy the higher living standards, rather than to return home where their abilities are needed so badly.

There are several ways to deal with this. For example, one can require students to return to their homelands for at least some number of years after completion of the educational program or offer higher wages as an incentive for trained persons from the LDCs to return. The large number of doctors, teachers, and other skilled personnel from LDCs who are seeking jobs in the developed countries suggests that this is not a negligible problem.

A second major contribution that the wealthier countries can make to the LDCs is to supply them with trained technicians and technical advice from their own populations. Such counseling and personnel can be very helpful as a temporary measure, but in the long run can prove detrimental if provision for the training of local personnel for the ultimate replacement of the foreign technicians and advisers is not built into the program.

Third, the world can help the LDCs through research. One of the hardest problems in heavily populated rural areas of Asia and Africa is what to do about persistent drought. New dry-farming techniques are badly needed and until some are discovered, poverty will increase as the population grows. An international research organization devoted to food production in problem areas in the LDCs would have much to contribute.

Fourth, the developed countries can help by encouraging freedom of trade and investment and the elimination of trade barriers. Exports of sugar, meat, cotton, and other agricultural products are inhibited by industrialized countries' tariffs and other restrictions. LDCs would also benefit substantially from a lifting of tariffs and quotas upon imports into industrial countries of processed or manufactured goods. Such restrictive measures make it difficult for LDCs to export anything but raw materials and impede their industrialization and modernization. All in all, increased freedom of trade is a top priority for the LDCs. It will probably also prove beneficial to the wealthier countries, as improved incomes in the LDCs make the latter better customers for the exports of the former.[16]

A last, and very important, type of assistance from the developed to the less developed countries takes the form of money or physical resources provided either as loans made on favorable terms or as outright grants (gifts).

LOANS AND GRANTS BY THE UNITED STATES AND OTHERS

Since World War II a number of countries have provided capital to the LDCs. The International Bank for Reconstruction and Development (which, along with a closely related institution, the International Development Association, makes up the *World Bank*) was created largely for this purpose. It has 177 member countries, each providing an amount of capital related to its wealth; for instance, the United States has contributed about 20 percent of the total, while Japan and Germany have supplied 14 percent and 11 percent, respectively. The bank makes loans that finance its bonds and has acted as guarantor of repayment to encourage some private lending. Since its inception the bank has approved loans totaling $333.8 billion to 162 countries, mostly for infrastructure, dams, communications, and transportation. In addition, it has provided technical assistance and planning advice.[17]

United States loans and grants have exceeded the total given by all other countries and international agencies, with U.S. interest and repayment terms generally far more generous than those of other governments. However, the bulk

---

[16]Not everyone agrees with this conclusion. There are those who have argued that it is bad for LDCs to participate in international trade because it weakens their capacity to develop as self-reliant, mature economies. It is believed that new manufacturing industries in the LDCs will not take off without protection from foreign competition, that development of raw material exports creates a politically powerful vested interest that inhibits manufacturing, and that foreign participation in trade and production of exports inhibits domestic investment and the development of local entrepreneurship.

In this view, LDCs are therefore held back by international trade and they would do better to integrate regionally and develop their own home markets without foreigners, who also bring unsuitable habits, tastes, and technology and impart crippling inferiority complexes to the LDCs.

[17]World Bank, *The World Bank Annual Report 1994* (Washington, D.C., 1994).

of the assistance provided by the United States has gone to a small number of countries, such as India, Pakistan, South Korea, and Turkey.

During the 1960s, our expenditures on aid ran to more than $3 billion per year. In the past decade, expenditures on foreign aid have become less popular politically and have gone down from about 0.5 percent of U.S. GDP in 1965 to about 0.3 percent of GDP in 1992.[18] France, Great Britain, Germany, Japan, and other industrialized countries now provide approximately $70 billion per year, which is about 1.0 percent of their combined GDPs.

Many economists have advocated greater generosity in our assistance to LDCs. It is argued that, by making those countries more stable economically and politically, we can contribute to our own economic tranquility. By increasing the LDCs' power to buy and sell, we contribute to the prosperity of the entire world.

CAN LDCs BREAK AWAY FROM POVERTY?

It is easy to jump to the conclusion that the economic problems of the LDCs are staggering and that the prospects of their ever catching up with the industrialized countries are negligible. Yet a number of LDCs and former LDCs have made enormous progress. In Africa, Nigeria, Senegal, and Ghana increased their GDPs during the late 1980s at a rate of about 5 to 6 percent a year, which is considerably faster than their population growth. In the Americas, Costa Rica's performance has been comparable. Even more striking is the expansion of output in a number of places in the Far East—particularly Hong Kong, Taiwan, South Korea, and Singapore, where prosperity is unprecedented and economic activity is expanding at an astonishing rate. Here, per-capita GDPs have been growing at a rate of 6 percent a year and more. These economies have progressed to a point that makes it inappropriate to continue to classify them as LDCs.

But the most impressive case is that of Japan. Many of your professors will remember clearly when U.S. business feared the flood of goods produced by cheap Japanese labor, and when the label "made in Japan" suggested inexpensive and shoddy merchandise. From one of the world's impoverished countries, Japan has risen to one of the world's richest. Its goods are now feared by American manufacturers not because they are produced and sold so cheaply, but because their quality is so high. Japanese cars and sophisticated electronic equipment find a ready market in the United States. And as a result, per-capita income in Japan has surpassed that in Great Britain.

Clearly, a less developed country need not lag behind forever.

[18]Bureau of the Census, *Statistical Abstract of the United States, 1995,* 115th ed. (Washington, D.C.: U.S. Government Printing Office, 1995), pp. 451 and 810.

SUMMARY

1. Productivity growth over the past century has made a tremendous contribution to *standards of living*. Real U.S. per-capita income is more than 9 times as large as it was in 1870. Never in previous history have economic conditions improved so much.
2. For the first time in history, famine is no longer a constant threat in the world's industrialized countries. That is because productivity in agriculture has increased greatly. In 1800 about 90 percent of the U.S. labor force was needed to feed the nation poorly. Today, less than 3 percent of the labor force works on farms and yet produces great abundance.
3. Because of compounding, over longer periods a small increase in rate of productivity growth can

make an enormous difference in the economic well-being of a nation. This is one of the **Ideas for Beyond the Final Exam.**

4. There is evidence suggesting that at least a small set of the world's leading economies are converging toward similar living standards and similar productivity levels.
5. All nations learn about new technological developments from one another. The international spread of inventions means that research in one country also benefits inhabitants in much of the rest of the world.
6. Since the 1970s, there has been a substantial slowdown in productivity growth in most industrial countries.
7. The growth of productivity in U.S. manufacturing shows no sign of a long-term slowdown.
8. The growth rate of U.S. productivity has for many decades been slower than that of a number of other industrial countries. However, at least in part, that reflects the fact that the United States is still the world's productivity leader; so that while we have much to learn from others, they have even more to learn from us.
9. The share of the U.S. labor force employed in the services has increased substantially. But so has that of every industrial, free-market economy. A major cause is probably the rapid rise of manufacturing productivity, which means that fewer workers are needed in the manufacturing sector.
10. Lagging productivity holds back real wages and per-capita incomes in a country. However, in the long run it will generally not cause unemployment or inability to export enough to pay for the nation's imports.
11. Increases in growth depend heavily on entrepreneurship, accumulation of capital equipment, and research and development.
12. Saving is necessary for the accumulation of resources with which to produce factories, machinery, and other capital equipment. Thus, saving is a critical requisite for growth, particularly in less developed countries.
13. A rapidly rising population poses a threat to growth of per-capita income.
14. On our finite planet, **exponential growth** (growth at a constant percentage rate) is, in general, impossible except for relatively brief periods of time.
15. Many observers argue that even if continued growth does not lead to catastrophically rapid depletion of resources (as some have predicted), it nevertheless has some questionable effects such as pollution and overcrowding.
16. Those who favor growth argue that without it there is no chance of ridding the world of poverty.
17. Standards of living in many *LDCs* are extremely low; per-capita incomes that are equivalent to $1,500 a year are not uncommon. Life expectancy is low and daily living is very difficult, particularly for women.
18. The gap between *per-capita* incomes in the less developed and the industrialized countries has continued to widen.
19. Growth in the LDCs is impeded by shortages of capital caused by poverty, traditions that do not encourage investment, rapid population growth, poor education, unemployment, lack of *entrepreneurship,* and government impediments to business.
20. Industrialized countries can help the LDCs by providing capital through loans and grants, by offering training and education to people from those lands, and by encouraging freedom of trade with the LDCs.
21. In the period after World War II many countries provided large amounts of money to the LDCs in the form of loans and grants.
22. Several international organizations, most notably the *World Bank,* have been organized to provide economic assistance to the LDCs.

KEY TERMS

Labor productivity
Standard of living
Exponential growth
GDP per capita
Deindustrialization
Embodied growth
Disembodied growth
Less developed countries (LDCs)
Disguised unemployment
Entrepreneurship
Brain drain
World Bank

QUESTIONS FOR REVIEW

1. Try to describe what family budgets were like 120 years ago when U.S. income per person (GDP per capita) was about one-ninth as high as it is today.
2. List some of the inventions that have increased agricultural output in the past century.
3. List some of the inventions that have increased manufacturing output in the last century.
4. List some of the new consumer products of the past century. Which of them became generally available only since World War II?
5. If growing productivity has vastly reduced the amount of labor needed to produce a given output, why has it not caused massively growing unemployment?
6. Which do you think are more similar?
   a. Production methods in a U.S. and a German factory today
   b. Production methods in a U.S. factory today and the methods used in that same U.S. factory 25 years ago
7. Which do you think has the higher total GDP, Pakistan or Luxembourg? Which has the higher per-capita GDP? In which do you think people are better off economically?
8. Suppose population grows at a constant, exponential rate and doubles every 12 years. How many times will it have grown in 36 years? How many years does it require to expand to 32 times its initial level?
9. Can you think of any innovations that permit growth without proportionate increases in use of inputs?
10. List as many undesirable consequences of growth as you can think of.
11. Are the undesirable consequences of growth more likely to be considered serious in a less developed country or in an industrialized country? Why?
12. To many families living in less developed countries, an income equivalent to $2,000 per year is considered a high standard of living. Can you make up a budget for a U.S. family of four earning $2,000 a year?
13. Explain how it is possible for the per-capita income of an LDC to grow at a faster rate than that in the United States and yet for the dollar difference between the incomes of average families in both countries to increase. Can you give a numerical example showing how this happens?
14. It has been noted that crime overlords who organize drug empires and the managements of law firms that specialize in stimulation of litigation are often, in fact, successful entrepreneurs. Discuss whether these persons contribute to the growth of their economies.

CHAPTER 21

COMPARATIVE ECONOMIC SYSTEMS: WHAT ARE THE CHOICES?

They pretend to pay us, and we pretend to work.
Polish folk definition of communism

There is no worthy alternative to the market mechanism as the method for coordinating economic activities.
Leonid Abalkin (Deputy Prime Minister of the Soviet Union, 1989)

There can be little doubt that, when the history of the late 20th century is written, the fall of communism will stand out as its defining event. For decades, the rivalry between Western capitalism and Soviet-style socialism had dominated the world's geopolitical scene. This competition had important economic, political, and military dimensions. But economic disarray in the planned socialist economies ultimately took its toll. When the end came, it came quickly. Within a few years the Iron Curtain fell, the Soviet Union disintegrated, and the economies of Eastern Europe began a painful *transition* from socialist planning to capitalist markets.

The transition process starkly illustrates that a society can in fact *choose* its economic system. In somewhat less dramatic fashion, the same thing is now going on in other parts of the world, including China, India, and parts of Latin America.

Here in the United States, we tend to take economic institutions as given and immutable. But they are not. In fact, there are many ways to practice capitalism, as the differing economic structures of Japan and Western Europe illustrate. A century ago, our country had no Social Security system, no income tax, no central bank, no antitrust laws, and hardly any labor unions. More than likely, the structure of the U.S. economy will change at least as much in the next century as it did in the last. But in which directions?

In this chapter we examine how a society might choose among *alternative economic systems.* The first parts of the chapter analyze the two major choices that every society must make: Should economic activity be organized through *markets* or by government *plan?* And should industry be *privately* or *publicly* owned? As we shall see, there are arguments on both sides of each question; so it is not surprising that different countries at different times have made different choices.

In the last sections of the chapter, we describe some of the actual choices that have been made in the contemporary world. We examine changes in Russia and in the People's Republic of China, two socialist nations that are transforming themselves in quite different ways. Then we turn to a notable example of a successful capitalist country that does things rather differently than we do: Japan. Does the United States have much to learn from the experiences of these other countries, or they from us? Read this chapter and then decide.

ECONOMIC SYSTEMS: TWO IMPORTANT DISTINCTIONS

Economic systems can be distinguished along many lines, but two are most fundamental.

The first is: *How is economic activity coordinated—by the market or by the plan?* The question does not, of course, demand an "either, or" answer. Rather the choice extends over a wide range from pure laissez-faire to rigid central planning. Society must decide which decisions it wants made in markets by individual businesses and consumers acting in their own self-interests, and which decisions it wants centrally planned so that businesses and consumers act more "in the national interest."

The second crucial distinction among economic systems concerns *who owns the means of production.* Specifically, are they privately owned by individuals or publicly owned by the state? Again, there is a wide range of choice and, to our knowledge, there are no examples of nations at either the **capitalist** extreme where all property is privately owned or at the **socialist** extreme where no private property whatever is permitted.

CAPITALISM is a method of economic organization in which private individuals own the means of production, either directly or indirectly through corporations.

SOCIALISM is a method of economic organization in which the state owns the means of production.

For example, while most industries are privately owned in the United States, a few are not. And many business owners face restrictions on what they can do with their capital. Automobile companies must comply with environmental and safety regulations. Private communication and transportation companies may have both their prices and conditions of service regulated by the government. And even in China, where large enterprises are publicly owned, anyone who can afford it can own a car, a bank account, or even a small business.

People tend to merge the two distinctions and think of capitalist economies as those with both a great deal of privately owned property *and* heavy reliance on free markets. By the same token, socialist economies typically are thought of as highly planned, as were those in the former Soviet bloc. However:

While there is an undeniable association between private ownership in a country and the degree to which it relies on markets, it is a mistake to regard these two features as equivalent. Socialism can exist with markets and capitalism can exist with rigid state planning. So, in thinking abstractly about a society's *choice* among economic systems, it is best to keep the two distinctions separate.

History holds examples of planned, capitalist economies—such as Germany under Hitler, Italy under Mussolini, and Argentina under Juan Peron. To a much lesser extent, Japan and the other "Asian tigers" have also planned their capitalist economies—apparently with great success.

We are not trying to suggest that capitalist economies are typically as heavily planned as socialist ones. In fact, they are not. But it is useful to view the choices between planning and markets and between capitalism and socialism as two choices, not one. We take them up in turn.

THE MARKET OR THE PLAN? SOME ISSUES

The choice between *planning* and reliance on *free markets* requires an understanding of just what the market accomplishes and where its strengths and weaknesses lie. Since these issues have been discussed in earlier chapters, we can review them quickly and proceed to a comparison with central planning.

What goods to produce and how much of each. In a market economy, consumers determine which goods and services will be provided, and in what quantities, by registering their dollar votes. Items that are overproduced will fall in price, while items in short supply will rise in price. These price movements act as *signals* to profit-seeking firms, which then produce more of the goods whose prices rise and less of the goods whose prices fall. This mechanism is called **consumer sovereignty.**

CONSUMER SOVEREIGNTY means that consumer preferences determine what goods shall be produced and in what amounts.

Of course, consumers are not absolute monarchs, even in market economies. Governments interfere with the price mechanism in many ways—taxing some goods and services and subsidizing others. Such interferences certainly alter the bill of goods that the economy produces. We have also learned that in the presence of externalities the price system may send out false signals, leading to inappropriate levels of output for certain commodities.

Under central planning, the bill of goods that society produces is selected by planners rather than by consumers. Which system works better? Certainly, consumer sovereignty can lead to some bizarre products, the kinds of things that social reformers find offensive: designer jeans, junk food, low-quality television programming, and the like. But few of us would prefer the old Soviet-style system, which seemed incapable of providing what people wanted. Chronic shortages of ordinary consumer goods were a consistent feature of life in Eastern Europe and the Soviet Union—and one of the major causes of discontent.

How to produce each good. In a market economy, firms choose the production technique, guided by the price system. Inputs that are in short supply will be assigned high prices by the market. This will encourage producers to use them sparingly. Other inputs whose supply is more abundant will be priced lower, which will encourage firms to use them.

Once again, the same two qualifications apply: Government taxes and subsidies alter relative prices, and externalities may make the price system malfunction. But on the whole, the market system has no serious competitor as an engine of productive efficiency, as the formerly socialist economies learned.

Planned economies can allow either plant managers or central planners to choose the production techniques. In the former Soviet Union, plant managers had little discretion—which led to monumental inefficiencies including production curtailments, poor quality, and high costs. Indeed, such problems were among the most serious weaknesses of socialist planning. The truth is that no incentive system has yet been designed that can match the profit motive of competitive firms for keeping costs down.

How income is distributed. In a market economy, the price system determines the distribution of income among individuals by setting the levels of wages, interest rates, and profits. As we have stressed, there is no reason to expect the resulting income distribution to be ethically appealing. And, in fact, the evidence shows that capitalist market economies produce sizable inequalities.

Income inequality is certainly one of capitalism's weak points. However, the government has many ways to mitigate inequality without destroying either free markets or private property (for example, through redistributive taxes and transfer payments). In practice, governments in all market economies intervene in the marketplace to alter the distribution of income.

So do governments in planned economies, only more so. For example, they may try to tamper directly with the income distribution by having planners, rather than the market, set relative wage rates. But doing so leads to shortages and surpluses of particular types of labor. So even in the former Soviet Union relative wages were established more or less by supply and demand, and there was considerable inequality in the distribution of wages.

Economic growth. The rate of economic growth depends fundamentally upon how much society decides to save and invest. In a free-market economy, these decisions are left to private firms and individuals, who determine how much of their current income they will consume today and how much they will invest for the future. Once again, however, government policies can influence these choices by, for example, making investment more or less attractive through tax incentives.

Planned economies have more direct control over their growth rates because the state can determine the volume of investment. They can therefore engineer periods of very high growth if they choose to—an option which both Stalin's Russia and Mao's China exercised successfully, though at great human cost. More recently, Singapore's planned market economy has grown rapidly by forcing individuals to save. One may wonder, however, whether rapid growth is desirable when it is paid for by loss of personal freedom, or even by bloodshed.

Furthermore, the economies of the Soviet Union and Eastern Europe turned in extremely poor growth performances in the 1970s and 1980s, while some of the fastest growth rates were recorded in the market economies of Japan, Taiwan, and Hong Kong. All told, history suggests that no other system can match market incentives for sustaining growth over long periods of time. Indeed, China has become the fastest-growing major economy on earth as it has moved away from planning toward markets (see pages 486–488).

Business fluctuations. A market economy is subject to periods of boom and bust, to inflation and unemployment. This holds true not only in capitalist market economies like the United States, but also in socialist market economies. So even though Marx dubbed the business cycle one of the fundamental flaws of *capitalism,* it is really a problem for *market economies,* be they capitalist or socialist.

Business fluctuations are not much of a problem in highly planned economies because total spending is controlled by the planners and is not permitted to get far out of line with the economy's capacity to produce. So the business cycle was not traditionally a serious problem in, say, the former Soviet Union or China. However, now that these two nations are transforming themselves into market economies, macroeconomic issues have become critical.

THE MARKET OR THE PLAN? THE SCOREBOARD

As we look back over this list, what do we find?

- Concerning *what to produce,* adherents to Western values will give a clear edge to the market, though conceding the need to curb some of its more flagrant abuses. And, apparently, this view has now swept the former Soviet bloc as well.

- As to *productive efficiency*, almost everyone now seems to recognize the superiority of the market mechanism—as the opening quotations of this chapter suggest.
- But when we consider the *distribution of income*, we find that all societies have decided to plan; they differ only in degree.
- *High growth*, it seems, can be achieved—at least temporarily—with or without planning. Here an advanced nation will pause to question whether faster is always better, especially if growth comes from hard work and forced saving rather than through technological innovation. But in the poorer nations, the goal of rapid development is typically of paramount importance. Years ago, the urgent need for growth often led these countries toward central planning. Nowadays, however, more and more of them are becoming convinced that market systems, not planning, offer the best hope for long-run growth.
- Finally, in managing *business fluctuations*, there is no question that planned economies can do much better.

The results of our scoreboard are not entirely one-sided. But they do on balance point clearly toward market solutions—which is one reason why one country after another has switched from planning to markets. In sum:

The market has both strengths and weaknesses. Different countries—with their different political systems, value judgments, traditions, and aspirations—will draw the boundaries between the plan and the market in different places. But it now appears that almost all countries believe that the market mechanism should bear the primary burden of deciding which products to produce and how best to produce them.

CAPITALISM OR SOCIALISM?

Although the choice between capitalism and socialism seems to excite more ideological fervor, many observers believe it is less important than the choice between the market and the plan.

If it could design an appropriate incentive structure, a socialist *market* economy could do just as well as a capitalist market economy in terms of producing the right set of goods in the most efficient way. However, we have emphasized the word *if* to underscore the fact that designing such an incentive system may be quite difficult under socialism, even when markets are free.

Lacking the profit motive, a socialist society must provide incentives for its plant managers to perform well. This has proved difficult enough. But a still deeper problem is the need to maintain inventiveness, innovation, and risk-taking in an ever-changing world. Socialist nations, in which large accumulations of personal wealth are impossible, are noticeably low on "high rollers." This, many people feel, is why they were left behind in the 1980s.

Income distribution under socialism is naturally more equal than under capitalism simply because the profits of industry do not go to a small group of stockholders but instead are dispersed among the workers or among the populace as a whole. However, if supply and demand rules the labor market, a socialist nation may have as much inequality in the distribution of labor income as a capitalist economy does—and for the same reasons: to attract workers into risky, or highly skilled, or difficult occupations.

The capitalist–socialist divergence is much more pronounced in regard to the issue of economic growth. To oversimplify, under capitalism it is the capitalists who determine the growth rate, while under socialism it is the state. Still, government incentives can prod capitalists to invest more; and socialist bureaucrats may squander resources on ill-advised investments. Examples of both fast and slow growth can be found under both systems.

Finally, as we have said, the severity of business fluctuations in a country depends much more on whether its economy is planned or unplanned than on whether its industries are publicly or privately owned.

SOCIALISM, PLANNING, AND FREEDOM

There is, however, a *noneconomic* aspect that is of the utmost importance in choosing between capitalism and socialism, or between the market and the plan, an issue whose importance was dramatized by the collapse of communism in Europe: *individual freedom.*

Planning must by necessity involve some degree of coercion; if it does not, then the plan may amount to little more than wishful thinking. In the extreme case of a command economy (such as Stalinist Russia or Nazi Germany), the abridgment of personal freedom is both painful and obvious. Less rigid forms of planning involve commensurately smaller infringements of individual rights, infringements that many people find tolerable.

Even in a market economy, some activities may be banned—such as prostitution and selling liquor to minors. Other economic activities may be compelled by law; safety devices in automobiles and labeling requirements on foods and drugs are two good examples. Each of these is planning of sorts, and each limits the freedom of some people. Yet most of these restrictions command broad public support in the United States.

Taxation is a still more subtle form of coercion. Many people do not view taxes as seriously impairing personal freedom because citizens remain free to choose the courses of action that suit them best. Indeed, this is one major reason why economists generally favor taxes over quotas and outright prohibitions. However, taxation can be a potent tool for changing individual behavior. As Chief Justice John Marshall pointed out with characteristic insight, "The power to tax involves the power to destroy."

Individual freedom is also involved in the choice between capitalism and socialism. After all, socialism imposes many more restrictions on what a person can do with his or her wealth. On the other hand, the poorest people in a capitalist society may find little joy in their "freedom" to go homeless and hungry.

Once again, it would be a mistake to paint the issue in black and white. Under rigid, authoritarian planning, the restrictions on individual liberties are so severe that they are probably intolerable to most people with Western values. That, presumably, is why many people in Eastern Europe reacted so strongly to the whiff of freedom. But more moderate and relaxed forms of planning—such as in some of the "Asian tigers"—seem compatible with personal freedoms.

Similarly, a doctrinaire brand of socialism that bans all private property (even the clothes on your back?) would entail a major loss of liberty. But a country with a large socialized sector can be basically free; the French, for example, do not feel notably less free than do Americans. And citizens of some countries with largely capitalist economies, such as South Korea or Taiwan, did not enjoy political freedom until quite recently.

The real question is not *whether* we want to allow elements of socialism or planning to abridge our personal freedoms, but by *how much.*

Just as your freedom to extend your arm is limited by the proximity of your neighbor's chin, the freedom to build a factory need not extend to building it in the midst of a residential neighborhood. Just as freedom of speech does not justify yelling "Fire!" in a crowded movie theater when there is no fire, freedom of enterprise does not imply the right to monopolize trade. So, not surprisingly, different societies have struck the balance between the market and the plan, and between socialism and capitalism, in different places.

Most nations of Eastern Europe and the former Soviet Union are still in the midst of a difficult transition from plan to market, and from socialism to capitalism. But we cannot hope to understand this complex process unless we first learn how the old, centrally planned system of the Soviet Union functioned.

THE ADMINISTRATIVE COMMAND ECONOMY: THE OLD SOVIET UNION

In November of 1917, a determined group of Bolsheviks led by V. I. Lenin overthrew a short-lived democratic government to establish a new government dominated by the Communist party. The Soviet Union was a relatively backward country then, and its economy was exhausted by a civil war. Seeing the new nation on the verge of both political and economic collapse by 1921, Lenin ushered in his New Economic Policy: a brief era of open discussion and dialogue in which markets returned and the economy prospered.

But his successor, Joseph Stalin, chose a very different—and costly—course when he rose to power. Starting in 1928, Stalin implemented one of the most brutal regimes of modern times. He made two major decisions. First, he forcibly introduced socialized agriculture in a process known as *collectivization.* Second, he nationalized the means of production and eliminated markets. *Central planning* was installed as the preeminent mechanism for allocating resources.

These events left a lasting mark on the Soviet economy. Indeed, several notable characteristics defined the Soviet system from Stalin's day right up to its demise in 1991:

- The economic system was *hierarchical* and *centralized.* The basic goals of economic activity were determined by the Communist party and left to be fulfilled by local enterprise managers.
- Stalinist economic policies stressed maximal economic growth, with emphasis on *heavy industry* and, especially, on the *military.* Consumer goods and agriculture were considered less important.
- The system was largely *quantity-directed,* with only limited use of the price mechanism.

CENTRAL PLANNING IN THE COMMAND ECONOMY

Let us see, briefly, how the old central-planning system worked. Ironically, the structure of the Soviet economic system resembled the hierarchy of a giant corporation. At the top was a single strongman or a ruling clique. The political leadership functioned like the chairman of the board, setting overall policy objectives, but had much more absolute authority than the chairman of any corporation. Next came the State Planning Commission (*Gosplan*) which translated the goals and priorities established by the top echelons of the Communist party into Five-Year and One-Year Plans.

The *Five-Year Plans* set the nation's basic strategy for resource allocation: How much for investment? How much for military procurement and for scientific research? Would there be more cars or more refrigerators? Observers in both the West and the Soviet Union paid close attention to the numerical goals in these plans—and to the Soviet Union's failure to meet them.

The Five-Year Plans were too vague to serve as blueprints for action, however. This job was left to the *One-Year Plans*—enormous sets of documents that covered almost every facet of Soviet economic life. Planners translated broad national goals into specific directives for subordinate ministries, agencies, and regional authorities. But the One-Year Plans were so detailed and complex that they were rarely completed until well into the year, if then.

Several more layers of bureaucracy intervened before reaching the level of the enterprise managers, who acted more like bureaucrats than entrepreneurs in the Soviet system. Communications within the hierarchy were predominantly vertical. Orders flowed down from top to bottom, while data flowed up from bottom to top. Since the data requirements were immense and the number of layers within the bureaucracy so large, the problems of accurate data transmission and processing were monumental. It is precisely this problem, of course, that the market mechanism solves so neatly: Prices convey most of the information that anyone needs.

THE ROAD TO *PERESTROIKA:* WHY DID THE SOVIET ECONOMY FAIL?

The economic system that we have just briefly described was plagued by many problems. Together they stunted productivity growth and consequently slowed the growth of output in the Soviet Union. While it is difficult to pinpoint the precise causes of the Soviet growth slowdown, several contributing factors are clear.

First, while central planning was powerful, it was also crude. It did not adapt well to either changing technology or the increasing complexity of modern economic life. The system, in a word, became ossified.

Second, Soviet planning emphasized high levels of output, with little attention to issues like product quality, low cost, and catering to consumer desires. Because managerial bonuses depended on fulfilling the plan, managers would do dysfunctional things to meet their quotas. For example, scarce materials were routinely hoarded, thus worsening chronic shortages. Or, if shoe leather was in short supply, factory managers might produce only children's shoes rather than adult shoes.

Third, the Soviet system inhibited change, since change threatened fulfillment of the plan. Even when new technology could be imported, diffusion of these new ideas often did not take place. There were simply no incentives to innovate.

Fourth, as time passed, workers became increasingly irritated that their earnings were not translated into better consumer goods and improved standards of living. (Refer back to the first opening quotation of this chapter.) Modern telecommunications exacerbated this problem by enabling Soviet workers to learn about the goods and services enjoyed in the West.

Attempts to reform the command economy date back to the Khrushchev era of the 1950s. But they were almost always superficial in character—designed to sustain the basic features of the planning system. And they were always imple-

FIGURE 21-1 THE SLOWDOWN OF SOVIET ECONOMIC GROWTH

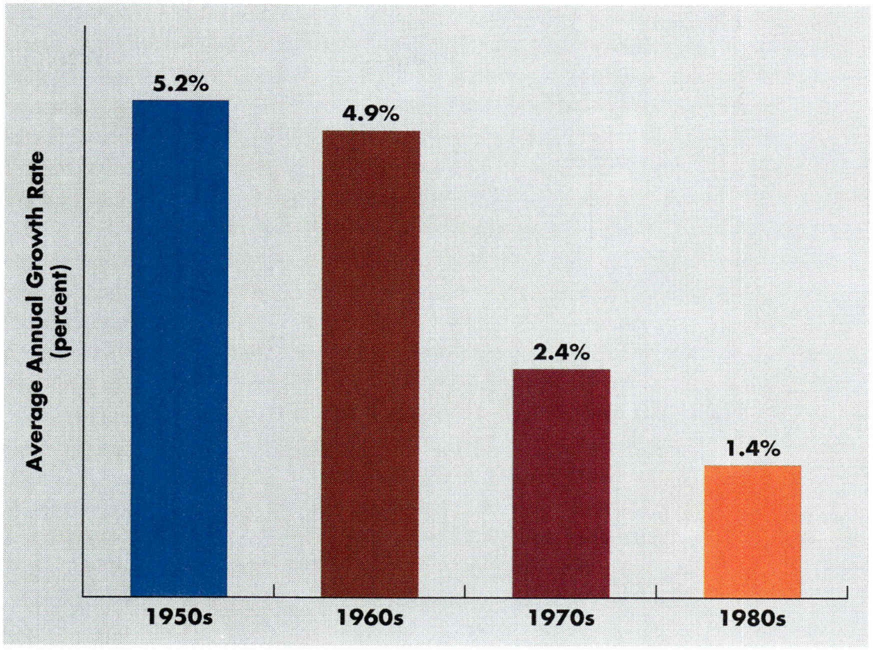

This chart shows that rapid Soviet economic growth in the 1950s and 1960s dwindled rapidly in the 1970s and 1980s.

SOURCE: Central Intelligence Agency.

mented on a limited scale. As a result, several waves of "reform" had little effect on the performance of the Soviet economy. Thus, from the 1960s onward, the rate of growth of productivity and output declined almost continuously. (See Figure 21-1.)

In 1985, Mikhail Gorbachev generated genuine excitement when he assumed power and announced both *perestroika* (restructuring) and *glasnost* (openness). Each seemed to call for fundamental changes in the Soviet system. Cast against the authoritarian background of the Soviet Union, the concept of *glasnost*, which involved the expansion of democratic ideas in both the political and economic spheres, seemed to be a major departure. Moreover, combined with *perestroika*, which involved major changes in the Soviet economy, ranging from less planning to greater managerial autonomy to decentralization of foreign trade decisions, the Gorbachev concept of radical reform seemed to be an appropriate prescription.

But in the end, *perestroika* failed because, in a sense, it was another partial reform designed to shore up the shaky socialist edifice. Moreover, as with previous attempts at reform, implementation encountered fierce resistance from the entrenched bureaucracy. Only when Boris Yeltsin asserted his authority and made clear his support for the transition to markets did the old Soviet system come to an end.

ECONOMIES IN TRANSITION: RUSSIA AND HER NEIGHBORS

The demise of central planning left the former Soviet Union and much of Eastern Europe with a daunting task: to build a system of capitalism and markets atop the wreckage of socialist central planning. In the West, market capitalism as we know it evolved gradually over hundreds of years; no one ever designed it. So there was no instruction book that the leaders of the formerly socialist countries could consult for advice about the transition process.

Not surprisingly, each country followed a different route, and experiences since the 1989 to 1991 period have differed greatly. Some countries, like the Czech Republic and Poland, decided to move as quickly as possible. The Czechs, in particular, handled the transition remarkably smoothly and are now mostly through it. Others, like Hungary and especially Russia, took a more cautious and piecemeal—some might say, uncertain—approach. Russia's prodigious economic problems were (and to some extent still are) complicated by considerable political instability and a breakdown of law and order. So progress was slow at first, and has been quite stressful; their transition is far from over. Nonetheless, despite these differences, the transition processes in the formerly socialist countries have had some common elements:

PRIVATIZATION means transferring publicly owned property to private hands.

1. *Privatization.* If socialism (public ownership) is to give way to capitalism (private ownership), the government must find some way to place assets in private hands—a process known as **privatization.** This was no easy task in a country like Poland or the Czech Republic, where the state had confiscated the means of production from individual owners decades ago. And it was even harder in Russia, which never really experienced capitalism.

   To establish a viable system of private ownership, several major questions needed to be addressed. How were ownership "rights" to be identified and parceled out? How could assets be valued in a country without a functioning price system? What was to be done about loss-making enterprises—businesses that might well have negative value under capitalism?[1] Where would the necessary business managers be found?

   In Russia, privatization proceeded slowly and unevenly at first, but has lately picked up speed. Some assets were directly distributed—for example, by giving shares to workers and apartments to tenants. Others were distributed by variants of the famous voucher system pioneered in what was then Czechoslovakia. Under this system, citizens are given a kind of fictitious money ("vouchers"), which they use to bid for shares in companies being sold at auction. So many companies were privatized in this way that Russia now has more citizen-shareholders than the United States!

2. *Establishing markets and prices.* Developing a price system virtually from scratch is also complicated. Most planned, socialist economies had made only minimal use of prices for allocating resources. So the prices that existed when the planning systems ended bore little resemblance to market prices and, in particular, did not reflect relative scarcities. For example, bread was priced so cheaply in the old Soviet Union that farmers used it instead of wheat to feed their cows.

   Although it was agreed that privatization would eventually lead to the development of markets, the process would take time. In the meantime, something had to be done about the inappropriate prices that existed. Those that had previously been held at ludicrously low levels were freed from control, though in varying degrees in different countries. The predictable result in most countries was inflation, which sharply reduced the real standards of living of most people.

[1]In one famous case, a major Italian auto company was offered an East German automobile factory for free. It turned the "gift" down!

3. *Macroeconomic stabilization.* As noted earlier in this chapter, neither inflation nor unemployment were serious problems in the planned economies. In consequence, few of them had ever used monetary or fiscal policy in the manner typical of market economies. This led to some serious problems when the old systems began to disintegrate. As just mentioned, inflation leaped upward in most transition economies. Government budget deficits increased because revenues could not be maintained with inappropriate tax structures and collapsing political systems.

   The large state enterprises posed a particularly cruel dilemma. If they were cut adrift to fend for themselves in world markets, most would have failed, leading to mass unemployment. None of the formerly socialist nations were willing to do this. Instead, subsidies to many loss-making enterprises were maintained—which widened government budget deficits. Since there were no financial markets as we know them, large budgets led to rapid expansion of the money supplies—which, of course, fueled inflation.
4. *Disruption of international trade.* One of the major features of the planned socialist systems was central control of international trade. In practice, they traded mostly with one another. When the planning system collapsed, trade decisions had to be decentralized. Worse yet, with the economies of its trading partners contracting rapidly, each country found its traditional export markets shrinking.

Any one of these four problems, by itself, would pose a major hurdle for an advanced Western economy. For example, the United Kingdom under Margaret

A TALE OF TWO COUNTRIES

After the Berlin Wall fell, the formerly socialist nations scrambled to implement economic reforms. The ensuing 6 years witnessed both stunning success stories and colossal debacles as nations long accustomed to command economies struggled to cope with free markets.

POLAND: TWO STEPS FORWARD, ONE BACK
No former Soviet satellite embraced economic reform more firmly in the late 1980s than Poland. But by 1995, President Lech Walesa, once a national icon, had lost a reelection bid to a former communist apparatchik. Walesa's repudiation was not, however, a signal that voters were ready to return to a planned economic system. Ironically, public opinion polls suggested that Poles were growing increasingly impatient with the slow pace of reform!

Nonetheless, reformers could find ample cause for concern. New laws stretched out the timetable for privatizing state-owned enterprises. And industries deemed "strategic," such as energy and telecommunications, could not be privatized without parliamentary approval. The state also began flexing more regulatory muscle. Free-market purists were worried that, when privatization resumes, political cronyism may count for more than economic efficiency.

THE CZECH REPUBLIC: FULL SPEED AHEAD
The Czech Republic adopted capitalism seemingly without breaking stride. Mass privatization there is now nearly complete. In 1995, the economy was growing at a steady 4 percent clip, with inflation at 10 percent and falling, minuscule unemployment, and a budget surplus.

The Czech success story combined both luck and skill. The Civic Democratic Party (CDP) of Prime Minister Vaclav Klaus, an ardent free marketeer, has assumed popular control. And there has yet to be any serious suggestion of returning to socialism, despite the fact that 40 percent of the people consider themselves poor.

Top CDP officials have taken a hands-on approach to ensuring that the free-market playing field remains level by rooting out corrupt officeholders and identifying conflicts of interests.

SOURCE: "Into the Trough," *The Economist*, July 15, 1995, p. 38; Casey Bukro, "Eyes Are Looking East to Former Soviet Bloc," *Chicago Tribune*, July 12, 1995, p. 1; Bob Williams, "Looking East for Salvation," *The News & Observer*, April 10, 1995, p. A1; and "Paradox Explained," *The Economist*, July 22, 1995, p. 52.

Thatcher took years to privatize a relatively small share of its economy—and made some mistakes along the way. Now try to imagine tackling all four problems—plus others we have not even mentioned—at once, and doing so in a nation that has just gone through a political revolution. That was the task facing the economies in transition. Every one of these countries suffered a severe contraction of output that lasted several years. By now all are growing again; but the transition process is far from over.

CHINA UNDER MAO: REVOLUTIONARY COMMUNISM

The People's Republic of China makes a good case study for this chapter because it has spent nearly 50 years experimenting with different economic models. In the process, the Chinese have vividly confronted the fundamental questions of this chapter. Socialism or capitalism? Market or plan? And they have come up with different answers at different times.

After the communist takeover in 1949, the Chinese economy was patterned on the Russian model. It was a Soviet-style command economy with emphasis on rapid economic growth, particularly industrial growth. But there were important differences. Probably the most important of these was the decision by Mao Tse-tung *not* to rely on *material incentives* to motivate the work force. Mao and the Chinese leadership were disdainful of such "bourgeois" motives; they preferred exhortation, patriotism, and, where necessary, force.

Russian communism bent socialist doctrine to accommodate human nature. But Chinese communism at first insisted on bending human nature to accommodate Maoist doctrine—to create "the new man in the new China," an effort that was abandoned more than 20 years ago.

A second, and more lasting, difference is that China was always less centralized than Russia. This has been true for centuries and, under central planning, provincial authorities in China had more power and discretion than they did in the Soviet Union. Even today, the leaders in Beijing often have trouble controlling the provinces.

Chinese economic growth has proceeded in fits and starts.

The immediate problem after the Maoist takeover was to lift China out of wartime devastation and to establish communist institutions and values in a vast and semiliterate land. With Soviet assistance, the plan succeeded. But then Mao changed course.

China's next step, the *Great Leap Forward* (1958–1960), turned out to be a giant step backward. The Maoist regime set unrealistically ambitious production goals and selected means for implementing them that were more romantic than rational. Material incentives were deemphasized. Ideologically pure "Reds" were supposed to replace technocratic "experts." Massive applications of brute labor were supposed to compensate for shortages of machinery and advanced technology.

It was a pipe dream or, more accurately, a nightmare for China. National income fell substantially and took years to recover (see Figure 21-2). The ideological excesses of the period also raised tensions with the Soviet Union.

Finally, the Chinese leadership threw out the "Reds" and brought back the "experts," signaling a return to rational economic calculation. The early 1960s were marked by a return to the Soviet planning model, though more decentralized. Economic growth resumed.

FIGURE 21-2 REAL GDP IN THE PEOPLE'S REPUBLIC OF CHINA[a]

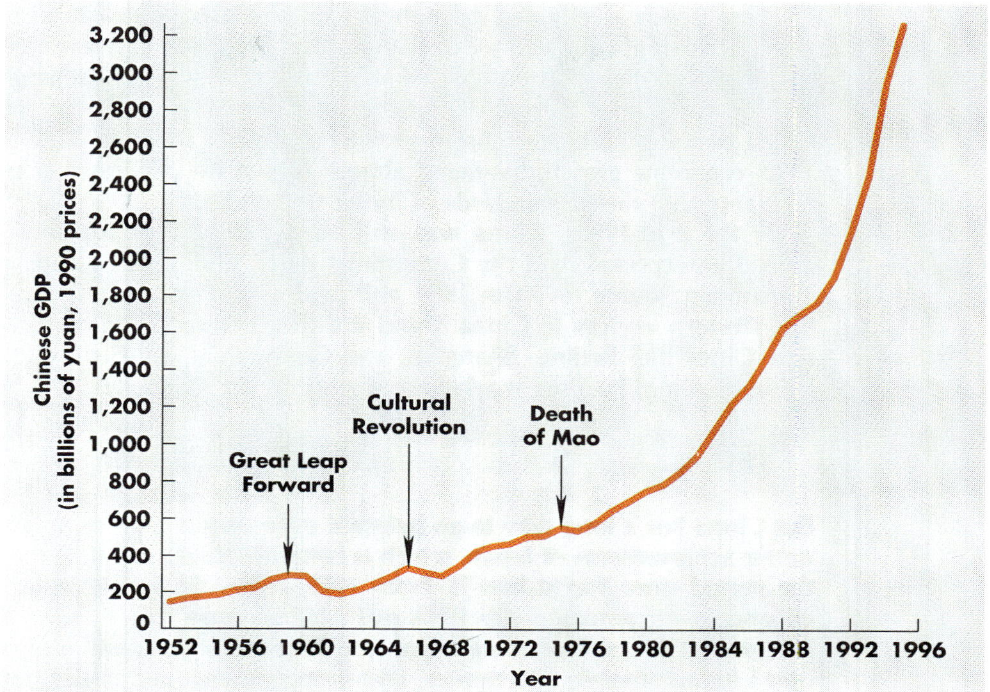

While Chinese economic statistics are notoriously inaccurate, the official data are portrayed here. The Great Leap Forward and the Cultural Revolution stand out as major blemishes on the record of Chinese economic growth. Growth has been extremely rapid since the 1980s.

[a]Data are the net material product for 1952–1977 and real GDP for 1978–1996.

SOURCE: *International Financial Statistics* and *China Statistical Yearbook*.

Then, inexplicably, Mao changed China's course once again with the *Great Proletarian Cultural Revolution* (1965–1969). The "Reds" were in and the "experts" were out as never before. The infamous Red Guards were sent out to purge rightist elements from Chinese society, organize revolutionary cadres, and spread the teachings of Chairman Mao. If anyone worried about economic productivity in this environment, it did not show. By the summer of 1967, both the Chinese economy and other elements of Chinese society were in disarray. Output fell again, but recovered more quickly than it had from the Great Leap (see again Figure 21-2).

Finally, in Mao's last years, Chinese revolutionary fever receded and the "experts" were rehabilitated once again. Material incentives and rational economic calculation returned to China, as did economic growth.

CHINA SINCE MAO: EXPLOSIVE GROWTH

The leaders who succeeded Mao were less doctrinaire about their communism and far more interested in results. China began, cautiously at first, to step away from the Soviet model and adopt important features of the market economy in its place. It welcomed Western tourism, trade, and technology. Chinese managers, engineers, and economists went to study in the West. Material incentives were emphasized and even small-scale capitalism was allowed back on the Chinese mainland.

These trends accelerated dramatically in the 1980s and 1990s, as market forces were increasingly allowed to supplant central planning. Farmers were given land to do with as they pleased. Private shops and other small businesses flourished. Foreign companies were invited to set up operations in China, and many did. China became the biggest Asian growth miracle of them all. Between 1981 and 1992, economic growth averaged almost 10 percent per year—a stunning performance that raised standards of living tremendously.

By the mid-1990s, China was still burdened with many inefficient, state-owned enterprises. And the Communist party, both scarred and scared by the Tiananmen Square revolt in 1989, still held a firm grip on the political system. But Western visitors to China found it difficult to see much evidence of socialism. Cities like Beijing, Shanghai, and Guangzhou gave every appearance of being hustling, bustling market economies on the make.

JAPAN'S UNIQUE BRAND OF CAPITALISM

But China has a long way to go before it even comes close to matching the economic achievements of Japan, which is certainly *the* outstanding success story of the period since World War II. From 1955—when Japan began its productivity enhancement campaign—to 1989, real GNP in Japan rose by an astounding 836 percent.[2] (The corresponding expansion of the U.S. economy was only 177 percent.) Its automobile, electronics, and semiconductor industries, to name just a few, lead the world in technological and manufacturing prowess. Its banks and other financial institutions are the world's largest.

How did Japan do it? It is true, but far too simple, to say that Japan succeeded by adopting free-market capitalism—for both free markets and capitalism look quite different in Japan than in the United States. We devote most of the rest of this chapter to describing some of these differences.

EXPORT-LED GROWTH

Japan is a crowded, island nation far removed from the world's major markets. Almost totally devoid of natural resources, it must import large amounts of raw materials, energy, and foodstuffs just to survive. And yet, by concentrating on manufacturing and exporting, it has managed not just to prosper but to propel itself into the forefront of nations.

EXPORT-LED GROWTH refers to the strategy of emphasizing the production of goods for export.

One secret to Japanese economic success has certainly been its emphasis on both high levels of investment and **export-led growth.** From 1955 to 1989, Japanese exports in real terms grew an astounding 3,227 percent. Indeed, Japan's export machine has been so successful that its huge trade surplus has been the cause of international trade frictions for years. (See the box on the next page.)

There is no single secret to Japan's exporting success. High levels of investment have certainly facilitated the adoption of the latest technology. Japanese industry is clearly outward looking in a way that American industry is not. Many organizations, such as the fabled Ministry of International Trade and Industry (MITI), work to promote exports. Japanese business has also shown a remarkable ability to adapt to changing world markets. As one industry (say, ship-

[2]We stop the comparison in 1989 because Japan has experienced a protracted recession in the 1990s.

U.S.-JAPANESE TRADE: IS EVERYONE PLAYING FAIR?

Japan's huge trade surpluses with the United States have threatened friendly relations between the two countries. Several rounds of trade negotiations during the Bush and Clinton administrations have reduced the surplus only slightly. Why? One former trade negotiator believes that leaders of both nations incorrectly assume that the Japanese and U.S. economies are organized in the same way.

As long as this assumption is accepted, there are only two possible explanations for our problems: Someone is cheating or someone is performing poorly. . . .

There is a third explanation: The two sides do not share the same economic views. The U.S. runs its economy for the consumer, prevents or strictly regulates aggregation of corporate power, eschews industrial policy, views the government role as that of referee and calls for a laissez-faire brand of free trade. Japan emphasizes the interest of the producer, promotes agglomeration of corporate power, pursues an active industrial policy, sees the government as a coach and practices a mercantilistic brand of free trade.

In effect, Japan is playing football while the U.S. is playing baseball. Japan is not playing unfairly, and the U.S. team is trying as hard as it can. But football is a rougher game than baseball, and the baseball players are taking a beating. They will continue to do so as long as their leaders insist that the games are really the same.

SOURCE: Clyde Prestowitz, "George and Toshiki—The Odd Couple," *The New York Times*, March 10, 1990.

building) declines, the Japanese shift into another (say, consumer electronics) whose star is rising. Above all, the major Japanese companies seek always to grow—and that means exporting.

"JAPAN, INC."

Unlike the United States, but like much of Western Europe, Japan has no tradition of enforcing antitrust laws. Indeed, at times the government has seemed to promote rather than oppose bigness, perhaps as a way to catch up to the West. In consequence, Japanese industry is far more concentrated than American industry, especially in manufacturing and financial services. Industrial concentration, barriers to imports, inefficient retailing, and an expensive currency combine to keep domestic prices of consumer goods astoundingly high.

The cozy relationship between the big Japanese corporations and the Japanese government has acquired the nickname "Japan, Inc.," to indicate that economic policy there is geared more to producer than to consumer interests. Indeed, for decades Japan was said to be ruled by an "iron triangle" consisting of giant corporations, powerful career bureaucrats, and politicians from the dominant Liberal Democratic Party (LDP).

Lately, however, this system has shown unmistakable signs of strain. The severe and protracted recession of the 1990s weakened many Japanese companies, especially the banks. The government's inability to set things right tarnished the reputations of the prestigious ministries. And then, in 1993, the LDP lost control of the government for the first time since its ascendancy in the 1950s. As this text is written, both political reform and financial reform stand high on the Japanese agenda.

JAPANESE MANAGEMENT METHODS

The internal organization of a Japanese company also looks quite different from an American corporation.[3] An industrial giant like Toyota may be surrounded

[3]However, in recent years, more and more American companies have adopted Japanese management techniques.

by satellite companies that supply parts and help it operate its famous "just-in-time" inventory system, a highly efficient way of organizing the factory floor to minimize delays. These smaller companies live at the mercy of the corporate giants and act as shock absorbers when demand declines.

In addition, members of Japan's manufacturing combines (*keiretsu*) own chunks of each other's stock and forge tight links with Japanese banks, the world's largest. This gives Japanese industry access to cheap, "patient" capital that is willing to wait for a return on its investment. Japanese managers pay scant attention to daily movements of the stock market and never worry about hostile takeovers. All this helps Japanese industry maintain its long-run focus.

Japan also differs from the United States in the way its work force is organized and paid. For one thing, many employees of large Japanese corporations have *lifetime employment* guarantees and are never laid off. These features help align the interests of labor and management, build loyalty to the company, and make Japanese workers less resistant to change than their American counterparts. For example, if a Japanese plant automates, most employees know they will not only keep their jobs but share in any gains automation may bring.

The Japanese workplace is also less hierarchical. Pay differentials between executives and production workers are a fraction of those in the United States; so, naturally, the Japanese distribution of income is much more equal. Managers eat in the same cafeterias, drink in the same bars, and sometimes even wear the same uniforms as blue-collar workers. Japanese workers are also consulted closely on how the factory is to be run. Decision making is by consensus—even if consensus takes a long time to build. American management, by contrast, exercises more top-down control.

For these reasons, and perhaps also because of strong conformist tendencies within Japanese society, labor-management relations in Japan are less adversarial and more cooperative than those in the United States or Europe.

IS JAPAN A PLANNED ECONOMY?

All this did not happen by the invisible hand alone. The system was consciously designed to raise industrial productivity, keep it growing fast, and turn Japan into an industrial powerhouse that would rival the Western nations. Many Japanese innovations, such as "just-in-time" manufacturing, originated in the private sector. But elite government bureaucrats played an active role in promoting what they saw as good ideas, discouraging bad ones and, in general, lending a helping and guiding hand.

The role of the government, and especially MITI, in Japan's economic success is highly controversial. Ardent free-marketeers downplay its contribution and point to episodes in which MITI clearly got in the way—such as its ill-conceived attempt to drive Honda out of the automobile business in the 1960s. Protectionists seeking to limit Japanese imports exaggerate the role of MITI and portray Japan, Inc., as a monolith, which it certainly is not. In their eyes, Japan's *industrial policy* is the key to its success.

A balanced view of the matter seems hard to strike, especially since few Westerners really fathom the clubby ways of Japanese businesses. But a few things seem clear. First, the Ministry of Finance and the Bank of Japan (the central bank) have exercised far more comprehensive control over the Japanese financial system than the Treasury and the Federal Reserve have ever done here. Second, Japanese industrial policy, while far from infallible, seems to have had consid-

CAN AMERICA IMPORT JAPANESE MANUFACTURING METHODS?

Most [Japanese] firms [in the United States] have adopted something like joint consultation and related Japanese practices, including an elaborate screening of job applicants. . . . [S]ome U.S. workers who were hired at Honda in Ohio were reportedly surprised both at the many questions they were asked that seemed unrelated to work and at the length of the interviews, which were attended by executives and vice presidents. . . . Once hired, these workers reported attending frequent meetings with the management on production matters. Such frequent meetings at the Honda plant in Ohio are signified by the slogan, "let's Y-gaya," which means in fractured Japanese, "let's have a bull session." In these operations management and workers share the same tables for lunch, thereby creating an informal setting for communication. . . .

Productivity at Nummi [a joint Toyota-General Motors factory in Fremont, California] after only one year of operation was reported to have increased by 48.5 percent over what it was at the old Fremont plant under GM management. Absenteeism and drug use, which plagued the old Fremont plant, dropped dramatically after Nummi took over. Nummi's efforts at productivity enhancement continue with the slogan "let's kaizen," or "let's improve." Also, in contrast to the old Fremont plant, the quality of the automobiles produced at Nummi has been rated highly. . . .

. . . Honda in Japan is known for its emphasis on nurturing the sense of cooperative teamwork among its workers. This emphasis was imported to Honda's operation in Ohio. At the Ohio plant workers, referred to as *associates*, are encouraged to acquire skills and training by continual interactions with one another on the shop floor rather than through formal training sessions. Productivity at the plant reportedly approaches that of Honda's plants in Japan, and the quality of the automobiles produced in Ohio is said to equal that of Japanese-made Hondas.

SOURCE: Masanori Hashimoto, "Employment and Wage Systems in Japan and Their Implications for Productivity," in Alan S. Blinder (ed.), *Paying for Productivity: A Look at the Evidence* (Washington, D.C.: Brookings Institution, 1990), pp. 292–293.

erable success in assisting winners and shutting down losers. Third, Japanese industry benefits enormously from a work force that may be the best educated and most cooperative in the world; this is certainly a substantial achievement of government.

WHAT CAN THE UNITED STATES LEARN FROM (AND TEACH) JAPAN?

Learning is a two-way street. The Japanese have learned much from American industry and continue to do so; their famed "quality circles," for example, orginated here. Economywide productivity continues to be higher in the United States than in Japan. Nonetheless, the Japanese seem to be the technological leader in some important industries—such as automobiles and robotics. There, we can "play catch-up" by observing them, just as they did years ago by observing us.

Many people feel, however, that the most important things we can learn from the Japanese are not the latest innovations in robotics or chip manufacturing, but rather their ways of organizing and motivating *people.* The process begins with an education system that has virtually abolished illiteracy, continues through Japan's unique labor-relations system, and includes production and management techniques that are being emulated all over the world. (See the box on the previous page for some examples of importing Japanese management methods to America.)

Some observers predict that, as the Japanese get richer, they will come to behave more like Americans. Already, for example, there are signs that Japanese households are saving less, Japanese workers are changing jobs more frequently, and there is strong sentiment to "deregulate" their economy somewhat along American lines. Others, however, stress basic cultural differences between the two societies that change very slowly, if at all. The two brands of capitalism are indeed different. Only time will tell which system adapts more successfully to our ever-changing world.

SUMMARY

1. Economic systems differ in the amount of planning they do and in the extent to which they permit private ownership of property. However, **socialism** (state ownership of the means of production) need not go hand in hand with central planning, and **capitalism** need not rely on free markets. The two choices are distinct, at least conceptually.
2. *Free markets* seem to do a good job of selecting the bill of goods and services to be produced and at choosing the most efficient techniques for producing these goods and services. Planned systems have difficulties with both of these choices.
3. Market economies, however, do not guarantee an equitable distribution of income and are often plagued by business fluctuations. In these two areas, *planning* seems to have some advantages.
4. A major problem for socialism is how to motivate management to achieve maximal efficiency and to maintain inventiveness in the absence of the profit motive.
5. Individual freedom is a noneconomic goal that is of major importance in the choice among economic systems. Any element of planning or of socialism infringes upon the freedoms of some individuals. Yet complete freedom does not exist anywhere, and certain limitations on individual freedom command wide popular support.
6. From the days of Stalin until its dissolution in 1991, the Soviet Union followed a rigid system of *central planning* which emphasized heavy industry and armaments and deemphasized consumer needs.
7. Planning in the Soviet Union was bureaucratic and hierarchical and encountered monumental difficulties in adapting to modern technology, motivating workers and managers, and achieving satisfactory productivity.
8. While Soviet consumers were free to spend their money as they pleased, there was little **consumer sovereignty.** Planners, not consumers, decided what would be produced. The labor market, however, operated much as it does in America—using wage rates to equate supply and demand.
9. With the end of centrally planned socialism in Eastern Europe and the former Soviet Union, planned systems are being replaced by market systems, a difficult process generally described as *transition.*
10. This transition process involves difficult problems like privatizing assets, freeing prices from controls, stabilizing the macroeconomy, and reestablishing international trade.
11. The Chinese economic system has changed several times since the communist takeover in 1949, passing through several periods of intense revolutionary fervor and little economic progress. Planning there was similar to that in Russia, although somewhat less centralized.
12. Beginning in the late 1970s, the Chinese introduced important aspects of the market economy—and even elements of capitalism—into their economic system. Lately, Chinese growth rates have been the highest in the world.

13. Japan has used **export-led growth** to propel itself to the forefront of nations; but lately its single-minded concentration on exporting has been a source of international trade tensions.
14. Japan has more industrial concentration than the United States, a less adversarial system of labor-management relations, tighter links between manufacturing companies and banks, and more active cooperation between government and industry. Observers disagree about the relative importance of each of these influences in accounting for Japan's industrial success.

KEY TERMS

Capitalism
Socialism
Planning
Free markets
Consumer sovereignty
Collectivization
Perestroika
Privatization
Material incentives
Great Leap Forward
Great Proletarian Cultural Revolution
Export-led growth
Industrial policy

QUESTIONS FOR REVIEW

1. Explain why the choice between capitalism and socialism is not the same as the choice between markets and central planning. Cite an example of a socialist, market economy and of a planned, capitalist economy.
2. If you were the leader of a small, developing country, what are some of the factors that would weigh heavily in your choice of an economic system?
3. Which type of economic system generally has the most trouble achieving each of the following goals? In each case, explain why.
   a. An equal distribution of income
   b. Adequate incentives for industrial managers
   c. Eliminating business fluctuations
   d. Balancing supply and demand for inputs
4. If you were a plant manager under old-style Soviet planning, what are some of the things you might do to make your life easier and more successful? (Use your imagination. Russian plant managers did!)
5. What are some of the major issues involved in the transition from plan to market, and why is this transition so difficult in practice?
6. Do you think the U.S. government should take a more active role in guiding American industry? If so, is Japan a good model? If not, why is Japan not a good model?
7. During the early 1990s, Japan and the United States engaged in talks on "structural impediments" designed to achieve more balanced trade between the two nations. As part of these talks, U.S. government representatives told the Japanese how they could make their economy more like ours, while Japanese negotiators told their American counterparts how to make the United States more like Japan. Does this make sense to you? Who should be emulating whom?

GLOSSARY

Absolute Advantage One country is said to have an absolute advantage over another in the production of a particular good if it can produce that good using smaller quantities of resources than can the other country. (p. 379)

Abstraction Abstraction means ignoring many details in order to focus on the most important elements of a problem. (p. 9)

Aggregate Demand Aggregrate demand is the total amount that all consumers, business firms, and government agencies are willing to spend on final goods and services. (p. 143)

Aggregate Demand Curve The aggregate demand curve shows the quantity of domestic product that is demanded at each possible value of the price level. (p. 98)

Aggregate Supply Curve The aggregate supply curve shows, for each possible price level, the quantity of goods and services that all the nation's businesses are willing to produce during a specified period of time, holding all other determinants of aggregate quantity supplied constant. (pp. 98, 206)

Aggregation Aggregation means combining many individual markets into one overall market. (p. 96)

Allocation of Resources Allocation of resources refers to the society's decision on how to divide up its economy's scarce input resources among the different outputs produced in the economy and among the different firms or other organizations that produce those outputs. (p. 60)

Appreciate A nation's currency is said to appreciate when exchange rates change so that a unit of its own currency can buy more units of foreign currency. (p. 400)

Asset An asset of an individual or business firm is an item of value that the individual or firm owns. (p. 260)

Automatic Stabilizer An automatic stabilizer is any arrangement that automatically serves to support aggregate demand when it would otherwise sag and to hold down aggregate demand when it would otherwise surge ahead. In this way, an automatic stabilizer reduces the sensitivity of the economy to shifts in demand. (p. 313)

Autonomous Increase in Consumption An autonomous increase in consumption is an increase in consumer spending without any increase in incomes. It is represented on a graph as a shift of the entire consumption function. (p. 193)

Balance of Payments Deficit The balance of payments deficit is the amount by which the quantity supplied of a country's currency (per year) exceeds the quantity demanded. Balance of payments deficits arise whenever the exchange rate is pegged at an artificially high level. (p. 408)

Balance of Payments Surplus The balance of payments surplus is the amount by which the quantity demanded of a country's currency (per year) exceeds the quantity supplied. Balance of payments surpluses arise whenever the exchange rate is pegged at an artificially low level. (p. 409)

Balance Sheet A balance sheet is an accounting statement listing the values of all the assets on the left-hand side and the values of all the liabilities and *net worth* on the right-hand side. (p. 260)

Barter Barter is a system of exchange in which people directly trade one good for another, without using money as an intermediate step. (p. 251)

Budget Deficit The budget deficit is the amount by which the government's expenditures exceed its receipts during a specified period of time, usually 1 year. (p. 326)

Capital Gain A capital gain is the difference between the price at which an asset is sold and the price at which it was bought. (p. 130)

Capital Good A capital good is an item that is used to produce other goods and services in the future, rather than being consumed today. Factories and machines are examples. (p. 58)

Capitalism Capitalism is a method of economic organization in which private individuals own the means of production, either directly or indirectly through corporations. (p. 476)

Central Bank A central bank is a bank for banks. America's central bank is the *Federal Reserve System.* (p. 274)

Closed Economy A closed economy is one that does not trade with other nations in either goods or assets. (pp. 28, 430)

Commodity Money A commodity money is an object in use as a medium of exchange, but which also has a substantial value in alternative (nonmonetary) uses. (p. 253)

Comparative Advantage One country is said to have a comparative advantage over another in the production of a particular good relative to other goods if it produces that good less inefficiently as compared with the other country. (p. 379)

Consumer Expenditure Consumer expenditure, symbolized by the letter *C*, is the total amount spent by consumers on newly produced goods and services (excluding purchases of new homes, which are considered investment goods). (p. 143)

Consumer Sovereignty Consumer sovereignty means that consumer preferences determine what goods shall be produced and in what amounts. (p. 477)

Consumption Function The consumption function is the relationship between total consumer expenditures and total disposable income in the economy, holding all other determinants of consumer spending constant. (p. 149)

Consumption Good A consumption good is an item that is available for immediate use by households, one that satisfies wants of members of households without contributing directly to future production. (p. 58)

Correlated Two variables are said to be correlated if they tend to go up or down together. But correlation need not imply causation. (p. 12)

Crowding In Crowding in occurs when government spending, by raising real GDP, induces increases in private investment spending. (p. 339)

Crowding Out Crowding out occurs when deficit spending by the government forces private investment spending to contract. (p. 339)

Cyclical Unemployment Cyclical unemployment is the portion of unemployment that is attributable to a decline in the economy's total production. Cyclical unemployment rises during recessions and falls as prosperity is restored. (p. 121)

Deflation Deflation refers to a sustained decrease in the general price level. (p. 103)

Demand Curve A demand curve is a graphical depiction of a demand schedule. It shows how the quantity demanded of some product during a specified period of time will change as the price of that product changes, holding all other determinants of quantity demanded constant. (p. 70)

Demand Schedule A demand schedule is a table showing how the quantity demanded of some product during a specified period of time changes as the price of that product changes, holding all other determinants of quantity demanded constant. (p. 70)

Deposit Insurance Deposit insurance is a system that guarantees that depositors will not lose money even if their bank goes bankrupt. (p. 258)

Depreciate The currency is said to depreciate when exchange rates change so that a unit of its currency can buy fewer units of foreign currency. (p. 400)

Devaluation A devaluation is a reduction in the official value of a currency. (p. 401)

Discount Rate The discount rate is the interest rate the Fed charges on loans that it makes to banks. (p. 281)

Discouraged Worker A discouraged worker is an unemployed person who gives up looking for work and is therefore no longer counted as part of the labor force. (p. 120)

Disposable Income Disposable income is the sum of the incomes of all the individuals in the economy after all taxes have been deducted and all transfer payments have been added. (p. 144)

Division of Labor Division of labor means breaking up a task into a number of smaller, more specialized tasks so that each worker can become more adept at a particular job. (p. 60)

Dumping Dumping means selling goods in a foreign market at lower prices than those charged in the home market. (p. 395)

Econometric Model An econometric model is a set of mathematical equations that embody the economist's model of the economy. (p. 315)

Economic Growth Economic growth occurs when an economy is able to produce more goods and services for each consumer. (p. 57)

Economic Model An economic model is a simplified, small-scale version of some aspect of the economy. Economic models are often expressed in equations, by graphs, or in words. (p. 13)

Equation of Exchange The equation of exchange states that the money value of GDP transactions must be equal to the product of the average stock of money times velocity. That is:

$$M \times V = P \times Y \quad \text{(p. 296)}$$

Equilibrium An equilibrium is a situation in which there are no inherent forces that produce change. Changes away from an equilibrium position will occur only as a result of "outside events" that disturb the status quo. (pp. 74, 171)

Excess Reserves Excess reserves are any reserves held in excess of the legal minimum. (p. 261)

Exchange Rate The exchange rate states the price, in terms of one currency, at which another currency can be bought. (p. 400)

Expenditure Schedule An expenditure schedule shows the relationship between national income (GDP) and total spending. (p. 173)

Exponential Growth Exponential growth is growth at a constant percentage rate. (p. 460)

Export-Led Growth Export-led growth refers to the strategy of emphasizing the production of goods for export. (p. 488)

Export Subsidy An export subsidy is a payment by the government to exporters to permit them to reduce their selling prices of their goods so they can compete more effectively in foreign markets. (p. 387)

Fiat Money Fiat money is money that is decreed as such by the government. It is of little value as a commodity, but it maintains its value as a medium of exchange because people have faith that the issuer will stand behind the pieces of printed paper and limit their production. (p. 253)

Final Goods and Services Final goods and services are those that are purchased by their ultimate users. (p. 100)

Fiscal Policy The government's fiscal policy is its plan for spending and taxation. It is designed to steer aggregate demand in some desired direction. (p. 227)

Fixed Exchange Rates Fixed exchange rates are rates set by government decisions and maintained by government actions. (p. 408)

Fixed Taxes Fixed taxes are taxes that do not vary with the level of GDP. (p. 228)

Floating Exchange Rates Floating exchange rates are rates determined in free markets by the law of supply and demand. (p. 401)

45° Line Diagram An income-expenditure diagram, also called a 45° line diagram, plots total real expenditure (on the vertical axis) against real income (on the horizontal axis). The 45° line marks off points where income and expenditure are equal. (p. 176)

Fractional Reserve Banking Fractional reserve banking is a system under which bankers keep as reserves only a fraction of the funds they hold on deposit. (p. 257)

Frictional Unemployment Frictional unemployment is unemployment that is due to normal turnover in the labor market. It includes people who are temporarily between jobs because they are moving or changing occupations, or for similar reasons. (p. 120)

Government Purchases Government purchases, symbolized by the letter *G*, refer to the goods (such as airplanes and paper clips) and services (such as school teaching and police protection) purchased by all levels of government. (p. 143)

Gross Domestic Product (GDP) Gross domestic product (GDP) is the sum of the money values of all final goods and services produced in the domestic economy during a specified period of time, usually 1 year. (pp. 27, 99)

Income-Expenditure Diagram An income-expenditure diagram, also called a 45° line diagram, plots total real expenditure (on the vertical axis) against real income (on the horizontal axis). The 45° line marks off points where income and expenditure are equal. (p. 176)

Indexing Indexing refers to provisions in a law or a contract whereby monetary payments are automatically adjusted whenever a specified price index changes. Wage rates, pensions, interest payments on bonds, income taxes, and many other things can be indexed in this way, and have been. Sometimes such contractual provisions are called *escalator clauses*. (p. 369)

Induced Increase in Consumption An induced increase in consumption is an increase in consumer spending that stems from an increase in consumer incomes. It is represented on a graph as a movement along a fixed consumption function. (p. 193)

Induced Investment Induced investment is the part of investment spending that rises when GDP rises and falls when GDP falls. (p. 173)

Inflation Inflation refers to a sustained increase in the general price level. (pp. 29, 98)

Inflation Accounting Inflation accounting means adjusting standard accounting procedures for the fact that inflation lowers the purchasing power of money. (p. 331)

Inflationary Gap The inflationary gap is the amount by which equilibrium real GDP exceeds the full-employment level of GDP. (p. 180)

Inputs Inputs or factors of production are the labor, machinery, buildings, and natural resources used to make outputs. (p. 26)

Intermediate Good An intermediate good is a good purchased for resale or for use in producing another good. (p. 100)

Investment Spending Investment spending, symbolized by the letter *I*, is the sum of the expenditures of business firms on new plant and equipment and households on new homes. Financial "investments" are not included, nor are resales of existing physical assets. (p. 143)

Labor Productivity Labor productivity refers to the amount of output a worker turns out in an hour (or a week or a year) of labor. It can be measured as total national output (GDP) in a given year divided by the total number of hours of work performed for pay in the country during that year. That is, labor productivity is defined as GDP per hour of labor. (p. 445)

Law of Supply and Demand The law of supply and demand states that, in a free market, the forces of supply and demand generally push the price toward the level at which quantity supplied and quantity demanded are equal. (p. 75)

Leading Indicator A leading indicator is a variable that, experience has shown, normally turns down before recessions start and turns up before expansions begin. (p. 316)

Liability A liability of an individual or business firm is an item of value that the individual or firm owes. Many liabilities are known as *debts*. (p. 260)

Liquidity An asset's liquidity refers to the ease with which it can be converted into cash. (p. 256)

M1 The narrowly defined money supply, usually abbreviated M1, is the sum of all coins and paper money in circulation, plus certain checkable deposit balances at banks and savings institutions. (p. 254)

M2 The broadly defined money supply, usually abbreviated M2, is the sum of all coins and paper money in circulation, plus all types of checking account balances, plus most forms of savings account balances, plus shares in money market mutual funds, and a few other minor items. (p. 255)

Marginal Propensity to Consume (MPC) The marginal propensity to consume (MPC) is the ratio of the change in consumption to the change in disposable income that produces the change in consumption. On a graph, it appears as the slope of the consumption function. (p. 150)

Market System A market system is a form of organization of the economy in which decisions on resource allocation are left to the independent decisions of individual producers and consumers acting in their own best interests without central direction. (p. 62)

Medium of Exchange The medium of exchange is the standard object used in exchanging goods and services. (p. 252)

Mixed Economy A mixed economy is one in which there is some public influence over the workings of free markets. There may also be some public ownership mixed in with private property. (p. 41)

Monetarism Monetarism is a mode of analysis that uses the equation of exchange to organize and analyze macroeconomic data. (p. 300)

Monetary Policy Monetary policy refers to actions that the Federal Reserve System takes in order to change the equilibrium of the money market; that is, to alter the money supply, move interest rates, or both. (p. 285)

Monetize the Deficit The central bank is said to monetize the deficit when it purchases the bonds that the government issues. (p. 336)

Money Money is the standard object used in exchanging goods and services. In short, money is the medium of exchange. (p. 252)

Multiplier The multiplier is the ratio of the change in equilibrium GDP (Y) divided by the original change in spending that causes the change in GDP. (p. 188)

National Debt The national debt is the federal government's total indebtedness at a moment in time. It is the result of previous deficits. (p. 326)

National Income National income is the sum of the incomes that all individuals in the economy earned in the forms of wages, interest, rents, and profits. It excludes transfer payments and is calculated before any deductions are taken for income taxes. (p. 144)

Natural Rate of Unemployment The economy's self-correcting mechanism always tends to push the unemployment rate back toward a specific rate of unemployment that we call the natural rate of unemployment. (p. 358)

Near Moneys Near moneys are liquid assets that are close substitutes for money. (p. 256)

Net Exports Net exports, symbolized by $(X - IM)$, is the difference between exports and imports. It indicates the difference between what we sell to foreigners and what we buy from them. (p. 143)

Net Worth Net worth is the value of all assets minus the value of all liabilities. (p. 260)

Nominal GDP Nominal GDP is GDP calculated by valuing all outputs at current prices. (p. 99)

Nominal Rate of Interest The nominal rate of interest is the percentage by which the money the borrower pays back exceeds the money that he borrowed, making no adjustment for any fall in the purchasing power of this money that results from inflation. (p. 129)

Open Economy An open economy is one that trades with other nations in goods and services, and perhaps also in financial assets. (pp. 28, 423)

Open-Market Operations Open-market operations refer to the Fed's purchase or sale of government securities through transactions in the open market. (p. 277)

Opportunity Cost The opportunity cost of some decision is the value of the next best alternative which you have to give up because of that decision (for example, working instead of going to school). (pp. 4, 51)

Outputs Outputs are the goods and services that consumers want to acquire. (p. 26)

Paradox of Thrift The paradox of thrift is the fact that an effort by a nation to save more may simply reduce national income and fail to raise total saving. (p. 197)

Phillips Curve A Phillips curve is a graph depicting the rate of unemployment on the horizontal axis and either the rate of inflation or the rate of change of money wages on the vertical axis. Phillips curves are normally downward sloping, indicating that higher inflation rates are associated with lower unemployment rates. (p. 353)

Potential (GDP) Potential (GDP) is the real GDP that the economy would produce if its labor and other resources were fully employed. (p. 118)

Price Ceiling A price ceiling is a legal maximum on the price that may be charged for a commodity. (p. 83)

Price Floor A price floor is a legal minimum on the price that may be charged for a commodity. (p. 86)

Principle of Increasing Costs The principle of increasing costs states that as the production of a good expands, the opportunity cost of producing another unit generally increases. (p. 54)

Privatization Privatization means transferring publicly owned property to private hands. (p. 484)

Production Possibilities Frontier A production possibilities frontier shows the different combinations of various goods that a producer or an economy can turn out, given the available resources and existing technology. (p. 53)

Productivity Productivity is the amount of output produced by a unit of input. (p. 209)

Progressive Tax A tax is progressive if the ratio of taxes to income rises as income rises. (p. 40)

Purchasing Power The purchasing power of a given sum of money is the volume of goods and services that it will buy. (p. 124)

Quantity Demanded The quantity demanded is the number of units that consumers want to buy over a specified period of time. (p. 70)

Quantity Supplied The quantity supplied is the number of units that sellers want to sell over a specified period of time. (p. 71)

Quota A quota specifies the maximum amount of a good that is permitted into the country from abroad per unit of time. (p. 387)

Rational Decision A rational decision is one that best serves the objectives of the decision maker, whatever those objectives may be. Such objectives may include a firm's desire to maximize its profits, a government's desire to maximize the welfare of its citizens, or another government's desire to maximize its military might. The term *rational* connotes neither approval nor disapproval of the objective itself. (p. 51)

Rational Expectations Rational expectations are forecasts which, while not necessarily correct, are the best that can be made given the available data. Rational expectations, therefore, cannot err systematically. If expectations are rational, forecasting errors are pure random numbers. (p. 364)

Real GDP Real GDP is the value of all the goods and services produced by an economy in a year, evaluated in dollars of constant purchasing power. Hence, inflation does not raise real GDP. (p. 29, 100)

Real Rate of Interest The real rate of interest is the percentage increase in purchasing power that the borrower pays to the lender for the privilege of borrowing. It indicates the increased ability to purchase goods and services that the lender earns. (p. 129)

Real Wage Rate The real wage rate is the wage rate adjusted for inflation. It indicates the volume of goods and services that money wages will buy. (p. 124)

Recession A recession is a period of time during which the total output of the economy falls. (pp. 30, 98)

Recessionary Gap The recessionary gap is the amount by which the equilibrium level of real GDP falls short of potential GDP. (p. 179)

Relative Price An item's relative price is its price in terms of some other item rather than in terms of dollars. (p. 126)

Required Reserves Required reserves are the minimum amount of reserves (in cash or the equivalent) required by law. Normally, required reserves are proportional to the volume of deposits. (p. 259)

Resources Resources are the instruments provided by nature or by people that are used to create goods and services. Natural resources include minerals, the soil, water, and air. Labor is a scarce resource partly because of time limitations (the day has only 24 hours), and partly because the number of skilled workers is limited. Factories and machines are resources made by people. These three types of resources are often referred to as *land, labor,* and *capital.* They are also called inputs or factors of production. (p. 50)

Revaluation A revaluation is an increase in the official value of a currency. (p. 401)

Run on a Bank A run on a bank occurs when many depositors withdraw cash from their accounts all at once. (p. 250)

Scatter Diagram A scatter diagram is a graph showing the relationship between two variables (such as consumer spending and disposable income). Each year is represented by a point in the diagram. The coordinates of each year's point show the values of the two variables in that year. (p. 147)

Shortage A shortage is an excess of quantity demanded over quantity supplied. When there is a shortage, buyers cannot purchase the quantities they desire. (p. 74)

Socialism Socialism is a method of economic organization in which the state owns the means of production. (p. 476)

Specialization Specialization means that a country devotes its energies and resources to only a small proportion of the world's productive activities. (p. 377)

Stabilization Policy Stabilization Policy is the name given to government programs designed to prevent or shorten recessions and to counteract inflation (that is, to *stabilize* prices). (p. 110)

Stagflation Stagflation is inflation that occurs while the economy is growing slowly ("stagnating") or having a recession. (pp. 109, 218)

Store of Value A store of value is an item used to store wealth from one point in time to another. (p. 252)

Structural Budget Deficit The structural budget deficit is the hypothetical deficit we *would have* under current fiscal policies if the economy were operating near full employment. (p. 329)

Structural Unemployment Structural unemployment refers to workers who have lost their jobs because they have been displaced by automation, because their skills are no longer in demand, or for similar reasons. (p. 120)

Supply Curve A supply curve is a graphical depiction of a supply schedule. It shows how the quantity supplied of some product during a specified period of time will change as the price of that product changes, holding all other determinants of quantity supplied constant. (p. 73)

Supply-Demand Diagram A supply-demand diagram graphs the supply and demand curves together. It depicts the equilibrium price and quantity. (p. 73)

Supply Schedule A supply schedule is a table showing how the quantity supplied of some product during a specified period of time changes as the price of that product changes, holding all other determinants of quantity supplied constant. (p. 72)

Surplus A surplus is an excess of quantity supplied over quantity demanded. When there is a surplus, sellers cannot sell the quantities they desire to supply. (p. 74)

Tariff A tariff is a tax on imports. (p. 387)

Theory A theory is a deliberate simplification of relationships whose purpose is to explain how those relationships work. (p. 12)

Time-Series Graph A time-series graph is a type of two-variable diagram in which time is the variable measured along the horizontal axis. It shows how some variable changed as time passed. (p. 28)

Trade Adjustment Assistance Trade adjustment assistance provides special unemployment benefits, loans, retraining programs, and other aid to workers and firms that are harmed by foreign competition. (p. 392)

Transfer Payments Transfer payments are sums of money that certain individuals receive as outright *grants* from the government rather than as payments for services rendered to employers. (p. 145)

Unemployment Rate The unemployment rate is the number of unemployed people, expressed as a percentage of the labor force. (p. 117)

Unit of Account The unit of account is the standard unit for quoting prices. (p. 252)

Variable Taxes Variable taxes are taxes that do vary with the level of GDP. (p. 228)

Velocity Velocity indicates the number of times per year that an "average dollar" is spent on goods and services. It is the ratio of nominal GDP to the number of dollars in the money stock. That is:

$$\text{Velocity} = \frac{\text{Nominal GDP}}{\text{Money stock}}$$ (p. 296)

Vertical (Long-Run) Phillips Curve The vertical (long-run) Phillips curve shows the menu of inflation/unemployment choices available to society in the long run. It is a vertical straight line at the natural rate of unemployment. (p. 359)

Wage-Price Controls Wage-price controls are legal restrictions on the ability of industry and labor to raise wages and prices. (p. 369)

CREDITS

Page 13, London School of Economics and Political Science; p. 22, Hiking Map & Guide of The Grand Teton National Park. ©1993 Earthwalk Press, La Jolla, CA; p. 36, ©Don Couch Photography, Houston; p. 61, ©UPI/Bettmann; p. 68, Courtesy of The Metropolitan Museum of Art, Bequest of Charles Allen Munn, 1924. (24.90.1828). All rights reserved, The Metropolitan Museum of Art; p. 84, ©Jim Levitt/Impact Visuals, p. 104, ©1993 C. Rob Badger/FPG International; p. 107, Culver Pictures, Inc.; p. 108, ©The Bettmann Archive; p. 126, From *The Wall Street Journal*—Cartoon by Cochran, reprinted with permission of Cartoon Features Syndicate; p. 134, Mario Tapia/NYT Pictures; p. 135, Camera Press—Photo Trends/Globe Photos, Inc.; p. 167, Burlington Industries/PhotoEdit; p. 252, Used by Permission of Johnny Hart and Creators Syndicate, Inc.; p. 259, ©Tony Freeman/PhotoEdit; p. 276, ©John Neubauer/PhotoEdit; p. 305, "Daddy's not mad at you, dear—Daddy's mad at the Fed," by Baloo, January 19, 1994, *The Wall Street Journal;* p. 324, From *The Wall Street Journal*—Reprinted with permission of Cartoon Features Syndicate; p. 340, From *The Wall Street Journal*—Reprinted with permission of Cartoon Features Syndicate; p. 380, ©Culver Pictures; p. 388, ©1996 Don Couch Photography, Houston; p. 394, ©1994 David Burnett/Contact Press Images; p. 396, ©Culver Pictures; p. 406, ©1996 Don Couch Photography, Houston; p. 406, "Big MacCurrencies," from *Finance and Economics* "The Hamburger Stand," *The Economist,* April 15, 1995, p. 74. ©1995 The Economist Newspaper Group, Inc. Reprinted with permission; p. 416, "Then it's agreed. Until the dollar firms up, we let the clamshell float." Drawing by Ed Fisher, ©1971—The New Yorker Magazine, Inc.; p. 439, ©Alan Levenson/Tony Stone Images; p. 444, ©Bettmann Newsphotos; p. 491, Photo Courtesy of Honda, Marysville, Ohio; pp. 55, 257 ©1995 PhotoDisc, Inc.

INDEX